THE CANADIAN YEARBOOK OF INTERNATIONAL LAW

2010

ANNUAIRE CANADIEN DE DROIT INTERNATIONAL

The Canadian Yearbook of International Law

VOLUME XLVIII   2010   TOME XLVIII

Annuaire canadien de droit international

Published under the auspices of
THE CANADIAN BRANCH, INTERNATIONAL LAW ASSOCIATION
AND
THE CANADIAN COUNCIL ON INTERNATIONAL LAW

Publié sous les auspices de
LA BRANCHE CANADIENNE DE L'ASSOCIATION DE DROIT INTERNATIONAL
ET
LE CONSEIL CANADIEN DE DROIT INTERNATIONAL

UBCPress · Vancouver · Toronto

Printed in Canada on acid-free paper

ISBN 978-0-7748-2303-6
ISSN 0069-0058

Canadian Cataloguing in Publication Data

The National Library of Canada has catalogued this publication as follows:

The Canadian yearbook of international law — Annuaire canadien de droit international

 Annual.
 Text in English and French.
 "Published under the auspices of the Canadian Branch, International Law Association and the Canadian Council on International Law."
 ISSN 0069-0058

  1. International Law — Periodicals.
 I. International Law Association. Canadian Branch.
 II. Canadian Council on International Law.
 III. Title: The Canadian yearbook of international law.
  JC 21.C3   341'.05   C75-34558-6E

Données de catalogage avant publication (Canada)

Annuaire canadien de droit international — The Canadian yearbook of international law

 Annuel.
 Textes en anglais et en français.
 "Publié sous les auspices de la Branche canadienne de l'Association de droit international et le Conseil canadien de droit international."
 ISSN 0069-0058

  1. Droit international — Périodiques.
 I. Association de droit international. Branche canadienne.
 II. Conseil canadien de droit international.
 III. Titre: Annuaire canadien de droit international.
  JC 21.C3   341'.05   C75-34558-6E

UBC Press
University of British Columbia
2029 West Mall
Vancouver, BC V6T 1Z2
(604) 822-5959
www.ubcpress.ca

The Board of Editors, the Canadian Branch of the International Law Association, the Canadian Council on International Law, and the University of British Columbia are not in any way responsible for the views expressed by contributors, whether the contributions are signed or unsigned.

Les opinions émises dans le présent *Annuaire* par nos collaborateurs, qu'il s'agisse ou non d'articles signés, ne sauraient aucunement engager la responsabilité du Comité de rédaction, de la Branche canadienne de l'Association de droit international, du Conseil canadien de droit international ou de l'Université de la Colombie-Britannique.

Communications to the *Yearbook* should be addressed to:
Les communications destinées à *l'Annuaire* doivent être adressées à:

The Editor/Le directeur
Canadian Yearbook of International Law/
Annuaire canadien de droit international
Faculty of Law, Common Law Section/
Faculté de droit, Section common law
University of/Université d'Ottawa
57 Louis Pasteur
Ottawa, Ontario K1N 6N5 Canada

Contents / Matière

Book Reviews / Recensions de livres

Preface / Préface

The publication of volume 48 marks an important turning point in the history of the *Canadian Yearbook of International Law*. In November 2010, Professors Donald M. McRae and Armand L.C. de Mestral, the *Yearbook*'s long-serving Editor-in-Chief and Associate Editor respectively, announced to the Board of Editors that they were stepping down from their positions upon publication of the forty-seventh volume. As Don McRae was only the *Yearbook*'s second Editor-in-Chief and Armand de Mestral its third Associate Editor since its inception in 1963, this is a change that cannot pass without notice.

"Long-serving" hardly does justice to Don McRae's and Armand de Mestral's remarkable records of service to the *Canadian Yearbook of International Law* over the years. Both were first named as Assistants to the Editors with volume 12 (1974),

La publication du 48e tome marque un tournant important dans l'histoire de l'*Annuaire canadien de droit international*. En novembre 2010, les professeurs Donald M. McRae et Armand L.C. de Mestral, directeur et directeur adjoint de longue date de l'*Annuaire*, annonçaient au Comité de rédaction leur départ de leurs postes dès la publication du 47e tome. Don McRae n'est que le deuxième directeur et Armand de Mestral le troisième directeur adjoint depuis l'avènement de l'*Annuaire* en 1963, un fait qui souligne l'importance de cette nouvelle.

La simple mention de longévité ne rend guère justice aux contributions remarquables de Don McRae et Armand de Mestral au service de l'*Annuaire*. Les deux furent d'abord nommés assistants à la rédaction avec la publication du 12e tome (en 1974) alors que Charles Bourne était

at a time when Charles Bourne and Donat Pharand were Editor-in-Chief and Associate Editor respectively. Armand de Mestral subsequently became Associate Editor with volume 21 (1983) and Don McRae Editor-in-Chief with volume 31 (1993). The astonishing result is that each has been involved, in one capacity or another, in editing at least thirty-six volumes of the *Yearbook* — seventeen under Don McRae's leadership as Editor-in-Chief, and twenty-seven with the benefit of Armand de Mestral's guidance as Associate Editor. As Peter Milroy, director of UBC Press, has aptly described it, this "must be one of the most extraordinary editorial partnerships in the history of serial publishing."

Such longevity of service also underscores the extent to which the reputation, prominence, and influence of the *Yearbook* are intimately bound up with the wise and skilful leadership of both Don McRae and Armand de Mestral. Indeed, their names have become synonymous with the *Yearbook*. Under their guidance, and building upon the sound foundations established by founding Editor-in-Chief Charles Bourne and prior Associate Editors Jacques-Yvan Morin and Donat Pharand, the *Yearbook* has become an

directeur et Donat Pharand directeur adjoint. Armand de Mestral devint ensuite directeur adjoint avec la publication du 21ᵉ tome (en 1983), et Don McRae directeur avec la publication du 31ᵉ tome (en 1993). Chacun a donc été impliqué, d'une façon ou d'une autre, dans la publication d'au moins 36 tomes de l'*Annuaire* — dont dix-sept sous la direction de Don McRae et vingt-sept sous la direction associée d'Armand de Mestral. Comme l'a si bien dit Peter Milroy, directeur de UBC Press, cela "doit constituer l'un des partenariats éditoriaux les plus exceptionnels de l'histoire de l'édition de collections."

Ce long service souligne également la mesure dans laquelle la réputation, l'importance et l'influence de l'*Annuaire* sont intimement liés au leadership plein de sagesse et de doigté de Don McRae et Armand de Mestral. En effet, leurs noms sont aujourd'hui intimement liés à l'*Annuaire*. Sous leur direction, et en s'appuyant sur les solides fondations établies par le directeur fondateur de l'*Annuaire* Charles Bourne ainsi que les anciens directeurs adjoints Jacques-Yvan Morin et Donat Pharand, l'*Annuaire* est devenu un forum international renommé pour les contributions canadiennes à l'étude

internationally respected forum for Canadian contributions to the understanding and development of international law. Under their leadership, the *Yearbook* has, in short, become an indispensable institution of the Canadian international legal academy and profession.

In succeeding Don McRae and Armand de Mestral, we are keenly aware of the standard they have set and of the magnitude of the responsibility they have bequeathed us. As Don McRae stated when he became Editor-in-Chief, "an important element in any change is continuity."[1] We are therefore committed to continuing the *Yearbook*'s fine tradition of promoting the development and dissemination, to Canadians and the larger international community, of Canadian research and practice in matters of international law. Yet, as Don McRae also observed, "a yearbook must also reflect its times."[2] We are therefore just as committed to adapting the *Yearbook* to the realities of twenty-first-century scholarly publishing. In light of the globalization of scholarly communities, for example,

et au développement du droit international. Sous leur houlette, l'*Annuaire* est devenu, en un mot, une institution indispensable de l'académie et la profession juridiques internationales au Canada.

En prenant la relève de Don McRae et Armand de Mestral, nous sommes forts conscients des standards qu'ils ont établis pour l'*Annuaire* et de l'ampleur de la responsabilité qu'ils nous ont léguée. Comme l'a dit Don McRae en assumant en 1993 le rôle de directeur, "un élément important dans tout changement est la continuité."[1] Nous nous engageons donc à continuer la tradition d'excellence de l'*Annuaire* dans la promotion, le développement et la diffusion de la recherche et de la pratique canadienne en matière de droit international, tant auprès des Canadiens que de la communauté internationale. Pourtant, comme Don McRae a aussi observé, "un annuaire doit également refléter son temps."[2] Nous sommes donc tout aussi engagés à adapter l'*Annuaire* aux réalités de l'édition savante au 21e siècle. À la lumière de la mondialisation des communautés savantes, par exemple, nous comptons accueillir,

---

1 Donald M. McRae, "Preface" (1993) 31 Can YB Int'l L xiii.

2 *Ibid.*

we look forward to welcoming, into the pages of the *Yearbook*, the very best thinking from around the world on problems of international law. The advent of electronic publishing also presents exciting opportunities for accelerating and extending the dissemination of the *Yearbook*'s content — opportunities we are keen to take advantage of in collaboration with UBC Press.

We are joined, in facing these challenges and opportunities, by Nicole LaViolette and Frédéric Mégret, both of whom become Assistants to the Editors with the publication of this volume. We look forward, with their support and with that of all members of the Board of Editors, to working in the service of the *Yearbook* over the years to come and, in so doing, honouring the fine legacy left by Don McRae, Armand de Mestral, and their predecessors.

dans les pages de l'*Annuaire*, la meilleure recherche du monde entier sur les problèmes du droit international. L'avènement de l'édition électronique présente également des opportunités excitantes pour accélérer et étendre la diffusion du contenu de l'*Annuaire*, opportunités dont nous souhaitons profiter en collaboration avec UBC Press.

Se joignent à nous pour relever ces défis et opportunités, dès la publication du 48e tome, les professeurs Nicole LaViolette et Frédéric Mégret à titre d'assistants à la rédaction. Avec leur soutien ainsi que celui de tous les membres du Comité de rédaction, nous accueillons avec enthousiasme cette chance de travailler au service de l'*Annuaire* dans les années à venir et, ce faisant, d'honorer l'héritage d'excellence qui nous est légué par Don McRae, Armand de Mestral et leurs prédécesseurs.

JOHN H. CURRIE
Editor-in-Chief / Directeur

RENÉ PROVOST
Associate Editor / Directeur adjoint

THE CANADIAN YEARBOOK OF INTERNATIONAL LAW

2010

ANNUAIRE CANADIEN DE DROIT INTERNATIONAL

Obeying Restraints:
Applying the Plea of Superior Orders to Military Defendants before the International Criminal Court

CHRISTOPHER K. PENNY

INTRODUCTION

It is not surprising that the plea of "just following orders" might be raised by military defendants accused of committing war crimes or other serious violations of international law. Indeed, one would expect military personnel, particularly low-ranking soldiers, to invoke superior orders frequently in justification of (otherwise) criminal behaviour committed during armed conflict. Armed forces are necessarily structured on the immediate obedience of orders by subordinates, and significant penalties can and do result from disobedience. In fact, compliance with orders is an inherent part of being a soldier.

Contemporary international law rightly addresses this situation by at times relieving soldiers of criminal responsibility by virtue of their legal obligation to follow the commands of their superiors.[1]

Christopher K. Penny is an assistant professor in the Norman Paterson School of International Affairs at Carleton University, Ottawa. The author would like to thank Stephen Garvey, Josh Chandler, and an anonymous reviewer for insightful comments on earlier drafts. This article has been substantially revised and updated since its presentation at the seventh Canadian Conference on Ethical Leadership. *Ethical Behaviour in an Environment of Complexity and Chaos* (presentation at the Canadian Conference on Ethical Leadership, Royal Military College, Kingston, ON, 29 November 2006).

1 This article focuses on the plea of superior orders as it relates to national military hierarchies. However, while this doctrine has historically been addressed in this context, as a matter of contemporary international law, the invocation of superior orders is not confined to military personnel. This plea is available to any defendant under a legal obligation to obey the commands of a superior, whether military or civilian. See, eg, *Rome Statute of the International Criminal Court*, 17 June 1998, 2187 UNTS 90, 37 ILM 1002 (entered into force 1 July 2002), art 33 [*Rome Statute*] ("[s]uperior orders and prescription of law"). The term "soldiers"

However, by permitting the invocation of superior orders as a full defence to war crimes charges before the International Criminal Court (ICC), the *Rome Statute of the International Criminal Court (Rome Statute)* has expanded the potential reach of this doctrine beyond its (arguably) more limited post-Second World War application as a factor to be considered only in mitigation of a sentence following conviction.[2] This recent return to the pre-war scope of the doctrine raises challenging questions concerning the manner in which superior orders should be assessed and applied by the ICC.

This article addresses the content and ramifications of the plea of superior orders, illustrating the complexities and risks of justifying otherwise criminal behaviour on this basis as well as the legitimate rationale for doing so in certain cases. Following this introductory section, the second part of this article discusses the general legal obligation for soldiers to obey commands. The third part outlines the historical development and legal content of the corresponding plea of superior orders, while the fourth part then details the incorporation of this plea into the *Rome Statute* itself. Finally, the fifth part turns to the potential future application of this plea by the ICC, arguing that in light of its moral and practical ramifications it should be treated by the court as both a full defence and a factor in mitigation of sentence, in a manner conceptually distinct from duress.

While recognizing the importance of considering superior orders as a full defence to war crime charges in certain circumstances, this article argues that its uncritical acceptance by the ICC could at times allow individuals who should bear responsibility for their actions to escape criminal sanction. Instead, a full defence should only remain open to soldiers who have acted under a reasonable, albeit mistaken, belief in the legality of their orders. In other cases, the ICC will better be able to address the moral nuances of human behaviour by continuing to consider superior orders only as a possible factor in the mitigation of a sentence following conviction.

This doctrine must be applied carefully to ensure that the ICC does not reward soldiers who consciously refuse to even consider the ramifications of questionable wartime actions. Although military hierarchies necessarily impose substantial limitations on individual autonomy, which should be reflected in the corresponding

---

is used in a generic sense to refer to all military personnel, whether members of an army, navy, air force, or other national military service.

[2] *Ibid.*

responsibility of soldiers, this requirement should not condone the creation of amoral automatons. Nor, however, should it be equated with illegitimate duress.

OBLIGATION TO OBEY

National armed forces are invariably organized as rigid hierarchies in which subordinates are under a strict obligation to obey the commands of their superiors. In fact, without the imposition of this duty on individual soldiers, armed forces would likely not be able to fulfil their legitimate responsibilities. Military operations frequently involve the central co-ordination of large groups of soldiers without providing (or being able to provide) each individual with detailed explanations for specific decisions, particularly when orders are conveyed through a lengthy chain of command to low-ranking soldiers. Battle itself often requires that commanding officers order soldiers into situations where their lives, or the lives of third parties, will be placed at serious risk. At times, the deaths of soldiers themselves will be the likely, or even inevitable result of compliance with their orders.[3] Nevertheless, military success may, and often does, depend upon soldiers complying with such orders without wavering. Military training emphasizes the importance of obedience, and professional soldiers generally recognize this obligation as part of their duty.

As acknowledged by the Supreme Court of Canada, "[t]he whole concept of military organization is dependent upon instant, unquestioning obedience to the orders of those in authority ... This requirement of instant obedience to superior order applies right down to the smallest military unit."[4] The Court characterized the nature of, and rationale for, this requirement as follows:

Military tradition and a prime object of military training is to inculcate in every recruit the necessity to obey orders instantly and unhesitatingly. This is in reality the only way in which a military unit can effectively operate. To enforce the instant carrying out of orders, military discipline is directed

---

3 See, eg, discussion of related issues in Yoram Dinstein, *The Defence of "Obedience to Superior Orders" in International Law* (Leyden, Netherlands: AW Sijthoff, 1965) at 5.

4 *R v Finta*, [1994] 1 SCR 701 at 828, 112 DLR (4th) 513 (Cory J., speaking for the majority; Gonthier and Major JJ., Lamer C.J.C. concurring) [*Finta*, cited to SCR].

at punishing those who fail to comply with the orders they have received. In action, the lives of every member of a unit may depend upon the instantaneous compliance with orders even though those orders may later, on quiet reflection, appear to have been unnecessarily harsh.[5]

Obedience to orders is typically ensured through the imposition of a legal duty backed by formal sanction (underpinning complementary military tradition and training). For example, in Canada, section 83 of the *National Defence Act* (*NDA*) prescribes the offence of insubordination as follows: "Every person who disobeys a lawful command of a superior officer is guilty of an offence and on conviction is liable to imprisonment for life or to less punishment."[6] Many other provisions of the *NDA* reiterate this general obligation in specifically defined circumstances.[7] Other armed forces impose upon their soldiers similar legal obligations of obedience to superior orders.[8]

Punishments for disobedience can be severe. In Canada, the *NDA* prescribes a maximum life sentence for insubordination.[9] Many other states (including the United States) retain the potential imposition of the death penalty in such circumstances, particularly when disobedience occurs during actual armed conflict.[10]

---

[5] *Ibid.*

[6] *National Defence Act,* RSC 1985, c N-5, s 83 [*NDA*].

[7] Eg, reiterations of this obligation are found in the following sections of the *NDA*: s 74(c), failing to use "utmost exertion" to carry out orders relating to operations of war in the presence of the enemy; s 76(a), being made a prisoner of war through, *inter alia,* disobedience of orders; s 106(1), disobedience of captain's orders when in a ship; and s 110(1), disobedience of captain's orders when in an aircraft.

[8] See, eg, the review of national legislation and military practice in Jean-Marie Henckaerts and Louise Doswald-Beck, *Customary International Humanitarian Law* (Cambridge: Cambridge University Press, 2005), volume 2, *Practice,* at 3800-14.

[9] The *NDA* also provides for a maximum life sentence of imprisonment for all of the related offences detailed earlier. The death penalty no longer applies to any military offences in Canada following its revocation from the *NDA* in 1998. *An Act to Amend the National Defence Act and to Make Consequential Amendments to Other Acts,* SC 1998, c 35. For civilian criminal offences, the death penalty was abolished over twenty years earlier, with the passage of Bill C-84 in 1976. This dichotomy illustrates the differences between conceptions of appropriate criminal sanctions for soldiers versus civilians. Soldiers are subject to separate and often more severe punishments for the same acts by virtue of the need to maintain discipline in, and the operational effectiveness of, military forces.

[10] Eg, the *Uniform Code of Military Justice,* 10 USC § 890 at art 90(2), in the United States provides that "[a]ny person subject to this chapter who wilfully disobeys

Nonetheless, militaries generally recognize that a soldier's obedience cannot and should not be absolute, incorporating into their policies and training a qualification that no one is required to follow a clearly illegal order.[11] Courts have played a key role in formulating this limitation, qualifying the otherwise obligatory nature of obedience. Reflecting the rationale for this restriction, the United States Military Tribunal (USMT) asserted in 1948 in *In re Ohlendorf and Others* (*Einsatzgruppen* case) that "[t]he obedience of a soldier is not the obedience of an automaton. A soldier is a reasoning agent. He does not respond, and is not expected to respond, like a piece of machinery."[12] Realistically, however, the lower a soldier's position in a military hierarchy, the less ability he or she will have to question orders (and the more orders there will likely be to obey).[13]

Although a soldier is required to disobey an obviously illegal order, in almost all circumstances a clear legal presumption in favour of obedience remains. For example, explanatory notes to the *Queen's Regulations and Orders for the Canadian Forces* establish that "[u]sually there will be no doubt as to whether a command or order is lawful or unlawful. In a situation, however, where the subordinate does not know the law or is uncertain of it he shall, even though he doubts the lawfulness of the command, obey unless the command

---

a lawful command of his superior commissioned officer shall be punished, if the offense is committed in time of war, by death or other such punishment as a court-martial may direct, and if the offense is committed at any other time, by such punishment, other than death, as a court-martial may direct."

[11] For instance, this limitation is enunciated in the *NDA, supra* note 6, s 83 (requiring obedience to "lawful" orders). It is reiterated in art 19.015 of the *Queen's Regulations and Orders for the Canadian Forces* [*Queen's Regulations and Orders*], enacted pursuant to the *NDA*, s 12. The official version of the *Queen's Regulations and Orders* is published electronically. See National Defence and the Canadian Forces: Queen's Regulations and Orders, online: <http://www.admfincs.forces.gc.ca/qro-orf/index-english.asp>. See also Henckaerts and Doswald-Beck (practice), *supra* note 8.

[12] *In re Ohlendorf and Others (Einsatzgruppen Trial)*, Judgment 217 (10 April 1948) (United States Military Tribunal (USMT), Nuremberg), 15 ILR 656 at 665 [*Einsatzgruppen* case]. Two years earlier, the International Military Tribunal had rejected the "mythical requirement of soldierly obedience at all costs" in the trial of Alfred Jodl. *In re Goering and Others*, Judgment (30 September – 1 October 1946) (International Military Tribunal (IMT), Nuremberg), reproduced in 22 *Trial of the Major War Criminals before the International Military Tribunal* 411 at 571 [*IMT Judgment*].

[13] See, eg, related discussion in *Finta, supra* note 4 at 838.

is manifestly unlawful."[14] In the absence of obvious illegality, other militaries also generally resolve the issue of uncertainty in favour of obedience.[15]

Some theorists on military obedience have argued that individual soldiers should be provided substantially greater autonomy to question orders and that this personal freedom would not only decrease the incidence of war crimes but could also actually increase the military effectiveness of the forces in question.[16] However, whatever doctrinal merit one ascribes to these controversial arguments, they have not been reflected in the actual legal obligations of obedience owed by most soldiers, even those serving advanced democracies such as Canada and the United States.[17]

TREATMENT OF THE PLEA OF SUPERIOR ORDERS AT INTERNATIONAL LAW

While obedience by subordinates remains a standard requirement of military forces, an obvious problem therefore arises when soldiers are ordered to act in a manner that leads to the commission

[14] *Queen's Regulations and Orders, supra* note 11, art 19.015, n(B). This obligation is reiterated in Canada, National Defence: Office of the Judge Advocate General, *Code of Conduct for Canadian Forces (CF) Personnel,* Doc B-GG-005-027/AF-023, online: National Defence and the Canadian Forces: Office of the Judge Avocate General: Operational Law <http://www.forces.gc.ca/jag/publications/Training -formation/CFCC-CCFC-eng.pdf> [*CF Code of Conduct*]. As LC Green notes, however, these provisions are silent with respect to the ramifications if a soldier complies with an order in such circumstances "and it transpires that it was in fact illegal." LC Green, "Superior Orders and the Reasonable Man," in LC Green, ed, *Essays on the Modern Law of War,* 2nd edition (Ardsley, NY: Transnational, 1999) 245 at 248.

[15] See, eg, Mark J Osiel, *Obeying Orders: Atrocity, Military Discipline and the Law of War* (New Brunswick, NJ: Transaction, 1999) at 54-55; Jordan J Paust, "Superior Orders and Command Responsibility," in M Cherif Bassiouni, ed, *International Criminal Law,* 2nd edition (Ardsley, NY: Transnational, 1999) volume 1, *Crimes,* 223 at 224-25. See also Henckaerts and Doswald-Beck (practice), *supra* note 8.

[16] See, eg, Osiel, *supra* note 15. Osiel focuses, in particular, on providing greater autonomy to officers and more senior non-commissioned members of armed forces (see, eg, at 8). This may be particularly relevant for peace enforcement operations fought by Western democracies where military disobedience does not pose an obvious threat to state stability and the armed forces in question are generally well trained and educated (see, eg, at 269-70).

[17] As a result, while the conclusions of this article generally complement those offered by Osiel, *supra* note 15, they focus on how the ICC should address the plea of superior orders in light of the current obligations of obedience owed by soldiers.

of criminal acts. In such circumstances, it is not unusual or surprising for soldiers subsequently charged with criminal offences to argue that their obedience to orders should reduce or even negate their individual responsibility. The following section provides an overview of the historical treatment of the plea of superior orders, addressing its legal content and illustrating its scope and exceptions.[18]

Before turning to an analysis of the substantive content of the plea of superior orders, two cautions are in order. First, this plea has received varying judicial treatment and political acceptance over the course of the twentieth century. While superior orders was accepted as a full defence in the wake of the First World War, it was formally confined to consideration in mitigation of sentence in the statutes governing the military tribunals established by the Allied powers following the Second World War.[19] This formal limitation

18 For a more detailed overview of the historical evolution and content of the plea of superior orders, see, eg, Dinstein, *supra* note 3; LC Green, *Superior Orders in National and International Law* (Leyden, The Netherlands: AW Sijthoff, 1976). For a more recent overview of this plea, see, eg, Green, "Superior Orders and the Reasonable Man," *supra* note 14; Matthew R Lippman, "Humanitarian Law: The Development and Scope of the Superior Orders Defense" (2001) 20 Penn St Int'l L Rev 153. See also Jean-Marie Henckaerts and Louise Doswald-Beck, *Customary International Humanitarian Law* (Cambridge: Cambridge University Press, 2005), volume 1, *Rules*, at 563-67.

19 Art 8 of the *Charter of the Military Tribunal at Nuremberg*, annexed to the *Agreement for the Prosecution and Punishment of Major War Criminals of the European Axis*, 8 August 1945, 82 UNTS 279, 59 Stat. 1544, expressly prohibits the invocation of superior orders as a defence: "The fact that the defendant acted pursuant to order of his Government or of a superior shall not free him from responsibility, but may be considered in mitigation of punishment if the Tribunal determines that justice so requires." Allied Control Council of Germany, *Allied Control Council Law no 10: Punishment of Persons Guilty of War Crimes, Crimes against Peace and against Humanity* (20 December 1945), 3 Official Gazette Control Council for Germany 50-55 (1946), art II(4)(b) [*Control Council Law no 10*], which establishes a similar limitation for national war crimes trials conducted by the Allied powers. See also, eg, *In re Von Leeb and Others (German High Command Trial)*, Judgment 119 (28 October 1948) (USMT, Nuremberg), 15 ILR 376 [*High Command* case] (discussing the nature of Hitler's authority in Nazi Germany as the rationale for the Allied denial of superior orders as a full defence). As early as 1943, the scholar Edwin Dickinson noted that a failure to limit this defence would mean that the "only war criminals available for punishment ... [would be] Hitler and Tojo, neither of whom is likely to be available alive when the victory is finally won." Charles Cheney Hyde, "Punishment of War Criminals" (1943) 37 Am Soc Int'l L Proc 39 at 49 (comment from Edwin Dickinson); see also Dinstein, *supra* note 3 at 144-47. In *Finta*, *supra* note 4 at 840, Cory J. even suggested

is, however, somewhat misleading as the actual practice of the tribunals belied it.[20] While the United Nations Security Council nevertheless followed the restrictive formal precedent when establishing ad hoc criminal tribunals in the mid-1990s, the *Rome Statute* has once again expanded the potential application of the doctrine so as to expressly permit superior orders as a full defence to some international criminal charges.

Second, while the plea of superior orders recognizes the limited ability of soldiers to act contrary to their orders, it does not necessarily mean that international law allows the commission of wartime criminal acts with impunity. Liability for such acts may instead rest further up the military chain of command — for example, on the individuals who actually ordered the acts or were otherwise responsible for their commission. This accountability may result either from the assessment of individual criminal responsibility for directly ordering the commission of a criminal offence or through the related doctrine of command responsibility.[21] While beyond the scope

---

that an unqualified defence of superior orders might have applied to Hitler himself (arguably misunderstanding the Fuhrer principle as it applied to the domestic law of Germany, as described, eg, in Dinstein, *supra* note 3 at 140-43). Restriction of the plea of superior orders was less absolute in the context of post-war trials conducted in the Far East, where it was not sufficient "of itself" to establish a defence. See, eg, discussion in Dinstein (at 156-59).

[20] This judicial practice is discussed in greater detail later in this article. In addition, these tribunals were arguably intended to address conduct already considered to be manifestly illegal and committed by high-ranking individuals with policy-making discretion. See, eg, Dinstein, *supra* note 3 at 154-55; Lippman, *supra* note 18 at 180-81. Although Dinstein does not himself accept this characterization, he notes its adoption by many involved with the IMT itself. See also Antonio Cassese, *International Criminal Law* (Oxford: Oxford University Press, 2003) at 232, n 3; Paola Gaeta, "The Defence of Superior Orders: The Statute of the International Criminal Court versus Customary International Law" (1999) 10:1 EJIL 172 at 180. In practice, however, this presumption was not accurate (see, eg, assessment of legal uncertainty concerning the use of prisoners for construction of fortifications by the USMT in the *High Command* case, *supra* note 19; and discussed in more detail in note 73 in this article).

[21] See, eg, *Rome Statute, supra* note 1, art 25 ("individual criminal responsibility") and art 28 ("responsibility of commanders and other superiors"). See also Robert Cryer et al., *An Introduction to International Criminal Law and Procedure*, 2nd edition (Cambridge: Cambridge University Press, 2010) at 417; Henckaerts and Doswald-Beck (*Rules*), *supra* note 18 at 556-63. Nonetheless, even individuals in very senior military positions have at times sought refuge in the plea of superior orders, albeit usually without success. Eg, Alfred Jodl argued obedience to superior orders in answer to charges of war crimes, crimes against humanity,

of this article, these heads of responsibility establish a necessary and important conceptual counterbalance to the plea of superior orders. They recognize that individual criminal responsibility may, and often should, attach to a person in *de jure* or *de facto* command of others whose actions lead, either directly or indirectly, to the commission of an offence. In addition, whether or not the plea of superior orders is accepted in individual criminal cases, the state itself may also attract international legal responsibility through the attribution to it of the acts of its military personnel.[22]

LATE NINETEENTH AND EARLY TWENTIETH CENTURIES

The plea of superior orders has a lengthy historical pedigree, reaching back over many centuries.[23] A classic formulation is found in *R v Smith*, a 1900 South African case involving the intentional killing of a South African native by a soldier during the Boer War.[24] In addressing the soldier's claim of obedience to superior orders, a special court concluded that although "it is monstrous to suppose that a soldier would be protected where the order is grossly illegal," the alternative argument:

---

and crimes against peace before the IMT in Nuremberg. Throughout the Second World War, Jodl held the position of chief of the operation staff of the high command of the German armed forces. In spite of this powerful position, he claimed that he was simply following the orders of his head of state, Adolf Hitler. The tribunal nonetheless found him guilty on all counts and rejected his plea of superior orders in mitigation of sentence. *IMT Judgment, supra* note 12 at 568-71. On 16 October 1946, Jodl was hanged.

22 There is no doubt that as a matter of international law a state bears responsibility for internationally wrongful acts committed by its armed forces. See, eg, *Application of the Convention on the Prevention and Punishment of the Crime of Genocide (Bosnia and Herzegovina v Serbia and Montenegro)*, Judgment, ICJ General List no 91 (26 February 2007) at 142; Henckaerts and Doswald-Beck(*Rules*), *supra* note 18 at 530-36.

23 Eg, in 1474, Peter von Hagenbach, the governor of the Upper Rhine appointed by Charles, Duke of Burgundy, was placed on trial for using methods such as murder and rape to force the submission of the town of Breisach. He argued obedience to superior orders, submitting that he "had no right to question the order which he was charged to carry out, and it was his duty to obey." Hagenbach then asked: "Is it not known that soldiers owe absolute obedience to their superiors?" This defence was rejected, and Hagenbach was sentenced to death. See discussion of this and other historical cases in *Finta, supra* note 4 at 830. See also Green, *National and International Law, supra* note 18 at 263-64; Osiel, *supra* note 15 at 2.

24 *R v Smith*, [1900] 17 SC 561 (Cape Prov. Div.) (Solomon J.) [*Smith*].

[that he] is responsible if he obeys an order [that is] not strictly legal ... is an extreme proposition which the Court cannot accept... [E]specially in time of war immediate obedience ... is required... I think it is a safe rule to lay down that if a soldier honestly believes he is doing his duty in obeying the commands of his superior, and if the orders are not so manifestly illegal that he must or ought to have known that they were unlawful, the private soldier would be protected by the orders of his superior officer.[25]

This case introduced the objective conception of manifest illegality as a limitation to the defence of superior orders.[26]

In the trials of German sailors following the First World War, the content of the doctrine of manifest illegality further approached its current formulation. Two cases before the German Reichsgericht in Leipzig served to illustrate the limits of this concept, helping to draw a line between acceptable obedience to orders and criminal behaviour. Both cases, *The Judgment in the Case of Commander Karl Neuman: Hospital Ship "Dover Castle" (Dover Castle)*[27] and *Judgment in the Case of Lieutenants Dithmar and Boldt: Hospital Ship "The Llandovery Castle" (Llandovery Castle)*,[28] involved the sinking of hospital ships by German submarines. In the first case, a German submarine commander faced trial for sinking the British hospital ship *Dover Castle*. He argued that his action resulted from obedience to superior orders. At the time of the sinking, the German Admiralty had concluded that the British were illegally using hospital ships for military purposes in violation of the laws of war governing the use of protected symbols (that is, the Red Cross). The German Supreme Court, while refusing to comment on the validity of the German Admiralty position, found that in light of this information the commander

---

25 *Ibid* at 567-68; also cited by the Supreme Court of Canada in *Finta, supra* note 4 at 831.

26 *Finta, supra* note 4 (relying on LC Green, "Superior Orders and Command Responsibility" (1989) 27 CYIL 167 at 174-75).

27 *Judgment in the Case of Commander Karl Neuman: Hospital Ship "Dover Castle,"* (1921) (Reichsgericht), cited in "Judicial Decisions Involving Questions of International Law" (1921) 16 AJIL 647 at 704 [*Dover Castle*]; discussed in *Finta, supra* note 4 at 832. See also Dinstein, *supra* note 3 at 12-14.

28 *Judgment in the Case of Lieutenants Dithmar and Boldt: Hospital Ship "The Llandovery Castle,"* (1921) (Reichsgericht), cited in "Judicial Decisions Involving Questions of International Law" (1921) 16 AJIL 647 at 708 [*Llandovery Castle*]; discussed in *Finta, supra* note 4 at 832-34.

was justified in viewing his attack as a legitimate reprisal rather than the illegal sinking of a protected ship.[29] As a result, the court accepted his defence and ordered his acquittal.

The case of the German submariners involved in the attack on the hospital ship *Llandovery Castle* stands in sharp contrast. Following the torpedoing of the *Llandovery Castle* (outside of the zone of reprisals authorized by the German Admiralty), the submarine commander ordered his junior officers to open machine gun fire on survivors as they climbed into lifeboats (apparently in order to eliminate witnesses to the initial criminal attack). Although the commander evaded capture after the war, the junior officers responsible for carrying out his order faced trial for their part in this attack. In their defence, these men argued obedience to the orders of their superior officer.[30] Commenting on the horrific nature of the acts in question, the court in *Llandovery Castle* concluded that attacking men as they clambered into lifeboats was an "offence against the law of nations" and that "international law, which is here involved, is simple and is universally known."[31] It therefore found that the junior officers could have had no confidence in the legality of the order to open fire, rejecting the defence of superior orders "if such an order is universally known to everybody, including also the accused, to be without any doubt whatever against the law."[32] Nonetheless, the court also recognized that, in general, "[i]t is certainly to be urged in favor of the military subordinates, that they are under no obligation to question the order of their superior officer, and they can count upon its legality."[33]

---

[29] The doctrine of reprisal permitted (and still permits, in some circumstances) the commission during wartime of certain types of otherwise unlawful acts as a mechanism to compel an enemy to resume compliance with the laws of war. See, eg, discussion of this doctrine in Henckaerts and Doswald-Beck(*Rules*), *supra* note 18 at 513-29; and in note 82 in this article. See also Lippman, *supra* note 18 at 213-14 (discussing post-Second World War treatment of superior orders in the context of reprisals).

[30] See, eg, discussion in Dinstein, *supra* note 3 at 14-16. See also Andreas Zimmermann, "Superior Orders," in Antonio Cassese, Paulo Gaeta, and John RWD Jones, eds., *The Rome Statute of the International Criminal Court: A Commentary* (Oxford: Oxford University Press, 2002), volume 1, 957 at 961-62.

[31] *Llandovery Castle, supra* note 28 at 721.

[32] *Ibid* at 722.

[33] *Ibid.*

SECOND WORLD WAR

The doctrine of superior orders received further extensive treatment in the wake of the Second World War, both in the arguments before, and in the judgments of, the International Military Tribunal (IMT) at Nuremberg and also in related proceedings conducted by the United States pursuant to *Control Council Law no. 10*.[34] Although the plea of superior orders was formally limited to a mitigating factor in sentencing when these tribunals were established, the resulting trials nonetheless built upon earlier judicial treatment of this doctrine, giving it further legal content and expanding upon the concept of manifest illegality.

Indeed, in the actual decisions of these tribunals, the plea of superior orders does not appear to have been confined solely to the role of post-conviction mitigation.[35] For example, the USMT in *In re List and Others (Hostages Trial)*(*Hostages* case) commented that "if the illegality of the order was not known to the inferior and he could not reasonably have been expected to know of its illegality, no wrongful intent necessary to the commission of a crime exists and the inferior will be protected."[36] Addressing the conduct of wartime extermination squads operating in occupied territories, the USMT in the *Einsatzgruppen* case nonetheless concluded that

[t]he subordinate is bound only to obey the lawful orders of his superior and if he accepts a criminal order and executes it with a malice of his own, he may not plead Superior Orders in mitigation of his offence. If the nature of the ordered act is manifestly beyond the scope of the superior's authority, the subordinate may not plead ignorance of the criminality of the order.[37]

Other post-war decisions applied similar tests regarding manifest illegality.[38]

---

[34] *Control Council Law no 10, supra* note 19. The plea of superior orders also received extensive treatment in separate national level trials conducted by various Allied powers in subsequent years, some of which are discussed later in the third part of this article. See, eg, Dinstein, *supra* note 3, and Green, *National and International Law, supra* note 18, for more detailed discussion of these historical proceedings.

[35] See, eg, Osiel, *supra* note 15 at 42-43.

[36] *In re List and Others (Hostages Trial)*, Judgment 215 (19 February 1948) (USMT, Nuremberg), 15 ILR 632 at 650 [*Hostages* case].

[37] *Einsatzgruppen* case, *supra* note 12 at 666.

[38] In a number of instances, high-ranking officials from Nazi Germany attempted, without success, to seek shelter behind this doctrine. See, eg, *High Command* case, *supra* note 19. See also discussion about Jodl in note 21 in this article.

However, when assessing superior orders, these trials often have focused on the existence of moral choice, at times effectively treating this plea as a military-specific doctrine of duress.[39] For example, the IMT itself has concluded that "[t]he true test, which is found in varying degrees in the criminal law of most nations, is not the existence of the order, but whether moral choice was in fact possible."[40] Expressions of opposition to the order in question at times furthered the mitigating effect of the plea of superior orders.[41]

JUDICIAL TREATMENT SINCE THE SECOND WORLD WAR

Over the latter half of the twentieth century, superior orders have continued to be raised both in national and international criminal forums. While some of these cases have reached back to address Second World War atrocities, others have dealt with crimes committed in more recent conflicts. For example, in 1973, the United States Court of Military Appeals addressed the plea of superior orders in the context of the Vietnam War when reviewing the conviction of Lieutenant William Calley for his role in the My Lai massacre. Consistent with historical practice, the court recognized both the subjective and objective elements to the doctrine. Although noting disagreement over the precise objective standard to be applied, the majority upheld the original conviction, which rested on a finding that a defence of superior orders could not apply to an order that "a man of ordinary sense and understanding would, under the circumstances, know to be unlawful, or if the order in question is actually known to be unlawful."[42]

---

[39] See, eg, discussion of treatment of superior orders by the IMT in Lippman, *supra* note 18 at 184, 203-4. See also Dinstein, *supra* note 3 at 147; Zimmermann, *supra* note 30 at 962-64. This is not surprising given the significant formal limitations placed on the consideration of the plea of superior orders by these tribunals. The problematic nature of this analogy is discussed in greater detail in the fifth part of this article.

[40] *IMT Judgment, supra* note 12 at 466. See discussion in Dinstein, *supra* note 3 at 147-50.

[41] See, eg, Lippman, *supra* note 18 at 204.

[42] *United States v William Calley Jr,* 22 CMA 534 at 542 (CMA 1973), aff'g 46 CMR 1131 (CMR 1973), rev'd on other grounds; *Calley v Callaway,* 382 F Supp 650 (MD Ga. 1974), rev'd 519 F 2d 194 (5th Cir 1975), cert denied, 425 US 911 (1976) [*Calley*]. This result is consistent with the standard established in *United States v Kinder,* 14 CMR 742 (CMR 1953) (in relation to an unlawful killing committed during the Korean War). See, eg, related discussion in Lippman, *supra* note 18 at 215-16.

Other national decisions addressing the concept of manifest illegality indicate that this standard will likely only be met in the most extreme circumstances. For instance, in the 1994 case of Imre Finta, a former Hungarian gendarme accused of aiding the deportation of thousands of Hungarian Jews to Auschwitz during the Second World War, the Supreme Court of Canada adopted the test that a manifestly unlawful order is one that "offends the conscience of every reasonable, right-thinking person; it must be an order which is obviously and flagrantly wrong. The order cannot be in a grey area or be merely questionable; rather it must patently and obviously be wrong."[43]

The case *R v Finta* cited an earlier decision of the District Military Court of Israel, *Chief Military Prosecutor v Lance Corporal Ofer, Major Malinki Shmuel and Others, Case Concerning the Events of 29 October 1956 in Kafr Qassem*, which had adopted a similarly high standard and provided the following colourful content to the concept of manifest illegality:

The identifying mark of a "manifestly unlawful" order must wave like a black flag above the order given, as a warning saying: "forbidden." It is not formal unlawfulness, hidden or half-hidden, not unlawfulness that is detectable only by legal experts, that is the important issue here, but an overt and salient violation of the law, a certain and obvious unlawfulness that stems from the order itself, the criminal character of the order itself or of the acts it demands to be committed, an unlawfulness that pierces and agitates the heart, if the eye be not blind nor the heart closed or corrupt. That is the degree of "manifest" illegality required in order to annul the soldier's duty to obey and render him criminally responsible for his actions.[44]

The standard for manifest illegality established in these latter cases is extremely high. Where this standard is applied, only the most egregious violations of international law will be captured and therefore excluded from the potential ambit of the plea of superior orders. Not surprisingly, national and international prosecutions have tended to focus on such obvious cases. This focus has in turn

---

[43] *Finta, supra* note 4 at 834 (Cory J.).

[44] *Chief Military Prosecutor v Lance Corporal Ofer, Major Malinki Shmuel and Others, Case Concerning the Events of 29 October 1956 in Kafr Qassem*, Judgment, Appeal no 279-283/58 (3 April 1959), 44 Psakim (Judgments of the District Courts of Israel) 362 [*Ofer*], cited in *Finta, supra* note 4. For an english language translation of *Ofer*, see (1985) 2 Palestine YB Int'l L 69.

severely restricted the development of legal precedent concerning the commission of less flagrant criminal acts pursuant to superior orders.[45] For example, the majority in *United States v William Calley Jr* concluded that disagreement over the precise objective standard applicable to the plea of superior orders was not material to the underlying conviction, given the nature of the specific acts in question (that is, the deliberate killing of unarmed civilians, including young children).[46]

Many recent decisions have continued to highlight the existence of "moral choice" as a factor material to accepting or rejecting the plea of superior orders. For example, in *Finta*, the Supreme Court of Canada recognized the availability of such choice as a key element in applying the plea of superior orders, effectively viewing it in the same light as duress.[47] In establishing the International Criminal Tribunal for the Former Yugoslavia (ICTY) and its sister tribunal for Rwanda (ICTR), the United Nations Security Council followed post-Second World War precedent and expressly rejected superior orders as a complete defence, restricting its consideration to a mitigating factor in sentencing.[48] Although judicial treatment of superior orders has been limited in these ad hoc international tribunals, the ICTY has also unnecessarily comingled superior orders with the concept of duress.[49]

---

[45] See, eg, Osiel, *supra* note 15 at 71-74. Osiel raises concerns that the resulting lack of legal clarity renders the manifest illegality rule an ineffective exception — that is, it is only in the most extreme cases where the plea of superior orders will be precluded on this basis (*ibid*). This critique regarding under-litigation of legal principles also applies to many other areas of international law governing armed conflict (see, eg, discussion at 324-25).

[46] *Calley, supra* note 42.

[47] See, eg, *Finta, supra* note 4 (reasons of La Forest J. at 778 and Cory J. at 828).

[48] See, respectively, *Statute of the International Criminal Tribunal for the Former Yugoslavia*, SC Res 827, 3217th Mtg, UN Doc S/RES/827 (1993), art 7(4); *Statute of the International Criminal Tribunal for Rwanda*, SC Res 955, 3453d Mtg, UN Doc S/RES/955 (1994), art 6(4). Indeed, there is a reasonable argument that the unqualified nature of this restriction went beyond existing precedent. See, eg, Osiel, *supra* note 15 at 43. See also Gaeta, *supra* note 20 at 181, and Zimmermann, *supra* note 30 at 961, noting the continued reservation of the United States to the adoption of an absolute standard for the ICTY.

[49] See, eg, *Prosecutor v Drazen Erdemovic*, Judgment IT-96-22-A (7 October 1997) (International Criminal Tribunal for the Former Yugoslavia (ICTY), Appeals Chamber) [*Erdemovic*] and its various separate and dissenting opinions. This issue is discussed in greater detail later in this article.

SUPERIOR ORDERS AND THE *ROME STATUTE*

In contrast to the ICTY and the ICTR, the *Rome Statute* recognizes superior orders as a potential full defence to some charges before the ICC. It provides as follows:

Article 33
Superior orders and prescription of law

(1) The fact that a crime within the jurisdiction of the Court has been committed by a person pursuant to an order of a Government or of a superior, whether military or civilian, shall not relieve that person of criminal responsibility unless:

    (a) The person was under a legal obligation to obey orders of the Government or the superior in question;

    (b) The person did not know that the order was unlawful; and

    (c) The order was not manifestly unlawful.[50]

In keeping with historical precedent, the *Rome Statute* thus incorporates both objective and subjective tests when addressing superior orders.[51] An accused may only be exonerated for conduct undertaken pursuant to orders that he did not know were illegal. Regardless of the existence of a legally binding superior/subordinate relationship, if it can be established that an accused soldier subjectively knew, or should have known, that his conduct was unlawful, a defence cannot rest on the existence of superior orders.

Despite its acceptance in the *Rome Statute*, the actual scope of the defence of superior orders is substantially more limited than it first

---

[50] *Rome Statute, supra* note 1, art 33.

[51] See, eg, Henckaerts and Doswald-Beck (*Rules*), *supra* note 18 at 563-67 ("practice that solely refers to the unlawfulness of the act ordered, without the requirement of knowledge of such unlawfulness, is not sufficiently widespread and uniform as to establish a rule of customary international law"). See also Cryer et al., *supra* note 21 at 416-17; Zimmermann, *supra* note 30 at 965-66, 972 (supporting the customary legal status of these tests and noting the "doubtful" existence of an absolute customary prohibition on invocation of superior orders as a full defence, particularly in light of its national judicial treatment). However, see Cassese, *supra* note 20 at 232-33, 241; Gaeta, *supra* note 20 at 190 (arguing that "it departs from customary international law without any well-grounded motivation" and that national treatment is distinguishable from an absolute international prohibition). However, Cassese himself notes that there may be an exception "where the law on a particular matter is obscure or highly controversial, in which case the defence of mistake of law may be raised." Cassese, *supra* note 20 at 233.

appears. Article 33(2) provides that "[f]or the purposes of this article, orders to commit genocide or crimes against humanity are manifestly unlawful."[52] As the effective jurisdiction of the ICC is at present limited to cases of genocide, crimes against humanity, and war crimes, the defence of superior orders is currently restricted to war crime charges alone. Since ICC jurisdiction with respect to war crimes is itself focused (albeit not formally restricted) to such offences "when committed as part of a plan or policy or as part of a large-scale commission of such crimes," the practical application of this defence may be further limited.[53]

The potential reach of the defence of superior orders will be extended once the ICC is able to exercise its jurisdiction over the crime of aggression. The 2010 Review Conference of the *Rome Statute* formally adopted a definition of this crime, which will allow the ICC to exercise jurisdiction one year following formal acceptance of related amendments to the *Rome Statute* by at least thirty states parties.[54] The *Rome Statute* does not expressly deem orders to commit the crime of aggression to be manifestly unlawful, nor did the review conference propose such an amendment.

Nonetheless, given the specific nature of this newly defined offence, it remains unlikely that the defence of superior orders would be material to most related proceedings before the ICC. Article 8*bis* restricts the crime of aggression to acts committed "by a person in a position effectively to exercise control over or to direct the political or military action of a State."[55] This limitation is generally consistent with the historical restriction of individual criminal responsibility for aggression (crimes against peace) to persons in policy-making positions.[56] By definition, it should limit (albeit not necessarily

---

[52] *Rome Statute, supra* note 1, art 33(2).

[53] *Ibid*, art 8(1).

[54] For further detail on various provisions concerning the crime of aggression, see Review Conference of the Rome Statute, *The Crime of Aggression,* 13th Plenary Meeting, ICC Doc RC/Res.6 (11 June 2010). Prior to the 2010 review conference, the *Rome Statute* included reference to the crime of aggression but provided that the ICC would only be able to exercise its jurisdiction over this crime following the formal adoption of a definition of the offence. *Rome Statute, supra* note 1, art 5(2).

[55] *Ibid.*, art 8*bis*(1). Art 25(3*bis*) also restricts the various heads of individual criminal responsibility for the crime of aggression, including aiding and abetting, to persons in such positions.

[56] See, eg, *High Command* case, *supra* note 19.

eliminate[57]) the invocation of the defence of superior orders in this context.[58]

The ICC is presumably required to consider — and, arguably, must be open to accept — superior orders as a full defence to at least some charges in some circumstances, given its express inclusion as such in the *Rome Statute*. However, in light of the ICC's recent establishment, and its limited number of ongoing investigations and cases, the plea of superior orders and the related concept of manifest illegality have not yet been tested in this forum.

APPLYING THE PLEA OF SUPERIOR ORDERS AT THE ICC: RECONCILING MORALITY AND LEGALITY

Inclusion of the plea of superior orders in the *Rome Statute* is a positive development that recognizes the legitimate restrictions placed on (and generally accepted by[59]) individual soldiers serving in military hierarchies. However, as this part demonstrates, the ICC must be encouraged to develop and apply this doctrine in a nuanced manner that truly reflects and promotes the ongoing individual moral responsibility of these soldiers. In many circumstances, this understanding should mean continuing to limit the application of this doctrine to the potential mitigation of a sentence following conviction. While Article 33 of the *Rome Statute* has rightly established its availability as a full defence, the practical and moral implications of the plea of superior orders cannot adequately be captured by accepting or rejecting it *solely* on this basis.

REJECTION OF DEFENCE FOR MANIFESTLY ILLEGAL ACTS

In cases involving the commission of manifestly illegal acts, the ICC should necessarily reject the defence of superior orders outright,

---

[57] Eg, as discussed in note 21, such a position did not prevent Alfred Jodl (chief of the operation staff of the high command of the German armed forces) from arguing obedience to superior orders in the context of crimes against peace, albeit unsuccessfully.

[58] Furthermore, art 8*bis*(1) establishes that the crime of aggression applies only to "an act of aggression which, by its character, gravity and scale, constitutes a manifest violation of the Charter of the United Nations." Review Conference of the Rome Statute, *supra* note 54. In at least some circumstances, it may be reasonable to equate reference to a "manifest violation of the Charter" with "manifest illegality" (although the former refers to *jus ad bellum* considerations while the latter has, instead, to this point, addressed gross violations of *jus in bello*).

[59] Moral and legal differences, if any, between applying the plea of superior orders to volunteer soldiers and to conscripts are beyond the scope of this article.

whether or not such conduct is subjectively known by the soldier to be unlawful. This approach is generally consistent with the legal precedents outlined earlier and is, in any event, expressly required by the *Rome Statute*. It is nevertheless appropriate for the ICC to adopt a high standard for assessing manifest illegality to ensure that the potential defence of superior orders is precluded in only the most egregious cases.

The concept of manifest illegality raises challenging moral questions. It introduces an objective element into the examination of superior orders in a context where the denial of the plea will likely lead to labelling as a war criminal.[60] On this basis, a soldier will be denied the defence because she "should have known" that her conduct was wrong regardless of whether she had any actual knowledge of wrongdoing (though at least some of the historical cases noted earlier maintained an element of subjectivity in this test).[61]

Given the focus of international criminal law on acts frequently involving mass atrocities, the incorporation of meta-ethical principles into this area is not surprising. As such, the application of this objective component will in many instances be uncontroversial. For example, there are few who would balk at denying this defence to those involved in the use of machine guns against the helpless crew of the hospital ship *Llandovery Castle*, as they attempted to gain the safety of lifeboats, for the purpose of concealing an earlier crime. The same can likely be said with respect to genocide, crimes against humanity, and aggression (at least as these crimes are defined in the *Rome Statute*).[62]

With respect to certain war crimes, however, precluding the defence of superior orders solely on the basis of objective factors may

---

[60] *Smith, supra* note 24 at 567-68, recognized the objective nature of the concept of manifest illegality and its application in cases where an accused "must or ought to have known that they were unlawful." The defence would not be necessary if the individual in question had not committed an otherwise criminal act.

[61] Eg, an element of subjectivity was maintained by the USMT in the *Einsatzgruppen* case, *supra* note 12 at 666, which focused on execution of a criminal order by a soldier "with malice of his own." Similarly, the Leipzig Court decision in the *Llandovery Castle, supra* note 28 at 722 [emphasis added], addressed conduct "universally known to everybody, *including the accused*, to be without any doubt whatever against the law."

[62] Eg, genocide requires specific intent to destroy an identified group, in whole or in part, while a crime against humanity requires widespread or systematic conduct directed specifically against an identifiable group. See, respectively, *Rome Statute, supra* note 1, Arts. 6, 7. For discussion of aggression, see notes 54-58 in this article and related text.

be more problematic given the nature of these offences. In contrast to genocide and crimes against humanity, war crimes are often somewhat technical and specific and relate to the actual conduct of hostilities in addition to the treatment of non-combatants.[63] The scope of this problem will depend in large part on the nature of the test applied by the ICC to determine manifest illegality and the extent to which the court is willing to address war crimes that are not large scale or policy based. The more inclusive the standard of manifest illegality applied (that is, the greater the number of situations in which the defence of superior orders is rejected on objective grounds), the greater the concerns that will arise.

The standards adopted by the Supreme Court of Canada in *Finta*[64] or the District Military Court of Israel in *Ofer*[65] incorporate an extremely high bar that precludes findings of manifest illegality in all but the most flagrant of circumstances. Such a high standard for manifest illegality is nonetheless justifiable even though it will more frequently support the potential acceptance of a defence of superior orders.[66] This result is especially warranted in light of the often dire ramifications of obedience to entirely legal commands. Unpalatable and potentially disastrous consequences for innocent third parties

---

[63] See, eg, *Rome Statute, supra* note 1, art 8, in particular, conduct of hostilities crimes such as: "[e]xtensive destruction and appropriation of property, not justified by military necessity and carried out unlawfully and wantonly" (art 8(2)(a)(iv)); or "[d]estroying or seizing the enemy's property unless such destruction or seizure be imperatively demanded by the necessities of war" (art 8(2)(b)(xiii), international conflict, and art 8(2)(e)(xii), non-international conflict). See, eg, related discussion in Osiel, *supra* note 15 at 151.

[64] *Finta, supra* note 4. Subsequent legislation in Canada has restricted the domestic precedential value of *Finta*, among other things, by further broadening the circumstances in which the plea of superior orders will be denied to an accused. See, eg, discussion in note 75 in this article.

[65] *Ofer, supra* note 44.

[66] Here one must remember that a successful defence of superior orders may relieve the individual soldier of criminal responsibility, but it does not (necessarily) lead to impunity for the acts in question. Individual criminal liability will — or, at least should — arise for persons further up the chain of command that ordered, or were otherwise responsible for, the commission of the crimes in question. However, see Paust, *supra* note 15 at 227-28, who maintains that the Supreme Court of Canada "set improper thresholds" with the judgment in *Finta*. See also Cassese, *supra* note 20 at 241, who argues that, in general, "the [International Criminal] Court should begin from the assumption that an order to engage in such violations [that is, war crimes] is by definition 'manifestly unlawful'" (on the basis of his (controversial) assertion that art 33 is inconsistent with prior existing customary law).

do not necessarily provide an effective or accurate benchmark for measuring the morality or legality of conduct in wartime, even though such measurements generally do fulfil such a function with respect to peacetime civilian actions.[67] For example, in an armed conflict, a necessary attack on an otherwise lawful military target is not rendered unlawful simply because there was a harmful impact on civilians or civilian infrastructure, so long as feasible precautions were taken to avoid this collateral effect and the civilian harm anticipated from the attack was not excessive in light of the military advantage expected from it.[68] Put simply, the death of (potentially high numbers of) innocent civilians is not necessarily an indication that an attack is unlawful. In practice, apart from the most severe circumstances, it may be extremely difficult for military personnel, particularly low-ranking soldiers, to distinguish accurately between internationally lawful and unlawful conduct during actual armed conflict.[69]

ACCEPTING SUPERIOR ORDERS AS A DEFENCE

Nonetheless, a full defence should not apply automatically once the existence of superior orders and the absence of manifest illegality are established. Clearly, the ICC is required to reject a defence of superior orders if the criteria in Article 33 are not met (that is, if there was no legal duty to obey or if there was subjective knowledge of illegality or manifest illegality). However, it is not expressly required always to accept the defence in the event that they are.[70] Indeed, there are substantial grounds militating against the automatic application of superior orders as a defence in all such cases.

Rather, the defence of superior orders should properly be considered by the ICC as a specialized form of mistake-of-law defence.[71]

---

[67] See, eg, related discussion in Osiel, *supra* note 15 at 114, 118.

[68] See, eg, *Protocol Additional to the Geneva Conventions of 12 August 1949, and Relating to the Protection of Victims of International Armed Conflicts*, 8 June 1977, 1125 UNTS 3, 16 ILM 1391 (1977) (entered into force 7 December 1979), art 51 [*Additional Protocol I*].

[69] See, eg, related discussion in Osiel, *supra* note 15 at 64-65, 92-93, 135. To these issues, one must add the often difficult task of assessing reasonable conduct through the fog of war (that is, with incomplete information in a dynamic and hostile environment).

[70] Art 33 provides only that superior orders "shall not relieve ... criminal responsibility unless" these factors are met. *Rome Statute*, supra note 1.

[71] See, eg, Cryer et al., *supra* note 21 at 418, 420. The existence of superior orders may also be a relevant factor in a mistake of fact argument. Eg, a soldier may be

This more limited reading appears consistent with Article 32(2) of the *Rome Statute:*

A mistake of law as to whether a particular type of conduct is a crime within the jurisdiction of the Court shall not be a ground for excluding criminal responsibility. *A mistake of law may, however, be a ground for excluding criminal responsibility if it negates the mental element required by such a crime, or as provided for in article 33.*[72]

When applying the defence of superior orders recognized by Article 33, the mistake of law in question therefore need not have actually negated the mental element required by the crime.[73] However, the burden of proof to demonstrate such a mistake should

---

misinformed by a superior concerning the factual nature of a target in the course of being ordered to attack it. See, eg, related discussion in Osiel, *supra* note 15 at 49-50, concerning an order to attack a protected cultural building on the mistaken basis that it is being used to store ammunition (which would have eliminated its protection). See also Dinstein, *supra* note 3 at 83-87. Mistake of fact may be accepted as a defence before the ICC "only if it negates the mental element required by the crime." *Rome Statute, supra* note 1, art 32. See also Lippman, *supra* note 18 at 209, for a discussion of the successful invocation of superior orders in defence of mistake of fact in national trials following the Second World War.

[72] *Rome Statute, supra* note 1, art 33(2) [emphasis added]. The use of "may" (rather than "shall") further supports arguments that the criteria in art 33 need not automatically establish a valid defence of superior orders in all cases. While Cryer et al, *supra* note 21 at 415, argue against this permissive reading of "may," they do so only with respect to general mistakes of law on the ground that mistakes negate *mens rea* and therefore necessarily found a legitimate defence. However, this argument does not apply to the defence of superior orders.

[73] See, eg, Cryer et al., *supra* note 21. This also appears consistent with judicial treatment of the plea of superior orders. See, eg, the findings of the USMT in the *Hostages* case, *supra* note 36 and related text. However, see Dinstein, *supra* note 3 at 76, 87-88 (advocating treatment of superior orders as a circumstantial factor in a mistake of law defence relying on negation of the requisite *mens rea*). Cassese, *supra* note 20 at 238-39, also interprets the USMT decision in the *High Command* case as establishing a defence of "lack of *mens rea* due to uncertainty of law." However, the specific passage cited in support of this assertion suggests instead that the issue for the USMT was not a general mistake of law establishing lack of *mens rea* but, rather, a mistake founded on the existence of superior orders and a valid *presumption* of legality in this context. With respect to a charge of unlawfully using prisoners for construction of fortifications, the USMT in the *High Command* case found the accused not responsible on the basis that the orders requiring them to do this "were not criminal upon their face, but a matter which a field commander *had the right to assume was properly determined by the legal authorities upon higher levels*" (cited Cassese, *supra* note 20 at 238-39 [emphasis added]).

nonetheless remain with the accused, and it should not be met simply by establishing the existence of superior orders.

Even if Article 33 is taken to establish a basis for automatic application of the defence of superior orders once its three conditions are met, it nonetheless remains open to the ICC to limit its application through the interpretation of these requirements (particularly the absence of subjective knowledge of illegality).[74] Indeed, failure to impose any further interpretive restrictions on this provision could, among other things, problematically render wilful blindness a legitimate basis for a lack of subjective knowledge of illegality. Instead, in order to justify acceptance of superior orders as a full defence to charges involving conduct that is illegal, but not manifestly so, there is a strong argument that a soldier should be able to demonstrate that he did all that he could reasonably be expected to do to seek clarification and raise concerns regarding questionable orders or that he had an honest (albeit obviously mistaken) belief in the legality of the orders from the outset. In other words, the accused soldier should be able to demonstrate that his mistake of law was *reasonable*.[75]

---

[74] Eg, Zimmermann, *supra* note 30 at 967, argues that, as an exception to the general rule against acceptance of superior orders as a defence, the requirements of art 33 must be "interpreted narrowly."

[75] Canada's domestic implementation of the *Rome Statute* lends support to such a reading. Section 14(1) of the *Crimes against Humanity and War Crimes Act*, SC 2000, c 24, establishes that the plea of superior orders "is not a defence ... unless" these three requirements are met and expressly provides in s 14(2) that "orders to commit genocide or crimes against humanity are manifestly unlawful." Although it thus generally incorporates the language of the *Rome Statute* concerning superior orders, the act then places further significant restrictions on the application of this defence in Canadian courts by providing in s 14(3) that "[a]n accused cannot base their defence under subsection (1) on a belief that an order was lawful if the belief was based on information about a civilian population or an identifiable group of persons that encouraged, was likely to encourage or attempted to justify the commission of inhumane acts or omissions against the population or group." Unlike s 14(2), relating to crimes against humanity and genocide, this provision does not characterize such a belief as "manifestly unlawful." Instead, s 14(3) appears to address the reasonableness of the absence of subjective knowledge of illegality. In the alternative, it establishes a fourth substantive requirement for the application of the defence of superior orders. In either case, this provision therefore places limits on the defence of superior orders beyond those expressly established by the *Rome Statute*. Eg, an accused may act on a belief concerning an "identifiable group of persons" yet not commit a crime against humanity (which requires widespread or systematic conduct directed specifically against that group) or an act of genocide (which requires specific intent to destroy the identified group in whole or in part).

Reasonableness in specific cases must necessarily be qualified in light of the rank of the soldier and the circumstances of conflict ruling at the time. For example, a low-ranking soldier directly engaged in ongoing combat is clearly not in the same position to assess or seek clarification of superior orders as is a junior officer involved in deliberative operational targeting decisions in a military headquarters.[76] In this context, it must be stressed that the soldier is operating under a reasonable mistake of international law. As outlined earlier, applicable domestic law is generally clear — obey in the absence of manifest illegality, following initial clarification of questionable orders.[77] For the individual soldier, it is not a case of weighting military considerations over legal obligations.[78] Instead, it is about being placed in circumstances involving conflicting legal duties where the domestic obligation is both known and clear and the international obligation is, by definition, neither.

As a result, there is a strong argument that the existence of superior orders establishes a different foundation for a defence of mistake of law than applies absent a formal hierarchical relationship.[79] Although domestic law is not generally a valid justification

[76] See, eg, related discussion in Osiel, *supra* note 15 at 289. Cryer et al., *supra* note 20 at 419, argue instead that such variations (eg, in rank, training, occupation, and experience) may support the application of "different standards" of manifest illegality when assessing the plea of superior orders. However, these variable factors are arguably better applied in an assessment of subjective knowledge of illegality rather than in the application of an objective standard.

[77] In many cases, there may also be a conflict between the known domestic obligation (that is, obey in the absence of manifest illegality) and other domestic obligations that remain unclear (eg, whether the conduct in question constitutes a war crime under domestic legislation).

[78] Osiel, *supra* note 15, characterizes the situation in precisely this manner and downplays the actual legal dilemma faced by soldiers (and thus more easily supports arguments for greater accountability). See also similar arguments in Cassese, *supra* note 20 at 231; Cryer et al, *supra* note 21 at 415-16. Though Osiel, *supra* note 15 at 94, recognizes that soldiers may be faced with conflicting legal duties, this is discussed in relation to the substantive content of the law governing specific conduct rather than the general obligation of obedience to orders itself. In contrast, this may be an accurate characterization of the choice made by states that establish and uphold domestic legal obligations of obedience and corresponding presumptions of legality. However, it should be noted that this is a very widespread state practice that may support the existence of a customary international law exception to this general presumption applicable to states themselves (that is, supporting the international legality of establishing domestic obligations of obedience and presumptions of legality).

[79] For the reasons outlined in the preceding paragraph, this article therefore disagrees with the contention by Dinstein, *supra* note 3 at 36, 76-77, 87-88, that

for breach of an international legal obligation, the defence of superior orders is a case where the international law in question has specifically established an exception to this general presumption, which is applicable to individual soldiers. Whether or not it results from a formal domestic obligation to do so, asking for clarification of a questionable order should not, and would not appear to, rise to the level of subjective *knowledge* of international illegality.[80]

Here, it is important to note that (apart from cases of manifest unlawfulness) soldiers engaged in armed conflict are unlikely actually to possess accurate, subjective knowledge of the international legal status of their actions outside of assessments provided through their chain of command. International humanitarian law — the law of armed conflict — is a complex body of law, and specific legal determinations require expertise beyond the training of most individual soldiers. In many cases, such assessments also require access to information that is restricted for security reasons and consideration of factors extending well beyond the immediate tactical environment. For example, the characterization of a conflict as either international or non-international will have a significant impact on the applicable international law, yet such a determination generally cannot be made solely at the tactical level on the basis of information available to an ordinary soldier. Although the *Rome Statute* has reduced the impact of this distinction, it has not eliminated it (nor have recent revisions resulting from the 2010 review conference). In Article 8, war crimes remain separately — and differently — delineated in each context.[81]

The very existence of this continued distinction supports arguments that at least some war crimes are not manifestly unlawful

---

there should be no distinction between the plea of superior orders and other arguments based on mistakes of law that do not rest on legally mandated obedience and presumptions of legality.

80 Eg, the *CF Code of Conduct, supra* note 14 at A-41, instructs soldiers that in cases of subjective doubt, the "first step of course must be to seek clarification." Despite encouraging clarification, there remains a clear presumption in favour of obedience. The *Code of Conduct* further establishes that "if after doing so the order still seems to be questionable you should obey the order — unless — the order is manifestly unlawful."

81 Eg, "making improper use of the military insignia and uniform of the enemy ... resulting in death or serious personal injury" is criminalized only in the context of international armed conflicts. *Rome Statute, supra* note 1, art 8(2)(b)(vii). See also related discussion in Osiel, *supra* note 15 at 64, 104-5.

(particularly when coupled with the absence of such a characterization in the *Rome Statute* itself). The doctrine of belligerent reprisal also poses a serious challenge for such an automatic characterization.[82] The assertion that all internationally proscribed war crimes are manifestly unlawful nonetheless underpins substantial criticism of Article 33.[83] Indeed, some commentators have implied that, regardless of any historical uncertainty, the very codification of war crimes in the *Rome Statute* (along with the subsequent enumeration of their elements) should itself lead to this result.[84] If accepted, this argument would render Article 33 essentially meaningless.[85]

Soldiers are (generally) not lawyers, and they should not be expected to act as such when assessing their orders. Nor should they

[82] In limited circumstances, the doctrine of reprisal permits the commission of certain types of otherwise unlawful acts during armed conflict — particularly those not directed against civilians — as a mechanism to compel an enemy to resume compliance with the laws of war. See, eg, discussion of this doctrine in Henckaerts and Doswald-Beck(*Rules*), *supra* note 18 at 513-29. Indeed, not all states even accept an absolute legal prohibition on reprisals against civilians themselves (see, eg, at 520-23). For an example of historical discussion of this doctrine in the context of the defence of superior orders, see *Dover Castle, supra* note 27 and related text (though modern international humanitarian law now establishes clearer prohibitions concerning reprisal against medical vessels (as outlined, eg, in Henckaerts and Doswald-Beck(*Rules*), *supra* note 18 at 524)). For an interesting, albeit controversial, discussion of this doctrine, particularly its modern content and potential application to the campaign against terrorism, see Mark Osiel, *The End of Reciprocity: Terror, Torture and the Law of War* (Cambridge: Cambridge University Press, 2009).

[83] See, in particular, Gaeta, *supra* note 20 at 190-91. Eg, Gaeta argues that "[i]t should not be difficult for the Court to hold that orders to commit any of the crimes enumerated in Article 8 are always manifestly illegal and consequently can never provide a defence for subordinates"(at 191). See also Cassese, *supra* note 20 at 82.

[84] See, eg, Cassese, *supra* note 20 at 241. As a result, he argues that "at present any serviceman is expected and required to *know* whether the act he is about to commit falls under the category of war crimes and must be aware of whether or not the execution of a superior order involves the commission of such a crime" (*ibid* [emphasis in original]). Gaeta, *supra* note 20 at 190, also makes a similar argument based on reference in the *Rome Statute* preamble to "the most serious crimes of concern to the international community as a whole."

[85] Though Cassese, *supra* note 20 at 241, himself notes that one may continue to be "faced with the exceptional or rare occurrence that the substantive law on the matter (that is, a particular provision of the ICC Statute) is unclear and the agent may usefully plead the defence of mistake of law."

be encouraged to do so in the absence of specialized legal knowledge and training.[86] In fact, it is usually not feasible for individual soldiers at the tactical level even to seek legal advice prior to compliance with their orders. Nor is it appropriate for the ICC to encourage the unworkable belief that such action is required. However, most states have a formal obligation to make legal advice available to their military commanders, where necessary, and also to provide relevant training in international humanitarian law to the members of their armed forces.[87] Being informed of such advice, whether specifically or through general military training — and acting consistently with it — should provide a solid basis for application of the defence of superior orders (assuming, of course, that such advice does not itself advocate manifestly unlawful actions).[88]

[86] The USMT in the *High Command* case expressly noted that soldiers should not be equated with lawyers. See, eg, discussion in Dinstein, *supra* note 3 at 185. See also the statement of the judge advocate in the *Peleus* trial, before a British military court in Germany, that "[i]t is quite obvious that no sailor and no soldier can carry with him a library of International Law, or have immediate access to a professor in that subject who can tell him whether or not a particular command is a lawful one." *Trial of Kapitanleutenant Heinz Eck and Four Others for the Killing of Members of the Crew of the Greek Steamship Peleus, Sunk on the High Seas (Peleus Trial)*, Judgment 1 (17-20 October 1945) (British Military Court for the Trial of War Criminals Held at the War Crimes Court, Hamburg), cited in *Law Reports of Trials of War Criminals: Selected and Prepared by the United Nations War Crimes Commission* (London: His Majesty's Stationery Office, 1947), volume 11 at 12.

[87] *Additional Protocol I, supra* note 68, art 82, establishes that states "shall ensure that legal advisers are available, when necessary, to advise military commanders at the appropriate level on the application of the [Geneva] Conventions and this Protocol and on the appropriate instruction to be given to the armed forces on this subject." Art 83 establishes a corresponding obligation to include the study of international humanitarian law (specifically, the 1949 *Geneva Conventions* and *Additional Protocol I*) in military training. As Osiel, *supra* note 15 at 345, notes in *Obeying Orders*, "[t]he presence of legal counsel inevitably raises the standard of care required of commanders, in assessing the reasonableness of their errors after the fact." Similarly, he submits that reasonable reliance on such advice should make acquittal easier (at 346).

[88] Obviously, this places a corresponding and substantial moral — and arguably legal — burden on military lawyers. See, eg, Osiel, *supra* note 15 at 346-47, for a brief discussion of this issue. While the extent of this obligation is beyond the scope of this article, it is clearly an issue that deserves more detailed assessment. Dinstein, eg, *supra* note 3 at 167, argues that this consideration should also extend to reliance on the legal opinions offered by non-military lawyers. Indeed, he argues that this would be more justified than reliance on the orders of

As a result, the more comprehensive the legal and practical training provided to soldiers, the less viable a plea of superior orders becomes. It is through such training that the plea of superior orders can and should be restricted rather than attempting to limit its application to individual soldiers where it remains factually and legally justified.[89] In other circumstances, there is certainly a reasonable argument that establishing an honest belief in the legality of orders should generally require the actual testimony of the accused soldier herself (despite the seemingly contrary conclusion of the Supreme Court of Canada in *Finta*).[90] Otherwise, considerable moral hazard will arise from accepting the plea of superior orders as a full defence. In the absence of such testimony, the defence of superior orders could remain available regardless of whether the soldier ever turned her mind to the morality or legality of the act or its consequences for third parties, as long as there was an order requiring the conduct in question and there was no external evidence supporting her subjective knowledge of illegality.

A full defence based on superior orders should only be available to soldiers who are able to demonstrate more than the mere existence of superior orders that are not manifestly unlawful. They should also be required to establish their continued engagement as individual moral actors when assessing the orders. In addition to individuals who have sought clarification regarding questionable orders, this standard will also encompass individuals who have not

---

superiors who are likely not themselves legal experts. The modern obligation to provide legal advice to military commanders may mitigate this latter concern. In any event, the obligation to obey superiors does not generally extend to persons outside of the military chain of command, however knowledgeable they may be, nor is it limited by reference to such outside opinions. The existence of such an opinion may nonetheless be relevant both to the reasonableness of compliance with orders without seeking prior clarification and to a general defence of mistake of law in the event of non-compliance.

[89] Eg, the judge advocate in the *Calley* prosecution, *supra* note 42 at 542 and related text, argued before the court that, "[i]n determining whether or not Lt. Calley had knowledge of the unlawfulness of any order ... you may consider all relevant facts and circumstances, including Lt. Calley's rank, *educational background, OCS [Officer Candidate School] schooling, other training while in the Army, including Basic Training, and his training in Hawaii and Vietnam,* his experience on prior operations involving contact with hostile and friendly Vietnamese, his age, and any other evidence tending to prove or disprove that [at the time], Lt. Calley knew the order was unlawful"[emphasis added].

[90] *Finta, supra* note 4. See, eg, related arguments in Osiel, *supra* note 15 at 292.

voiced concerns due to an honest but mistaken belief that the order was not questionable in the first place (that is, in its legality).[91] Without requiring this additional element, treating superior orders as a full defence could actually *encourage* soldiers to act as automatons, blindly accepting the validity of their orders, by rewarding absolute obedience unless the conduct in question surpasses the extremely high threshold of manifest illegality.[92]

SUPERIOR ORDERS AND THE MITIGATION OF SENTENCE

In many circumstances, consideration of superior orders in the mitigation of sentence is a more appropriate response to the moral and practical nuances of this doctrine than its acceptance as a full defence. This approach provides a mechanism for reducing the potentially unreasonable impact of assigning full individual criminal responsibility in specific cases while preventing the absolute exoneration of illegal conduct based on total and unquestioning obedience of orders. Absolving individuals who have committed *prima facie* war crimes is not (necessarily) in their own best interests — let alone those of society as a whole — particularly when they have unquestionably accepted the illegal orders that led to this result.[93]

---

[91] As Osiel, *supra* note 15 at 136, n 27, recognizes, "[t]here would, of course, remain the question of whether the defendant is telling the truth regarding his professed belief in the legality of the orders he received from his superiors."

[92] Nonetheless, this will involve a lower threshold than that proposed by Osiel, *supra* note 15 at 325, who advocates a general presumption against compliance with unlawful orders with a corresponding defence arising from a reasonable belief in their legality. He argues that "[t]he soldier would no longer be expected to resolve any and all doubts about the legality of superior orders in favor of obeying them" (at 288). In contrast, recognizing the continued existence of mandatory presumptions of order legality, this article suggests only that for the full defence to apply soldiers must either make reasonable efforts to seek clarification of questionable orders or demonstrate that their failure to do so was itself reasonable.

[93] See Stephen P Garvey, "Punishment as Atonement" (1999) 46 UCLA L Rev 1801, for an analysis of the need for both punishment and atonement following the commission of a criminal act. For individuals who do obey immoral commands, significant feelings of responsibility and remorse may arise when they are finally removed from the hierarchy in question. See, eg, Stanley Milgram, *Obedience to Authority: An Experimental View* (New York: Harper and Row, 1974) at 164. In contrast to absolute acquittal, punishment and atonement may provide a method to overcome this result, allowing for the full and effective reintegration of the individual into society.

The defence of superior orders is not available to a soldier who knew that his conduct was illegal, whether it was manifestly so or not. In so far as this principle prevents the application of this defence to a conscious and deliberate wrongdoer who willingly defies the laws of war, it is not controversial. In essence, in these circumstances, the criminal act in question has not arisen as a result of the issuance of orders but, rather, from the criminal preference of the accused. In some respects, the order may thus be viewed as the initiation of a criminal conspiracy rather than as the imposition of a duty on an otherwise unwilling actor. In such a case, there is no reason for consideration of superior orders in mitigation of sentence either.

However, rejection of the defence of superior orders on the basis of subjective knowledge of wrongdoing may also arise in circumstances where a soldier did not otherwise actually desire to act contrary to the law, with vastly different consequences. It is certainly possible that a soldier may know her conduct to be wrong at the time and feel remorseful after the fact, yet be unwilling to make the difficult and costly decision to disobey the orders of her commanding officer. The potential that such a situation could arise is not surprising given the clear presumption in favour of obedience in the structure and training of armed forces and the severe penalties applicable in the event of insubordination.[94]

Although still deserving of punishment, it may be that such a morally weak individual, who has knowingly committed war crimes under orders, should be treated less harshly following conviction than her wilful and malicious counterpart.[95] Still different considerations will apply to individuals who deliberately avoid any self-

---

[94] This is particularly true in times of armed conflict. Failure to obey orders immediately and without question may at times result in serious threats to the soldier's comrades or to national security. However, knowing compliance with illegal orders for these reasons is not an example of moral weakness but, rather, the adoption of a different moral standard by the soldier, in which less weight is given to compliance with the laws of war than to these other considerations.

[95] For the reasons outlined earlier, questioning and outright refusal of orders by soldiers is difficult. This is compounded by a seemingly natural human inclination to obey when placed in hierarchical relationships as exemplified in experiments conducted by Stanley Milgram in the early 1970s. Milgram, *supra* note 93 at 131, suggests that overcoming individualism is necessary for any hierarchy to function, arguing that "[b]ecause people are not all alike, in order to derive the benefit of hierarchical structuring, readily effected suppression of local control is needed at the point of entering the hierarchy, so that the least efficient unit does not determine the operation of the system as a whole." Profound attitudinal shifts may result from such a hierarchical relationship, leading to a situation

examination at all beyond conformity with orders, whether due to amorality, negligence, or indifference. In all such cases, applying the plea of superior orders in the (potential) mitigation of sentence rather than as a defence will allow for appropriate societal condemnation of the criminal actions in question, while retaining the possibility of moderating individual sanctions to reflect actual moral blameworthiness.[96]

In order to reflect these distinctions properly, however, it is important that subjective knowledge of illegality or objective manifest illegality not *automatically* preclude acceptance of the plea of superior orders as a mitigating factor in sentencing. While the *Rome Statute* requires rejection of superior orders as a full defence in such cases, it is silent with respect to its use as a mitigating factor following conviction.[97]

---

where "the person entering an authority system no longer views himself as acting out of his own purposes but rather comes to see himself as an agent for executing the wishes of another person. Once an individual conceives his action in this light, profound alterations occur in his behavior and his internal functioning. These are so pronounced that one may say that this altered attitude places the individual in a different *state* from the one he was in prior to integration into the hierarchy" (at 133 [emphasis in original]).Even absent any pronounced outside coercion or lawful authority, these experiments highlighted the disturbing ease with which a "substantial proportion" of otherwise normal individuals would inflict pain at the behest of a superior, even one with very little actual power (at 189). This phenomenon was recently illustrated by a similar experiment conducted for a French television documentary. "Contestants Turn Torturers in French TV Experiment: Four of Five Players in Fake Game Show Willingly 'Shocked' Man to 'Death,'" *Ottawa Citizen* (17 March 2010) A7. See discussion of Milgram experiments and their relevance to the plea of superior orders for military personnel in Green, *National and International Law, supra* note 18 at 256-61.

96 Although Milgram, *supra* note 93 at 164, noted that disobedience was difficult, it was not impossible, and not all experimental subjects obeyed the immoral commands of their superiors. However, he observed that "[t]he price of disobedience is a gnawing sense that one has been faithless. Even though he has chosen the morally correct action, the subject remains troubled by the disruption of the social order he brought about, and cannot fully dispel the feeling that he deserted a cause to which he had pledged support. It is he, and not the obedient subject, who experiences the burden of his action." Avoiding uncritical acceptance of superior orders as a defence may serve, in part, to reallocate this burden, shifting it to those morally responsible for the commission of criminal acts (along with potential individual criminal responsibility for issuing the order in question and through the doctrine of command responsibility).

97 Indeed, art 76 specifically requires that the ICC consider evidence or submissions that are "relevant to the sentence," whether presented at trial or on further hearing. *Rome Statute, supra* note 1, art 76.

SUPERIOR ORDERS AND DURESS

When assessing claims of superior orders, whether as a defence or a factor in mitigation of sentence, "moral choice" is not always the most appropriate test to apply, despite some earlier case law to this effect.[98] The plea of superior orders should not necessarily require that a soldier have acted against his own inclinations and due to the threat of punishment (though such inclinations or threats are clearly relevant to any such claim). While this motivation may be the case, an honest belief of legality — whether from the outset or after seeking clarification of an order — should itself also be sufficient to support such a plea. Although national and international judicial decisions often appear to confuse and comingle these concepts, superior orders should simply not be equated with duress.[99]

Underlying the plea of superior orders is a valid hierarchical relationship based on legal obligations and justifiable professional and practical expectations of military obedience.[100] This legitimate foundation is not the case with duress, which instead suggests the temporary existence of undue and illegitimate influence. While the two doctrines have much in common, superior orders would serve no positive purpose if it simply constituted "duress in uniform."

In the event that the ICC rejects a plea of superior orders, a separate claim of duress may instead remain open to a soldier accused of war crimes or other international criminal offences. Duress is also accepted as a full defence in the *Rome Statute*, although its consideration as such is expressly limited to circumstances involving the threat of "imminent death" or "continuing or imminent bodily harm" to the accused or a third party.[101] An additional proportionality

---

98 Reference to moral choice largely involved situations of manifest illegality where the underlying issue was not superior orders but duress based on illegitimate coercion. This reference arguably permitted post-Second World War tribunals to consider superior orders in the context of a defence despite the formal prohibition on doing so in their founding authority.

99 See, eg, post-Second World War decisions incorporating the concept of "moral choice" and the opinion of the ICTY in *Erdemovic, supra* note 49.

100 This type of relationship has nevertheless been characterized by at least one defendant as acting "on the orders of his superiors and under hierarchical duress." *Prosecutor v Goran Jelisic,* Judgment IT-95-10-T (14 December 1999) at para 12 (ITCY).

101 *Rome Statute, supra* note 1, art 31(1)(d). This defence is in theory available with respect to all crimes within the ICC's effective jurisdiction, although the

requirement has also been maintained in the contemporary inter-national law conception of duress.[102] This balancing requirement reflects the USMT conclusion in the *Einsatzgruppen* case that "[i]f one claims duress in the execution of an illegal order it must be shown that the harm caused by obeying the illegal order is not disproportionately greater than the harm which would result from not obeying the illegal order."[103]

Recent judicial treatment of duress nonetheless clearly demon-strates its potential application in a military context. In *Prosecutor v Drazen Erdemovic*, the ICTY was faced with a defendant soldier who admitted killing dozens of innocent civilians in the 1995 Srebrenica massacre.[104] In uncontested evidence, Erdemovic submitted that he would have been killed, alongside the victims, had he not par-ticipated in the slaughter as ordered. He initially refused to follow this order, submitting only when faced with the stark choice of either lining up with the victims or with their executioners.

While upholding the validity of considering duress in mitigation of punishment in these circumstances, the ICTY rejected its applica-tion as a full defence on the ground that the case involved killing innocent third parties.[105] In the tribunal's majority view, such a defence was not supported by international law and could never be justified on moral grounds.[106] While highlighting the practical

---

majority opinion in *Erdemovic, supra* note 49, will severely constrain its applica-tion in practice, given that these crimes often — if not usually — involve the killing of innocents.

[102] See *Erdemovic, supra* note 49, and related discussion later in this article. As a result, it appears difficult, if not impossible, to support such a claim when the soldier in question faced nothing more than a prison sentence for disobedience.

[103] *Einsatzgruppen* case, *supra* note 12 at 666.

[104] *Erdemovic, supra* note 49.

[105] Unlike superior orders, the ICTY was permitted to accept duress as a full defence.

[106] See, eg, *Erdemovic, supra* note 49 (joint separate opinion of McDonald J. and Vohrah J. at para. 75; and separate and dissenting opinion of Li J. at para. 12). The majority decision accepted a Kantian view of moral responsibility where punishment should always result from the killing of innocents, even when re-sulting from duress involving threats to the life of the soldier. This view appears consistent with Garvey's, *supra* note 93, arguments concerning punishment and atonement. However, in a strongly argued dissent, Stephen J. recognized the rationality of Erdemovic's choice under the circumstances given that his victims were going to be killed whether or not he participated in the massacre. The only question was whether Erdemovic would die as well (*Erdemovic, supra* note 49 (separate and dissenting opinion of Stephen J. at para. 54)).

distinction between superior orders and duress (albeit not explicitly), *Erdemovic* also clearly illustrates that a plea that is rejected as a full defence may nonetheless still be considered in mitigation of the resulting sentence.

CONCLUSION

Morality, like law, is not rendered irrelevant with the outbreak of armed conflict. In undertaking one of the first efforts to codify the laws of war in 1863, Franz Lieber recognized that "[m]en who take up arms against one another in public war do not cease on this account to be moral beings, responsible to one another and to God."[107] Nonetheless, the horrific nature of war and the existence of obligatory command structures render individual morality in the context of armed conflict significantly different in appearance and content from its peacetime counterpart. War, by its very nature, involves conduct that, if committed in peacetime, would be both immoral and criminal.

The laws of war recognize this distinction, providing immunity for lawful combatants who kill or commit other violent acts in accordance with the accepted international rules of wartime conduct.[108] Similarly, the *Rome Statute* rightly recognizes that the legitimate obedience owed by soldiers may, in some circumstances, reduce or even negate their responsibility for otherwise illegal acts committed pursuant to superior orders. However, such orders should not *necessarily* serve as a basis for the complete absolution of individual soldiers in such situations. Instead, they should do so only where the individual has operated under a reasonable, albeit mistaken, belief in their legality. In other cases, they may still provide a potential basis for mitigation of sentence following conviction.

---

[107] *Instructions for the Government of the Armies of the United States in the Field,* Prepared by Francis Lieber, promulgated as General Orders no. 100 by President Lincoln (24 April 1863), art 15, cited in Dietrich Schindler and Jiri Toman, eds, *The Laws of Armed Conflicts: A Collection of Conventions, Resolutions and Other Documents* (Leiden, The Netherlands: Martinus Nijhoff, 1988) at 6.

[108] See, eg, *Additional Protocol I, supra* note 68, art 43(2) (recognizing "the right to participate directly in hostilities" for members of the armed forces). There is no express combatant immunity in internal armed conflict, although there is an obligation for states to consider the widest possible amnesty. *Protocol Additional to the Geneva Conventions of 12 August 1949, and Relating to the Protection of Victims of International Armed Conflict,* 8 June 1977, 1125 UNTS 609, 16 ILM 1442 (1977) (in force 7 December 1978), art 6(5).

Considering superior orders is clearly justified when determining appropriate sanctions for the wartime conduct of soldiers (particularly in light of potential superior or state liability). In doing so, however, the ICC must be careful to encourage, rather than discourage, individual moral autonomy to the extent possible. Especially on the modern battlefield, soldiers must continue to act and be judged as "reasoning agents" and not as mere automatons.

Sommaire

Obéissance restreinte: l'application du plaidoyer d'ordre hiérarchique aux accusés militaires devant la Cour pénale internationale

Cet article porte sur le contenu et les enjeux du plaidoyer particulier d'ordre hiérarchique, illustrant la complexité d'absoudre sur cette base le comportement en temps de conflit armé ainsi que la justification à le faire dans certains cas. L'article traite de l'obligation juridique générale pour les soldats d'obéir aux ordres; présente l'évolution historique et le contenu juridique du plaidoyer relié d'ordre hiérarchique, y compris son incorporation dans le Statut de Rome de la Cour pénale internationale (CPI); et évalue l'éventuelle application par la CPI de cette doctrine spécialisée d'"erreur de droit." L'auteur soutient qu'à la lumière de ses enjeux moraux et pratiques, la Cour devrait le qualifier et de moyen de défense et de facteur pouvant atténuer la peine, d'une manière qui diffère conceptuellement du plaidoyer de la contrainte. Cependant, l'auteur avertit que la CPI doit être prudent afin d'encourager, plutôt que décourager, dans la mesure du possible, l'autonomie morale individuelle. Un soldat ne doit pouvoir se prévaloir d'ordre hiérarchique comme moyen de défense que si il ou elle était d'avis raisonnable quoiqu'erronée que l'ordre en question était licite. Surtout sur le champ de bataille moderne, les soldats doivent continuer à agir et à être jugés comme des "agents rationnels" et non comme de simples automates.

Summary

Obeying Restraints: Applying the Plea of Superior Orders to Military Defendants before the International Criminal Court

This article addresses the content and ramifications of the unique plea of superior orders, illustrating the complexities of absolving wartime behaviour on this basis as well as the legitimate rationale for doing so in certain cases.

The article discusses the general legal obligation for soldiers to obey commands; outlines the historical development and legal content of the corresponding plea of superior orders, including its incorporation into the Rome Statute of the International Criminal Court *(ICC); and assesses the potential future application by the ICC of this specialized "mistake of law" doctrine. The author argues that in light of its moral and practical ramifications it should be considered by the court as both a full defence and a factor in mitigation of sentence, in a manner conceptually distinct from duress. However, the author cautions that the ICC must be careful to encourage, rather than discourage, individual moral autonomy, to the extent possible. A full defence should remain open to soldiers only when they have acted under a reasonable albeit mistaken belief in the legality of their orders. Especially on the modern battlefield, soldiers must continue to act and be judged as "reasoning agents" and not as mere automatons.*

The Rogue Civil Airliner
and International Human Rights Law:
An Argument for a Proportionality
of Effects Analysis within the Right to Life

ROBIN F. HOLMAN

INTRODUCTION

B y now, it has become trite to state that the terrorist attacks of
11 September 2001 (9/11) had a paradigm-shifting effect on
the approaches taken by states to aviation security, to national defence, and to law enforcement. In their efforts to prevent similar
attacks by rogue civil aircraft — that is, civil aircraft under the effective control of one or more individuals who apparently intend
to use the aircraft as a weapon against persons and/or property on
the surface — the responses of states have been as varied as their
respective national legal traditions and political histories. State
members of the International Civil Aviation Organization (ICAO)
have collectively implemented stricter security standards for international flights and agreed to extend measures relating to the unlawful interference with international civil aviation to domestic civil
aviation operations "to the extent practicable."[1] Aviation security

---

Robin F. Holman is a legal officer in the Office of the Judge Advocate General for
the Canadian Forces. The author is grateful to René Provost, who supervised the
thesis upon which this article is based, who was involved in a number of lengthy
discussions of the ideas contained therein, and who provided helpful suggestions
regarding its content. The views expressed in this article are the author's alone.
They do not necessarily reflect, nor should they be taken to reflect, the views of the
Government of Canada, the Department of National Defence, the Canadian Forces,
or the Office of the Judge Advocate General.

1 See *Convention on International Civil Aviation*, 7 December 1944, 15 UNTS 295,
Can TS 1944 No 36 (entered into force 4 April 1947) [*Chicago Convention*];
International Civil Aviation Organization (ICAO), *Security: Safeguarding International Civil Aviation against Acts of Unlawful Interference, Annex 17 to the Convention
on International Civil Aviation*, 8th edition (entered into force 1 July 2006), in
particular, para 2.2.2 [*Annex 17 to the Chicago Convention*].

worldwide has taken on a multi-faceted, layered, "defence-in-depth" approach by incorporating such elements as "no fly" lists, more stringent physical security screening, the installation of armoured cockpit doors, and the placement of armed, undercover "air marshals" on some commercial flights.[2] States have also agreed upon amendments to existing international instruments that seek to deter (through state assertion of criminal jurisdiction) unlawful interference with civil aviation. Such amendments will require ratifying states parties to criminalize the use of "an aircraft in service for the purpose of causing death, serious bodily injury, or serious damage to property or the environment."[3]

Still, while the likelihood of, and risks posed by, a rogue civil aircraft incident can be mitigated through active security measures and, perhaps, through the deterrent effect of after-the-fact criminal measures, these responses, which are consistent with a paradigmatic "law enforcement" approach, are not capable of eliminating the risks entirely. Thus, as a last resort, to prevent attacks by rogue civil aircraft against targets on the surface, a number of states have implemented, either through legislation or under the authority of executive prerogative, procedures under which officials may, under particular circumstances (not all of which have been made public), authorize military personnel to shoot down rogue civil aircraft.[4]

---

[2] See, eg, US Department of Homeland Security, *National Strategy for Aviation Security* (Washington, DC: Department of Homeland Security, 2007) at 16, 18-20, online: Department of Homeland Security <http://www.dhs.gov/xlibrary/assets/laws_hspd_aviation_security.pdf>. More generally, see *Annex 17 to the Chicago Convention, supra* note 1.

[3] *Convention on the Suppression of Unlawful Acts Relating to International Civil Aviation,* 10 September 2010, art 1(f) [not yet in force] [*Beijing Convention*]. As noted at art 24, this convention is intended to supersede, as between states parties, the *Convention for the Suppression of Unlawful Acts against the Safety of Civil Aviation,* 23 September 1971, 974 UNTS 178, Can TS 1973 No 3 (entered into force 26 January 1973), as amended by the *Protocol for the Suppression of Unlawful Acts of Violence at Airports Serving International Civil Aviation, Supplementary to the Convention of 23 September 1971,* 24 February 1988, 1589 UNTS 474, 27 ILM 627.

[4] In North America, Canadian and American fighter aircraft controlled by NORAD are permanently on alert to intercept and, under particular (and classified) circumstances, shoot down rogue civil aircraft. See Ian MacLeod, "Canada's 'Unthinkable Protocol' for Shooting Down a Hostile Airliner, *Ottawa Citizen* (10 July 2011), online: Ottawa Citizen <http://www.ottawacitizen.com/news/Canada+unthinkable+protocol+shooting+down+hostile+airliner/5079275/story.html>; Craig Mellow, "Don't Cross That Line," *Air and Space Magazine* (1 March 2010), online: Air and Space Magazine <http://www.airspacemag.com/flight-today/dont-cross-that-line.html>; Rebecca Grant, *The War of 9/11: How the*

The possibility that some of these circumstances might properly be characterized as armed attacks or as associated with armed conflict — such that the *lex specialis* of international humanitarian law (IHL) would regulate the state's use of force in response — is beyond question. Less clear, but legally more interesting, is the international law framework governing state responses to circumstances that do not fall within the armed attack/armed conflict paradigm but constitute a mere criminal act.

This article examines the obligations of states under international human rights law (IHRL) to respect and ensure the rights of persons subject to their jurisdiction not to be arbitrarily deprived of life. It does so in the specific context of possible state responses to a particular combination of circumstances, a subset of the problem posed by rogue civil aircraft, which I will call the "rogue civil airliner problem." These circumstances are:

- the rogue civil aircraft is airborne;
- in addition to the person or persons who are effectively in control of it, the rogue civil aircraft also carries innocent persons[5] — that is, passengers and crew who are not involved in any plan to use the aircraft as a weapon and who are presumed to be unable to influence the conduct of the persons effectively in control;[6]

World Conflict Transformed America's Air and Space Weapon (Arlington, VA: Air Force Association, 2005) at 19-20. For a fairly forthcoming description of the process followed in the United Kingdom in respect of rogue civil aircraft, see Richard Norton-Taylor, "RAF Jets Scrambled after Two Passenger Plane Terrorist Alerts," *The Guardian* (29 March 2010), online: Guardian Unlimited <http://www.guardian.co.uk/uk/2010/mar/29/raf-jets-scrambled-terrorist-alerts>.

5   I use the term innocent to denote persons who "have done nothing, and are doing nothing that entails the loss of their rights." See Michael Walzer, *Just and Unjust Wars*, 4th edition (New York: Basic Books, 1977) at 146.

6   It is this circumstance — the presence of innocent persons on board — that, for the purposes of my analysis, most defines the a rogue civil airliner subset. This distinction between rogue civil aircraft and rogue civil airliner is based upon a similar one drawn in the recently published Program on Humanitarian Policy and Conflict Research at Harvard University, *Commentary on the Humanitarian Policy and Conflict Research Manual on International Law Applicable to Air and Missile Warfare*, version 2.1 (March 2010), online: Program on Humanitarian Policy and Conflict Research <http://ihlresearch.org/amw/Commentary%20on%20the%20HPCR%20Manual.pdf> [*Harvard Manual*]. The intention of the distinction is to emphasize that aircraft carrying innocent ("civilian") passengers are to be treated with "particular care in terms of precautions" (see rules 1(h) and 1(i)).

- the incident is a crime, albeit one of potentially significant proportion, and occurs in a pure "law enforcement" context such that the only relevant international law framework engaged is IHRL; and
- the state possesses the capability to destroy the rogue civil airliner either immediately or, at least, in a timely manner — before the persons effectively in control are able to successfully perfect their attack.

Taken to the most extreme case, where attempts to use less forceful measures to deter the attack have been exhausted or are no longer practicable, the rogue civil airliner problem presents the state (and the officials authorized to make and carry out decisions on the state's behalf) with a dilemma: either use deadly force to shoot down the aircraft or refrain from such use of force. A decision to shoot down the aircraft will protect persons and property on the surface from both the direct and indirect effects of the use of the aircraft as a weapon. The costs of these positive effects, however, are the negative effects caused or contributed to by the state's actions — the destruction of the airliner and its cargo and, most significantly, the likely deaths of everyone aboard it, including its innocent passengers and crew. Conversely, a decision to refrain from the use of force will have the positive effect of preserving (for at least some period of time) the airliner, its cargo, and the lives of all persons on board. Yet this effect will come at the cost of allowing the persons effectively in control of the airliner to carry out their intended acts, possibly (and in the most extreme case, certainly) resulting in the deaths not only of all those on board the aircraft but also in deaths and injuries among innocent persons on the surface along with direct or indirect destruction and damage to property.

I argue that IHRL's existing approach to the right to life fails to provide a satisfactory analytical framework for considering the legal aspects of the rogue civil airliner problem — one that is principled, effective, and in line with the rule of law and human rights.[7] A more

---

[7] This definition of what constitutes a satisfactory framework for legal analysis is based upon a formulation employed by Kai Möller in discussing legal challenges posed by the threat of terrorism. See Kai Möller, "On Treating Persons as Ends: The German Aviation Security Act, Human Dignity, and the German Federal Constitutional Court" (2006) 51 PL 457 at 465. Nils Melzer uses a similar definition of satisfactory — namely that the normative standards under discussion "meet the demands of both operational reality and humanity in that they entail

satisfactory framework — one that more completely accounts for the moral, political, and legal complexities of the problem — is provided by adding a norm requiring proportionality of positive to negative effects. Such a norm would be analogous to those that have been developed within the frameworks of IHL and modern constitutional rights law as well as by some schools of moral philosophy, to address what would otherwise be irreconcilable state duties arising from irreconcilable rights claims. This proposed norm of proportionality of effects would supplement — not replace — the existing IHRL normative framework only in specific circumstances: where all of the options available to the state may be expected inevitably to cause or to contribute to innocent persons being deprived of life — circumstances such as those of the rogue civil airliner problem. I argue that, under such circumstances, incidental deaths of innocent persons that are consistent with existing IHRL norms and that also display a proportionality of effects should not be considered to be arbitrary deprivations of life. Given the social reality following the 9/11 attacks — that (at least some) states appear willing, under particular circumstances and as a final resort, to consider shooting down a rogue civil aircraft, even a rogue civil airliner carrying innocent persons — a proportionality of effects norm would provide states with an additional tool of legal analysis in addressing a morally, politically, and legally complex dilemma.

ANALYSIS

Before launching into my analysis, I will provide a brief exposition of some additional assumptions I have made in order to isolate the essential elements of the rogue civil airliner problem. First, I recognize that Article 3*bis* of the *Convention on International Civil Aviation* (*Chicago Convention*)[8] provides that (subject to the rights and obligations set forth in the *Charter of the United Nations*)[9] "every State must refrain from resorting to the use of weapons against civil aircraft in

---

neither unreasonable restraints for the operating States nor unacceptable risks for the individuals exposed to their authority or power." Nils Melzer, *Targeted Killing in International Law* (Oxford: Oxford University Press, 2008) at 82; see also at 431.

8   *Chicago Convention, supra* note 1; *Protocol Relating to an Amendment to the Convention on International Civil Aviation*, 10 May 1984, 2122 UNTS 337, 23 ILM 7045 (entered into force 1 October 1998) [Article 3*bis*].

9   *Charter of the United Nations*, 26 June 1945, Can TS 1945 No 7 [*UN Charter*].

flight and that, in case of interception, the lives of persons on board and the safety of aircraft must not be endangered." However, for present purposes, I also accept the view that Article 3*bis* does not preclude a state's use of weapons for law enforcement purposes, at least within its own sovereign airspace, against a civil aircraft on its own registry.[10] Second, while recognizing that any practical analysis of a particular rogue civil airliner incident must account for uncertainties regarding, *inter alia*, the intent of those effectively in control of the aircraft and its possible targets, I assume for the purposes of this article the most extreme case — that a failure of the state to shoot down the rogue civil airliner will result in its striking its target on the surface, causing significant death and destruction.

THE RIGHT TO LIFE IN IHRL

Notwithstanding the modern prominence of human rights discourses, international law dealing with human rights is a product of relatively recent times, first finding common expression in the years immediately following the adoption of the *Charter of the United Nations*[11] and the end of the Second World War.[12] The extensive and ever-expanding collection of international instruments — binding treaties and non-binding declarations, codes of conduct, guidelines, and the like (some of which have become a settled basis for the practice of states) — represents an attempt to create a normative structure that captures values shared across societies and cultures.

The nature of state duties under IHRL instruments differs from the nature of the duties under most international treaties, which are generally limited to the direct performance of reciprocal obligations between two or more states. While the obligations set out in

---

[10] Michael Milde, who was the director of the ICAO Legal Bureau at the time of its adoption, argues that Article 3*bis*, *supra* note 8, was intended to limit states' use of weapons only in respect of aircraft registered in other states. See Michael Milde, "Interception of Civil Aircraft versus Misuse of Civil Aviation" (1986) 11 Ann Air & Sp L 105 at 126. See also Robin Geiß, "Civil Aircraft as Weapons of Large-Scale Destruction: Countermeasures, Article 3*bis* of the Chicago Convention, and the Newly Adopted German 'Luftsicherheitsgesetz'" (2005) 27:1 Mich J Int'l L 227 at 250-51.

[11] *UN Charter, supra* note 9.

[12] René Provost, *International Human Rights and Humanitarian Law* (Cambridge: Cambridge University Press, 2002) at 201; David Kretzmer, "Rethinking the Application of IHL in Non-International Armed Conflicts" (2009) 42:1 Israel LR 8 at 9-10.

IHRL instruments are also undertaken in agreements among states, the performance of these obligations is internal to each state, taking place in the context of the relationship between the state and the persons who are subject to its jurisdiction. The state's obligation to its fellow states parties is to "respect and ensure," *vis-à-vis* those persons subject to its jurisdiction, the rights set out in the instruments.[13] The obligation may be broader still. Obligations derived from the "principles and rules concerning the basic rights of the human person" have been cited by the International Court of Justice as examples of obligations *erga omnes* — that is, obligations that a state owes to the international community as a whole and not simply reciprocally to other state parties.[14]

The right to life is seen by many (but not all) scholars as being pre-eminent among human rights. As Yoram Dinstein notes, "[w]hen life is deprived, it is impossible to enjoy any fundamental freedom."[15] The right to life, however — even in the eyes of those who rank it above all other rights — is not an absolute right, and its existence does not impose unlimited duties upon the state. Again in the words of Dinstein, it is "in effect, the right to be safeguarded against (arbitrary) killing."[16]

[13] See, eg, *International Covenant on Civil and Political Rights*, 19 December 1966, 999 UNTS 171, art 2(1), Can TS 1976 No 47 (entered into force 23 March 1976) [*ICCPR*]; *Convention for the Protection of Human Rights and Fundamental Freedoms*, 4 November 1950, 213 UNTS 221, art 1, Eur TS 5 (entered into force 3 September 1953) [*ECHR*].

[14] *Barcelona Traction, Light and Power Company, Limited (Belgium v Spain)*, [1970] ICJ Rep 3 at paras 33-34.

[15] See, eg, Yoram Dinstein, "Terrorism as an International Crime" (1987) 19 Israel YB on Human Rights 55 at 63, quoted in Kenneth Watkin, "Assessing Proportionality: Moral Complexity and Legal Rules" (2005) 8 YB Int'l Human L 3 at 14. This view of the pre-eminence of the right is also shared by the United Nations Human Rights Committee, which calls the right to life "the supreme right." See *General Comment No 6: Article 6 (The Right to Life)*, UN Human Rights Committee, 16th Sess, (1982) in *Compilation of General Comments and General Recommendations Adopted by Human Rights Treaty Bodies*, UN Doc HRI/GEN/1/Rev.1, (1994) at 128. See, cf, Saskia Hufnagel, "German Perspectives on the Right to Life and Human Dignity in the 'War on Terror'" (2008) 32 Criminal LJ 100 at 101: "Human rights lawyers typically disclaim any hierarchy of rights."

[16] Yoram Dinstein, "The Right to Life, Physical Integrity and Liberty" in Louis Henkin, ed, *The International Bill of Human Rights: The Covenant on Civil and Political Rights* (New York: Columbia University Press, 1981) 114 at 115, quoted in BG Ramcharan, "The Concept and Dimensions of the Right to Life," in BG Ramcharan, ed, *The Right to Life in International Law* (Dordrecht: Martinus Nijhoff Publishers, 1985) 1 at 4.

Different international human rights instruments define individual rights and state duties in respect of human life in different ways. For the purposes of the present analysis, I will focus upon the formulation of the right to life as it appears in the most widely accepted IHRL instrument, the *International Covenant on Civil and Political Rights (ICCPR)*.[17] It provides that every person has the right not to be *arbitrarily* deprived of life[18] and imposes a correlative obligation upon state parties to respect that right and to ensure that persons subject to their jurisdiction are not arbitrarily deprived of their lives.[19] Similar protections against arbitrary deprivation of life appear in the *American Convention on Human Rights*,[20] the *African Charter on Human and Peoples' Rights*,[21] and the League of Arab States' *Revised Arab Charter on Human Rights*.[22] While the European *Convention for the Protection of Human Rights and Fundamental Freedoms (ECHR)*, which predates the *ICCPR*, contains a different formulation that sets out an exhaustive list of permitted limitations to the right to life,[23] the Grand Chamber of the European Court of Human Rights (ECtHR) has, on at least one occasion, implied that these limitations would constitute at least a subset of non-arbitrary deprivations of life, speaking of the *ECHR* as providing "a general legal prohibition of arbitrary killing by agents of the State."[24]

17 *ICCPR, supra* note 13. As of 27 September 2011, the Covenant has 167 states parties. See United Nations Treaty Collection, online: <http://treaties.un.org/Pages/ViewDetails.aspx?src=TREATY&mtdsg_no=IV-4&chapter=4&lang=en>.

18 *ICCPR, supra* note 13, art 6(1) [emphasis added]: "Every human being has the right to life ... No one shall be arbitrarily deprived of his life."

19 *Ibid*, art 2(1): "Each State Party ... undertakes to respect and ensure to all individuals within its territory and subject to its jurisdiction the rights recognized in the present Covenant."

20 *American Convention on Human Rights,* 22 November 1969, 1144 UNTS 123, art 4(1), OAS TS No 36, 9 ILM 99 (1969) (entered into force 18 July 1978).

21 *African Charter on Human and Peoples' Rights,* 27 June 1981, 1520 UNTS 217, art 4, 21 ILM 58 (1981) (entered into force 21 October 1986).

22 See *Arab Charter on Human Rights,* 22 May 2004, art 5(2), reprinted in (2005) 12 Int'l Human Rights Rep 893 (entered into force 15 March 2008).

23 *ECHR, supra* note 13, art 2(2): "Deprivation of life shall not be regarded as inflicted in contravention of this article when it results from the use of force which is no more than absolutely necessary:
a. in defence of any person from unlawful violence;
b. in order to effect a lawful arrest or to prevent the escape of a person lawfully detained;
c. in action lawfully taken for the purpose of quelling a riot or insurrection."

24 See *McCann and Others v United Kingdom* (1995), 324 ECHR (Ser A) 4 at para 161, 21 EHRR 97 [*McCann and Others,* cited to ECHR], where the court, in

The use of the term "arbitrary" in defining the scope of individual protection and state duty has been criticized for lacking precise legal meaning. It seems clear from the *travaux préparatoires* to the *ICCPR*, however, that the drafters' much-debated choice to adopt the term was intended, first, to reflect a realistic approach to the right to life by recognizing that there do exist circumstances under which the taking of life by the state may be justified and, second, to ensure sufficient flexibility so that the content of the right to life (and exceptions and limitations to it) could be developed over time without the constraint of a fixed enumeration of specific exceptions that would necessarily be incomplete.[25] The obligation to respect and ensure the right not to be arbitrarily deprived of life imposes two different types of duties upon the state, both of which are relevant to the rogue civil airliner problem. These are generally called negative duties and positive duties, and, respectively, they enjoin the state from acting or from omitting to act in certain ways.

Negative duties "require states not to interfere in the exercise of rights"— that is, to refrain from particular acts.[26] Violation of these duties comes about as a result of state action. Thus, the state's negative duty in respect of the right to life is to refrain from acts that would arbitrarily deprive a human being subject to its jurisdiction of life.

Positive duties, on the other hand, require states to take positive actions ("reasonable and suitable measures") to protect the rights of the individual.[27] Positive duties are not unlimited. States must

finding that the right to life imposes a positive obligation upon states to conduct an effective official investigation into deaths caused by the State's use of lethal force, noted that in the absence of such a requirement, "a general legal prohibition of arbitrary killing by the agents of the State would be ineffective."

[25] BG Ramcharan, "The Drafting History of Article 6 of the International Covenant on Civil and Political Rights," in Ramcharan, *supra* note 16, 42 at 43, 51-52. As CK Boyle points out, the negotiators of the *ICCPR* appear to have arrived at the concept of an arbitrary deprivation of life as a compromise, with the expectation that its substantive content would emerge from future jurisprudence, soft law developments and state practice: "No reading of the *travaux* [*préparatoires*] of Article 6 of the Covenant could possibly conclude that there was any consensus as to the meaning of arbitrary or as to its appropriateness in that Article." CK Boyle, "The Concept of Arbitrary Deprivation of Life," in Ramcharan, *supra* note 16, 221 at 225.

[26] Jean-Francois Akandji-Kombe, *Positive Obligations under the European Convention on Human Rights: A Guide to the Implementation of the European Convention on Human Rights* (Strasbourg: Council of Europe, 2007) at 5; Daniel D Nsereko "Arbitrary Deprivation of Life: Controls on Permissible Deprivations" in Ramcharan, *supra* note 16, 245 at 246.

[27] Akandji-Kombe, *supra* note 26 at 7, 11.

"exercise due diligence to prevent, punish, investigate or redress the harm caused by ... acts by private persons or entities" that would impair individual rights.[28] Violation of positive duties is brought about by state inaction (or an omission to act). Thus, the state's positive duties in respect of the right to life include an obligation to take practical "preventative operational measures" to prevent persons subject to its jurisdiction from attacking the physical integrity or taking the life of another individual where there is a real and immediate threat to that individual of which the state is aware or ought to be aware.[29] Positive human rights duties underlie many of the specific duties of state officials in the law enforcement context — a fact recognized in the considerable body of IHRL surrounding state uses of force (including deadly force) in the context of law enforcement operations.

NORMS PROVIDING FOR NON-ARBITRARY DEPRIVATION OF LIFE

Scholarly and judicial analysis of IHRL in relation to state uses of deadly force in a law enforcement (that is, non-armed conflict) context has tended to assume a narrow paradigm case — that of individual state law enforcement personnel defending themselves or others by using deadly force against one or more individuals who pose a grave and imminent threat of death or serious bodily injury through violence. Analysis has been, for the most part, silent on the human rights implications of using force that causes foreseeable and incidental (as opposed to accidental) injury or death to innocent persons who do not pose a threat.

This assumption of the paradigm case is reflected in the IHRL framework that governs state uses of deadly force in a purely law enforcement context, which includes a series of commonly held requirements for a state deprivation of life to be considered not arbitrary. This framework applies to all state law enforcement authorities, including military personnel employed in a law enforcement,

---

28 *General Comment no 31: Nature of the General Legal Obligation on States Parties to the Covenant*, UN Human Rights Committee, 80th Sess, UN Doc CCPR/C/21/Rev.1/Add.13 (2004) at para 8 [*General Comment no 31*].

29 Gloria Gaggioli and Robert Kolb, "A Right to Life in Armed Conflicts?: The Contribution of the European Court of Human Rights" (2007) 37 Israel YB on Human Rights 115 at 129; *Osman v United Kingdom* (1998), 95 ECHR (Ser A) 3124 at para 115ff, 29 EHRR 245. See also Philip Alston, *Interim Report on the Worldwide Situation in Regard to Extrajudicial, Summary or Arbitrary Executions*, UNGAOR, 61st Sess, UN Doc A/61/311 (2006) at para 37.

or assistance to a law enforcement, role.[30] In its broad strokes, this framework has received near universal acceptance among states, judicial authorities, and scholars.

To be non-arbitrary, any limitation of the right to life must "be regarded as an extraordinary exception that requires special justification."[31] However, the very acceptance in IHRL of a formulation of the right to life that allows for state deprivations that are not "arbitrary" reflects a recognition that extraordinary exceptions can and do exist — that "[t]he individual's right to life cannot ... be considered in isolation. It must be considered together with the rights of the rest of the members of the community."[32] The substantive content of what comprises an IHRL-permitted, non-arbitrary deprivation of life is found in a variety of sources. Much follows from the practice of states in accepting and adhering to various "codes of conduct" or "statements of basic principles" developed by groups of experts, either with or without official state involvement. These instruments seek to expand upon and provide substantive content to the deliberately broad formulations incorporated in legally binding instruments such as the *ICCPR*.[33] Other "softer"

---

[30] *Code of Conduct for Law Enforcement Officials*, GA Res 34/169, UNGAOR, 34th Sess, UN Doc A/34/169 (1979), commentary to art 1, paras (a) and (b).

[31] Kretzmer, *supra* note 12 at 24.

[32] Nsereko, *supra* note 26 at 246.

[33] The norms are drawn, to a considerable degree, from the *Code of Conduct for Law Enforcement Officials*, *supra* note 30, and from the *Basic Principles on the Use of Force and Firearms by Law Enforcement Officials*, 8th UN Congress on the Prevention of Crime and Treatment of Offenders, UN Doc A/CONF.144/28/Rev.1 (1990). Alston points out that their value lies in the fact that these documents were "developed through intensive dialogue between law enforcement experts and human rights experts" and that the "process of their development and adoption involved a very large number of States and provides an indication of the near universal consensus on their content." See Alston, *supra* note 29 at para 35. More broadly, the norms are also consistent with the *Siracusa Principles on the Limitation and Derogation of Provisions in the International Covenant on Civil and Political Rights*, ECOSOC, 41st Sess, UN Doc E/CN.4/1984/4 (1984) [*Siracusa Principles*], see particularly arts 5, 10, and 11, and with the approach to limitations captured within the term "arbitrary" in the context of other protected rights that are similarly not subject to an internal limitation clause. See, for instance, *Toonen v Australia*, UN Human Rights Committee, 50th Sess, UN Doc CCPR/C/50/D/488/1992 (1994). The committee opined that in order to not be arbitrary, "any interference with privacy [as protected by art 17 of the Covenant] must be proportional to the end sought and be necessary in the circumstances of any given case" (at paras 8.3-8.6).

sources of relevant IHRL comprise such diverse elements as reports and comments of supervisory bodies and special rapporteurs, those portions of internationally developed codes of conduct and guidelines that have not crystallized into customary IHRL, scholarly analyses, and judicial decisions that have persuasive value outside of the *espace juridique* of the issuing tribunal.

A review of existing IHRL reveals the following generally accepted norms with respect to state uses of deadly force in a law enforcement context. They provide indicia of circumstances where the state is relieved at international law of the negative duty not to deprive a human being of life — situations where, in the eyes of IHRL, the positive duty to protect the lives of other persons outweighs the duty not to take life. Deaths resulting from state uses of deadly force in a law enforcement context that do not comply with these norms will generally be considered to be arbitrary deprivations of life. As will become clear, different international law sources organize and express the norms in different terms. Thus, the norms summarized in the following sections are all interrelated and overlapping.

Authorized by Law

Consistent with the rule of law, there exists a general requirement that the use of deadly force by the state be authorized according to the law of that state.[34] It cannot be, to use a commonly held lay definition of arbitrariness, "based on ... random choice; capricious."[35] A discussion of the various forms that such authorization can take[36] or the procedural and substantive requirements it must meet[37] is beyond the scope of the present analysis.

---

[34] Gaggioli and Kolb, *supra* note 29 at 134; Melzer, *supra* note 7 at 100; Boyle, *supra* note 25 at 239.

[35] *Concise Oxford Dictionary of Current English*, 9th edition (Oxford: Oxford University Press, 1995), *sub verbo* "arbitrary."

[36] Depending upon the constitutional framework of the state concerned, the form of such authorization can include: primary legislation enacted by a legislative body; secondary legislation enacted by the executive pursuant to authority granted in primary legislation or a constitutional document; exercises of discretionary authority granted in legislation; or authority derived from constitutionally permitted exercises of residual executive (or "Crown") prerogative powers.

[37] See, for instance, Nsereko, *supra* note 26 at 248, positing that a law authorizing a deprivation of life must not, *inter alia*, be "despotic, tyrannical and in conflict with international human rights standards or international humanitarian law."

Triggered by Positive Duties to Protect

As discussed earlier, IHRL imposes upon the state positive duties to protect the lives of persons subject to its jurisdiction against the threat of grave and imminent violence.[38] Building upon the idea that providing for common security is one of the bases for the state's very existence,[39] the obligation to protect individual human beings can be extended and generalized to a broader obligation (or, indeed, a right against other states) to protect persons subject to the state's jurisdiction from threats to "law and order"[40] or to "the security of all."[41] Some care is required, however. While IHRL recognizes that the duty to protect security constitutes a component of the positive duty to protect life,[42] the term "security," like the term "terrorism," is one that brings with it both theoretical uncertainties and considerable emotional baggage. One must avoid allowing the use of broad terms such as "security" to cloud our understanding of the substance of state duties in respect of the individual's right to life in a purely law enforcement context. These duties are not significantly different in the context of a "terrorist" threat to "security"

---

[38] *Code of Conduct for Law Enforcement Officials, supra* note 30, arts 1, 3 (see also commentary to art 3, para a).

[39] See, eg, Kimmo Nuotio, "Security and Criminal Law: The Difficult Relationship," in Martin Scheinin et al, eds, *Law and Security: Facing the Dilemmas,* Working Paper (Florence: European University Institute Department of Law, 2009-11) 23 at 23, online: Social Sciences Research Network <http://papers.ssrn.com/sol3/Delivery.cfm/SSRN_ID1555686_code97794.pdf?abstractid=1555686&mirid=1>; Lucas Lixinski, "The Rights/Security Debate in the Inter-American System," in Scheinin et al., 97 at 97.

[40] Melzer, *supra* note 7 at 101.

[41] Inter-American Commission on Human Rights, *Report on Terrorism and Human Rights,* Doc OEA/Ser.L/V/II.116/Doc.5 (2002), rev 1, corr, at para 88 [*Report on Terrorism and Human Rights*]. See also *American Convention on Human Rights, supra* note 20, art 32(2), which provides that "[t]he rights of each person are limited by the rights of others, by the security of all, and by the just demands of the general welfare, in a democratic society."

[42] *Permissibility of Shooting Down a Passenger Aircraft in the Event of a Danger That It Has Been Used for Unlawful Acts, and Where State Security Is Threatened,* Case K44/07 (2008) (Constitutional Tribunal of the Republic of Poland) [*Permissibility of Shooting Down a Passenger Aircraft* (English summary)]. Although a complete translation does not exist, an English summary contains excerpts. See Polish Constitutional Tribunal, online: <http://www.trybunal.gov.pl/eng/summaries/documents/K_44_07_GB.pdf> at para 15.

from what they are in "normal" times.[43] Their content must always be considered in the context not of labels but, rather, of particular fact situations. The point to be made here is that it is only in the context of protecting select rights (most particularly the right to life) that state deprivations of life may even be contemplated.[44] The standard of care in fulfilling positive duties is one of "due diligence,"[45] which means that where the state is in an immediate position to fulfil its protective duties it may (provided that all other conditions are met) be permitted (perhaps even obligated) to deprive one or more human beings of life without such deprivation being "arbitrary."[46]

Distinction

One of the foundational concepts in modern IHL, "distinction" is a term that is not commonly associated with IHRL. Nevertheless, state uses of deadly force in a law enforcement context are, in effect, constrained by a similar concept — the requirement to distinguish between persons "who, by their actions, constitute an imminent threat of death or serious injury, or a threat of committing a particularly serious crime involving a grave threat to life and persons who do not present such a threat"[47] as well as the related requirement to "use force only against the former."[48] Unlike IHL, distinction in IHRL is made on the basis not of status (that is, "combatant"

---

[43] Lixinski, *supra* note 39 at 97.

[44] See, eg, *Universal Declaration of Human Rights*, GA Res 217 (III), UNGAOR, 3d Sess, Supp No 13, UN Doc A/810 (1948), art 29(2): "In the exercise of his rights and freedoms, everyone shall be subject only to such limitations as are determined by law solely for the purpose of securing due recognition and respect for the rights and freedoms of others and of meeting the just requirements of morality, public order and the general welfare in a democratic society."

[45] Phillip Alston, *Report on Extrajudicial, Summary or Arbitrary Executions: Addendum: Study on Targeted Killings*, UNHRC, 14th Sess, UN Doc A/HRC/14/24/Add. 6 (2010) at para 33.

[46] Liora Lazarus, "Mapping the Right to Security," in Benjamin J Goold and Liora Lazarus, eds, *Security and Human Rights* (Oxford: Hart, 2007) 325 at 342. See Alston, *supra* note 29 at para 37.

[47] *Report on Terrorism and Human Rights*, *supra* note 41 at para 111.

[48] *Ibid.* See also *Declaration of Minimum Humanitarian Standards*, art 5(1), reprinted in *Report of the Sub-Commission on Prevention of Discrimination and Protection of Minorities on its Forty-Sixth Session*, UNESCOR, 51st Sess, UN Doc E/CN.4/1995/116 (1995) [*Declaration of Minimum Humanitarian Standards*]; *ECHR*, *supra* note 13, art 2; Kretzmer, *supra* note 12 at 24.

versus "civilian") but, rather, on the basis of particular conduct or the imminent threat thereof.[49] The standard of care in distinction is one of reasonableness — a use of deadly force cannot be based upon a mere suspicion that an individual or object poses a threat.[50]

Necessity

The use of deadly force by state law enforcement officials must be necessary on three separate axes: qualitative, quantitative, and temporal.[51] It must be a last resort — that is, "strictly unavoidable"[52] or "strictly necessary"[53] for the state to achieve the purpose of fulfilling its positive duties to protect life (qualitative necessity).[54] That is to say, the use of deadly force is only permitted "if other means remain ineffective or without any promise of achieving the intended [and otherwise permitted] result" (for example, self-defence or the defence of others).[55] The amount of force used must not be more than is "absolutely necessary" to achieve that result (quantitative necessity).[56] Finally, the threat against which deadly force is used must be immediate or imminent (temporal necessity).[57]

[49] Kretzmer, *supra* note 12 at 24, argues against introducing an IHL-like principle of distinction into the law enforcement paradigm, arguing that doing so would defeat the humanitarian purpose that the principle plays in IHL: "[F]orbidding the use of force against some persons ... would by implication be legitimizing use of force against others." This is a valid concern, but it is not one that arises from the conduct-based distinction discussed earlier. It does, however, point to the importance of clarity in the language used to express related but different (indeed, distinct) concepts.

[50] Melzer, *supra* note 7 at 102.

[51] This characterization of necessity is Melzer's, *supra* note 7 at 101.

[52] *Basic Principles on the Use of Force and Firearms by Law Enforcement Officials*, *supra* note 33, art 9. Alston asserts that the substance of art 9 reflects customary international law. Alston, *supra* note 29 at para 35.

[53] *Code of Conduct for Law Enforcement Officials*, *supra* note 20, art 3. Alston asserts that the substance of art 3 reflects customary international law. Alston, *supra* note 29 at para 35.

[54] *Report on Terrorism and Human Rights*, *supra* note 40 at para 88; Gaggioli and Kolb, *supra* note 29 at 136.

[55] *Basic Principles on the Use of Force and Firearms by Law Enforcement Officials*, *supra* note 33, art 4. See also Gaggioli and Kolb, *supra* note 29 at 137.

[56] *Code of Conduct for Law Enforcement Officials*, *supra* note 30, commentary to art 3; *ECHR*, *supra* note 13, art 2(2). See also *Isayeva, Yusupova and Bazayeva v Russia*, Case nos 57947/00, 57948/00, and57949/00 (24 February 2005) (ECtHR) at para 169 [*Isayeva I*]; *Isayeva v Russia*, Case no 57950/00 (24 February 2005) (ECtHR) at para 173 [*Isayeva II*].

[57] Melzer, *supra* note 7 at 101.

Precaution

The state must take all feasible precautions to avoid resorting to deadly force and must, in any event, minimize the amount of force used.[58] Such feasible precautions may include warnings, attempts to arrest, and the use of non-lethal measures.[59] The state must also avoid, and in any event minimize, the amount of damage and injury caused by its use of force.[60] The norm of precaution provides that *all* damage and injury is to be avoided or at least minimized. It is, therefore, neutral on the question to which I will soon turn: whether any non-accidental injury or death may be permitted to persons other than those who constitute the imminent threat. If such "collateral damage" is permitted by existing IHRL, it too must be avoided and in any event minimized.[61]

Proportionality (of Force)

The amount of force used by the state must be proportionate (or, indeed, "strictly proportionate"[62]) to the seriousness of the threat and to the legitimate objective to be achieved.[63] In general, IHRL's approach to limitations of human rights is to balance the negative effects of the limiting measure with the importance of the aim that

---

58 Note that these first two elements of the principle of precaution simply reflect the principles of qualitative and quantitative necessity.

59 Melzer, *supra* note 7 at 102. See also Alston, *supra* note 29 at para 41.

60 *Code of Conduct for Law Enforcement Officials, supra* note 30, art 3; *Basic Principles on the Use of Force and Firearms by Law Enforcement Officials, supra* note 33, arts 4, 5.

61 *Isayeva II, supra* note 56 at para 176; Gaggioli and Kolb, *supra* note 29 at 134.

62 *Isayeva I, supra* note 56 at para 169; *Isayeva II, supra* note 56 at 173. Interestingly, the European Court of Human Rights's (ECtHR) approach shows a strong relationship between the concept of force that is "no more than absolutely necessary" to achieve a legitimate aim and force that is "strictly proportional" to the achievement of the same. The first term appears in art 2(2) of the *ECHR*; the second does not. The court treats "the concept of proportionality as being inherent in the idea of necessity" and, in fact, uses "absolute necessity" and "strict proportionality" interchangeably. See Boyle, *supra* note 25 at 239 and discussion in note 95 and associated text. For an approach that does assert a distinction between necessity and proportionality of force, see Alston, *supra* note 29 at paras 40-44.

63 *Declaration of Minimum Humanitarian Standards, supra* note 48, art 5(2); *Code of Conduct for Law Enforcement Officials, supra* note 30, commentary to art 3 at para b; *Basic Principles on the Use of Force and Firearms by Law Enforcement Officials, supra* note 33, art 5(a); Melzer, *supra* note 7 at 101.

the limitation seeks to achieve. This is the case also with its approach to limitations to the right to life. The norm of proportionality of force deals with the importance of the aim to be achieved by the use of force and "the question of how much force might be permissible" to achieve it.[64] The state may only use deadly force to respond to a threat of the same magnitude — that is, force that may cause death or serious bodily injury.[65]

Effective Investigation

Any use of force by the state that results in any deprivation of life must be thoroughly and effectively investigated.[66] The purpose of such an investigation is to determine whether a deprivation of life complies with the norms set out earlier — that is, to determine whether it was arbitrary or not. It serves the additional purpose of deterring those officials who might otherwise be tempted to subscribe to a less restrictive standard of care in considering the use of deadly force.[67] As the ECtHR has noted, "a general legal prohibition of arbitrary killing by the agents of the State would be ineffective, in practice, if there existed no procedure for reviewing the lawfulness of the use of lethal force by State authorities."[68] The hallmarks of an adequate investigation include: the investigator's formal and practical independence from the persons or organizations being investigated; the possibility that the investigation will lead to effective remedies, including criminal proceedings; the timeliness of the investigation; and the availability of public scrutiny.[69]

---

[64] Alston, *supra* note 29 at para 42.

[65] Leaving aside other potentially legitimate aims for the use of deadly force in a law enforcement context, some scholars argue that the only permissible reason for the state to deprive a person of life is to prevent that person from taking other lives. See Boyle, *supra* note 25 at 241-42 (who, in 1985, saw this standard as *lex ferenda* — a "goal" towards which IHRL should strive to evolve). See also Alston, *supra* note 29 at para 44 (where Alston asserts the standard as *lex lata*).

[66] *Basic Principles on the Use of Force and Firearms by Law Enforcement Officials, supra* note 33, art 22; *General Comment no 31, supra* note 28 at para 6. See also Kretzmer, *supra* note 12 at 26, 36.

[67] See Boyle, *supra* note 25 at 241.

[68] *McCann and Others v United Kingdom, supra* note 24 at para 161.

[69] *Isayeva I, supra* note 56 at paras 208-13; *Isayeva II, supra* note 56 at paras 209-14. See also Amichai Cohen, *Proportionality in Modern Asymmetrical Wars* (Jerusalem: Jerusalem Center for Public Affairs, 2010) at 33, online: Jerusalem Center for Public Affairs <http://www.jcpa.org/text/proportionality.pdf>.

Of the seven norms that I have described, those that will be of most interest going forward are the four whose substantive legal content has an impact upon operational decisions as to whether, and how, the state resorts to the use of deadly force in the law enforcement context: distinction, necessity, precaution, and proportionality of force. It is these IHRL norms that will form the basis for my comparisons with other normative frameworks. Nevertheless, it is important to remain cognizant of the existence and content of the more procedurally oriented norms, since they will continue to be a part of any IHRL legal framework governing the use of deadly force. It is only through the collective operation of all of these norms that IHRL addresses arbitrary deprivations of life.

IHRL's approach to the use of deadly force in law enforcement is notable for its asymmetry. While it fully accounts for negative state duties by strictly constraining the uses of force intended to deprive individuals of life, its approach to positive state duties to protect the right to life actively, particularly when the state is in a position to do so, is incomplete. The IHRL framework governing state uses of deadly force in a law enforcement context clearly defaults to the avoidance or at least the minimization of the use of force. However, while it focuses on circumscribing state uses of deadly force, it pays considerably less attention to the impact of state non-uses of force — that is, situations where violence to innocent persons results from a state decision, despite having an immediate capability to do so, to refrain from the use of force. This approach leaves a normative gap in respect of situations where deaths of innocent persons are inevitable.

COLLATERAL DAMAGE AND IHRL

One cannot help but notice that the commonly accepted set of IHRL norms applicable to state uses of deadly force in the law enforcement context, not to mention the sources from which they are drawn, are silent regarding the possibility of collateral damage, particularly in the form of the deaths of innocent persons that are foreseeable, but incidental, to state uses of deadly force.[70] The

---

[70] For the purposes of the present analysis, the definition of collateral damage is that used by the group of experts who drafted the *Harvard Manual, supra* note 6, rule 1 (l): "'Collateral damage' means incidental loss of civilian life, injury to civilians and damage to civilian objects or other protected objects or a combination thereof, caused by an attack on a lawful target." This definition is derived from language set out in *Protocol Additional to the Geneva Conventions of 12 August*

framework does not indicate or imply that foreseeable incidental innocent deaths may be acceptable. Nor does it indicate or imply that foreseeable incidental civilian deaths would be treated as arbitrary. The best that can be said of the existing framework is that it simply does not account for incidental deaths but leaves a gap that, to the extent that it is filled at all, is filled only with non-binding commentary. Such commentary as exists, however, assumes the paradigm case of law enforcement and is unpersuasive in that it fails to provide a coherent analytical accounting of situations such as the rogue civil airliner problem — situations in which innocent persons will inevitably be deprived of life, regardless of how the state responds.

The Prevailing View: A Categorical "No"

In 2006, the German Federal Constitutional Court struck down as "completely unconstitutional and consequently ... void" provisions of the German *Aviation Security Act* (*Luftsicherheitsgesetz*) that authorized, as a last resort, the shooting down of "renegade" civil aircraft in a "non-warlike" context.[71] One of its bases for doing so was a finding that, to the extent that it authorized the shooting down of an aircraft carrying innocent passengers and crew (whom the court recognized to be "victims of an attack on the security of air traffic"),[72] the impugned provisions were inconsistent with the German Constitution's (the *Basic Law for the Federal Republic of Germany*) protection

---

1949, and Relating to the Protection of Victims of International Armed Conflicts (Protocol I), 8 June 1977, 1125 UNTS 3, arts 51(5)(b), 57(2), Can TS 1991 No 2 (entered into force 7 December 1979) [*Additional Protocol I*].

71 *Dr H v s 14.3 of the Aviation Security Act of 11 January 2005*, [2006] 1 BvR 357/05 at para 153 (German Federal Constitutional Court) [*Dr H*]. An English translation of the complete judgment may be found online: Das Bundesverfassungsgericht <http://www.bundesverfassungsgericht.de/en/decisions/rs20060215 _1bvr035705en.html>. Under the impugned legislation, the resort to shooting down the aircraft was subject to several conditions: the measures had to be necessary; cause the least impairment to individuals and the general public; and not result in a "detriment that is recognisably out of proportion to the aspired success." *Aviation Security Act (Luftsicherheitsgesetz – LuftSiG) of 11 January 2005*, Federal Law Gazette (Bundesgesetzblatt) I at 78, para 14(2). A similar decision by the Polish Supreme Court striking down a similar law has attracted virtually no international attention. See *Permissibility of Shooting Down a Passenger Aircraft* (English summary), *supra* note 42.

72 *Dr H, supra* note 71 at para 116.

of the right to life of the innocent persons on board the aircraft,[73] read in conjunction with its guarantee of human dignity.[74] The decision, which adopts an absolutist approach to human dignity and the right to life but considers only the rights of those persons aboard the aircraft, without carrying out a similar analysis of the rights of those on the surface, has been the subject of considerable academic discussion. Commentators are divided between praising and criticizing the result and the reasoning underlying it.[75] Nils Melzer, in a brief analysis, attempts to extend the German court's constitutional rights conclusions to IHRL, characterizing the case as confirming a "[f]ailed legalization of 'collateral damage.'"[76] This apparent view of the *lex lata* — that foreseeable and incidental deaths of innocent persons are not permitted by IHRL — is supported by a number of eminent scholars of international

---

[73] See *Basic Law for the Federal Republic of Germany*, 23 May 1949, art 2 (Official English translation), online: Deutscher Bundestag <https://www.btg-bestellservice.de/pdf/80201000.pdf>, which provides:

> Every person shall have the right to free development of his personality insofar as he does not violate the rights of others or offend against the constitutional order or the moral law.

> Every person shall have the right to life and physical integrity ... These rights may be interfered with only pursuant to a law.

[74] *Ibid*, art 1 (1): "Human dignity shall be inviolable. To respect and protect it shall be the duty of all state authority." Möller, *supra* note 7 at 458, notes that the official translation of the *Basic Law* may lack nuance. The German word used in this provision, "unantasbar," is more appropriately translated as "untouchable," a term that Möller suggests implies an even stronger degree of protection — that is, one where "any interference will automatically amount to a violation of the right" — than "inviolable."

[75] See, eg, Oliver Lepsius, "Human Dignity and the Downing of Aircraft: The German Federal Constitutional Court Strikes Down a Prominent Anti-Terrorism Provision in the New Air-Transport Security Act" (2006) 7:9 German LJ 761 (praising the decision as "remarkable" and criticizing the act as "pretend[ing] to prevent something which will hardly happen again in this way" (at 775); and Tatjana Hörnle, "Shooting Down a Hijacked Plane: The German Discussion and Beyond" (2009) 3:2 Crim L & Phil 111 (particularly critical of the court's absolutist approach to human dignity). In an earlier article, Hörnle provides a lengthy list of articles approving of the decision. See Tatjana Hörnle, "Hijacked Airplanes: May They Be Shot Down?" (2007) 10:4 New Criminal L Rev 582 at 584, n 7. In contrast, the bulk of the English-language literature (much of it written from the perspective of Anglo-American legal culture) seems to be more critical of the decision. See, eg, Michael Bohlander, "In Extremis: Hijacked Airplanes, 'Collateral Damage' and the Limits of Criminal Law" (2006) Crim L Rev 579 at 589-90.

[76] Melzer, *supra* note 7 at 15.

law. The predominant view appears to be that any death of an innocent person that is foreseeable and yet incidental to an otherwise lawful state use of deadly force in a non-armed conflict/law enforcement context would constitute an arbitrary deprivation of life. Some of the more prominent expressions of this view are described briefly in the text that follows. It is notable that each of these expressions occurs almost as an afterthought, as if the author views the proposition as trite law that does not require further explanation.[77]

Theodor Meron, in a seminal and much cited article, implies that a norm against incidental innocent death exists, pointing out that "despite the growing convergence of various protective trends" one of the significant differences remaining between IHRL and IHL is that, "[u]nlike human rights law, the law of war allows, or at least tolerates, the killing and wounding of human beings not directly participating in armed conflict, such as civilian victims of lawful collateral damage."[78] Similarly, Philip Alston, writing as United Nations special rapporteur on extrajudicial, summary, or arbitrary executions, summarily rejects the possibility that IHRL might accept as lawful any deaths of innocent persons that are incidental to a targeted killing in a law enforcement context: "[K]illing of anyone other than the target (family members or others in the vicinity, for example) would be an arbitrary deprivation of life under human rights law and could result in State responsibility and individual criminal liability."[79] Thomas Smith extends the comparison between

---

[77] Eg, Melzer uses the *Aviation Security Act* case as an example in the introductory portion of his book on targeted killings but does not revisit it (*ibid* at 15-18). Kretzmer, *supra* note 12 at 28, also makes brief use of the outcome of the case to buttress an argument but does not analyze it. Similarly, Lazarus, *supra* note 46 at 343, uses the case to illustrate the limits to positive duties of the state to protect security, but she does not critique it. One might speculate as to whether this scholarship suffers from an availability heuristic — that is, "a mental shortcut by which individuals correlate the probability of an event to their ability to call to mind an example of that event" (see "Responding to Terrorism: Crime, Punishment and War" (2002) 115:4 Harv L Rev 1217 at 1230) — in that the "paradigm" law enforcement case involves small-scale, low-level, tactical policing and extreme cases such as the rogue civil airliner are less available (or at least were in the pre-9/11 era when the existing framework of IHRL was developed). It would, however, require significantly more research (into *travaux préparatoires*, conference proceedings, and so on) to determine whether the heuristic exists and to exclude other possible explanations for IHRL's relative silence on the issue.

[78] Theodor Meron, "The Humanization of Humanitarian Law" (2000) 94:2 AJIL 239 at 240.

[79] Alston, *supra* note 46 at para 86. Note that in the preceding paragraph, Alston also expresses the view that a targeted killing within a state's own territory in a

IHL and IHRL. In pointing out that the relationship between IHL and IHRL is an uneasy one in the best of circumstances, he points specifically to the contrast in their treatment of collateral deaths:

> Where is the common ground between the dignity represented by human rights and the tragedy represented by the "necessary" violence, including collateral violence against civilians, that is sanctioned by the law of war? The utilitarianism of humanitarian law sets it apart from the "absoluteness" of human rights. For military lawyers the central question about the use of force is "Is it worth it?" Can civilian casualties be justified by the military advantage anticipated? Human rights law drives a harder bargain. Certain acts — killing innocent civilians ... — are never worth it; at least that norm is inescapable.[80]

David Kretzmer, in the context of a discussion of the IHL norm of proportionality of effects, argues that IHRL has no parallel doctrine that would allow state authorities to decide to attack "a legitimate target in full knowledge that innocent persons will also be hit."[81] He does suggest one possible exceptional situation where IHRL might permit incidental innocent deaths: "[I]f the innocent persons are those whom the authorities are aiming to protect by attacking the target."[82] He uses as an example incidental deaths of hostages that occur in an attempt to free them.[83] He limits even this exception, however, by distinguishing it from cases where force is used to protect persons other than those innocent persons who may foreseeably be harmed.[84]

The opinion of the International Court of Justice (ICJ) in *Legality of the Threat or Use of Nuclear Weapons* might also be understood as

---

law enforcement context "would be very unlikely to meet human rights law limitations on the use of lethal force."

[80] Thomas W Smith, "Can Human Rights Build a Better War?" (2010) 9:1 J Human Rights 24 at 25. See also Cohen, *supra* note 69 at 14-19, pointing out that some human rights advocates seek to extend this approach even into the armed conflict context.

[81] Kretzmer, *supra* note 12 at 27. This view forms the foundation of a broader argument that international human rights law (IHRL) alone should govern the conduct of non-international armed conflicts since its rejection of collateral damage and of a norm of proportionality of effects would provide greater protection to innocent persons.

[82] *Ibid* at 27, n 52.

[83] *Ibid.*

[84] *Ibid* at 29, n 58.

further authority for the proposition that IHRL does not allow for incidental deaths of innocent persons in a law enforcement context.[85] The ICJ's observation that what constitutes an arbitrary deprivation of life during armed conflict not only cannot be decided by IHRL alone as *lex generalis* but also requires reference to IHL as *lex specialis* implies that IHRL does not generally incorporate such IHL norms as acceptance of incidental deaths of innocent persons, provided there is proportionality of effects. If such a norm existed within IHRL as *lex generalis*, there would be no requirement to refer to IHL in such a situation. The IHRL framework is structured to address the classical law enforcement paradigm, constraining the state from using deadly force in a manner inconsistent with its negative duty not to take life. It is less effective in accounting for the state's positive duty to protect life against deprivations by third parties — a duty that is particularly strong when the state has the immediate capability to intervene and prevent the deprivation.

The effect of the existing IHRL's apparent rejection, as arbitrary, of any foreseeable and incidental deaths of innocent persons in the law enforcement context is to categorically prohibit, regardless of the consequences, the state use of deadly force if it is foreseeable that such use will incidentally deprive any innocent person (or, in Kretzmer's approach, any innocent person other than those whom the use of deadly force is intended to protect) of life. This approach seems radically, even absurdly, absolutist. In its extreme form, it would prohibit the state from using deadly force where even one incidental innocent death is foreseeable, even if that use of force could save thousands of other innocent lives.[86] There may be some moral attraction to such a norm as part of the pacifist, idealistic strain that animates at least some aspects of both human rights law

---

85 *Legality of the Threat or Use of Nuclear Weapons*, Advisory Opinion, [1996] ICJ Rep 226 at para 25. William Schabas hints at such an argument. See William Schabas, "*Lex Specialis?* Belt and Suspenders?: The Parallel Operation of Human Rights Law and the Law of Armed Conflict, and the Conundrum of *Jus ad Bellum*" (2007) 40:2 Israel LR 592 at 604. Marko Milanović discusses appeals to the *lex specialis* as a means of avoiding conflicts between norms of IHRL and international humanitarian law (IHL), similarly implying that in the absence of a conflict, no appeal to the *lex specialis* would be required. See Marko Milanović, "A Norm Conflict Perspective on the Relationship between International Humanitarian Law and Human Rights Law" (2009) 14:3 J Conflict & Security 459.

86 Möller makes a similar argument in respect of the extreme consequences of the German Federal Constitutional Court's absolutist approach to human dignity. See Möller, *supra* note 7 at 458-59.

and the deontological school of moral philosophy, but it is an approach that seems inconsistent with social and political reality — at least beyond the point where the possible effects of adhering to it cross some qualitative or quantitative threshold.

More important than its lack of consistency with social and political reality, an approach to IHRL that categorically rejects the possibility of incidental death or injury to innocent persons leads to a result that is logically and legally unsatisfactory when applied to circumstances such as those of the rogue civil airliner problem. Applying an absolutist approach to the right to life of the individuals on both sides of that problem leads to an irreconcilable conflict in state duties to respect and ensure life — no matter what course of action the state selects, innocent persons will be deprived of life through the state's failure to fulfil one or more of its duties.

ECtHR: A Conditional "Yes"?

There exists some limited authority, however, for a different approach, at least in respect of the right to life as it is protected by the *ECHR*. This is the view that "strict HRL proportionality [that is, proportionality of force used] does not imply that 'collateral damages' are not acceptable"[87] and that, at the extreme boundaries of the law enforcement paradigm, IHRL must account in some way for state decisions regarding the use or non-use of deadly force when the deaths of innocent persons are unavoidable. This view finds some support in two recent ECtHR decisions that address the issue of incidental deaths of innocent persons in the context of the right to life as formulated in the *ECHR*.[88] The four cases decided in those decisions arose in Chechnya during events that the court characterized not as an armed conflict but, rather, as operations by Russian law enforcement authorities[89] in response to a situation that, as the court accepted, "called for exceptional measures by the State in order to regain control over the Republic and to suppress

---

[87] Gaggioli and Kolb, *supra* note 29 at 137. Boyle, *supra* note 25 at 240, in discussing IHRL's approach to proportionality also appears to advocate a comparison of end-states that looks very much like a proportionality of effects analysis, requiring that "it be evident that greater damage or harm will result unless the purpose is achieved" when using force for a legitimate purpose. He does this, however, at the conclusion of a discussion in which he makes clear his rejection of incidental deaths of innocent persons.

[88] See *ECHR, supra* note 13, art 2.

[89] *Isayeva II, supra* note 56 at para 191.

the illegal armed insurgency."[90] While holding that these exceptional measures "could presumably include" the deployment and employment of military units, including aviation units equipped with heavy combat weapons,[91] the court also held that given the circumstances, the employment of these measures had to be judged against a "normal legal background" — that is to say, against the standards of IHRL, specifically the *ECHR*, and not against the standards of IHL.[92]

All four cases arose out of aerial attacks made by Russian Air Force aircraft that resulted in the deaths of a significant number of innocent persons who took no part in any use or threat of violence. In the first three cases, decided in *Isayeva, Yusupova and Bazayeva v Russia* (*Isayeva I*), the Russian pilots claimed to have acted in self-defence after having been fired upon by two trucks that they said were travelling within a convoy of civilian vehicles.[93] In the final case, *Isayeva v Russia* (*Isayeva II*), the deaths occurred during the Russian bombardment of a village in which a large number of insurgents had taken refuge.[94]

The *Isayeva* cases were decided in the context of Article 2 of the *ECHR*, which, in contrast to the *ICCPR* and other major IHRL instruments, does not protect a right not to be arbitrarily deprived of life but, rather, sets out an explicit (and exhaustive) list of allowable limitations to the right to life:

Deprivation of the right to life shall not be regarded as inflicted in contravention of this article when it results from the use of force which is no more than absolutely necessary:

(a) in the defence of any person from unlawful violence ...[95]

What is particularly significant about the court's analysis of the *Isayeva* cases is that it does not categorically reject any possibility of

---

[90] *Ibid* at para 180; *Isayeva I, supra* note 56 at para 178.

[91] *Isayeva I, supra* note 56 at para 178; *Isayeva II, supra* note 56 at para 180.

[92] *Isayeva II, supra* note 56 at para 191. The court declined to consider or apply IHL despite evidence that could have supported a characterization of the situation as a non-international armed conflict and the submissions of the applicants and third party interveners urging it to do so.

[93] *Isayeva I, supra* note 56.

[94] *Isayeva II, supra* note 56.

[95] *ECHR, supra* note 13, art 2(2).

incidental deaths of innocent persons as being absolutely inconsistent with state duties to protect life, even in a pure law enforcement context (which was the context within which it purported to decide the cases). Instead, the court recognizes and accepts the possibility that there may exist circumstances under which incidental deaths of innocent persons would not violate a state's *ECHR* obligations.

The court held that "article 2 covers not only intentional killing but also situations where it is permitted to 'use force' which may result, as an unintended outcome, in the deprivation of life."[96] In other words, provided that it complies with the generally accepted IHRL restrictions on the use of force, a state may use deadly force for a "permitted aim" such as "the defence of any person from unlawful violence," even if that use of force results in unintended, but presumably foreseeable, deaths of innocent persons.[97] The only limitation that the court placed on such deaths in addition to commonly held IHRL standards was a logically related expansion in the scope of the norm of precaution — that is, states must avoid and, in any event, minimize incidental deaths of innocent persons.[98]

The only proportionality requirement discussed and applied by the court in the *Isayeva* cases was the commonly held IHRL requirement of proportionality of force — that is, that the force used be "strictly proportionate" to (or, to use the convention's language, "no more than absolutely necessary" for) the achievement of the permitted aim of defending persons from unlawful violence.[99] While assuming in one decision[100] and accepting in the other[101] that the use of force may have been justified in order to protect persons from unlawful violence, the court noted that "a balance must be achieved between the aim pursued and the means employed to achieve it."[102]

The court made no reference to, and did not incorporate into its analysis of human rights law, a proportionality of effects analysis such as that developed within the framework of IHL or in constitutional human rights law. This approach might be seen as an indication that

---

[96] *Isayeva I, supra* note 56 at para 169; *Isayeva II, supra* note 56 at para 173.

[97] *Ibid.*

[98] *Isayeva II, supra* note 56 at para 176. See also *Isayeva I, supra* note 56 at para 171.

[99] *Isayeva I, supra* note 56 at para 169; *Isayeva II, supra* note 56 at para 173.

[100] *Isayeva I, supra* note 56 at paras 181, 199.

[101] *Isayeva II, supra* note 56 at paras 180, 200.

[102] *Ibid* at paras 181, 191.

it did not view such a test as being appropriate in the law enforcement context of the cases. It might equally be because the *ECHR*, lacking a broad, flexible standard that allows for "non-arbitrary" deprivations of life, deprived the court of jurisdiction to consider a balancing approach. Just as likely, however, is the possibility that given the facts of the cases, where the amounts of force used were not just excessive but also so excessive as to be indiscriminate, there was, in effect, no need for the court to extend its analysis to the point that such an approach might have become relevant. In both cases, the court found that the Russian military's uses of force had not been "planned and executed with the requisite care for the lives of the civilian population."[103] The force used was more than absolutely necessary and therefore failed the standard of strict proportionality of force.[104] Moreover, the authorities had not taken the precautions required to avoid, and in any event to minimize, incidental casualties to innocent persons.[105]

Some scholars have been critical of the ECtHR's "Ivory Tower" approach to the *Isayeva* cases and to other similar cases that arose out of circumstances that might well have been characterized as non-international armed conflicts[106] — an approach that has resisted any explicit reference to IHL.[107] Others have chosen to ignore the court's characterization of the cases as not arising in the context of an armed conflict (a characterization that was made in the face of contrary submissions by the claimants and third parties[108]) and to treat the cases as illustrative of their argument that IHRL can provide protection to victims of non-international armed conflicts that is superior to that provided by IHL.[109] Yet another has gone so far as to suggest that the *Isayeva* decisions must be distinguished

---

[103] *Isayeva I, supra* note 56 at para 199; *Isayeva II, supra* note 56 at para 200.

[104] *Isayeva I, supra* note 56 at paras 194-98; *Isayeva II, supra* note 56 at paras 189-90, 198-99.

[105] *Isayeva I, supra* note 56 at paras 186, 189, 195-96; *Isayeva II, supra* note 56 at paras 184-96.

[106] Eg, *Ergi v Turkey* (1998), 81 ECHR (Ser A) 1751, 32 EHRR 18; *Ahmet Özkan and Others v Turkey*, No 21689/93 (6 April 2004).

[107] See, eg, Gaggioli and Kolb, *supra* note 29 at 124ff.

[108] See, eg, *Isayeva I, supra* note 56 at paras 157, 162-67; *Isayeva II, supra* note 56 at para 167.

[109] See William Abresch, "A Human Rights Law of Internal Armed Conflict: The European Court of Human Rights in Chechnya" (2005) 16:4 EJIL 74; Kretzmer, *supra* note 12 at 30-31.

from other ECtHR decisions since they took place in the context of hostilities and presumably, therefore, reflect the influence of IHL as *lex specialis* on IHRL in the specific context of an armed conflict.[110] However, the court itself was clear: it dealt with the cases strictly under IHRL, judging them against a "normal legal background."[111] Thus, its acceptance of the possibility of incidental deaths of innocent persons in the pursuit of a legitimate goal must be taken as an acceptance of such within IHRL.

Implications of the ECtHR's Approach

The ECtHR's approach, in recognizing the possibility of lawful incidental deaths of innocent persons, shows some promise of alleviating the irreconcilable conflicts in state duties that can arise at the extreme boundaries of the right to life. This promise extends to situations such as the rogue civil airliner problem where any course of action elected by the state will result in innocent persons being deprived of life. Even if the possibility of incidental deaths is accepted, however, the existing IHRL framework governing state uses of force in the law enforcement context may not be entirely satisfactory because its limited approach to proportionality may not account for the complexities of situations such as the rogue civil airliner problem. As a result, it may not provide a sufficiently nuanced or "surgical" approach to resolving irreconcilable conflicts in state duties to respect and ensure the right to life. Indeed, limiting the proportionality analysis to proportionality of force may, in some circumstances, prove to be less protective of individual claims to the right to life and overly deferential to the state's choices.

One cannot ignore the possibility that there may exist circumstances where the threat posed or the importance of the state's objective is sufficient to warrant the use of deadly force on the existing proportionality of force analysis, where deadly force is necessary because no equally effective alternatives are available and where all feasible precautions have been taken to avoid and in any event minimize collateral damage, and, yet, despite being consistent with the full spectrum of existing IHRL norms governing state uses of deadly force, the expected collateral damage (including incidental deaths of innocent persons that would be permitted but not accounted for in the proportionality of force analysis) would exceed

110 Melzer, *supra* note 7 at 386-92.
111 *Isayeva II, supra* note 56 at para 191.

the advantages anticipated from the use of force.[112] Under such circumstances, the ECtHR's approach would not only allow for the possibility of incidental deaths but would also allow for the use of deadly force even though the negative effects of that use of force would be expected to exceed the anticipated positive effects. In failing to account for this possibility, the approach taken by the ECtHR in the *Isayeva* cases, while showing the promise of an improved analytical framework for state uses of deadly force that accounts for what would otherwise be irreconcilable conflicts in state duties arising from irreconcilable claims to the right to life, remains incomplete and, therefore, unsatisfactory.

I conclude that, because of its inability to address the irreconcilable conflicts in state duties and individual rights, IHRL's absolutist approach to the right to life is unsatisfactory as a framework within which to consider the rogue civil airliner problem. Rather than providing a principled approach to the problem, the existing IHRL framework leads to arbitrary, capricious results — results that vary depending upon which side of the equation one begins one's analysis and that are reached without reference to any coherent legal standard. Such results are inconsistent with the rule of law and fail to fully account for all of the relevant human rights interests.

Indeed, it would appear from this analysis that if IHRL is to accept the possibility of incidental deaths of innocent persons, its concern for the protection of human life also requires, as a matter of logic, that it incorporate a requirement of proportionality of positive and negative effects. Only this sort of additional norm will fill the protective gap that could be left if legal analysis were to be limited to the existing substantive IHRL factors of distinction, necessity, precaution, and proportionality of force and will thereby ensure that competing claims to the right to life are properly accounted for. If IHRL is to account for the reality that, in some circumstances, any course of action involving the use (or non-use) of deadly force by a state will result in incidental deaths of innocent persons, then it appears that it must incorporate a legal analysis comparing the effects of different courses of action.[113]

---

112 For a judicial elaboration of this concern in a constitutional rights context, see *Dagenais v Canadian Broadcasting Corp*, [1994] 3 SCR 835 at paras 92-95, 120 DLR (4th) 12 [*Dagenais*].

113 See Kretzmer, *supra* note 12 at 28-29, for a critique of this approach from an absolutist IHRL perspective.

PROPORTIONALITY OF EFFECTS: A COMPARATIVE ANALYSIS

Having concluded that a satisfactory legal framework for the analysis of the rogue civil airliner problem requires the addition of a norm of proportionality of effects, I turn to a comparative analysis of the role of proportionality of effects norms in balancing competing interests in three non-IHRL normative frameworks: IHL, moral philosophy, and constitutional human rights law. I conclude that the premises underlying each framework's approach to proportionality of effects are sufficiently similar to the factual circumstances inherent in the rogue civil airliner problem in a law enforcement context to indicate that a similar approach, carefully tailored so as to be minimally intrusive to the existing framework, will provide IHRL with a satisfactory analytical approach to the problem.

IHL

Although at least from a Western perspective, IHL and IHRL share similar roots in theology and moral philosophy[114] and although, in many ways, they respond to similar humanitarian concerns, each has, for the most part — and at least until recently — developed and evolved independently of the other: "[T]hey advanced on parallel tracks; different personalities were involved in the projects of IHL and IHRL and represented different state interests."[115] IHL and IHRL approach their shared humanitarian concerns from different perspectives: IHL from the pragmatic, accepting "that … it is too late to prevent the use of armed violence between the various parties to [a] conflict"[116] and seeking instead "the maximization of humanitarian protections from harms of inevitable wars,"[117] and IHRL from the idealistic.

IHL's norm of proportionality weighs the anticipated positive effects of a state use of military force against at least some of the expected negative effects. The state must refrain from launching

114 Watkin, *supra* note 15 at 34.

115 Kretzmer, *supra* note 12 at 10 [footnotes omitted].

116 International Committee of the Red Cross (ICRC), *International Humanitarian Law and Other Legal Regimes: Interplay in Situations of Violence*, Summary Report of the XXVIIth Round Table on Current Problems of International Humanitarian Law (November 2003), online: ICRC <http://www.icrc.org/Web/eng/siteengo.nsf/htmlall/5UBCVX/$File/Interplay_other_regimes_Nov_2003.pdf> at 13.

117 Gabriella Blum, "The Laws of War and the 'Lesser Evil'" (2010) 35:1 Yale J Int'l L 1 at 44.

(or continuing) an attack that may be expected to cause incidental loss of civilian life, injury to civilians, damage to civilian objects, or a combination thereof (collateral damage), which would be excessive in relation to the concrete and direct military advantage anticipated.[118] It is important to note that this norm of proportionality of effects imposes a legal obligation that is distinct from, and complementary to, IHL's other fundamental norms of distinction, military objectives, and precaution. Once military objectives have been identified and all feasible precautions have been taken to avoid or at least minimize collateral damage, a separate assessment of proportionality of effects must be carried out.[119] As Amichai Cohen notes,

instead of military necessity justifying any damage to civilians, [the norm of proportionality] … orders the attacking power to audit his proposed operation, comparing the foreseeable damage to the civilian population with the expected military advantage … [and] to relinquish the effort to gain a military advantage if its attainment threatens to cause disproportionate harm to the civilian population.[120]

The IHL norm of proportionality of effects responds to a set of circumstances that shares similarities with those that exist in the rogue civil airliner problem. In both sets of circumstances, the violent deaths of innocent persons are inevitable, and attacks that harm innocent persons are allowed only because no possible alternative exists.[121] In the armed conflict context, the IHL norm of proportionality of effects seeks to minimize those deaths to the extent practicable by balancing those deaths (and other elements of collateral damage) against the constellation of conflicting interests that is captured by the phrase "military advantage." In the law enforcement context, a norm of proportionality of effects would also seek to minimize innocent deaths. The degree of pragmatism

---

118 Jean-Marie Henckaerts and Louise Doswald-Beck, eds, *Customary International Humanitarian Law* (Cambridge: International Committee of the Red Cross, 2005) vol 1 (*Rules*), rule 14 at 46; *Additional Protocol I, supra* note 70, arts 51(5) (b), 57(2)(a)(iii).

119 Judith Gardam, *Necessity, Proportionality and the Use of Force by States* (Cambridge: Cambridge University Press, 2004) at 102 and 112; Kretzmer, *supra* note 12 at 27.

120 Cohen, *supra* note 69 at 9.

121 *Ibid* at 14. See also Watkin, *supra* note 15 at 47.

implicit in an IHRL balancing would, however, have to be considerably more limited, with the conflicting interests being limited in a manner consistent with IHRL's focus upon protecting human rights rather than the gaining of military advantages.

The recently published *Program on Humanitarian Policy and Conflict Research at Harvard University Manual on International Law Applicable to Air and Missile Warfare (Harvard Manual)* provides a convenient mechanism to consider how an IHL-like norm of proportionality of effects could be applied to the rogue civil airliner problem.[122] The manual addresses itself directly to the situation of the rogue civil airliner, albeit in the context of armed conflict. In its approach to collateral damage and proportionality, however, it provides an illustration of how an analysis of proportionality of effects can be integrated into a legal analysis that is, in all other relevant operational respects, effectively identical to the analysis that is required by IHRL in the law enforcement context.

The *Harvard Manual* holds that there are circumstances during armed conflict under which a civil airliner, ordinarily protected from attack as a civilian object, may, by virtue of its use, location, or purpose, lose its protection and become a military objective despite the fact that innocent persons — that is, civilians — are on board.[123] These circumstances include the use of the aircraft as a means of attack[124] and its refusal to comply with orders from state authorities or otherwise resisting interception.[125] The manual recognizes, however, that the presence of innocent crew members and passengers on board the aircraft makes the rogue civil airliner a special case in targeting, which requires particular care in decision making and that must be analyzed using a more nuanced approach than IHL ordinarily requires. As a result, the circumstances under which the rogue civil airliner may lawfully be shot down in an armed attack/armed conflict context are very strictly prescribed through the addition of norms that are ordinarily applicable only in the

---

[122] The *Harvard Manual* is not a binding legal instrument. Its authority is persuasive. It was prepared by a group of experts in the IHRL and IHL fields and is intended to be an elaboration of international law as applicable specifically to air and missile warfare. See *Harvard Manual, supra* note 6, rule 2.

[123] *Ibid*, rule 10(b)(ii). See also *Additional Protocol I, supra* note 70, art 52.

[124] *Harvard Manual, supra* note 6, rule 1(t), commentary to rule 27(a) at para 2, commentary to rule 58 at paras 7, 10.

[125] *Ibid*, rule 63, commentary to rule 27(a).

non-armed conflict/law enforcement context.[126] These additional norms are:

- necessity — the use of deadly force against a rogue civil airliner must be necessary in the sense that "no other method is available for exercising military control" of the aircraft (that is, for preventing the rogue civil aircraft from accomplishing its aim);[127]
- precaution — all feasible precautions (including verifying that the aircraft is a military objective,[128] the issuing of warnings (when circumstances permit),[129] and making all feasible attempts to divert the aircraft for landing, inspection, and possible capture[130]) must be taken prior to a use of force in order to avoid and in any event minimize both the use of force itself and incidental effects of any use of force;[131] and
- proportionality of force — the circumstances under which its use, location, or purpose make the rogue civil airliner a military objective must be "sufficiently grave to justify an attack"[132] (in other words, any use of deadly force must only be in response to a sufficiently grave threat).

These norms represent an innovation in the approach of international law to armed conflict, at least in respect of the rogue civil airliner, in that they incorporate legal restrictions on the use of deadly force that traditional IHL would not require, strictly speaking, as a matter of law. The addition of these norms contributes to a more nuanced framework for legal analysis and also reflects the influence upon international law norms of the moral and political dilemmas associated with the rogue civil airliner problem.

The *Harvard Manual*'s approach to a rogue civil airliner in the context of an armed conflict is to employ an analytical framework that consists of the core, substantive norms of the IHRL use of deadly force framework (distinction, necessity, precaution, and

---

[126] *Ibid*, rule 58; see also section J(III).

[127] *Ibid*, rule 68(b).

[128] *Ibid*, rule 40.

[129] *Ibid*, rules 38, 70.

[130] *Ibid*, rule 68(a). See also generally Section G, rule 58, commentary to rule 10.

[131] *Ibid*, rules 68(a), 68(d).

[132] *Ibid*, rule 68(c).

proportionality of force) along with the added IHL norm requiring proportionality of effects — that "the expected collateral damage will not be excessive in relation to the military advantage anticipated."[133] This approach confirms that there are circumstances where a pragmatic proportionality of effects analysis can be integrated with IHRL's more idealistic approach to strictly limiting state uses of deadly force.

When it comes to the pure law enforcement context, however, some of the substantive content of the IHL proportionality analysis remains inappropriate in analyzing the rogue civil airliner problem. While the two contexts share the significant similarity that the loss of innocent lives is inevitable, there remains a significant difference in how the dilemma of choosing which lives to end must be addressed. The IHL norm of proportionality allows a state to accept foreseeable and innocent deaths of innocent persons in the achievement of an anticipated "military advantage" that is not limited to the protection of other lives. Thus, human lives may be "balanced" against a broad range of interests other than other human lives — anything that might provide a military advantage, including the destruction of equipment, weapons, and other items of military value or the advantage of gaining or denying to the enemy the use of a particular piece of geography. IHRL, on the other hand, to the extent that it accepts any state use of deadly force, accepts it only for the limited purpose of protecting human life.

This distinction between the IHL and IHRL frameworks, while significant, is not irreconcilable, particularly in the circumstances of the rogue civil airliner. Part of the difference is narrowed by the factual circumstances. Any use of deadly force against a rogue civil airliner, regardless of context, will have a defensive purpose. The advantage to be gained from it will be primarily preventative. In an armed conflict context, it lies in preventing the enemy from achieving its own military advantage, while, in a law enforcement context, it lies, similarly, in preventing the person(s) in effective control of the aircraft from achieving their suicidal/homicidal and destructive objective. While the set of possible military advantages in an armed conflict context is thus more limited than it would be in the case of an offensive attack, it still includes matters that go beyond protecting the lives of those on the surface and may, in fact, have no rational connection at all to any goal of saving innocent lives. Thus, the "balancing" that takes place in the context of the rogue civil

---

133 *Ibid*, rule 68(d).

airliner problem in armed conflict still incorporates other factors not related to the right to life and can involve balancing lives against those factors. Such balancing is anathema to the idealistic foundation of IHRL.

IHRL's restrictive approach to the use of force in a law enforcement context is one that must not be interfered with lightly. Its legal framework has proven to be satisfactory in respect of the vast majority of circumstances that might arise in the law enforcement context. As a result, there is no requirement, nor any justification, for a radical amendment to the framework. Indeed, any general incorporation of a proportionality of effects analysis might have the effect of seriously weakening IHRL's protective framework by increasing the scope within which state deprivations of life might be considered acceptable.[134] Thus, any use of a proportionality of effects norm in a law enforcement context to resolve the irreconcilable conflicts of state duties and individual claims to the right to life must differ from the IHL approach to the norm by ensuring that the right to life remains at the centre of its analysis.

This effect can be achieved through a combination of three constraints. First, the circumstances under which a law enforcement proportionality of effects analysis is permitted must be carefully constrained. The addition of a proportionality of effects analysis to the existing IHRL framework must only occur under circumstances that cannot be coherently and satisfactorily addressed by that framework. Second, while recognizing that other interests will factor into state decision making, even in a law enforcement context, the proportionality of effects analysis must respect the significant value that IHRL places on the right to life and assign the lives of persons (particularly innocent persons) a more significant "weight" in the balancing exercise than might be the case in the armed conflict context. Third, and in a similar vein, the analysis must also ensure that valid state interests that do not have a rational connection to the state's duties to respect and ensure the right to life are assigned a minimal value — one that ensures that decision makers do not lose focus on the lives involved.

Moral Philosophy

The moral dimension of the rogue civil airliner problem was of particular importance to the German Federal Constitutional Court

---

[134] See Kretzmer, *supra* note 12 at 29.

in its striking down of portions of the *Aviation Security Act* in 2006.[135] Indeed, its approach to the problem was strongly rooted in the Kantian, categorical view that human lives are of incommensurable worth and in an absolutist, deontological approach that holds that nothing, even the saving of innumerable other lives, can justify the taking of even one innocent life. The practical implications of such an approach are clear in the result — namely an irreconcilable conflict in state duties, the practical resolution of which is arbitrary and capricious.

While many moral theorists continue, like the Constitutional Court did, to hew to an absolutist approach whatever the consequences, others argue that in circumstances such as the rogue civil airliner problem, where deprivations of innocent life are inevitable, the conflict can be resolved by reference to the most fundamental premise upon which Kantian deontology is built: individual free will and self-determination. In other words, "[t]he overriding value Kantian moral philosophy places on the rational autonomy of individuals does not support indifference to how many individuals survive. That would not be in harmony with the value of individual human beings whose personhood rational autonomy defines."[136]

Thus, in such a truly exceptional situation, where innocent persons will inevitably be deprived of life, there is a claim to be made in moral philosophy that a course of action that preserves the rational autonomy, dignity, and lives of more, rather than fewer, persons would be in keeping with Kant's fundamental premise.[137] If one is committed to the goal of protecting life, one must also be committed to the goal of protecting the most lives. One cannot hide behind "question-begging claims about the distinction between state actions and state omissions or between killing and letting die."[138]

Another strong moral claim, and one that is more broadly accepted than the consequentialist reading of Kant set out above, is

---

135 *Dr H, supra* note 71. See Möller, *supra* note 7 at 464: "The problem of whether it is permissible to kill some in order to save others from being killed is at the centre of much contemporary debate in moral theory."

136 Tom Stacy, "Acts, Omissions and the Necessity Killing of Innocents" (2002) 29:3 Am J Crim L 481 at 508.

137 *Ibid* at 507-12. See David Cummiskey, "Kant's Consequentialism" 100:3 Ethics 586, which makes a similar argument. See also Blum, *supra* note 117 at 40-44.

138 Cass R Sunstein and Adrian Vermeule, "Is Capital Punishment Morally Required?: Acts, Omissions and Life-Life Tradeoffs" (2005) 58:3 Stan L Rev 703 at 708.

made by the school of "threshold deontology," which recognizes "that at some extreme points, one cannot avoid some consequentialist analysis that would require departure from the absolute proscription" and "responds to the accusation that pure deontology would allow catastrophic outcomes for the sake of moral narcissism."[139] The approach of threshold deontology is to seek a theory that is strongly protective of life (and, for some theorists, of dignity) but that nevertheless justifies and authorizes limited departures from deontological absolutes once a particular threshold is reached. One such theory is the doctrine of double effect (DDE). This doctrine is of long-standing, deriving from St. Thomas Aquinas's writings on self-defence and just-war theory[140] and is generalized and elaborated not only by Catholic theologians but also by secular moral philosophers. It has been applied to the context of armed conflict as an analytical framework capable of resolving a number of key moral dilemmas, justifying not only killing in self-defence or the defence of others but also killings of innocent persons that are incidental to the achievement of a sufficiently important military objective.[141] DDE provides that an act that is likely to have "evil" consequences is morally permissible provided that each of the following conditions hold:

- the act is good in itself or at least indifferent;
- the direct effect of the act is morally acceptable;
- the intentions of the actors are good — that is, they aim only at the acceptable effect and the evil effect is not one of their ends, nor is it a "mere means" to their ends; and
- there is a proportionality of effects — that is, the good effect is sufficiently good to compensate for allowing the evil effect.[142]

Some describe the IHL norm of proportionality as being rooted in DDE.[143] The analytical similarities are certainly not difficult to

---

[139] Blum, *supra* note 117 at 43ff.

[140] See Sophie Botros, "An Error about the Doctrine of Double Effect" (1999) 74:1 Philosophy 71 at 72-73.

[141] See, eg, Joseph M Boyle, Jr, "Toward Understanding the Principle of Double Effect" (1980) 90:4 Ethics 527 at 528-29.

[142] These elements paraphrase those set out by Walzer, *supra* note 5 at 153 and 129. For an alternative formulation, see Botros, *supra* note 140 at 72-73.

[143] See, eg, Watkin, *supra* note 15 at 26. Blum, *supra*, note 117 at 40, equates IHL's norm of proportionality of effects with the doctrine of double of effect (DDE);

perceive. However, even a cursory review of current scholarly debates in moral philosophy demonstrates that DDE has proven to be a useful theoretical tool far beyond the confines of armed conflict. It plays a prominent role in many theoretical analyses of moral dilemmas, such as the well-known "trolley" and "transplant" problems that mirror many of the features of the rogue civil airliner problem,[144] including the inevitable deaths of innocent persons, *prima facie* irreconcilable conflicts between duties and claims to rights, and the requirement for an analytical framework that will assist in resolving those conflicts in a principled, rather than an arbitrary or capricious, manner.

Far from being the consequentialist "sham" that some suspect it of being,[145] DDE provides a theoretical device that, in contrast to broader "maximization of good" consequentialism, recognizes the particular weight of some moral duties and claims and provides an analytical framework to address conflicts that would, in a pure, absolutist deontology, be irresolvable.[146] As Joseph Boyle, Jr., points out in discussing the role of the doctrine in moral philosophy, a commitment to "a normative theory demanding respect for a set of basic goods" (that is, human rights) also requires a commitment

---

Kretzmer, *supra* note 12 at 26, also notes the conceptual similarity. On the other hand, note that Gardam, *supra* note 119, who describes the history of the norm of proportionality in considerable detail, makes little mention of any influence of DDE in the emergence of IHL's rule.

[144] In the trolley problem, a runaway trolley travels towards five people on the track in front of it, all of whom will be killed if it strikes them. However, a bystander is able to use a switch that will divert the trolley onto another track where it will only kill one person. A variation on the problem posits that there is no switch, but that the bystander can stop the trolley before it kills the five people on the track by pushing another person (sometimes a "fat person") into the trolley's path. See the description (albeit without a discussion of DDE) in Mattias Kumm, "Political Liberalism and the Structure of Rights: On the Place and Limits of the Proportionality Requirement," in George Pavlakos, ed, *Law, Rights and Discourse: The Legal Philosophy of Robert Alexy* (Oxford: Hart, 2007) 131 at 153. The transplant problem is the "fat person/trolley" problem in a different context: A doctor has five ill patients who will all die unless they receive transplanted organs. The doctor also has a healthier patient whose organs, if harvested, will save the ill patients. See Botros, *supra* note 140 at 75.

[145] See Hörnle, "Hijacked Airplanes" *supra* note 75 at 592: "I doubt that this doctrine is much more than a sham to hide pockets of consequentialist reasoning in states of emergency or other situations when the consequences of deontological thinking might seem too harsh."

[146] Botros, *supra* note 140 at 73, 82-83.

to a proportionality of effects approach such as that in DDE: "Otherwise respecting the goods becomes an impossibility, since any performance can — and many performances do — bring about what is contrary to one or more basic goods."[147] To put it in the terms of our rogue civil airliner problem, a commitment to the protection of the lives of innocent persons means that where a deprivation of innocent life is unavoidable, a morally principled response requires that some sort of proportionality-based, balancing approach be adopted.

Constitutional Human Rights

Building upon the work of Ronald Dworkin and based upon a study of the German constitutional order, Robert Alexy has posited an influential theory of constitutional protection of human rights that has relevance across a broad range of state constitutional orders, particularly those that have emerged in the post-Second World War era of human rights and that feature extensive guarantees of those rights.[148] The theory will appear familiar to scholars of Canadian law, who will recognize, albeit in different terms, the elements of the analysis undertaken by Canadian courts to determine whether a limit to a right protected by the *Canadian Charter of Rights and Freedoms* is reasonable and can be demonstrably justified in a free and democratic society.[149]

Alexy conceives of rights as "principles" that, according to his theory, are "optimization requirements," expressions of "ideal oughts" that are valid across the legal order as a whole but apply in a "more-or-less" fashion.[150] Within such a conception of rights, where broadly defined principles are certain to come into conflict,

---

[147] Boyle, *supra* note 141 at 538.

[148] See Robert Alexy, *A Theory of Constitutional Rights*, translated by Julian Rivers (Oxford: Oxford University Press, 2002). See also Kai Möller, "The Right to Life between Absolute and Proportional Protection" (2010) LSE Law Society and Economy Working Papers 13/2010 at 2, online: SSRN <http://papers.ssrn.com/sol3/papers.cfm?abstract_id=1620377>.

[149] *Canadian Charter of Rights and Freedoms*, Part I of the *Constitution Act, 1982*, being Schedule B to the *Canada Act 1982* (UK), 1982, c 11, s 1. For an elaboration of the analytical framework, see *R v Oakes*, [1986] 1 SCR 103 at paras 69-70, 26 DLR (4th) 200; *Dagenais*, *supra* note 112 at paras 92-96.

[150] Alexy, *supra* note 148 at 57-66. For useful paraphrasing and summaries of the basic building blocks of the theory, see Martin Scheinin, "Terrorism and the Pull of 'Balancing' in the Name of Security," in Scheinin et al, *supra* note 39, 55 at 58; Kumm, *supra* note 144 at 136-37.

a "balancing" test based on proportionality is required as an "analytical structure for assessing whether limits imposed on the realization of a principle in the particular [factual] context are justified."[151] The balancing process weighs the importance of the competing principles to the situation at hand, favouring the "weightier" principle while also seeking to apply the other principle to the extent legally and factually possible.[152] Alexy describes a "proportionality test" that uses the following elements to analyze whether a particular limit should be permitted:

- legitimate ends — the limitation of rights must serve a legitimate objective;
- suitability — the limitation must be suitable to achieve the legitimate objective (in other words, it must be capable of achieving it);
- necessity — the limitation must be necessary to achieve the legitimate objective in that there are no other, less limiting means of achieving it; and
- balancing — there must be proportionality *stricto sensu* between the limitation's positive effects and its negative effects (that is, the costs must not clearly outweigh the benefits).[153]

The heart of the constitutional proportionality framework is the proportionality of effects analysis that Alexy calls "balancing." As Alexy conceives of it, the balancing test is flexible, allowing for different principles to be assigned different "weights" depending upon the particular circumstances in which they conflict. This is a very flexible theory, one that is capable of accounting for the different approaches to various rights and interests that are taken by the constitutional orders of different states, including even categorical approaches to particular rights that can be accounted for by assigning absolute rights an infinite weight in the balancing exercise so as to preclude any countervailing interest.[154]

---

151 Kumm, *supra* note 144 at 137.

152 This description is drawn from the work of Scheinin in summarizing and paraphrasing Alexy. See Scheinin, *supra* note 150.

153 See generally Alexy, *supra* note 148 at 57-66. See also Möller, *supra* note 148 at 3; Möller, *supra* note 7 at 458; Kumm, *supra* note 144 at 137. McCrudden provides another useful description of the common elements among similar proportionality analyses. Christopher McCrudden, "Human Dignity and Judicial Interpretation of Human Rights" (2008) 19:4 EJIL 655 at 715.

154 See Alexy, *supra* note 148 at 102; Robert Alexy, "Thirteen Replies," in Pavlakos, *supra* note 144, 333 at 344.

Alexy's constitutional rights theory also provides a useful analogy to IHRL in that both constitutional human rights law and IHRL are concerned with the protection of similar rights and both are capable of doing so in a non-armed conflict context. Moreover, the proportionality-based constitutional and legislative approaches to the protection of human rights taken by states whose constitutional orders are reflected in Alexy's theory might be seen as providing some indication (in the form of both state practice and *opinio juris* in respect of the implementation by those states of their obligations under IHRL) of the possibility of an emerging customary IHRL acceptance of a proportionality of effects analysis where irreconcilable conflicts of state duties and individual rights claims exist.[155]

DEFINING AN IHRL NORM OF PROPORTIONALITY OF EFFECTS

The fact that constitutional rights theory, widely held theories of moral philosophy, and IHL all converge upon a similar analytical framework — proportionality of effects — as a means of resolving conflicting claims to protection of strongly held, "weighty" rights such as the right not to be arbitrarily deprived of life, along with the fact that such an approach is not limited to an armed conflict context, supports the use of such an approach to provide a satisfactory theoretical approach to the rogue civil airliner problem in a pure law enforcement context. The strongly IHRL-influenced approach to the rogue civil airliner problem that is taken by the *Harvard Manual* is perhaps the closest analogy that is available, but, as suggested earlier, some adjustments are required. A theoretical basis for these adjustments is suggested in the theories of moral philosophy and constitutional human rights discussed earlier. With these thoughts in mind, I turn to defining an IHRL norm of proportionality of effects.

---

[155] Both Möller and Kumm imply that Alexy's theory might be applicable in the IHRL context (at least within the *ECHR*, which, in the case of many rights, provides a clearer textual basis for "balancing" than does the *ICCPR*'s language of "arbitrary"). Such an approach also seems to be common in balancing competing rights (at least those that are susceptible to limitations or derogations) within the *ICCPR*. See *Siracusa Principles, supra* note 33. Scheinin, *supra* note 150 at 63, argues that because it lacks a strong central structure for review of state decisions and actions in balancing human rights principles, "international human rights law [in contrast to 'stable' constitutional systems] still needs to emphasize the existence of absolute rules that are not subject to 'balancing' against competing interests" in order to maximize the protection of individual rights on a practical level. Scheinin's approach, however, does not provide any

The "Threshold" — Triggering the Application of the Norm

Drawing on the idea of a "threshold" beyond which categorical approaches to moral or legal questions are no longer appropriate, under what circumstances should a proportionality of effects test be added to the existing IHRL framework governing the use of deadly force in a purely law enforcement context? This is a question that is closely related to the issue of whether an increase in the permissiveness of the IHRL framework might constitute the top of a "slippery slope" of other modifications to the framework that could weaken its overall ability to protect the right to life.

The existing IHRL framework that governs state uses of deadly force in a law enforcement context has proven itself to be both coherent and effective in most situations. Thus, any modification to it should be limited to what is required to achieve coherence and effectiveness in the circumstances at hand while preserving, to the greatest extent possible, IHRL's absolutist, idealistic core. This aim is achieved, *prima facie*, by limiting the application of an IHRL proportionality of effects norm to situations where the existing IHRL framework is not satisfactory — that is, where there exists a conflict between state duties to ensure and respect the right to life that arises from irreconcilable claims to that right — situations where, in other words, innocent persons will be deprived of life no matter the state's chosen course of action.

It is only when the deaths of innocent persons are inevitable, regardless of the state's course of action, that a proportionality of effects analysis should be added to the existing IHRL framework. It is only under these circumstances that the existing approaches to IHRL become incoherent, and some additional analytical framework is required.

A Proposed Formulation of the Norm

I have already suggested that, in contrast to the IHL norm of proportionality, any IHRL proportionality of effects analysis must, as IHRL itself does, place particular weight upon the right to life. However, once it has been triggered, any proportionality analysis will be ineffective if it perpetuates the theoretical shortcomings that

---

alternative mechanisms to account for the irreconcilable conflicts of duties and rights claims that are inherent in situations such as the rogue civil airliner problem.

have led to its being required in the first place. Therefore, the "weight" placed on the right to life of innocent persons cannot be infinite. Any legal analysis of the rogue civil airliner problem must both accept the reality that innocent deaths are inevitable and then provide a mechanism that will assist state decision makers in choosing an appropriate course of action. To categorically assign infinite weight to human lives would, in the circumstances of the rogue civil airliner problem, simply "break the scale," so to speak, with infinite weights on both sides rendering any attempt to "balance" through a proportionality analysis nugatory and leaving the irreconcilable conflicts in place.

While the balancing analysis can (and indeed must) account for interests other than lives, the additional interests accounted for should be limited to those that are significant to the overall public interest, bearing in mind the pre-eminent weight given to the right to life by IHRL. In other words, the interests that can be given positive weight in the analysis are those that are rationally connected to the state's duty to ensure and respect the right to life. These additional interests might include environmental effects and damage to infrastructure of a sort that would have an effect upon public and individual health (as opposed to mere convenience or comfort) along with more policy-oriented concerns (also related to the protection of health and life) such as the sustaining of public confidence in the state's ability to provide security and protection of individual rights and the deterence of future incidents of similar scale and seriousness. These are all matters habitually balanced by governments in making policy decisions with legal implications and by courts in reviewing such decisions. As such, they should not pose insurmountable challenges to the effectiveness of the modified IHRL framework.

With these caveats in mind, how should the proportionality of effects norm in the particular circumstance of the rogue civil airliner in the law enforcement context be formulated? I propose the following norm:

Select a course of action that is not expected to result in incidental loss of life to innocent persons, injury to innocent persons, damage to other interests rationally connected to the protection of human life, or any combination thereof, that is excessive in relation to the anticipated concrete and direct advantages that are rationally connected to the protection of human life.

This formulation takes a neutral approach to the available courses of action both in refraining from any reference to a direct use of force and in not modifying the term "excessive" with adjectives such as "clearly" that would suggest a default position with respect to the use of force. Its focus upon "innocent" persons is a reflection of the fact that the right to life of "non-innocent" persons is already accounted for in the existing IHRL framework. The requirement that any advantages to be balanced against human life be rationally connected to the protection of human life reflects and retains the pre-eminent value placed upon human life by IHRL.

The Proposed Norm in Context

For ease of comparison, a table summarizing and comparing the existing, IHRL-based law enforcement approach to the rogue civil airliner with both the *Harvard Manual*'s armed conflict approach and the proposed law enforcement approach, which includes my proposed addition of the proportionality of effects analysis, is set out in Table 1. While Table 1 compares the three legal frameworks in respect to what I have called the operationally relevant norms of IHL and IHRL, it must also be understood that my proposal does not modify any of the other norms of the existing IHRL framework. Thus, any use of deadly force against a rogue civil airliner in a law enforcement context must also be authorized by law and subjected to an effective investigation.

Practical Challenges in Application of the Norm

The mere acceptance of a modified legal framework leaves unaddressed a number of issues that will arise in most, if not all, real world manifestations of the rogue civil airliner problem. While I will introduce some of these issues in the following discussion, their potential variations are infinite and will depend upon the particular factual circumstances of each case. My point in introducing them is not to resolve them — this challenge will have to wait until actual situations with actual facts arise. The modified framework that I advocate provides a framework within which these issues can be raised and analyzed — a framework that would not otherwise exist.

The first set of issues that will arise in any "real world" rogue civil airliner incident is that of dealing with "prognostic difficulty" — that is, how the state authorities "will be able to know with sufficient certainty the factual foundation" for any decision-making

Table 1
COMPARISON OF LEGAL FRAMEWORKS

Existing IHRL	Proposed IHRL	Existing IHL (Harvard Manual)
Distinction: Distinguish between persons who, by their actions, constitute an imminent threat of death or serious injury, or a threat of committing a particularly serious crime involving a grave threat to life and persons who do not present such a threat and use force only against the former.	*Distinction:* Distinguish between ordinary civil aircraft and rogue civil aircraft. Direct attacks only against rogue civil aircraft that constitute a grave and imminent threat of death or serious injury.	*Distinction:* Distinguish between ordinary civil aircraft and those that have become military objectives (rogue civil aircraft). Direct attacks only against the latter.
Necessity: Employ deadly force only when absolutely necessary to protect life.	*Necessity:* Employ deadly force against a rogue civil airliner only if no other method is available to protect the life of persons on the surface.	*Necessity:* Attack a rogue civil airliner only if "no other method is available for exercising military control."
Precaution in Using Force: Take all feasible precautions to avoid and in any event minimize the use of force.	*Precaution in Using Force:* Take all feasible precautions to avoid the use of force.	*Precaution in Using Force:* Take all feasible precautions to avoid the use of force.
Precaution in Amount of Force: Take all feasible precautions to avoid and in any event minimize death or injury to innocent persons (ECtHR only)	*Precaution in Amount of Force:* Take all feasible precautions to avoid and in any event minimize collateral damage.	*Precaution in Amount of Force:* Take all feasible precautions to avoid and in any event minimize collateral damage.

▲ Table 1
COMPARISON OF LEGAL FRAMEWORKS

Existing IHRL	Proposed IHRL	Existing IHL (Harvard Manual)
Proportionality of Force: Use only force that is strictly proportionate to the threat and the legitimate objective to be attained.	*Proportionality of Force:* Use force against a rogue civil airliner if the circumstances are "sufficiently grave to justify an attack."	*Proportionality of Force:* Use force against a rogue civil airliner only if the circumstances are "sufficiently grave to justify an attack."
Proportionality of Effects: not applicable	*Proportionality of Effects:* Where, regardless of the state's course of action, both using and refraining from using deadly force will foreseeably result in casualties to innocent persons, select a course of action that is not expected to result in incidental loss of life to innocent persons, injury to innocent persons, damage to other interests rationally connected to the protection of human life, or any combination thereof that is excessive in relation to the anticipated concrete and direct advantages that are rationally connected to the protection of human life.	*Proportionality of Effects:* In any event, refrain from carrying out an attack where the expected collateral damage would be excessive in relation to the military advantage anticipated.

exercise.[156] As indicated earlier, for the purposes of developing my analysis, I have assumed the extreme case — that without state intervention, the person in effective control will, in fact, crash the aircraft into his or her target. Such a degree of certainty will be impossible to replicate in any "real world" case. The existence of an additional analytical tool such as the proportionality of effects test will not change this issue. Nor will it provide certainty as to the effects of a successful rogue civil airliner attack. Thus, while the likely success and incidental effects of a state use of deadly force against the rogue civil airliner can be divined with some degree of confidence (although not in respect of damage likely to be caused by the aircraft's wreckage on the surface),[157] decision makers will always be faced with considerable uncertainty as to the intention of the persons in effective control of the aircraft and of the effects if they are successful in perpetuating their attack.

An additional set of issues will also be inherent in any rogue civil airliner situation — that is, how to value the lives of the persons affected by it. For instance, are the lives of the innocent passengers and crew to be given a lower weight in the balancing exercise because they are expected to die in any event? Such an approach would be problematic from both a fundamental philosophical perspective (in that human lives are of inestimable value regardless of their quality or anticipated duration) and from a practical one (in the sense that if the persons in effective control intend only to perform a "low pass" over the apparent target area, shooting the aircraft down will result in death and destruction that would have been unnecessary, while refraining from stopping an eventually successful attack could have the effect of undervaluing the lives of persons on the surface). Further, what number of immediate deaths and what degree of other effects on the surface that are related to the right to life will justify shooting down the aircraft?[158] In the

---

[156] Bohlander, *supra* note 75 at 583.

[157] The group of experts that drafted the *Harvard Manual, supra* note 6, could not agree on whether to account for such damage in applying the IHL rule of proportionality to the shooting down of an aircraft. The majority rejected such an accounting as impractical, but they conceded that some exceptional circumstances might warrant considering the potential for collateral damage on the surface, such as where the state has air supremacy and can choose the time and place of an attack on an airborne aircraft. See Section G(III), commentary to chapeau at para 4, commentary to rule 68(d) at para 3.

[158] For another description of the situation, see Kumm, *supra* note 144 at 156, n 58. See also Hörnle, "Shooting Down a Hijacked Plane,"*supra* note 75 at 121-22,

extreme case, does preventing a single death on the surface justify shooting down the aircraft (since those on board will die in either event)? What if that person is a particularly important individual, a political leader or a scientist possessing irreplaceable knowledge?[159]

The weighing of various interests, particularly the lives of the persons on each side of the rogue civil airliner problem, is not simple: it is complex and requires that a large number of factors be assimilated and analyzed. In any rogue civil airliner situation, the factors of time and space will play a significant role. A decision will have to be made quickly and likely without all of the information that might be desirable. And a decision cannot be avoided. Given the consequences, a non-decision (or a non-timely decision) is, in effect, a decision. The elements and interests implicated in the rogue civil airliner problem, therefore, must be analyzed in as much detail as possible before an actual incident occurs. Decision makers must understand the policy, legal, and operational landscapes. Exercising the various operational response and communications mechanisms that are available in order to identify and rectify shortcomings is also necessary to ensure that decision makers, those who advise them and those who execute their decisions can focus their attention and efforts on the specific circumstances of each incident.[160]

The manner in which decision makers address these issues is of some importance since, in the law enforcement context, any deaths caused by a state use of deadly force must be the subject of an effective investigation within the state. It seems reasonable to conclude that the requirement of an investigation will have a positive influence upon state decision makers from the perspective of protecting human rights. A decision maker "who is aware that his actions will be monitored after the fact is likely to take care that he gives due

---

for a brief discussion of different approaches to valuing the lives of those aboard the aircraft and their apparent relationship to different legal traditions.

[159] An example from an entirely different context may clarify this point. In an article that analyzes empirical evidence suggesting that eighteen lives were saved for every state execution of a convicted murderer, Sunstein and Vermeule suggested that this ratio (where eighteen lives could be saved by ending one) might represent a threshold at which execution might be not merely morally justified but morally required. Sunstein and Vermeule, *supra* note 138 at 719, 727. See also Blum, *supra* note 117 at 60-62.

[160] These sort of exercises do, in fact, appear to take place on a regular basis. See, eg, Mellow, *supra* note 4, and Dan Elliott, "Russia, U.S. Chase Jet in Hijack Drill," *Associated Press* (9 August 2010), online: MSNBC<http://www.msnbc.msn.com/id/38628835/ns/world_news-europe/t/russia-us-chase-jet-hijack-drill/>.

consideration to all possibilities when reaching a decision."[161] Since there are no objectively correct ways in which to respond to a particular rogue civil airliner situation, it is impossible for any investigation, tribunal, or other state to judge the lawfulness of the ultimate result. The best that can be done is to investigate and judge the decision-making process.[162]

POSSIBLE ALTERNATIVE APPROACHES

Before concluding, I will consider briefly whether alternative approaches might provide a satisfactory framework for considering the rogue civil airliner problem. The two clearest possibilities both involve retaining, without changes, the existing IHRL framework and using different mechanisms to resolve the conflict of irreconcilable duties and claims to the right to life.

Political Question

One alternative is to accept that the legal conflict between state IHRL duties in respect of the lives of the innocent persons on board the rogue civil airliner and the lives of the innocent persons on the surface is one that cannot be resolved by the law and to choose a course of action on the basis of political and moral factors alone. Assuming that there is no factual basis to claim that another framework of international law applies (that is, there is no armed attack and no armed conflict), the state employing this first alternative might support its choice before the international community on a number of bases, each employing some element of legal reasoning. The state might simply argue that the conflict in duties indicates that the appropriate approach to resolving the problem is a political one — one with which the law should not concern itself.[163] As a matter of law, the point seems to be easier to make in the context of a domestic legal system. Indeed, some legal systems do admit doctrines of "political questions" or "non-justiciability" in certain

---

[161] Cohen, *supra* note 69 at 32.

[162] *Ibid* at 30-31.

[163] See Milanović, *supra* note 85, particularly at 477-81; Miguel Beltran de Felipe and Jose Maria Rodriguez de Santiago, "Shooting Down Hijacked Airplanes? Sorry We're Humanists: A Comment on the German Constitutional Court Decision of 2.15.2006, Regarding the Luftsicherheitsgesetz (2005 Air Security Act)" (2007) Berkeley Electronic Press 1983 at 21-25, online: Berkeley Electronic Press <http://law.bepress.com/expresso/eps/1983>. See also McCrudden, *supra* note 153 at 715.

circumstances.[164] As a matter of practicality, it seems less likely to be persuasive in the context of international law regulating the relations between sovereign states or in the context of obligations *erga omnes*.

Internationally, the state might assert that law enforcement is a matter that is essentially within its domestic jurisdiction — a purely internal matter. This argument operates on a political level seeking to convince other states to forego claims of a legal nature. It may, indeed, prove to be effective, depending upon a number of factors, including, for example, the number of foreign citizens affected by a particular rogue civil aircraft situation and its outcome. Outcomes that might be expected to be of greater concern to foreign states include those where the rogue civil airliner is shot down and contains a large number of foreign citizens (states may be more willing to accept deaths of their citizens that can be attributed to criminal acts of the persons effectively in control of the aircraft than those that are attributable to the state shooting the aircraft down) or where the attack is successful but causes widespread environmental damage affecting other states.[165] Both general international law and the *ICCPR* impose particular obligations upon the state, and acts or omissions of the state that breach those obligations entail state responsibility at international law.[166] If foreign states pursue claims of international responsibility, a more nuanced response is required.

Circumstances Precluding International Responsibility

A second alternative would involve an assertion by the state of a circumstance such as distress or necessity, which would preclude

---

[164] Eg, *Baker v Carr*, 369 US 186 at 210-11 (1962). Where a determination of constitutionally protected human rights is at stake, see, cf, *Operation Dismantle v The Queen*, [1985] 1 SCR 441 at paras 51-68 (Wilson J.) and para 38 (Dickson J.), 18 DLR (4th) 481.

[165] See, eg, *Trail Smelter Case (United States v Canada)* (1938 and 1941), III UNRIAA 1905.

[166] *Draft Articles on Responsibility of States for Internationally Wrongful Acts, with Commentaries*, contained in *Report of the International Law Commission, Fifty-Third Session*, UN ILC, 56th Sess, Supp No 10, UN Doc A/56/10 (2001), ch IV.E.1, arts 1-3 [*Draft Articles on Responsibility*]. The issue that seems more likely to arise as a result of a rogue civil airliner problem is not whether there is state responsibility for a breach of an international obligation undertaken pursuant to the *ICCPR* but, rather, whether another state would raise the issue in an international dispute resolution forum.

its being held internationally responsible.[167] The pleas of distress and necessity both present specific difficulties, however. While the claim of distress, on its face, seems to require only that there be "no other reasonable way ... of saving ... the lives of ... persons entrusted to the ... care" of the author of the otherwise internationally wrongful act,[168] most cases where distress has been claimed have involved breaches of sovereignty by aircraft or ships due to threats to life caused by bad weather or mechanical failure.[169] Moreover, the claim requires a "special relationship" of responsibility between the author of the act and the persons in danger that appears to go beyond the general duty of state agents to protect all persons subject to the state's jurisdiction and, thus, does not extend to "more general cases of emergencies, which are more a matter of necessity than distress."[170]

The possibility of a claim of necessity as a circumstance precluding wrongfulness is somewhat more intriguing. The claim of necessity acts as a justification or excuse for acts or omissions "where there is an irreconcilable conflict between an essential interest [of the state] on the one hand and an [international] obligation ... on the other,"[171] and the act or omission "is the only way for the State to safeguard an essential interest against grave and imminent peril."[172] The difficulty in asserting such a claim with respect to the rogue civil airliner problem is that it involves not simply a conflict between an essential interest and an international obligation but, rather, conflicts between two interests that might be seen to be essential to the state (the right to life of those persons on board the aircraft and the right to life of those on the surface) and between two international obligations (to ensure and respect the right to life of each group of individuals). Necessity provides the state with a justification for an act or omission that breaches an obligation in international law under circumstances where the requirements of international law are inconsistent with the social and political reality of a particular

---

[167] See, eg, the discussion of such possibilities in Darren C Huskisson, "The *Air Bridge Denial Program* and the Shootdown of Civil Aircraft under International Law" (2005) 56 AFL Rev 109 at 152-54 (dealing with distress), 154-63 (dealing with necessity).

[168] *Draft Articles on Responsibility, supra* note 166, art 24.

[169] *Ibid*, commentary to art 24 at paras 2, 5.

[170] *Ibid* at para 7.

[171] *Ibid*, commentary to art 25 at para 2.

situation. It is not clear that it provides a justification for a choice between competing obligations.

In any event, two other arguments militate against reliance on either distress or necessity in preference to adopting a proportionality of effects approach within the existing IHRL framework that governs the use of deadly force in the law enforcement context. The first is that the nature of the international obligation that is primarily at stake in the rogue civil airliner problem may either preclude a claim of necessity or render it superfluous. The wrongfulness of an act or omission that violates a peremptory norm of general international law — part of *jus cogens* — cannot be excused or justified under any circumstances.[173] There are some who assert that the right to life (and the state's obligation to ensure and respect that right) form part of *jus cogens*, although the particular substantive content of the *jus cogens* right and duty is not clear.[174] This would appear to leave open three possibilities in the context of the rogue civil airliner problem. The first is that the act or omission breaches *jus cogens*, in which case neither distress nor necessity is available as a justification or excuse. The second is that the act or omission breaches neither *jus cogens* nor any of the substantive content of the obligation to ensure and respect the right to life that is legally binding but resides outside of *jus cogens*, in which case there is no need to resort to a justification or excuse. The third is the only possibility in which a plea of necessity as a circumstance precluding responsibility is available, and it arises where there is no breach of *jus cogens* but a breach of an international obligation nonetheless. Thus, while distress and necessity may remain relevant to an analysis of the situation, they may play less of a role than might have been expected.

---

172 *Ibid*, art 25(1)(a).

173 *Ibid*, art 26.

174 See Ramcharan, *supra* note 25 at 14-15, making the argument that the right to life, "subject to certain controlled exceptions" (which presumably fall within the scope of "non-arbitrary"), is part of *jus cogens*. See also *General Comment no. 29: States of Emergency (Article 4)*, UN Human Rights Committee, 72nd Sess, UN Doc CCPR/C/21/Rev.1/Add.11(2001) at para 11. While the negative duty might be sufficiently well defined to allow for legal debate as to whether it has been breached and whether it is of peremptory character, the extent of the state's positive duties is considerably less certain. Thus, it seems premature at least to claim that there is any clearly defined right to life in *jus cogens*. It seems that the most that might be said is that some of the specific use of force obligations that define the negative aspect of the right form part of customary international law.

The second and more important argument is that invoking circumstances precluding wrongfulness still requires a legal analysis of the situation. Indeed, both distress and necessity can both only be invoked where there exists a proportionality of effects. A claim of distress cannot be made where the otherwise wrongful act or omission is "likely to create a comparable or greater peril" than the situation of distress to which it responds.[175] Indeed, the ILC's commentary to its *Draft Articles on Responsibility of States for Internationally Wrongful Acts* argues that "[d]istress can only preclude wrongfulness where the interests sought to be protected ... clearly outweigh the other interests at stake in the circumstances. If the conduct sought to be excused endangers more lives than it may save or is otherwise likely to create a greater peril it will not be covered by the plea of distress."[176] Similarly, the requirement that an act or omission in respect of which necessity is invoked "not seriously impair an essential interest of the State or States towards which the obligation exists, or the international community as a whole"[177] is said to require that "the interest relied on must outweigh all other considerations, not merely from the point of view of the acting State but on a reasonable assessment of the competing interests, whether these are individual or collective."[178]

The point to be made here is that the sort of legal analysis that must be carried out in contemplation of any claim of distress or necessity in regard to a rogue civil airliner in the law enforcement context will strongly resemble the sort of analysis that will be required under the IHRL-centred approach that I have proposed. Even if distress or necessity is claimed, international obligations can only be breached to the extent required by the circumstances, which implies conditions additional to those that the act or omission be necessary and proportionate, such as the taking of all feasible precautions to avoid, and in any event minimize, wrongful acts and omissions and their effects. Applied to its fullest extent, pleading a circumstance precluding wrongfulness would seem to require that the state carry out, in full, the legal analysis that would be required under my proposed norm of proportionality of effects.

---

[175] *Draft Articles on Responsibility, supra* note 166, art 24(2)(b).

[176] *Ibid*, commentary to art 24 at para 10.

[177] *Ibid*, art 25(1)(b).

[178] *Ibid*, commentary to art 25 at para 17.

The foregoing discussion is not an outright rejection of pleas of distress or necessity as an alternative approach to addressing the legal dimension of the rogue civil airliner problem in a law enforcement context. It is, rather, a recognition that adopting this approach may have only minimal impact (if any) on the sort of legal analysis that will be required in assessing a state's operational response to a rogue civil airliner situation. There is one important legal distinction between the approaches, however. Under a distress/necessity approach, there is no substantive change to the existing IHRL framework governing the use of deadly force by the state in a law enforcement context. By its acts or omissions, the state breaches an international law obligation to ensure and respect the right of innocent persons not to be arbitrarily deprived of life, but, at the same time, it excuses or justifies its acts or omissions through a claim of distress or necessity. Thus, the idealism of IHRL is (apparently) preserved, although with a recognition that states may attempt to escape responsibility for their breaches of its idealistic, absolutist values.

Under my proposed approach, there is a substantive change to IHRL, in that there is an expansion of what constitutes a non-arbitrary deprivation of life — although under very limited, pre-scribed circumstances. This approach to the rogue civil airliner problem is more realistic and respectful of the rule of law. The rogue civil airliner problem is one of a small set of realistically foreseeable circumstances under which the state cannot abdicate its responsibilities and accept an irreconcilable conflict in its international law duties. Given that the possibility of a rogue civil airliner is one that has now been recognized (and, indeed, there is sufficient information available to support a presumption that, at the very least, some states will not, in practice, reject out of hand the possibility of shooting down a rogue civil airliner), respect for the rule of law favours the development of a principled yet effective legal analytical framework within substantive IHRL rather than a premeditated and standing intention to breach an international obligation while invoking a circumstance precluding responsibility.[179]

Some would surely argue that IHRL must retain an idealistic, pacifist approach to individual rights and resist any acceptance of

---

[179] See Victor V Ramraj, "Between Idealism and Pragmatism: Legal and Political Constraints on State Power in Times of Crisis," in Goold and Lazarus, *supra* note 46, 185 at 189. The idea is one introduced by David Dyzenhaus.

deaths of innocent persons that are incidental to state uses of force.[180] However, if IHRL norms are to be universally respected and effectively implemented, there must be some degree of practicality to them — they must respond to and reflect social reality.[181] Otherwise, they risk irrelevance. Thus, "it might be better to have *some* rules which are effective than rules which satisfy our moral intuitions but are honoured only by their breach."[182]

CONCLUSION

The addition of a proportionality of effects analysis to the existing IHRL framework governing state uses of deadly force in a law enforcement context provides a modified framework within which to consider the rogue civil airliner problem that is principled, effective, and in line with the rule of law and with human rights — a framework, in other words, that is satisfactory. The modified framework is principled in that it accounts, under the circumstances where the proportionality of effects norm is intended to apply, for the reality that any state course of action will result in the deaths of innocent persons and provides a legal mechanism that can contribute effectively to the state's decision-making process. It is impossible under such circumstances to maintain an idealistic "purity" in IHRL and ignore the conflicting rights claims and duties that arise from categorical approaches. Such an approach is naive, irrational, and ultimately unprincipled since it deprives the decision maker of any legal analytical framework and results in the choice of a course of action that is based purely on extra-legal factors.

The modified use of force approach is effective because it accounts for the reality that some states are prepared, in appropriate circumstances, to consider shooting down a rogue civilian airliner, yet

---

180 See Schabas, *supra* note 85.

181 See Lon L Fuller, "Human Interaction and the Law" (1969) 14 Am J Juris 1 at 27.

182 Milanović, *supra* note 85 at 479. See also Heiner Bielefeldt, "Philosophical and Historical Foundations of Human Rights," in Caterina Krause and Martin Scheinin, eds, *International Protection of Human Rights: A Textbook* (Turku/Abo: Abo Akademe University Institute for Human Rights, 2009) 3 at 8-9. Kretzmer, *supra* note 12 at 27, also rejects, in very strong terms, an IHL-like proportionality of effects rule in IHRL: "[A] *rule*, which makes it lawful in advance to use force with the full knowledge that innocent persons will be killed or injured if their death or injury is not excessive in relation to the anticipated advantage of using that force" [emphasis in original].

provides them with a rational, legal framework within which to make decisions. The "balancing" approach that I propose is one that is accepted by IHL, constitutional human rights theory, and moral theory. It has proven to provide an effective analytical framework within each of these fields and brings with it a rich body of theoretical scholarship and practical application that can assist state decision makers.

The proposed framework is also consistent with the rule of law. By providing a legal framework for decision making, it ensures that state decision making is based upon something more than extralegal factors and provides protection against decisions that are arbitrary and capricious. The proportionality of effects test itself is flexible, allowing for adjustment of the weight assigned to particular interests under particular circumstances. As such, it is able to account for different state approaches to such individual interests as human dignity and the right to life. The addition of a proportionality of effects analysis under the limited circumstances proposed in no way modifies the procedural protections that already exist under the IHRL framework. Any course of action in response to the rogue civil airliner problem must be authorized by law, and any use of force that results in a deprivation of life must be the subject of an effective investigation.

Finally, the addition of a proportionality of effects analysis to the existing framework is consistent with human rights. This conclusion is, to some extent, a matter of definition. It is inherent in the rogue civil airliner problem that lives will be lost. An individual is only deprived of a protected right, however, if he or she is deprived of life arbitrarily. The modification of the existing IHRL framework governing the use of deadly force also modifies the conditions under which a deprivation of life is permitted by IHRL as not being arbitrary. This acknowledgement would seem to be entirely consistent with the apparent intention of the drafters of the *ICCPR* when they decided to adopt the more flexible language of "arbitrary" in describing the limits of the right to life. While it is important not to weaken IHRL's strong rights protections in a manner that would lead to them becoming less relevant and/or less protective under other circumstances, such a concern can be addressed by strictly limiting the circumstances in which the proportionality of effects analysis is admissible.

The proposed framework is consistent with human rights on a broader level as well. By considering the rights of all individuals implicated in the problem, a balancing approach respects and values their lives in a manner that a less principled, more arbitrary decision-making process would not. It at least does them the dignity of considering whether there exists any benefit that can justify their foreseeable deaths. Moreover, where it is accepted as inevitable that some persons will be deprived of life, the addition of a proportionality of effects analysis provides more "granularity" to the decision-making process. It allows a more nuanced assessment and fills the analytical gap created by the possibility that even though all of the other use of force norms are complied with, the deleterious effects of a course of action will still be excessive in comparison with the salutary effects.

The proposed test should not be seen as being simple window dressing to justify a decision to shoot down a rogue civil airliner. That is not its intent. The intent behind the proposal is to provide a tool for the legal analysis of the problem — one that neither provides conflicting results depending upon the group of individuals to which it is applied nor predetermines the outcome of the political, moral, and legal dilemma facing the state. Nor should the proposal be seen as an attempt to weaken human rights protections in a law enforcement context. Rather, it should be seen as advocating limited modification to a generally satisfactory legal framework that will bring increased coherence to that framework's approach to a particular set of factual circumstances.

The proportionality of effects norm that I propose is not perfect, but there is no perfect solution (legal or otherwise) to the rogue civil airliner problem. The addition of the norm to the existing IHRL framework governing state uses of deadly force in a law enforcement context does, however, provide decision makers (and their legal advisors) with a more flexible, nuanced analytical framework than would otherwise be available — one that allows a possible basis for resolution of what would otherwise be irreconcilable conflicts in the state's duties to respect and ensure the right to life arising from irreconcilable claims to that right. To refuse to consider such a balancing approach — one that incorporates an analysis of the proportionality of effects — is to deprive IHRL of a useful tool — one that is ultimately protective of the sanctity of human life.

Sommaire

L'avion de ligne civil dévoyé et le droit international de la personne: un argument pour une analyse de la proportionnalité des effets dans le cadre du droit à la vie

Les approches théoriques actuelles du droit international de la personne en ce qui a trait à l'obligation de l'État de respecter et garantir le droit de ne pas être arbitrairement privé de la vie ne fournissent pas un cadre analytique adéquat pour traiter du problème d'un avion de ligne civil dévoyé — un avion avec des passagers civils mais sous le contrôle effectif d'un ou plusieurs individus qui ont l'intention d'utiliser l'avion lui-même comme une arme contre des personnes ou des immeubles à la surface. Une approche plus utile est fournie par l'ajout d'une norme de proportionnalité des effets, par analogie à celles qui ont été développées dans le cadre du droit international humanitaire, la philosophie morale moderne et le droit constitutionnel des droits de la personne. Cette norme supplémentaire s'appliquerait seulement où il y a un conflit irréconciliable entre les devoirs de l'État à l'endroit du droit à la vie qui découle du fait que tous les cours d'action disponibles à l'État se traduiront en la mort de personnes innocentes.

Summary

The Rogue Civil Airliner and International Human Rights Law: An Argument for a Proportionality of Effects Analysis within the Right to Life

Existing theoretical approaches to international human rights law governing the state's duty to respect and ensure the right not to be arbitrarily deprived of life fail to provide a satisfactory analytical framework within which to consider the problem of a rogue civil airliner — a passenger-carrying civil aircraft under the effective control of one or more individuals who intend to use the aircraft itself as a weapon against persons or property on the surface. A more satisfactory approach is provided by the addition of a norm of proportionality of effects that is analogous to those that have been developed within the frameworks of international humanitarian law, moral philosophy, and modern constitutional rights law. This additional norm would apply only where there is an irreconcilable conflict between the state's duties in respect of the right to life such that all of the courses of action available will result in innocent persons being deprived of life.

Regional Arrangements and the Maintenance of International Peace and Security: The Role of the African Union Peace and Security Council

CHARLES RIZIKI MAJINGE

Introduction

The adoption of the *Constitutive Act of the African Union* (*Constitutive Act*) in 2000 was not only an act that paved the way for reconstituting Africa's political and economic framework, but it also ushered in a new era in which there is a compelling need for African countries to assume greater responsibility for addressing the peace and security challenges confronting the African continent.[1] Thus, the new African Union (AU) framework made provision for the

Charles Riziki Majinge, LL.B. (University of Dar Es Salaam), LL.M. (Northwestern University School of Law, Chicago), is a doctoral candidate in the London School of Economics and Political Science. I am grateful to Dr. Tim Murithi of the Institute for Justice and Reconciliation in Cape Town, South Africa, and external anonymous reviewers whose comments and suggestions were extremely useful. It was also a great pleasure working with the editors of the *Canadian Yearbook of International Law*, whose meticulous support helped get this article into its current form. I gratefully acknowledge the insightful discussion with Judge James L. Kateka of the International Tribunal for the Law of the Sea and former member of the United Nations International Law Commission. I am most grateful to my joint doctoral supervisors Chaloka Beyani and Christine Chinkin, whose constant support in the preparation of my doctoral thesis continues to be outstanding and a source of inspiration. The author is solely responsible for any errors.

1 *Constitutive Act of the African Union*, 11 July 2000, OAU Doc CAB/LEG/23.15 (2000) (entered into force 26 May 2001) [*Constitutive Act*]; Corrine A Packer and Donald Rukare, "The African Union and Its Constitutive Act" (2002) 96 AJIL 365. See also Tiyanjana Maluwa, "The Constitutive Act of the African Union and Institution-Building in Post-Colonial Africa" (2003) 16:1 Leiden J Int'l L 157 at 157-70; Tiyanjana Maluwa, "Reimagining African Unity: Some Preliminary Reflections on the Constitutive Act of the African Union" (2001) 9 Afr YB Int'l L 3 at 3-15.

creation of the Peace and Security Council (PSC),[2] an organ specifically conceived to address African peace and security issues.[3] The establishment of the AU PSC is significant not only because it assumes the powerful role of determining and addressing threats to African peace and security but also because it is the supreme organ responsible for peace and security issues specifically related to Africa.

The creation of the AU PSC raises several important questions relating to the maintenance of international peace and security, especially from an African perspective. For example, does the organization's power to determine threats to peace and security interfere with the primary role of the United Nations (UN) Security Council?[4] If not, what happens when the AU PSC determines the existence of threats to international peace and security but fails to act? And, perhaps most crucially, how does the UN Security Council ensure that regional arrangements that receive mandates under Article 53 of the *Charter of the United Nations* (*UN Charter*) are sufficiently empowered to discharge their functions on its behalf?[5] It is this latter question that is the focus of this article. I will attempt to demonstrate that, although the AU PSC clearly has a mandate to maintain peace and security on the African continent, its capacity

---

[2] *Constitutive Act, supra* note 1, art 5(2). The African Union Peace and Security Council (AU PSC) was established under the *Protocol Relating to the Establishment of the Peace and Security Council of the African Union*, 9 July 2002,online: <http://www.au.int/en/sites/default/files/997Peace_and_Security.pdf> (entered into force 26 December 2003) [*AU PSC Protocol*].

[3] The AU PSC is composed of fifteen members. As of January 2011, its members are: Rwanda, Burundi, Benin, Ivory Coast (suspended in December 2010), Chad, Mauritania, Namibia, South Africa, Kenya, Djibouti, Zimbabwe, Nigeria, Libya, Equatorial Guinea, and Mali. See African Union, online: <http://www.africa-union.org/root/au/AUC/Departments/PSC/PSC.htm>. See further Jakkie Cilliers, "Hopes and Challenges for the Peace and Security Architecture of the African Union," in Hany Besada, ed, *Crafting an African Security Architecture: Addressing Regional Peace and Conflict in the Twenty-First Century* (Surrey: Ashgate, 2010) 37 at 37-50.

[4] Art 24(1) of the *Charter of the United Nations*, 26 June 1945, Can TS 1945, No 7 [*UN Charter*], designates the UN Security Council as the primary body responsible for determining threats to, and maintaining, international peace and security. See also David M Malone, ed, *The UN Security Council: From the Cold War to the Twenty-First Century* (Boulder, CO: Lynn Rienner, 2004).

[5] Art 53 of the *UN Charter, supra* note 4, provides that the UN Security Council may delegate enforcement action in international peace and security matters to regional arrangements or agencies, such as the AU PSC.

to do so has been, and continues to be, constrained by inadequate financial and logistical capabilities. Given the existence of these challenges, it remains the responsibility of the UN to improve funding of international peace and security initiatives in Africa.[6]

Challenges to international peace and security in Africa were especially prevalent during the post-independence period of many African countries, beginning in the 1960s.[7] Indeed, during this period, many African countries experienced successive military coups, cross-border and intra-state conflicts, influxes of refugees, and military interventions from both within and beyond the continent.[8] Collectively, these events eroded the capacity of most African states to guarantee peace and security within their own borders. Institutions that were specifically created to address these challenges, such as the Organization of African Unity (OAU), were haplessly ill-positioned to do so because of inherent limitations in their institutional and legal frameworks and, perhaps more importantly, because they were more interested in the liberation struggle than the outcome of the struggle itself.[9] In this post-independence period, African countries viewed Western countries that had colonized the continent for much of its history as a common enemy that posed an existential threat to their well-being. As such, the role of the OAU was to mobilize resources and defend the continent against this common enemy. Threats to peace and security were considered matters best handled within the domestic framework of each state. Consequently, OAU member states agreed on the

---

6 Njunga-Michael Mulikita, "Cooperation versus Dissonance: The UN Security Council and the Evolving African Union (AU)?" (2001) 9 Afr YB Int'l L 75 at 75-77.

7 See generally Adekeye Adebajo, *The Curse of Berlin: Africa after the Cold War* (New York: Columbia University Press, 2010). See also Francis Deng et al, *Sovereignty as Responsibility: Conflict Management in Africa* (Washington, DC: Brookings Institution, 1996) 1-30; Solomon Gomes, "The OAU, State Sovereignty, and Regional Security," in Edmond J Keller and Donald Rothchild, eds, *Africa in the New International Order: Rethinking State Sovereignty and Regional Security* (Boulder, CO: Lynne Rienner, 1996) 37.

8 See UN Security Council, *Report of the Secretary-General: The Causes of Conflict and the Promotion of Durable Peace and Sustainable Development in Africa*, UN Doc A/52/871-S/1998/31 (1998).

9 Samuel M Makinda and F Wafula Okumu, *The African Union: Challenges of Globalization, Security, and Governance* (London and New York: Routledge, 2008) at 22-24. See also Christopher Clapham, *Africa and the International System: The Politics of State Survival* (Cambridge: Cambridge University Press, 1996) at 8-32.

principle of non-intervention in the internal affairs of other states.[10] With this principle's entrenchment in the *OAU Charter*, countries could abuse human rights with impunity, and OAU leaders refrained from speaking out against such abuses for fear of being seen as interfering in the internal affairs of their peers.[11] It is under this provision that dictators such as Mobutu in Zaire, Bokassa in the Central African Republic, Idi Amin in Uganda, and Siad Barre in Somalia survived and perpetrated serious violations of human rights against their citizens.[12]

Admittedly, during this period, the OAU did involve itself in conflict resolution, but it restricted itself to addressing border disputes that were considered to pose a threat to peace among newly independent countries who had committed themselves through the *Cairo Declaration on Border Disputes among African States Legitimizing National Borders Inherited from Colonial Times* to respect colonial borders bequeathed to Africa upon independence.[13] The doctrines of sovereign equality among states, non-interference in internal affairs, and inviolability of the borders left by the departing colonial powers constituted cardinal principles that defined the modalities and parameters of multilateral co-operation within the OAU.[14]

---

[10] *OAU Charter*, 25 May 1963, online: African Union <http://www.au.int/en/sites/ default/files/OAU_Charter_1963_0.pdf> art 3 [*OAU Charter*]. See also P Mweti Munya, "The Organization of African Unity and Its Role in Regional Conflict Resolution and Dispute Settlement: A Critical Evaluation" (1999) 19 BC Third World LJ 537 at 537-51.

[11] *OAU Charter*, *supra* note 10.

[12] Abdulqawi A Yusuf, "Reflections on the Fragility of State Institutions in Africa" (1994) 2 Afr YB Int'l L 3 at 9. For an account of the human rights situation in Africa during this period, see Rachel Murray, *Human Rights in Africa: From the OAU to the African Union* (Cambridge: Cambridge University Press, 2004).

[13] *Cairo Declaration on Border Disputes among African States Legitimizing National Borders Inherited from Colonial Times*, reproduced in Ian Brownlie, *African Boundaries: A Legal and Diplomatic Encyclopaedia* (London: C. Hurst and Company, 1979) at 11 [*Cairo Declaration*]. See Garth Abraham, "'Lines upon Maps': Africa and the Sanctity of African Boundaries" (2007) 15 Afr J Int'l & Comp L 61. See also EKM Yakpo, "The African Concept of Uti Possidetis: Need for Change?" in Emile Yakpo and Tahar Boumedra, eds, *Liber Amicorum: Judge Mohammed Bedjaoui* (The Hague: Kluwer Law International, 1999) 272 at 274-77; Jeremy I Levitt, "Africa: A Maker of International Law," in Jeremy I Levitt, ed, *Africa: Mapping New Boundaries in International Law* (Oxford: Hart, 2008) 1 at 1-3.

[14] *OAU Charter*, *supra* note 10, art 3. See Solomon Gomes, "The Peace Making Role of the OAU and AU: A Comparative Analysis," in John Akokpari, Angela Ndinga-Muvumba, and Tim Murithi, eds, *The African Union and Its Institutions* (Sunnyside,

With the end of the Cold War and the disintegration of the Soviet Union, African countries had to wake up to the reality of new common threats facing them. Threats to their existence and well-being were no longer confined to external interference from Western countries. The genocide in Rwanda, which claimed almost a million lives, provided a devastating reality check. Africa had to confront security challenges emanating from within. Intra-state conflicts within African states, rather than external intervention, were causing much of the insecurity on the continent.[15] Continued dictatorship, complete disregard for, and abuse of, human rights, unconstitutional changes of government, sham and inconclusive elections, and the flow of refugees all posed a greater threat to the continent than the traditional enemy — that is, former colonial powers. With this realization came the need to address these challenges collectively, mainly because it was in the interests of all countries to pull together to achieve change. For example, neighbouring states would bear many of the consequences of conflict within Somalia or Liberia, whether through hosting refugees or dealing with increased cross-border criminal activity. Consequently, in 1993, the OAU decided to create a security framework to address peace and security challenges on the continent.[16]

Yet, mainly because of the failure of African states to commit to this framework, it did not achieve its intended objectives. This failure was caused not only by the lingering unwillingness of African countries to allow any possibility of external intervention in what they considered their domestic affairs but also by their inability to commit adequate resources to operationalize the framework. These developments allowed states to continue their practices of abusing human rights and disregarding the international rule of law with impunity.

South Africa: Fanele, 2008) 113 at 113-17. See also Pierre Englebert, *Africa: Unity, Sovereignty and Sorrow* (Boulder, CO: Lynne Rienner, 2009).

15 OAU, *Report of the Secretary General on the Establishment of an International Panel of Eminent Personalities to Investigate the Genocide in Rwanda and the Surrounding Events*, Doc CM/2048 (LXVII) (1997). The panel's report was released on 7 July 2000. International Panel of Eminent Personalities (IPEP), "Report of the 1994 Genocide in Rwanda and Surrounding Events, 2000 (Selected Sections)" (2007) 40 ILM 141.

16 *Declaration of the Assembly of Heads of State and Government on the Establishment within the OAU of a Mechanism for Conflict Prevention, Management and Resolution*, OAU Assembly, 29th Sess, OAU Doc AHG/DECL.3 (XXIX) (1993) [*Mechanism for Conflict Prevention*].

It is also important to acknowledge that, despite the far-reaching political and social implications of the profound security challenges that were dominating the African continent, the UN Security Council did not fully live up to its responsibility as guarantor of international peace and security either.[17] This observation is made in light of the many conflicts in Africa that have claimed millions of lives without intervention by the UN Security Council. In cases where the UN Security Council did intervene, it did so either too late or without adequate resources to carry out the missions successfully.[18] There are different explanations for the absence of, or reluctant, involvement of the UN Security Council in some African conflicts. These include, among others, the dynamics of the UN's internal functioning; inadequate resources (or the unwillingness of powerful countries to provide adequate resources); and the threat or use of the veto by permanent members whose own interests would be threatened by external involvement in such conflicts.[19]

As a result, African countries recognized that they faced a stark choice: either develop their own peace and security framework or continue to depend on the UN Security Council, whose assistance was neither predictable nor assured. The AU decided to pursue the former course. As Ambassador Said Djinnit, former AU commissioner for peace and security, stated:

Africans cannot ... watch the tragedies developing in the continent and say it is the UN's responsibility or somebody else's responsibility ... [W]e cannot as Africans remain indifferent to the tragedy of our people.[20]

Despite these and similar words from senior African diplomats such as Ambassador Djinnit, who have expressed optimism and political will, the challenge has been to translate these commitments

---

[17] For an account of UN failures in Africa, see, for example, UN Security Council, *Report of the Independent Inquiry into the Actions of the United Nations during the 1994 Genocide in Rwanda*, UN Doc S/1999/1257 (1999). See also IPEP, *supra* note 15.

[18] *Ibid.*

[19] JPD Dunbabin, "The Security Council in the Wings: Exploring the Security Council's Non-Involvement in Wars," in Vaughan Lowe et al, eds, *The United Nations Security Council and War: The Evolution of Thought and Practice since 1945* (Oxford: Oxford University Press, 2008) 494 at 500-3.

[20] Ambassador Said Djinnit, address delivered at Addis Ababa, 28 June 2004, quoted in Kristiana Powell, "The African Union's Emerging Peace and Security Regime: Opportunities and Challenges for Delivering on *The Responsibility to Protect*" (2005) 119 North-South Institute 1 at 4.

into reality. The decision to establish the AU PSC to address threats to peace and security was the hallmark of the AU's new vision and desire to provide African solutions for African problems.[21] It can be argued that while the mechanism may be imperfect, it reaffirms Africa's willingness to take measures to address the challenges it is facing without having to depend on international assistance — the record of which on the African continent is a mixture of abysmal success and spectacular failure. Yet despite these bold measures, as this article will show, the capacity of the AU PSC to address peace and security challenges continues to be highly constrained by the inability of AU member states to resource the organization adequately.

The remainder of this article proceeds in five parts. The next section examines the role of the UN Security Council in the maintenance of international peace and security. Following this examination, a detailed analysis is provided of the role of regional arrangements in securing peace and stability under Article 53 of the *UN Charter*. Next, the mandate of the AU PSC, and particularly its function as the primary security actor on the African continent, is examined. The capacity of the AU PSC to secure peace and security in Africa is then evaluated by reflecting on various initiatives it has undertaken. Finally, some observations are offered on how the role of the AU PSC can be enhanced so that it can perform its functions effectively and thereby contribute to peace and stability in Africa.

The UN Security Council and the Maintenance of International Peace and Security

The *UN Charter* bestows upon the UN Security Council the primary, albeit not exclusive, mandate to maintain international peace and security. Article 24(1) of the *UN Charter* provides that this responsibility is conferred on the Security Council by member states in order to ensure prompt and effective action by the UN. UN members also agree that the UN Security Council, in carrying out its

---

21 For an introduction to the subject "African solutions for African problems," see Matthias Goldmann, "Sierra Leone: African Solutions to African Problems?" (2005) 9 Max Planck YB UN Law 457 at 468-71. See also Hany Besada, Ariane Goetz, and Karolina Werner, "African Solutions for African Problems and Shared R2P" in Besada, *supra* note 3, 1 at 1-10; Ulf Engel and João Gomes Porto, eds, *Africa's New Peace and Security Architecture: Promoting Norms, Institutionalizing Solutions* (Farnham, UK: Ashgate, 2010).

duties under this responsibility, acts on their behalf.[22] Unlike the UN General Assembly, the Security Council can take decisions that are binding on all UN members.[23] When viewed in the overall, historical context of UN decision making, it is clear that the UN Security Council has played the dominant role in determining the existence of threats to international peace and security since the *UN Charter*'s adoption in 1945.[24]

The UN Security Council's primary role as guarantor of international peace and security is underpinned by Article 39 of the *UN Charter*, which empowers the Security Council to "determine the existence of any threat to the peace, breach of the peace, or act of aggression and ... make recommendations, or decide what measures shall be taken ... to maintain or restore international peace and security."[25] Reading this provision, it is clear that the Security Council has authority to characterize any situation as constituting a threat to international peace and security — whether in a particular region of the world or within individual states. Interestingly, the *UN Charter* neither provides criteria for such determinations nor compels the Security Council to intervene in any particular situation. Rather, it leaves decisions as to whether and on what basis to intervene within the prerogative of the Security Council. Nor does Article 39 specify the mechanisms to be used by the Security Council when intervening. Rather, the choice of such mechanisms is also left to the discretion of the Security Council (subject, however, to the broad but non-exhaustive parameters set out in Articles 41 and 42).

While it is therefore clear that the UN Security Council has the primary role in determining threats to international peace and security, with broad powers to match, its perennial failure to exercise this responsibility effectively, or its selectivity in doing so, have raised concerns in some quarters as to its willingness and ability to tackle

---

22 *UN Charter, supra* note 4, art 24(1).

23 Paul C Szasz, "The Security Council Starts Legislating" (2002) 96 AJIL 901. For detailed discussion of the powers of the UN Security Council, see Erika De Wet, *The Chapter VII Powers of the United Nations Security Council* (Oxford: Hart, 2004); Bruno Simma, *The Charter of the United Nations: A Commentary*, 2nd edition (Oxford: Oxford University Press, 2002).

24 Edward C Luck, "A Council for All Seasons: The Creation of the Security Council and Its Relevance Today," in Lowe et al, *supra* note 19, 61 at 61-82. See also Mohammed Bedjaoui, *The New World Order and the Security Council: Testing the Legality of Its Acts* (Dordrecht: Martinus Nijhoff, 1994).

25 *UN Charter, supra* note 4, art 39.

pressing global challenges relating to peace and security issues.[26] The question that therefore arises is: when and how should the UN Security Council exercise its powers to maintain or restore international peace and security? This question is especially relevant *vis-à-vis* Africa, which for a long time has experienced tragic events that have claimed millions of lives with minimal commitment from the Security Council to address these situations.[27] As noted earlier, the *UN Charter* does not provide express benchmarks to be applied by the UN Security Council when deciding whether to determine the existence of a threat to international peace and security. Rather, as experience has shown, Security Council intervention in most cases only occurs when the permanent five members — who not only enjoy veto powers but also wield unchallenged military capabilities — are on the same page or when their interests are threatened.

It is not by coincidence that the permanent members of the UN Security Council are the countries with the most powerful military capabilities, as these were the powers that emerged victorious in the aftermath of the Second World War. Their victory ensured that their military and economic capabilities were unrivalled and that they could shape the global peace and security framework to their own liking, at least to the extent that their interests were aligned.

Furthermore, given the tragic history of colonialism, the permanent members of the UN Security Council have their own "spheres of influence." All UN Security Council interventions have reflected this unofficial balance of powers. For example, while the United Kingdom's intervention in Sierra Leone and France's interventions in the Democratic Republic of the Congo (DRC), Chad, and Ivory Coast were undertaken under the UN umbrella, it is clear that these powers took a leading role in intervening in these countries due to their past colonial linkages.[28] This claim is made in light of the

---

26 Dapo Akande, "The International Court of Justice and the Security Council: Is There Room for Judicial Control of the Decisions of the Political Organs of the United Nations?" (1997) 46:2 ICLQ 309. See also Christine M Chinkin, "Kosovo: A 'Good' or 'Bad' War?" (1999) 93 AJIL 841 at 845-47; Bedjaoui, *supra* note 24 at 9-20, 37-50.

27 Ike Minta, "The Rwanda Conflict: With the Failure of Peacekeeping, Is Peacemaking Still Possible?" (1996) 4 Afr YB Int'l L 19 at 19-25. See also Mohammed Ayoob, *The Third World Security Predicament: State Making, Regional Conflict, and the International System* (Boulder, CO: Lynne Rienner, 1995).

28 John Quigley, "The 'Privatization' of Security Council Enforcement Action: A Threat to Multilateralism" (1996) 17 Mich J Int'l L 249 at 270-73. See also

failure of the same powers to commit their resources in places such as Somalia or Darfur.[29]

Admittedly, intervention by the UN Security Council has traditionally occurred within the larger UN framework, whether through direct military intervention or the authorization of peacekeeping missions. Despite this practice, it is indisputable that the Security Council has only taken action when its members are willing to commit their troops and other financial resources to the cause of peace. Whether such a commitment is made often depends on whether the intervention will serve particular states' strategic interests.[30] This practice has meant that countries considered of no strategic value to major powers have had to endure long spells of devastating conflict with inadequate or no intervention by the UN Security Council. These countries are left with few options: they must either turn to regional arrangements or seek out states capable of offering bilateral assistance outside of the UN peace and security framework.

REGIONAL ARRANGEMENTS AND THE MAINTENANCE OF INTERNATIONAL PEACE AND SECURITY

An examination of the engagement of the UN Security Council in addressing peace and security issues on the African continent reveals that the practice of the UN Security Council has been to delegate its Chapter VII powers to regional arrangements where necessary for the maintenance or restoration of international peace and security.[31] The *UN Charter* explicitly recognizes such a role for regional

---

Michael Barnett, *Eyewitness to a Genocide: The United Nations and Rwanda* (Ithaca, NY: Cornell University Press, 2002).

[29] Alex Belamy, "Responsibility to Protect or Trojan Horse? The Crisis in Darfur and Humanitarian Intervention after Iraq" (2005) Ethics & Int'l Affairs 31 at 31-42. See also Thomas G Weiss, "The Sunset of Humanitarian Intervention? The Responsibility to Protect in a Unipolar Era" (2004) 35:2 Security Dialogue 135 at 136-42.

[30] Simon Chesterman, *Just War or Just Peace? Humanitarian Intervention and International Law* (Oxford: Oxford University Press, 2003) at 163-251. See also Eric Heinze, *Waging Humanitarian War: The Ethics, Law, and Politics of Humanitarian Intervention* (Albany, NY: State University of New York Press, 2009).

[31] Danesh Sarooshi, *The United Nations and the Development of Collective Security: The Delegation by the UN Security Council of Its Chapter VII Powers* (Oxford: Oxford University Press, 2000) at 253.

organizations.[32] While Chapter VIII of the *UN Charter* authorizes the UN Security Council to delegate peace enforcement action to regional arrangements, it is important to note that Chapter VIII does not in and of itself delegate such power to regional arrangements. Rather, context-specific delegation by the Security Council is needed. Article 53(1) of the *UN Charter*, in particular, provides that "[t]he Security Council shall, where appropriate, utilize such regional arrangements or agencies for enforcement action under its authority. But no enforcement action shall be taken under regional arrangements or by regional agencies without the authorization of the Security Council."[33] In thus allowing the UN Security Council to make use of regional mechanisms to carry out peace enforcement activities in some cases but not in others, Article 53(1) inherently reaffirms the UN Security Council's ultimate power to determine the best way to deal with threats to international peace and security.[34]

In addition to the requirement of case-by-case authorization by the UN Security Council for military enforcement action by a regional arrangement, the UN Security Council must also be able to continue to exercise its overall authority and control over the use of its delegated powers. This is because the delegation of powers is not the same as the transfer of powers *in toto*.[35]

Although Article 53(1) foresees that peace enforcement powers may be delegated to a regional arrangement, state practice shows that such powers are often in fact exercised by individual states acting within the regional arrangement framework rather than by the regional arrangement itself. For example, during the civil wars in Liberia and Sierra Leone, the UN Security Council delegated its powers to maintain and restore peace and security in these countries

---

[32] *UN Charter, supra* note 4, c VIII. See also generally Sarooshi, *supra* note 31.

[33] *UN Charter, supra* note 4, art 53(1).

[34] Sarooshi, *supra* note 31 at 248-52; *UN Charter, supra* note 4.

[35] See Danesh Sarooshi, *The United Nations and the Development of Collective Security: The Delegation by the UN Security Council of its Chapter VII Powers* (Oxford: Oxford University Press, 1999) at 7. There have been instances where the UN Security Council has retroactively "validated" regional arrangements' interventions undertaken without prior UN Security Council authorization — for example, the intervention by the Economic Community of West African States (ECOWAS) in West Africa. The legality of such retroactive validation will not be addressed here, however, given that the focus of this article is advance resource provision to the AU PSC by the UN Security Council and, hence, on the prior authorization scenario.

to the Economic Community of West African States Monitoring Group (ECOMOG). However, those powers were exercised by Nigeria and a handful of other regional states acting under and within the framework of that regional arrangement.

In this connection, the distinction between regional and sub-regional organizations is significant. In UN practice, the AU is classified as a regional arrangement within the meaning of Chapter VIII of the *UN Charter*, while regional mechanisms such as the Economic Community of West African States (ECOWAS) and the South African Development Community (SADC) are recognized as sub-regional arrangements. Sub-regional arrangements in Africa have undertaken responsibility to maintain peace and security at times more successfully than regional arrangements such as the OAU and its successor the AU. For example, when comparing ECOWAS initiatives in Sierra Leone and Liberia, on the one hand, and OAU intervention in Chad or Rwanda, on the other, it is clear that the former performed much better. Similarly, the SADC intervention in Lesotho and Burundi was significantly more successful than the AU's efforts in Somalia.[36] This contrast in the success of regional and sub-regional organizations may be attributable to a number of factors, but chief among them is that sub-regional arrangements have often been able to rely on the capabilities of sub-regionally dominant member states that consider themselves vulnerable to the threats posed by local conflicts. Thus, in ECOWAS, Nigeria has often taken the lead to address peace and security challenges within the region partly for fear of the destabilizing effects on its economy that might result from regional instability.[37] The same can be said of South Africa and its dominant role within the SADC.[38]

It should also be noted that the growing practice of the UN Security Council in responding to threats to peace and security in Africa

---

[36] Devon Curtis and Gilbert Nibigirwe, "Complementary Approaches to Peacekeeping? The African Union and the United Nations in Burundi," in Besada, *supra* note 3, 109 at 109-25. See also Emma Svensson, *The African Mission in Burundi: Lessons Learned from the African Union's First Peace Operation* (Stockholm: Swedish Defence Research Agency, 2008) at 8-17; Cedric de Coning, "The Evolution of Peace Operation in Africa: Trajectories and Trends" (2010) 14 J Int'l Peacekeeping 6 at 6-12.

[37] Adekeye Adebajo and Christopher Landsberg, "South Africa and Nigeria as Regional Hegemons," in Mwesiga Baregu and Christopher Landsberg, eds, *From Cape to Congo: Southern Africa's Evolving Security Challenges* (Boulder, CO: Lynne Rienner, 2003) 171 at 171-84.

[38] *Ibid.*

has largely followed one of two options. The first option has been to use regional or sub-regional arrangements to take up the entire responsibility of maintaining peace on behalf of the UN Security Council. This mechanism was used in West Africa with ECOWAS,[39] in Central Africa with the SADC,[40] and in East Africa with the African Union Mission in Somalia.[41] The second option has been to deploy non-regional peacekeeping forces as well. While these latter missions tend arguably to be dominated by African troops, they have also included troops from countries outside Africa including Bangladesh, Pakistan, India, and Sri Lanka. Examples of the use of this second option include the interventions in Darfur and Congo.

However, the major question and focus of this article is not whether the UN Security Council can give mandates to regional arrangements to address threats to peace and security, but, rather, whether the UN Security Council provides or ought to provide adequate resources to these arrangements so that they can exercise their mandates successfully. The competence of the UN Security Council to delegate its Chapter VII powers to a regional arrangement does not in itself mean that the regional arrangement has the institutional capacity or competence to exercise these powers.[42] It has been, and continues to be, a major challenge for the use of regional arrangements to address threats to peace and security in Africa, as the UN Security Council has from time to time authorized regional entities to undertake collective efforts to maintain peace and security without providing resources for such undertakings.[43] Yet, while these regional arrangements exercise powers that have been delegated to them by the UN Security Council, the Security Council still retains primary responsibility under the *UN Charter* to secure global peace and security.

The fact that the history of the UN Security Council's commitment to fulfilment of its *UN Charter* responsibility to maintain peace and

[39] Binaifer Nowrojee, "Joining Forces: United Nations and Regional Peacekeeping — Lessons from Liberia" (1995) 8 Harv Hum Rts J 129 at 129-45. See also Adekeye Adebajo, *Liberia's Civil War: Nigeria, ECOMOG, and Regional Security in West Africa* (Boulder, CO: Lynne Rienner, 2002).

[40] Charles Riziki Majinge, "The Future of Peacekeeping in Africa and the Normative Role of the African Union" (2010) 2:2 Goettingen J Int'l L 463 at 481-83.

[41] *Ibid* at 495-99.

[42] See, eg, Sarooshi, *supra* note 31 at 246.

[43] Jane Boulden, "United Nations Security Council Policy on Africa," in Jane Boulden, ed, *Dealing with Conflicts in Africa: The United Nations and Regional Organizations* (New York: Palgrave Macmillan, 2003) 11 at 11-23.

security has not been positive, especially in Africa, is readily illustrated. For example, the ECOMOG intervention in Sierra Leone
to restore the government of Tejan Kabbah was undertaken without
a commitment by the UN Security Council to provide financial resources. Rather, ECOMOG was compelled to rely on resources from
its own members, some of whom happened to be embroiled in
conflicts of their own that required, conversely, the assistance of
ECOMOG.[44]

Similarly, the ECOWAS mission in Liberia in the 1990s relied
primarily on its own resources with little help from the UN Security
Council. Admittedly, the UN did take over both missions after they
were established.[45] However, the UN did not start taking an active
role in the Liberian conflict until it escalated in 1993 and the *Cotonou
Agreement* had been signed.[46] Internal squabbles within ECOWAS,
which saw different countries supporting different factions involved
in the conflict, cannot be considered as a compelling excuse for
the UN Security Council's dithering response. Irrespective of the
conflicting interests of the states or factions involved in the conflict,
the UN Security Council, as the guarantor of international peace
and security, has the responsibility to use its powers to maintain
peace. Yet the lukewarm response of the UN Security Council was
vivid even when ECOMOG had sent in more than 16,000 troops.
The Security Council did not pick up the tab. Rather, it only provided full funding when it took over the mission from ECOMOG.[47]
And notwithstanding this ultimate assumption of responsibility for
the mission, the motive behind the initial reluctance of the UN to
support the effort of the regional organization is questionable. The
perennial challenge of mobilizing adequate resources would have
been addressed if the Security Council had provided sufficient financial and logistical support to ECOWAS to enable it to discharge
its duties. Indeed, the conflict would likely have been resolved more
swiftly while minimizing the long-term suffering of civilians.

In yet another example, the AU decided to send troops to Somalia
in 2007 to secure peace and stability there by supporting the

---

[44] Adekeye Adebajo, "The Security Council and Three Wars in West Africa," in
Lowe et al, *supra* note 19, 465 at 476-80.

[45] *Ibid.*

[46] *Cotonou Agreement* [Liberia], 25 July 1993, UN Doc S/26272 (9 August 1993),
Annex, online: <http://www.unhcr.org/refworld/docid/3ae6b5796.html>
[*Cotonou Agreement*].

[47] Adebajo, *supra* note 44 at 472-75, 489.

Transitional Federal Government.[48] While the UN Security Council had adopted Resolution 1744, reaffirming its support for the establishment of the mission by the AU and asking the secretary-general to send a technical assessment mission to look into the possibility of a UN peacekeeping operation to follow the AU deployment, the AU mission, which is essentially fulfilling the UN Security Council's responsibilities, has faced continuing challenges of inadequate and sometimes unavailable resources for the discharge of its functions.[49] And while the UN Security Council has continued to adopt resolutions reaffirming the willingness of the international community to resolve the conflict in Somalia, it has also continued to fail to provide adequate resources to the mission.[50] The current situation in Somalia is a powerful reminder of what happens when the UN Security

---

[48] AU-PSC, *Communiqué of the Sixty-Ninth Meeting of the Peace and Security Council,* 69th Meeting, Doc PSC/PR/Comm (LXIX) (2007) [*Communiqué of the Sixty-Ninth Meeting*].

[49] UN Security Council Resolution 1744, UNSC, 5633rd Meeting, UN Doc S/Res/1744 (2007).

[50] See, eg, Security Council Resolution 1910, UNSC, 6266th Meeting, UN Doc S/Res/1910 (2010). This resolution reiterates the UN Security Council's and international community's commitment to support the African Union Mission in Somalia's (AMISOM) peacekeeping efforts. See also UN Security Council Resolution 751, UNSC, 3069th Meeting, UN Doc S/Res/751 (1992); UN Security Council Resolution 1356, UNSC, 4332nd Meeting, UN Doc S/Res/1356 (2001); UN Security Council Resolution 1425, UNSC, 4580th Meeting, UN Doc S/Res/1425 (2002); UN Security Council Resolution 1519, UNSC, 4885th Meeting, UN Doc S/Res/1519 (2003); UN Security Council Resolution 1725, UNSC, 5579th Meeting, UN Doc S/Res/1725 (2006); UN Security Council Resolution 1772, UNSC, 5732nd Meeting, UN Doc S/Res/1772 (2007); UN Security Council Resolution 1801, UNSC, 5842nd meeting, UN Doc S/Res/1801 (2008); UN Security Council Resolution 1811, UNSC, 5879th Meeting, UN Doc S/Res/1811 (2008); UN Security Council Resolution 1814, UNSC, 5893rd Meeting, UN Doc S/Res/1814 (2008); UN Security Council Resolution 1844, UNSC, 6019th Meeting, UN Doc S/Res/1844 (2008). The Security Council has also adopted various presidential statements on Somalia that reaffirm its commitment to finding a lasting peace in Somalia. See, eg, Statement by the President of the UN Security Council, UNSC, 5486th Meeting, UN Doc S/PRST/2006/31 (2006); Statement by the President of the Security Council, UNSC, UNSC, 5611th Meeting, UN Doc S/PRST/2006/59 (2006); Statement by the President of the UN Security Council, UNSC, 5671st Meeting, UN Doc S/PRST/2007/13 (2007); Statement by the President of the UN Security Council, UNSC, 5695th Meeting, UN Doc S/PRST/2007/19 (2007); Statement by the President of the UN Security Council, UNSC, 5812th Meeting, UN Doc S/PRST/2007/49 (2007); Statement by the President of the Security Council, UNSC, 5970th meeting, UN Doc S/PRST/2008/33 (2008).

Council abdicates its responsibility to maintain international peace and security and leaves the task to under-resourced regional organizations.

In Darfur, the peacekeeping mission struggled until it was hybridized to include both UN and AU forces. Yet, while it can be argued that the hybridization of the UN Mission in Darfur has brought significant improvement in security in the region, at the time of writing the number of those displaced by conflict continues to swell, and rebels opposed to the government continue to pose security challenges to civilians, peacekeepers, and humanitarian personnel.[51] These situations demonstrate that the willingness of the UN Security Council to delegate its powers to regional arrangements in Africa has in most cases not been matched by a willingness to provide sufficient accompanying support to allow such mandates to be carried out effectively.

Finally, mention must be made of Rwanda, where the UN failed to provide assistance when almost a million people were slaughtered in one hundred days.[52] Indeed, it is the atrocities in Rwanda that most compelled African countries to re-evaluate their relationship with the UN Security Council and what can realistically be expected from it in resolving peace and security challenges on the African continent. Their frustration is eloquently summed up by Ambassador Sam Ibok who stated:

The UN has global responsibility for the maintenance of international peace and security. In spite of this, genocide took place in Rwanda. It took place in Rwanda because Africans had to wait for more than six months for the deployment of UN peacekeeping forces. The same thing happened in Somalia, in the DRC, in Burundi, in Liberia and in Côte D'Ivoire.[53]

This repeated failure by the UN Security Council to address some of Africa's most profound security challenges has progressively

---

[51] Tim Murithi, "The African Union's Foray into Peacekeeping: Lessons from the Hybrid Mission in Darfur" (2009) 14 J of Peace, Conflict & Development, online: <http://www.peacestudiesjournal.org.uk/dl/Issue%2014%20Article%2015%20 Revised%20copy%201.pdf>.

[52] IPEP, *supra* note 15.

[53] Sam Ibok, "The OAU/AU: Records, Challenges and Prospects," in Abdalla Bujra and Hussein Solomon, eds, *Perspectives on the OAU/AU and Conflict Management in Africa* (Tripoli, Addis Ababa: African Center for Applied Research and Training in Social Development, Community of Sahel-Sahara States, Development Policy Management Forum, 2004) 11 at 16.

reinforced the AU's desire for greater autonomy in finding solutions for the continent's most pressing peace and security issues. Similarly, sub-regional arrangements in Africa have expressed their willingness to address peace and security issues. Yet equally true is the fact that they have faced difficult challenges in carrying out this vision. The issue is no longer whether these entities enjoy adequate mandates from the UN Security Council but, rather, how the required resources can be mobilized to undertake these responsibilities. As the situation in Somalia has demonstrated, the UN Security Council must go beyond the procedural formalities of adopting resolutions or delegating enforcement authority as a mechanism of addressing peace and security challenges. It must allocate adequate resources to assist regional organizations in carrying out their mandates.

The challenges that the African regional arrangements have faced in maintaining peace and security can be contrasted with the situation in other parts of the world and in Europe in particular. The practice of UN Security Council has not been to delegate its Chapter VII powers to the North Atlantic Treaty Organization (NATO) in specific terms, but, rather, to delegate these powers more generally to UN member states, with the provision that these powers be exercised through regional arrangements.[54] This practice has been so notwithstanding the fact that NATO had previously not been regarded as a regional arrangement for the purpose of Chapter VIII of the *UN Charter* but, rather, as a collective self-defence pact.[55] Yet, from the practice of the UN it is clear that the Security Council has effectively taken to delegating enforcement authority to NATO under the regional arrangement mechanism.[56]

The major difference between the effectiveness of regional arrangements rests on the capabilities of these arrangements to carry out their mandates without having to rely heavily on the UN Security Council to provide the required resources. Indeed, during the Balkan conflict, NATO provided all of the required resources for its mission within the region. The role of the UN Security Council was limited to legitimating NATO's acts. This is in contrast to ECOWAS or the SADC, whose ability to execute their missions independently

---

54 Sarooshi, *supra* note 31 at 253.

55 *Ibid* at 251. Indeed, this view was reaffirmed by the German Constitutional Court in its decision that NATO can be classified as a type of collective security system. *Deployment of the Federal Armed Forces [Bundeswehr] in International Operations* (1994), BVerfGE 90, 286 (Constitutional Court of Germany).

56 Sarooshi, *supra* note 31 at 251-52.

was greatly constrained and therefore required not only a legalizing mandate from the UN Security Council but also material support.

As suggested earlier, it is partly frustration caused by the practice of the UN Security Council of delegating mandates to regional arrangements without allocating adequate resources to carry them out that caused Africa to establish its own mechanism to deal with peace and security challenges on the continent. Still, among the profound questions raised by such an initiative was whether it might *further* marginalize Africa's place on the agenda of the UN Security Council by causing the latter to assume that Africa would deal with its own problems without the need for UN involvement. To forestall such a possibility, the new AU peace and security architecture reaffirmed the crucial role of the UN Security Council in maintaining international peace and security.[57] Yet, as will be seen in the following discussion, the effect of this recognition of the primacy of the UN Security Council in maintaining international peace and security has been more symbolic than substantive. In particular, it has not heralded a new era of strong-willed commitment by the UN Security Council to assume a greater role in addressing the security challenges faced by Africa.

THE MANDATE OF THE AU PEACE AND SECURITY COUNCIL

As part of its efforts to promote peace and stability on the African continent, the AU launched the AU PSC in 2004.[58] It is interesting to note that this AU organ was not part of the original treaty, adopted in 2000, that established the AU.[59] Rather, the AU PSC was incorporated into the AU's structure by way of an amending protocol adopted in 2002, the *Protocol Relating to the Establishment of the Peace*

---

[57] *AU PSC Protocol, supra* note 2, art 17.

[58] The Fourth Ordinary Session of the AU Executive Council, meeting in Addis Ababa in March 2004, and acting on behalf of the AU Assembly, elected the fifteen members of the AU PSC and decided that it should be operationalized on 25 May 2004. See *Decision on Election of Members of the Peace and Security Council*, AU Executive Council, Fourth Sess, AU Doc EX/CL/Dec.81 (IV) (2004); and *Decision on the Operationalization of the Peace and Security Council*, AU Executive Council, Fourth Sess, AU Doc EX/CL/Dec.79 (IV) (2004), online: AU <http://www.africa-union.org/official_documents/council%20of%20minsters%20 meetings/4th%20ordinarysession%20AAEthiopia/ex%20cl%20dec%2075%20 -%2092%20iv.pdf>.

[59] *Constitutive Act, supra* note 1.

and Security Council of the African Union (AU PSC Protocol).[60] This fact raises a preliminary question: why was the AU PSC not provided for during the negotiation and eventual adoption of the AU's *Constitutive Act?* Why did the AU rather choose to amend the *Constitutive Act* less than two years after its adoption in order to incorporate this body?

In fact, this development can be attributed to a number of factors. While AU members had initially assumed that the *Mechanism for Conflict Prevention, Management and Resolution*, which was adopted by the OAU in 1993,[61] would be sufficient to address security challenges in Africa, the proliferation of conflicts following the adoption of the *Constitutive Act* highlighted a compelling need for a more comprehensive security architecture for the continent. Further, reform of the 1993 mechanism was necessitated by its inability to address existing and emerging trends of conflict. In particular, it had failed to prevent genocide in Rwanda or to provide comprehensive solutions to the unrest in Liberia, Sierra Leone, or Sudan. The practice of relying on preventive diplomacy, which was at the heart of the 1993 mechanism, was not equal to the task of addressing conflicts on the continent.[62] A new framework that could take into account the security challenges confronting Africa in the new century was needed.[63]

The AU PSC was specifically established as one of the organs of the AU pursuant to Article 5(2) of the *Constitutive Act.*[64] Its main objectives include the promotion of peace, security, and stability in Africa;[65] the anticipation, prevention, and resolution (through

---

[60] The *AU PSC Protocol, supra* note 2, entered into force on 26 December 2003 after ratification by twenty-seven AU member states.

[61] *Mechanism for Conflict Prevention, supra* note 16.

[62] Paul D Williams, "The Peace and Security Council of the African Union: Evaluating an Embryonic International Institution" (2009) 47:4 J Modern African Studies 603 at 605.

[63] Abdulqawi A Yusuf, "The Right of Intervention by the African Union: A New Paradigm in Regional Enforcement Action?" (2003) 11 Afr YB Int'l Law 3 at 3-17. See generally Monde Muyangwa and Margaret A Vogt, *An Assessment of the OAU Mechanism for Conflict Prevention, Management and Resolution, 1993-2000* (New York: International Peace Academy, 2002); Joram Mukama Biswaro, *Perspectives on Africa's Integration and Cooperation from OAU to AU: "Old Wine in a New Bottle"?* (Dar Es Salaam: Tanzania Publishing House, 2006).

[64] *Constitutive Act, supra* note 1, art 5(2).

[65] *AU PSC Protocol, supra* note 2, art 3(a).

peacemaking and peacebuilding efforts) of conflict;[66] the promotion and implementation of post-conflict reconstruction activities;[67] and the co-ordination and harmonization of continental efforts to prevent terrorism.[68] It also bears responsibility for developing a common defence policy; encouraging respect for democratic practices, good governance, the rule of law, and humanitarian law; and protecting human rights and fundamental freedoms.[69] Among its guiding principles are the peaceful settlement of disputes and conflicts,[70] early response in order to contain crises,[71] and respect for the rule of law.[72] It is also guided by the principles of respect for the sovereignty and territorial integrity of member states;[73] non-interference by one member state in the internal affairs of another;[74] the inalienable right to independent existence;[75] and respect for borders inherited upon independence.[76] On the question of intervention, it is notable that the AU does not rely exclusively on the request of a member state to intervene.[77] Rather, it can do so with AU Assembly authorization in cases of war crimes, crimes against humanity, or genocide.[78]

AU PSC membership comprises fifteen members elected by the AU Assembly, five of which are elected for three-year terms and ten for two-year terms.[79] Membership is determined on the basis of regional representation and rotation.[80] The *AU PSC Protocol* also lists other criteria that are to be taken into account by the Assembly when electing members to the AU PSC.[81] These include capacity

[66] *Ibid*, art 3(b).

[67] *Ibid*, art 3(c).

[68] *Ibid*, art 3(d).

[69] *Ibid*, art 3(e)-(f).

[70] *Ibid*, art 4(a).

[71] *Ibid*, art 4(b).

[72] *Ibid*, art 4(c).

[73] *Ibid*, art 4(e).

[74] *Ibid*, art 4(f).

[75] *Ibid*, art 4(h).

[76] *Ibid*, art 4(i).

[77] *Ibid*, art 4(k).

[78] *Ibid*, art 4(j); *Constitutive Act, supra* note 1, art 4(h).

[79] *AU PSC Protocol, supra* note 2, art 5(1).

[80] *Ibid*, art 5(2).

[81] *Ibid*.

and commitment to shoulder the responsibilities entailed by membership;[82] contribution to the Peace Fund and/or special funds created for specific purposes;[83] respect for constitutional governance as well as the rule of law and human rights;[84] and a commitment to honouring financial obligations to the AU.[85] Similarly, the *AU PSC Protocol* provides that periodic review shall be undertaken to assess whether the members elected to the AU PSC continue to satisfy these criteria.[86] Retiring members are eligible for re-election.[87]

Examining the AU members who have been elected and re-elected to serve on the AU PSC since its inception demonstrates that most, if not all, of these countries have not lived up to the criteria specified in the *AU PSC Protocol*. For example, Algeria, Togo, Gabon, Cameroon, and Sudan were all elected to serve on the AU PSC from 2004 to 2006. Collectively, these countries either have a questionable record on human rights or are experiencing conflicts that should disqualify them from being members of the AU PSC. Sudan, as a case in point, has been embroiled in conflict since 2003,[88] and from time to time its human rights record has been condemned both by the UN and by individual states.[89] Yet despite this record, which is in stark contrast with the values articulated in the *AU PSC Protocol*, Sudan was elected a member of this powerful decision-making body on peace and security issues. Similarly, from 2008 to 2010, Uganda, Chad, Rwanda, and Swaziland were members. Examining the human rights record of Uganda or Rwanda shows

[82] *Ibid*, art 5(2)(c).

[83] *Ibid*, art 5(2)(f).

[84] *Ibid*, art 5(2)(j).

[85] *Ibid*.

[86] *Ibid*, art 5(4).

[87] *Ibid*, art 5(3).

[88] This excludes the period of conflict in the South, which dates from 1956 when Sudan attained its independence. This conflict ended in 2005 after the signing of the *Comprehensive Peace Agreement* (Government of the Republic of Sudan and the Sudan People's Liberation Movement/Sudan People's Liberation Army), 31 December 2004. For a comprehensive account of the conflict in southern Sudan and the South's self-determination claim, see Charles Riziki Majinge, "Southern Sudan and the Struggle for Self-Determination in Contemporary Africa: Examining Its Basis under International Law" (2010) 53 German YB Int'l L 541.

[89] For example, see Resolution 6/34, UNHRC, 6th Sess, UN Doc A/HRC/RES/6/34 (2007); Resolution 6/35, UNHRC, 6th Sess, UN Doc A/HRC/RES/6/35 (2007); Resolution 7/16, UNHRC, 7th Sess, UN Doc A/HRC/RES/7/16 (2008).

that both countries have committed, and continue to commit, human rights abuses with impunity. This fact is exemplified by the practice of these states of dealing arbitrarily with dissenting voices or those who question the democratic credibility of their respective regimes.[90] Similarly, Swaziland is a constitutional monarchy whose credibility on democracy and rule of law has been questioned on several occasions by its own citizens and the international community.[91]

A related concern arises from the *AU PSC Protocol*'s requirement that membership shall be based on equitable regional representation of member states.[92] This can have the effect of undermining the application of other criteria. If member states in a particular region defer to one of their colleagues, it will be difficult for members of the Assembly to reject the latter's candidacy. It is no wonder, then, that Zimbabwe has been a member of the AU PSC despite its poor record on human rights and the rule of law — and the same could be said of Libya, Uganda, or Cameroon. These realities, when coupled with such factors as the poverty of many AU member states (making contributions to the Peace Fund extremely difficult[93]) as well as ongoing conflicts and democratic deficits in many parts of the continent, suggest that the AU has adopted standards for AU PSC membership that it perhaps knew would be difficult for much of its membership to meet.[94]

---

90 Human Rights Watch, "Rwanda: Silencing of Dissent Ahead of Elections" (2 August 2010), online: Human Rights Watch <http://www.hrw.org/en/news/2010/08/02/rwanda-attacks-freedom-expression-freedom-association-and-freedom-assembly-run-presi>. See also Timothy Longman, "Limitations to Political Reform: The Undemocratic Nature of Transition in Rwanda," in Scott Straus and Lars Waldorf, eds, *Remaking Rwanda: State Building and Human Rights after Mass Violence* (Wisconsin: University of Wisconsin Press, 2011) 25.

91 See, eg, the 2008 US State Department report on human rights in Swaziland. The report documents various abuses of human rights that are sometimes condoned by the state and the lack of accountability of leadership (it being an absolute monarchy). Bureau of Democracy, Human Rights, and Labor, "2008 Human Rights Report" (25 February 2009), online: US Department of State <http://www.state.gov/g/drl/rls/hrrpt/2008/af/119027.htm>.

92 *AU PSC Protocol, supra* note 2, art 5(2).

93 *Ibid*, art 5(2)(f).

94 Charles Riziki Majinge, "The Concept of Global Governance in Public International Law: Addressing Democratic Deficit and Enhancing Accountability in Decision-Making of the AU" (2010) 3:1 J Afr & Int'l L 1 at 6-19.

The AU PSC has a wide range of powers. It can authorize intervention in member states, approve modalities of intervention, institute sanctions with respect to unconstitutional changes of government, and co-ordinate the harmonization of regional economic communities.[95] It also has a role in promoting partnerships for peace and security and ensuring that any external initiatives in the field of peace and security on the continent take place within the framework of the AU's objectives and priorities.[96] Finally, it has the power to decide on any other issue that has implications for the maintenance of peace, security, and stability on the African continent and to exercise any power that may be delegated to it by the AU Assembly.[97] Just as in the case of the UN Security Council, AU member states agree that the AU PSC acts on their behalf in carrying out its duties. They also agree to accept and implement the decisions of the AU PSC in accordance with the *Constitutive Act*.[98]

However, the AU PSC also differs significantly from the UN Security Council in a number of significant ways. Notably, decisions are generally taken on a consensual basis with a provision, where consensus cannot be reached, for simple majority voting on procedural matters and two-thirds majority voting on all other matters.[99] Thus, the nature of decision making in the AU PSC eliminates the likelihood of any country enjoying the equivalent of a veto power or the ability to dominate other members in the decision-making process.

There are also notable differences between the functional powers of the AU PSC and the UN Security Council respectively in addressing threats to peace and security. The *AU PSC Protocol* states that the AU PSC has primary responsibility for promoting peace, security, and stability *on the continent*,[100] while reaffirming the role of the UN Security Council as the organ with primary responsibility to promote and maintain *international* peace and security.[101] This provision may seem rather contradictory or even appear to encroach on the powers of the UN Security Council, particularly in light of the following statement by the Legal Counsel of the AU Commission:

---

95 *AU PSC Protocol, supra* note 2, art 7(1).

96 *Ibid*, art 7(1)(l).

97 *Ibid*, art 7(1)(r).

98 *Ibid*, art 7(3).

99 *Ibid*, art 8(13).

100 *Ibid*, art 16(1).

101 *Ibid*, art 17(1).

[W]hen questions were raised as to whether the Union could possibly have an inherent right to intervene other than through the Security Council, they were dismissed out of hand. This decision reflected a sense of frustration with the slow pace of reform of the international order, and with instances in which the international community tended to focus attention on other parts of the world at the expense of more pressing problems in Africa.[102]

Despite this apparent willingness of the AU PSC to tackle African security challenges without relying on UN Security Council involvement (which is neither predictable nor assured), consensus on the need to clarify the ambiguity concerning the primacy of the mandates of the two bodies grew. Consequently, during its meeting on the common African position on the proposed reform of the UN, commonly known as the Ezulwini consensus, the AU specified that, in general, interventions by regional organizations necessarily require the prior approval of the UN Security Council.[103] Yet it also maintained that "in certain situations, such approval [of the UN Security Council] could be granted 'after the fact' in circumstances requiring urgent action."[104] This position by the AU can be explained simply as a way of avoiding disagreements with the world body rather than as an expression of faith that the world body will indeed take up the primary responsibility for addressing peace and security challenges facing the African continent.

Notwithstanding the potentially conflicting precedence of the UN Security Council and the AU PSC in maintaining international peace and security in Africa, the AU PSC is nevertheless mandated to work closely with the UN Security Council and other relevant UN bodies in carrying out its functions.[105] Where necessary, the AU

---

[102] Ben Kioko, "The Right of Intervention under the African Union's Constitutive Act: From Non-Interference to Non-Intervention" (2003) 85 Int'l Rev Red Cross 807 at 821. See also Edward Ansah Akuffo, "Cooperating for Peace and Security or Competing for Legitimacy in Africa? The Case of the African Union in Darfur" (2010) 19:4 African Security Review 74.

[103] *Common African Position on the Proposed Reform of the United Nations: "The Ezulwini Consensus,"* AU Executive Council, 7th Sess, Doc Ext/EX/CL/2 (VII) (2005) at 6.

[104] *Ibid.* Besides the question of intervention, the Ezulwini consensus reaffirms the long-standing demand of Africa for two permanent seats and five non-permanent seats on the UN Security Council. As to who would occupy these seats, this would be determined on the basis of criteria to be established by the AU. *Ibid* at 9-10.

[105] *AU PSC Protocol, supra* note 2, art 17.

PSC will seek financial or military assistance from the UN Security Council on behalf of the AU when the latter is undertaking activities related to the maintenance of peace and security on the continent in accordance with Chapter VIII of the *UN Charter*.[106] In addition, the AU PSC and the AU chairperson are required to keep close contact with the UN secretary-general and his or her representatives on matters of mutual concern to both parties.[107]

There are also significant differences between the AU PSC and its predecessor, the 1993 OAU Mechanism for Conflict Prevention, Management and Resolution. The differences are vivid in terms of its composition, its governing rules, the scope of its mandate, and the manner in which it pursues this mandate. With particular reference to the latter, while the 1993 mechanism decentralized peace and security issues by dividing Africa into regions and relying heavily on existing regional economic community (REC) mechanisms, the newly adopted AU PSC provides for centrally co-ordinated responses to peace and security issues. This is not to say that the role of the RECs in addressing peace and security issues has been entirely displaced. Rather, as with regional arrangements under Chapter VIII of the *UN Charter*, the RECs now act under the aegis of, and pursuant to, mandates delegated by the AU PSC. The preservation of this role for the RECs stems from a recognition that their proximity to different conflicts may provide them with a better understanding of the dynamics, key players, and context-specific management and resolution options relevant to such conflicts.[108]

Also, unlike its predecessor, the *AU PSC Protocol* recognizes that addressing threats to peace and security on the African continent requires collaboration among a number of different bodies within the AU. For example, the AU PSC is required to maintain a close working relationship with the Pan African Parliament, the African Commission on Human and Peoples' Rights, and civil society organizations.[109] This development is crucial and highlights the extent to which human rights protection in Africa has evolved. It recognizes that human rights protection and promotion is at the core of peace and security. Where human rights are abused or disregarded, it is likely that peace and security will be endangered. It is on this basis

---

[106] *Ibid*, art 17(2).

[107] *Ibid*, art 17(3).

[108] Funmi Olonisakin, "Liberia," in Boulden, *supra* note 43, 111 at 111.

[109] *AU PSC Protocol*, *supra* note 2, arts 18-20.

that the *AU PSC Protocol* requires that the African Commission on Human and Peoples' Rights bring any information relevant to the AU PSC's mandate to the latter's attention.[110]

Yet, even this apparent willingness of the AU PSC to take human rights seriously faces some practical challenges. For example, the *African Charter on Human and Peoples' Rights* requires that the annual report of the African Commission on Human and Peoples' Rights activities be submitted to the AU Assembly before its publication.[111] Indeed, the Assembly has on occasion rejected the commission's annual activity report, requiring that it be amended.[112] This practice highlights one of the challenges facing the AU PSC in treating human rights as a continental peace and security issue. Ultimately, the AU PSC, as an AU organ, is subject to the overall authority of the AU Assembly as the AU's highest decision-making body.[113]

The relationship between the AU PSC and the Pan African Parliament can be viewed as being less influential on the decisions undertaken by the former. The Pan African body is neither involved in the decision making of, nor can it adopt resolutions binding on, the AU PSC. The same can be said of the relationship between the AU PSC and civil society organizations in Africa. However, as part of its overall efforts to involve civil society organizations in its decision making, the AU PSC agreed in 2008 to designate the AU's Economic, Social and Cultural Council (ECOSOCC) as the focal point for interaction between the AU PSC and civil society.[114] This agreement specifies potential areas of co-operation including technical support to the AU PSC in undertaking fact-finding missions across the continent, early warning reporting, mediation, post-conflict reconstruction, environmental rehabilitation, and public advocacy on actions taken by the AU PSC.[115] Despite this arrangement's potential for fostering co-operation between the AU PSC

---

110 *Ibid*, art 19.

111 *African Charter on Human and Peoples' Rights*, 6 June 1981, 21 ILM 58, art 59 (entered into force 21 October 1986).

112 See, eg, AU Assembly, *Decision on the 17th Annual Activity Report of the African Commission on Human and Peoples' Rights*, 3rd Sess, AU Doc EX.CL/109 (V) (2004) (suspending the publication of the commission's report).

113 *Constitutive Act, supra* note 1, art 6(2).

114 Benedikt Franke, *Security Cooperation in Africa: A Reappraisal* (Boulder, CO: First Forum Press, 2009) at 142-43.

115 *Ibid* at 143. See also Isaac Olawale Albert, "The African Union and Conflict Management" (2007) 32:1 Africa Development 41 at 47-55.

and ECOSOCC on behalf of civil society, it is clear that the inter-action between the two has been minimal given the opaque nature of decision making within the AU PSC and the fragmentary nature of civil society organizations in Africa.

The *AU PSC Protocol* is also innovative in a number of other respects — for example, its approach to gathering information and advice relevant to the AU PSC's work. Instead of relying solely on the input of bureaucrats within the AU Commission, Secretariat, and Assembly, it also calls for the establishment of a "Panel of the Wise" to support the work of the AU PSC in the areas of peacemaking and conflict prevention.[116] The panel can make use of personal mediation, diplomacy, and good offices to avoid resumption or escalation of conflicts.[117] The specific inclusion of the panel in the *AU PSC Protocol* reaffirms the long-standing African practice of relying on eminent personalities with international stature to mediate conflicts. Indeed, looking at the inaugural members of the panel shows that it was dominated by persons who have occupied senior positions at both the national and international levels. For example, the first panel included Ben Bella, former president of Tunisia; Salim Ahmed Salim, former OAU secretary-general and president of the UN General Assembly; Brigalia Bam, chairperson of the South Africa Independent Electoral Commission; and Miguel Trovaoda, former president of São Tomé and Principe. As with most organs of the AU, the Panel of the Wise is constituted on a rotating geographical representation basis.[118]

The establishment of the Panel of the Wise is particularly significant in light of the AU's need to prevent escalation of conflict rather

---

[116] The Panel of the Wise was established pursuant to the *AU PSC Protocol, supra* note 2, art 11. The current members (as of January 2011) are Ahmed Ben Bella (North Africa), Salim Ahmed Salim (East Africa), Kenneth Kaunda (Southern Africa), Marie Madeleine Kalala-Ngoy (Central Africa), and Mary Chinery Hesse (West Africa). On the work of the Panel of the Wise, see Jegede Ademola Oluborode, "The African Union Peace and Security Architecture: Can the Panel of the Wise Make a Difference?" (LL.M. dissertation, University of Pretoria, 2008). See also Laurie Nathan, *Mediation and the African Union's Panel of the Wise,* Crisis States Development Research Centre Discussion Paper no. 10, (2005), online: <http://eprints.lse.ac.uk/28340/1/dp10.pdf>.

[117] *Modalities for the Functioning of the Panel of the Wise,* as adopted by the Peace and Security Council at its 100th Meeting on 12 November 2007, art III, online: AU <http://www.africa-union.org/root/au/publications/PSC/Panel%20of%20the%20wise.pdf> [*Panel of the Wise Modalities*].

[118] *AU PSC Protocol, supra* note 2, art 11(2).

than resolve it once it has erupted. Since the AU enjoys limited resources — especially of a military nature — it must seek alternative means of addressing these challenges peacefully. The Panel of the Wise is one such means. In its interventions, it is guided by five criteria.[119] These are: the degree to which a conflict situation has already received regional or international attention; whether the AU PSC is already seized of a particular conflict situation and whether additional attention by the panel may add value to existing efforts; whether a given situation has been mired in conflict for a considerable amount of time or is in danger of descending into conflict despite ongoing mediation; whether a conflict situation has experienced a sudden and speedy deterioration; and whether implementation of a peace agreement has encountered difficulties such that there is a risk that the situation will revert to conflict.

Although the AU PSC is a permanent organ with a permanent secretariat, it is required to meet a minimum of two times a month.[120] Meetings are chaired by the AU PSC chairperson, a position that rotates on a monthly basis in alphabetical order according to the state's name.[121] The requirement to meet at least twice a month is a reflection of the realities and nature of conflicts in Africa. With multiple conflicts ongoing in different parts of the continent, it is in the interests of the AU PSC to meet frequently to assess the situation and make recommendations or take appropriate measures as the situation may require.

EVALUATING THE ABILITY OF THE AU PSC TO CONFRONT THREATS TO PEACE AND SECURITY

THE CHALLENGES CONFRONTING THE AU PSC

Since its establishment in 2004, the AU PSC has adopted and promoted various means of addressing threats and real challenges to peace and security on the African continent. It has supported mediation efforts conducted primarily under the aegis of the AU, in particular by the Panel of the Wise. It has also supported the use

---

119 *Panel of the Wise Modalities, supra* note 117, art III.

120 *AU PSC Protocol, supra* note 2, art 8(2). Note that the minimum twice monthly meetings need only be at the ambassadorial level, whereas the AU PSC must meet at least yearly at the ministerial and heads-of-state-or-government levels. *Ibid.*

121 *Ibid,* art 8(6).

of military force and peacekeeping forces to restore international peace and security. In addressing threats to peace and security, the AU PSC, acting within its powers, has recommended and approved the establishment of peacekeeping missions in Sudan and Somalia, and it has also recommended that the AU chairperson appoint special envoys to mediate conflicts across the continent. In Sudan, the AU PSC has made use of its full arsenal, both on the diplomatic and military fronts. It has appointed special envoys to foster peace and stability in the country, sent in the Panel of the Wise to mediate between warring parties, and supported the setting up of military forces to protect civilians.

Yet, despite the eloquence of African leaders in affirming their commitment to addressing African peace and security issues within a "home grown" legal and institutional framework, the AU PSC's efforts have also faced a myriad of challenges.[122] This is evidenced by the fact that, since the adoption of the *AU PSC Protocol*, several threats and real challenges to peace and security in Africa have continued to proliferate with little or no effective intervention by the AU PSC.[123] The continent has witnessed a rise in unconstitutional changes of government, mass uprisings against dictatorial regimes, intrastate conflicts, sham and inconclusive elections, continued poor governance, and abuse of the rule of law, among other challenges. While addressing all of these developments would require, in the best of circumstances, engagement of the full range of the AU PSC's powers, its effectiveness in exercising such powers has been highly constrained. In some cases, the best it has been able to do is to issue resolutions that at times have been ignored by the states concerned.[124] The extent of these challenges, and some of the reasons underlying them, can best be understood by examining a number of specific situations in greater detail, beginning with Somalia.

---

[122] Jeremy Sarkin, "The Role of the United Nations, the African Union and Africa's Sub-Regional Organizations in Dealing with Africa's Human Rights Problems: Connecting Humanitarian Intervention and the Responsibility to Protect" (2009) 53:1 J African L 1.

[123] Africa's conflicts continue to proliferate, affecting even countries previously considered peaceful: see Jeffrey Gettleman, "Africa's Forever Wars" (2010) 178 Foreign Policy 73.

[124] See, eg, AU Assembly, *Resolution on Zimbabwe*, 11th Sess, AU Doc Assembly/AU/Res.1 (XI) (2008).

SOMALIA

As seen earlier, the *AU PSC Protocol* empowers the AU PSC to recommend intervention in the internal affairs of AU member states when doing so would be in the interests of peace and stability.[125] It is pursuant to this mandate that the AU PSC recommended a peacekeeping mission in Somalia to support the Transitional Federal Government appointed in 2004, a recommendation that was adopted by the AU in 2007.[126] This decision was made on the understanding that the UN, as the primary guarantor of international peace and security, would take over the mission within six months.[127] This expectation has never been fulfilled. Part of the mission's mandate is to support the Transitional Federal Government in its efforts to stabilize the situation in the country; further dialogue and reconciliation among different factions involved in the conflict; assist in the implementation of national security; support training of Somali security forces; provide security to key infrastructure; and assist in delivery of humanitarian aid.[128]

Despite the fact that the African Union Mission in Somalia (AMISOM) has the blessing of the UN Security Council, it has been struggling. The mission has even had difficulty paying its soldiers, who have put their lives on the line in one of Africa's most hostile regions. Yet despite these challenges, the fact remains that the AU decided to authorize and commit its troops in one of the most dangerous hotspots on the continent without the explicit commitment of the UN Security Council in terms of resources. Uganda and Burundi have taken a leading role in AMISOM despite security challenges within their own countries.[129] This is a remarkable development on the African continent, and it illustrates the continent's willingness to fend for itself, even without the support of the UN Security Council.

Arguably, the UN Security Council has made a significant contribution towards resolving the political crisis in Somalia through both

---

[125] *AU PSC Protocol, supra* note 2, art 7(e).

[126] *Communiqué of the Sixty-Ninth Meeting, supra* note 48.

[127] AU PSC, *Report of the Chairperson of the Commission*, AU Doc PSC/PR/2 (CV) (2008).

[128] *Communiqué of the Sixty-Ninth Meeting, supra* note 48.

[129] See AMISOM, Military Component, online: AU <http://www.africa-union.org/root/au/auc/departments/psc/amisom/AMISOM_MILITARY_COMPONENT.htm>.

diplomatic and financial means. Indeed, in various resolutions, it has demonstrated its willingness to help the Transitional Federal Government and AMISOM perform their functions. For example, it has urged member states, international organizations, and humanitarian bodies to facilitate, notwithstanding the economic and financial embargoes imposed on Somalia, the delivery of essential items for urgent humanitarian assistance in the country.[130] It is also noteworthy that in 2010-11, UN support for enhancing the capabilities of AMISOM was set at approximately US $174 million.[131] Similarly, some Western states have extended financial and technical support to the mission, demonstrating the willingness of these countries to "do something" in Somalia.[132]

Yet while this assistance is notable, it is clear that it is insufficient. Given the complex nature of the Somali conflict and the reluctance of the major powers to get involved, a disproportionate burden is thus placed on both Uganda and Burundi — countries that face serious economic and political challenges within their own borders. The insufficiency of the budgetary allocation by the UN Security Council is plain when one considers that Somalia has been without a central government for the past two decades. The allocation of these funds without concrete steps by UN Security Council members to increase technical and financial support to AMISOM can hardly make a difference in a country that has known anarchy for most of its post-independence period.[133]

Moreover, despite continued affirmations by the UN Security Council of the international community's unflinching support for the peaceful resolution of the Somali conflict,[134] AMISOM continues to struggle to garner support from the international community

130 UN Security Council Resolution1972, 6496th Meeting, UN Doc S/RES/1972 (2011).

131 *Fifth Committee Takes up Financing for Peacekeeping Missions in Haiti, Sudan, Hybrid Operation in Darfur, Support for African Union Mission in Somalia*, UNGAOR, 65th Sess, UN Doc GA/AB/3990 (2011).

132 Cecilia Hull and Emma Svensson, *African Union Mission in Somalia (AMISOM): Exemplifying African Union Peacekeeping Challenges* (Stockholm: Swedish Defence Research Agency, 2008) at 29-30.

133 Ken Menkhaus, "Stabilization and Humanitarian Access in a Collapsed State: The Somali Case" (2010) 34:3 Disasters 320.

134 See, eg, UN Security Council Resolution 1872, UNSC, 6127th Meeting, UN Doc S/Res/1872 (2009). Among other things, this resolution reiterates the Security Council's commitment to "a comprehensive and lasting settlement of the situation in Somalia."

and from African countries in particular.[135] As of May 2011, Uganda and Burundi remained the only two states to have troops on the ground. As to why other AU countries have been unwilling to commit troops to Somalia despite the AU PSC's explicit request that they do so, the answer may be due in part to the dangerous nature of the mission itself. As with the African Union Mission in Darfur (UNAMID), the mission in Somalia continues to operate in a war zone, which is a disincentive for contributions by AU member states to peacekeeping efforts in the country. However, the hesitancy of AU states may also be related to the reluctance of the broader international community to provide requisite resources to support the mission. Successive UN special envoys and AU officials have lobbied for stronger commitments to the Somalia mission by the UN Security Council, without success.[136] Indeed, even the secretary-general has not hidden his disappointment with the great powers over their reluctance to commit resources to the cause of peace in Somalia.[137]

The experience of AMISOM demonstrates that the challenge has little to do with the inadequacy of the mandate that it enjoys. Rather, the challenge has been one of mobilizing resources to put boots on the ground and, in particular, dealing with the (un)willingness of the UN Security Council to adequately support the mission's operations.

SUDAN

In 2004, the AU PSC authorized the African Union Mission in Sudan (AMIS) to restore peace and security in Darfur.[138] In the face of UN reticence, the AU PSC authorized the mission with the understanding that African states would most likely have to meet the costs

---

[135] Hull and Svensson, *supra* note 132 at 27-28. See also Andre Le Sage, "Somalia's Endless Transition: Breaking the Deadlock" (2010) 257 Strategic Forum 1; Nicoletta Pirozzi, "Towards an Effective Africa-EU Partnership on Peace and Security: Rhetoric or Facts?" (2010) 45:2 International Spectator 85.

[136] Hull and Svensson, *supra* note 132 at 40.

[137] See comments of the secretary general during the UN Security Council's 6407th meeting, UN Doc S/PV.6407 (2010). See also Alex Vines, "Rhetoric from Brussels and Reality on the Ground: The EU and Security in Africa" (2010) 86:5 International Affairs 1091.

[138] AU PSC, *Communiqué on the Solemn Launching of the Tenth Meeting of the Peace and Security Council*, 10th Meeting, AU Doc PSC/AHG/Comm (X) (2004).

associated with the mission.[139] This undertaking proved to be financially challenging for most African countries.

Examining the work of AMIS, it is clear that the operation was unique and complex. It was unique in the sense that it was the first and largest mission authorized by the AU PSC, and it was complex because its troops were under-equipped and did not enjoy adequate support from the host government, which was hostile to its presence from the moment of its creation.[140] Indeed, the AU PSC's efforts were deliberately frustrated by the government, which refused to extend its co-operation as required by both the *Constitutive Act* and the *AU PSC Protocol*.[141]

In light of these challenges, the mission was later rehatted as a "blue helmet" mission, for which the UN picked up the bill. In contrast to the level of UN support to AMISOM, UN Security Council sanctioned missions such as UNAMID or the UN Mission in Sudan enjoy a comparative advantage in terms of resources allocated.[142] Though even this level of support may not be adequate to address the peace and security challenges facing these regions, it may nevertheless be argued that it reflects the UN Security Council's willingness to tackle some of the most serious security challenges confronting Africa and Sudan in particular.

However, the takeover of the mission in Darfur by the UN raises some profound concerns pertaining to the overall vision of African solutions for African problems. If the AU cannot mobilize the resources to carry out this vision, it is clear that the best it can do is

---

[139] *Ibid.*

[140] Seth Appiah-Mensah, "The African Union Mission in Sudan: Darfur Dilemmas" (2006) 15:1 African Security Rev 2.

[141] In December 2010, the Sudanese government pulled out of the UN- and AU-supported Doha peace talks, contrary to the advice of the joint AU-UN mediator, Djibril Bassolé. See "Sudan Recalls Its Team from Doha but Says It's Still Committed to Peace in Darfur," *Sudan Tribune* (30 December 2010), online: Sudan Tribune <http://www.sudantribune.com/Sudan-recalls-its-team-from-Doha,37446>. As a result, Ambassador Bassolé resigned from his position as the joint UN/AU mediator in April 2011. See Statement of the AUC Chairperson, "Resignation of the Joint Chief Mediator, Djibril Bassolé," 29 April 2011, online: African Press Organization <http://appablog.wordpress.com/2011/04/29/statement-of-the-auc-chairperson-resignation-of-the-joint-chief-mediator-djibril-bassole/>.

[142] In 2010-11, the African Union Mission in Sudan's assessed budget was US $1 billion while that of the African Union Mission in Darfur was US $1.8 billion dollars. See *General Assembly Calls for Intensified Effort towards Goal of Conflict-Free Africa*, UNGAOR, 65th Sess, UN Doc GA/11o6 (2011).

to mobilize troops that will require financial and logistical support from the "international community" to discharge their functions. Yet such a practice will continue to raise questions concerning the capability of African countries to address their own security issues without the involvement of the international community — whether through the UN or regional entities such as the European Union or NATO.

One of the major issues facing the AU PSC in Sudan has been how to handle the ongoing Darfur investigation by the International Criminal Court (ICC) and the issuance by the ICC of an indictment against the Sudanese president.[143] The AU PSC has issued several communiqués reaffirming its position that the ICC should defer its indictment against Omar al-Bashir until the conflict in Darfur is resolved.[144] An alternative proposed by the AU PSC — one that would have allowed for the establishment of an ad hoc tribunal composed of judges from Sudan and other African countries — was rejected outright by the Sudanese government.[145] This rejection not only demonstrates the limited influence of the AU PSC among AU member states, which appear only to implement or respect its decisions or recommendations when these are aligned with their own national interests. The practice of member states such as Sudan of ignoring or rejecting outright decisions of the AU PSC also undermines its credibility at the international level. This practice, in turn, has the ironic effect of eroding the AU PSC's ability to

---

[143] *Prosecutor v Omar Hassan Ahmad Al Bashir (Omar Al Bashir)*, Case ICC-02/05-01/09, Warrant of Arrest for Omar Hassan Ahmad Al Bashir (Public) (4 March 2009). See also Dapo Akande, "The Legal Nature of Security Council Referrals to the International Criminal Court and Its Impact on Al Bashir's Immunities" (2009) 7:2 J Int'l Crim Just 333; Paola Gaeta, "Does President Al Bashir Enjoy Immunity from Arrest?" (2009) 7:2 J Int'l Crim Just 315.

[144] AU PSC, *Communiqué of the 142nd Meeting of the Peace and Security Council*, 142nd Meeting, AU Doc PSC/MIN/Comm (CXLII) (2008). Indeed, during its ordinary session held in Kampala in July 2010, the AU Assembly expressed its disappointment over the refusal of the UN Security Council to defer the International Criminal Court (ICC) arrest warrant against President Bashir of Sudan. See *Decision on the Progress Report of the Commission on the Implementation of Decision Assembly/AU/Dec.270 (XIV) on the Second Ministerial Meeting on the Rome Statute of the International Criminal Court (ICC)*, AU Assembly, 15th Sess, AU Doc Assembly/AU/10(XV) (2009) at para 4.

[145] See "Sudan Reiterates Rejection of Darfur Hybrid Courts," *Sudan Tribune* (31 October 2009) online: Sudan Tribune <http://www.sudantribune.com/spip.php?page=imprimable&id_article=32973>.

defend the interests of those AU member states that fail to abide by its decisions or recommendations in the first place.

For example, had Sudanese president Omar al-Bashir accepted the recommendation of the AU PSC to establish an ad hoc tribunal to try crimes in Darfur, the case against ICC intervention in Sudan would have been strengthened on the basis of the complementarity principle of the *Rome Statute of the International Criminal Court* (*Rome Statute*).[146] As it turns out, the AU PSC has had to pursue its attempts to convince the UN Security Council to defer the al-Bashir indictment without anything tangible to show in terms of the willingness or ability of Sudan to undertake credible trials for crimes committed in Darfur.

It is important to acknowledge that the practice of ignoring AU PSC decisions has not been limited to recalcitrant AU member states. Rather, even the UN Security Council has on different occasions deliberately ignored the AU PSC's decisions or recommendations. For example, the indictment of al-Bashir by the ICC has been one of the thorny issues on which the UN Security Council and the AU PSC have disagreed. The AU PSC has repeatedly requested that the UN Security Council invoke its powers under Article 16 of the *Rome Statute* to defer al-Bashir's indictment, without success.[147] In fact, it is frustration over this rejection of AU PSC requests by the UN Security Council that prompted the AU to adopt a resolution stating a collective position rejecting any kind of co-operation between the AU and the ICC.[148] Yet despite this collective stance, there

---

146 *Rome Statute of the International Criminal Court*, 17 June 1998, 2187 UNTS 90, art 17, 37 ILM 1002 (entered into force 1 July 2002) [*Rome Statute*]. See also generally Steve Odero, "Politics of International Criminal Justice: The ICC's Arrest Warrant for Al Bashir and the African Union's Neo-Colonial Conspirator Thesis," in Chacha Murungu and Japhet Biegon, eds, *Prosecuting International Crimes in Africa* (Pretoria, South Africa: Pretoria University Law Press, 2011) 145. See also Jann K Kleffner, "The Impact of Complementarity on National Implementation of Substantive International Criminal Law" (2003) 1:1 J Int'l Crim Just 86; William W Burke-White, "Complementarity in Practice: The International Criminal Court as Part of a System of Multi-Level Global Governance in the Democratic Republic of Congo" (2005) 18:3 Leiden J Int'l L 557.

147 *Rome Statute, supra* note 146, art 16.

148 See, eg, *Decision on the Report of the Commission on the Meeting of African States Parties to the Rome Statute of the International Criminal Tribunal (ICC)*, AU Assembly, 13th Sess, AU Doc Assembly/AU/Dec.245 (XIII) Rev (2009). In 2010, during the AU Assembly ordinary session in Kampala, the AU rejected the request of the ICC to open a liaison office in Ethiopia. See *Decision on the Progress Report of the Commission on the Implementation of Decision Assembly/AU/Dec.270(XIV) on the Second*

has been sharp disagreement between the AU members, some of whom feel bound by their obligations under the *Rome Statute*.[149]

IVORY COAST

The situation in Ivory Coast has been another major test for the AU PSC in addressing peace and security challenges on the African continent. While the UN and the Ivory Coast Electoral Commission concluded that incumbent Laurent Gbagbo had lost the November 2010 presidential election to his opponent, Gbagbo was unwilling to relinquish power.[150] The AU PSC issued carefully worded statements calling upon the parties to abide by the election results as pronounced by the Electoral Commission.[151] When Gbagbo persisted, the AU PSC suspended Ivory Coast from the AU.[152] This decision was in line with the requirements of the unconstitutional change of government clause adopted by the AU.[153]

Ministerial Meeting on the Rome Statute of the International Criminal Court (ICC), AU Assembly, 15th Sess, AU Doc Assembly/AU/10(XV) (2010). For growing concerns regarding the ICC and its activities in Africa, see Charles C Jalloh, Dapo Akande, and Max du Plessis, "Assessing the African Union Concerns about Article 16 of the Rome Statute of the International Criminal Court" (2011) 4:1 African J Legal Studies 5; Ifeonu Eberechi, "'Rounding Up the Usual Suspects': Exclusion, Selectivity and Impunity in the Enforcement of International Criminal Justice and the African Union's Emerging Resistance" (2011) 4:1 African J Legal Studies 51.

[149] Botswana and South Africa have publicly disagreed with the AU's decision not to co-operate with the ICC, by reaffirming their international obligations under the *Rome Statute*. See, eg, "South Africa Reverses Course on ICC Arrest Warrant for Bashir," *Sudan Tribune* (30 July 2009), online: Sudan Tribune <http://www.sudantribune.com/South-Africa-reverses-course-on,31986>. See also Dire Tladi, "The African Union and the International Criminal Court: The Battle for the Soul of International Law" (2009) 34 SAYB Int'l L 57; Lee Stone, "Implementation of the Rome Statute in South Africa," in Murungu and Biegon, *supra* note 146, 305.

[150] The UN mission in Ivory Coast certified the election on 3 December 2010 and declared Alassane Ouattara the winner in accordance with UN Security Council Resolution 1765, UNSC, 5716th Meeting, UN Doc S/Res/1765 (2007). See also "Ban Reaffirms the UN's Unwavering Support for Poll Result in Côte d'Ivoire," *UN News Centre* (2 January 2011) online: UN News Centre <http://www.un.org/apps/news/story.asp?NewsID=37191&Cr=Ivoire&Cr1>.

[151] AU PSC, *Communiqué of the 252nd Meeting of the Peace and Security Council*, 252nd Meeting, AU Doc PSC/PR/COMM.1 (CCLII) (2010).

[152] *Ibid* at para 4.

[153] *AU PSC Protocol, supra* note 2, art 7(1)(g).

The question that this episode raises is whether the AU PSC can go beyond issuing statements and suspensions in order to resolve electoral impasses of the sort witnessed in Ivory Coast or elsewhere — for example, in Kenya or Zimbabwe. The answer would be difficult to predict mainly because throughout its history the AU has learned that military intervention is a costly undertaking that should be pursued only as a last resort and where there is a clear willingness on the part of its members to provide the necessary resources to ensure success.

Moreover, while the *AU PSC Protocol* requires that its members conduct free and fair elections and respect their outcomes, the electoral records of most African countries are hardly without blemish in this regard.[154] For example, Rwanda has been a member of the AU PSC since 2010.[155] In 2010, Rwanda held an election in which the incumbent won by more than 90 percent. Opponents of the governing regime were accused of terrorism and imprisoned, while others were barred from participating in the election.[156] Similarly, recent elections in Egypt and Ethiopia were marred by irregularities and voter intimidation, and incumbents also won by more than 90 percent. Indeed, in examining the records of the AU PSC members, both past and present, it becomes clear that most do not live up to the ideals they purport to promote. The fact that member states with the responsibility of defending and promoting the AU PSC's values are often the very countries violating them does not bode well for its effective functioning.

---

154 *Ibid*, art 5(2).

155 During the sixteenth ordinary session of the Executive Council of the AU, Rwanda was elected to serve on the council for a two-year term with effect from April 2010. Other members elected were Chad and Burundi (Central Africa), Mauritania (North Africa), Benin, Mali, and Ivory Coast (West Africa), Namibia and South Africa (Southern Africa), Djibouti (East Africa). See *Election of the Members of the Peace and Security Council of the African Union Decision*, AU Executive Council, 16thSess, AU Doc EX.CL/Dec.553 (XVI) (2010).

156 For example, the opposition candidate running for the Office of the President in Rwanda was disqualified from running in 2010 and imprisoned. She was charged with terrorism offences, among others. See "Rwanda: Opposition Leader Charged with Terrorism," *New York Times* (26 October 2010), online: Afrika.no <http://www.afrika.no/Detailed/20012.html>. Similarly, in January 2011, some high ranking military officers who disagreed with the government and went into exile were sentenced to prison for committing terrorist acts against the state. See Kezio-Musoke David and Norman S Miwambo, "Nation Jails Nyamwasa for Twenty-Four Years for Terrorism," *The Monitor* (17 January 2011), online: All Africa <http://allafrica.com/stories/201101170007.html>.

However, the situation in Ivory Coast does demonstrate some important features of the manner in which the AU PSC addresses peace and security challenges facing Africa. First, it is notable that the AU PSC did not recommend or authorize military options against the Gbagbo regime. Rather, it invested efforts in mediation through the appointment of special representatives and the high-level, direct involvement of selected African heads of state as mediators.[157] Second, the efforts of the AU PSC were consistent with Article 52 of the *UN Charter*, which requires that "[t]he Members of the United Nations entering into [regional] arrangements or constituting [regional] agencies shall make every effort to achieve pacific settlement of local disputes through such regional arrangements or by such regional agencies before referring them to the Security Council."[158] Third, the AU PSC allowed ECOWAS to take centre stage in addressing the Ivory Coast electoral debacle. In particular, ECOWAS issued strong statements requiring the incumbent Gbagbo to quit and hand over power to the widely recognized winner of the election, Alassane Ouattara, and also threatened military intervention if necessary.[159]

---

[157] In January 2011, the AU PSC established a High-Level Panel for the Resolution of the Crisis in Ivory Coast. The panel was composed of the heads of state of South Africa, Mauritania, Burkina Faso, Chad, and the United Republic of Tanzania as well as the chairperson of the AU Commission and the president of ECOWAS. It was chaired by the president of Mauritania, Mohamed Ould Abdel Aziz. The panel was mandated to "evaluate the situation and formulate, on the basis of the relevant decisions of the AU and ECOWAS, an overall political solution." It was required to conclude its work in a period not exceeding one month. See AU PSC, *Communiqué of the 259th Meeting of the Peace and Security Council*, 259th Meeting, AU Doc PSC/AHG/COMM(CCLIX) (2011). See also generally the AU PSC, *Report of the Chairperson of the Commission on the Situation in Côte d'Ivoire*, 273rd Meeting, AU Doc PSC/PR/2 (CCLXXIII) (2011).

[158] *UN Charter, supra* note 4, art 52(2). It can also be argued that the UN Security Council's decision to support the AU's mediation efforts was consistent with art 52(3) of the *UN Charter*, which states that "[t]he Security Council shall encourage the development of pacific settlement of local disputes through such regional arrangements or by such regional agencies either on the initiative of the states concerned or by reference from the Security Council" (*ibid*, art 52(3)). See also UN Security Council Resolution 1975, UNSC, 6508th Meeting, UN Doc S/Res/1975 (2011), which, among other things, noted "the constructive efforts of the African Union High-level Panel for the resolution of the crisis in Côte d'Ivoire" and reiterated the UN Security Council's "support to the African Union and the Economic Community of West African States (ECOWAS) for their commitment to resolve the crisis in Côte d'Ivoire."

[159] See ECOWAS, Heads of State and Government, *Final Communiqué on the Extraordinary Session of the Authority of Heads of State and Government on Côte d'Ivoire*, Extraordinary Session, ECOWAS Doc 188/2010 (2010).

Arguably, the experience in Ivory Coast has shown that the AU PSC is capable of effective action when its members agree that such action is imperative. The AU PSC's swift decision to recommend suspension of the membership of Ivory Coast from the AU, backed by concrete measures by ECOWAS such as the imposition of limited sanctions on key figures of the Gbagbo regime, demonstrates that the AU PSC has the potential to address security challenges facing the continent if supported by its members, including those acting through RECs.

ZIMBABWE, COMOROS, AND BURUNDI: THE ROLE OF SUB-REGIONAL MECHANISMS

As has been suggested earlier, it is clear that the AU, in addressing peace and security challenges, has been willing to defer elements of its mandate to sub-regional mechanisms when it has felt that the latter are in a better position to discharge that role. For example, during the Zimbabwe crisis of 2008, when the incumbent president Robert Mugabe rejected the outcome of the presidential election, the AU Assembly recommended that the SADC handle the media-tion process in order to resolve the impasse peacefully.[160] Indeed, since 2008, it has been the SADC that has taken the lead in resolving Zimbabwe's crisis with the support and on behalf of the AU. With the signing of the *Global Political Agreement*, imperfect as it may be, one can argue that the SADC has achieved modest success by bring-ing the parties together to form the Government of National Unity.[161]

In 2008, the AU PSC supported the military intervention in Com-oros to restore the government of President Ahmed Abdallah Sambi, which was threatened by the breakaway of the island of Anjouan.[162]

---

160 *Resolution on Zimbabwe*, AU Assembly, 11th Sess, AU Doc Assembly/AU/Res.1 (XI) (2008), online: <http://www.africa-union.org/root/AU/Conferen-ces/2008/june/summit/dec/ASSEMBLY%20DECISIONS%20193%20-%20 207%20(XI).pdf>.

161 *Global Political Agreement* (Zimbabwe African National Union-Patriotic Front and the Movement for Democratic Change), 15 September 2008, online: Zimbabwe African National Union-Patriotic Front and the Movement for Democratic Change <http://www.zimfa.gov.zw/index.php?option=com_docman&task= doc_details&gid=12&Itemid=91>.

162 See *Decision on the Situation in Comoros*, AU Assembly, 10th Sess, AU Doc Assem-bly/Dec.186 (X) (2007), requesting "all Member States capable of doing so to provide the necessary support to the Comorian Government in its efforts to restore, as quickly as possible, the authority of the Union in Anjouan." This mission, which was code named "Operation Democracy in the Comoros," was

This intervention, although undertaken under the auspices of the AU PSC, was in fact carried out by several African countries, such as Tanzania, Senegal, and Sudan, which felt the need to restore calm in the islands. Similarly, in Burundi, the AU PSC authorized military intervention that was carried out by South Africa and other states under the auspices of the SADC. It has been widely acknowledged that both interventions achieved their objectives.[163]

It may be wondered why the AU PSC has relied so heavily on subregional mechanisms such as the SADC, the Intergovernmental Authority for Development (IGAD), and ECOWAS to maintain peace and security across the continent. The most likely answer is that the capacity of the AU PSC to mobilize resources to undertake these missions itself is highly constrained. Furthermore, it is highly likely that conflicts or threats to peace and security can best be addressed by states within the region that stand to suffer the consequences most directly if they are allowed to escalate.

LIBYA

The AU PSC first discussed the situation in Libya at its 261st meeting in February 2011, where, among other things, it expressed "deep concern" at developments in the country and "strongly condemn[ed] the indiscriminate and excessive use of force and lethal weapons against peaceful protestors, in violation of human rights and International Humanitarian Law."[164] The AU PSC also called on the Libyan authorities to "ensure the protection and security of the citizens and also ensure the delivery and provision of humanitarian assistance to the injured and other persons in need."[165] Moreover,

---

hailed by the African Union chairperson as a success. See AU PSC, *Report of the Chairperson of the African Union Commission on the Situation in the Comoros Since the 10th Ordinary Session of the Assembly of the African Union Held in Addis Ababa from 31 January to 2 February 2008*, 124th Meeting, AU Doc PSC/PR/2 (CXXIV) (2008).

163 AU Central Organ of the Mechanism for Conflict Prevention, Management, and Resolution at Ambassadorial Level, *Communiqué of the Ninety First Ordinary Session of the Central Organ of the Mechanism for Conflict Prevention, Management, and Resolution at Ambassadorial Level*, 91st Sess, AU Doc Organ/MEC/AMB/Comm. (XCI) (2003).

164 AU, *Communiqué of the 261st Meeting of the Peace and Security Council*, AU Doc PSC/PR/COMM (CCLXI) (2011) at para 2.

165 *Ibid* at para 3.

the AU PSC underscored that "the aspirations of the people of Libya for democracy, political reform, justice and socio-economic development are legitimate."[166] This is interesting in that it represents the first occasion on which an AU-mandated organ — the AU PSC — has directly linked political and governance issues with violations of human rights in a specific country. Subsequently, the AU PSC established a High-Level Committee to lead efforts to resolve the Libyan crisis.[167]

However, unlike the situation in Ivory Coast, in Libya the AU PSC did not assume a prominent role in finding African solutions for African problems. Rather, the League of Arab States (LAS) assumed the lead role in addressing the Libyan situation. In fact, it was this body that adopted a decision requesting that the UN Security Council impose a no-fly zone on Libya to protect civilians and facilitate humanitarian assistance.[168] In what may be seen as a recognition that it would only be one of many actors involved in finding a solution to the crisis in Libya, the AU PSC asked the High-Level Committee to "engage AU's partners [*sic*], in particular the League of Arab States (LAS), the Organization of the Islamic Conference (OIC), the European Union (EU) and the United Nations, to facilitate coordination of efforts and seek their support for the early

---

166 *Ibid* at para 5.

167 AU, *Communiqué of the 265ᵗʰ Meeting of the Peace and Security Council*, AU Doc PSC/PR/COMM.2 (CCLXV) (2011), online: AU <http://www.au.int/en/dp/ps/sites/default/files/2011_mar_11_psc_265theeting_libya_communique_en.pdf>. The High-Level Panel is composed of the heads of state of Mali, Congo, Mauritania, South Africa, and Uganda. See *Report of the Chairperson of the Commission on the Activities of the AU High Level ad hoc Committee on the Situation in Libya*, AU Doc PSC/PR/2 (CCLXXV) (2011) at para 6, online: AU <http://www.au.int/en/dp/ps/sites/default/files/275%20-%20Report%20on%20 Libya%20_Eng%20_%20(3).pdf>. It is worth noting the declaration issued by the AU Assembly on the state of peace and security in Africa on 25 May 2011, in which the Assembly reiterated "the need to assess the status of implementation of the AU instruments relating to democracy, good governance and the rule of law, in order to enhance their effectiveness and to adapt them, if necessary, to changing circumstances in the historical evolution of the African people and the progress made in the achievement of the strategic objectives of the AU." See *Declaration on the State of Peace and Security in Africa: Enhancing Africa's Leadership, Promoting African Solutions*, AU Assembly, Extraordinary Session on the State of Peace and Security in Africa, AU Doc EXT/ASSEMBLY/AU/DECL/ (01.2011) (2011).

168 Council of the League of Arab States Resolution 7360, 12 March 2011, UN Doc S/2011/137 (Annex) (2011) at para 1, online: UN <http://daccess-dds-ny.un.org/doc/UNDOC/GEN/N11/263/05/PDF/N1126305.pdf?OpenElement>.

resolution of the crisis."[169] This state of affairs may be attributed to many factors, such as the proximity of Arab states to Libya — states that are most likely to be affected by events taking place there.

What was the contribution of the AU PSC in addressing the Libyan conflict? What the AU PSC's efforts in Libya demonstrate is that it was keen to resolve the conflict through political dialogue between the Libyan government and the rebels (although this option was rejected by the rebels, whose condition for dialogue was the removal of Muammar Gaddafi and his associates from power). Further, the AU PSC condemned the military intervention by NATO as exceeding its mandate, which was limited to protecting civilians and facilitating humanitarian assistance.[170] As such, it may be argued that the AU PSC's approach to the crisis in Libya was to support dialogue between the warring parties within a wider international framework that included the UN, the European Union, and the LAS.

Yet in these efforts too it was undermined. For example, the AU High-Level Committee was, at the time of writing, unable to travel to Libya due to the refusal by the UN Security Council to allow its flight mission. This refusal greatly impacted the AU PSC's potential role in resolving the conflict by inhibiting necessary missions to liaise with the government and rebels.[171] This result was particularly damaging in that, as illustrated by its efforts to address peace and security challenges in Libya and Ivory Coast, one of the AU PSC's biggest challenges has been to establish its credibility with the warring

---

169 AU High Level *Ad Hoc* Committee on Libya, *Communiqué of the Meeting of the AU High Level Ad Hoc Committee on Libya,* 19 March 2011, at para 2, online: AU <http:// au.int/en/dp/ps/sites/default/files/COMMUNIQUE_EN_19_MARCH_2011 _PSD_MEETING_AU_HIGH_LEVEL_AD_HOC_COMMITTEE_LIBYA_ NOUAKCHOTT_ISLAMIC_REPUBLIC_MAURITANIA.pdf>.

170 See, eg, the press release by the AU on 3 May 2011, stressing the need for a "political solution in Libya and the importance for NATO to respect the letter and spirit of UN Security Council Resolution 1973/2011." AU, *The AU Intensifies its Efforts towards a Political Solution in Libya and Stresses the Importance of the Respect of the Letter and Spirit of Resolution 1973 (2011),* Press Release (3 May 2011). See also *Decision on the Peaceful Resolution of the Libyan Crisis,* Extraordinary Session of the Assembly of the Union on the State of Peace and Security in Africa, AU Doc EXT/ASSEMBLY/AU/DEC/(01.2011) (2011) at para 5.

171 See AU PSC, *Report of the Chairperson of the Commission on the Activities of the AU High Level Ad Hoc Committee on the Situation in Libya,* 275th Meeting, AU Doc PSC/PR/2 (CCLXXV) (2011). On 25-26 May 2011, the AU Assembly held an extraordinary session devoted to discussion of the work of the High-Level Committee on Libya and collective African responses to the situation there. See *Decision on the Peaceful Resolution of the Libyan Crisis, supra* note 170.

parties. In both Libya and Ivory Coast, the AU PSC's efforts were significantly hampered by the rejection, by both sides to the conflicts, of the mediators or terms of mediation it proposed.[172]

ASSESSING THE AU PSC's SUCCESSES AND CHALLENGES

Based on the foregoing survey, it is arguable that, while the AU PSC's capacity to address peace and security challenges is highly constrained, it has managed in its short existence to have a positive impact on efforts to resolve conflicts in Africa. These limited successes have been achieved partly through the AU PSC's reliance on mediators and partly due to the ability and willingness of sub-regional mechanisms such as ECOWAS, the SADC, and the IGAD to address security challenges under the overall authority of the AU PSC. Most notably, when one examines the AU PSC's efforts in Sudan and Somalia, one can fairly conclude that the measures undertaken by the AU PSC have helped defuse the escalation of those conflicts by fostering an atmosphere of dialogue among the various factions involved.

However, examining the decisions taken by the AU PSC reveals a mixed record of success and failure. There has been success in the sense that, as suggested earlier, the AU PSC has managed to provide leadership in addressing some threats to peace and security on the African continent — for example, through authorizing peacekeeping missions and mediation efforts. On the other hand, there has been failure in the sense that some AU members have failed to respect and implement the AU PSC's decisions or recommendations. This situation is paradoxical. Given that AU PSC decisions are taken in the name of all AU members, it would be expected that the latter would comply with them, as indeed is required by the *AU PSC Protocol*.[173] However, the record clearly shows that member states in whose territories the AU PSC decisions are to be implemented have often been reluctant to carry out their

---

172 In Libya, the Transitional National Council rejected the "peace plan" advanced by the AU precisely because it did not provide for the removal of Muammar Gaddafi and his associates from power. In Ivory Coast, the Gbagbo regime rejected the "peace plan" advanced by the AU on the basis that it favoured the opposition. The opposition, led by Alassane Ouattara, rejected the AU's appointment of the former foreign minister of Cape Verde as the mediator in the Ivorian crisis, accusing him of being too close to the regime of Laurent Gbagbo.

173 *AU PSC Protocol, supra* note 2, art 7(2)-(4).

obligations, unless doing so is perceived to be in their national interests.

Indeed, this reluctance is symptomatic of a growing tendency among African states to view the AU as a shield against external criticism or intervention. Such states claim that any problems must be solved within the AU framework without external intervention, yet the AU's attempts to address the situations are not followed by concrete action by member states. Few African states are willing to criticize or take stern measures against their peers, whether for violations of human rights, stolen elections, or general violations of the provisions of the *Constitutive Act*.[174] The reality is that few countries in Africa can accuse others of violating their obligations under the *Constitutive Act* because most countries are in the same boat when it comes to non-observance of their commitments. This is a pattern that has undermined the AU PSC's credibility. Indeed, it may in part explain why the response of the international community, and of the UN Security Council in particular, to the AU PSC's efforts to maintain peace and security in Africa has been lukewarm at best.

Enhancing the Capacity of the AU PSC to Respond to Threats to Peace and Security

Recognizing the challenges that continue to face the AU PSC in its quest to maintain peace and security on the African continent, it is worth examining how the capacity of this institution to discharge its functions effectively can be enhanced. In my view, there are four specific areas that require addressing if such progress is to be made. First, as the experiences in Sudan, Somalia, and elsewhere make clear, challenges relating to the mobilization of resources are likely to continue to inhibit the AU PSC's effectiveness. As amply demonstrated in this article, international partners cannot be relied upon to provide requisite resources for peace initiatives on the continent. Their assistance is neither predictable nor assured but, rather, depends on their own national interests.[175] The UN Security Council's

---

[174] Rhoda E Howard-Hassmann, "Mugabe's Zimbabwe, 2000-2009: Massive Human Rights Violations and the Failure to Protect" (2010) 32 Human Rts Q 898 at 909-12.

[175] This argument is made in light of the fact that most donors do not keep their promises to fund the activities or peace missions of the AU. For example, out of the total US $213 million pledged in April during the AU/UN Donor

record in responding to African security challenges, in particular, suggests that it would be counterproductive for the AU to authorize peacekeeping missions in the expectation that the UN Security Council will pick up the tab. Ideally, of course, the UN Security Council would indeed provide financial and logistical resources to regional peacekeeping missions, particularly where its members were not willing to send in their own troops to maintain international peace and security. Yet, experience has shown that the UN Security Council only acts when it is within the broader interests of its permanent members to do so.[176] This lesson in *realpolitik* suggests that it would be in the interests of the AU and its peoples to realize that, if the AU wishes to claim a role in finding African solutions for African problems, it must do so on the understanding that it will bear the ultimate burden of mobilizing the required resources to do so.

In an attempt to address this challenge, the *AU PSC Protocol* establishes a special Peace Fund with the primary goal of mobilizing resources from both within and outside the continent to support peace and security initiatives in Africa.[177] At present, the main source of funding for the Peace Fund is an annual contribution from the AU's regular budget, which effectively amounts to contributions by member states and international partners. Unfortunately, this means that as the AU's main budget continues to face budgetary constraints due to the inability of some of its members to pay, so does the fund.[178] Thus, whether it is sending peacekeeping missions to secure

---

Conference to support AMISOM and the Transitional Federal Government, by November 2009 only US $77.7 million had been received, of which AMISOM received US $25 million and the AU received US $16.6 million. See Eki Yemisi Omorogbe, "Can the African Union Deliver Peace and Security?" (2011) 16 J Conflict & Security L 35 at 58-59, who contends that between 2008 and 2010 there was a decline in funding to Somalia to the tune of US $178 million. See also "Donor Fatigue, Conflict Worsen Humanitarian Disaster in Somalia," *Afrique en ligne*, 19 May 2011, online: <http://www.afriquejet.com/news/africa-news/donor -fatigue,-conflict-worsen-humanitarian-disaster-in-somalia-2011051912438. html>.

[176] For example, China voted down the decision to support peacekeeping missions in Macedonia and Guatemala mainly because these two countries had recognized Taiwan. See Dunbabin, *supra* note 19 at 502. See also Joel Wuthnow, "China and the Processes of Cooperation in UN Security Council Deliberations" (2010) 3:1 Chinese J. Int'l Politics 55.

[177] The Peace Fund is established under the *AU PSC Protocol, supra* note 2, art 21.

[178] The AU budget for 2010 was approximately US $250 million. Of this amount, less than half, or US $118 million, was to be contributed by AU member states

peace and stability, as was done in Somalia, or undertaking mediation efforts, as happened in Zimbabwe, Ivory Coast, or Guinea
Bissau, the AU PSC requires alternative sources of funding. This
could be accomplished through various continental initiatives, such
as the imposition of mandatory taxation on airlines flying to Africa
or increased contributions from African states with significant
economies as compared to those of their peers who are less well
off. At all events, it is encouraging to note that the AU has sought
to increase its budget on peace and security issues while, at the same
time, continuing to lobby international partners both within and
beyond the continent to contribute to the fund.

Second, as we have seen earlier, the *AU PSC Protocol* stipulates that
the AU PSC is premised on respect for human rights, the rule of
law, and good governance, yet these ideals are hardly upheld by its
own members. As previously discussed, this fact seriously undermines the AU PSC's credibility and raises questions as to its ability
to promote ideals that are not upheld by its own members. For
example, when a country such as Zimbabwe — which has committed widespread abuses of human rights — is elected to the AU PSC
and is thus placed in a position where it can participate in making
decisions with far-reaching consequences for other states, it raises
legitimate questions about the seriousness of the AU's commitment
to combating human rights abuses. Similarly, when countries such
as Rwanda or Ethiopia — where opponents of the incumbent regime
are imprisoned or barred from running for public office, allowing
the incumbents or their preferred candidates to "win" elections
with more than 90 percent of the vote — are elected to the AU PSC
and thus assume responsibility for monitoring the electoral processes
of other countries, profound concerns over the seriousness of the
AU to promote the rule of law and good governance are raised.

---

through normal assessment. The remainder, or $133 million, was to be secured
from international partners. The approved budget for the AU PSC was only US
$695,000. This budget was adopted during the sixteenth ordinary session of
the Executive Council in Addis Ababa, Ethiopia, on 1 February 2010. See AU
Executive Council, *Decision on the Budget for the African Union*, 16th Sess, AU Doc
EX.CL/537 (XVI) (2010). Indeed, it is recognition of these inherent challenges
facing the AU that has led the UN secretary-general to call for increased funding
of the AU's peace initiatives by the international community. See "Ban Calls for
Predictable Funding for African Union Peace Initiatives," *UN News Centre* (22
October 2010), online: UN News Centre <http://www.un.org/apps/news/story.
asp?NewsID=36545&Cr=african+union&Cr1>.

In order to address these difficulties, the AU PSC should explore the possibility of adopting a transparent mechanism for vetting AU PSC nominations. Moreover, consideration should be given to maintaining the human rights, rule of law, and good governance criteria while eliminating the requirements of regional representation and ability to pay into the Peace Fund. The danger of the latter criteria is that they facilitate, on the basis of geographic or financial considerations, the nomination of states otherwise notorious for flouting the provisions of the *Constitutive Act* and the *AU PSC Protocol.*

Third, to further enhance the AU PSC's capacities and effectiveness, there is a need for a fundamental shift in how member states implement its directives. As seen in the cases of Sudan or Ivory Coast, AU member states often ignore AU PSC directives with few or no consequences. For example, the fact that President al-Bashir of Sudan brushed aside, without consequence, the AU PSC's recommendation to form a hybrid tribunal to try crimes committed in Darfur set a precedent to the effect that member states can ignore such directives without major repercussions. The AU PSC must reassert its authority. It must make clear that member states must comply with its directives, failing which punitive measures will be imposed on the defaulting member.

Fourth and notwithstanding observations made under the first point, we have also seen that the UN Security Council has a pivotal role to play, under the *UN Charter,* in ensuring that international peace and security are maintained, including in Africa. All African countries are UN members and therefore have a legitimate claim to the protections of the *UN Charter.* Yet as shown earlier, time and again the UN Security Council has shown that it is not willing to send troops into the most hostile regions of the African continent or to adequately resource AU PSC initiatives in this regard. As argued by Ambassador Nicholas Bwakira, it is greatly unfair that the UN Security Council should enjoy the privilege of being the sole organ to determine threats to international peace and security without bearing corresponding responsibility.[179]

The UN Security Council's record in this regard has a compound detrimental effect, as experience has shown that most African states are reluctant to participate in AU peacekeeping missions when they know that the AU has limited resources and that the UN is not fully committed to the effort. They fear that they will be required to bear

---

[179] See Majinge, *supra* note 40 at 496.

the double burden of both providing soldiers and also paying for them. It cannot be right that a poor country such as Burundi, which faces serious economic and political challenges and is just emerging from a long and protracted conflict of its own, is willing to commit its troops to a peacekeeping mission, yet major powers fail to reciprocate by funding the mission. Similarly, it cannot be right that, since sending its troops to Somalia, Uganda has suffered various terrorist attacks allegedly committed by Al Shaabab militants without being able to count on international assistance in terms of investigating and bringing the perpetrators to justice. Collectively, these challenges hamper the willingness of African countries to contribute to peace efforts on the African continent.

With the UN Security Council's decision to hybridize various missions between the UN and the AU, it was expected that it would be willing to provide accompanying resources to ensure that such missions could perform their functions effectively. Contrary to these expectations, Darfur has shown that hybrid missions are no panacea to peacekeeping issues on the African continent precisely because the UN Security Council has lacked the decisive resolve to provide sufficient tools to such missions.

It is therefore argued that, if the AU PSC is to make an effective contribution to peace and security in Africa, the UN must fulfil its responsibility as the primary guarantor of international peace and security. This means that there should be a division of labour between the UN and regional arrangements such as the AU. If the AU can provide troops to venture into hostile spots such as Mogadishu or Darfur, the UN Security Council should be willing to play its role as a reliable partner. If the UN Security Council is not willing to send troops to the most hostile regions of the African continent, it should at least be prepared to provide adequate resources to allow those regional organizations that are willing to do so to discharge such functions on its behalf.

Yet it is important to note that the UN Security Council's role should not be limited to extending *financial* assistance to AU PSC authorized missions. An undue focus on funding individual missions could eclipse required assistance in other crucial areas such as the training of peacekeepers; the provision of equipment, such as aircraft, armoured vehicles, and medical facilities; and the support of experts in the AU itself in order to enhance its capacity to deploy and manage missions. Such "in-kind" support can be crucial given the hostile nature of missions in such places as Somalia, where some inexperienced and under-equipped troops have had to battle Al Shaabab militias on a regular basis.[180]

Moreover, envoys and officials appointed by the UN tend to be better resourced in comparison with their AU counterparts. As such, UN contributions to the work of the AU PSC should be directed not only towards peacekeeping missions but also towards strengthening the capabilities and effectiveness of AU mediators and mediation processes. In particular, there is a need for UN and AU envoys to work together rather than apart as competitors. Such competition not only harms mediation efforts but also creates mistrust between mediators themselves and the parties involved in the conflict. Overcoming this tendency would help in ensuring that available resources are used optimally in the interests of effective mediation efforts.[181]

CONCLUSION

As the preceding discussion shows, the *UN Charter* recognizes the pivotal role of regional arrangements in the maintenance of international peace and security. The UN Security Council, however powerful it might be, cannot effectively take measures to maintain international peace and security in all corners of the world. This reality compels the UN Security Council to rely upon regional arrangements to carry out elements of its mandate on its behalf. Yet, as its practice in the African context demonstrates, the UN Security Council has tended to do so without providing corresponding resources for the task, despite the differing capabilities of regional arrangements to fulfil such mandates.

For the AU, the question of adequate resources is perhaps more crucial than for any other organization of its type anywhere in the world. Unlike the European Union or NATO, the AU's members are among the world's most economically challenged and politically unstable states. Indeed, most AU members are either embroiled in,

---

[180] For example, in February and March 2011, more than fifty peacekeepers from Burundi were killed in Mogadishu while trying to secure the city from Al Shaabab. Katherine Houreld, "Fifty-Three African Union Peacekeepers Killed in Somalia Offensive," *Associated Press* (5 March 2011), online: The Independent <http://www.independent.co.uk/news/world/africa/53-african-union-peacekeepers-killed-in-somalia-offensive-2233169.html>).

[181] For example, there has been a sense of competition between mediators in Darfur because of the differing interests of the various countries involved. See, eg, "Arab Competition over Roles Slowing Darfur Initiative: Qatar," *Sudan Tribune* (12 January 2009), online: Sudan Tribune <http://www.sudantribune.com/Arab-competition-over-roles,29849>.

or emerging from, conflicts that require the intervention of the AU or are completely poor and hence unable to contribute meaningfully to the cause of international peace and security. It is highly unrealistic to expect countries such as Somalia, Chad, Guinea Bissau, or Liberia, to name but a few, to contribute meaningfully to efforts to maintain continental peace and security when these same countries, apart from being poor, are also experiencing varying levels of conflict or instability within their own borders.

This article has argued that there is a need for the UN Security Council to re-examine its engagement with regional bodies that carry out its mandate in circumstances where it is unwilling or unable to do so. The UN Security Council should adopt a policy to the effect that, when it authorizes a regional body to undertake enforcement action in accordance with the *UN Charter*, it will require UN member states to provide sufficient accompanying resources to permit the regional authority to perform its functions effectively. It is tragic that, since 2007, when the AU authorized AMISOM to intervene in Somalia with the strong support of the UN Security Council, AMISOM continues to struggle to attract financial and logistical support from the international community. At times, the mission has gone months without paying its soldiers. Similarly, in Darfur, the hybridization of the mission has not resolved its issues. The mission has continued to face traditional problems ranging from the unwillingness of countries to commit troops to the mission to the inability of the UN Security Council to provide adequate funding. Privileges clearly entail responsibilities. The UN Security Council cannot expect to call the shots on peace and security-related matters when it is not willing or prepared to discharge the obligations that come with that power. The UN Security Council must recognize that, in addressing African peace and security issues, the AU PSC is simply performing functions that are ultimately the responsibility of the UN Security Council as the primary guarantor of international peace and security.

There is therefore a profound need for a permanent mechanism, supported by both the UN and the AU, to fund peace and security initiatives on the African continent. Such a mechanism would have to acknowledge that it is the primary responsibility of the UN Security Council to maintain international peace and security and that whatever is done by regional arrangements such as the AU in that regard is undertaken on behalf of the former. Without such a mechanism, any other progress, whether political or economic, cannot be achieved.

It has also been underscored that both the *Constitutive Act* of the AU and the *AU PSC Protocol* provide that the promotion of human rights, the rule of law, and good governance are obligations of all AU members and, in particular, of those who want to be elected to the AU PSC. Yet the African continent continues to be plagued by the reality of perennially venal governance. If countries such as Rwanda, Ethiopia, Sudan, or Zimbabwe can be members of the AU PSC — an institution entrusted with upholding human rights and the rule of law — it is difficult to see how the AU PSC can assume a leadership role in transforming these values into living reality. It is against this background that this article has argued that, if it is to be taken seriously both within and outside Africa, the AU PSC must be seen to uphold the values that it claims to advance by closely scrutinizing the records of states vying to occupy its seats.

Moreover, despite the call for the UN Security Council to expend more resources to resolve peace and security issues on the African continent, it has been argued that African states must take proactive measures to be able, ultimately, to address this challenge on their own. This argument has been made in light of the fact that the UN Security Council only acts swiftly when the interests of major powers are at stake or when it is within its members' collective interests to do so. Unfortunately, in Africa, it is hardly possible to think of any conflict that has attracted unanimous action by the UN Security Council. Rather, most conflicts have been addressed either in light of the interests of the former colonial power, which can effectively lobby for UN Security Council action, or on "humanitarian grounds" where the UN Security Council requests that the international community provide humanitarian assistance to refugees or those affected by the conflict. In either case, it is Africa that has continued to pay the heavy price of these conflicts because of the inaction, or selective action, of the UN Security Council.

Thus, while it is acknowledged that the AU operates on a tight budget, the organization must explore alternative ways of mobilizing additional resources to fund the implementation of the AU PSC's decisions. For example, the AU should explore the possibility of convincing the private sector, especially multinational enterprises with substantial investments on the continent, to contribute to African peace and security through the Peace Fund. Admittedly, the effectiveness of this suggestion will largely depend on the image that African leaders and administrators project to the business world, both within and outside Africa. It will be difficult to win the support of private sector actors if their day-to-day experience of doing business in Africa is tainted by deeply entrenched governmental corruption, abuse of human rights, and a general disregard for the rule of law, which are all antithetical to conditions required for their businesses' success. Of course, there may be other avenues to explore in seeking to secure the resources necessary to permit the AU PSC to address Africa's peace and security challenges. In any event, the ultimate goal must be to transform "African solutions to African problems," particularly in the area of peace and security, from a slogan into a reality.

Sommaire

Les organismes régionaux et le maintien de la paix et de la sécurité internationales: le rôle du Conseil de paix et de sécurité de l'Union africaine

Cet article examine le rôle des organismes régionaux dans le maintien de la paix et de la sécurité internationales selon la Charte des Nations Unies. *Le Conseil de paix et de sécurité (CPS), l'organe de l'Union africaine (UA) chargée de lutter contre les menaces contre la paix et la sécurité internationales sur le continent africain, sert d'étude de cas. L'auteur soutient que les défis majeurs auxquels sont confrontés les organismes régionaux dans l'exercice de mandats en vertu de l'article 53 de la* Charte des Nations Unies *ont plus à voir avec l'insuffisance de leurs ressources financières et logistiques que la nature des mandats eux-mêmes. Examinant le rôle de l'UA en Somalie, le Soudan et d'autres pays africains à titre d'exemples, l'article démontre que le CPS n'a pas atteint son objectif de maintenir la paix et la sécurité précisément parce que le Conseil de sécurité de l'Organisation des Nations Unies (ONU), organe plus puissant et mieux financé, n'était pas à la hauteur de sa responsabilité d'étendre le soutien nécessaire pour permettre au CPS d'exercer ses fonctions. L'auteur en conclut que, lorsque le Conseil de sécurité de l'ONU délègue ses pouvoirs à des organismes régionaux pour le maintien de la paix et de la sécurité internationales, il devrait également fournir des ressources adéquates à ces organismes régionaux, en particulier à ceux qui n'auront autrement que peu ou pas de chance de s'acquitter de leurs mandats avec succès.*

Summary

Regional Arrangements and the Maintenance of International Peace and Security: The Role of the African Union Peace and Security Council

This article examines the role of regional arrangements under the Charter of the United Nations (UN Charter) in the maintenance of international peace and security. The African Union Peace and Security Council (AU PSC), the organ within the AU charged with addressing threats to international peace and security on the African continent, is used as a case study. The author contends that the major challenges facing regional arrangements in exercising mandates under Article 53 of the UN Charter of the United Nations have more to do with inadequate financial and logistical resources than the nature of those mandates. Taking the AU's role in Somalia, Sudan, and other African countries as examples, the article demonstrates that the AU PSC has failed to achieve its objective of maintaining peace and security precisely because the United Nations (UN) Security Council — a more powerful and better resourced organ — has failed to live up to its responsibility of extending the assistance necessary to enable the AU PSC to perform its functions. Consequently, the author concludes that the UN Security Council, when delegating powers to regional arrangements to maintain international peace and security, should provide adequate resources to such regional arrangements, especially those that will otherwise have minimal or no capacity to fulfil their mandate effectively.

Les piliers économique et environnemental du développement durable: conciliation ou soutien mutuel? L'éclairage apporté par la Cour internationale de Justice dans l'*Affaire des Usines de pâte à papier sur le fleuve Uruguay (Argentine c Uruguay)*

GÉRAUD DE LASSUS SAINT-GENIÈS

INTRODUCTION

Alors qu'il vise la prévisibilité et la sécurité, le droit international regorge de notions floues au sens indéterminé. De telles notions ne laissent à ceux qui veulent les appréhender qu'une seule solution: les interpréter. Et plus l'indétermination de l'objet à interpréter est grande, plus la contribution de l'interprète à la détermination de son sens s'avère décisive. Ainsi en est-il avec le concept de développement durable. Notion indéterminée par excellence,[1] le développement durable ne peut être défini sans recourir au jeu de l'interprétation. Son sens n'étant en effet pas "donné" par la norme, celui-ci doit par conséquent être "construit" par la voie de l'herméneutique juridique. Or, l'étude de cette herméneutique fait

Géraud de Lassus Saint-Geniès est Doctorant à la Faculté de droit de l'Université Laval et à l'Université Paris 1 Panthéon-Sorbonne, membre de la Chaire de recherche du Canada en droit de l'environnement. L'auteur tient à remercier les professeurs Ivan Bernier, Paule Halley et Véronique Guèvremont pour leurs commentaires ainsi que le Conseil de recherches en sciences humaines du Canada pour le soutien financier dont il bénéficie dans le cadre de ses travaux.

[1] Sur la difficulté de définir le développement durable, voir par ex "Sustainable Development: The Challenge to International Environmental Law: Report of a Consultation Held at Windsor 27 to 29 April 1993" (1993) 2:4 RECIEL 1; voir aussi Michael Redclift, "Reflections on the 'Sustainable Development' Debate" (1994) 1:1 Int'l J Sustainable Dev & World Ecol 3; Chantal Cans, "Environnement et développement durable" dans Yves Petit, dir, *Droit et politiques de l'environnement*, Paris, La Documentation française, 2009.

aujourd'hui ressortir l'existence de deux paradigmes qui déterminent chacun une manière distincte et opposée de concevoir le développement durable en droit international.

S'il est traditionnellement admis que le développement durable se compose d'au moins trois piliers[2] — économique, environnemental et social — cette divergence d'interprétation porte sur la façon d'envisager la relation entre ces différents piliers. En effet, la conception de cette relation peut considérablement varier en fonction de la perception qu'ont les interprètes de ce qu'est, ou devrait être, le développement durable. Ainsi, selon un premier paradigme, la relation entre les piliers du développement durable, et plus particulièrement la relation entre les piliers économique et environnemental, serait caractérisée par la recherche d'une conciliation. Selon un second, elle serait caractérisée par l'existence d'un soutien mutuel. L'objectif de cet article est donc de mettre en lumière l'existence de ces deux conceptions opposées du développement durable qui sont actuellement présentes au sein de l'ordre juridique international, en revenant sur les circonstances de leur émergence, les présupposés sur lesquels elles se fondent ainsi que sur les contextes dans lesquels les différents acteurs du droit international y ont souscrit.

Sur le plan chronologique, l'interprétation du développement durable a tout d'abord été guidée par le premier paradigme, qui peut être qualifié de paradigme de la conciliation. La Cour internationale de Justice a joué un rôle important dans son apparition en reconnaissant en 1997 dans l'*Affaire relative au Projet Gabčíkovo-Nagymaros* que le développement durable traduit la "nécessité de concilier développement économique et protection de l'environnement."[3] Pourtant, à partir du milieu des années 1990, la référence

---

[2] La précision s'impose dans la mesure où semble actuellement émerger un quatrième pilier culturel du développement durable. La *Convention sur la protection et la promotion de la diversité des expressions culturelles*, 20 octobre 2005, 2440 RTNU 32 [*UNESCO*], incite en effet à considérer la culture comme un pilier du développement durable puisque son article 2.6 reconnaît que "[l]a protection, la promotion et le maintien de la diversité culturelle sont une condition essentielle pour un développement durable." Si la notion de "pilier" fait désormais partie du vocabulaire usuel du développement durable, sa définition et son contenu demeurent encore assez imprécis. Sans doute la notion comprend-t-elle au *minimum* l'idée d'objectif à poursuivre. C'est d'ailleurs dans cette perspective qu'elle sera employée au cours de cette étude. Interprétée plus largement, elle pourrait également intégrer l'ensemble des valeurs et préoccupations relatives à la nature de chacun des piliers.

[3] *Affaire relative au Projet Gabčíkovo-Nagymaros* (*Hongrie c Slovaquie*), [1997] CIJ rec 7 au para. 140 [*Affaire relative au Projet Gabčíkovo-Nagymaros*].

au principe du soutien mutuel dans les travaux portant sur les relations entre les normes du système commercial multilatéral et les Accords environnementaux multilatéraux (AEM), a progressivement conduit à l'éclosion d'une autre lecture du développement durable. Selon celle-ci, le développement économique et la protection de l'environnement ne seraient plus deux objectifs à concilier car, au lieu d'être en opposition, ceux-ci se soutiendraient mutuellement, la poursuite de l'un étant *ipso facto* favorable à la poursuite de l'autre. Consacré lors du Sommet mondial pour le développement durable de Johannesburg en 2002, ce paradigme du soutien mutuel, qui conduit ainsi à extraire du développement durable toute idée de tension entre l'économie et l'environnement, fait depuis sentir son influence sur la façon dont ce concept est interprété au sein de l'ordre juridique international.

C'est dans ce contexte que mérite d'être souligné l'arrêt rendu par la Cour internationale de Justice le 20 avril 2010 dans l'*Affaire relative à des Usines de pâte à papier sur le fleuve Uruguay*.[4] En rappelant que le développement durable traduit la nécessité de concilier le développement économique et la protection de l'environnement, la Cour a réaffirmé, treize ans après l'affaire du *Projet Gabčíkovo-Nagymaros*, son adhésion au paradigme de la conciliation. Toutefois, compte tenu du contexte international dans lequel s'inscrit cet arrêt, la réaffirmation de cette conception du développement durable ne semble ni présager la fin, ni même annoncer un recul, de la conception du développement durable fondée sur le paradigme du soutien mutuel. Au contraire, elle semble indiquer une coexistence de ces deux paradigmes au sein de l'ordre juridique international et donc de deux conceptions opposées du développement durable.

LA RELATION ENTRE LES PILIERS ÉCONOMIQUE ET ENVIRONNEMENTAL DU DÉVELOPPEMENT DURABLE: DU PARADIGME DE LA CONCILIATION AU PARADIGME DU SOUTIEN MUTUEL

La façon dont a été interprété le développement durable en droit international depuis son apparition atteste d'une évolution. Considéré dans un premier temps comme un concept visant à concilier des objectifs économique et environnemental perçus comme étant en opposition, il a par la suite été appréhendé comme un concept

---

4 *Affaire relative à des Usines de pâte à papier sur le fleuve Uruguay* (*Argentine c Uruguay*), [2010] en ligne: CIJ <http://www.icj-cij.org> [*Affaire des Usines de pâte à papier sur le fleuve Uruguay*].

impliquant l'existence d'un soutien mutuel entre ces deux objectifs, sous-entendant ainsi leur absence totale d'opposition. Cette évolution de la perception du développement durable, qui reflète par conséquent un changement dans les paradigmes utilisés par les acteurs de l'ordre juridique international pour interpréter ce concept, s'est notamment manifestée par un renouvellement des termes employés par ces acteurs dans la construction de leurs "discours" sur le développement durable.

LE PARADIGME DE LA CONCILIATION

D'abord perçu comme synonyme de croissance économique, "l'idée de développement s'est peu à peu complexifiée pour se transformer en un concept pluridimensionnel grâce à l'importance grandissante des dimensions sociales, politiques, culturelles et environnementales face à la dimension économique."[5] Ce processus d'agrégation de problématiques différentes au sein d'un concept unique, débuté à partir des années 1970,[6] a conduit les États à chercher les moyens d'élaborer des politiques intégrées visant à poursuivre conjointement et simultanément, entre autres, les objectifs de développement économique et de protection de l'environnement.[7] Or, en rapprochant ces deux objectifs auparavant appréhendés par le biais de politiques sectorielles distinctes, cette démarche intégrée a stimulé le développement de la problématique de leur articulation. Certes, la poursuite conjointe et simultanée des objectifs économique et environnemental n'implique pas automatiquement l'existence d'un conflit entre ces objectifs.[8] Mais elle ne l'exclut pas non plus. Et

---

[5] Ignacy Sachs, "Développement de la culture, culture du développement" (2005) 68 Liaison énergie-francophone — culture et développement durable 25 à la p 25.

[6] Alexandre S Timoshenko, "From Stockholm to Rio: The Institutionalization of Sustainable Development" dans Winfried Lang, dir, *Sustainable Development and International law*, Londres (R-U), Boston, Graham & Trotman, Martinus Nijhoff, 1995, 143.

[7] Voir le Principe 4 de la Déclaration de Rio sur l'environnement et le développement, Doc off CNUED, 47ᵉ sess, Annexe I, Doc NU A/CONF.151/26 (Vol I) (1992) [Déclaration de Rio] qui énonce que "[p]our parvenir à un développement durable, la protection de l'environnement doit faire partie intégrante du processus de développement et ne peut être considérée isolément."

[8] Un conflit d'objectifs désigne une situation dans laquelle la poursuite d'un objectif a pour effet de porter atteinte à la poursuite d'un autre objectif ou de rendre impossible sa réalisation. Pour certains auteurs, il existerait nécessairement un conflit entre la poursuite des objectifs économique et environnemental. En ce

lorsque surgit un tel conflit d'objectifs, la question est dès lors de savoir comment articuler leur poursuite.

En 1972, lors de la Déclaration finale adoptée à l'issue de la Conférence mondiale sur l'environnement humain de Stockholm, les États ont considéré que cette articulation devait être caractérisée par la recherche de "conciliation" et de "compatibilité."[9] Le choix de ces deux termes n'est pas neutre et leur emploi constitue un éclairage pour comprendre la façon dont les États ont à cette époque conçu la relation entre les futurs piliers économique et environnemental du développement durable. Puisque "concilier" signifie "faire aller ensemble, rendre harmonieux (ce qui était très différent, contraire)"[10] et "compatible" désigne ce "[q]ui peut s'accorder avec autre chose, exister en même temps,"[11] l'usage de ces deux termes traduisait trois idées: d'abord, qu'il pouvait exister une contradiction entre la poursuite des objectifs économique et environnemental, puisque selon la définition du terme "concilier," ne peut être concilié que ce qui est contraire; ensuite, que cette opposition pouvait être dépassée, sinon il n'y eu aucun sens à vouloir rendre ces deux objectifs compatibles ; et enfin, que la poursuite de ces deux objectifs ne pouvait être absolue, faute de quoi leur poursuite simultanée eut été impossible. C'est d'ailleurs cette "idée de limitation"[12] dans la poursuite des objectifs économique et environnemental qui,

---

sens voir Agathe Van Lang, *Droit de l'environnement,* 2ᵉ éd, Paris, Presses Universitaires de France, 2007 (selon l'auteure, il "semble en effet peu douteux que la croissance économique et la protection de l'environnement soient des objectifs contradictoires"), à la p 188.

9 Voir le Principe 13 de la *Déclaration de la Conférence des Nations Unies sur l'environnement,* Doc off CNUEH, 21ᵉ séance, Doc NU A/CONF.48/14/Rev 1 (1972), qui énonce que "les Etats devraient adopter une conception intégrée et coordonnée de leur planification du développement, de façon que leur développement soit compatible avec la nécessité de protéger et d'améliorer l'environnement dans l'intérêt de leur population" et le Principe 14 qui note que la "planification rationnelle est un instrument essentiel si l'on veut concilier les impératifs du développement et la nécessité de préserver et d'améliorer l'environnement." Voir aussi la résolution de l'Assemblée générale des Nations Unies Développement et environnement, Doc off AGNU, 26ᵉ sess, 2026ᵉ séance, Doc NU A/RES/2849/(XXVI) (1971) (l'Assemblée dit "[c]onvaincue que les plans de développement doivent être compatibles avec une saine écologie") alinéa 7.

10 *Le Grand Robert de la langue française,* 2001, *sub verbo* "concilier."

11 *Ibid sub verbo* "compatible."

12 Commission mondiale sur l'environnement et le développement, *Notre avenir à tous,* Doc off CMED, 42ᵉ sess, Doc NU A/42/427 (1987) à la p 55.

quinze ans plus tard, a été considérée par les membres de la Commission mondiale sur l'environnement et le développement comme un concept inhérent au développement durable.

En revanche, lors de la déclaration adoptée à Rio de Janeiro en 1992, dans laquelle le concept de développement durable se trouvait pour la première fois consacré dans un texte juridique international de portée générale,[13] les États sont restés silencieux sur la façon de coordonner la poursuite des objectifs économique et environnemental. La déclaration ne contient en effet ni le terme "conciliation" et/ou "compatibilité," ni aucune autre indication relative à l'articulation de ces deux objectifs. Cette absence de précision a certainement permis de conférer au développement durable des vertus fédératrices au sein d'une communauté internationale en proie aux divergences d'intérêts, en évitant notamment de remettre en cause le droit souverain de chaque État de décider de son propre mode de développement.[14] Néanmoins, cette indétermination ouvrait une large voie pour l'interprétation du concept. C'est ainsi qu'en 1997, dans l'affaire du *Projet Gabčíkovo-Nagymaros*, la Cour internationale de Justice a interprété le développement durable comme traduisant la "nécessité de concilier développement économique et protection de l'environnement."[15] À l'instar de la conception qui avait prévalu lors de la Déclaration de Stockholm, la Cour reconnaissait donc que l'articulation entre ces deux objectifs devait être effectuée à travers le prisme de la conciliation. Par cette interprétation, elle contribuait ainsi à l'émergence d'un premier paradigme, d'une première matrice, pour le décodage du concept de développement durable.

Envisager la relation entre les piliers économique et environnemental du développement durable sous l'angle de la conciliation revenait dès lors à reconnaître qu'il était nécessaire d'établir une limite dans la poursuite des objectifs économique et environnemental ainsi qu'un choix dans la priorité à leur accorder. En effet, les notions de limite et de choix sont toutes les deux intrinsèquement liées à la logique qui régit le fonctionnement du mécanisme de la

---

[13] Déclaration de Rio, *supra* note 7.

[14] Voir Pierre-Marie Dupuy, "Où en est le droit international de l'environnement à la fin du siècle ?" (1997) 101:4 RGDIP 873 ("les mérites diplomatiques comme les faiblesses techniques [du développement durable] tiennent précisément à son extrême généralité comme aux frontières imprécises sensées l'embrasser sans trop la définir") à la p 886.

[15] *Affaire relative au Projet Gabčíkovo-Nagymaros*, *supra* note 3 au para140.

conciliation et à ce titre, celles-ci constituent des pièces maitresses dans l'ensemble des représentations qui structurent le paradigme de la conciliation.

La conciliation est une opération qui vise à résoudre un conflit entre des objectifs (ou des principes, des normes, des valeurs, etc.) dont la poursuite simultanée et intégrale est impossible. Or, dans la mesure où la conciliation doit permettre de poursuivre simultanément deux objectifs, le conflit entre ces objectifs ne peut être résolu que grâce à une limitation de leur poursuite.[16] En effet, parce qu'elle repose sur l'idée de prise en compte simultanée, la conciliation ne peut fonctionner selon un raisonnement de type binaire dans lequel un objectif est soit poursuivi, soit non poursuivi. Aussi, la conciliation implique de recourir à la logique floue pour faire varier, et donc limiter, l'intensité de la poursuite d'au moins l'un des deux objectifs qu'elle met en rapport.[17]

Mais concilier n'est pas non plus "un jugement de Salomon coupant exactement en deux moitiés parfaites l'objet du litige."[18] Autrement dit, si la conciliation conduit à limiter l'intensité de la poursuite des objectifs, il est peu probable que cette intensité soit parfaitement identique pour chacun des deux objectifs. Dès lors, concilier conduit à établir un choix en fonction des circonstances de l'espèce (mais aussi de la subjectivité de celui qui est amené à

---

[16] Sur l'idée de limite dans le mécanisme de la conciliation voir par ex Véronique Champeil-Desplats, "Raisonnement juridique et pluralité des valeurs: les conflits axio-téléologiques de normes" (2001) Analisi e Diritto 59 (pour l'auteure, la conciliation permet "l'application partielle des deux normes qui entrent en conflit" à la p 66); voir aussi Georges Vedel, " La place de la Déclaration de 1789 dans le 'bloc de constitutionnalité'" dans *La déclaration des droits de l'homme et du citoyen et la jurisprudence de 1789*, Paris, Presses Universitaires de France, 1990, 35 ("La conciliation entre des exigences contraires mais de valeur formellement égale doit se comprendre comme faisant partiellement droit à l'une et à l'autre," à la p 59).

[17] Sur la logique floue voir Mireille Delmas-Marty et Marie-Laure Izroche, "Marge nationale d'appréciation et internationalisation du droit: réflexions sur la validité formelle d'un droit commun pluraliste" (2001) 46:4 RD McGill 923 ("Le passage de cette logique binaire (interrupteur ouvert ou fermé, lampe allumée ou éteinte) à la logique floue se traduit *non pas par un changement de structure* du circuit mais par le remplacement des interrupteurs par des rhéostats, qui vont permettre de faire *varier continûment* l'intensité du courant électrique entre la valeur 0 et la valeur 1, en déplaçant le curseur … [L]es valeurs de l'intensité du courant électrique ne sont plus réduites à deux possibilités (le courant passe ou le courant ne passe pas), mais varient entre 0 et le maximum, représenté par la valeur 1" à la p 946).

[18] Vedel, *supra* note 16 à la p 59.

résoudre le conflit) dans la priorité à accorder à la poursuite des objectifs en conflit, tout en essayant de maintenir entre eux un certain équilibre.[19] L'exercice de la conciliation par les juridictions, tant nationales qu'internationales, s'accompagne d'ailleurs du recours à certaines opérations judiciaires telles que la mise en balance (ou pesée) des intérêts et la proportionnalité qui permettent d'établir une priorité dans la poursuite des objectifs à concilier.[20]

Bien avant l'affaire du *Projet Gabčíkovo-Nagymaros*, la nécessité de cette limite et de ce choix dans la relation entre le développement économique et la protection de l'environnement avait déjà été identifiée en 1971 par les auteurs du rapport de Founex qui visait à préparer la Conférence des Nations Unies sur l'environnement de Stockholm. Ceux-ci avaient en effet reconnu que "lorsque surgit une incompatibilité [entre les objectifs environnementaux et la croissance économique], notamment lorsqu'il s'agit d'établir un ordre de priorité à court ou à moyen terme, il y aura des choix plus difficiles à faire pour établir un compromis entre ces objectifs et des objectifs de croissance plus étroitement conçus."[21] Pourtant, un autre courant d'interprétation du développement durable allait soutenir que ce concept n'impliquait ni limite, ni choix.

LE PARADIGME DU SOUTIEN MUTUEL

L'émergence d'un courant d'interprétation du développement durable fondé sur un paradigme distinct de celui de la conciliation découle de l'attention particulière dont a fait l'objet le principe du soutien mutuel — ou du renforcement mutuel — au sein de la communauté internationale à partir du milieu des années 1990. L'existence de ce principe du soutien mutuel résulte de la spécificité de l'ordre juridique international. Fragmenté, celui-ci est composé

---

[19] Voir Sylvie Caudal-Sizaret, *La protection intégrée de l'environnement en droit public français*, thèse de doctorat en droit, Université Lyon III Jean Moulin, 1993 [non publiée] (l'approche intégrée fait apparaître des conflits d'objectifs dont la résolution conduit "à opérer des choix, à faire prévaloir tel élément sur tel autre, tout en essayant de conserver un certain équilibre" à la p 637).

[20] Voir par ex en droit suisse Charles-Albert Morand, dir, *La pesée globale des intérêts: Droit de l'environnement et de l'aménagement du territoire*, Bâle, Helbing & Lichtenhahn, 1994; en droit français voir Xavier Philippe, *Le contrôle de proportionnalité dans les jurisprudences constitutionnelle et administrative française*, Paris, Économica, 1990; en droit international voir *L'Arbitrage du Rhin de fer (Belgique c Pays-Bas)* [2005] en ligne: CPA <http://www.pca-cpa.org>.

[21] PNUD, "Développement et environnement: le rapport de Founex" dans *Sauvegarde, les textes fondamentaux sur l'environnement*, Nairobi, PNUE, 1981 à la p 5.

de différents systèmes juridiques qui visent chacun à poursuivre un objectif d'intérêt commun relatif à une problématique déterminée. Mais dans la mesure où ces objectifs sont souvent interdépendants, il peut arriver que les champs d'application des systèmes se chevauchent. Dès lors, la mise en œuvre d'une norme appartenant à un système devient susceptible de perturber ou de rendre impossible la mise en œuvre d'une norme appartenant à un autre système. Par exemple, les mesures commerciales inscrites dans les AEM destinées à restreindre les conditions de circulation de certains produits ou à interdire leur commerce peuvent présenter un risque d'incompatibilité avec les règles du système commercial multilatéral élaborées afin de libéraliser les échanges commerciaux.[22]

Face à une telle situation, au lieu de chercher à faire prévaloir une norme sur une autre, le principe du soutien mutuel vise à assurer la "pleine réalisation des droits et obligations [inscrits dans chacune des normes et à garantir] l'intégrité et … la non-modification des droits et obligations qui sont négociés au sein de fora internationaux distincts."[23] L'objectif de ce principe est donc de coordonner l'application simultanée et intégrale de deux traités dont les obligations sont potentiellement conflictuelles.[24] Il s'agit ainsi d'assurer, par le biais de l'interprétation des textes, "la cohérence et la coexistence entre instruments n'appartenant pas au même *corpus juris* mais susceptibles de poursuivre un ou des objectifs juridiques plus ou moins similaires."[25]

Même si le principe du soutien mutuel définit aujourd'hui les relations entre les règles du système commercial multilatéral, intimement liées au développement économique,[26] et certains traités

---

[22] Voir par ex Winfried Lang, "Les mesures commerciales au service de la protection de l'environnement" (1995) 99:3 RGDIP 545.

[23] Laurence Boisson de Chazournes et Makane M Mbengue, "À propos du principe du soutien mutuel — Les relations entre le Protocole de Cartagena et les Accords de l'OMC" (2007) 111:4 RGDIP 830.

[24] Commission du droit international, *Fragmentation du droit international: difficultés découlant de la diversification et de l'expansion du droit international*, Doc off AGNU, 58e sess, Doc NU A/CN.4/L.682 (2006) au para 272.

[25] Boisson de Chazournes et Mbengue, *supra* note 23 (les auteurs relèvent que le principe du soutien mutuel "dicte" une "lecture" particulière des divers instruments juridiques qu'il met en rapport, à la p 831).

[26] Déclaration ministérielle de Doha du 20 novembre 2001, OMC Doc WT/MIN(01)/DEC/1, en ligne: OMC <http://docsonline.wto.org> [Déclaration ministérielle] (La Déclaration adoptée à Doha le 4 novembre 2001 à l'issue de la quatrième Conférence ministérielle des États membres de l'Organisation

multilatéraux relatifs à des domaines autres que la protection de l'environnement,[27] c'est néanmoins dans le cadre des relations entre les règles de ce système commercial et les AEM que ce principe a émergé. Présent dans l'Agenda 21 adopté à Rio en 1992,[28] il a imprégné les travaux du Comité du commerce et de l'environnement mis en place à l'issue des négociations du cycle d'Uruguay instituant l'Organisation mondiale du commerce (OMC).[29] La décision créant ce comité indiquait en effet "qu'il ne devrait pas y avoir, et qu'il n'y a pas nécessairement, de contradiction au plan des politiques entre la préservation et la sauvegarde d'un système commercial multilatéral ouvert, non-discriminatoire et équitable d'une part et les actions visant à protéger l'environnement et à promouvoir le développement durable d'autre part."[30] Depuis, le principe du soutien mutuel constitue un guide au sein de l'OMC pour définir les relations entre les normes commerciales et environnementales.[31]

---

mondiale du commerce reconnaît que "[l]e système commercial multilatéral qu'incarne l'Organisation mondiale du commerce a largement contribué à la croissance économique" et que "[l]e commerce international peut jouer un rôle majeur dans la promotion du développement économique" aux para 1-2).

[27] Voir par ex le Préambule du Traité sur les ressources phytogénétiques pour l'alimentation et l'agriculture, 3 novembre 2001, 2010 RTNU 303 [FAO]; voir aussi l'article 20 de la *Convention sur la protection et la promotion de la diversité des expressions culturelles, supra* note 2.

[28] Selon l'article 2.10.d de l'Agenda 21, Doc off CNUED, 47e sess, Annexe I, Doc NU A/CONF.151/26 (Vol I) (1992), la communauté internationale doit avoir pour objectif de "garantir la synergie des politiques environnementales et commerciales, en vue d'assurer un développement durable." La version anglaise énonce: "[e]nsure that environment and trade policies are mutually supportive, with a view to achieving sustainable development." Au niveau régional, le concept de soutien mutuel a été évoqué dès 1979 dans les travaux de l'Organisation de coopération et de développement économique (OCDE). Voir OCDE, "Communiqué des Ministres de l'environnement réunis à la Conférence de Paris les 7 et 8 mai 1979," dans *Politique de l'environnement pour les Années 1980*, Paris, OCDE, 1980, 6 ("Les Ministres ont conclu qu'à long terme la protection de l'environnement et le développement économique sont non seulement compatibles mais interdépendants et se renforcent mutuellement" au para 3).

[29] Håkan Nordström et Scott Vaughan, *Trade and Environment, Special Studies 4*, Geneva, World Trade Organization, 1999 à la p 72; voir aussi Caroline London, *Commerce et environnement*, Paris, Presses Universitaires de France, 2001 à la p 36.

[30] OMC, *Décision sur le Commerce et Environnement*, 14 avril 1994, en ligne: OMC <http://docsonline.wto.org>.

[31] Ce principe oriente notamment l'action de l'OMC en matière de lutte contre les changements climatiques. Voir OMC et PNUE, *Commerce et changement climatique, rapport établi par l'OMC et le PNUE*, Genève, OMC, 2009.

Réciproquement, il a également conduit l'insertion de clauses dites de soutien mutuel dans certains AEM.[32]

Pourtant, si ce principe a vocation à s'appliquer dans le cadre des relations normatives *inter-* et *intra-*systémiques,[33] l'attention dont il a fait l'objet a progressivement conduit les États à "dénormativiser" son champ d'application pour en faire un nouveau paradigme pour l'interprétation du développement durable. Ainsi, les piliers, et non plus seulement les normes, économique et environnemental seraient eux aussi caractérisés par un soutien mutuel. Si cette lecture du concept a émergé dans la doctrine dès 1995,[34] elle n'a formellement été consacrée par les États qu'en 2002, lors du Sommet mondial pour le développement durable de Johannesburg. Dans la Déclaration et le Plan de mise en œuvre adoptés lors de ce sommet, les États ont en effet affirmé que le développement économique, le développement social et la protection de l'environnement sont trois piliers "qui sont interdépendants et qui se renforcent mutuellement."[35] Il est difficile de ne pas voir dans le Sommet de

---

[32] Si l'on tient compte des différentes "tendances de soutien mutuel" identifiées par Boisson de Chazournes et Mbengue, *supra* note 23 aux pp 832-36, il convient de citer la Convention de Rotterdam sur la procédure de consentement préalable en connaissance de cause applicable à certains produits chimiques et pesticides dangereux qui font l'objet d'un commerce international, 10 septembre 1998, 2244 RTNU 337; la Convention de Stockholm sur les polluants organiques persistants, 22 mai 2001, 2256 RTNU 119; ainsi que le Protocole de Cartagena sur la prévention des risques biotechnologiques relatif à la Convention sur la diversité biologique, 29 janvier 2000, 2226 RTNU 208.

[33] Le principe du soutien mutuel peut également s'appliquer dans le cadre des relations entre les AEM comme l'illustre l'articulation entre la Convention-cadre des Nations Unies sur les changements climatiques, 9 mai 1992, 1771 RTNU 191 et la Convention sur la diversité biologique, 5 juin 1992, 1760 RTNU 79. Sur ce point voir Harro Van Asselt, Francesco Sindico et Michael A Mehling, "Global Climate Change and the Fragmentation of International Law" (2008) 30:4 Law & Pol'y 423.

[34] Commission du développement durable des Nations Unies, *Report of the Expert Group Meeting on Identification of Principles of International Law for Sustainable Development*, Doc off CDD-ONU, 4e sess, Paper N° 3, Principles of International Law for Sustainable Development (1995) (Selon le groupe d'experts réuni pour l'identification de principes du développement durable à l'invitation du secrétariat de la Commission du développement durable des Nations Unies, "economic development, social development and environmental protection are interdependent and mutually reinforcing components of sustainable development" au para 37).

[35] Déclaration de Johannesburg sur le développement durable, Doc off Sommet mondial pour le développement durable, chap I, rés 1, annexe, Doc NU

Johannesburg l'influence de la Conférence ministérielle des États membres de l'OMC réunie à Doha en novembre 2001.[36] Dans la Déclaration finale adoptée à l'issue de cette conférence, les ministres se sont dits "convaincus que les objectifs [et non plus les politiques ou les normes] consistant à maintenir et à préserver un système commercial multilatéral ouvert et non discriminatoire, et à œuvrer en faveur de la protection de l'environnement et de la promotion du développement durable peuvent et doivent se renforcer mutuellement."[37]

La reconnaissance de ce soutien mutuel entre les piliers économique et environnemental du développement durable traduit l'émergence d'une nouvelle conception du développement durable en droit international. Selon celle-ci, il n'existerait aucune opposition entre la poursuite des objectifs économique et environnemental. Mais le paradigme du soutien mutuel n'implique pas simplement de concevoir la relation entre les piliers du développement durable comme étant fondée sur une sorte de neutralité passive garantissant une absence de conflit dans la mise en œuvre de ces piliers. De manière plus ambitieuse, ce paradigme repose sur la reconnaissance d'une interdépendance, d'une imbrication, d'un entrelacement entre ces piliers, de telle sorte que la poursuite de l'objectif de développement économique serait nécessairement favorable à la poursuite de l'objectif de protection de l'environnement et vice-versa.[38]

A/CONF.199/20 (2002) au para 5 [Déclaration de Johannesburg]. *Plan de mise en œuvre du Sommet mondial pour le développement durable,* Doc off Sommet mondial pour le développement durable, chap I, rés 2, annexe, Doc NU A/CONF.199/20 (2002) au para. 2. Pour un commentaire de ce sommet voir Sandrine Maljean-Dubois "Environnement, développement durable et droit international. De Rio à Johannesburg: et au-delà ?" (2002) 48 AFDI 592.

[36] Voir Virginie Barral, "Johannesburg 2002: quoi de neuf pour le développement durable?" (2003) 107:2 RGDIP 413; sur la portée de cette déclaration voir Laurence Boisson de Chazournes et Makane M Mbengue, "La déclaration de Doha de la Conférence Ministérielle de l'Organisation mondiale du commerce et sa portée dans les relations commerce/environnement" (2002) 106:4 RGDIP 855.

[37] Déclaration ministérielle, *supra* note 26.

[38] Ce paradigme du soutien mutuel pose inévitablement la question de sa traductibilité dans la réalité. Car dans les faits, comment parvenir à un tel soutien mutuel entre le développement économique et la protection de l'environnement ? À défaut de réponse, ce "discours" du soutien mutuel semble constituer un parfait exemple de "fabulation juridique," c'est-à-dire d'une fabrication juridique de la réalité par le juriste, dont la fonction principale est "de créer un espace imaginaire, expérimental, où les contradictions peuvent se résoudre et

Ainsi, la mise en œuvre de chaque pilier du développement durable viendrait "soutenir," "renforcer," la mise en œuvre de tous les autres.[39]

Dès lors, selon ce paradigme du soutien mutuel, le conflit entre les objectifs économique et environnemental — dont la reconnaissance constituait l'élément caractéristique du paradigme de la conciliation — disparaît au profit de l'affirmation par l'interprète du développement durable d'une sorte de compatibilité "naturelle" entre le développement économique et la protection de l'environnement. Contrairement au paradigme de la conciliation, cette lecture du développement durable repose ainsi sur un postulat qui prétend qu'il n'existe aucune contradiction entre la poursuite des objectifs économique et environnemental. En ce sens, il convient de souligner que dans la Déclaration et le Plan de mise en œuvre adoptés à Johannesburg, les États n'ont employé ni les termes "conciliation" et/ou "compatibilité" lorsqu'il s'est agi de définir les relations entre les piliers du développement durable. Ainsi les États ont-ils fait fi de l'interprétation du développement durable livrée par la Cour internationale de Justice en 1997. Le paradigme du soutien mutuel repose donc lui aussi sur deux idées centrales, mais contraires à celles du paradigme de la conciliation: l'absence de limitation et l'absence de choix. En effet, il n'est pas nécessaire de poursuivre les objectifs économique et environnemental de manière limitée dès lors que ceux-ci ne sont plus considérés comme pouvant entrer en contradiction. Et il n'est pas non plus nécessaire d'établir entre ces objectifs une priorité si leur poursuite simultanée

---

les conflits s'apaiser." Voir Bernard Edelman, *Quand les juristes inventent le réel. La fabulation juridique*, Paris, Hermann, 2007 à la p 285.

[39] Sur le plan normatif, le soutien mutuel semble aller au-delà de la simple reconnaissance de la coexistence de règles potentiellement conflictuelles ou de leur complémentarité. En effet, la Convention sur la promotion et la protection de la diversité des expressions culturelles distingue le soutien mutuel de la simple complémentarité. Sur ce point voir Ivan Bernier, "Les relations entre la Convention de l'UNESCO sur la protection et la promotion de la diversité des expressions culturelles et les autres instruments internationaux: l'émergence d'un nouvel équilibre dans l'interface entre la culture et le commerce," en ligne: Ministère de la Culture, de la Communication et de la Condition Féminine du Québec <http://www.diversite-culturelle.qc.ca>. Le soutien mutuel impliquerait donc une harmonie et une synergie entre les règles que n'impliquerait pas la complémentarité. Transposé aux relations entre les piliers du développement durable, le soutien mutuel sous-entendrait par conséquent davantage qu'une neutralité entre ces piliers.

et intégrale n'est pas perçue comme étant susceptible de s'avérer incompatible.[40]

S'intéresser à la perception du développement durable en droit international permet de constater qu'au sein de cet ordre juridique, ce concept a été au fil du temps interprété de deux manières distinctes et contradictoires. Dans un premier temps, le paradigme de la conciliation a conduit à appréhender le développement durable comme un concept visant à concilier les objectifs économique et environnemental dans la mesure où ceux-ci étaient considérés comme incompatibles, chacun pouvant entraver la réalisation de l'autre. Interprété selon le paradigme du soutien mutuel, le développement durable est par la suite devenu un concept exprimant la synergie entre les objectifs économique et environnemental puisque ceux-ci ont cessé d'être considérés comme contradictoires et que leur poursuite a été perçue comme étant nécessairement mutuellement bénéfique. Pourtant, cette évolution ne semble pas traduire le remplacement du paradigme de la conciliation par le paradigme du soutien mutuel. En effet, au lieu de s'être substitués l'un à l'autre, il apparaît plutôt que ces deux paradigmes sont désormais simultanément utilisés au sein de l'ordre juridique international.

L'affaire des Usines de pâte à papier sur le fleuve Uruguay: la coexistence des paradigmes de la conciliation et du soutien mutuel

Alors que les États ont manifesté leur adhésion au paradigme du soutien mutuel pour interpréter le développement durable, la Cour internationale de Justice a récemment eu l'occasion de réaffirmer son attachement au paradigme de la conciliation. Aussi, il semble que ces paradigmes soient tous deux en mesure de guider l'interprétation du développement durable. Et si cette coexistence des

---

[40] Plus récemment, l'influence de ce paradigme du soutien mutuel s'est faite sentir lors des préparatifs diplomatiques précédant les Conférences des États Parties à la *Convention-cadre des Nations Unies sur les changements climatiques* et au *Protocole de Kyoto à la Convention-cadre des Nations Unies sur les changements climatiques*, 11 décembre 1997, 2333 RTNU 162, tenues à Copenhague en décembre 2009. Au cours de cette période le Président français, Nicolas Sarkozy, a ainsi déclaré: "[t]out l'intérêt de Copenhague, c'est qu'on ne demande pas aux pays de choisir [*sic*] entre la croissance et la protection de l'environnement." Cité dans Arnaud Le Parmentier, "Nicolas Sarkozy veut aider financièrement l'Inde pour la rallier à un accord à Copenhague," *Le Monde* (27 novembre 2009), en ligne: <http://www.lemonde.fr/recherche>.

paradigmes, qui fait apparaître un risque de conflit entre des interprétations divergentes, semble résulter de l'indétermination du développement durable, sans doute son origine peut-elle être expliquée autrement. En effet, cette coexistence apparaît moins comme la conséquence d'une indétermination du concept que de son caractère "caméléon," son sens et sa fonction étant susceptibles de varier selon les contextes de son utilisation.

LA RÉAFFIRMATION DU PARADIGME DE LA CONCILIATION

La question de l'articulation entre les objectifs de développement économique et de protection de l'environnement s'est récemment trouvée posée à la Cour internationale de Justice lors d'un différend soumis par l'Argentine relatif à l'*Affaire des Usines de pâte à papier sur le fleuve Uruguay*. Dans cette affaire, l'Argentine contestait la légalité de l'autorisation accordée par l'Uruguay de construire et de mettre en service sur son territoire deux usines de pâte à papier à proximité du fleuve Uruguay au regard des obligations découlant du *Statut du fleuve Uruguay*, un traité relatif à l'utilisation du fleuve conclu en 1975 entre les deux parties et entré en vigueur l'année suivante. L'Argentine invoquait notamment la violation de l'obligation de notifier la construction de ces projets à la Commission administrative du fleuve Uruguay, organisme chargé de la coopération entre ces deux États créé en vertu du traité, ainsi que de l'obligation de contribuer à "l'utilisation rationnelle et optimale du fleuve" énoncée à l'article 1er du traité, dans la mesure où les activités envisagées auraient eu pour effet de modifier l'équilibre écologique du fleuve.[41]

Après avoir rejeté les demandes en indication de mesures conservatoires présentées par chacune des parties au différend,[42] la Cour a rendu son arrêt sur le fond le 20 avril 2010 alors que l'une des deux usines, l'usine Orion, avait été mise en service par l'Uruguay. Opérant une distinction entre les obligations de nature procédurale et les obligations de fond, la Cour a reconnu la violation des premières sans toutefois reconnaître la violation des secondes. De l'avis

---

[41] *Affaire relative à des Usines de pâte à papier sur le fleuve Uruguay (Argentine c Uruguay)*, requête introductive d'instance enregistrée au Greffe de la Cour le 4 mai 2006, en ligne: CIJ <www.icj-cij.org> aux pp 18-19.

[42] *Affaire relative à des Usines de pâte à papier sur le fleuve Uruguay (Argentine c Uruguay)*, ordonnance du 13 juillet 2006, [2006] CIJ rec 113; voir aussi *Affaire relative à des Usines de pâte à papier sur le fleuve Uruguay (Argentine c Uruguay)*, ordonnance du 23 janvier 2007, [2007] CIJ rec 3.

de la Cour "les éléments de preuve versés au dossier [n'ont pas permis] d'établir de manière concluante que l'Uruguay n'a pas agi avec la diligence requise ou que les rejets d'effluents de l'usine Orion (Botnia) ont eu des effets délétères ou ont porté atteinte aux ressources biologiques, à la qualité des eaux ou à l'équilibre écologique du fleuve depuis le démarrage des activités de l'usine."[43]

Au cours de cette affaire, la Cour s'est appuyée sur le concept de développement durable pour préciser le sens à attribuer à certaines dispositions du traité de 1975. Elle a ainsi considéré que "l'utilisation rationnelle et optimale du fleuve" énoncée à l'article 1er du traité "devrait permettre un développement durable qui tienne compte 'de la nécessité de garantir la protection continue de l'environnement du fleuve ainsi que le droit au développement économique des États riverains.'"[44] La Cour s'est également fondée sur le développement durable pour définir la portée et les implications de l'article 27 du traité relatif au droit de chacune des parties d'utiliser les eaux du fleuve à l'intérieur de sa juridiction. Selon la Cour, cet article reflétait "non seulement la nécessité de concilier les intérêts variés des États riverains dans un contexte transfrontière et, en particulier, dans l'utilisation d'une ressource naturelle partagée, mais aussi celle de trouver un équilibre entre l'utilisation et la protection des eaux du fleuve qui soit conforme à l'objectif de développement durable."[45] La Cour a ainsi reconnu que cet article "traduit ce lien étroit entre l'utilisation équitable et raisonnable d'une ressource partagée et la nécessité de concilier le développement économique et la protection de l'environnement qui est au cœur du développement durable."[46]

Par le biais de cette référence au développement durable — la deuxième de son histoire[47] — la Cour internationale de Justice a tout d'abord entendu confirmer le rôle central joué par ce concept

---

[43] *Affaire des Usines de pâte à papier sur le fleuve Uruguay, supra* note 4 au para 265.

[44] *Ibid* au para 75.

[45] *Ibid* au para 177.

[46] *Ibid.*

[47] Il s'agit de la deuxième affaire contentieuse dans laquelle la Cour se réfère à la notion de développement durable. Elle avait toutefois cité le Principe 24 de la Déclaration de Rio, *supra* note 7, qui contient la notion dans l'Avis consultatif rendu dans l'*Affaire de la Licéité de la menace ou de l'emploi d'armes nucléaires,* Avis consultatif 1996 CIJ rec 226 au para 30. La Cour aura sans doute l'occasion de faire à nouveau référence au développement durable puisque le 1er juin 2010, l'Australie a introduit une instance contre le Japon pour violation alléguée des obligations internationales relatives à la chasse à la baleine. Cette affaire risque

dans les différends mettant en cause des atteintes à l'environnement, réelles ou alléguées, du fait d'activités économiques. Le développement durable constitue ainsi une sorte de cadre conceptuel au sein duquel les relations entre les préoccupations économiques et environnementales doivent nécessairement être appréhendées.[48] Et de l'avis de la Cour, ce cadre doit conduire les États à "concilier le développement économique et la protection de l'environnement."[49] Ce faisant, en reconnaissant que la notion de conciliation est "au cœur du développement durable,"[50] et en confirmant la définition du développement durable énoncée dans l'arrêt relatif au *Projet Gabčíkovo-Nagymaros*,[51] la Cour a réaffirmé son attachement à une conception du développement durable fondée sur le paradigme de la conciliation. Cette réaffirmation se révèle d'autant plus significative qu'elle s'inscrit en rupture avec la perception que les États reconnaissent avoir du développement durable depuis le Sommet de Johannesburg.

De plus, l'arrêt rendu dans l'*Affaire des Usines de pâtes à papier sur le fleuve Uruguay* intervient dans un contexte où l'idée de soutien mutuel semble progressivement se répandre au sein de l'ordre juridique international, tout particulièrement au sein de la sphère juridictionnelle. Dans une sentence rendue par le tribunal arbitral constitué sous les auspices de la Cour permanente d'arbitrage en 2005 dans l'affaire relative à la *Ligne du Rhin de fer*, les arbitres ont considéré que "[l]e droit de l'environnement et le droit applicable au développement ne constituent pas des alternatives, mais des concepts intégrés se renforçant mutuellement."[52] Certes, le soutien mutuel semble ici renvoyer aux règles du droit de l'environnement

---

donc de voir s'opposer les préoccupations environnementales et économiques des États ainsi que, probablement, leurs préoccupations culturelles.

48 *Affaire relative à des Usines de pâte à papier sur le fleuve Uruguay,* opinion individuelle de M le juge Cançado Trindade, [2010] en ligne: CIJ <http://www.icj-cij.org>. (Dans son opinion individuelle le juge Cançado Trindade considère que "[t]here are strong reasons for recognizing sustainable development as a guiding general principle for the consideration of environmental and developmental issues" au para 139).

49 *Affaire des Usines de pâte à papier sur le fleuve Uruguay, supra* note 4 au para 177.

50 *Ibid.*

51 *Ibid* au para 76.

52 *L'Arbitrage du Rhin de fer, supra* note 20 au para 59. Pour un commentaire de cette sentence voir Philippe Weckel, "Chronique de jurisprudence internationale" (2006) 109:3 RGDIP 715.

et du droit applicable au développement[53] (dimension normative *inter*-systémique) et ne paraît pas constituer pour les arbitres un paradigme pour l'interprétation du développement durable. Mais le fait qu'ils aient utilisé le terme "concept" dans la même phrase suscite une ambiguïté sur l'objet de ce soutien mutuel. Est-ce seulement les règles qui se soutiennent mutuellement ou est-ce également les concepts de protection de l'environnement et de développement économique? Cette ambiguïté inciterait à croire que pour les arbitres, le champ d'application du soutien mutuel ne se limite pas seulement aux règles mais qu'il peut également s'étendre à ces deux concepts qui correspondent chacun à un pilier du développement durable. Ainsi, sans toutefois aller jusqu'à énoncer une conception du développement durable fondée sur le paradigme du soutien mutuel — les arbitres se réfèrent à l'interprétation livrée dans l'arrêt relatif au *Projet Gabčíkovo-Nagymaros*[54] — cette sentence semble néanmoins opérer une "dénormativisation" de l'objet du soutien mutuel et constitue par conséquent un premier pas vers la reconnaissance d'un soutien mutuel entre les piliers du développement durable par le juge international.

Au-delà de la réaffirmation du paradigme de la conciliation, l'*Affaire des Usines de pâte à papier sur le fleuve Uruguay* se révèle fort peu éclairante pour résoudre les zones d'ombres dont continue d'être entouré le développement durable. Tout d'abord, l'apport de cet arrêt en ce qui concerne la compréhension du concept reste très limité. D'une part, il ne permet pas d'en cerner davantage le sens puisque la Cour n'apporte aucune précision supplémentaire par rapport à la définition donnée dans son arrêt de 1997. Elle confirme sa position adoptée dans l'affaire du *Projet Gabčíkovo-Nagymaros* selon laquelle il ne lui appartient pas de se substituer aux parties pour déterminer une solution au litige qui soit conforme au développement durable.[55] Si cette approche, qui s'inspire de

---

[53] La version officielle anglaise de la sentence arbitrale énonce: "[e]nvironmental law and the law on development stand not as alternatives but as mutually reinforcing, integral concepts." *Arbitration regarding the Iron Rhine Railway (The Kingdom of Belgium v The Kingdom of the Netherlands)* [2005], en ligne: CPA <http://www.pca-cpa.org> au para 59.

[54] *L'Arbitrage du Rhin de fer*, *supra* note 20 au para 59.

[55] *Affaire des Usines de pâte à papier sur le fleuve Uruguay*, *supra* note 4 au para 77. *Affaire relative au Projet Gabčíkovo-Nagymaros*, *supra* note 3 (la Cour a considéré qu'il ne lui appartenait pas "de déterminer quel sera le résultat final des négociations à mener par les Parties. Ce sont les Parties elles-mêmes qui doivent trouver d'un commun accord une solution qui tienne compte des objectifs du

celle adoptée par la Cour dans d'autres types de différends,[56] permet de respecter la souveraineté des États et de leur ménager une marge de manœuvre dans l'appréciation de ce qui constitue une solution "conciliée," elle représente néanmoins un obstacle aux éclaircissements que la Cour pourrait apporter sur la signification concrète du concept de développement durable.[57]

D'autre part, en demandant aux États de parvenir à un "équilibre entre l'utilisation et la protection des eaux du fleuve qui soit conforme à l'objectif de développement durable," la Cour contribue à alimenter l'indétermination du développement durable. En effet, il n'est pas douteux que le contenu de "l'objectif de développement durable" ne fasse pas l'unanimité entre les États et que son interprétation puisse considérablement varier en fonction des circonstances nationales dans lesquelles se trouvent placées les parties au différend. Or, si cette indétermination du concept peut être un atout dans un contexte de négociations multilatérales dans la mesure où elle permet d'éviter de cristalliser les divergences entre États sur les questions de développement et d'environnement, elle apparaît au contraire comme une faiblesse dans le cadre de la résolution d'un différend interétatique puisqu'elle ne permet pas

---

traité — qui doivent être atteints de façon conjointe et intégrée — de même que des normes du droit international de l'environnement et des principes du droit relatif aux cours d'eau internationaux" au para 141).

56 Voir *Affaire du Plateau continental de la mer du Nord (République fédérale d'Allemagne c Danemark), (République fédérale d'Allemagne c Pays-Bas)*, [1969] CIJ rec 3 (Dans les différends relatifs à la délimitation du plateau continental, la Cour a reconnu que sa tâche se limitait uniquement à fournir des directions sans prescrire des méthodes à utiliser pour parvenir à la délimitation du plateau continental, au para 84).

57 Néanmoins, si la Cour laisse le soin aux parties d'aboutir par la négociation à une solution conforme au développement durable, elle précise, lorsqu'elle rappelle que le développement durable traduit la nécessité de concilier le développement économique et la protection de l'environnement, que la conciliation constitue une condition pour garantir la conformité d'une solution à l'objectif de développement durable. Ce faisant, on peut se demander si, en matière de développement durable, la Cour ne s'autorise pas quand même à indiquer une méthode, certes très sommaire, pour déterminer la solution au litige et qui impliquerait à tout le moins une démarche intégrée et la recherche d'un équilibre entre des préoccupations opposées. Sur ce point voir Philippe Sands, "International Courts and the Application of the Concept of 'Sustainable Development'" (1999) 3 Max Planck UNYB 389 (pour l'auteur "the term 'sustainable development' appears useful as a means of bridging two views without necessarily having to provide close reasoning as to method or outcome," à la p 396).

d'ériger le développement durable en une référence suffisamment précise pour guider les parties au litige vers une solution. Plus encore, cette référence incite les États à définir eux-mêmes ce qui, de leur point de vue, est conforme à l'objectif de développement durable, au risque de multiplier les interprétations contraires du concept. Il semblerait donc que la conformité d'une solution à l'objectif de développement durable dépende davantage de son processus d'élaboration — la solution doit avoir fait l'objet d'une conciliation entre le développement économique et la protection de l'environnement — que de son résultat, étant donné que le contenu de cet objectif reste encore largement indéterminé.

En outre, la Cour ne s'est pas saisie de l'opportunité offerte par ce différend pour se prononcer sur la valeur juridique du développement durable en droit international. Certes, elle n'a pas pris soin de réaffirmer la qualification qu'elle avait donnée du développement durable dans l'affaire du *Projet Gabčíkovo-Nagymaros*.[58] En qualifiant le développement durable de concept, la Cour s'était alors assurée de ne pas ouvrir la voie à une éventuelle juridisation de la notion. Mais à l'inverse, elle n'a pas non plus avancé de nouveaux éléments permettant de conclure à la formation d'une norme de "développement durable." En fait, il semble plutôt que la Cour ait voulu dans cette affaire éviter de se prononcer sur la valeur juridique du développement durable. Cette position, qui contraste avec celle adoptée par les arbitres dans la sentence de la *Ligne du Rhin de fer*,[59] pourrait témoigner d'un essoufflement de l'intérêt suscité

---

[58] Même si elle cite le passage de l'arrêt *Affaire relative au Projet Gabčíkovo-Nagymaros, supra* note 3, qui qualifie le développement durable de concept (au para 76), la Cour n'a pas elle-même confirmé cette interprétation dans l'*Affaire des Usines de pâte à papier sur le fleuve Uruguay, supra* note 4.

[59] Dans cette affaire les arbitres ont vraisemblablement cherché un ancrage juridique au développement durable en conférant au principe d'intégration une valeur coutumière. En effet, les arbitres semblent avoir considérés le principe d'intégration et le développement durable comme des concepts interchangeables. Voir *L'Arbitrage du Rhin de fer, supra* note 20. En ce sens voir Virginie Barral, "La sentence du Rhin de fer, une nouvelle étape dans la prise en compte de l'environnement par la justice internationale" (2006) 110:3 RGDIP 647; voir aussi Sandrine Maljean-Dubois, *Quel droit pour l'environnement?* Paris, Hachette, 2008 aux pp 64-65. On peut d'ailleurs s'étonner du contraste entre cette sentence et l'arrêt rendu par la CIJ dans *Affaire des Usines de pâte à papier sur le fleuve Uruguay, supra* note 4, puisque les juges Tomka et Simma ont siégé sur les deux affaires. Il convient toutefois de relever que dans son opinion dissidente rédigée avec le juge Al-Khasawneh, le juge Simma inclut un "principe" de développement durable dans une liste de principes, applicables à la gestion des ressources naturelles

par le concept et inviterait par conséquent à relativiser l'importance de son rôle en droit international. En effet, si les juges avaient considéré le développement durable comme un concept susceptible de constituer une base juridique pour résoudre le différend en cause, et non simplement une orientation à suivre pour les États, sans doute auraient-ils cherché à en affirmer la positivité en droit international.

Le principal apport de l'*Affaire des Usines de pâte à papier sur le fleuve Uruguay* en ce qui concerne le développement durable n'a donc pas été de préciser le sens de ce concept ou de clarifier son statut juridique mais plutôt de réaffirmer sa dimension conciliatrice dans un contexte juridique international marqué par l'essor d'une conception du développement durable fondée sur le paradigme du soutien mutuel. Et puisque l'émergence de ce second paradigme n'a pas conduit à la disparition ou à la marginalisation du premier, cet arrêt permet ainsi de conclure à leur coexistence.

LA CAUSE DE LA COEXISTENCE DES PARADIGMES: DIVERSITÉ DES INTERPRÈTES ET DES CONTEXTES D'INTERPRÉTATION DU DÉVELOPPEMENT DURABLE EN DROIT INTERNATIONAL

Cette coexistence des paradigmes de la conciliation et du soutien mutuel, qui conduit à des interprétations antinomiques de la relation entre les piliers économique et environnemental du développement durable, peut *a priori* se présenter comme la conséquence directe de l'indétermination qui affecte ce concept. En effet, l'impossibilité d'en faire émerger une seule et unique définition en droit international, et donc d'en déterminer la substance,[60] semble constituer la cause à l'origine de l'apparition de ces deux lectures divergentes du développement durable. N'ayant aucun sens précis, chacun serait par conséquent autorisé à lui en attribuer un et libre de choisir lequel. Finalement, le développement durable ne serait qu'une coquille vide laissée à la disposition de l'interprète,

---

et aux dommages transfrontières, comprenant d'autres principes dont la valeur juridique est incontestable tels que la souveraineté permanente sur les ressources naturelles et l'obligation de ne pas causer de dommage à l'environnement. Voir *Affaire relative à des Usines de pâte à papier sur le fleuve Uruguay,* opinion dissidente commune de MM les juges Al-Khasawneh et Simma, [2010], en ligne: CIJ <http://www.icj-cij.org> au para 26.

[60] Sur l'absence de contenu du concept voir par ex Michael McCloskey "The Emperor Has No Clothes: The Conundrum of Sustainable Development" (1999) 9:2 Duke Envtl L & Pol'y F 153.

un concept "auberge espagnole"[61] condamné à errer dans les limbes de l'indétermination, cette caractéristique pouvant ainsi expliquer la pluralité des définitions dont il fait l'objet.

Pourtant, l'origine de la coexistence entre les paradigmes de la conciliation et du soutien mutuel gagne peut-être à être recherchée ailleurs que dans cette thèse. Car considérer la coexistence des paradigmes comme une conséquence de la nature indéterminée du développement durable procède d'un raisonnement qui postule à son départ la nécessité de ne pouvoir attribuer à ce concept qu'une seule définition. Or, mise à part "notre commune tendance spontanée au réductionnisme,"[62] rien ne prédispose à ce que ce concept soit enfermé dans une définition unique. Ainsi, par ce changement de perspective, le développement durable n'apparaît plus comme un concept nécessairement homogène dont le sens est susceptible d'être circonscrit par une seule définition et ne devant posséder dans l'ordre juridique international qu'un rôle bien déterminé, mais comme un concept malléable, polymorphe, pouvant varier de signification selon ses contextes d'utilisation et remplir différentes fonctions. Une telle appréhension du développement durable peut alors justifier que ce concept fasse l'objet de différentes interprétations, construites à partir de différents paradigmes.

Aussi, cette pluralité de sens qui passait pour être la preuve d'une indétermination pourrait en réalité être la caractéristique d'un concept évolutif et adaptable, un concept à contenu variable dont la variabilité résulterait moins de "l'ambiguïté ou des doutes sur les caractères constituant [s]a définition"[63] que du contexte dans lequel il se trouve être employé et de l'objectif poursuivi par les acteurs qui y font référence. Et l'étude des paradigmes de la conciliation et du soutien mutuel invite à une telle conclusion dans la mesure où elle tend à montrer que ces lectures contraires du développement durable sont chacune le fruit d'interprètes distincts (dans un cas les États, dans l'autre le juge international) placés dans des circonstances différentes (un cadre de négociations multilatérales pour les États, un cadre juridictionnel pour le juge international). En somme, le développement durable serait un concept "caméléon"

---

61 Voir Jean JA Salmon, "Les notions à contenu variable en droit international public"dans Chaïm Perelman et Raymond Vander Elst, dir, *Les notions à contenu variable en droit*, Bruxelles, Bruylant, 1984 à la p 254.

62 Denys de Béchillon, "L'ordre juridique est-il complexe ?" dans Denys de Béchillon, dir, *Les défis de la complexité*, Paris, L'Harmattan, 1994 à la p 44.

63 Salmon, *supra* note 61, à la p 254.

revêtant les teintes les plus adaptées à l'environnement juridique dans lequel il évoluerait et la coexistence des paradigmes de la conciliation et du soutien mutuel ne serait qu'une conséquence de cette particularité.

Comme l'illustrent les arrêts rendus par la Cour internationale de Justice dans les affaires du *Projet Gabčíkovo-Nagymaros* et des *Usines de pâte à papier sur le fleuve Uruguay*, le paradigme de la conciliation correspond à la conception que les juges de cette instance se forgent du développement durable. Dans ce cadre juridictionnel, le concept apparaît alors comme un instrument de résolution des différends interétatiques au cours desquels s'opposent les préoccupations économiques et environnementales des parties au litige. Et c'est précisément pour résoudre ce type de différends que le développement durable est interprété comme traduisant la nécessité de concilier les objectifs de développement économique et de protection de l'environnement.

La sentence rendue dans l'affaire de la *Ligne du Rhin de fer* tend d'ailleurs à renforcer cette thèse. Même si les arbitres y ont évoqué la notion de soutien mutuel, ils ont néanmoins procédé à une mise en balance des préoccupations économiques et environnementales pour déterminer la solution du litige.[64] Par cette opération, ils ont ainsi fait la démonstration de l'impossibilité de résoudre un différend fondé sur une opposition entre de telles préoccupations sans opérer de conciliation. Il convient à ce titre de souligner la contradiction lorsque les arbitres énoncent que "[l]e droit de l'environnement et le droit applicable au développement ne constituent pas des alternatives, mais des concepts intégrés se renforçant mutuellement" et que, en conséquence, "lorsque le développement risque de porter atteinte de manière significative à l'environnement, [il] doit exister une obligation d'empêcher, ou au moins d'atténuer, cette pollution."[65] Si les deux concepts se renforçaient mutuellement, la poursuite du développement économique ne porterait pas atteinte à la protection de l'environnement et ne justifierait donc pas une telle obligation de prévention ou d'atténuation. De fait, les différends au cours desquels s'opposent des considérations économiques et environnementales surgissent parce qu'il n'existe aucun

---

64 Sur cette mise en balance voir Virginie Barral, "L'affaire du *Chemin de fer du "Rhin de fer,"* *entre fragmentation et unité du droit international*"dans Hélène Ruiz Fabri et Lorenzo Gradoni, dir, *La circulation des concepts juridiques: Le droit international de l'environnement entre mondialisation et fragmentation*, Paris, Société de législation comparée, 2009 aux pp 366-67.

65 *L'Arbitrage du Rhin de fer, supra* note 20 au para 59.

soutien mutuel entre celles-ci. Ce passage laisse ainsi présager tout le décalage qui peut exister entre un développement durable conçu comme impliquant un soutien mutuel entre les piliers économique et environnemental et sa traductibilité sur le plan du raisonnement juridictionnel, et démontre par conséquent l'impossibilité pour le juge international de concevoir le développement durable à travers le paradigme du soutien mutuel, compte tenu de la nature même de la fonction juridictionnelle qu'il exerce.

Le paradigme du soutien mutuel est quant à lui apparu au cours de processus de négociations multilatérales visant à définir des objectifs d'intérêt commun susceptibles d'être atteints par l'ensemble des États. Dans ce contexte, le développement durable n'a donc pas été conçu comme un instrument de résolution des différends interétatiques mais comme un objectif à atteindre par la communauté internationale. C'est d'ailleurs en tant qu'objectif que le renforcement entre les piliers du développement durable a été évoqué dans la Déclaration et le Plan de mise en œuvre du Sommet mondial pour le développement durable.[66] Et compte tenu des divergences qui opposent les États développés et en développement quant à l'importance à accorder au développement économique et à la protection de l'environnement, il n'est pas étonnant que dans un contexte multilatéral, où l'enjeu réside dans l'atteinte d'un consensus et d'une large adhésion des États à l'action internationale, le développement durable ait été interprété comme un concept délivré de tout antagonisme entre l'économie et l'environnement. Aussi, en extrayant du développement durable les idées de limite et de choix inhérentes au mécanisme de la conciliation, le paradigme du soutien mutuel a certainement permis de faire de ce concept un élément fédérateur, une référence commune susceptible de transcender les divergences de points de vue entre les États relatives à l'articulation des objectifs de développement économique et de protection de l'environnement.

Si les paradigmes de la conciliation et du soutien mutuel se démarquent par leur contexte d'utilisation, ils se distinguent également par le rôle qu'ils conduisent chacun à conférer au développement durable. Instrument de résolution des conflits interétatiques devant les juridictions internationales lorsqu'il est interprété selon le paradigme de la conciliation, le développement durable devient un facteur de consensus dans les négociations internationales dès lors qu'il est appréhendé à travers le paradigme du soutien mutuel. La

---

[66] Déclaration de Johannesburg, *supra* note 35.

divergence de perception du développement durable fait ainsi apparaître la diversité des fonctions que ce concept peut être amené à remplir au sein de l'ordre juridique international, fonction juridictionnelle d'une part et fonction politique d'autre part.

Présenter le développement durable comme un concept indéterminé résistant à l'unicité d'une définition peut constituer un moyen pour tenter d'expliquer les interprétations divergentes dont il fait l'objet et les différentes fonctions qu'il est amené à remplir. Mais à mesure que le développement durable s'enracine dans le droit international, ce discours de l'indétermination gagne à être dépassé pour laisser place à une appréhension du concept davantage en adéquation avec sa véritable nature. Et pour l'instant, il semble que le développement durable soit un concept hétérogène, multiforme et multifonctionnel, son sens et sa fonction pouvant s'adapter au gré des circonstances. Sans doute est-ce en raison de cette nature particulière que coexistent actuellement au sein de l'ordre juridique international les deux lectures opposées de ce concept.

CONCLUSION

En rendant son arrêt dans l'*Affaire des Usines de pâte à papier sur le fleuve Uruguay*, la Cour internationale de Justice ne semble pas avoir voulu ouvrir la "boîte de pandore" que constitue le développement durable. Si elle a bien évoqué le concept, elle ne s'est pas pour autant penchée sur sa valeur juridique, son sens ou ses implications concrètes. En laissant ces points en suspens, les juges ont ainsi donné l'impression qu'il ne s'agissait pas là de questions essentielles, leur absence de réponse n'empêchant pas de faire référence au développement durable. Serait-ce alors le signe d'un essoufflement de l'intérêt suscité par ce concept, ou peut-être, de la nécessité d'en relativiser l'importance? Quoiqu'il en soit, en le citant à nouveau dans sa jurisprudence, la Cour a contribué à accentuer davantage son ancrage dans le paysage juridique international sans pour autant en préciser la nature et le contenu.

Même s'il se révèle insuffisant pour lever les nombreuses interrogations dont le développement durable continue de faire l'objet, cet arrêt présente toutefois un intérêt certain en ce qui concerne la compréhension de ce concept. En effet, en rappelant que la conciliation est au cœur de ce modèle de développement, la Cour a apporté un éclairage intéressant — peut-être à son insu — sur la façon de concevoir la relation entre les piliers économique et environnemental du développement durable au sein de l'ordre juridique international. Alors que celle-ci a été au cours des dernières années, conçue comme impliquant un soutien mutuel entre ces piliers, la réaffirmation d'une dimension conciliatrice du développement durable incite à considérer qu'il existe aujourd'hui en droit international une *summa diviso* dans la façon de concevoir le développement durable.

L'existence de cette *divisio* ne doit toutefois pas faire oublier que ces deux conceptions partagent un dénominateur commun dans la mesure où elles visent chacune à envisager conjointement et simultanément les objectifs de développement économique et de protection de l'environnement. Ce point commun, à l'origine du développement durable,[67] constitue ainsi une passerelle, une zone de superposition, entre les paradigmes de la conciliation et du soutien mutuel qui a pour effet de limiter leur divergence à la seule question de la relation entre les piliers économique et environnemental du développement durable.

Finalement, la présence simultanée de ces deux paradigmes dans l'ordre juridique international pourrait participer à l'émergence d'une vision plus nuancée et plus complète des différentes formes que peut prendre l'articulation entre ces deux piliers. Certes, cette articulation peut être uniquement appréhendée à travers le prisme de la conciliation. Mais dès lors, le développement durable est voué à être un concept dont le seul but n'est que de résoudre les incompatibilités qui apparaissent entre la poursuite des objectifs économique et environnemental et non d'éviter que celles-ci ne surgissent. À l'inverse, le risque qui résulte de l'usage du paradigme du soutien mutuel est que soient délibérément occultés les cas d'incompatibilité entre ces objectifs. Dans les faits, une telle approche pourrait conduire à condamner "toute politique de l'environnement ne faisant pas 'partie intégrante du processus de développement,' c'est-à-dire, incompatible avec les impératifs du développement économique."[68] Reconnaître la coexistence des paradigmes de la

---

[67] Mohammed A Bekhechi, "Le droit international à l'épreuve du développement durable: Quelques réflexions à propos de la Déclaration de Rio sur l'environnement et le développement" (1993) 6 Hague YB Int'l L 57.

[68] Sur cette question voir Marc Pallemaerts, "La Conférence de Rio: bilan et perspectives" dans *L'actualité du droit de l'environnement*, Bruxelles, Bruylant, 1995 aux pp 83-84. En effet, il ne suffit pas de prophétiser la disparition de toute contradiction entre les piliers économique et environnemental du développement durable pour que celle-ci se réalise. Il ressort d'ailleurs de l'affaire de la *Ligne du Rhin de fer* que devant les juridictions, l'idée de soutien mutuel ressemble davantage à un mantra ou à une profession de foi qu'à un modèle d'articulation entre les préoccupations économiques et environnementales susceptible d'être traduit sur le plan du raisonnement juridictionnel.

conciliation et du soutien mutuel constituerait donc peut-être une condition préalable pour faire sortir le développement durable du flou dans lequel il est encore trop souvent maintenu et l'appréhender enfin comme un concept véritablement opérationnel.

Summary

The Economic and Environmental Pillars of Sustainable Development: Reconciliation or Mutual Support? Clarification from the International Court of Justice in the *Case Concerning Pulp Mills on the River Uruguay (Argentina v Uruguay)*

There has been a major change in the way actors in the international legal system interpret the relationship between the economic and environmental pillars of sustainable development. As these pillars were originally perceived to conflict, an initial interpretation suggested that they had to be reconciled. However, according to another interpretation that emerged later, these pillars were seen as mutually reinforcing. This second conception, which seeks to remove the notion of a tension between environment and economy from the concept of sustainable development, has recently become more influential. However, the International Court of Justice has recently reasserted its commitment to the first interpretation of sustainable development in the Case Concerning Pulp Mills on the River Uruguay. *It therefore appears that two opposing conceptions of sustainable development are currently operative in international law; one based on the reconciliation paradigm and the other on the paradigm of mutual support.*

Sommaire

Les piliers économique et environnemental du développement durable: conciliation ou soutien mutuel? L'éclairage apporté par la Cour internationale de Justice dans l'*Affaire des Usines de pâte à papier sur le fleuve Uruguay (Argentine c Uruguay)*

La façon dont les divers acteurs de l'ordre juridique international ont appréhendé la relation entre les piliers économique et environnemental du développement durable témoigne d'une évolution: alors qu'une première interprétation estimait que cette relation se fondait sur la recherche d'une conciliation, une seconde interprétation a par la suite considéré qu'elle était au contraire caractérisée par l'existence d'un soutien mutuel. Si cette seconde *conception, qui conduit à extraire du développement durable toute idée de tension entre l'environnement et l'économie, a connu une influence grandissante au cours des dernières années, la Cour internationale de Justice a réaffirmé dans l'*Affaire des Usines de pâte à papier sur le fleuve Uruguay *son attachement à la première interprétation de la relation entre les piliers économique et environnemental. Il semble donc actuellement coexister en droit international deux lectures opposées du développement durable, l'une se fondant sur le paradigme de la conciliation, l'autre sur le paradigme du soutien mutuel.*

Notes and Comments /
Notes et commentaires

Does the *Charter* Float?
The Application of the *Canadian Charter of Rights and Freedoms* to Canada's Policing of High Seas Fisheries

INTRODUCTION

The majority decision of the Supreme Court of Canada in *R v Hape*[1] sought to clarify the extraterritorial reach of the *Canadian Charter of Rights and Freedoms* (*Charter*).[2] One issue that was not addressed by the Court, and remains uncertain, is whether the *Charter* applies to a high seas interdiction, by Canadian officials, of a foreign-flagged vessel. This question is worth considering, particularly in light of Canadian fisheries protection officers' authority to interdict foreign-flagged fishing vessels located in high seas Regional Fisheries Management Organization (RFMO) areas. The nature of these interdictions could engage protections under the *Charter* such as the right to life, liberty, and security of the person, freedom from unreasonable search and seizure, freedom from arbitrary detention, the right to counsel, and other protections applicable in cases of arrest or detention.[3]

This comment considers whether or not the *Charter* should apply to interdictions by Canadian officials of foreign-flagged fishing vessels located in RFMO areas. In particular, it explores the majority decision of the Supreme Court of Canada in *Hape* and considers whether its rule against the extraterritorial application of the *Charter* should apply to Canada's enforcement of RFMO measures. Canada's

---

[1] *R v Hape*, [2007] 2 SCR 292 [*Hape*].

[2] *Canadian Charter of Rights and Freedoms*, Part I of the *Constitution Act 1982*, being Schedule B to the *Canada Act 1982* (UK), 1982, c 11 [*Charter*].

[3] *Ibid*, ss 7-12.

interdiction of foreign-flagged fishing vessels in RFMO areas is governed by established international legal regimes and comprehensive domestic legislation, which provide a concrete backdrop against which the applicability of the majority's reasons in *Hape* may be considered. In addition, Canada is active in the policing of high seas fisheries, making the issue of practical importance.

This comment is divided into three parts. The first part discusses the majority decision in *Hape*. The second part reviews the legal rules pertaining to non-flag state enforcement of high seas fisheries regulations under international and Canadian domestic law. The third part explores the potential application of the rule in *Hape* to high seas fisheries law enforcement. It examines who, in general, may possess a *Charter* right and considers whether the majority decision in *Hape* on the extraterritorial application of the *Charter* should apply, *mutatis mutandis,* to high seas interdictions, by Canadian officials, of foreign-flagged fishing vessels.

This comment does not consider the application of the *Charter* to government actions against foreign-flagged vessels in a Canadian port or in Canada's internal waters, territorial sea, contiguous zone, or exclusive economic zone. It also does not consider the application of the *Charter* in other high seas interdiction contexts, such as during an armed conflict. Lastly, it does not consider the application of specific *Charter* rights. Rather, it only considers whether or not the *Charter* in general should apply.

THE RULE IN *HAPE*

In 2002, the Ontario Superior Court of Justice found Lawrence Hape guilty of money laundering. At trial, Hape asked the court to exclude evidence from his office in the Turks and Caicos Islands that had been collected by officers of the Royal Canadian Mounted Police (RCMP), arguing that their search of his office had breached his *Charter* rights.[4] The Turks and Caicos Islands had granted the RCMP permission to conduct their investigation in its territory on the condition that the investigation proceed under the supervision and authority of a local police official, Superintendant Detective Lessemun, who was "in charge" to the extent that the investigation occurred within the Turks and Caicos Islands.[5] In February 1998, RCMP officers and technical experts, accompanied by Detective

---

[4] *Hape, supra* note 1 at para 1.

[5] *Ibid* at para 3.

Lessemun, entered the premises of Hape's investment company without a warrant.[6] The RCMP officers testified at trial that they knew they had no warrant but that they had relied on Detective Lessemun to ensure the legality of the investigation.[7] In March 1998, RCMP investigators and Detective Lessemun twice more entered Hape's office.[8] At trial, the RCMP officers testified that they understood that Detective Lessemun had obtained warrants for these entries, but these were not introduced at trial.[9] Almost a year after their initial investigation, the investigators returned to seize and copy a large quantity of documents from Hape's office. Again, the investigators claimed to believe that Detective Lessemun had procured the necessary warrant for the seizure, but it was not produced at trial.[10] The trial judge rejected Hape's argument that the *Charter* applied to the search of his office in the Turks and Caicos Islands, and copies of the seized documents were entered as evidence.

The question of the *Charter*'s application to the RCMP officers' actions in the Turks and Caicos Islands eventually reached the Supreme Court of Canada. The nine justices of the Court split three ways on how to address the question of whether the *Charter* applies to government agents' extraterritorial conduct. Justice Ian Binnie advocated maintaining the Court's earlier ruling in *R v Cook*.[11] Three other justices advocated a presumption that the *Charter* applies to the extraterritorial actions of Canadian agents, including the RCMP officers in the instant case, but held that Hape's *Charter* rights were not violated.[12] The majority, however, instituted a rule that the *Charter* does not apply to Canadian agents operating in foreign territory, subject to some limited exceptions, thereby effectively overruling the court's earlier judgment in *Cook*.[13]

---

6 *Ibid* at paras 5-7.

7 *Ibid* at para 7.

8 *Ibid* at para 9.

9 *Ibid* at paras 9, 10.

10 *Ibid* at para 11.

11 *Ibid* at para 183; *R v Cook*, [1998] 2 SCR 597 [*Cook*].

12 *Hape, supra* note 1 at paras 160-61, 174, 178, 179.

13 The majority in *Cook, supra* note 11 at para 48, held: "The *Charter* applies on foreign territory in circumstances where the impugned act falls within the scope of s. 32(1) of the *Charter* on the jurisdictional basis of the nationality of the state law enforcement authorities engaged in governmental action, and where the application of *Charter* standards will not conflict with the concurrent territorial jurisdiction of the foreign state."

The majority reasoned that a territorial constraint on the *Charter*'s reach is prescribed by international law and is consistent with section 32 of the *Charter*. The majority held that the *Charter* can only apply where it can be enforced[14] and that because international legal principles prohibit the extraterritorial enforcement of Canada's laws, including the *Charter*, in another state's territory, the *Charter* is not applicable in another state's territory either.[15] Pointing to the Permanent Court of International Justice's majority judgment in the *Case of the SS "Lotus" (France v Turkey)* (*SS Lotus* case), the majority in *Hape* held that Canada's jurisdiction is restricted by the principles of sovereignty, non-intervention, and territoriality.[16] As a consequence, according to the majority, no Canadian legislature has the authority, under international law, to authorize the enforcement of its statutes over "matters in the exclusive territorial jurisdiction of another state."[17] Instead, the law of the foreign state governs the actions of Canadian agents while they are present within its territory.[18]

With this interpretation of international law in hand, the majority in *Hape* turned to section 32 of the *Charter*, which reads: "This Charter applies ... to the Parliament and government of Canada in respect of all matters within the authority of Parliament."[19] The majority noted that section 32 is silent on its territorial application, and, therefore, it was for the Court to interpret its jurisdictional reach.[20] In the majority's view, the fact that a Canadian agent is involved in the extraterritorial action is not sufficient to attract the *Charter*'s application. Rather, the action under review must also fall within

---

[14] *Hape, supra* note 1 at paras 85, 91, 92.

[15] *Ibid* at paras 40-46, 57-65, 69. There are two types of jurisdiction under international law: prescriptive and enforcement. Malcolm N Shaw, *International Law*, 6th edition (New York: Cambridge University Press, 2008) at 645. Prescriptive jurisdiction is the capacity to pass laws regulating a subject or object (*ibid* at 645). It is usually based on territorial links, although it may also be based on other grounds, such as nationality (*ibid* at 646, 664, 666-68). Enforcement jurisdiction is the capacity to enforce laws, and its scope is typically restricted to state territory (*ibid* at 646). Some would add adjudicative jurisdiction as a third category. See, for example, *Hape, supra* note 1 at para 58.

[16] *Case of the SS "Lotus" (France v Turkey)* (1927), PCIJ (Ser A) No 10 [*SS Lotus* case].

[17] *Hape, supra* note 1 at paras 65, 85, 105.

[18] *Ibid* at para 90.

[19] *Charter, supra* note 2, s 32(1)(a).

[20] *Hape, supra* note 1 at para 33.

the "authority of Parliament."[21] The majority reasoned that to determine the *Charter*'s extraterritorial scope of application, the Court "should seek to ensure compliance with Canada's binding obligations under international law where the express words are capable of supporting such a construction."[22] In particular, it held that section 32 should be read in a manner consistent with customary international legal principles pertaining to jurisdiction, namely the sovereignty and equality of states and non-interference.[23] Accordingly, it reasoned, because international law prohibits Canada from exercising enforcement jurisdiction over subjects within another sovereign state, such subjects are outside "matters within the authority of Parliament" and, therefore, also outside the scope of application of the *Charter*.[24] Consequently, the majority held that the *Charter* does not apply to the extraterritorial actions of Canadian police officers because Canada cannot enforce compliance with its requirements when they are within another state's territory.[25]

The majority set out two exceptions to the non-extraterritorial application of the *Charter*. First, the *Charter* may apply to Canadian agents in other jurisdictions if they act contrary to Canada's international obligations, particularly its human rights obligations.[26] The Court subsequently applied this exception in *Canada (Justice) v Khadr*.[27] Second, the *Charter* may apply to Canadian agents' actions in the territory of another state if that state consents to its application.[28] Unfortunately, the Court did not explain what it meant by "consent." Must the other state merely consent to Canada's enforcement actions generally or must it consent to application of the *Charter* specifically?[29] In addition, the majority noted that evidence obtained extraterritorially by Canadian agents may be excluded at trial if its inclusion would be unfair.[30] This is not, however, an exception to

21 *Ibid* at para 94.

22 *Ibid* at para 56.

23 *Ibid* at paras 41, 45, 56.

24 *Ibid* at para 94; *Charter, supra* note 2, s 32(1)(a).

25 *Hape, supra* note 1 at paras 91-92, 105.

26 *Ibid* at paras 52, 101.

27 *Canada (Justice) v Khadr*, [2008] 2 SCR 125 at para 18 [*Khadr* 2008]. See also *Canada (Prime Minister) v Khadr*, [2010] 1 SCR 44 at paras 16, 18 [*Khadr* 2010].

28 *Hape, supra* note 1 at para 106.

29 Amir Attaran, "Have Charter, Will Travel? Extraterritoriality in Constitutional Law and Canadian Exceptionalism" (2009) 87 Can B Rev 515 at 519.

30 *Hape, supra* note 1 at paras 91, 108.

the non-extraterritorial application of the *Charter.* Instead, it is a means of maintaining a fair trial in Canada, as guaranteed by the *Charter.*[31]

The majority judgment in *Hape* is not without its critics.[32] It has been said that the majority conflated prescriptive jurisdiction and enforcement jurisdiction,[33] misinterpreted the *S.S. Lotus* case on the issue of extraterritorial jurisdiction,[34] misunderstood the relationship between domestic and international law,[35] and, in breathtaking fashion, elevated customary international law to a constitutional norm.[36]

The latter criticism is particularly compelling. The principle that domestic legislation is presumed consistent with international law is not novel.[37] It is, however, only a presumption. It must be kept in mind that, from the perspective of the Canadian legal system, Canada's Constitution is not subordinate to international law.[38] As one commentator has pointed out, "[i]nternational law does not

---

[31] *Ibid* at para 108.

[32] See Attaran, *supra* note 29; John H Currie, "Weaving a Tangled Web: *Hape* and the Obfuscation of Canadian Reception Law" (2007) 45 Can YB Int'l Law 55; Donald J Rennie et al, "The Canadian Charter of Rights and Freedoms and Canadian Officials Abroad" (2009) 47 Sup Ct L Rev 127; K. Roach, "*R. v. Hape* Creates Charter-Free Zones for Canadian Officials Abroad" (2007) 53 Crim LQ 1.

[33] Currie, *supra* note 32 at 87, n 138.

[34] Attaran, *supra* note 29 at 525. Attaran points out that Lebel J., writing for the majority, cited the *S.S. Lotus* case for the principle that "jurisdiction 'cannot be exercised by a State outside its territory except by virtue of a permissive rule derived from international custom or from a convention,'" but it failed to consider the subsequent paragraph in the *SS Lotus* case where the Permanent Court of International Justice held: "It does not, however, follow that international law prohibits a State from exercising jurisdiction in its own territory, in respect of any case which relates to acts which have taken place abroad, and in which it cannot rely on some permissive rule of international law" (*ibid; SS Lotus* case, *supra* note 16 at 19.

[35] See Attaran, *supra* note 29 at 521; Currie, *supra* note 32 at 63-69.

[36] See Attaran, *supra* note 29; Currie, *supra* note 32 at 91.

[37] Ruth Sullivan, *Statutory Interpretation,* 2nd edition (Toronto: Irwin Law, 2007) at 241.

[38] Canada's Parliament and Constitution are not subordinate to international law. Rights and obligations found in international treaties must be transformed into domestic law by a legislature before they have legal effect in Canada. John H Currie, *Public International Law,* 2nd edition (Toronto: Irwin Law, 2008) at 235; *Capital Cities Communications v CRTC,* [1978] 2 SCR 141 at 172-73. In addition, pursuant to the principles of constitutional and parliamentary sovereignty, Parliament has the authority to enact legislation that is inconsistent with customary

normally preclude the application of Canadian laws, any more than a sovereign sitting in some foreign land can vouchsafe whether or not a particular Canadian law is valid."[39] Nevertheless, the Court used customary international law to restrain the application of the *Charter*, thereby effectively raising customary international law to constitutional status.[40]

Moreover, the *Charter* is not like other laws. As acknowledged by the majority in *Hape*, it applies only to those exercising the authority of the state, namely Parliament and the executive government, and its function is to limit the state's coercive power.[41] Further, agents of a state present in foreign territory are not like other visitors. While Canadian agents must comply with the laws of a host state when present in its territory, as state agents they maintain state immunity before the host state's courts.[42] This is distinct from the case of a non-state agent, such as an ordinary Canadian citizen, who enters the host state's territory and is subject to the enforcement jurisdiction of its courts. Thus, while the principle of territoriality may provide a host state's courts with enforcement jurisdiction over Canadian police officers present within its borders, international law will generally prohibit their exercise of enforcement jurisdiction. Nonetheless, in the majority's view, it is inappropriate for the *Charter* to apply to actions attributable to a Canadian authority in such circumstances.[43]

---

and conventional international law. *Hape, supra* note 1 at paras 39, 53, 68; *Reference re Secession of Quebec*, [1998] 2 SCR 217 at para 72. Conversely, it is generally accepted that customary international law may be incorporated into the common law, "so far as it is not inconsistent with rules enacted by statutes or finally declared by their tribunals." *Cheung Chi Cheung v The King*, [1939] AC 160 at 168; Currie, *supra* note 32 at 234. This necessarily implies that Parliament has the authority to pass legislation that is inconsistent with customary international law (for further discussion of *Hape* and the reception of customary international law, see Currie, *supra* note 32 at 59-71). Thus, Parliament has the authority, under Canadian constitutional law, to decide if international law — whether conventional or customary — is received into Canada's domestic law. If legislatures are not subordinate to international law, neither is the Constitution that governs their authority.

[39] Attaran, *supra* note 29 at 521.

[40] See *ibid*; Currie, *supra* note 32 at 91.

[41] *Hape, supra* note 1 at para 32.

[42] Hazel Fox, *The Law of State Immunity*, 2nd edition (Toronto: Oxford University Press, 2008) at 462-64; *Tritt v United States of America* (1989), 68 OR (2d) 284 at 287 (HCJ).

[43] *Hape, supra* note 1 at paras 68-69, 97.

In addition to criticisms of the Court's interpretation and application of international law, it has also been argued that the decision

creates a dangerous precedent that once Canadian police officers, security intelligence officers and soldiers leave Canadian air space, they can wave the restraints of the Charter goodbye ... [W]hile most Canadians would not expect an imperialistic imposition of the Charter on foreign officials, they would expect that the basic values of the Charter would apply to our officials when they act abroad.[44]

FLAG STATE JURISDICTION AND HIGH SEAS FISHERIES

In light of the majority's reasoning in *Hape*, the question of the *Charter*'s application to high seas interdictions in RFMO areas is fundamentally tied to the issue of enforcement jurisdiction over vessels located on the high seas. This section therefore explores international and Canadian law pertaining to state jurisdiction over vessels on the high seas and the interdiction of foreign-flagged vessels in RFMO areas.

FLAG STATE JURISDICTION

Flagged Vessels

Pursuant to the customary international legal principle *mare liberum* (freedom of the high seas) and the 1982 *United Nations Convention on the Law of the Sea* (*UNCLOS*), the high seas are open to all states.[45] While no state enjoys sovereignty over the high seas, a vessel on the high seas is subject to the exclusive jurisdiction of the state whose

---

44 Roach, *supra* note 32 at 3-4.

45 Shaw, *supra* note 15 at 609; Natalie Klein, "The Right of Visit and the 2005 Protocol on the Suppression of Unlawful Acts against the Safety of Maritime Navigation" (2006) 35 Denv J Int'l L & Pol'y 287 at 291. The high seas consist of "all parts of the sea that are not included in the exclusive economic zone, in the territorial sea or in the internal waters of a State, or in the archipelagic waters of an archipelagic State." *United Nations Convention on the Law of the Sea*, 10 December 1982, 1833 UNTS 3, art 86 [*UNCLOS*]. The freedom of the high seas includes, *inter alia*, the freedom of navigation, overflight, laying of submarine cables and pipelines, construction of artificial islands and other installations, and the conduct of scientific research (*ibid*, art 87(1)). It also includes the freedom to fish, which must be exercised "with due regard for the interests of other states in their exercise of the freedom of the high seas, and also with due regard for the rights under this Convention with respect to activities in the Area" (*ibid*, art 87(1)-(2)).

flag it flies, a principle recognized by the Permanent Court of International Justice in the *SS Lotus* case and codified in Article 92 of *UNCLOS*.[46] A state's exclusive jurisdiction over vessels sailing under its flag on the high seas should not be equated with the concept of state sovereignty over territory, however. The view that a ship on the high seas is the "territory" of its flag state, a relic of prize law, has fallen into disrepute.[47] Rather, the flag state has exclusive prescriptive and enforcement jurisdiction over vessels bearing its nationality, meaning that it is the prerogative of the flag state to regulate, and, where necessary, interdict, vessels bearing its nationality.[48] Flag state jurisdiction is recognized as the "foundation of the maintenance of order on the high seas" and the starting point of high seas law enforcement.[49]

A high seas interdiction is an exercise of extraterritorial enforcement jurisdiction.[50] Generally speaking, it may involve two distinct exercises of enforcement jurisdiction. The first is stopping, boarding, and inspecting or searching a vessel for evidence of prohibited conduct ("boarding").[51] The second is the arrest of persons or the seizure of the vessel where prohibited conduct is found ("seizure").[52] A state only has the lawful right to exercise enforcement jurisdiction over a foreign-flagged vessel if the vessel's flag state consents or if

[46] Klein, *supra* note 45 at 291; *SS Lotus* case, *supra* note 16 at 25: "It is certainly true that — apart from certain special cases which are defined by international law — vessels on the high seas are subject to no authority except that of the State whose flag they fly. In virtue of the principle of the freedom of the seas, that is to say, the absence of any territorial sovereignty upon the high seas, no State may exercise any kind of jurisdiction over foreign vessels upon them."

[47] Rosemary Gail Rayfuse, *Non-Flag State Enforcement in High Seas Fisheries* (Boston: Martinus Nijhoff Publishers, 2004) at 21; Ian Brownlie, *Principles of Public International Law*, 7th edition (New York: Oxford University Press, 2008) at 318. In contrast, see Asia N Wright, "High Seas Crimes" (2009) 7 Loy Mar LJ 1 at 26.

[48] Klein, *supra* note 45 at 296; Robert CF Reuland, "Interference with Non-National Ships on the High Seas: Peacetime Exceptions to the Exclusivity Rule of Flag State Jurisdiction" (1989) 22 Vand J Transnat'l L 1161 at 1196.

[49] Douglas Guilfoyle, "Interdicting Vessels to Enforce the Common Interest: Maritime Countermeasures and the Use of Force" (2007) 56 Int'l & Comp LQ 69 at 80-81; Shaw, *supra* note 15 at 611. See also Reuland, *supra* note 48 at 1164; Klein, *supra* note 45 at 291.

[50] Douglas Guilfoyle, *Shipping Interdiction and the Law of the Sea* (New York: Cambridge University Press, 2009) at 9.

[51] *Ibid*. See also Francisco Orrego Vicuñña, *The Changing International Law of High Seas Fisheries* (New York: Cambridge University Press, 2004) at 252.

[52] Guilfoyle, *supra* note 50 at 9. See also Vicuñña, *supra* note 51 at 252.

a specific rule of international law provides an exception to the exclusivity of the flag state's jurisdiction.[53]

Exceptions to Exclusive Flag State Jurisdiction

International law permits state interference with foreign-flagged vessels, up to and including interdiction, in a limited number of circumstances.[54] First, the customary international legal right of reconnaissance or approach allows state vessels to approach any merchant vessel on the high seas for the purpose of ascertaining its identity and nationality.[55] This action includes requesting that the vessel show its "colours" or flag, which is *prima facie* evidence of its nationality.[56]

Second, the right of visit allows officers from a state vessel to board a foreign-flagged vessel if the boarding state has reasonable grounds to believe that the vessel is engaged in piracy, unauthorized broadcasting, or the slave trade, the ship is stateless, or the vessel shares its nationality.[57] The purpose of the visit is to ascertain the ship's right to fly its flag.[58] The right of visit does not, however, itself provide the boarding state with jurisdiction to inspect, search, seize, arrest, or prosecute the vessel, although such rights may exist pursuant to other rules of customary or conventional international law.[59]

Third, a vessel involved in piracy or unauthorized broadcasting on the high seas is subject to the enforcement jurisdiction of non-flag states.[60] Fourth, the right of hot pursuit permits a state to

---

[53] Guilfoyle, *supra* note 50; Rayfuse, *supra* note 47 at 17; Reuland, *supra* note 48 at 1163; Anne Bardin, "Coastal States' Jurisdiction over Foreign Vessels" (2002) 14 Pace Int'l L Rev 27 at 46; Daniel H Joyner, "The Proliferation Security Initiative: Nonproliferation, Counter Proliferation, and International Law" (2005) 30 Yale J Int'l L 507 at 536.

[54] Rayfuse, *supra* note 47 at 17; Reuland, *supra* note 48 at 1163; Bardin, *supra* note 53 at 46.

[55] Reuland, *supra* note 48 at 1169; Brownlie, *supra* note 47 at 232; Rayfuse, *supra* note 47 at 62.

[56] Reuland, *supra* note 48 at 1170.

[57] *UNCLOS, supra* note 45, art 110(1). The right of visit of a foreign ship, originally a belligerent right, has an uncertain status under customary international law. Brownlie, *supra* note 47 at 232; Rayfuse, *supra* note 47 at 63; Reuland, *supra* note 48 at 1170.

[58] *UNCLOS, supra* note 45, art 110(2).

[59] *Ibid,* art 110.

[60] *UNCLOS, supra* note 45, art 105, and customary international law provide all states with universal jurisdiction to stop, seize, arrest, and prosecute a ship and

interdict a foreign-flagged vessel on the high seas, but only for violations of the interdicting state's laws that occurred within its jurisdiction and only if certain conditions are met.[61] Lastly, one state may consent to another state's exercise of enforcement jurisdiction over a vessel bearing the former's nationality.[62] Consent may be ad hoc or pursuant to a treaty and is usually partial or limited.[63] For example, a state may consent to the boarding and inspection of a ship but not to its seizure.[64] A flag state's consent to a foreign interdiction does not deprive the flag state of jurisdiction over the vessel.[65] Instead, the flag state waives the exclusivity of its jurisdiction, thereby providing the non-flag state with the right to exercise enforcement jurisdiction over the vessel to the extent of the waiver.[66]

Stateless Vessels

A stateless vessel is any vessel without a claim to nationality under Article 91 of *UNCLOS*.[67] Any flagged vessel may be rendered stateless

---

61   its crew involved in piracy on the high seas (see *SS Lotus* case, *supra* note 16 at 70 (per Judge Moore in dissent)). Article 109 provides some non-flag states with concurrent jurisdiction over a vessel engaged in unauthorized broadcasting. The flag state (or the state of registry for the installation making the unauthorized broadcast), a state receiving the broadcast, a state whose radio communication is suffering interference from the unauthorized broadcast, and the state of which the unauthorized broadcaster is a national all have jurisdiction to prosecute the unauthorized broadcasting (*UNCLOS*, *supra* note 45, art 109(3)). Piracy and unauthorized broadcasting do not result in loss of nationality for the vessel (*ibid*, art 104). Rather, the flag state loses its exclusive jurisdiction over the vessel in favour of one or more additional states sharing concurrent or parallel jurisdiction over the vessel (*ibid*, art 109(3)); Guilfoyle, *supra* note 50 at 9, 297-98.

61   *UNCLOS*, *supra* note 45, art 111.

62   Rosemary Rayfuse, "Regulation and Enforcement in the Law of the Sea: Emerging Assertions of a Right to Non-Flag State Enforcement in the High Seas Fisheries and Disarmament Contexts" (2005) 24 Aust YB Int'l L 181 at 183; Klein, *supra* note 45 at 303. *UNCLOS*, *supra* note 45, art 110, both anticipates state consent to non-flag state enforcement and is an example of such consent. Guilfoyle, *supra* note 50 at 276; Joyner, *supra* note 53 at 537.

63   Klein, *supra* note 45 at 303; Rayfuse, *supra* note 62 at 183; Guilfoyle, *supra* note 50 at 9.

64   Guilfoyle, *supra* note 50 at 9.

65   *Ibid.*

66   *Ibid.*

67   Guilfoyle, *supra* note 50 at 16. Each state determines the conditions necessary for it to grant its nationality or flag to a ship. *UNCLOS*, *supra* note 45, art 91.

by law, such as when it sails under two flags.[68] A state may also revoke a vessel's registration or nationality, including while it is at sea.[69] However, a state's inability or refusal to regulate a vessel flying its flag does not render that vessel stateless.[70] Only flagged vessels have the freedom to navigate the high seas free from non-flag state interference.[71] Consequently, the interdiction of a stateless vessel on the high seas is not a breach of international law, in part because no state can claim it was wronged by the ship's seizure.[72]

International law's treatment of stateless vessels raises a question about the appropriate characterization of state jurisdiction over vessels on the high seas. The conclusion that a state can interfere with and seize a stateless vessel suggests that, but for the principle

---

While *UNCLOS* dictates that "[t]here must be a genuine link between the State and the ship" for a state to grant its nationality to the vessel, custom provides states with discretion in choosing ships to which to accord their nationality and a tenuous link does not render a vessel stateless (*ibid*, art 91(1); Reuland, *supra* note 48 at 1202, 1204; Shaw, *supra* note 15 at 611). Nevertheless, a ship may only sail under one flag at any given time and risks being treated as a stateless vessel if it sails under two or more flags (*ibid*, art 92).

68   UNCLOS, *supra* note 45, art 92(2).

69   Rayfuse, *supra* note 47 at 133.

70   *M/V "Saiga" (No 2) Case (Saint Vincent and the Grenadines v Guinea)*, (Merits) ITLOS Case no 2, Judgment of 1 July 1999 at paras 76, 82 [*M/V Saiga* case]. In the *M/V Saiga* case, Guinea argued that a state is not required to recognize the exclusive jurisdiction of the flag state over a vessel if the flag state cannot exercise its jurisdiction as required by *UNCLOS*. *UNCLOS*, *supra* note 45, art 94, requires flag states to, *inter alia*, exercise their jurisdiction over vessels flying their flag. Article 94(6) establishes what a state may do if it believes another state is not properly exercising its jurisdiction as required and the acquisition of enforcement jurisdiction is not included. The International Tribunal on the Law of the Sea held that Article 94(6) is conclusive on the matter and that a state's failure to exercise jurisdiction does not render a vessel stateless. It should be noted, however, that some states take jurisdiction over crimes committed against their nationals aboard a foreign-flagged vessel on the high seas. Wright, *supra* note 47 at 27. Such exercises of jurisdiction fall under the passive personality principle. Shaw, *supra* note 15 at 664. This does not mean, however, that the state claiming jurisdiction ceases to recognize the nationality of the vessel.

71   *Molvan v Attorney-General for Palestine*, [1948] AC 351 at 369-70 [*Asya* case]; Brownlie, *supra* note 47 at 228; Klein, *supra* note 45 at 295; Bardin, *supra* note 53 at 49.

72   *Asya* case, *supra* note 71. See also Herman Meyers, *The Nationality of Ships* (The Hague: Martinus Nijhoff, 1967) at 318, 320-21. A stateless vessel is also not entitled to many of the rights, benefits, and freedoms prescribed by the law of the sea. Shaw, *supra* note 15 at 611.

providing for exclusive flag state jurisdiction, all states possess concurrent enforcement jurisdiction over vessels located on the high seas.[73] Therefore, it may be argued, the principle of exclusive flag state jurisdiction provides flagged vessels with immunity from foreign states' exercises of enforcement jurisdiction.[74] This characterization of exclusive flag state jurisdiction as an immunity is also supported by the rule that a non-flag state may exercise enforcement jurisdiction over a foreign-flagged vessel with the consent of the vessel's flag state. In other words, a flag state's consent to foreign-state interdiction is in fact a waiver of the vessel's immunity from foreign-state enforcement jurisdiction, thereby allowing both the flag state and boarding state to exercise their concurrent or parallel jurisdiction over the vessel — albeit only to the extent of the flag state's consent or waiver.[75]

HIGH SEAS FISHERIES

International Regulation of High Seas Fisheries

The international regulation of high seas fishing has faced challenges. Particularly prior to the entry into force of the *Agreement for the Implementation of the Provisions of the United Nations Convention on the Law of the Sea of 10 December 1982 Relating to the Conservation and Management of Straddling Fish Stocks and Highly Migratory Fish Stocks (Fish Stocks Agreement)*,[76] fishing vessels could avoid complying with RFMO measures in a RFMO area by re-flagging to a state that was not a party to the RFMO convention governing that region of the high seas.[77] Moreover, some states have not adequately regulated

---

[73] Guilfoyle, *supra* note 50 at 296. This view is also held by David D Caron, "Ships, Nationality and Status," in Rudolf Bernhardt, ed, *Encyclopedia of Public International Law*, vol. 4 (New York: North-Holland, 1992) at 404. Meyers also recognizes that non-flag states may exercise jurisdiction over flagged vessels but questions whether two states can maintain concurrent jurisdiction over a vessel. Meyers, *supra* note 72 at 41-42.

[74] Guilfoyle, *supra* note 50 at 296.

[75] *Ibid* at 297. Guilfoyle, *supra* note 50, prefers the term "parallel jurisdiction" but does not explain the significance of the difference, if any, between the two terms in the context of interdictions.

[76] *Agreement for the Implementation of the Provisions of the United Nations Convention on the Law of the Sea of 10 December 1982 Relating to the Conservation and Management of Straddling Fish Stocks and Highly Migratory Fish Stocks*, 2167 UNTS 3 (entered into force 11 December 2001) [*Fish Stocks Agreement*].

[77] Rayfuse, *supra* note 47 at 34-35.

their fishing vessels bearing their flag.[78] Reasons for inadequate regulation have included the failure by states to ratify conservation and management treaties or to implement treaties to which they are a party as well as a lack of political will on the part of some states to exercise their enforcement jurisdiction.[79] Other states have simply lacked the capacity to exercise enforcement jurisdiction over vessels bearing their flag.[80] Consequently, illegal, unreported, and un-regulated (IUU) fishing has flourished into a billion dollar industry and contributed to a decline in fish stocks.[81]

In response, co-operative international enforcement schemes have been developed.[82] Notably, the international community has chosen not to follow the piracy or unauthorized broadcasting model, whereby all states would maintain universal, concurrent enforcement jurisdiction to interdict and prosecute IUU fishing on the high seas.[83] Instead, states have favoured agreements that provide for consensual and reciprocal interdiction of each other's fishing vessels for the limited purpose of carrying out inspections.[84] While these agreements permit a state to exercise limited enforce-ment jurisdiction (for example, boarding and inspection) over foreign-flagged fishing vessels on the high seas, none authorizes a non-flag state to prosecute a vessel for violations of conservation measures — although each state remains free to consent to such a prosecution.[85]

Interdictions under Fisheries Conventions and the Canadian Coastal Fisheries Protection Act (CFPA)

Canadian agents' authority to interdict foreign-flagged vessels is found in several international treaties and the *CFPA*, in which vari-ous treaty provisions are transformed into Canadian domestic law.[86]

---

[78] *Ibid* at 34.

[79] *Ibid* at 24.

[80] *Ibid*.

[81] Fisheries and Oceans Canada, "Illegal, Unreported and Unregulated (IUU) Fishing," online: <http://www.dfo-mpo.gc.ca/international/isu-iuu-eng.htm>.

[82] Vicunña, *supra* note 51 at 240.

[83] Guilfoyle, *supra* note 50 at 25. Guilfoyle notes that this is likely to do with states' distrust about who may do the enforcing against whom.

[84] Vicunña, *supra* note 51 at 241.

[85] *Ibid*.

[86] *Coastal Fisheries Protection Act*, RSC 1985, c C-33 [*CFPA*].

This section discusses Canada's jurisdiction to interdict foreign-flagged vessels pursuant to these international agreements and the *CFPA*.

Fish Stocks Agreement

The purpose of the *Fish Stocks Agreement* is to add detail to some of the more general *UNCLOS* fisheries provisions and establish a sustainable international fisheries regulatory framework.[87] The *Fish Stocks Agreement* provides RFMOs with a central role in the co-operative management of fish stocks.[88] For example, Article 8 provides that coastal and fishing states must co-operate in the management of fish stocks through RFMOs.[89] It also provides that vessels flagged by a party to the agreement may only access a fish stock managed by a RFMO if the party is either a member of the RFMO or co-operates with it by applying its conservation measures.[90]

The *Fish Stocks Agreement*'s enforcement and compliance measures are found at Articles 19 through 23. They provide that a party to the agreement must ensure that vessels flying its flag comply with RFMO measures.[91] Further, parties are required to co-operate in the investigation of violations.[92] To facilitate co-operation, the *Fish Stocks Agreement* includes a non-flag state boarding and inspection scheme.[93] Pursuant to the scheme, inspectors from a party to a RFMO are authorized by the agreement to board and inspect any vessel present in the RFMO area that is flagged by a party to the *Fish Stocks Agreement*.[94] Where boarding and inspection raise the belief that a violation of a RFMO conservation measure has occurred, the investigators must notify the vessel's flag state.[95] Upon such

---

87 Guilfoyle, *supra* note 50 at 103. Seventy-eight states, including Canada, are parties to the *Fish Stock Agreement*. United Nations, "Chronological Lists of Ratifications of, Accessions and Successions to the Convention and the Related Agreements as at 15 November 2010," online: <http://www.un.org/Depts/los/convention_agreements/convention_overview_fish_stocks.htm>.

88 Guilfoyle, *supra* note 50 at 103.

89 *Fish Stocks Agreement, supra* note 76, art 8(1).

90 *Ibid*, arts 8(3), 8(4).

91 *Ibid*, art 19(1); Vicunña, *supra* note 51 at 237.

92 *Fish Stocks Agreement, supra* note 76, arts 20(1)-(6).

93 *Ibid*, art 21.

94 *Ibid*, art 21(1).

95 *Ibid*, art 21(5).

notice, the flag state may take over the investigation or authorize the inspecting state to investigate further.[96] Any enforcement actions taken by a party to an RFMO against a foreign-flagged vessel must be proportionate to the seriousness of the violation.[97] The *Fish Stocks Agreement* is silent on prosecution by non-flag states.[98]

RFMOs

Canada is a party to several RFMOs, including the Northwest Atlantic Fisheries Organization (NAFO), the International Commission for the Conservation of Atlantic Tunas (ICCAT), and the North Pacific Anadromous Fish Commission (NPAFC).[99] While the three RFMOs share many similarities, the rules pertaining to interdictions vary across RFMO agreements as does Canada's involvement in enforcing the respective RFMO measures against foreign-flagged vessels.

(a) NAFO

NAFO comprises twelve parties, including Canada and the European Union (EU).[100] Pursuant to Article XVIII of the *Convention on Future Multilateral Cooperation in the Northwest Atlantic Fisheries (NAFO Convention)*, NAFO parties agree to implement an enforcement scheme that includes, *inter alia*, reciprocal boarding and inspection rights.

---

[96] *Ibid*, art 21(6).

[97] *Ibid*, art 21(16). Investigators must comply with certain procedures and safety standards, either the default procedures under the *Fish Stocks Agreement* or procedures set out under the RFMO conventions (*ibid*, arts 21(2), 21(10), 22).

[98] Vicunña, *supra* note 51 at 254.

[99] *Convention on Future Multilateral Cooperation in the Northwest Atlantic Fisheries*, 24 October 1978, Can TS 1979 no 11 (entry into force 1 January 1979) [*NAFO Convention*]; *International Convention for the Conservation of Atlantic Tunas*, Can TS 1969 no 18 (entry into force 21 March 1969) [*ICCAT Convention*]; *Convention for the Conservation of Anadromous Stocks in the North Pacific Ocean*, 11 February 1992, Can TS 1993 no 13 (entry into force 16 February 1993) [*NPAFC Convention*].

[100] The NAFO parties are: Canada, Cuba, Denmark (with respect to the Faroe Islands and Greenland), the European Community, France (with respect to Saint Pierre and Miquelon), Iceland, Japan, Korea (Republic of), Norway, Romania, the Russian Federation, Ukraine, and the United States. See online: NAFO <http://www.nafo.int/about/frames/about.html>. The NAFO area covers the Atlantic Ocean's waters north of 35 degrees north and west of 42 degrees west to Cape Farewell, Greenland, and the Gulf of Saint Lawrence. *NAFO Convention*, *supra* note 99, art 1; Rayfuse, *supra* note 47 at 225. NAFO manages eleven species, totalling nineteen stocks. See online: NAFO <http://www.nafo.int/fisheries/frames/fishery.html>.

The scheme is embodied in the *Conservation and Enforcement Measures* of the *NAFO Convention* (*NAFO CEM*).[101] The boarding and inspection scheme between NAFO parties is found in Articles 28-43 of the *NAFO CEM*. Four non-armed inspectors of a NAFO party may board and inspect a fishing vessel flagged to another NAFO party.[102] Inspectors may examine "all relevant areas, decks and rooms of the fishing vessels, processed and unprocessed catches, nets or other gear, equipment, and any relevant documents which inspectors deem necessary to verify compliance with NAFO Conservation and Enforcement Measures."[103] An inspector is to record observed NAFO

---

[101] *NAFO Conservation and Enforcement Measures 2011*, NAFO/FC, Doc 11/1 (2011), Serial no N5867 [*NAFO CEM*]. Historically, NAFO parties have been active in non-flag state inspections, particularly in the 1980s and early 1990s. In 1990, there was a total of 807 inspections by non-flag states, while there were only 193 in 2000. Rayfuse, *supra* note 47 at 246, Table 1. The average between 1987 and 2001 was 389. Although the number of inspections decreased throughout the 1990s, the percentage of "apparent infringements" (AI) per inspection increased overall, ranging from a low of 1 percent in 1990 to a high of 27.5 percent in 2000 (*ibid* at 246, Table 1). The average AI per inspection was 10 percent between 1990 and 1995 and 14 percent between 1996 and 2001. Boardings of non-NAFO party vessels also varied, as did their presence in the NAFO area. In 1989, forty-seven non-NAFO party vessels were reported in the NAFO area, while none were reported in 2000 (*ibid* at 252, Table 5). Boardings of vessels flagged by non-NAFO parties reached a high in 1993 when thirty-three non-party vessels were boarded a total of seventy-six times (*ibid.*). From the early 1990s through 2001, Canada conducted the majority of non-flag inspections (*ibid* at 248, Table 4). The most recent data on inspections is for 2008. NAFO, *Annual Compliance Review 2009*, NAFO/FC, Doc 09/16 (2009). Between 2004 and 2008, non-flag state inspections of NAFO party vessels continued. In 2004, the 134 NAFO-flagged vessels in the NAFO area were boarded and inspected by other NAFO parties a total of 401 times, with twelve vessels cited for one or more AIs. NAFO, *Annual Compliance Review 2008*, NAFO/FC, Doc 08/20 (2008), Table 5-2004, Part 1. In 2007, the total number of NAFO vessels in the area and the number of non-flag state inspections fell to seventy-six and 294 respectively (*ibid*, Table 5-2007, Part 1). However, because the number of fishing days and vessels in the NAFO area decreased over the 2004-7 period, the at-sea inspection rate of vessels per fishing day actually increased from 2.4 percent to 4.5 percent over the period (*ibid* at 7). The number of vessels and inspections continued to fall in 2008 (NAFO, *Annual Compliance Review 2009*, Table 5-2008, Part 1). No data is available detailing the number of non-flag state inspections conducted by each NAFO party for the 2004-8 period. Similarly, no data is available for at-sea inspections of non-NAFO party vessels in the NAFO area during the 2004-8 period. No information was available with respect to the inspection of stateless vessels during any period.

[102] *NAFO CEM*, *supra* note 101, arts 29(1), 29(8), 33(4).

[103] *Ibid*, art 33(5).

infringements.[104] If a specified "serious infringement" is found, the inspector is to notify the vessel's flag state.[105] Following notification of a serious infringement, the flag state must ensure the vessel is investigated within seventy-two hours, during which time an inspector may remain on board the interdicted vessel.[106] An inspecting NAFO party is not authorized to seize and prosecute a vessel flagged by another NAFO party. Instead, each party is obliged to prosecute its own vessels.[107] However, as discussed later in this comment, Canadian legislation provides that it is an offence for a vessel flagged to a "participating state" to breach a NAFO measure, and, in some circumstances, the legislation deems a participating state's consent to Canada's arrest and prosecution of vessels bearing the former's flag. Thus, it is foreseeable that, notwithstanding the *NAFO Convention*, evidence collected by Canadian inspectors during a high seas interdiction may be used by Canada or another NAFO party to prosecute NAFO violations.[108]

The enforcement measures applicable to vessels flagged by a non-party to the *NAFO Convention* are found in Articles 51-59 of the *NAFO CEM*. Article 53 provides that, "if appropriate," NAFO inspectors may request to board and inspect a vessel flagged to a non-NAFO party, suggesting that vessels or flag states may decline inspections. Article 51(2) of the *NAFO CEM*, however, provides that "[n]othing in this Scheme shall affect the sovereign rights of Contracting Parties to impose additional measures to promote compliance by [non-contracting parties'] vessels, in accordance with international law." This article would appear to provide a state that is a party to both NAFO and the *Fish Stocks Agreement* with the authority to enforce NAFO's conservation measures in the NAFO area by boarding and inspecting a fishing vessel flagged by any state party to the *Fish Stocks Agreement*.[109]

---

[104] *Ibid*, art 36.

[105] *Ibid*, arts 37(1)-(2).

[106] *Ibid*, arts 37(3), 37(5).

[107] *Ibid*, art 40.

[108] *Ibid*, arts 37, 40-41.

[109] Canada appears to take advantage of this provision in the *CFPA*, *supra* note 86. Interestingly, both Guilfoyle's and Rayfuse's discussions of NAFO's enforcement provisions against vessels flagged to non-NAFO parties only mention consensual boarding under Article 53 and not the potential implications of Article 51(2). Guilfoyle, *supra* note 50 at 137-38; Rayfuse, *supra* note 47 at 242-43.

(b) ICCAT

ICCAT was established in the 1960s and covers the entire Atlantic Ocean.[110] There are presently forty-eight parties to the *International Convention for the Conservation of Atlantic Tunas (ICCAT Convention)*, including the EU and Canada.[111] ICCAT developed a non-flag inspection regime in 1975, but it only came into force with respect to a single species, bluefin tuna, in 2008.[112] The ICCAT Scheme of Joint International Inspection (ICCATSJII) provides that inspectors from ICCAT party states may board each other's vessels to inspect gear, catch, and documents.[113] Flag states must "consider and act upon" the reports of inspectors from other states parties and "collaborate in order to facilitate judicial or other proceedings arising from a report of an inspector under these arrangements."[114] In the case of a foreign inspector discovering a specified "serious infringement," the flag state must order the fishing vessel into port for further investigations.[115] ICCAT does not provide for non-flag state prosecution.

(c) NPAFC

NPAFC, the successor to the International North Pacific Fishery Commission, was established in 1993.[116] The contracting parties

---

[110] Rayfuse, *supra* note 47 at 158.

[111] ICCAT, "Contracting Parties," online: <http://www.iccat.int/en/contracting.htm>. See also *ICCAT Convention, supra* note 99.

[112] ICCAT Commission, *Recommendation Amending the Recommendation by ICCAT to Establish a Multiannual Recovery Plan for Bluefin Tuna in the Eastern Atlantic and Mediterranean*, ICCAT Doc 08-05 (2008) at paras 97-98, Annex 8; ICCAT, *ICCAT Scheme of Joint International Inspection*, ICCAT Doc 75-02 (1975). Note that, pursuant to Article VIII of the *ICCAT Convention*, Commission recommendations become binding on the parties. *ICCAT Convention, supra* note 99, art VIII.

[113] ICATT Commission, *supra* note 112, Annex 8, paras 4, 7-8. At the time of writing, no data on non-flag boardings and inspections was available.

[114] *Ibid,* Annex 8, para 11.

[115] *Ibid,* Annex 8, paras 1-3.

[116] Rayfuse, *supra* note 47 at 117. The NPAFC area includes "the waters of the North Pacific Ocean and its adjacent seas, north of 33 degrees North Latitude beyond 200 nautical miles from the baselines from which the breadth of the territorial sea is measured" and the organization is only concerned with anadromous fish, particularly salmon. *NPAFC Convention, supra* note 99, arts I-II and Annex, Part I.

are Canada, the United States, Russia, Japan, and South Korea.[117] China is not a party, but it does co-operate with the organization.[118] Article IV of the *Convention for the Conservation of Anadromous Stocks in the North Pacific Ocean* (*NPAFC Convention*) provides that each state must take measures to ensure its nationals comply with the convention and that the parties shall "invite the attention" of non-parties to the actions of their flagged vessels in the NPAFC area.[119] Article IV also anticipates the enforcement of NPAFC measures against non-party vessels, as it calls on NPAFC parties to "cooperate in taking action, consistent with international law and their respective domestic laws, for the prevention by any state or entity not party to this Convention of any directed fishing for, and the minimization by such state or entity of any incidental taking of, anadromous fish by nationals, residents or vessels of such state or entity in the Convention Area."[120]

Article V provides that parties may board and inspect each other's vessels on the basis of a reasonable belief that the vessel is engaged in directed fishing or the incidental taking of anadromous fish.[121] If a violation is found, the boarding state may arrest and seize a vessel flagged to a NPAFC party.[122] The arrested vessel is to be turned over to its flag state for further investigation and prosecution as the *NPAFC Convention* also does not provide the arresting state with the authority to prosecute vessels flagged to other NPAFC parties.[123]

---

[117] NPAFC, "About NPAFC," online: <http://www.npafc.org/new/about_convention.html>.

[118] Guilfoyle, *supra* note 50 at 118. China's co-operation includes a 1993 ship-rider and boarding agreement with the United States that allows both states to board and inspect one another's vessels located in the NPAFC area.(*ibid* at 119).

[119] *NPAFC Convention, supra* note 99, arts IV(1)-(3).

[120] *Ibid*, art IV(4).

[121] *Ibid*, art V(2)(a).

[122] *Ibid*, art V(2)(b).

[123] *Ibid*, arts V(2)(c)-(d). NPAFC parties have been active with respect to boardings and inspections. While data on the total number of boardings and inspections is not available, between 1993 and 2009 forty-one vessels were detected driftnet fishing in the area and sixteen vessels were apprehended. NPAFC, "Enforcement Activities," online: <http://www.npafc.org/new/enforcement_activities.html>. Apprehended vessels were flagged by Honduras, Indonesia, China, Taiwan, and Russia. NPAFC, "List of Apprehended Illegal Salmon Fishing Vessels in NPAFC Convention Area (1993-2007)," online: <http://www.npafc.org/new/about/

Canada's *CFPA*

The *CFPA* transforms Canada's boarding and inspection rights under the *Fish Stocks Agreement* and RFMOs into domestic law.[124] The *CFPA* and its regulations take an aggressive approach to the enforcement of RFMO measures. In a bold assertion of authority over the high seas, the *CFPA* and its regulations ban vessels flagged to Belize, the Cayman Islands, Honduras, Panama, Saint-Vincent and the Grenadines, and Sierra Leone from fishing in the NAFO area (NAFO prohibited states).[125] The *CFPA* also prohibits vessels flagged to fifty-one states (participating states) — which are all parties to the *Fish Stocks Agreement* — from contravening NAFO and ICCAT measures in the respective areas.[126] Similarly, the *CFPA* and its regulations prohibit vessels flagged to NPAFC parties from contravening the *NPAFC Convention*.[127] Lastly, the act also prohibits all stateless vessels from fishing in the NAFO, ICCAT, or NPAFC areas.[128]

The *CFPA* lists several actions by foreign vessels on the high seas that constitute an offence. For example, it is an offence for a fishing vessel flagged to a prohibited state to enter the NAFO area,[129] for a vessel flagged to a prescribed state to contravene NAFO or ICCAT conservation measures in the respective areas,[130] for a vessel flagged to a party to the *NPAFC Convention* to contravene that convention

---

Apprehended(web).pdf>. Some apprehended vessels were stateless, either by assimilation or by the flag state refuting a vessel's registration (see also Rayfuse, *supra* note 47 at 130-33). In addition, at least two non-parties have consented to the arrest and prosecution of their flagged vessels by a NPAFC party for violations of the *NPAFC Convention* (*ibid* at 133-34). It should be noted that it is not always clear whether enforcement actions by NPAFC members are under the *NPAFC Convention* or the UN driftnet moratorium (*ibid* at 134-35; Guilfoyle, *supra* note 50 at 117; *Large-Scale Pelagic Drift-Net Fishing and Its Impact on the Living Marine Resources of the World's Oceans and Seas*, GA Res 46/215, UNGAOR (1991)).

124 *CFPA, supra* note 86.

125 *Ibid*, s 5.2; *Coastal Fisheries Protection Regulations*, CRC, c 413, s 21(2)(b), Table III [*CFPR*].

126 *CFPA, supra* note 86, s 5.3; *CFPR, supra* note 125, ss 22, 23(1), 39(1), Schedule IV. The fifty-one listed states were the parties to the *Fish Stocks Agreement* as of 2004. United Nations, *supra* note 87.

127 *CFPA, supra* note 86, s 5.4; *CFPR, supra* note 125, ss 43-44.

128 *CFPA, supra* note 86, s 5.5; *CFPR, supra* note 125, ss 23(2), 39(2), 43(2).

129 *CFPA, supra* note 86, s 18(1).

130 *Ibid*, s 18(2).

in the NPAFC area,[131] and for a stateless vessel to fish in the NAFO, ICCAT, or NPAFC areas.[132] The penalties for these offences include fines of up to CDN $750,000.[133]

The *CFPA* and its regulations provide designated "protection officers," such as RCMP or fisheries officers, with extensive enforcement powers. A protection officer may board and inspect "any vessel" in the NAFO area but only for the purpose of enforcing the *CFPA* and its regulations, thereby limiting its jurisdiction to vessels flagged to a NAFO-prohibited state or a prescribed state.[134] Similarly, a protection officer may board and inspect a vessel flagged to one of the fifty-one prescribed states that is found in the ICCAT area or a vessel flagged to a NPAFC party that is found in the NPAFC area.[135] A protection officer may also board and inspect a stateless vessel in any of the three RFMO areas.[136] In the case of stateless vessels and vessels flagged to a NPAFC party, a protection officer who is investigating the vessel and who believes on reasonable grounds that an offence has been committed under the act may arrest the vessel.[137] In the case of a vessel flagged to a participating state and located in the NAFO or ICCAT areas respectively, a protection officer who believes an offence has occurred must notify the flag state and may only arrest, seize, or prosecute the vessel if the flag state consents or is deemed to have consented by either not responding within the prescribed period or not "fully investigating" the alleged contravention.[138]

Pursuant to international law, however, a flag state's inadequate exercise of enforcement jurisdiction over one of its flagged vessels does not give rise to an exception to the exclusivity of that flag state's jurisdiction.[139] Moreover, a foreign state is not subject to the authority of Canada's Parliament, meaning that the *CFPA* cannot *deem* its

---

[131] *Ibid.*

[132] *Ibid.*

[133] *Ibid,* ss 18(1)-(3).

[134] *Ibid,* ss 7(a), 16.1-16.2. With a warrant, however, a protection officer may inspect any fishing vessel found within the NAFO area (*ibid,* s 7(b)).

[135] *Ibid,* ss 16.1-16.2.

[136] *Ibid,* s 16.1(c).

[137] *Ibid,* ss 8-9, 16.1.

[138] *Ibid,* ss 8-9, 16.1-16.2.

[139] *M/V Saiga* case, *supra* note 70 at para 82. Conversely, Rayfuse has argued that there is an emerging customary rule that flag states may only authorize their nationals to fish where the flag state can exercise its supervisory responsibilities,

consent at international law. It follows that the arrest and prosecution of a foreign-flagged vessel under the *CFPA*'s deemed consent provision would exceed the consent provided by the flag state in the applicable RFMO convention.[140]

Notwithstanding the issue of consent, pursuant to the powers granted to protection officers by the *CFPA*, it is foreseeable that a high seas interdiction of a foreign-flagged fishing vessel could involve activities that engage protections under the *Charter*, including the right to life, liberty, and security of the person, freedom from unreasonable search and seizure, freedom from arbitrary detention, the right to counsel, and other protections applicable in cases of arrest or detention.

The *Charter* and the High Seas

As discussed earlier, Canadian protection officers may, pursuant to international and domestic law, exercise extraterritorial enforcement jurisdiction over foreign-flagged fishing vessels on the high seas in certain circumstances. Such enforcement actions, including the boarding, inspection, arrest, seizure, and prosecution of a foreign-flagged fishing vessel, may involve coercive actions that would attract *Charter* protections if they occurred within Canada.

There are two reasons why the *Charter* may not apply to high seas fisheries interdictions. First, a vessel's non-Canadian crew members may not fall within the category of persons entitled to protection under specific *Charter* provisions. Second, for the reasons set out by the majority in *Hape*, the *Charter* may not apply to the actions of Canadian fisheries protection officers aboard vessels flagged to another state.

---

and, in turn, flag states implicitly consent to enforcement actions against their vessels bearing their flag by RFMO members "where their vessels are fishing in contravention of the measures adopted by that RFMO and where the flag state is unwilling or unable to act, regardless of the existence or otherwise of an established scheme for non-flag state enforcement within the RFMO or the application of the FSA." Rayfuse, *supra* note 62 at 194-95. Rayfuse does not, however, point to any specific instance of state practice where a state interdicted a foreign-flagged vessel in such circumstances and claimed a customary right to do so (although the *CFPA* could be held out as an example of relevant state practice). Moreover, it is questionable whether there is sufficient *opinio juris* to the effect that a state may use force against a foreign-flagged vessel because its flag state has not adequately regulated the vessel.

140 *NAFO CEM, supra* note 101, arts 29-31, 33-34, 36-37, 40; ICCAT Commission, *supra* note 112, Annex 8, paras 11, 13-16.

NON-CANADIANS AND THE MEANING OF "EVERYONE"

The question of whether the *Charter* applies to Canada's policing of high seas fisheries is moot if persons subject to an interdiction do not fall within a category of persons entitled to relevant protections under the *Charter*. Setting aside for the moment the issue of extraterritorial jurisdiction, a person may only enforce a breach of a *Charter* right against the government if the person falls within a category of persons entitled to that right.[141] Some *Charter* rights apply to "everyone" and some only to a "citizen of Canada."[142] "Everyone" does not mean all persons on the planet.[143] Nonetheless, "everyone" may include non-Canadians, even those outside Canada. For example, in *Cook*, a US citizen interrogated in the United States by Canadian police officers fell within the category of "everyone."[144] The majority of the Supreme Court of Canada in *Hape* did not, however, provide any further guidance as to when non-Canadians outside Canada fall within the category.

The question of when non-Canadians fit within the category of "everyone" as set out in section 7 of the *Charter* was recently considered by the Federal Court and Federal Court of Appeal. In *Amnesty International Canada v Canada (Chief of the Defence Staff)*, the Federal Court of Appeal held that the meaning of "everyone" depends on the circumstances of the particular case, but it did not explain what circumstances should be considered or how they should be weighed.[145] Subsequently, in *Slahi v Canada (Justice)*, the Federal Court of Canada held that to come within the category of "everyone" under section 7 of the *Charter*, "circumstances must connect the claimant with Canada, whether it be by virtue of their presence in Canada, a criminal trial in Canada, or Canadian citizenship."[146] In the court's view, Canadian citizens in Canada, non-Canadians in Canada, non-Canadians subject to a criminal trial in Canada, and, in exceptional circumstances, Canadian citizens abroad fall within the category.[147]

---

141 *Cook, supra* note 11 at paras 85-87 (per L'Heureux-Dubé J. dissenting).

142 Compare *Charter, supra* note 2, ss 6, 7.

143 *Cook, supra* note 11 at para 86 (per L'Heureux-Dubé J. dissenting).

144 *Ibid* at paras 23, 25. See also *ibid* at paras 85-87 (per L'Heureux-Dubé J. dissenting).

145 *Amnesty International Canada v Canada (Chief of the Defence Staff)*, 2008 FCA 401 at para 20 [*Amnesty International*].

146 *Slahi v Canada (Justice)*, 2009 FC 160 at para 47, aff'd 2009 FCA 259 [*Slahi*].

147 *Ibid*.

Although not mentioned by the Court in *Slahi*, non-Canadians who are within Canada's enforcement jurisdiction and are charged with a regulatory offence, such as an offence under the *CFPA*, are also entitled to *Charter* protection, meaning they too fall within the category of "everyone."[148] Similarly, non-Canadian crew members whose vessel is detained, searched, or arrested on the high seas but are not brought into Canada for trial ought to fall within the category of "everyone." The fact that the vessel and crew are subject to coercive actions specifically provided for by an act of Parliament and that evidence has been collected by Canadian boarding agents for the purpose of prosecution, either in the vessel's flag state or under the *CFPA*, should establish a sufficient nexus to Canada to bring the crew within the category of "everyone," regardless of whether they are arrested or charged. Consequently, if the *Charter* applies to Canadian agents that board and inspect a foreign-flagged or stateless vessel pursuant to the *CFPA*, the crew should come within the *Charter* category of "everyone."

EXTRATERRITORIAL APPLICATION OF THE *CHARTER* ON
THE HIGH SEAS

As mentioned earlier, section 32 of the *Charter* provides that the *Charter* applies "to the Parliament and government of Canada in respect of all matters within the authority of Parliament."[149] Insofar as protection officers' actions under the *CFPA* occur within Canadian territory, there is no doubt that the *Charter* applies to such actions.[150] Similarly, in light of *Hape*, the issue of whether the *Charter* applies to the actions of Canadian protection officers present in another state's territory is subject to little doubt. Whether the *Charter* applies to their interdiction of a foreign-flagged fishing vessel on the high seas, however, remains uncertain.

Stateless Vessels

The majority's reasons in *Hape* do not prohibit the application of the *Charter* to Canada's high seas interdiction of stateless vessels.

---

[148] See, *eg, R v Ramalheira*, 2009 NLCA 4, 243 CCC (3d) 72, where the master of a Portuguese fishing vessel was charged with a regulatory offence under the *CFPA, supra* note 86.

[149] *Charter, supra* note 2, s 32(1)(a).

[150] See Peter Hogg, *Constitutional Law of Canada*, 5th edition (looseleaf) (Toronto: Carswell, 2007) at para 37.18.1.

The majority's concern about *Charter* enforcement infringing the sovereignty of another state does not arise when Canada interdicts a stateless vessel on the high seas, because there is no sovereignty to infringe and such interdictions are not prohibited by international law.[151] Moreover, the *CFPA*, an act of Parliament, specifically provides for Canadian enforcement jurisdiction over stateless vessels in specified areas of the high seas, leaving no question as to whether the actions of Canadian protection officers fall within the purview of Parliament as required by the majority's interpretation of section 32 of the *Charter*.[152]

Foreign-Flagged Vessels

Arguments favouring the non-application of the *Charter* to high seas interdictions

It may be argued that the rule in *Hape* limiting the extraterritorial application of the *Charter* applies, *mutatis mutandis,* to Canadian protection officers' interdiction of a foreign-flagged fishing vessel on the high seas. As a preliminary matter, it must be recognized that the majority judgment in *Hape* was focused on the extraterritorial application of the *Charter* to actions occurring within a foreign state's territory and that a vessel on the high seas is not a portion of the territory of its flag state. Nonetheless, the crux of the majority decision in *Hape* was that Canada cannot enforce its laws against a subject or object that is under the exclusive enforcement jurisdiction of another state. Thus, if the majority's reasons for limiting the extraterritorial application of the *Charter* in foreign territory — respect for the exclusive enforcement jurisdiction of sovereign states and the principle of non-interference — also apply to interdictions of foreign-flagged vessels, the *Charter* should, similarly, not apply in the latter situation.

Arguably, the law and circumstances surrounding the interdiction of a foreign-flagged vessel raise similar concerns and issues to those discussed by the majority in *Hape*. Like states' exclusive enforcement jurisdiction in their sovereign territory, exclusive flag state jurisdiction is recognized as a rule of both customary and conventional international law.[153] Moreover, as with the extraterritorial exercise

---

[151] *Asya* case, *supra* note 71 at 370.

[152] Hogg, *supra* note 150 at para 37.18; *CFPA, supra* note 86 at s 16.1.

[153] Guilfoyle, *supra* note 49 at 80-81; Shaw, *supra* note 15 at 611. See also Reuland, *supra* note 48 at 1164; Klein, *supra* note 45 at 291.

of enforcement jurisdiction over a subject within the borders of a foreign state, a state may only exercise enforcement jurisdiction over a foreign-flagged vessel if its flag state consents. Lastly, the flag state maintains primary jurisdiction over the vessel throughout the interdiction.[154] This jurisdiction includes the right to decide if any other state may prosecute the vessel and crew.[155] As such, it may be argued that because the flag state has the authority to determine who may sanction the crew for violations of conservation measures, it also maintains the authority to determine the rights ascribed to the crew. If this argument is accepted, it follows that the *Charter* should not apply to Canadian agents that board foreign-flagged vessels on the high seas unless the flag state consents to the *Charter*'s application.

Applying *Hape* in this manner to high seas interdictions does raise some uncertainties and practical difficulties, however. For example, while Canadian protection officers board and inspect the foreign fishing vessel with the consent of the flag state, it is not clear whether the consent provided within RFMO conventions or the *Fish Stocks Agreement* implies consent to the application of the *Charter*. In addition, strictly applying *Hape* raises a question as to what law Canadian boarding agents must follow in the course of an interdiction. The majority in *Hape* held that the host state's laws govern the conduct of Canadian agents when operating in the territory of that host state.[156] If this view is applied to the high seas context, it stands to reason that the actions of Canadian boarding agents must comply with the relevant laws of the flag state throughout an interdiction. Such a mandate would require that Canadian protection officers be familiar with the laws of each RFMO party as well as the fifty-one prescribed states whose vessels Canada may interdict pursuant to the *Fish Stocks Agreement* and the *CFPA*. To add to this challenge, unlike the RCMP officers in *Hape*, protection officers operating under the *CFPA* are unlikely to have the equivalent of a Detective Lessemun to guide them through the flag state's legal procedures.

Conversely, Douglas Guilfoyle argues that boarding agents are subject to the boarding state's police procedures throughout an interdiction.[157] This view is consonant with provisions in the *NAFO*

---

154 Guilfoyle, *supra* note 50 at 297-98.

155 *Ibid.*

156 See Rennie, *supra* note 32 at 129. See also *R v Terry*, [1996] 2 SCR 207 at para 19.

157 Guilfoyle, *supra* note 50 at 298-99. Guilfoyle argues that a flag state, in principle, maintains jurisdiction over the conduct of foreign boarding agents throughout

and *ICCAT Conventions* discussed later in this comment, which affirm that a boarding state maintains control and responsibility over its boarding agents throughout an interdiction.[158] If Guilfoyle's view is applied, Canadian boarding agents would be required to comply with Canadian law when boarding a foreign-flagged vessel and must only voluntarily respect the flag state's laws to the extent possible.[159] Requiring Canadian boarding agents to comply with Canadian law throughout an interdiction of a foreign-flagged vessel, however, begs the question of the *Charter*'s application in the circumstances.

Arguments favouring application of the *Charter* to high seas interdictions

The preferable view is that the *Charter* applies to Canadian protection officers' high seas interdictions authorized by the RFMO conventions and the *Fish Stocks Agreement*. First, presumably valid Canadian legislation specifically provides for Canadian enforcement jurisdiction over foreign-flagged vessels located on the high seas. This authority is in contrast with *Hape*, where Canada had no legislation providing Canadian protection officers with the express authority to conduct a search and seizure of a private office in the Turks and Caicos Islands.[160] If extraterritorial actions are specifically authorized by valid legislation enacted by Parliament, it is difficult to

---

a consensual interdiction (albeit concurrent with that of the boarding state) and that, while boarding agents are under a duty not to breach the flag state's laws, they are obliged to comply with the boarding state's police procedures. The boarding agents are, however, likely entitled to state immunity for any breach of the flag state's laws (*ibid* at 303-4; Fox, *supra* note 42 at 462-64). The implications of this conclusion are discussed later in this comment.

[158] *NAFO CEM, supra* note 101, s 31(2); ICCAT Commission, *supra* note 112, Annex 8, para 10. NAFO's Joint Inspection and Surveillance Scheme provides: "Inspectors shall carry out their duties in accordance with the rules set out in this Scheme, but they shall remain under the operational control of the authorities of their Contracting Parties and shall be responsible to them."

[159] See note 157 in this article.

[160] The *Royal Canadian Mounted Police Act* provides that the RCMP may be employed outside Canada and that the force may address breaches of its code of conduct outside Canada, but no Canadian legislation specifically authorized the RCMP to search Hape's office in the Turks and Caicos Islands. *Royal Canadian Mounted Police Act*, RSC 1985, c R-10, ss 4, 39(1). Instead, the RCMP operated under the jurisdiction of the Turks and Caicos Islands and under the supervision of Detective Lessemun.

see how those actions do not qualify as "matters within the authority of Parliament" as provided in section 32 of the *Charter*. Moreover, not applying the *Charter* would create a vacuum whereby, contrary to section 32, the *Charter* does not apply to state police actions specifically authorized by Canadian legislation.

Second, it may be argued that Canada's jurisdiction to interdict and search a vessel under a RFMO convention or the *Fish Stocks Agreement* is different from the jurisdictional circumstances faced by the RCMP officers in *Hape*. As discussed earlier, Guilfoyle argues that a state's consent to the interdiction of a vessel bearing its flag by another state is a waiver of the exclusivity of the flag state's jurisdiction, permitting the other state to exercise its concurrent jurisdiction over the vessel to the extent of the waiver.[161] If this view is accepted, it follows that when Canadian agents board and inspect a foreign-flagged vessel pursuant to an RFMO convention or the *Fish Stocks Agreement*, Canada enjoys enforcement jurisdiction concurrent with, or parallel to, that of the flag state to the extent of the latter's waiver. Exercising concurrent jurisdiction over a vessel is distinct from the jurisdictional paradigm in *Hape*, where the RCMP investigators were operating within the territory of another state and, hence, pursuant to its exclusive enforcement jurisdiction. The fact that both states would enjoy concurrent enforcement jurisdiction in the high seas context negates many of the *Hape* majority's concerns about Canada unlawfully exercising enforcement jurisdiction over a subject within the exclusive jurisdiction of another state. In particular, Canada's exercise of enforcement jurisdiction over a foreign-flagged vessel in such circumstances would not conflict with the sovereignty, independence, or exclusive jurisdiction of the flag state. Moreover, this exercise of enforcement jurisdiction would not be contrary to Canada's international legal obligations.

Third, the concurrent jurisdiction argument rests on Canada interdicting a foreign-flagged vessel with the consent of the latter's flag state. What if Canada's enforcement actions exceed the consent provided by the flag state, such as the arrest of a vessel pursuant to the *CFPA*'s deemed consent provision? Despite the fact that international law would not recognize Canada's enforcement jurisdiction over the vessel in such circumstances, the *Charter* would likely still

---

161 Guilfoyle, *supra* note 50 at 9; Caron, *supra* note 73 at 404. Jurisdiction is limited to actions for which the flag state has provided consent. The boarding state's concurrent jurisdiction, throughout a consensual interdiction, is over both its boarding agents and the vessel (*ibid* at 298-99).

apply.[162] Any non-flag state enforcement action against a vessel without the consent of the flag state is an unlawful interference with the vessel and, in the view of some, may even amount to an unlawful use of force.[163] Nonetheless, the majority in *Hape* recognized that extraterritorial actions by Canadian agents that violate Canada's international obligations, particularly its international human rights obligations, may attract a *Charter* remedy.[164] This was confirmed by the Court in *Khadr* in 2008 and in *Khadr* in 2010.[165] Thus, irrespective of whether the rule set out in *Hape* applies, *mutatis mutandis*, to high seas law enforcement, the *Charter* may apply to an interdiction by Canadian agents where the interdiction is contrary to Canada's international legal obligations, namely where it violates the exclusivity

---

[162] While Canada would not have enforcement jurisdiction over the vessel under international law, Canadian protection officers would be acting under the authority of the *CFPA*. It is a long-standing principle that Canada's Parliament can enact legislation that is inconsistent with international law. *Cheung Chi Cheung v The King*, [1939] AC 160 at 168; Currie, *supra* note 38 at 234.

[163] Reuland, *supra* note 48 at 1164; Guilfoyle, *supra* note 49 at 82; Guilfoyle, *supra* note 50 at 9. There is debate as to whether an unlawful interdiction amounts to a breach of Article 2(4) of the *Charter of the United Nations*, 26 June 1945, Can TS 1945 No 7 [*UN Charter*]. Guilfoyle notes that an unlawful interdiction is a use of force but does not comment on whether it is a use of armed force contrary to the *UN Charter*. Guilfoyle, *supra* note 49 at 82. In *Fisheries Jurisdiction (Spain v Canada)* before the International Court of Justice, Spain argued that Canada's interdiction of a Spanish fishing vessel on the high seas was a use of force contrary to Article 2(4) of the *UN Charter*. *Fisheries Jurisdiction (Spain v Canada)*, Jurisdiction of the Court, Judgment, [1998] ICJ Rep 432 at para 78 [*Fisheries Jurisdiction* case]. While the International Criminal Court (ICC) held that it did not have jurisdiction to decide on the legality of Canada's interdiction, it did, however, reject Spain's argument that Canada's interdiction was a use of force that gave rise to a separate claim under the *UN Charter* (at para 84). In the court's view, the interdiction fell within Canada's reservation pertaining to the enforcement of conservation measures and that "[b]oarding, inspection, arrest and minimum use of force for those purposes are all contained within the concept of enforcement of conservation and management measures according to a 'natural and reasonable' interpretation of this concept" (*ibid*). On the question of minimal use of force for law enforcement purposes, the arbitral tribunal in *Guyana v Suriname* held that such use of force must be unavoidable, reasonable, and necessary. *Suriname v Guyana*, Award of the Arbitral Tribunal, Permanent Court of Arbitration, 17 September 2007, at para 445. For a recent discussion of the debate over Article 2(4) of the *UN Charter* and the use of force against merchant vessels, see Andrew Murdoch, "Forcible Interdiction of Ships Transporting Terrorists" (2009) 48 Mil L & L War Rev 287 at 291-98.

[164] *Hape, supra* note 1 at paras 52, 101.

[165] *Khadr* 2008, *supra* note 27 at 18; *Khadr* 2010, *supra* note 27 at 14.

of the flag state's jurisdiction and involves the exercise of coercive police actions against a foreign-flagged vessel contrary to international law.

Fourth, as noted earlier, NAFO and ICCAT's respective boarding and inspection schemes provide that a boarding state maintains "operational control" over its boarding agents and is responsible for their actions throughout an interdiction.[166] The *NPAFC Convention* and the *Fish Stocks Agreement* do not include a similar provision, although Guilfoyle's argument that boarding agents are obliged to abide by the boarding state's police procedure may lead to the same result.[167] On the one hand, it may be argued that the provisions of the *NAFO* and *ICCAT Conventions* merely confirm that the boarding state is liable under international law for the actions of its boarding agents and that the flag state has no authority to direct non-flag state boarding agents. Further, it may be argued that confirming the boarding state's responsibility and control over its boarding agents does not deprive the flag state of its primary jurisdiction over the vessel and crew, including the right to arrest and prosecute them, nor does it provide the boarding state with the jurisdiction to ascribe rights to the vessel's crew that could affect the collection of evidence or prosecution of a crew member.[168]

On the other hand, it may be argued that these provisions provide the boarding state with the necessary consent for its boarding agents to follow the laws of the boarding state rather than the flag state throughout the interdiction. According to this view, the provisions explicitly provide Canada with enforcement jurisdiction over the vessel and crew and therefore negate the *Hape* majority's concerns, such as the practical difficulties in having the *Charter* guide conduct where Canada has no enforcement jurisdiction or having Canada exercise enforcement jurisdiction over subject matter that is under the exclusive jurisdiction of another state.[169] Moreover, in the circumstances of a consensual interdiction, it is likely that the boarding state would be the only state practically able to enforce its laws against the boarding agents. While the flag state would maintain

---

166 *NAFO CEM, supra* note 101, s 31 (2); ICCAT Commission, *supra* note 112, Annex 8, para 10.

167 Guilfoyle, *supra* note 50 at 298. The *Fish Stocks Agreement* does, however, provide that a boarding state is liable for losses attributable to its enforcement actions if those actions are unlawful or unreasonable: *Fish Stocks Agreement, supra* note 76, arts 21(18), 35.

168 Guilfoyle, *supra* note 50 at 297-98.

169 See *Hape, supra* note 1 at paras 62, 69, 89, 91.

jurisdiction over the vessel in principle, by virtue of the principles of state immunity and the boarding state's concurrent jurisdiction, only the boarding state would have both the practical capacity and legal authority to enforce its laws against the boarding agents.[170] In addition, in enforcing the *Charter* against Canadian boarding agents, any rights bestowed upon the crew would be with respect to Canada and not the flag state.

Fifth, and as mentioned earlier, vessels on the high seas are distinct from territory.[171] This distinction is evident in Canada's treatment of foreign-flagged vessels when compared with its treatment of other objects located outside Canada. For example, while Canada has long had domestic laws authorizing extraterritorial enforcement actions over foreign-flagged vessels and crew on the high seas,[172] it does not, in general, have laws authorizing extraterritorial enforcement actions against non-Canadians located within the borders of another state.[173] In light of the reality that jurisdiction over vessels is of a different nature than jurisdiction over territory, and given the importance of *Charter* values, it may be argued that the rule in *Hape* should be limited to foreign territory and not applied to high seas enforcement actions.

A separate issue is whether the *Charter*'s application to high seas interdictions would have any tangible impact on the treatment accorded to non-Canadian crew members aboard an interdicted vessel. It would, potentially, in the case of a non-Canadian crew member brought to Canada for prosecution under the *CFPA*, as he or she could ask a court for a *Charter* remedy. Such a prosecution would, however, be highly unusual. In the case of non-Canadian crew members who are not brought to Canada, it is unlikely that a *Charter* breach occurring during a high seas interdiction would be subject to judicial scrutiny. The challenges faced by a non-Canadian crew

---

[170] Guilfoyle, *supra* note 50 at 297-98.

[171] Brownlie, *supra* note 47 at 318.

[172] For example, *Croft v Dunphy*, a seminal case in which the Privy Council held that Canada's Parliament could enact laws with extraterritorial reach, was a case in which Canada had exercised enforcement jurisdiction over a foreign vessel outside its territorial sea. *Croft v Dunphy*, [1933] 1 DLR 225 (PC).

[173] See *Hape*, *supra* note 1 at para 66. There are a few exceptions where Canadian legislation does provide for the exercise of enforcement jurisdiction over non-Canadians located outside Canada's territory. For example, an alleged spy for the enemy may be prosecuted outside Canada by a military tribunal established under the *National Defence Act*. *National Defence Act*, RSC 1985, c N-5, ss 60(1)(h), 68.

member located outside Canada in obtaining a remedy in a Canadian court for a *Charter* breach occurring on the high seas would almost always outweigh any benefit the crew member might derive therefrom. Any evidence collected by Canadian inspectors would likely have been passed to the flag state pursuant to the relevant RFMO convention before the non-Canadian crew member could file an application for *Charter* relief in a Canadian court. Consequently, a remedy provided by a Canadian court for a *Charter* breach that occurred on the high seas is unlikely to provide a non-Canadian crew member located outside Canada with anything more than personal or moral vindication.

The fact that the circumstances pertaining to the policing of high seas fisheries make it unlikely that non-Canadians outside Canada will seek a judicial remedy for a *Charter* breach occurring on the high seas does not render the issue unimportant or irrelevant. Canadians expect that Canadian government agents will respect the *Charter*'s values regardless of their physical location or non-Canadian crew members' practical ability to seek a judicial remedy.[174] Moreover, the unlikelihood of a non-Canadian crew member asserting his or her *Charter* rights before a Canadian court does not mean that crew members of interdicted vessels should be deprived of the *Charter*'s protections or that Canadian protection officers are entitled to ignore their obligation to respect the *Charter*.

CONCLUSION

Canada is a party to several treaties pursuant to which it is authorized to board and inspect foreign-flagged vessels on the high seas. In implementing the rights and responsibilities prescribed in these treaties, the *CFPA* provides for the exercise of enforcement jurisdiction over foreign-flagged vessels in RFMO areas, including the boarding, inspection, and, in some cases, the prosecution of foreign-flagged vessels. Thus, if the *Charter* applies to such interdictions, it is foreseeable that *Charter* rights would be engaged, including those relating to life, liberty, and security of the person, freedom from unreasonable search and seizure, and freedom from arbitrary detention.

If the *Charter* does not apply to the actions of Canadian boarding agents when they interdict a foreign-flagged vessel, a situation would be created whereby the *Charter* does not apply to Canadian police actions prescribed by an act of Parliament. Such a state of affairs is,

174 Roach, *supra* note 32 at 4.

on its face, inconsistent with a plain reading of section 32(1) of the *Charter*. The preferred approach is that Canadian agents must abide by the *Charter* whenever they are engaged in high seas enforcement actions. Unlike the RCMP investigators in *Hape*, Canadian protection officers on the high seas will generally be acting alone and engaged in actions specifically authorized by Canadian legislation. In addition, to the extent that Canadian agents' enforcement actions comply with the consent provided under an RFMO convention or the *Fish Stocks Agreement*, Canada's enforcement actions would not interfere with the enforcement jurisdiction of the flag state because Canada would enjoy concurrent jurisdiction over the vessel. Moreover, Canadians expect that Canadian government agents will respect the *Charter*'s values, regardless of whether they are acting inside or outside Canada.[175] However, the question of whether or not the *Charter* applies on the high seas will remain uncertain until the issue is brought before the courts or until the Supreme Court of Canada reconsiders its *Hape* rule on the extraterritorial application of the *Charter*.

DREW TYLER
LL.B., LL.M., University of Ottawa

Sommaire

Faire voguer la Charte? *L'application de la* Charte canadienne des droits et libertés *au contrôle canadien des pêches en haute mer*

Selon le jugement majoritaire de la Cour suprême du Canada dans l'arrêt R c Hape, *la* Charte canadienne des droits et libertés *ne s'applique pas, en général, aux agents du gouvernement canadien lorsqu'ils agissent en territoire étranger. Ce commentaire s'interroge sur la question à savoir si cette règle devrait s'étendre aux interdictions en haute mer, par des agents canadiens, de navires battant pavillon étranger. Plus particulièrement, il examine l'application potentielle de la* Charte *au contrôle par le Canada des pêches en haute mer. Il conclut que les régimes juridiques régissant les pêches en haute mer sont suffisamment différents de ceux se rapportant au territoire étatique que la règle dans l'arrêt* Hape *ne devrait pas s'appliquer aux interdictions en haute mer, et que la* Charte *devrait donc s'appliquer aux activités de contrôle des pêches en haute mer par le Canada.*

---

175 *Ibid.*

Summary

Does the Charter Float? The Application of the *Canadian Charter of Rights and Freedoms* to Canada's Policing of High Seas Fisheries

The majority judgment of the Supreme Court of Canada in R v Hape *held that, in general, the* Canadian Charter of Rights and Freedoms *does not apply to Canadian government agents when they are acting in foreign state territory. This comment considers whether this rule should extend to high seas interdictions, by Canadian agents, of foreign-flagged vessels. In particular, it considers the potential application of the* Charter *to Canada's policing of high seas fisheries. It concludes that the legal regimes governing high seas fisheries are sufficiently distinct from those pertaining to state territory, that the rule in* Hape *should not apply to high seas interdictions, and that the* Charter *should therefore apply to Canada's high seas fisheries policing activities.*

The International Court of Justice's *Kosovo* Case: Assessing the Current State of International Legal Opinion on Remedial Secession

INTRODUCTION

Remedial secession is one of the most controversial legal issues that arises in the context of secessionist conflicts involving oppression and human rights abuses. Advocates of remedial secession argue that where a "people" is either denied internal self-determination or faced with massive human rights violations, that people has a right to secede from the repressive parent state as a last resort. Due to a lack of state practice and the apparent conflict of remedial secession with the principle of territorial integrity, the debate surrounding remedial secession was largely confined to academia throughout the 1990s and much of the 2000s.

However, remedial secession received renewed international legal and political attention in 2008 when the UN General Assembly (UNGA) voted to request an advisory opinion from the International Court of Justice (ICJ) on the legality of Kosovo's unilateral declaration of independence (UDI) from Serbia. The ICJ did not directly address the issue of remedial secession in its advisory opinion. Instead, it focused on answering the specific question posed to it by the UNGA — that is, whether Kosovo's UDI was legal. Nevertheless, this case and the formal discourse it generated are significant developments in the debate surrounding the status of remedial secession in international law. In particular, for the first time, eleven states formally indicated, in their country submissions, support for remedial secession, and two sitting ICJ judges, in separate opinions,

The views expressed are the author's alone and do not necessarily reflect the views of the government of Canada. *Accordance with International Law of the Unilateral Declaration of Independence in Respect of Kosovo*, Advisory Opinion, [2010] ICJ General List No 141 [*Kosovo* case].

apparently endorsed the concept. This comment will demonstrate that advocates of remedial secession may plausibly argue that these developments have strengthened the soft law status of remedial secession. However, the impact of such developments should not be overstated, as a number of contrary indicators were also in evidence.

I begin by focusing on the legal dimensions of remedial secession, briefly discussing its theoretical origins and status in international law prior to the UNGA's request for an advisory opinion in the case *Accordance with International Law of the Unilateral Declaration of Independence in Respect of Kosovo* (*Kosovo* case). I then describe the ICJ's advisory opinion before analyzing and categorizing the various positions that states took on remedial secession during the proceedings. Separate or dissenting opinions by members of the ICJ specifically addressing remedial secession are then noted. Finally, I conclude by analyzing the international legal implications of these developments in the *Kosovo* case.

REMEDIAL SECESSION: ORIGINS AND CURRENT INTERNATIONAL LEGAL STATUS

Remedial secession arises from the legal principle of self-determination, which, in turn, has been animated in international law by a number of sources, including two reports to the League of Nations regarding the Aaland Islands,[1] the *Charter of the United Nations* (*UN Charter*),[2] UNGA resolutions,[3] the *International Covenant on Civil and Political Rights*,[4] the *International Covenant on Economic*,

---

[1] *Report of the International Committee of Jurists Entrusted by the Council of the League of Nations with the Task of Giving an Advisory Opinion upon the Legal Aspects of the Aaland Islands Question* (1920) 3 League of Nations Official Journal, Special Supplement [1920 *Aaland Islands report*]; League of Nations, *The Aaland Islands Question: Report Submitted to the Council of the League of Nations by the Commission of Rapporteurs*, Doc. B7.21/68/106 (1921) [1921 *Aaland Islands* report].

[2] *Charter of the United Nations*, 26 June 1945, Can TS 1945 No 7, arts 1(2), 55. Self-determination is also implicated in arts 73 and 76.

[3] See especially *Declaration on the Granting of Independence to Colonial Countries and Peoples*, GA Res 1514(XV), UNGAOR, 15th Sess, Supp No 16, UN Doc A/L.323 and Add.1-6 (1960); *Declaration on Principles of International Law Concerning Friendly Relations and Co-operation among States in Accordance with the Charter of the United Nations*, GA Res 2625, UNGAOR, 25th Sess, Supp No 28, UN Doc A/8082 (1970) [*Declaration on Friendly Relations*].

[4] *International Covenant on Civil and Political Rights*, 16 December 1966, 999 UNTS 171, art 1, Can TS 1976 No 47, 6 ILM 368 (entered into force 23 March 1976).

Social and Cultural Rights,[5] the Helsinki *Final Act,*[6] the *Vienna Declaration and Programme of Action,*[7] and four ICJ cases.[8] While the parameters of self-determination have not been clearly defined,[9] the ICJ in *East Timor (Portugal v Australia) (East Timor* case) and in *Legal Consequences of the Construction of a Wall in the Occupied Palestinian Territory (Israeli Wall* case), in particular, has recognized that self-determination is vested with an *erga omnes* character.[10] Moreover, a consensus has emerged in these sources: self-determination has "external" implications, potentially leading to independence, in the context of (1) colonial domination or (2) alien subjugation, domination, and exploitation.[11]

Self-determination is frequently separated into "internal" or "external" self-determination.[12] Internal self-determination broadly refers to a people's right to non-discriminatory treatment by a

---

[5] *International Covenant on Economic, Social and Cultural Rights,* 16 December 1966, 993 UNTS 3, art 1, Can TS 1976 No 46, 6 ILM 360 (entered into force 3 January 1976).

[6] *Conference on Security and Co-operation in Europe: Final Act,* 1 August 1975, 14 ILM 1292 [Helsinki *Final Act*].

[7] *Vienna Declaration and Programme of Action,* UNGAOR, UN Doc A/CONF.157.24 (1993) [*Vienna Declaration and Programme of Action*], endorsed by the UN General Assembly (UNGA) in *World Conference on Human Rights,* GA Res 48/121, UNGAOR, 48th Sess, UN Doc A/RES/48/121 (1994).

[8] *Legal Consequences for States of the Continued Presence of South Africa in Namibia (South West Africa) Notwithstanding Security Resolution 276 (1970),* Advisory Opinion, [1971] ICJ Rep 16; *Western Sahara,* Advisory Opinion, [1975] ICJ Rep 12; *East Timor (Portugal v Australia),* [1995] ICJ Rep 90 [*East Timor* case]; *Legal Consequences of the Construction of a Wall in the Occupied Palestinian Territory,* Advisory Opinion, [2004] ICJ Rep 136 [*Israeli Wall* case].

[9] See Lee C Buchheit, *Secession: The Legitimacy of Self-Determination* (New Haven, CT: Yale University Press, 1978), for a strong overview of the historical development and ambiguities of self-determination. As Buchheit explains, "[a]s a descriptive phrase, the title 'Holy Roman Empire' was defective … inasmuch as it denoted an entity neither holy, nor Roman, nor an empire. As a legal term of art, 'the right of self-determination' fails in much the same fashion. The expression itself gives no clue to the nature of the self that is to be determined; nor does it provide any enlightenment concerning the process of determination or the source and extent of the self's putative right to this process" (at 8-9).

[10] See *East Timor* case, *supra* note 8 at para 29; *Israeli Wall* case, *supra* note 8 at para 88.

[11] See especially *Declaration on Friendly Relations, supra* note 3.

[12] The first international institutional use of the terminology of "internal" and "external" self-determination can be found in the *Special Report of the United Nations Commission for Indonesia,* 4 UN SCOR, Spec Supp 6, UN Doc S/1417 (1949).

central government. Beyond ensuring equal treatment, internal self-determination entails that "each people should be given the opportunity to participate in the decision-making process of the state, in particular on the constitution and amendments thereto."[13] In other words, internal self-determination affirms "the right of all groups in a state to influence governmental behaviour in accordance with constitutional processes."[14] Internal self-determination may be ensured through, among other policies, the promotion of popular participation in public affairs, which includes full respect for human rights, the prevention of discrimination, and the granting of special protections to groups that may otherwise be excluded from genuine participation.[15] In contrast, external self-determination refers to a people's achievement of independent statehood, integration into another state, free association with another state, or any other sovereign status freely chosen by the people in question.[16]

Largely in response to the wave of ethnic conflicts that affected a number of states in the early to mid-1990s, a number of academic commentators sought to develop the external element of self-determination such that it would apply beyond the two broadly accepted situations of colonial domination and alien subjugation, domination, and exploitation. Dubbed "the right to secede" or "remedial secession," some academics characterized this third category of external self-determination as a last-resort remedy, entailing a right to secede that would be applicable in situations involving denial of internal self-determination or massive human rights abuses.[17]

---

[13] Jan Klabbers and Rene Lefeber, "Africa: Lost between Self-Determination and *Uti Possidetis*," in Catherine Brölmann, René Lefeber, and Marjoleine Zieck, eds, *Peoples and Minorities in International Law* (Dordrecht: Martinus Nijhoff Publishers, 1993) 37 at 43.

[14] Buchheit, *supra* note 9 at 16.

[15] Hurst Hannum, *Autonomy, Sovereignty, and Self-Determination: The Accommodation of Conflicting Rights*, revised edition (Philadelphia: University of Pennsylvania Press, 1996) at 113-14.

[16] Klabbers and Lefeber, *supra* note 13 at 42-43.

[17] See, eg, Allen Buchanan, "Self-Determination and the Right to Secede" (1992) 45:2 J Int'l Affairs 347 at 354; Umozurike Oji Umozurike, *Self-Determination in International Law* (Hamden, CT: Archon Books, 1972) at 199; Klabbers and Lefeber, *supra* note 13 at 48; Christian Tomuschat, "Secession and Self-Determination," in Marcelo G Kohen, ed, *Secession: International Law Perspectives* (Cambridge: Cambridge University Press, 2006) 23 at 42; Markku Suski, "Keeping the Lid on the Secession Kettle: A Review of Legal Interpretations Concerning Claims of Self-Determination by Minority Populations" (2005) 12 Int'l J Minority & Group Rights 189 at 225.

Advocates of remedial secession have frequently emphasized several key international legal documents to support their position. First, much attention has been devoted to the 1920 and 1921 Aaland Islands reports, in which a Commission of Jurists and subsequently a Commission of Rapporteurs appointed by the League of Nations "reported" on a dispute between Finland and Sweden regarding sovereignty over the Aaland Islands.[18] While the Commission of Jurists concluded in its report that positive international law did not recognize a right to national self-determination,[19] the Commission of Rapporteurs found in its subsequent report that secession may be available as a "last resort when the State lacks either the will or the power to enact and apply just and effective guarantees" of minority rights.[20] Advocates of remedial secession also cite the 1970 *Declaration on Principles of International Law Concerning Friendly Relations and Co-operation among States in Accordance with the Charter of the United Nations* (*Declaration on Friendly Relations*) to support their position. It states:

[A]ll peoples have the right freely to determine, without external interference, their political status ... Nothing in the foregoing paragraphs shall be construed as authorizing or encouraging any action which would dismember or impair, totally or in part, the territorial integrity or political unity of sovereign and independent *States conducting themselves in compliance with the principles of equal rights and self-determination as described above and thus possessed of a government representing the whole people belonging to the territory without distinction as to race, creed or colour.*[21]

18 1920 *Aaland Islands* report, *supra* note 1; 1921 *Aaland Islands* report, *supra* note 1.

19 The initial report concluded: "Positive International Law does not recognize the right of national groups, as such, to separate themselves from the State of which they form part by the simple expression of a wish, any more than it recognizes the right of other States to claim such a separation. Generally speaking, the grant or refusal of the right to a portion of its population of determining its own political fate by plebiscite or by some other method, is, exclusively, an attribute of the sovereignty of every State which is definitively constituted." See 1920 *Aaland Islands* report, *supra* note 1 at 5.

20 1921 *Aaland Islands* report, *supra* note 1 at 27-28.

21 *Declaration on Friendly Relations*, *supra* note 3 [emphasis added]. It should be further noted that the 1993 *Vienna Declaration and Programme of Action* from the World Conference on Human Rights essentially quotes the *Declaration on Friendly Relations* verbatim, though it replaces the phrase "without distinction as to race, creed or colour" with the phrase "without distinction of any kind." See *Vienna Declaration and Programme of Action*, *supra* note 7.

Commonly referred to as the "safeguard clause," this provision has been interpreted as authority for the proposition that territorial integrity is not assured where states do not comply with the principles of equal rights and self-determination.[22]

The issue of remedial secession has also been addressed in domestic legal settings. In perhaps the most cited example, the Supreme Court of Canada considered the issue of remedial secession in the 1998 *Reference re Secession of Quebec,* defining the concept as follows: "[W]hen a people is blocked from the meaningful exercise of its right to self-determination internally, it is entitled, as a last resort, to exercise it by secession."[23] However, the Court emphasized that "it remains unclear whether this ... proposition actually reflects an established international law standard,"[24] thereby explicitly leaving the issue of remedial secession unresolved.[25]

While a number of commentators have argued in favour of remedial secession, many (including several advocates of the concept) have acknowledged that remedial secession is not established in international law.[26] For example, following an exhaustive survey of state practice and international law pertaining to secession, James Crawford reached the following conclusion in 2006:

Since 1945 the international community has been extremely reluctant to accept unilateral secession of parts of independent states if the secession is opposed by the government of that state. In such cases the principle of territorial integrity has been a significant limitation. Since 1945 no state which has been created by unilateral secession has been admitted to the United Nations against the declared wishes of the predecessor state.[27]

---

[22] This interpretation was common to a number of states that took positions that were favourable to remedial secession in their submissions in the *Kosovo* case, first unnumbered footnote.

[23] *Reference re Secession of Quebec,* [1998], 2 SCR 217 at para 134, 161 DLR (4th) 385.

[24] *Ibid* at 135.

[25] It should be noted that the Supreme Court of Canada left this as an open question by neither confirming nor rejecting the existence of such a doctrine in international law. It then showed that its putative requirements were not met in any event in Quebec's case.

[26] See, eg, note 17 in this article.

[27] James Crawford, *The Creation of States in International Law,* 2nd edition (Oxford: Clarendon Press, 2006) at 390. Compare Antonio Cassese, *Self-Determination of Peoples: A Legal Reappraisal* (Cambridge: Cambridge University Press, 1995) at 122, 339. See also James Crawford, "State Practice and International Law in

One of the few areas of general consensus regarding self-determination is that secession in and of itself is "neither legal nor illegal in international law, but a legally neutral act the consequences of which are regulated internationally."[28]

THE ICJ AND THE *KOSOVO* CASE

The international debate over remedial secession was renewed with Kosovo's UDI from its parent state, Serbia, on 17 February 2008. In response, in October 2008, the UNGA adopted a resolution posing the following question to the ICJ for its advisory opinion: "Is the unilateral declaration of independence by the Provisional Institutions of Self-Government of Kosovo in accordance with international law?"[29] While, as noted earlier, the ICJ's majority opinion did not directly address the issue of remedial secession (preferring instead to answer very precisely the specific question posed by the UNGA), the *Kosovo* case remains a significant legal landmark in the development of remedial secession. This significance is twofold. First, thirty-six states prepared country submissions to the ICJ for this case, many of which contain explicit statements and detailed explanations of their views on the status and application of remedial secession in international law. Second, three sitting ICJ judges explicitly stated their views on remedial secession in separate and dissenting opinions. The country submissions, in particular, present a unique opportunity to gauge current international legal opinion among states on remedial secession, with potential implications for general or regional customary international law on the issue.

THE ICJ'S ADVISORY OPINION

In its majority opinion, the ICJ addressed the issue of remedial secession in the following terms:

Relation to Secession" (1999) 90 Br YB Int'l L 69 at 114, who states: "State practice since 1945 shows the extreme reluctance of states to recognise unilateral secession outside of the colonial context. That practice has not changed since 1989, despite the emergence during that period of twenty-three new states. On the contrary, the practice has been powerfully reinforced."

28 Crawford, *The Creation of States, supra* note 27 at 390. See also Cassese, *supra* note 27 at 340; Anne F Bayefsky, ed, *Self-Determination in International Law: Quebec and Lessons Learned* (The Hague: Kluwer Law International, 2000) at 241.

29 *Request for an Advisory Opinion on the International Court of Justice on Whether the Unilateral Declaration of Independence of Kosovo Is in Accordance with International Law,* GA Res 63/3, UNGA, 63rd Sess, UN Doc A/Res/63/3 (2008).

A number of participants in the present proceedings have claimed, although in almost every instance only as a secondary argument, that the population of Kosovo has the right to create an independent State either as a manifestation of a right to self-determination or pursuant to what they described as a right of "remedial secession" in the face of the situation in Kosovo.[30]

The ICJ went on to note:

[R]adically different views were expressed by those taking part in the proceedings and expressing a position on the question ... The Court considers that it is not necessary to resolve these questions in the present case. The General Assembly has requested the Court's opinion only on whether or not the declaration of independence is in accordance with international law. Debates regarding the extent of the right of self-determination and the existence of any right of "remedial secession," however, concern the right to separate from a State ... [T]hat issue is beyond the scope of the question posed by the General Assembly.[31]

The case, then, ultimately turned on the majority's holding that there is no general prohibition on UDIs in international law and that Kosovo's UDI was not in violation of UN Security Council Resolution 1244 (1999) or Kosovo's constitutional framework. The UDI was therefore found not to violate any applicable rule of international law.[32]

Several commentators have criticized the ICJ's handling of remedial secession in this way. Thomas Burri, for example, has argued that "one cannot credibly avoid dealing with the legality of secession, when asked to assess the legality of a declaration of independence in the circumstances of this case. It is, in my view, artificial to separate secession and the declaration of independence in the given case."[33] Others have concluded that the advisory opinion had little

---

[30] *Kosovo* case, *supra* first unnumbered note at para 82.

[31] *Ibid* at paras 82-83.

[32] *Ibid* at para 122.

[33] Thomas Burri, "The Kosovo Opinion and Secession: The Sounds of Silence and Missing Links" (2010) 11:8 German LJ 881 at 886 [footnotes omitted]. Compare Björn Arp, "The ICJ Advisory Opinion on the *Accordance with International Law of the Unilateral Declaration of Independence in Respect of Kosovo* and the International Protection of Minorities" (2010) 11:8 German LJ 847 at 847: "[T]he present Advisory Opinion might not enter into the judicial history of the Court for its answer to this question, but rather for what it did not say."

substantive impact on remedial secession. For example, Christian Pippan has opined that remedial secession "was effectively taken off the radar of the Court in the present case."[34] Hurst Hannum has argued that, "given the majority's conservative approach, the Advisory Opinion will have minimal legal significance either for the status of Kosovo or for our understanding of state formation and self-determination in the twenty-first century."[35]

COUNTRY SUBMISSIONS IN THE *KOSOVO* CASE

While much commentary has been published regarding the majority's advisory opinion, little substantive analysis has yet been conducted on the thirty-six country submissions that were tendered to the ICJ by various states. Yet, as suggested earlier, these statements are among the most legally interesting elements of the case. For ease of discussion, the thirty-six country submissions can be broken down into four general categories with regard to their stated positions on remedial secession: (1) states that regard remedial secession as established in international law, applicable in various circumstances (eleven states); (2) states that view Kosovo as a *sui generis* case while adopting different postures on remedial secession in international law more generally (six states); (3) states that either remain neutral or express ambiguous views on remedial secession (five states); and (4) states that are hostile to remedial secession as established in international law in varying degrees (fourteen states).[36] Figure 1 shows which states are associated with each of these categories, and it summarizes the nuances in country positions within each category, as described more fully in the following subsections.

Category 1: States That Regard Remedial Secession as Established in International Law, Applicable in Various Circumstances

The submissions of Albania, Estonia, Finland, Germany, Ireland, the Netherlands, Norway, Poland, Russia, Slovenia, and Switzerland

---

34 Christian Pippan, "The International Court of Justice's Advisory Opinion on Kosovo's Declaration of Independence: An Exercise in the Art of Silence" (2010) 3 Eur J Minority Issues 145 at 151-52.

35 Hurst Hannum, "The Advisory Opinion on Kosovo: An Opportunity Lost, or a Poisoned Chalice Refused?" (2011) 24:1 Leiden J Int'l L 155 at 159.

36 It should be noted that Kosovo also argued in favour of remedial secession as international law, but its status as a state is yet to be determined.

Figure 1

Country positions on remedial secession expressed in the *Kosovo* case

Category 1: States that regard remedial secession as established international law, applicable in various circumstances

1.1: A right to secede arises where a people is subjected to severe and long-standing refusal of internal self-determination and other possible ways to resolve the situation have been exhausted: *Albania, Estonia, Finland, Germany, Netherlands, Switzerland.*

1.2: A right to secede arises as a last resort where a people is subjected to gross and fundamental human rights abuses that involve discrimination: *Ireland, Poland, (Kosovo).*

1.3: A right to secede arises as a last resort where a people is subjected to truly extreme circumstances, such as an outright armed attack by the parent state that threatens the very existence of the people in question: *Russia, Norway.*

1.4: The right to self-determination is paramount. States must "earn" the protection of their territorial integrity: *Slovenia.*

Category 2: States that view Kosovo as a sui generis *case while adopting different postures on remedial secession in international law more generally*

2.1: Kosovo is a *sui generis* case, although declarations of independence may fulfil the right to self-determination: *Latvia.*

2.2: Kosovo is a *sui generis* case; remedial secession and self-determination are not mentioned: *Luxembourg, the Maldives.*

2.3: Kosovo is a *sui generis* case; some indications of hostility towards a general doctrine of remedial secession or emphasis that the Kosovo situation has no precedent value: *France, Japan, United Kingdom.*

Category 3: States that either remain neutral or express ambiguous views on remedial secession

3.1: The question before the court can be answered without addressing the contours of international law regarding self-determination: *Austria, Czech Republic, Sierra Leone, United States.*

3.2: There is no general prohibition in international law against declarations of independence; denial of internal self-determination is "not irrelevant" to such situations: *Denmark.*

▶

Category 4: States that are hostile to remedial secession as established international law in varying degrees

4.1: Remedial secession not explicitly addressed, but respect for the sovereignty and territorial integrity of states is emphasized as paramount: *Brazil, Libya, Venezuela.*

4.2: Remedial secession explicitly dismissed as not established in international law: *Argentina, Azerbaijan, Bolivia, China, Cyprus, Egypt, Iran, Romania, Serbia, Slovakia, Spain.*

---

fall into this category and can be broken down into four subcategories. Each will be considered in the following sections.

Category 1.1: A Right to Secede Arises Where a People Is Subjected to Severe and Long-Standing Refusal of Internal Self-Determination, and Other Possible Ways to Resolve the Situation Have Been Exhausted

In its submission to the ICJ, **Albania** argued that "the Supreme Court of Canada clearly recognized the right of a people to secede unilaterally when denied the right to exert their right to self-determination as in the case of Kosovo."[37] Albania concluded that "in a situation such as the one in Kosovo, where a system of officially sanctioned discrimination and unequal treatment was put into place and maintained through force and suppression of fundamental

---

[37] *Kosovo* case, *supra* first unnumbered note, "Written Statement of Albania" (14 April 2009), online: International Court of Justice (ICJ) <http://www.icj-cij.org/docket/files/141/15618.pdf> at 44. Albania emphasized that Kosovars were unable to achieve internal self-determination and that independence was a last resort following protracted internationally supervised negotiations that failed (*ibid* at 40, 44-48). It should be noted that Albania's interpretation of the Supreme Court of Canada's decision is incorrect. The Court left the existence of remedial secession under international law as an open question, and the Court went on to show that even if it were to exist it would not apply to Quebec in any event (see notes 23-25 in this comment). While the Albanian statement to the ICJ first maintained that the ICJ should exercise its discretion to decline giving the advisory opinion, Albania's primary substantive argument as to whether Kosovo's declaration of independence was in accordance with international law was grounded in the principle of self-determination.

human rights there is no unconditional claim to the maintenance of the *status quo*, territorial or otherwise."[38]

Estonia argued that "self-determination may exceptionally legitimise secession ... if the secession is the only remedy against a prolonged and rigorous refusal of internal self-determination ... whereby there exists no other possibility to solve the situation and the secession would be the only possibility to maintain or restore international peace, security and stability."[39] Estonia concluded that "Kosovo was, according to international law, entitled to use the right to external self-determination and justified to make a Declaration of Independence."[40]

Finland opened by arguing that self-determination is not limited to the "special case" of decolonization and examined the underlying rationale of self-determination in a modern context.[41] This analysis led it to argue that decolonization is not a prerequisite to the right to self-determination. Rather, the prerequisite to self-determination is an "abnormal" situation.[42] More specifically, Finland submitted that "[t]he rationale invoked in [self-determination] cases points to a distinction between normal situations and those of abnormality, or rupture, situations of revolution, war, alien subjugation, or the absence of a meaningful prospect for a functioning internal self-determination regime."[43] Finland argued that Kosovo's situation was "abnormal" in this sense because Kosovars were denied meaningful internal self-determination.[44] Therefore, "the only realistic

---

[38] *Kosovo* case, *supra* first unnumbered note, "Written Comments of Albania" (July 2009), online: ICJ <http://www.icj-cij.org/docket/files/141/15694.pdf> at 34. See also at 32, n 72, where Albania cites the criteria for remedial secession as noted earlier.

[39] *Kosovo* case, *supra* first unnumbered note, "Written Statement of Estonia" (13 April 2009), online: ICJ <http://www.icj-cij.org/docket/files/141/15648.pdf> at 5-6 ["Written Statement of Estonia"]. Estonia further noted that severe and long-standing refusal of internal self-determination is often accompanied by brutal violations of human rights, genocide, or ethnic cleansing and that other possible ways to resolve the situation must be exhausted (*ibid* at 6, 9).

[40] *Ibid* at 12. It should be noted that the Estonian statement primarily relied on remedial secession to justify its position. It would be inaccurate to characterize remedial secession as a secondary argument.

[41] *Kosovo* case, *supra* first unnumbered note, "Written Statement of Finland" (16 April 2009), online: ICJ <http://www.icj-cij.org/docket/files/141/15630.pdf> at 4 ["Written Statement of Finland"].

[42] *Ibid.*

[43] *Ibid.*

[44] *Ibid* at 5-7.

solution was to realize the right [to self-determination] by independent statehood."[45]

Germany opened by arguing that limiting the right to self-determination to the colonial context would "render the internal right of self-determination meaningless in practice. There would be no remedy for a group which is not granted the self-determination that may be due to it under international law."[46] Germany argued that, in exceptional circumstances, a right to remedial secession arises under two conditions. The first condition requires "an exceptionally severe and long-standing refusal of internal self-determination by the State in which a group is living."[47] The second condition requires "that no other avenue exists for resolving the resulting conflict."[48] Germany further noted that if the situation were to change or the repression were to cease, "whether or not such changes make the right to external self-determination disappear must be judged on the merits of each case, taking into account the severity of the situation prior to those changes."[49]

In perhaps the most technical and cogent argument in favour of remedial secession, the **Netherlands** submitted:

[T]he exercise of the right to external self-determination is subject to the fulfilment of substantive and procedural conditions that apply cumulatively. Such a right only arises in the event of a "serious breach" of (a) the obligation to respect and promote the right of self-determination, or (b) the

---

45 *Ibid* at 12. It should be noted that the Finnish statement to the court is different, in its general legal approach to remedial secession from most other statements that supported remedial secession. Its emphasis on "normal" and "abnormal" situations incorporates a more critical legal perspective on international law. Additionally, the Finnish statement focused on self-determination as the primary basis of its argument. It would be inaccurate to characterize the argument as secondary or alternative in nature.

46 *Kosovo* case, *supra* first unnumbered note, "Written Statement of Germany" (15 April 2009), online: ICJ <http://www.icj-cij.org/docket/files/141/15624.pdf> at 33-34 ["Written Statement of Germany"]. It should be noted that the first or primary German argument was that there is no general prohibition on declarations of independence in international law. Arguments about remedial secession appear to have been secondary in nature.

47 *Ibid* at 35. Germany further noted that this condition "will often coincide with severe violations of human rights, such as the right to life and freedom, but also the rights of association and assembly."

48 *Ibid.*

49 *Ibid* at 36.

obligation to refrain from any forcible action which deprives peoples of this right (substantive condition).[50]

The Netherlands argued that this obligation is breached when fundamental human rights are denied or the government does not represent all of the people belonging to its territory.[51] Before exercising the right to secession, "all effective remedies must have been exhausted to achieve a settlement (procedural condition)."[52]

Switzerland opened by arguing that the principle of territorial integrity is not protected to an unlimited extent. It contended that "a people may by way of exception exercise the right to external self-determination if the State systematically and gravely violates the right to internal self-determination on the basis of distinctive group traits."[53] Switzerland submitted that if a people were unable to exercise the right to external self-determination in such circumstances, self-determination would lose its intrinsic function.[54]

Category 1.2: A Right to Secede Arises as a Last Resort Where a People Is Subjected to Gross and Fundamental Human Rights Abuses That Involve Discrimination

Ireland opened its statement by noting that international law contains neither a general right to, nor a general prohibition of, UDIs or secession.[55] It then argued that a "right [to secession] may arise, as

---

50 *Kosovo* case, *supra* first unnumbered note, "Written Statement of the Netherlands" (17 April 2009), online: ICJ <http://www.icj-cij.org/docket/files/141/15652.pdf> at 9 ["Written Statement of Netherlands"]. It should be noted that the Netherlands placed primary emphasis on the absence of a prohibition of a declaration of independence in UN Security Council Resolution 1244. Remedial secession was addressed as one of several related arguments.

51 *Ibid.*

52 *Ibid.*

53 *Kosovo* case, *supra* first unnumbered note, "Written Statement of Switzerland" (25 May 2009), online: ICJ <http://www.icj-cij.org/docket/files/141/15614.pdf> at 17 ["Written Statement of Switzerland"].

54 *Ibid.* It should be noted that Switzerland first substantively focused on UN Security Council Resolution 1244 and its implementation. However, the balance of its submission on whether the declaration of independence was "in accordance with international law" primarily involved articulating a balance between self-determination and territorial integrity. Remedial secession was included in this discussion.

55 *Kosovo* case, *supra* first unnumbered note, "Written Statement of Ireland" (17 April 2009), online: ICJ <http://www.icj-cij.org/docket/files/141/15662.pdf?

a last resort, only in the case of gross and fundamental human rights abuses and, further, where an element of discrimination is involved (that is, where the central authorities exclude a defined group from the meaningful exercise of internal self-determination)."[56] Ireland concluded that Kosovo's UDI represented an exercise of self-determination in the context of gross and fundamental human rights abuses.[57]

Poland argued in favour of remedial secession in cases where "a state gravely violates international human rights and humanitarian law against peoples inhabiting its territory. Those violations may include, *inter alia*, genocide, crimes against humanity, war crimes and other massive violations of human rights and humanitarian law."[58] Poland argued that remedial secession arises only as a last resort and that Kosovo, having met the earlier criteria, was entitled to secede.[59]

Kosovo's submission consistently maintained that there was no need to consider self-determination in reaching a conclusion to the case, although it argued in favour of remedial secession in the alternative.[60] In doing so, Kosovo first invoked the 1970 *Declaration on Friendly Relations*, arguing that this text denies the right of states

---

PHPSESSID=c794ab64a6f225f0371804bbb07cd24a> at 5 ["Written Statement of Ireland"].

56 *Ibid* at 10.

57 *Ibid* at 12. It should be noted that Ireland's primary argument was that Kosovo's declaration of independence was not unlawful as international law does not prohibit unilateral declarations of independence. Ireland's arguments about remedial secession were expressly made as "further" or "alternative" arguments.

58 *Kosovo* case, *supra* first unnumbered note, "Written Statement of Poland" (15 April 2009), online: ICJ <http://www.icj-cij.org/docket/files/141/15632.pdf> at 25 ["Written Statement of Poland"].

59 *Ibid* at 26. It should be noted that Poland's statement first highlighted the *sui generis* nature of Kosovo's situation and went on to refer to self-determination and remedial secession as the primary substantive basis for its argument that Kosovo's declaration of independence was in accordance with international law.

60 *Kosovo* case, *supra* first unnumbered note, "Written Contribution of the Authors of the Unilateral Declaration of Independence" (17 April 2009), online: ICJ <http://www.icj-cij.org/docket/files/141/15678.pdf> at 157; *Kosovo* case, *supra* first unnumbered note, "Written Contribution of the Authors of the Unilateral Declaration of Independence Regarding the Written Statements" (17 July 2009), online: ICJ <http://www.icj-cij.org/docket/files/141/15708.pdf> at 75-82 ["Written Contribution of the Authors"].

to invoke sovereignty against a people deprived of its right of self-determination.[61] Kosovo then argued that "given the decade of deliberate exclusion from governing institutions and the violation of basic human rights, culminating, in 1998-99, in massive crimes against humanity and war crimes, the people of Kosovo had the right to choose independence" once it was clear that there was no alternative.[62]

Category 1.3: A Right to Secede Arises as a Last Resort Where a People Is Subjected to Truly Extreme Circumstances, Such As an Outright Armed Attack by the Parent State That Threatens the Very Existence of the People in Question

Russia was the main advocate of this formulation of remedial secession. It submitted that the 1970 *Declaration on Friendly Relations* "may be construed as authorizing secession under certain conditions. However, these conditions should be limited to truly extreme circumstances, such as an outright armed attack by the parent State, threatening the very existence of the people in question."[63] However, Russia went on effectively to nullify any value such a conception of remedial secession may have, by contradictorily requiring that it be invoked both contemporaneously with the extreme circumstances and also, only, as a last resort.[64] Russia concluded that Kosovo was not entitled to secede because its people were not under an extreme threat on 17 February 2008 when Kosovo declared independence.[65] As noted by both Germany and Switzerland, these requirements effectively meant that remedial secession would almost never be available to a secessionist entity because by the time secession became

---

[61] "Written Contribution of the Authors," *supra* note 60 at 79.

[62] *Ibid* at 80 [footnotes omitted]; see also at 86. It should be noted that Kosovo definitively used arguments about remedial secession as secondary or alternative arguments. Its primary argument was that the declaration of independence did not contravene any applicable rule of general international law.

[63] *Kosovo* case, *supra* first unnumbered note, "Written Statement of the Russian Federation" (16 April 2009), online: ICJ <http://www.icj-cij.org/docket/files/141/15628.pdf> at 31-32 ["Written Statement of Russia"]. It should be noted that the Russian Federation first focused on UN Security Council Resolution 1244. Its main argument about general international law revolved around reconciliation of territorial integrity, self-determination, and secession.

[64] *Ibid* at 31, 36-37.

[65] *Ibid* at 37.

a last resort, the atrocities would likely have ceased as they had in Kosovo.[66]

The position of **Norway** is somewhat difficult to categorize definitively, as Norway's initial statement offered no insight into its position on remedial secession. Nevertheless, Norway's subsequent comments on other states' submissions indicated that Norway "shares the extremely restrictive view expressed in many written statements submitted to the Court with regard to the existence of any right of secession under international law."[67] It also noted in a footnote that "this view is notably confirmed in the written statement by the Russian Federation, 16 April 2009, pp. 31-32, paragraphs 87-88."[68] The specific paragraphs of the Russian statement to which Norway referred in its footnote discuss an "outright armed attack by the parent State, threatening the very existence of the people in question."[69] However, Norway did not cite the subsequent Russian paragraphs that would severely limit the temporal availability of remedial secession.

Category 1.4: The Right to Self-Determination Is Paramount — States Must "Earn" the Protection of Their Territorial Integrity

Slovenia's statement and commentary were arguably the most strident position against territorial integrity and, by extension, in favour of remedial secession. Slovenia opened by stating: "The preservation of territorial integrity of states is often a reason for gross violations of human rights and the rights of minorities or small nations. It is even an excuse and the cause for war and hotbeds of crisis."[70]

---

66 *Kosovo* case, *supra* first unnumbered note, "Written Comments of Switzerland" (17 July 2009), online: ICJ <http://www.icj-cij.org/docket/files/141/15698.pdf> at 2 ["Written Comments of Switzerland"]; "Written Statement of Germany," *supra* note 46 at 36. Germany, for example, argued that "it would be both illogical and unjust to hold the time needed for these attempts against the group by holding that this lapse of time made the right of external self-determination disappear before it could even be used."

67 *Kosovo* case, *supra* first unnumbered note, "Written Comments of Norway" (6 July 2009), online: ICJ <http://www.icj-cij.org/docket/files/141/15682.pdf?PHPSESSID=boc86f1bbe1daofb1202f4e28d76b604> at 2 ["Written Comments of Norway"].

68 *Ibid.*

69 "Written Statement of Russia," *supra* note 63 at para 88.

70 *Kosovo* case, *supra* first unnumbered note, "Written Statement of Slovenia" (17 April 2009), online: ICJ <http://www.icj-cij.org/docket/files/141/15654.pdf?

Slovenia then reviewed the development of self-determination after the Cold War, arguing that "when the 'right of a state' to protect its territorial integrity and the 'right of people' to decide upon their own destiny are in conflict, the right of people prevails."[71] Therefore, Slovenia argued, "even a state, in particular an ethnically complex state, must 'earn' the protection of its territorial integrity. If a state does not respect the right to self-determination and its government does not enjoy representativity or if the [latter] is lost, it cannot count on having its territorial integrity assured."[72]

Category 2: States That View Kosovo as a Sui Generis *Case While Adopting Different Postures on Remedial Secession in International Law More Generally*

In their submissions to the ICJ, France, Japan, Latvia, Luxembourg, the Maldives, and the United Kingdom all argued that the case of Kosovo was fact-specific and, therefore, a *sui generis* case. However, their approaches to the general issue of remedial secession varied. These differing approaches can be grouped into three subcategories, described in the following sections.

Category 2.1: Kosovo Is a *Sui Generis* Case, although Declarations of Independence May Fulfil the Right to Self-Determination

In its very brief submission, **Latvia** argued that Kosovo was a *sui generis* case due to: (1) the breaches of human rights and war crimes that had occurred there; (2) the international administration of Kosovo; (3) the absence of a prohibition of a UDI in UN Security Council Resolution 1244; and (4) the exhaustion of other remedies.[73]

PHPSESSID=boc86f1bbe1daofb1202f4e28d76b604> at 2 ["Written Statement of Slovenia"]. It should be noted that Slovenia's primary stated bases for supporting Kosovo's declaration of independence were its belief that the unilateral declaration of independence (UDI) was in conformity with international law and its respect for the right to self-determination.

71   *Ibid.* Slovenia also stated: "[I]n recent decades, the right to self-determination as a human right has been given precedence over the principle of respect for the territorial integrity of states" (*ibid*).

72   *Kosovo* case, *supra* first unnumbered note, "Written Comments of Slovenia" (17 July 2009), online: ICJ <http://www.icj-cij.org/docket/files/141/15696.pdf> at 6-7.

73   *Kosovo* case, *supra* first unnumbered note, "Written Statement of Latvia" (17 April 2009), online: ICJ <http://www.icj-cij.org/docket/files/141/15656.pdf> at 1-2.

Latvia also somewhat ambiguously noted that "no rule of international law prohibits issuing of a declaration of independence as an outcome of the fulfilment of the right of self-determination," but it did not elaborate on this point.[74]

Category 2.2: Kosovo is a *Sui Generis* Case — Remedial Secession and Self-Determination Are Not Mentioned

Luxembourg argued that Kosovo was a *sui generis* case due to: (1) the violent breakup of Yugoslavia; (2) the crimes against humanity, repression of Kosovars, ethnic cleansing, and massacres that had occurred; (3) the international administration of Kosovo; and (4) the existing processes for determining Kosovo's status under UN auspices.[75] It did not refer to either self-determination or remedial secession.

The **Maldives** also recognized Kosovo as a *sui generis* case due to: (1) the history of ethnic cleansing and human rights violations that had occurred there; (2) the breakdown of its negotiations; (3) the political evolution of Kosovo; (4) the right to national self-determination entrenched in the *UN Charter*; and (5) the fulfilment of the criteria for statehood under international law.[76] The Maldives also submitted that the UDI was a last resort and provided the best prospects for regional peace and stability.[77] Again, it did not make submissions regarding the content of either of the doctrines of self-determination or remedial secession.

Category 2.3: Kosovo Is a *Sui Generis* Case — Some Indications of Hostility towards a General Doctrine of Remedial Secession or Emphasis That the Kosovo Situation Has No Precedent Value

France opened by noting that "the right of peoples to self-determination does not create a right to accede to independence outside colonial situations, but nor does the principle of territorial integrity stand in the way of the access to independence of

---

[74] *Ibid* at 1.

[75] *Kosovo* case, *supra* first unnumbered note, "Written Statement of Luxembourg (translation by the Registry)" (30 March 2009), online: ICJ <http://www.icj-cij.org/docket/files/141/15634.pdf> at 1-2.

[76] *Kosovo* case, *supra* first unnumbered note, "Written Statement of Maldives" (15 April 2009), online: ICJ <http://www.icj-cij.org/docket/files/141/15670.pdf> at 1.

[77] *Ibid.*

non-colonial peoples."[78] Notwithstanding this assertion, France argued that Kosovo was a *sui generis* case on the grounds that: (1) Kosovo had had a separate and distinct status from Serbia since 1999; (2) independence was a last resort; (3) Kosovo had committed to democracy, human rights, and the rule of law; and (4) international actors continued to support Kosovo.[79] Regarding precedent, France concluded that "these different factors very clearly preclude the case of Kosovo from establishing a precedent able to be cited in other situations."[80]

Japan's position was very similar to that of France — it noted that "no provision ... provides the general right of a group of people within a sovereign State, outside the colonial context, to seek secession from the State to which they belong and to create their own independent State."[81] However, Japan argued that Kosovo was a *sui generis* case on the grounds that Kosovo: (1) was denied internal self-determination and faced serious human rights violations; (2) received international attention; (3) seceded according to the desires of the Kosovar population; and (4) seceded as a last resort.[82]

The **United Kingdom** repeatedly highlighted the *sui generis* character of the situation in Kosovo, citing, among other factors: (1) the human rights atrocities that had occurred there; (2) the involvement of the UN Security Council; (3) the involvement of the international community; and (4) the absence of a credible alternative to independence.[83] The United Kingdom was also unique among other states in explicitly justifying its position on the need to maintain international peace and security:

---

[78] *Kosovo* case, *supra* first unnumbered note, "Written Statement of France (translation by the Registry)" (7 April 2009), online: ICJ <http://www.icj-cij.org/docket/files/141/15607.pdf> at 27.

[79] *Ibid* at 29.

[80] *Ibid.*

[81] *Kosovo* case, *supra* first unnumbered note, "Written Statement of Japan" (17 April 2009), online: ICJ <http://www.icj-cij.org/docket/files/141/15658.pdf> at 4.

[82] *Ibid* at 6-8. Japan concluded: "[W]e cannot, and should not, deduce any general rule or principle of international law from the legal assessment of the case of Kosovo" (*ibid* at 8).

[83] *Kosovo* case, *supra* first unnumbered note, "Written Statement of the United Kingdom of Great Britain and Northern Ireland" (17 April 2009), online: ICJ <http://www.icj-cij.org/docket/files/141/15638.pdf> at 11-14.

Stability in the international system is important and States in other parts of the world must have a clear understanding that events in the Balkans, and Kosovo's Declaration of Independence, do *not* create risks of internal instability for them ... Kosovo's independence does not open the door to the fracturing of States more generally. The independence of Kosovo cannot be relied upon as a template for secessionist or self-determination claims elsewhere.[84]

Category 3: States That Either Remain Neutral or Express Ambiguous Views on Remedial Secession

The submissions of Austria, the Czech Republic, Denmark, Sierra Leone, and the United States either declined to address the issue of self-determination or presented views on self-determination that are unclear or difficult to interpret. These submissions can be broken down into two subcategories, each of which is considered in the following sections.

Category 3.1: The Question before the Court Can Be Answered without Addressing the Contours of International Law Regarding Self-Determination

Austria maintained that secession is a legally neutral act: "[I]nternational law is silent with regard to declarations of independence, thus no prohibition of the Declaration can be derived from international law."[85] Since secession is not prohibited by international law, Austria argued that "secession in this sense needs no justification by the right to self-determination."[86]

The **Czech Republic** argued similarly that "international law neither prohibits nor promotes secession."[87] Interestingly, the Czech Republic also stated that "the principle of territorial integrity is an essential element of state sovereignty, but it is not an absolute rule and should be understood in the light of recent developments in

---

84 *Ibid* at 10 [emphasis in original].

85 *Kosovo* case, *supra* first unnumbered note, "Written Statement of Austria" (16 April 2009), online: ICJ <http://www.icj-cij.org/docket/files/141/15620.pdf> at 14.

86 *Ibid* at 22.

87 *Kosovo* case, *supra* first unnumbered note, "Written Statement of the Czech Republic" (15 April 2009), online: ICJ <http://www.icj-cij.org/docket/files/141/15605.pdf> at 7.

international law."[88] Advocates of remedial secession may interpret this statement as an indication that the Czech Republic may be sympathetic to the argument that self-determination outweighs territorial integrity in some cases, although such a reading is not self-evident.

Sierra Leone limited itself to stating that it "recognized Kosovo as an Independent State in June 2008 and the Government of Sierra Leone believed that Kosovo's independence itself ... was in accordance with International Law."[89]

The **United States** consistently argued that "declarations of independence, standing alone, present matters of fact, which are neither authorized nor prohibited by international law."[90] Regarding remedial secession, the United States noted:

The United States continues to believe that the question referred to the Court can be answered without addressing the contours of international law regarding self-determination. This Comment offers no view on the issues of who is a "people," whether there is a remedial/external right of self-determination in certain egregious situations, or to whom such a right could flow. Kosovo's declaration of independence need not be an exercise of the right of external self-determination to be consistent with international law.[91]

The United States also went on to state that, "should the Court find it necessary to examine Kosovo's declaration of independence through the lens of the right of self-determination ... then the Court should consider Kosovo's specific legal and factual circumstances,"[92] including the large-scale atrocities against the population of Kosovo and Kosovo's good faith participation in unsuccessful negotiations.[93] Clearly, the United States did not want to be seen as taking a position

---

88 *Ibid.*

89 *Kosovo* case, *supra* first unnumbered note, "Written Statement of Sierra Leone" (15 April 2009), online: ICJ <http://www.icj-cij.org/docket/files/141/15672.pdf> at 1.

90 *Kosovo* case, *supra* first unnumbered note, "Written Statement of the United States of America" (17 April 2009), online: ICJ <http://www.icj-cij.org/docket/files/141/15640.pdf> at 50.

91 *Kosovo* case, *supra* first unnumbered note, "Written Comments of the United States of America" (17 July 2009), online: ICJ <http://www.icj-cij.org/docket/files/141/15704.pdf> at 21 [footnotes omitted].

92 *Ibid* at 22.

93 *Ibid* at 22-23.

on remedial secession. Nonetheless, advocates of remedial secession may argue that the American citation of "large-scale atrocities" and unsuccessful negotiations may have been a tacit diplomatic nod to the commonly advanced criteria, for remedial secession, of the denial of internal self-determination and of secession as a last resort. However, such a reading of the American position would be somewhat tendentious.

Category 3.2: There Is No General Prohibition in International law against Declarations of Independence — Denial of Internal Self-Determination Is "Not Irrelevant" to Such Situations

Denmark's arguments principally revolved around the proposition that "no general prohibition exists in international law against declarations of independence."[94] While Denmark did not address remedial secession directly, it did state that "[w]hile there are implications of the right of self-determination not yet fully developed in international practice, the Danish Government sees no reason why denial of meaningful internal self-determination ... should be deemed irrelevant in relation to an otherwise legitimate claim of independence."[95] While proponents of remedial secession may interpret this statement as indicating some degree of recognition of the principles behind remedial secession, the Danish position that denial of internal self-determination "should not be deemed irrelevant" is ambiguous and was not further clarified in its submissions.

Category 4: States That Are Hostile to Remedial Secession as Established in International Law in Varying Degrees

The submissions of Argentina, Azerbaijan, Bolivia, Brazil, China, Cyprus, Egypt, Iran, Libya, Romania, Serbia, Slovakia, Spain, and Venezuela signalled varying degrees of hostility towards remedial secession. This hostility was expressed in one of two general ways: either implicitly, by emphasizing the paramountcy of sovereignty and territorial integrity or, explicitly, by directly disavowing the international legal status of remedial secession. Each of these two subcategories of submissions is considered in greater detail in the following sections.

---

[94] *Kosovo* case, *supra* first unnumbered note, "Written Statement of Denmark" (17 April 2009), online: ICJ <http://www.icj-cij.org/docket/files/141/15664.pdf> at 13.

[95] *Ibid* at 12.

Category 4.1: Remedial Secession Not Explicitly Addressed, but Respect for the Sovereignty and Territorial Integrity of States Is Emphasized as Paramount

Brazil submitted that "the right to self-determination does not stand in contradiction with the principle of territorial integrity and [the users of the right] must respect [Security Council] decisions."[96] Brazil's argument focused on the importance of territorial integrity, concluding that Kosovo's UDI "contradicts relevant provisions of ... international law, in particular the principle of territorial integrity of sovereign and independent States."[97]

Libya's one-page statement is somewhat difficult to categorize, but it also emphasized the importance of territorial integrity. Libya concluded that "the independence of the Province of Kosovo was proclaimed before negotiations had been completed with Serbia on self-determination, and therefore has no legal justification."[98] This statement probably implies Libya's opposition to non-consensual secession.

In its brief submission, **Venezuela** argued that Kosovo's UDI violated international law because it disrespected Serbia's territorial integrity.[99] Venezuela also argued that recognizing Kosovo's independent statehood was a "separatist ... [policy] promoted by the main powers to weaken the developing countries."[100]

Category 4.2: Remedial Secession Explicitly Dismissed as Not Established in International Law

Argentina argued that the international instruments that address self-determination also tend to reinforce the principle of territorial integrity.[101] Argentina contended that

---

96 *Kosovo* case, *supra* first unnumbered note, "Written Statement of Brazil" (17 April 2009), online: ICJ <http://www.icj-cij.org/docket/files/141/15660.pdf> at 2.

97 *Ibid.*

98 *Kosovo* case, *supra* first unnumbered note, "Written Statement of the Libyan Arab Jamahiriya (translation by the Registry)" (17 April 2009), online: ICJ <http://www.icj-cij.org/docket/files/141/15636.pdf> at 1.

99 *Kosovo* case, *supra* first unnumbered note, "Written Statement of Venezuela" (24 April 2009), online: ICJ <http://www.icj-cij.org/docket/files/141/15676.pdf> at 1.

100 *Ibid* at 2.

101 *Kosovo* case, *supra* first unnumbered note, "Written Statement of Argentina" (17 April 2009), online: ICJ <http://www.icj-cij.org/docket/files/141/15666.pdf> at 38.

the right [to secession], which is one of the possible outcomes of the exercise of the right to self-determination by those peoples entitled thereto, is not granted on the basis of the major or minor violence inflicted upon particular groups of individuals. The so-called theory of "remedial secession" is nothing more than an argument made in doctrine, which has not received any legal consecration.[102]

Azerbaijan opened its discussion of the issue by explicitly rejecting remedial secession: "[I]nternational law does not create grounds and conditions for legitimizing unilateral or non-consensual secession in any sense. Such secession from an existing sovereign State does not involve the exercise of any right conferred in international law."[103]

Bolivia argued that declarations of independence are exceptional cases, warning that such actions may also be motivated by foreign geopolitical interests intent on the disintegration of disfavoured states.[104] Bolivia explicitly stated that "[t]he fact that a State pursues a discriminatory policy against an ethnic group cannot, as such, give rise to a right to unilateral secession."[105]

China first argued that territorial integrity "has constituted the most important principle of international law and the basic norm governing international relations."[106] China then contended that "the right to self-determination is different in nature from the so-called right of secession. The exercise of the right of self-determination shall not undermine the sovereignty and territorial integrity of the State concerned."[107] China firmly concluded: "Secession is not recognized by international law and has always been opposed by the international community of States."[108]

---

[102] *Ibid* at 34.

[103] *Kosovo* case, *supra* first unnumbered note, "Written Statement of Azerbaijan" (17 April 2009), online: ICJ <http://www.icj-cij.org/docket/files/141/15668. pdf> at 5.

[104] *Kosovo* case, *supra* first unnumbered note, "Written Statement of Bolivia" (17 April 2009), online: ICJ <http://www.icj-cij.org/docket/files/141/15674.pdf> at 1.

[105] *Kosovo* case, *supra* first unnumbered note, "Written Comments of Bolivia" (17 July 2009), online: ICJ <http://www.icj-cij.org/docket/files/141/15700.pdf> at 4.

[106] *Kosovo* case, *supra* first unnumbered note, "Written Statement of China" (16 April 2009), online: ICJ <http://www.icj-cij.org/docket/files/141/15611.pdf> at 2-3.

[107] *Ibid* at 3-4.

[108] *Ibid* at 6.

Cyprus argued that remedial secession was not grounded in a positive source of international law: "[S]uch a major right as this would require a positive source, rather than a mere *a contrario* reasoning [from, for example, the 1970 *Declaration on Friendly Relations*]."[109] Cyprus concluded by arguing that

[w]hile the claim that there is a "right of secession of last resort" has been supported by some writers and by *a contrario* reasoning ... it is without support in State practice. It has not emerged as a rule of customary law. It is not found in any treaty. And it has no support from the practice of the UN.[110]

Egypt opened its discussion of the issue by highlighting the principle of territorial integrity as a "cornerstone of international relations."[111] Following an evaluation of the history of self-determination, Egypt concluded with two points. First, "[n]othing, so far, in international law would clearly lend assistance to accommodate arguments contending that the right to self-determination can only be exercised externally, *as long as there are adequate safeguards against discrimination*."[112] Second, "[t]he right to self-determination has evolved under customary international law, and become legally respected as a treaty-bound obligation after its inclusion in the UN Charter. Its application, however, should not lead to situations threatening international peace and security."[113] The Egyptian position is both sophisticated and difficult to categorize.[114] The words italicized earlier imply that Egypt may be sympathetic to a claim of secession in situations of discrimination, but since Egypt also expressed concern that remedial secession *writ large* may threaten international peace and security, its position on remedial secession in the future may be an interesting bellwether to observe.

After considering remedial secession, **Iran** came to a distinctly unambiguous conclusion:

109 *Kosovo* case, *supra* first unnumbered note, "Written Statement of Cyprus" (3 April 2009), online: ICJ <http://www.icj-cij.org/docket/files/141/15609.pdf> at 37.

110 *Ibid* [footnotes omitted].

111 *Kosovo* case, *supra* first unnumbered note, "Written Statement of Egypt" (16 April 2009), online: ICJ <http://www.icj-cij.org/docket/files/141/15622.pdf> at 8.

112 *Ibid* at 19 [emphasis added].

113 *Ibid* at 20.

114 The Egyptian statement was also highlighted as being of particularly high value. See "Written Comments of Norway," *supra* note 67 at 2, n 1.

Even a large scale and systematic violation of international humanitarian law and human rights law in some parts of the territory of the state concerned, does not create a right of unilateral secession for the victims ... Even in that case, the principle of territorial integrity must be respected, and has been respected in all similar occasions.[115]

The Iranian statement is arguably the most strident and explicit rejection of remedial secession in the country statements to the ICJ.

Romania argued that remedial secession is not established in international law and is also lacking in state practice.[116] However, Romania considered that it was of interest to apply a theoretical model of remedial secession to the case of Kosovo as an academic exercise. It accordingly proceeded to apply essentially the criteria for remedial secession articulated by Germany, focusing on denial of internal self-determination and secession as a last resort.[117] However, in similar fashion to the Russian submission, Romania also argued that Kosovo would not be entitled to remedial secession, even based on this model, as the people of Kosovo would need to have been subject to gross violations of human rights at the moment of their UDI in 2008.[118] As noted in the German statement and Swiss comments, this temporal requirement would nullify the efficacy of remedial secession as it was highly unlikely that the contemporaneity and last resort requirements could be concurrently met in any realistic situation.

Serbia examined the issue of remedial secession at length. Following a detailed analysis of the development of self-determination in international law, Serbia submitted that "the right to self-determination has become a legal right in international law, but in a carefully limited manner"[119] that is restricted to colonial

---

115 *Kosovo* case, *supra* first unnumbered note, "Written Statement of the Islamic Republic of Iran" (17 April 2009), online: ICJ <http://www.icj-cij.org/docket/files/141/15646.pdf> at 6-7. Iran went on to state that "the right to self-determination for minorities is an internal one and means their entitlement to democracy and human rights and does not involve any right to secession" (*ibid* at 7).

116 *Kosovo* case, *supra* first unnumbered note, "Written Statement of Romania" (14 April 2009), online: ICJ <http://www.icj-cij.org/docket/files/141/15616.pdf> at 40.

117 *Ibid.*

118 *Ibid* at 43-45.

119 *Kosovo* case, *supra* first unnumbered note, "Written Statement of Serbia" (17 April 2009), online: ICJ <http://www.icj-cij.org/docket/files/141/15642.pdf> at 189.

domination and foreign occupation.[120] Serbia maintained that "international law assuredly does not recognise a right of secession from independent States and no formulation of the principle of self-determination can be interpreted so to do."[121] Serbia also reviewed and dismissed other states' submissions that favoured remedial secession before reaching the following conclusion:

> States invoking the existence of a "right to remedial secession" have presented different conditions for its exercise. None of them has demonstrated how this doctrine has ever been incorporated into positive international law. None of them explains where the conditions for the exercise of this so-called "right" are depicted under international law. All of them have failed to establish its existence in international law.[122]

Slovakia opened its comments by noting that "few principles in present-day international law are so firmly established as that of the territorial integrity of States."[123] Regarding remedial secession, Slovakia concluded that

> the right to secede does not exist in international law ... Outside the colonial context, the principle of self-determination is not recognized in practice as giving rise to unilateral rights of secession by parts of independent states.[124]

Spain found itself in a difficult diplomatic situation. While a majority of its allies in the European Union had recognized Kosovo, it also had to consider the impact of its statement on secessionist groups within its own borders. Spain mainly argued that the UDI was contradictory to Serbia's sovereignty and territorial integrity, submitting that "there can be no doubt that respect for the sovereignty and

---

120 *Ibid* at 189-92.

121 *Ibid* at 207. Serbia also argued in the alternative that even if a right to remedial secession were found to exist, it would not apply to Kosovo on the grounds that Kosovars did not constitute a "people" (*ibid* at 215).

122 *Kosovo* case, *supra* first unnumbered note, "Written Comments of Serbia" (15 July 2009), online: ICJ <http://www.icj-cij.org/docket/files/141/15686.pdf> at 146.

123 *Kosovo* case, *supra* first unnumbered note, "Written Statement of Slovakia" (16 April 2009) online: ICJ <http://www.icj-cij.org/docket/files/141/15626.pdf> at 1.

124 *Ibid* at 2.

territorial integrity of States is inscribed in the essential, non-derogable core of the basic principles of international law."[125] Spain further argued that the "secession-as-sanction or secession-as-remedy formulas" do not have a "proper legal basis in international law," while also contending that the international community had already fashioned an appropriate remedy for the situation in Kosovo through the imposition of an international administration.[126]

DISSENTING AND SEPARATE JUDICIAL OPINIONS ON REMEDIAL SECESSION

While the ICJ's majority opinion did not directly address the issue of remedial secession, the dissenting and separate opinions of three ICJ judges substantively addressed the concept. The separate opinion of Judge Abdulqawi Ahmed Yusuf was the most explicit in supporting remedial secession. Judge Yusuf first found that "the right to self-determination chiefly operates inside the boundaries of existing States"[127] before stating the following:

[I]nternational law [does not turn] a blind eye to the plight of such groups, particularly in those cases where the State not only denies them the exercise of their internal right of self-determination (as described earlier) but also subjects them to discrimination, persecution, and egregious violations of human rights or humanitarian law. Under such exceptional circumstances, the right of peoples to self-determination may support a claim to separate statehood provided it meets the conditions prescribed by international law.[128]

Judge Yusuf went on to note:

To determine whether a specific situation constitutes an exceptional case which may legitimize a claim to external self-determination, certain criteria have to be considered, such as the existence of discrimination against a people, its persecution due to its racial or ethnic characteristics, and the

---

[125] *Kosovo* case, *supra* first unnumbered note, "Written Statement of Spain" (14 April 2009), online: ICJ <http://www.icj-cij.org/docket/files/141/15644.pdf> at 18; see also at 12.

[126] *Kosovo* case, *supra* first unnumbered note, "Written Comments of Spain" (July 2009), online: ICJ <http://www.icj-cij.org/docket/files/141/15706.pdf> at 6.

[127] *Kosovo* case, *supra* first unnumbered note at para 9 (separate opinion of Judge Yusuf).

[128] *Ibid* at para 11.

denial of autonomous political structures and access to government ... All possible remedies for the realization of internal self-determination must be exhausted before the issue is removed from the domestic jurisdiction of the State.[129]

Advocates of remedial secession may also find encouragement in the separate opinion of Judge Antônio A. Cançado Trindade, who indicated a degree of support for remedial secession, albeit indirectly. Judge Cançado Trindade cited the 1970 *Declaration on Friendly Relations* and the 1993 *Vienna Declaration and Programme of Action* in finding the following:

The principle of self-determination has survived decolonization, in order to face nowadays new and violent manifestations of systematic oppression of peoples ... It is immaterial, whether in the framework of these new experiments, self-determination is given the qualification of 'remedial,' or another qualification. The fact remains that people cannot be targeted for atrocities, cannot live under systematic oppression. The principle of self-determination applies in new situations of systematic oppression, subjugation and tyranny.[130]

Judge Cançado Trindade also noted that "[t]he government of a State which incurs grave and systematic violations of human rights ceases to represent the people or population victimized."[131] Regarding Kosovo, he found that "the entitlement to self-determination of the victimized population emerged, as the claim to territorial integrity could no longer be relied upon by the willing victimizers."[132]

Thus, while Judge Cançado Trindade does not explicitly affirm remedial secession, he appears to have adopted much of the language surrounding the concept. He does so by referring to a right to self-determination that arises in cases of systematic oppression, subjugation, and tyranny that in turn takes precedence over the principle of territorial integrity.[133]

---

[129] *Ibid* at para 16.

[130] *Ibid* at para 175 (separate opinion of Judge Cançado Trindade). *Vienna Convention on the Law of Treaties,* 8 ILM 679 (1969).

[131] *Kosovo* case, *supra* first unnumbered note at para 180.

[132] *Ibid* at 181.

[133] It should also be noted that Judge Cançado Trindade has generally taken a very distinctive approach to international law. For example, Judge Cançado

While such judicial statements may be significant, their import may be tempered by the dissenting opinion of Judge Abdul Koroma, who held that

> not even the principles of equal rights and self-determination of peoples as precepts of international law allow for the dismemberment of an existing State without its consent ... The [1970 *Declaration on Friendly Relations*] leaves no doubt that the principles of the sovereignty and territorial integrity of States prevail over the principle of self-determination.[134]

It is clear from this statement that Judge Koroma generally places great emphasis on the principle of territorial integrity and also does not take a favourable position towards remedial secession. It should also be noted that both Judge Bruno Simma and Judge Bernardo Sepúlveda-Amor indicated, in their separate opinions, that the ICJ should have directly addressed the scope of the right to self-determination and the issue of remedial secession. However, neither disclosed their opinions on these issues.[135]

LEGAL RAMIFICATIONS OF THE KOSOVO CASE AND ASSOCIATED COUNTRY SUBMISSIONS

In the immediate aftermath of the ICJ's ruling in the *Kosovo* case, there appeared to be some degree of consensus that the ruling would not have a major impact on the position of remedial secession in international law because the majority did not directly address the issue.[136] In addition, the separate opinions of Judges Yusuf and Cançado Trindade, which indicated support for remedial secession, received relatively little attention and media coverage. While this assessment of the effect of the ICJ majority opinion may or may

---

Trindade has advocated what he refers to as a "people-centred outlook on contemporary international law — reflecting the current process of its humanization" (*ibid* at para 170). In the event that Judge Cançado Trindade's remarks on remedial secession were to be referenced as evidence of customary international law in the future, it is unclear to what degree his more general views on international law would inform understandings of the specific concept of remedial secession.

[134] *Ibid* at para 22 (dissenting opinion of Judge Koroma).

[135] *Ibid* at paras 6-7 (separate opinion of Judge Simma); at para 35 (separate opinion of Judge Sepulveda-Amor).

[136] See, eg, Pippan, *supra* note 34; Hannum, *supra* note 35.

not be accurate, it is also worth considering whether the country submissions in particular may have had a significant impact on the status of remedial secession in international law.[137] I therefore turn to an evaluation of the potential legal implications of the *Kosovo* case and its associated country submissions, through the lenses of general and regional customary international law.

GENERAL CUSTOMARY INTERNATIONAL LAW

The formation of general customary international law requires two elements: (1) state practice and (2) accompanying *opinio juris* — that is, a belief on the part of states that their practice is legally sanctioned.[138] State practice, in turn, is generally required to be uniform, widespread, and continuous.[139] The quantity of time necessary to establish the legal criterion of state practice is flexible, depending on the quality and quantity of state practice, particularly the practice of specially affected states.[140] However, as noted by Judge Manfred Lachs in his dissenting opinion in the *North Sea Continental Shelf Cases (Federal Republic of Germany v Denmark; Federal Republic of Germany v Netherlands)* (*North Sea Continental Shelf* case), it is "an essential factor ... that States with different political, economic and legal systems, States of all continents, participate in the process."[141] Judge Lachs held that the practice need not be universal, but "evidence should be sought in the behaviour of a great number of States, possibly the majority of States, in any case the great majority of interested states."[142] Moreover, state practice requires a degree of continuity, such that "State conduct inconsistent with a given rule

---

137 See, *contra*, Sienho Yee, "Notes on the International Court of Justice (Part 4): The *Kosovo* Advisory Opinion" (2010) 9:4 Chinese J Int'l L 763.

138 John Currie, Craig Forcese, and Valerie Oosterveld, *International Law: Doctrine, Practice, and Theory* (Toronto: Irwin Law, 2007) at 121.

139 It should also be noted that mere silence or inaction by a state in the face of state practice by others may be considered to be acquiescence to that practice. See *Fisheries Case (United Kingdom v Norway)*, [1951] ICJ Rep 116 at 139.

140 *North Sea Continental Shelf Cases (Federal Republic of Germany v Denmark; Federal Republic of Germany v Netherlands)*, [1969] ICJ Rep 3 at paras 73-74 [*North Sea Continental Shelf* case]. The ICJ stated that "it might be that, even without the passage of any considerable period of time, a very widespread and representative participation in the convention might suffice of itself, provided it included that of States whose interests were specially affected" (*ibid* at 73).

141 *Ibid* at 227 (dissenting opinion of Judge Lachs).

142 *Ibid* at 229.

should generally have been treated as breaches of that rule, not as indications of the recognition of a new rule."[143]

In addition to state practice, the emergence of a new rule of customary international law also requires, as noted, *opinio juris*. As affirmed by the ICJ in the *North Sea Continental Shelf* case, state practice must not only be settled, but there must also be "evidence of a belief that this practice is rendered obligatory by the existence of a rule of law requiring it ... The frequency, or even habitual character of the act is not in itself enough."[144] The ICJ also found in its advisory opinion on the *Legality of the Threat or Use of Nuclear Weapons* that *opinio juris* is unlikely to be present when "the members of the international community are profoundly divided on the matter."[145] Evidence of *opinio juris* can be garnered from a number of sources including, "with all due caution,"[146] attitudes of states towards UNGA resolutions.[147]

Of course, the ascertainment of customary international law presents a number of methodological difficulties, including evaluating inconsistent acts, divining states' beliefs, and ascertaining the practice of almost 200 states.[148] Due to these difficulties, the country submissions in the *Kosovo* case present a unique and somewhat rare opportunity to establish the positions of the submitting states with respect to remedial secession.

Do the country submissions in the *Kosovo* case support the argument that remedial secession has achieved the status of a principle of general customary international law? It is evident that this is not the case for several reasons. First, as noted earlier, general customary international law requires widespread, uniform, and representative state practice accompanied by *opinio juris*. From this perspective, it is significant that the overall participation rate in the proceedings was relatively low (thirty-six of 192 UN member states). Of these,

---

143 *Military and Paramilitary Activities in and against Nicaragua (Nicaragua v United States of America)*, [1986] ICJ Rep 14 at para 186 [*Nicaragua v United States of America*].

144 *North Sea Continental Shelf* case, *supra* note 140 at para 77.

145 *Legality of the Threat or Use of Nuclear Weapons*, Advisory Opinion, [1996] ICJ Rep 226 at para 67.

146 *Nicaragua v United States of America*, *supra* note 143 at para 188.

147 *Ibid.*

148 For a more detailed survey of the methodological complications inherent in the ascertainment of customary international law, see Currie, Forcese, and Oosterveld, *supra* note 138 at 133.

only ten states, all European, have been willing not only to recognize Kosovo's independence in practice but also, arguably, to express a degree of belief that remedial secession is an established basis for such independence in international law.[149] Second, this limited state practice has occurred over too short a period of time to be considered uniform. New rules may emerge rapidly if the quantity and quality of state practice is high, but state practice in this case — only ten states in the period spanning from 2008 to 2011 — is drastically insufficient to ground the sudden emergence of a new rule of customary international law. Third, weighing state practice requires special emphasis on the practice of "specially affected" or "interested" states. In the case of remedial secession, "interested" states could be interpreted as states that currently face secessionist movements or other challenges to their territorial integrity. In contrast to some of those states that explicitly opposed remedial secession, none of the ten states that have recognized Kosovo and that supported remedial secession in their country submissions in the *Kosovo* case have hosted a major secessionist movement. It may also be significant that some states that might be considered "specially affected" by secessionism, such as Canada and Nigeria, did not make submissions in this case.

Moreover, the soft law impact of the practice and *opinio juris* of the ten states recognizing Kosovo and supporting remedial secession should not be overstated. While these ten states have shown a degree of support for remedial secession, their motivations for doing so are often unclear in their statements. Therefore, a firm conclusion that these statements necessarily represent *opinio juris* corresponding to a "belief" in the existence of a rule of law would be premature pending further analysis of these states' attitudes towards remedial secession. Also, it must be remembered that, while these ten states expressed support for remedial secession, a greater number of states (fourteen) expressed varying degrees of hostility to the concept.

It has been argued that the findings of the ICJ majority have also had a substantive negative impact on the legal status of remedial secession. For example, Sienho Yee has persuasively argued that the ICJ majority implicitly found against the existence of remedial secession:

---

[149] Of the eleven states making Category 1 country submissions, Russia has not recognized the independence of Kosovo (at the time of writing).

The fact, as pointed out by the Court, that radically different views were expressed on this question during the proceedings demonstrates the lack of any extensive and uniform *opinio juris* supporting this claimed right ... Although the Court did not say so expressly, and although the Court may not have intended to say so at all, the Court did manage to give a negative answer coincidentally or collaterally to the argument for external self-determination or remedial secession.[150]

It could also be argued that the ICJ's observation that states' arguments in favour of remedial secession were made "in almost every instance only as a secondary argument" casts doubt on the quality of support expressed by some states for remedial secession, with potentially negative implications for its customary status.[151] However, the ICJ's interpretation of the structure of states' arguments in this regard is somewhat questionable. Several states that expressed favourable views towards remedial secession clearly positioned such arguments as secondary or alternative,[152] but it appears that a greater number of states either placed primary emphasis on self-determination and remedial secession[153] or included them among several arguments in which a hierarchy is not readily evident.[154] On such closer scrutiny, this specific finding of the ICJ is therefore unlikely to play a significant role in determining the status of remedial secession.

To acknowledge the limited impact that the country submissions favouring remedial secession are likely to have on the customary status of the doctrine is not to say that these submissions are completely

---

150 Yee, *supra* note 137 at 777-78. See also Arp, *supra* note 33 at 853: "The Court briefly addressed [the issue] by stating that remedial secession was 'a subject on which radically different views were expressed by those taking part in the proceedings and expressing a position on the question.' From this it can be inferred that the Court may consider that there is no consolidated legal opinion (*opinio juris*) in international law on this topic."

151 *Kosovo* case, *supra* first unnumbered note at para 82.

152 See, eg, "Written Statement of Germany," *supra* note 46; "Written Statement of Ireland," *supra* note 55; "Written Contribution of the Authors," *supra* note 60.

153 See, eg, "Written Statement of Estonia," *supra* note 39; "Written Statement of Finland," *supra* note 41; "Written Statement of Poland," *supra* note 58; "Written Statement of Slovenia," *supra* note 70.

154 See, eg, "Written Statement of Albania," *supra* note 38; "Written Statement of Netherlands," *supra* note 50; "Written Statement of Russia," *supra* note 63. In fairness, it should be noted that analyzing whether an argument is "primary" or "secondary" is a highly subjective exercise.

inconsequential. As we have seen, in his 2006 survey of state practice regarding secession, James Crawford concluded that "state practice since 1945 shows the extreme reluctance of states to recognize unilateral secession outside of the colonial context."[155] The ten states that have extended recognition to Kosovo and that have also publicly expressed support for remedial secession now stand as a small but concrete counterpoint to this analysis. There was little to no evidence of any state practice or *opinio juris* supporting remedial secession prior to the *Kosovo* case. Following the *Kosovo* case, the ten country submissions that expressed explicitly positive views on remedial secession have elevated the soft law status of the concept. While remedial secession remains far from having the status of a principle of general customary international law, and the significance of the ten state submissions to the ICJ should not be overstated. At a minimum, it can be concluded that serious international legal attention to the issue has reached a new high.

REGIONAL CUSTOMARY INTERNATIONAL LAW

While remedial secession has not emerged as a new rule of general or universal customary international law, advocates of remedial secession may plausibly argue that remedial secession is in the process of emerging as a regional customary norm for those states that support it. As noted in the *Asylum Case (Colombia v Peru)*, regional groupings of states may create regional customary international law, the binding force of which is specific to that region.[156] Moreover, as noted in *Case Concerning Right of Passage over Indian Territory (Portugal v India)*, the formation of regional customary international law does not require participation by a sizable subset of the world's countries. This can come about as a result of participation by as few as two states, which do not even have to be geographically linked.[157]

In this case, advocates of remedial secession could plausibly argue that Albania, Estonia, Finland, Germany, Ireland, the Netherlands, Norway, Poland, Slovenia, and Switzerland may have laid the groundwork for a new regional customary rule, potentially binding on them, providing for remedial secession in certain circumstances. It could be argued that each of these states has recognized Kosovo as

---

155 Crawford, *The Creation of States, supra* note 27 at 390.

156 *Asylum Case (Colombia v Peru)*, [1950] ICJ Rep 266 at 276.

157 *Case Concerning Right of Passage over Indian Territory (Portugal v India)*, [1960] ICJ Rep 6 at 39.

a new state (that is, state practice) while also expressing a belief that remedial secession is a principle of law (that is, *opinio juris*). A plausible argument could therefore be made that, as a result of the recognition by these states of Kosovo and of the views expressed in their submissions in the *Kosovo* case, remedial secession has taken a substantive step towards becoming a rule of regional customary international law applicable to these states.

On the other hand, it must be acknowledged that such state practice and *opinio juris* are still emergent and have occurred within a very short time frame. Further observation of these states' practices and positions with respect to remedial secession would be required before the emergence of such a regional customary norm could be confirmed. In particular, it may be notable that these states have not gone on to recognize other secessionist entities that may also have claims to remedial secession, such as Somaliland.

CONCLUSION

As the principle of self-determination has developed in international law, a general consensus has emerged that self-determination has external implications in situations of colonial domination or foreign occupation. There is also a general consensus that secession is neither legal nor illegal in international law. Beginning mainly in the mid-1990s, some academics proposed a "third category" of external self-determination according to which, if a people were to be denied internal self-determination or subjected to massive human rights violations, that people would be entitled to remedial secession as a last resort. This concept did not receive support in state practice.

The *Kosovo* case may have impacted the development of remedial secession in international law in several ways. First, for the first time, two sitting ICJ judges have publicly stated their support for remedial secession and the principles that underlie it, while other ICJ judges have indicated a desire that the ICJ formally express an opinion on the issue. Second, in their country submissions in the case, eleven states — ten of which have recognized Kosovo as an independent state — formally and explicitly supported a doctrine of remedial secession in international law. While such developments fall far short of what would be required to evidence a new rule of general customary international law, they do increase the soft law status of remedial secession while also qualifying the prior record, which disclosed no state practice or state support for remedial secession. Third, while it remains implausible to argue that general customary international law on the topic has changed, advocates of remedial secession may plausibly argue that the ten states that have both recognized Kosovo and publicly supported an international legal doctrine of remedial secession may have sown the seeds for a regional customary rule on the issue. Whether such a conclusion is warranted, however, will depend on the behaviour of, and the opinions expressed by, such states in other instances.

Contrary indicators must also be emphasized. Opponents of remedial secession may note that while two ICJ judges explicitly supported remedial secession, another judge explicitly rejected it. Moreover, while eleven states explicitly indicated support for remedial secession, fourteen states either implicitly or explicitly opposed it, and a further 156 UN member states, including potential "specially affected" states such as Canada and Nigeria, expressed no opinion at all on the issue. Also, while ten states that indicated support for remedial secession have also recognized Kosovo as a state, their intent to be bound by such actions is unclear, and their practice is arguably inconsistent insofar as none of them has subsequently gone on to recognize other potential candidates for remedial secession, such as Somaliland. Moreover, it must be remembered that the ICJ majority opinion could be interpreted as implicitly finding a lack of consistent *opinio juris* favouring remedial secession.

Bearing these contrary indicators in mind, on balance, the *Kosovo* case appears to have improved the soft law status of remedial secession due to increased levels of state support and international judicial consideration of the concept. Bjorn Arp has wryly remarked that "the fact that the ICJ did not comprehensively analyze the issue of remedial secession will give leeway to both the partisans and detractors of this notion alike to include the Advisory Opinion into their argumentation in favour of their respective positions."[158] Advocates of remedial secession may therefore argue that the *Kosovo* case is a harbinger of a more concrete legal status for remedial secession in international law, whereas opponents of remedial secession may also find new legal tools in it to bolster their arguments.

Daniel H. Meester
JD, MA, BPAPM, Policy Analyst, Health Canada

---

[158] Arp, *supra* note 33 at 853.

Sommaire

Le cas du Kosovo à la CIJ : faire le point sur l'état actuel de l'opinion juridique internationale sur la sécession comme moyen de redressement

À la lumière du nombre de mouvements sécessionnistes à l'échelle mondiale, certains ont proposé une doctrine de sécession comme moyen de redressement de dernier recours qui serait applicable là où un peuple est soit nié l'auto-détermination interne ou est confronté à des violations massives des droits de la personne par un régime répressif. Alors que le manque de pratique étatique a voulu que cette doctrine ne soit prise au sérieux qu'en milieu académique pendant les années 1990 et la plupart des années 2000, la sécession comme moyen de redressement a suscité une attention accrue lors de la procédure relative à l'avis consultatif de 2008 de la CIJ dans l'affaire du Kosovo. En fait, onze États y ont exprimé leur soutien à cette doctrine, ainsi que, vraisemblablement, deux juges de la CIJ dans des opinions individuelles. Les partisans de la sécession comme moyen de redressement peuvent donc plausiblement prétendre que le statut "soft law" du concept a été affermi, et peut-être même qu'il est en voie d'émergence comme norme coutumière régionale pour les États qui l'ont appuyé. Toutefois, l'impact de l'affaire du Kosovo sur la solidification du statut juridique de la sécession comme moyen de redressement ne devrait pas être surestimé, car les opposants du concept pourront identifier, parmi les communications officielles dans cette affaire, certains courants en sens contraire.

Summary

The International Court of Justice's *Kosovo* Case: Assessing the Current State of International Legal Opinion on Remedial Secession

In light of the global prevalence of secessionist movements, some have proposed "remedial secession" as a last resort solution where a "people" is either denied internal self-determination or is faced with massive human rights violations by a repressive regime. While lack of state practice largely confined this concept to academic circles through the 1990s and much of the 2000s, remedial secession received renewed international legal attention in the proceedings concerning the International Court of Justice's (ICJ) 2008 advisory opinion in the case Accordance with International Law of the Unilateral Declaration of Independence in Respect of Kosovo *(Kosovo case). In light of support for remedial secession expressed in the submissions of eleven states, as well as its apparent endorsement in the separate opinions of two ICJ judges, advocates of remedial secession may plausibly argue that the soft law status of the concept has been strengthened and perhaps even that it is in the process of emerging as a regional customary norm for those states that supported it. However, the impact of the Kosovo case on solidifying the legal status of remedial secession should not be overstated, as opponents of the concept may point to a number of contrary indicators that also emerged from the formal discourse surrounding the case.*

Chronique de droit international économique en 2009 / Digest of International Economic Law in 2009

I Commerce

RICHARD OUELLET

I Introduction

Il serait inconvenant de débuter cette chronique en ne mentionnant pas que l'année 2009 marquait le 100ᵉ anniversaire du ministère des Affaires étrangères du Canada. L'évolution de ce ministère — qu'on appelle aujourd'hui ministère des Affaires étrangères et du Commerce international — au cours de ce siècle est notable à plus d'un point de vue. À ses débuts, "guère plus qu'un bureau de poste de prestige"[1] et situé au-dessus d'un salon de coiffure pour hommes à Ottawa, le ministère est devenu, au fil des ans, un haut lieu de la diplomatie et d'expérience avec plus de 9 000 employés

Richard Ouellet est professeur titulaire de droit international économique à la Faculté de droit et à l'Institut québécois des hautes études internationales de l'Université Laval et membre du Centre d'études interaméricaines (CEI). L'auteur tient à remercier le CEI pour son appui financier et Mme Sophie Lépine Zaruba pour sa collaboration dans la préparation de la présente chronique.

1 Affaires étrangères et Commerce international Canada, *"Jouer dans la cour des grands" Histoire du ministère des Affaires étrangères et du Commerce international. Des débuts modestes: 1909-1921*, en ligne: Affaires étrangères et Commerce international Canada <http://www.international.gc.ca/history-histoire/department-ministere/index.aspx?lang=fra>.

2 Affaires étrangères et Commerce international Canada, *"Jouer dans la cour des grands" Histoire du ministère des Affaires étrangères et du Commerce international. Un ministère intégré: De 1984 jusqu'au présent*, en ligne: Affaires étrangères et Commerce international Canada <http://www.international.gc.ca/history-histoire/department -ministere/1984-present.aspx?lang=fra>; Greg Donaghy, "Le ministère des Affaires étrangères souligne son centenaire" (2009) 32:4 Rev Parlementaire Canadienne

et 168 missions dans 109 pays.[2] On doit à ce ministère le développement d'une politique commerciale canadienne forte, basée sur une expertise professionnelle qui fait l'envie de plusieurs nations de par le monde.

Malgré les réjouissances qu'amène la célébration d'un centenaire, l'année 2009 en a été une de difficultés au plan commercial et celle du pire ralentissement économique depuis la Grande Crise de 1929. La croissance du PIB au niveau mondial est ainsi passée de 5,2% en 2007 à 3,0% en 2008, puis à −0,6% en 2009 alors que pour les économies avancées, le scénario était encore plus catastrophique, passant de 2,8% en 2007 à 0,5% en 2008 et à -3,2% en 2009.[3] Le Canada, avec un recul de 2,6% en 2009 serait le pays ayant connu le plus faible ralentissement du G-7, précédant tout juste les États-Unis.[4] Le dollar canadien a en outre connu une forte volatilité par rapport au dollar américain pour l'année 2009. Sa valeur aura fluctué de 76,9 cents à 97,2 cents pour une moyenne annuelle de 87,57 cents.[5] Tous ces chambardements économiques internationaux ont bien entendu eu des répercussions sur le volume des échanges au pays. Les exportations canadiennes sont ainsi passées en 2009 à 436,3 milliards de dollars, en baisse de 22,1% par rapport à 2008.[6] De cette baisse, 40% serait attribuable aux produits de l'énergie.[7] Dans ce contexte, les relations nord-américaines sont demeurées somme toute assez calmes. Mis à part le renforcement de la sécurité à la frontière canado-états-unienne[8], aucune avancée

---

9, en ligne: Revue parlementaire canadienne <http://www.revparl.ca/32/4/32n4_09f_Donaghy.pdf>.

[3] Affaires étrangères et Commerce international Canada, *Le commerce international du Canada: Le point sur le commerce et l'investissement, 2010*, Ottawa, Travaux publics et Services gouvernementaux Canada, 2010, à la p 10, en ligne: Affaires étrangères et Commerce international Canada <http://www.international.gc.ca/economist -economiste/assets/pdfs/SoT_2010_AR_FRA.pdf> [MAECI, *Le point*].

[4] *Ibid* aux pp 10, 31 et 34.

[5] *Ibid* à la p 40.

[6] *Ibid* à la p 41.

[7] *Ibid*.

[8] Parmi ces mesures, on note l'obligation de présenter un passeport valide (ou un autre document sécuritaire approuvé) lors du passage à la frontière canado-états-unienne depuis le 1er juin 2009: Agence des services frontaliers du Canada, *Communiqué National 2009*, Ottawa, 2009, en ligne: Agence des services frontaliers du Canada <http://www.cbsa-asfc.gc.ca/media/release-communique/2009/2009-06-01-fra.html>.

majeure à l'intégration nord-américaine ou à l'ALÉNA ne s'est manifestée au cours de l'année.

Si les relations nord-américaines n'ont pas connu le dynamisme souhaité pour le Canada, la réalité des relations commerciales avec le reste du monde est différente. En effet, les exportations à destination des marchés non américains ayant subi un recul moins rapide que celles vers les États-Unis, une diversification des échanges canadiens a ainsi pu avoir lieu.[9] Malgré un contexte mondial plus ou moins favorable, le Canada a ainsi poursuivi son action bilatérale visant à "assurer des conditions d'accès favorables aux entreprises, aux investisseurs et aux innovateurs canadiens."[10] En cohérence avec la *Stratégie commerciale mondiale* publiée en janvier 2009 et en accord avec les discours anti-isolationnistes du Directeur général de l'OMC,[11] la négociation et la signature de plusieurs ententes de libre-échange, de promotion et de protection des investissements étrangers, mais aussi d'accords relatifs aux services aériens a pu avoir lieu. Le tout effectué avec une attention particulière pour les marchés émergents et en croissance, tel que le proposait le *Rapport sur les plans et les priorités* de 2009-2010 du MAECI.[12] Cette préoccupation s'est d'ailleurs reflétée dans les accords contractés, mais aussi dans le choix des missions commerciales effectuées par le ministre, notamment en Asie, au Moyen-Orient et en Amérique latine.

On constate donc que même si le gouvernement conservateur de Stephen Harper prévoyait en début d'année des mesures d'austérité et de soutien aux investissements propices à la croissance à

---

9 MAECI, *Le point, supra* note 3 à la p 44.

10 Gouvernement du Canada, *Saisir les avantages globaux: La stratégie commerciale mondiale pour assurer la croissance et la prospérité du Canada*, Ottawa, Travaux publics et Services gouvernementaux Canada, 2009, à la p 5, en ligne: Affaires étrangères et Commerce international Canada <http://www.international.gc.ca/commerce/assets/pdfs/GCS-fr.pdf>.

11 Pascal Lamy notait dans un discours devant la Chambre de commerce internationale que: "Face à la crise économique mondiale, l'ennemi numéro un est l'isolationnisme": Pascal Lamy, "Le commerce fait partie de la solution à la crise économique mondiale," Chambre de commerce internationale, 2 février 2009, en ligne: OMC <http://www.wto.org/french/news_f/sppl_f/sppl114_f.htm>.

12 Affaires étrangères et Commerce international Canada, *Rapport sur les plans et les priorités 2009-2010: Affaires étrangères et du Commerce international Canada*, Ottawa, aux pp 4-5, 9-10, en ligne: Secrétariat du Conseil du Trésor du Canada <http://www.tbs-sct.gc.ca/rpp/2009-2010/inst/ext/exto1-fra.asp>.

long terme,[13] de nombreux efforts ont été déployés à court terme pour propager l'action canadienne à l'étranger et ainsi sortir de la récession. Le dynamisme canadien s'est également traduit en 2009 par une implication dans de nombreux différends commerciaux, essentiellement pris en charge par le système de règlement des différends de l'Organisation mondiale du commerce (OMC).

Nous observerons ainsi dans les prochains développements les activités commerciales canadiennes aux plans bilatéral et régional, puis dans une perspective multilatérale.

II Le commerce canadien aux plans bilatéral et régional

A Les négociations commerciales aux plans bilatéral et régional

1 *L'intégration nord-américaine*

Dès le début de 2009, les relations commerciales canado-américaines ont été mises à mal par la crise économique. Le 17 février 2009, le Congrès des États-Unis adoptait l'*American Recovery and Reinvestment Act of 2009*,[14] un vaste plan de relance économique par lequel 787 milliards étaient injectés sur deux ans dans l'économie américaine. De ce montant, environ 240 milliards étaient destinés à financer des marchés publics d'infrastructures. Or, ce qui devait être une bonne nouvelle pour les fournisseurs canadiens prêts à répondre aux appels d'offres provenant des États-Unis était en fait largement réservé aux fournisseurs états-uniens. La loi telle qu'adoptée en février 2009 comportait à son article 1605 une clause de type *Buy American* par laquelle il était prescrit que les fonds rendus disponibles par le plan de relance ne pouvaient être affectés à des travaux publics que si le fer, l'acier et les produits manufacturés utilisés dans le cadre de ces travaux étaient d'origine états-unienne. Le Canada s'est évidemment étonné de la présence d'une telle clause qui allait peut-être à l'encontre des termes du chapitre 10 de l'ALÉNA portant sur les marchés publics. Des négociations sur les marchés publics se sont donc engagées entre les deux gouvernements et un accord bilatéral sur la question est attendu début 2010.

---

13 Ottawa, Parlement du Canada, *Discours du Trône*, 40ᵉ lég, 2ᵉ sess (26 janvier 2009), en ligne: Discours du Trône <http://www.discours.gc.ca/fra/media.asp?id =1384>.

14 *American Recovery and Reinvestment Act of 2009*, Pub L No 111-5, 123 Stat 115, en ligne: U.S. Government Printing Office <http://www.gpo.gov/fdsys/pkg/PLAW -111publ5/pdf/PLAW-111publ5.pdf>.

Les 27 et 28 avril 2009, le ministre du commerce Stockwell Day s'est rendu à Washington où il a rencontré le représentant au Commerce, M Ron Kirk et le secrétaire au Commerce, M Gary Locke, pour discuter de questions relatives au commerce entre les deux pays, notamment l'étiquetage du pays d'origine, les dispositions du programme "*Buy American*," le bois d'œuvre résineux, le respect des droits de propriété intellectuelle et le crédit pour l'utilisation, comme carburant de remplacement, d'un résidu appelé "liqueur noire."

Le Partenariat Canada-Mexique (PCM) s'est aussi poursuivi en 2009 alors que la septième réunion annuelle du PCM s'est tenue le 24 mars à Cuernavaca, au Mexique. Rappelons que ce partenariat est composé de sept groupes de travail s'intéressant aux thèmes suivants: commerce, investissement, innovation, agro-industrie, habitation et viabilité urbaine, capital humain, énergie, mobilité de la main-d'œuvre et environnement et foresterie.

Au plan trilatéral, en octobre, s'est tenue à Dallas au Texas la réunion de 2009 de la Commission du libre-échange de l'ALÉNA. À l'issue de cette réunion sans éclat, le représentant au Commerce des États-Unis, l'ambassadeur Ron Kirk, le secrétaire à l'Économie du Mexique, M Gerardo Ruiz Mateos, et le ministre du Commerce international du Canada et ministre de la porte d'entrée de l'Asie-Pacifique, l'honorable Stockwell Day, ont publié une déclaration conjointe dans laquelle il était convenu de créer des groupes de travail pour renforcer l'intégration économique et commerciale entre les trois pays.[15]

2   *Les autres développements aux plans bilatéral et régional ou la prolifération d'accords bilatéraux et régionaux dans les marchés émergents et en croissance*

L'année 2009 a été faste pour le Canada quant à la négociation et à la conclusion d'accords économiques. Il va de soi que le point d'orgue de l'année a été le lancement de négociations avec l'Union européenne en vue d'en arriver à un accord de partenariat économique approfondi. À l'occasion du Sommet Canada-UE qui s'est tenu le 6 mai à Prague, en République tchèque, les dirigeants

---

15 Commission du libre-échange de l'ALÉNA, Réunion 2009, Déclaration conjointe, Dallas, Texas, 19 octobre 2009, en ligne: Affaires étrangères et Commerce international Canada <http://www.international.gc.ca/trade-agreements -accords-commerciaux/agr-acc/nafta-alena/js-dallas.aspx?lang=fr>.

européens et canadiens ont annoncé le lancement de négociations sur un accord économique de large portée. Il a alors été décidé que la première série de négociations devait avoir lieu dès que possible. Compte tenu de l'importance du marché européen, beaucoup est attendu de ces négociations auxquelles doivent participer les provinces canadiennes.

Des négociations en vue d'accords de libre-échange ont aussi été lancées avec le Maroc en juin et avec l'Ukraine en septembre.

D'autres accords de libre-échange ont été conclus quant à eux avec la Colombie, la Jordanie, l'Association européenne de libre-échange, le Pérou et le Panama.

Le Canada a aussi multiplié les accords de transport aérien, de coopération économique, de promotion et de protection des investissements.[16]

B   LES DIFFÉRENDS LIÉS À DES ACCORDS BILATÉRAUX OU
     RÉGIONAUX IMPLIQUANT LE CANADA

1   *Le bois d'œuvre résineux*

En application de l'Accord sur le bois d'oeuvre résineux de 2006,[17] la *London Court of International Arbitration* a rendu une décision le 26 février en réponse à une plainte des États-Unis contre le Canada. Donnant raison aux États-Unis, le tribunal a estimé que le Canada était en défaut d'appliquer correctement le facteur d'ajustement à l'égard du bois d'œuvre provenant des provinces de l'Ontario, du Québec, du Manitoba et de la Saskatchewan pour les six premiers mois de l'année 2007. Le tribunal a donc ordonné au gouvernement du Canada d'imposer des droits de 10% sur le bois d'œuvre provenant de ces quatre provinces jusqu'à ce qu'un montant de 68,26 millions de dollars ait été perçu.[18]

---

[16] On trouvera le détail de ces accords ou de l'état de ces négociations sur diverses pages du site du ministère des Affaires étrangères et du Commerce international du Canada, en ligne: <http://www.international.gc.ca/trade-agreements-accords -commerciaux/agr-acc/index.aspx?lang=fr>.

[17] *Accord sur le bois d'œuvre résineux entre le gouvernement du Canada et le gouvernement des États-Unis d'Amérique*, 12 septembre 2006, RT Can 2006 n⁰ 23 (entrée en vigueur: 12 octobre 2006).

[18] *United States of America, Claimant v Canada, Respondent, Award on Remedies, Case 7941* (23 février 2009)(London Court of International Arbitration), en ligne: Affaires étrangères et Commerce international Canada <http://www.international. gc.ca/controls-controles/assets/pdfs/softwood/USAvCanada0921 9Award onRemedies.pdf>.

En avril 2009, le Canada a requis une nouvelle décision arbitrale. Le Canada prétendait qu'un montant de 34 millions plus intérêts constituait une réparation correcte du manquement à l'Accord sur le bois d'œuvre constaté en février dans l'affaire 7941.[19] Dans une décision rendue en septembre, les prétentions canadiennes ont été rejetées.[20]

Aussi en 2009, se sont tenues à Ottawa des audiences relatives à une plainte des États-Unis contre divers programmes ontariens et québécois de crédits d'impôt, de prêts, de garanties de prêts ou d'aménagement forestier qui vont, aux dires des États-Unis, à l'encontre des termes de l'Accord sur le bois d'œuvre résineux de 2006.[21] Une décision dans cette affaire est attendue en 2010 ou 2011.

Enfin, une brève décision en lien avec l'Accord sur le bois d'œuvre résineux de 2006 a été rendue sous le chapitre 19 de l'ALÉNA le 30 janvier 2009. Dans une ordonnance de 11 pages, un groupe spécial binational constitué en vertu de l'article 1904 a accueilli une requête en rejet présentée par le département du Commerce des États-Unis. Cette requête visait à faire rejeter une instance en raison de son caractère théorique.[22] Le département du Commerce demandait qu'il soit mis fin à toute procédure administrative et examen d'entreprise en lien avec une ordonnance révoquée à la suite de la signature de l'Accord sur le bois d'œuvre résineux. Une entreprise, Gorman Bros. Ltd., s'opposait à cette requête en rejet, arguant qu'elle avait droit à un examen administratif accéléré, droit qui lui serait nié si la requête en rejet était acceptée. En raison de

---

19 *Canada, Claimant v United States of America, Respondent, Request for Arbitration* (2 avril 2009) (London Court of International Arbitration), en ligne: Affaires étrangères et Commerce international Canada <http://www.international.gc.ca/controls-controles/assets/pdfs/softwood/RequestforArbitration0304.pdf>.

20 *Canada, Claimant v United States of America, Respondent, Award, Case 91312* (27 septembre 2009) (London Court of International Arbitration), en ligne: Affaires étrangères et Commerce international Canada <http://www.international.gc.ca/controls-controles/assets/pdfs/softwood/CanadavUSA_Award21092009.pdf>.

21 *United States of America, Claimant v Canada, Respondent, Request for Arbitration, Case 81010* (18 janvier 2008) (London Court of International Arbitration), en ligne: Affaires étrangères et Commerce international Canada <http://www.international.gc.ca/controls-controles/assets/pdfs/softwood/jan18-ArbitrationRequest.pdf>.

22 *Certains produits de bois d'œuvre résineux en provenance du Canada: résultats finals de l'examen administratif en matière de droits compensateurs et annulation de certains examens individuels d'entreprises* (2009), USA-CDA-2005-1904-01 (Groupe spéc art 1904), en ligne: Secrétariat de l'ALÉNA <http://registry.nafta-sec-alena.org/cmdocuments/4d78e358-02e5-4dec-9e82-a0f36c876941.pdf>.

l'absence de portée pratique de la demande de Gorman, en raison de l'absence de compétence du Groupe spécial d'ordonner un quelconque redressement pour Gorman dans les circonstances, la requête en rejet a été accueillie.[23]

2   *Les autres affaires en lien avec des accords bilatéraux ou régionaux*

Deux décisions en matière de dumping qui sont indirectement en lien avec l'application de l'ALÉNA au Canada méritent ici une brève mention. Le 1er septembre, le Tribunal du commerce international des États-Unis a donné raison au Canada, à la Commission canadienne du blé et à trois gouvernements provinciaux et a ordonné le remboursement de droits antidumping et compensateurs perçus sur les importations de blé de force roux de printemps.[24] Le 20 novembre, les États-Unis en ont appelé de cette décision devant la Cour d'appel fédérale des États-Unis. Il sera intéressant de suivre la suite de cette affaire en 2010.

L'autre décision a été rendue sous le chapitre 19 de l'ALÉNA par un groupe spécial binational dans une affaire entre le Mexique et les États-Unis.[25] En novembre 2006, à la suite d'une enquête en dumping, la *Unidad de Practicas Comerciales Internacionales* du *Secretaria de Economia* du Mexique a rendu une détermination finale à l'encontre de pommes *"red and golden delicious"* importées des États-Unis et a imposé des droits antidumping. Ces droits antidumping allaient de 6,40% à 47,05% selon l'importateur en cause. Après examen, le groupe spécial binational a notamment conclu que la période de référence utilisée par les autorités dans leur enquête était trop éloignée dans le temps pour justifier l'application de droits. Il a aussi estimé entre autres que l'enquête avait été faite à partir de données insuffisantes. Il a donc renvoyé l'affaire devant les autorités mexicaines pour qu'une autre détermination mieux fondée soit rendue.[26]

---

[23] *Ibid*, conclusion.

[24] *Canadian Wheat Board and the Government of Canada v United States and the United States Department of Commerce* (2009) United States Court of International Trade, Consol. Court 07-00058, en ligne: United States Court of International Trade <http://www.cit.uscourts.gov/slip_op/Slip_op09/09-92.pdf>.

[25] *Re Antidumping Duty Investigation on Imports of Certain Red Delicious Apples and Golden Delicious Apples from the United States of America* (2009), MEX-USA-2006-1904-02 (Group spéc art 1904), en ligne: Secrétariat de l'ALÉNA <http://registry.nafta-sec-alena.org/cmdocuments/f5b4cb9b-0637-4e2f-9b73-32d09f971b36.pdf>.

[26] *Ibid* aux pp 31-32.

III LE COMMERCE CANADIEN ET L'ORGANISATION MONDIALE DU
   COMMERCE (OMC)

A   LES DÉVELOPPEMENTS DANS LE SYSTÈME COMMERCIAL
    MULTILATÉRAL EN 2009

Si l'année 2009 n'a pas permis d'avancées notables dans les négociations commerciales multilatérales, on verra qu'elle a tout de
même été une année de fébrile activité à l'OMC. Les principaux
acteurs et instances du système commercial multilatéral se sont
montrés dynamiques.

Dans les nouvelles touchant ces acteurs, on se sera réjoui du renouvellement de mandat du directeur général Pascal Lamy, décidé par
le Conseil général à sa réunion du 30 avril.[27] Le mandat de M Lamy
a été renouvelé pour quatre ans à compter du 1er septembre 2009.

L'Organe de règlement des différends, quant à lui, a décidé du
renouvellement de M David Unterhalter comme membre de
l'Organe d'appel et a désigné deux nouveaux membres en les personnes de Ricardo Ramirez Hernandez et d'un professeur de droit
international économique prolifique et très reconnu, M Peter Van
den Bossche.[28]

Enfin, parmi les nouvelles affectant en 2009 les principaux acteurs
du système commercial multilatéral, comment passer sous silence
la note verbale par laquelle le Président du Conseil de l'Union
européenne et le Président de la Commission des Communautés
européennes ont notifié l'OMC des effets du Traité de Lisbonne
qui allait entrer en vigueur le 1er décembre 2009:

Le Traité de Lisbonne modifiant le Traité sur l'Union européenne et le
Traité instituant la Communauté européenne entrera en vigueur le 1er
décembre 2009.

En conséquence, à compter de cette date, l'Union européenne se subs-
tituera et succédera à la Communauté européenne (article premier, troisième paragraphe du Traité sur l'Union européenne, tel qu'il résulte des
modifications apportées par le Traité de Lisbonne).

---

27 OMC, Conseil Général, *Compte rendu de la réunion tenue au Centre William Rappard
   les 29 et 30 avril 2009*, OMC Doc WT/GC/M/119 (23 juin 2009), en ligne: OMC
   <http://docsonline.wto.org/DDFDocuments/u/WT/GC/M119.doc>.

28 OMC, Organe de règlement des différends, *Compte rendu de la réunion tenue le 19
   juin 2009 au Centre William Rappard*, OMC Doc WT/DSB/M/270 (28 août 2009),
   aux para. 82 à 91, en ligne: OMC <http://docsonline.wto.org/DDFDocuments/u/
   WT/DSB/M270.doc>.

Par conséquent, à compter de cette date, l'Union européenne exercera tous les droits et assumera toutes les obligations de la Communauté européenne, y compris son statut au sein de l'Organisation, tout en continuant à exercer les droits et assumer les obligations existants de l'Union européenne.

En particulier, à compter de cette date, l'Union européenne succédera à la Communauté européenne pour tous les accords conclus et tous les engagements pris par elle avec votre Organisation et pour tous les accords et engagements adoptés au sein de votre Organisation et ayant force obligatoire pour la Communauté européenne.[29]

1   Les négociations commerciales multilatérales au niveau ministériel

Dans le contexte de la crise économique ayant sévi en 2009, le directeur de l'OMC, Pascal Lamy, a plusieurs fois prédit que la conclusion du Cycle de Doha serait favorable à une reprise économique. Pour lui, le cycle de négociations constitue le meilleur plan de relance mondial possible.[30] Un tel aboutissement des négociations a ainsi maintes fois été proposé pour 2010, tel que le calendrier des échéances le prévoyait.[31] Néanmoins, en juin, le Directeur général devait appeler les Membres à "passer de la musique d'ambiance à la piste de danse"[32] en intensifiant les négociations, l'engagement politique et ministériel et le travail technique à Genève.

---

[29] OMC, *Note verbale du Conseil de l'Union européenne et de la Commission des Communautés européennes*, OMC Doc WT/L/779 (30 novembre 2009), en ligne: OMC <http://docsonline.wto.org/DDFDocuments/u/WT/L/779.doc>.

[30] Pascal Lamy, "M. Lamy reçoit le prix du Mondialiste de l'année," Conseil international du Canada, présentée à Toronto, 3 novembre 2009, en ligne: OMC <http://www.wto.org/french/news_f/sppl_f/sppl141_f.htm>; Pascal Lamy, "M. Lamy: Le succès du Cycle de Doha peut rapporter un double dividende: relance mondiale et réforme structurelle", Sommet de l'Association allemande des constructeurs de machines et d'équipement, présentée à Berlin, 13 octobre 2009, en ligne: OMC <http://www.wto.org/french/news_f/sppl_f/sppl137_f.htm>; Pascal Lamy, "M. Lamy 'Le commerce fait partie de la solution à la crise économique mondiale,'" présentée à la Chambre de commerce internationale, 2 février 2009, en ligne: OMC <http://www.wto.org/french/news_f/sppl_f/sppl114_f.htm>.

[31] On observe qu'à la section Nouvelles 2009 de l'OMC, en ligne: <http://www.wto.org/french/news_f/news09_f/news09_f.htm>, Pascal Lamy propose à plus d'une dizaine de reprises la fin du Cycle de Doha pour 2010, soit notamment les 13 et 24 juillet, 3, 16 et 28 septembre, 20 octobre, 30 novembre, 1er, 2 et 17 décembre.

[32] Pascal Lamy, "M. Lamy: 'Nous devons passer de la musique d'ambiance à la piste de danse,'" conférence de presse, présentée à Paris, 25 juin 2009, en ligne: OMC <http://www.wto.org/french/news_f/news09_f/dgpl_25jun09_f.htm>.

Alors que les déclarations d'intention des hauts dirigeants fusaient en début d'année, celles-ci sont peu à peu tombées dans l'oubli après juin. L'Inde prend alors l'initiative d'organiser une réunion ministérielle informelle à New Delhi afin de préparer le terrain pour le Sommet du G-20 de Pittsburgh. Lors de ce dernier événement, aucun document officiel de fond ne sera déposé concernant l'importance de faire avancer les négociations multilatérales. Seule la déclaration finale du Sommet fera état de manière très générale de l'importance de faire progresser le Cycle de Doha et de lutter contre le protectionnisme.[33] M Lamy ayant néanmoins noté un changement d'attitude des dirigeants, le plan de travail des négociations de septembre à décembre 2009 s'annonçait alors assez chargé, montrant une certaine volonté de l'OMC et peut-être de ses Membres de faire mieux avancer les travaux.[34]

La 7e Conférence ministérielle de la fin novembre a ensuite été l'occasion de réaffirmer l'importance de la conclusion du Cycle de Doha pour 2010 par les ministres. Une forte convergence a d'ailleurs été relevée quant à l'importance du commerce et du Cycle pour la relance économique et la réduction de la pauvreté dans les pays en développement.[35] Le Président de la Conférence, M Andrés Velasco, ministre des Finances chilien, a également résumé les principales questions abordées lors de la rencontre, à savoir la prolifération des accords commerciaux régionaux, la transparence et l'inclusion, le renforcement des capacités, le système de règlement des différends et les changements climatiques. En déclaration plénière, le Canada, représenté par son ministre du Commerce

---

[33] G-20, "Leaders' Statement," Pittsburgh Summit, 24-25 septembre 2009, aux paras 28, 42 et 49, en ligne: <http://www.g20.org/Documents/pittsburgh_summit_leaders_statement_250909.pdf>.

[34] OMC, *DDA Work Plan September - December 2009*, en ligne: OMC <http://www.wto.org/english/news_e/news09_e/programme_dda_sept_dec09_e.doc>; Pascal Lamy, "Problèmes mondiaux, solutions mondiales: Vers une meilleure gouvernance mondiale", Forum public de l'OMC, 28 septembre 2009, en ligne: OMC <http://www.wto.org/french/news_f/sppl_f/sppl136_f.htm>.

[35] OMC, *Septième Conférence Ministérielle: Résumé du Président de la Conférence Ministérielle*, OMC Doc WT/MIN(09)/18 (2 décembre 2009), 7e Session, en ligne: OMC <http://docsonline.wto.org/GEN_highLightParent.asp?qu=%28%28+%40meta%5FSymbol+WT%FCMIN%2A%29+and+%28%40meta%5FTitle+Seventh+Session+and+NOT+ST%2A%29%29+&doc=D%3A%2FDDFDOCUMENTS%2FU%2FWT%2FMIN09%2F18%2EDOC%2EHTM&curdoc=20&popTitle=WT%2FMIN%2809%29%2F18>.

international Stockwell Day, rappelait l'importance de trouver des pistes d'action sur les questions des biens environnementaux et de la dimension commerciale des changements climatiques.[36] Rappelant les difficultés économiques mondiales, M Day affirme que *"The single most important thing we can do to help secure a recovery from the global economic crisis and build momentum for future growth and stability is to bring the Doha Development Round to a successful conclusion."*[37] Dans cette veine, le ministre canadien s'engageait de nouveau, en décembre 2009, à renforcer l'OMC en vue d'augmenter le commerce mondial tout en continuant à prendre une part active dans les négociations du Cycle de Doha.[38]

2   Les travaux des comités et groupes de travail

C'est évidemment dans un contexte de crise économique que les travaux des groupes de négociation ont débuté en 2009.

L'objectif à court terme du Cycle de Doha étant d'établir les modalités pour l'agriculture et l'accès aux marchés non agricoles (AMNA), beaucoup de travail restait à faire pour les délégations comme l'a rappelé le Président du Comité des négociations multilatérales en marge du Forum économique mondial de Davos.[39] Dans cette veine, plus d'une trentaine de documents de négociations[40] ont été soumis au cours de l'année dans le comité sur l'AMNA. Le Canada a poursuivi avec dynamisme son action dans ce comité en ce qui concerne la question des obstacles non tarifaires

---

[36] Stockwell Day, "The WTO, the Multilateral Trading System and the Global Economic Environment," Conférences ministérielles de l'OMC, 30 novembre 2009, à la 1, en ligne: OMC <http://www.wto.org/french/thewto_f/minist_f/min09_f/min09_statements_f.htm>.

[37] *Ibid.*

[38] Affaires étrangères et Commerce international Canada, communiqué n° 365, "Le Canada s'engage à renforcer l'OMC" (1er décembre 2009), en ligne: Affaires étrangères et Commerce international Canada <http://www.international.gc.ca/media_commerce/comm/news-communiques/2009/365.aspx?lang=fra>.

[39] OMC, Conseil général, *Rapport du Président du comité des négociations commerciales* (31 janvier 2009), en ligne: OMC <http://www.wto.org/french/news_f/news09_f/tnc_chair_report_03feb09_f.htm>.

[40] OMC, *Le Comité des négociations commerciales: Documents concernant les négociations, par sujet,* en ligne: OMC <http://www.wto.org/french/tratop_f/dda_f/tnc_f.htm>.

(ONT), en posant[41] ou répondant[42] à certaines interrogations sur le sujet. Néanmoins, l'année 2009 ne permettra pas de compléter les négociations de ce comité puisque bien peu a progressé selon les dires mêmes du Président du Comité des négociations multilatérales.

De son côté, le Groupe de négociation sur l'agriculture a connu des transformations au cours de l'année 2009. En effet, un changement de garde à la tête du comité s'est effectué en avril, quand M Crawford Falconer a été remplacé par l'Australien David Walker.[43] Aussi, l'action de fond de ce comité aura essentiellement eu lieu en 2008 même si un consensus n'avait alors pas été atteint.[44] Pour 2009, on ne dénombre, en fouillant sur le site de l'OMC, que huit documents de négociation, tous publiés par le Secrétariat, faisant par exemple la mise à jour de la valeur totale de la production agricole[45]

---

[41] Des questions sur les propositions concernant les ONT ont été posées dans le cadre de deux documents se recoupant: OMC, Groupe de négociation sur l'accès aux marchés, *Questions sur les propositions concernant les ONT,* OMC Doc JOB(09)/31 (30 mars 2009) et OMC, Groupe de négociation sur l'accès aux marchés, *Questions sur les propositions concernant les ONT (en anglais seulement),* OMC Doc JOB(09)/31/Corr.1 (2 avril 2009). Également, certaines questions concernant la transparence ont été adressées à une récapitulation des États-Unis: OMC, Groupe de négociation sur l'accès aux marchés, *Récapitulation établie par les États-Unis, contenant la dernière version de la proposition de texte sur les ONT pour l'Accord sur les obstacles non tarifaires se rapportant à la sécurité électrique et à la compatibilité électromagnétique (CEM) des produits électroniques, ainsi que l'historique des questions et réponses en rapport avec cette proposition,* OMC Doc TN/MA/W/125 (4 décembre 2009), en ligne: OMC <http://docsonline.wto.org/GEN_viewer window.asp?http://docsonline.wto.org:80/DDFDocuments/u/tn/ma/W125. doc>.

[42] Le Canada, en collaboration avec ses coauteurs, a répondu aux questions soulevées par la *Décision ministérielle sur les procédures visant à faciliter la recherche de solutions pour les ONT,* OMC Doc TN/MA/106 (9 mai 2008) dans le cadre du document OMC Doc TN/MA/W/110 (16 avril 2009) et de sa correction OMC Doc TN/MA/W/110/Corr.1 (24 avril 2009).

[43] OMC, *Rapport du Président, S.E. M. David Walker, au Comité des négociations commerciales aux fins du bilan dans le cadre du CNC,* OMC Doc TN/AG/25 (22 mars 2010), en ligne: OMC <http://www.wto.org/french/tratop_f/agric_f/negoti_tnc_22 march10_f.htm>; OMC, Comité de l'agriculture, Note du Secrétariat, *Rapport résumé de la trente-quatrième session extraordinaire formelle du comité de l'agriculture tenue le 22 avril 2009,* OMC Doc TN/AG/R/22 (14 mai 2009), sess extraordinaire.

[44] Richard Ouellet, "Chronique de Droit international économique en 2008" (2009) 47 ACDI 343 aux pp 356 à 359.

[45] OMC, Comité de l'agriculture, Note du Secrétariat: Révision, *Valeur totale de la production agricole,* OMC Doc TN/AG/S/21/Rev.3 (11 décembre 2009), sess extraordinaire.

ou observant la mise en oeuvre de certaines mesures d'aide reliées au coton.[46] Le Canada ne s'est pas montré particulièrement actif dans ce secteur en 2009. On note néanmoins que des travaux techniques relatifs au projet de modalités soumis en décembre 2008 ont été poursuivis par le biais de consultations et rencontres informelles.[47]

Le Groupe de négociation sur les règles, qui vise la clarification et l'amélioration des règles de l'Accord antidumping et de l'Accord sur les subventions et mesures compensatoires, a poursuivi ses discussions techniques de manière soutenue, notamment en matière de subvention à la pêche et de droits antidumping. Cependant, très peu de documents de négociation ont été élaborés, l'essentiel des travaux du comité ayant tourné autour d'une feuille de route présentée par le Président du Comité en début d'année.[48]

Le Groupe de négociation sur le développement a concentré ses efforts pour l'année 2009 sur des accords particuliers et sur le mécanisme de surveillance. À ce sujet, de nombreuses propositions informelles ont été présentées, notamment par le Canada.[49] Des différences conceptuelles entre les délégués sur l'objet d'un tel mécanisme empêcheraient les délégués d'obtenir consensus pour son préambule, mais l'avancement des travaux en ce qui concerne sa structure, sa portée et ses fonctions était satisfaisant.[50]

Au sein du Comité de négociation sur les aspects de propriété intellectuelle, les négociations ont bien progressé en 2009. En effet, des discussions ont entouré trois principales questions reliées au *Système multilatéral de notification et d'enregistrement des indications géographiques pour les vins et spiritueux.* Ces questions sont les suivantes:

---

[46] OMC, Sous-Comité du coton, Rapport de situation du Secrétariat, *Mise en œuvre des aspects relatifs à l'aide au développement des décisions se rapportant au coton de l'ensemble des résultats de juillet 2004 et du paragraphe 12 de la Déclaration ministérielle de Hong Kong,* OMC Doc TN/AG/SCC/W/11 et WT/CFMC/23 (7 septembre 2009).

[47] OMC, Notes d'information, *Agriculture: modalités de négociations,* en ligne: OMC <http://www.wto.org/french/tratop_f/dda_f/status_f/agric_f.htm>.

[48] OMC, Groupe de négociation sur les règles, *Réunion informelle ouverte avec les hauts-fonctionnaires — 25 novembre 2009,* OMC Doc TN/RL/W/246 (27 novembre 2009), à la 9, en ligne: OMC <http://docsonline.wto.org/DDFDocuments/u/tn/rl/W246.doc>.

[49] OMC, Comité du commerce et du développement, *Note sur la réunion du 23 juillet 2009,* OMC Doc TN/CTD/M/36 (24 août 2009), 36e sess extraordinaire.

[50] *Ibid* à la p 2.

- les effets juridiques de l'enregistrement et de la participation;
- les questions de la notification et de l'enregistrement;
- des questions comme les taxes, les frais et les charges administratives, en particulier pour les pays en développement et les pays les moins avancés Membres, ainsi que le traitement spécial et différencié.[51]

En novembre, le Président de ce comité, M Trevor Clarke, a quitté ses fonctions pour occuper un poste à l'OMPI. Il convient de souligner qu'avant de quitter, celui-ci a formulé cinq principes directeurs susceptibles de faire avancer les négociations, dans un document récapitulatif des négociations en cours concernant la propriété intellectuelle.[52] N'ayant pas recueilli l'unanimité au sein des délégués, ces principes ont été écartés et il a été entendu que les négociations se poursuivraient comme par le passé.[53] On remarque une forte participation canadienne aux travaux de ce comité alors que le pays prend une place importante dans trois des quatre comptes rendus de réunions publiés en 2009.[54]

Les négociations sur les services ont pris un nouvel élan à la suite de la présentation d'un projet de texte révisé sur la règlementation intérieure par le Président du Comité en mars. Cette question a ainsi occupé le groupe pour le reste de l'année,[55] laissant un peu

---

[51] OMC, Conseil des aspects des droits de propriété intellectuelle qui touchent au commerce, Rapport du Président, M l'Ambassadeur C Trevor Clarke (Barbade), *Système multilatéral de notification et d'enregistrement des indications géographiques pour les vins et spiritueux*, OMC Doc TN/IP/19 (25 novembre 2009), sess extraordinaire, à la p 2.

[52] *Ibid* aux pp 5 et 6.

[53] OMC, *Rapport du Président du Comité des négociations commerciales*, (22 février 2010), en ligne: OMC <http://www.wto.org/french/news_f/news10_f/tnc_chair_report_22feb10_f.htm>.

[54] OMC, Conseil des aspects des droits de propriété intellectuelle qui touchent au commerce, *Compte rendu de la réunion tenue au Centre William Rappard le 29 octobre 2008*, OMC Doc TN/IP/M/20 (26 février 2009); OMC, Conseil des aspects des droits de propriété intellectuelle qui touchent au commerce, *Compte rendu de la réunion tenue au Centre William Rappard le 5 mars 2009*, OMC Doc TN/IP/M/21 (28 mai 2009) ; OMC, Conseil des aspects des droits de propriété intellectuelle qui touchent au commerce, *Compte rendu de la réunion tenue au Centre William Rappard le 10 juin 2009*, OMC Doc TN/IP/M/22 (19 octobre 2009).

[55] OMC, *Rapport du Président du Comité des négociations commerciales*, (17 décembre 2009), en ligne: OMC <http://www.wto.org/french/news_f/news09_f/tnc_chair_report_17dec09_f.htm>.

de côté les trois autres questions devant être abordées.[56] Le Canada s'est fortement impliqué dans les négociations sur les services et a fréquemment fait entendre sa position lors des réunions en insistant sur l'importance d'éviter de faire avancer les travaux du comité en vase clos.[57]

Dans le Groupe sur la facilitation des échanges, un texte récapitulatif a été l'élément déclencheur d'une relance des négociations. Celui-ci ayant été publié en décembre, il permettra des progrès sur nombre de questions et donne un portrait plus clair de l'architecture du futur Accord sur la facilitation des échanges.[58] Le Canada apportera ici encore une contribution appréciable aux négociations, notamment par son implication dans la rédaction d'un *Guide d'auto-évaluation*.[59]

B   LES DIFFÉRENDS DEVANT L'OMC IMPLIQUANT LE CANADA

L'année 2009 aura été l'occasion d'un heureux constat pour les créateurs du mécanisme de règlement des différends de l'OMC. En effet, cette année aura été celle de l'introduction d'un 400ᵉ

---

[56] Les trois autres questions portent sur l'accès aux marchés, les règles de l'AGCS relatives aux mesures de sauvegarde d'urgence, aux marchés publics et aux subventions et la mise en œuvre des modalités pour les PMA: OMC, *Les négociations sur les services*, en ligne: OMC <http://www.wto.org/french/tratop_f/serv_f/s_negs_f.htm>; Pascal Lamy, "Rapport sur la deuxième Semaine des hauts fonctionnaires," Comité des négociations commerciales, 27 novembre 2009, en ligne: OMC <http://www.wto.org/french/news_f/news09_f/tnc_dg_stat_27nov09_f.htm>.

[57] OMC, Conseil du commerce des services, Note du Secrétariat, *Note sur la réunion du 6 avril 2009*, OMC Doc TN/S/M/30 (11 juin 2009), sess extraordinaire; OMC, Conseil du commerce des services, Note du Secrétariat, *Rapport de la réunion tenue le 29 juin 2009*, OMC Doc TN/S/M/31 (6 octobre 2009), sess extraordinaire, aux para. 3 à 6 essentiellement; OMC, Conseil du commerce des services, Note du Secrétariat, *Note sur la réunion du 9 octobre 2009*, OMC Doc TN/S/M/32 (6 novembre 2009), sess extraordinaire, notamment aux paras 35 à 37.

[58] OMC, Comité de négociation sur la facilitation des échanges, *Projet de texte de négociation récapitulatif*, OMC Doc TN/TF/W/165 (14 décembre 2009); OMC, Comité de négociation sur la facilitation des échanges, *Réunion du CNC du 22 mars 2010, Rapport du Président, M. l'Ambassadeur Sperisen-Yurt, au Comité des négociations commerciales aux fins du bilan dans le cadre du CNC*, OMC Doc TN/TF/7 (22 mars 2010).

[59] OMC, Comité de négociation sur la facilitation des échanges, *Négociations de l'OMC sur la facilitation des échanges. Guide d'autoévaluation: Révision*, OMC Doc TN/TF/W/143/Rev.3 (1er mai 2009).

différend commercial devant l'Organe de règlement des différends (ORD). Pour Pascal Lamy, il s'agit là d'un "vote de confiance qui plébiscite un système considéré par beaucoup comme un modèle à suivre pour le règlement pacifique des différends qui surgissent au niveau international dans d'autres domaines des relations politiques ou économiques."[60]

Des 400 premières affaires portées devant l'ORD, 33 ont été amenées par le Canada à titre de plaignant tandis que 15 demandes de consultation visaient une mesure canadienne. Ces données révèlent que le Canada est, parmi les Membres de l'OMC, le troisième plus actif devant l'ORD, derrière les États-Unis et les Communautés européennes.

Plusieurs des affaires impliquant le Canada connurent des développements notables au cours de l'année 2009. Ces développements sont présentés ici selon l'ordre numérique des différends.[61]

1   Communautés européennes – Mesures concernant les viandes et les produits carnés (hormones) (DS48)

Dans une communication déposée le 22 décembre 2008 et diffusée le 8 janvier 2009,[62] les Communautés européennes demandaient l'ouverture de consultations avec le Canada au titre des articles 21:5 et 4 du Mémorandum d'accord sur les règles et procédures régissant le règlement des différends. Ce recours constituait en quelque sorte la suite obligée des conclusions et recommandations du rapport de l'Organe d'appel adopté par l'ORD en 2008 dans l'affaire *Canada – Maintien de la suspension d'obligations dans le différend CE-Hormones (DS 321)*.[63]

60 OMC, communiqué PRESS/578 "Le nombre des différends portés devant l'OMC atteint la barre des 400" (6 novembre 2009), en ligne: OMC <http://www.wto.org/french/news_f/pres09_f/pr578_f.htm>.

61 Nous résumons ici les développements dans les affaires où le Canada est plaignant ou défendeur. Le format de la chronique ne permet pas de résumer les développements des affaires dans lesquelles le Canada est tierce partie.

62 *Communautés européennes – Mesures concernant les viandes et les produits carnés (hormones): Recours des Communautés européennes à l'article 21:5 du Mémorandum d'accord sur le règlement des différends* (8 janvier 2009), OMC Doc WT/DS48/21, en ligne: OMC <http://docsonline.wto.org/DDFDocuments/u/WT/DS/48-21.doc>.

63 Voir Richard Ouellet, "Chronique de droit international économique en 2008" (2009) 47 ACDI 343 aux pp 365 à 367.

L'objet de la demande des Communautés européennes est d'obtenir que le Canada mette fin à la suspension des concessions qu'il applique à l'égard des Communautés depuis une dizaine d'années. Pour bien comprendre ce recours européen, un bref retour en arrière s'impose.

On se rappellera qu'en 1996, le Canada et les États-Unis avaient demandé et obtenu l'établissement de groupes spéciaux pour juger de la conformité avec le GATT et l'Accord SPS de mesures européennes qui interdisaient ou restreignaient l'administration de six hormones à des animaux d'exploitation et interdisaient la mise sur le marché des animaux auxquels ces hormones avaient été administrées ainsi que la mise en marché des viandes de ces animaux.

Le 13 février 1998, l'Organe de règlement des différends a adopté le rapport de l'Organe d'appel dans lequel il est constaté que les mesures européennes dénoncées par le Canada et les États-Unis n'étaient pas établies sur la base d'une évaluation des risques au sens de l'article 5:1 et 5:2 de l'Accord SPS.[64]

Tenant compte des recommandations de l'ORD, les Communautés européennes ont ensuite entrepris et financé des études et des projets de recherche spécifiques sur les six hormones en cause. Elles ont demandé à des pays tiers leurs données et informations scientifiques sur ces hormones. Elles ont examiné les conclusions de rapports de groupes d'experts indépendants et les preuves et renseignements scientifiques disponibles au sujet des six hormones. Sur la base de ces évaluations de risque, les Communautés européennes ont adopté en 2003 la Directive 2003/74/CE.[65] Cette directive prévoit une interdiction permanente de la mise sur le marché des viandes et produits carnés provenant d'animaux traités à l'oestradiol-17β et une interdiction provisoire de la mise sur le marché des viandes et produits carnés provenant d'animaux traités aux cinq autres hormones en cause. Après l'adoption de cette directive, les Communautés européennes ont continué de recueillir et d'examiner les renseignements pertinents disponibles sur les cinq hormones en cause dans l'interdiction provisoire.

---

[64] Voir les constatations et recommandations du rapport *Communautés européennes – Mesures concernant les viandes et les produits carnés (hormones) (Canada)* (16 janvier 1998), OMC Doc WT/DS48/AB/R (Rapport de l'Organe d'appel), en ligne: OMC <http://docsonline.wto.org/DDFDocuments/r/WT/DS/48ABR-00.pdf>.

[65] CE, *Directive 2003/74/CE du Parlement européen et du Conseil du 22 septembre 2003 modifiant la Directive°96/22/CE du Conseil concernant l'interdiction d'utilisation de certaines substances à effet hormonal ou thyréostatique et des substances βagonistes dans les spéculations animales*, [2003] JO, L 262/17.

Dans le recours qu'elles ont déposé en janvier 2009, les Communautés européennes prétendent qu'en recueillant et en analysant toutes les preuves scientifiques pertinentes disponibles, en adoptant la Directive 2003/74/CE sur la base d'évaluations de risques et en s'efforçant d'obtenir des renseignements additionnels sur les hormones pour lesquelles elles ont prononcé une interdiction provisoire, les Communautés ont rendu conformes aux dispositions de l'Accord SPS les mesures qui avaient été jugées incompatibles en 1998.

Les Communautés européennes considèrent donc qu'elles se sont conformées sur le fond aux recommandations de l'ORD et que leurs mesures jugées incompatibles ont été éliminées. Selon les Communautés, le Canada n'est donc plus en droit de suspendre des concessions et d'imposer des droits d'importation plus élevés que les taux consolidés sur les importations en provenance des Communautés européennes.

2 *Communautés européennes – Mesures affectant l'approbation et la commercialisation des produits biotechnologiques (Plaignant: Canada) (DS292)*

Dans cette affaire qui durait depuis plus de six ans, et après avoir prorogé plusieurs fois le délai raisonnable de mise en œuvre du rapport du Groupe spécial, le Canada et l'Union européenne ont annoncé à la mi-juillet en être arrivés à une solution convenue d'un commun accord.[66] Au terme de l'accord intervenu et notifié à l'ORD, les Communautés européennes (CE) et le Canada ont convenu d'établir "un dialogue bilatéral sur les questions d'intérêt commun concernant l'accès aux marchés pour les produits agricoles biotechnologiques."[67] Des réunions doivent avoir lieu deux fois par an, en alternance à Bruxelles et à Ottawa. Le dialogue portera notamment sur les approbations de produits génétiquement modifiés (GM) sur le territoire du Canada ou des CE, les perspectives commerciales et économiques pour les approbations futures de produits GM, toute incidence sur le commerce liée à des approbations asynchrones de produits GM ou la dissémination accidentelle

---

66 *Communautés européennes – Mesures affectant l'approbation et la commercialisation des produits biotechnologiques: Notification d'une solution convenue d'un commun accord* (17 juillet 2009), OMC Doc WT/DS292/40, en ligne: OMC <http://docsonline. wto.org/DDFDocuments/u/G/TBT/D29A1.doc>.

67 *Ibid* à la p 2.

de produits non autorisés et, de façon générale, les mesures, pratiques et législations mises en place par les CE ou par le Canada en rapport avec la biotechnologie. Cette affaire semble enfin connaître son dénouement.

3   Chine – Mesures affectant les importations de pièces automobiles (Plaignant: Canada) (DS342)

Le rapport rendu par l'Organe d'appel à la toute fin de l'année 2008[68] dans cette affaire a été adopté par l'ORD dès sa première réunion de 2009.[69]

À la réunion de l'ORD du 31 août 2009, à la demande du Canada, des États-Unis et des Communautés européennes, la Chine a informé l'ORD et ses Membres que:

Le 15 août 2009, le Ministère de l'industrie et des technologies de l'information ainsi que la Commission nationale pour le développement et la réforme avaient publié un décret conjoint pour stopper la mise en œuvre des dispositions pertinentes concernant l'importation de pièces automobiles dans le cadre de la Politique de développement de l'industrie automobile. Le 28 août 2009, l'Administration générale des douanes et les organismes compétents avaient promulgué un décret conjoint afin d'abroger le Décret n° 125. Tous ces nouveaux décrets entreraient en vigueur le 1er septembre 2009. Par conséquent, la Chine était heureuse de déclarer qu'elle avait mis ses mesures en conformité avec les recommandations et décisions de l'ORD.[70]

4   États-Unis d'Amérique – Certaines prescriptions en matière d'étiquetage indiquant le pays d'origine (EPO) (Plaignant: Canada) (DS384)

Cette affaire concernant les prescriptions en matière d'étiquetage indiquant le pays d'origine s'était amorcée à la fin de l'année 2008

---

[68] Voir Richard Ouellet, "Chronique de droit international économique en 2008" (2009) 47 ACDI 343 aux pp 367-68.

[69] *Compte-rendu de la réunion tenue au Centre William Rappard le 12 janvier 2009*, OMC Doc WT/DSB/M/262 (Organe de règlement des différends), au para. 12, en ligne: OMC <http://docsonline.wto.org/DDFDocuments/u/WT/DSB/M262.doc>.

[70] *Compte-rendu de la réunion tenue au Centre William Rappard le 31 août 2009*, OMC Doc WT/DSB/M/273 (Organe de règlement des différends), au para. 90, en ligne: OMC <http://docsonline.wto.org/DDFDocuments/u/WT/DSB/M273.doc>.

par une demande de consultations du Canada. En début d'année 2009, des consultations entre le Canada et les États-Unis n'ont pas donné de résultats. En octobre, le Canada a demandé, puis obtenu, la formation d'un groupe spécial.[71] Il estime qu'un ensemble de mesures regroupées sous l'acronyme EPO ou, en anglais COOL (*Country of origin labelling*), est incompatible avec plusieurs dispositions de l'Accord OTC, de l'Accord SPS, du GATT et de l'Accord sur les règles d'origine.[72] La composition de ce groupe spécial devrait être connue au printemps 2010.

5   *République de Corée – Mesures visant l'importation de viande bovine et de produits à base de viande bovine en provenance du Canada (DS391)*

Le Canada a demandé l'ouverture de consultations avec la Corée au sujet de mesures visant l'importation de viande bovine et de produits à base de viande bovine en provenance du Canada. On sait que depuis 2003, la Corée, au motif de protéger sur son territoire les personnes et les animaux contre l'encéphalopathie spongiforme bovine (ESB), interdit l'importation de viande bovine et de produits à base de viande bovine canadiens.

Dans sa demande de consultations,[73] le Canada conteste deux mesures coréennes:

- l'Ordonnance administrative n° 51584476, qui est entrée en vigueur le 21 mai 2003 et qui interdit l'importation en Corée de viande bovine et de produits à base de viande bovine en provenance du Canada; et
- la Loi coréenne n° 9130 portant modification de la Loi sur la prévention des maladies animales contagieuses (également dénommée Loi sur la prévention des épidémies du bétail), qui est

---

[71] *États-Unis – Certaines prescriptions en matière d'étiquetage indiquant le pays d'origine (EPO) (Demande d'établissement d'un groupe spécial présentée par le Canada)* (9 octobre 2009), OMC Doc WT/DS/384/8, en ligne: OMC <http://docsonline.wto.org/DDFDocuments/u/WT/DS/384-8.doc>.

[72] *Ibid.* Pour le détail des prétentions canadiennes dans cette affaire que nous avons déjà résumées, voir Richard Ouellet, "Chronique de droit international économique en 2008" (2009) 47 ACDI 343 aux pp 364-65.

[73] *Corée – Mesures visant l'importation de viandes bovines et de produits à base de viande bovine en provenance du Canada (Demande de consultations présentée par le Canada)* (15 avril 2009), OMC Doc WT/DS/391/1, en ligne: OMC <http://docsonline.wto.org/DDFDocuments/u/G/SPS/GEN918.doc>.

entrée en vigueur le 11 septembre 2008 et qui énonce un certain nombre de conditions pour la levée de l'interdiction d'importer, parmi lesquelles l'obligation de soumettre à l'approbation de l'Assemblée nationale coréenne toutes prescriptions sanitaires relatives à l'importation de viande bovine et de produits à base de viande bovine en provenance du Canada.

Le Canada fait valoir que les mesures en cause sont incompatibles avec l'Accord SPS et le GATT de 1994, notamment les dispositions suivantes:

- les articles 2:2, 2:3, 3:1, 3:3, 5:1, 5:5, 5:6, 5:7, 6:1 et 8 et l'Annexe C de l'Accord SPS; et
- les articles I:1, III:4 et XI:1 du GATT de 1994.

À sa réunion du 31 août 2009, l'ORD a établi un groupe spécial.[74] Le Brésil, le Japon, le Taipei chinois, les États-Unis, l'Argentine, la Chine et les Communautés européennes participeront à titre de tierces parties. La composition du Groupe spécial a été arrêtée en novembre.[75]

6 *Communautés européennes – Mesures prohibant l'importation et la commercialisation de produits dérivés du phoque (Plaignant: Canada) (DS400)*

Le 27 juillet 2009, le Parlement européen a adopté un règlement qui balise et restreint de façon très importante l'importation et la mise sur le marché européen de produits dérivés du phoque.[76]

Les longs considérants que l'on trouve au début de ce règlement révèlent les objectifs des autorités européennes en mettant en place cette mesure.[77] Il y est fait référence au fait que "les phoques sont des animaux sensibles qui peuvent ressentir de la douleur, de la détresse, de la peur et d'autres souffrances." Il est aussi rappelé que

---

[74] *Corée – Mesures visant l'importation de viandes bovines et de produits à base de viande bovine en provenance du Canada (Constitution du Groupe spécial à la demande du Canada)* (16 novembre 2009), OMC Doc WT/DS/391/4, en ligne: OMC <http://docsonline.wto.org/DDFDocuments/u/WT/DS/391-4.doc>.

[75] *Ibid.*

[76] CE, *Règlement (CE) no 1007-2009 du Parlement européen et du Conseil du 16 septembre 2009 sur le commerce des produits dérivés du phoque*, [2009] JO, L 286/36.

[77] *Ibid.* Nous présentons et résumons brièvement ici les principales idées qui se trouvent dans les 21 paragraphes de considérants du règlement.

la chasse aux phoques soulève de vives inquiétudes auprès du public et des gouvernements européens en raison de la douleur infligée aux animaux lors de leur mise à mort et de leur écorchage. Or, des États membres de l'Union européenne "ont adopté, ou ont l'intention d'adopter, des mesures législatives réglementant le commerce des produits dérivés du phoque, en interdisant leur importation et leur production, alors que dans d'autres États membres le commerce de ces produits ne fait l'objet d'aucune restriction." Cela étant posé, il nous semble que les paragraphes 6, 7 et 8 des considérants sont assez révélateurs de l'objectif du règlement, au moins au plan commercial:

(6) Il existe donc des différences entre les dispositions nationales régissant le commerce, l'importation, la production et la commercialisation des produits dérivés du phoque. Ces différences perturbent le fonctionnement du marché intérieur des produits qui contiennent ou sont susceptibles de contenir des produits dérivés du phoque et constituent des obstacles au commerce de ces produits.

(7) Ces dispositions divergentes peuvent dissuader davantage les consommateurs d'acheter des produits qui ne sont pas dérivés du phoque, mais qu'il n'est peut-être pas aisé de distinguer de marchandises similaires dérivées du phoque, ou des produits qui peuvent inclure des éléments ou des ingrédients dérivés du phoque, sans que cela soit évident, comme les fourrures, les gélules et huiles oméga-3 et les produits en cuir.

(8) Les mesures prévues par le présent règlement devraient donc harmoniser les règles en vigueur dans la Communauté en matière d'activités commerciales liées aux produits dérivés du phoque et éviter ainsi une perturbation du marché intérieur des produits concernés, y compris les produits équivalents ou substituables aux produits dérivés du phoque.[78]

Le règlement ne compte ensuite que huit articles dont les trois premiers contiennent ce qui nous intéresse le plus du point de vue canadien au plan du commerce international.

L'article premier du règlement énonce que "le présent règlement établit des règles harmonisées concernant la mise sur le marché des produits dérivés du phoque."

L'article deux définit ce qu'est, aux termes du règlement, un "phoque," un "produit dérivé du phoque," la "mise sur le marché," un "Inuit" et une "importation."

---

[78] *Ibid* aux para 6, 7 et 8 des considérants.

Les deux premiers paragraphes de l'article trois sont ceux qui, pour l'essentiel affectent le plus le commerce international et donneront prise à la demande de consultation canadienne:

ARTICLE 3
Conditions de mise sur le marché

1. La mise sur le marché de produits dérivés du phoque est autorisée uniquement pour les produits dérivés du phoque provenant de formes de chasse traditionnellement pratiquées par les communautés inuites et d'autres communautés indigènes à des fins de subsistance. Ces conditions s'appliquent au moment ou au point d'importation pour les produits importés.

2. Par dérogation au paragraphe 1:

   a) l'importation de produits dérivés du phoque est autorisée lorsqu'elle présente un caractère occasionnel et concerne exclusivement des marchandises destinées à l'usage personnel des voyageurs ou des membres de leur famille. La nature et la quantité de ces marchandises ne peuvent pas pouvoir laisser penser qu'elles sont importées à des fins commerciales;

   b) la mise sur le marché de produits dérivés du phoque est également autorisée lorsqu'ils résultent d'une chasse réglementée par la législation nationale et pratiquée dans le seul objectif d'une gestion durable des ressources marines. Cette mise sur le marché est uniquement autorisée dans un but non lucratif. La nature et la quantité de ces marchandises ne peuvent pas pouvoir laisser penser qu'elles sont mises sur le marché à des fins commerciales.

L'application du présent paragraphe ne compromet pas la réalisation de l'objectif du présent règlement.[79]

Le règlement est entré en vigueur vingt jours après sa publication soit le 20 novembre 2009, à l'exception de l'article 3, applicable à partir du 20 août 2010.

Sans même attendre l'entrée en vigueur du règlement, le Canada, dont le commerce de produits dérivés du phoque allait être durement touché par ce règlement, a déposé début novembre une de-

---

[79] *Ibid*, art 3, aux para 1 et 2.

mande de consultations auprès de l'ORD.[80] Selon le Canada, les mesures européennes décrites ici sont incompatibles avec l'article 2.1 et 2.2 de l'Accord OTC; les articles I:1, III:4, et XI:1 du GATT de 1994 et l'article 4:2 de l'Accord sur l'agriculture.

Il sera intéressant de voir en 2010 comment sera appliqué le règlement européen et quelle tournure prendra cette affaire, surtout quand on sait que le Canada et l'Union européenne ont amorcé des négociations en vue d'en arriver à un accord de libre-échange bilatéral.

IV Conclusion

L'année 2009 aura été l'occasion de constater combien le Canada est un acteur important du système commercial. Il multiplie les accords économiques de tous ordres, il est très actif dans les négociations de Doha et est le Membre de l'OMC qui est impliqué dans le plus de différends après les géants états-unien et européen.

Ce qui est peut-être davantage de nature à inquiéter est l'état du système. Encore en 2009, les négociations de Doha ont piétiné. Au plan régional, l'effritement de l'ALÉNA comme accord unique et dynamique d'intégration se fait sentir. On voit bien la propension des pays signataires de cet accord à régler leurs différends en marge de l'ALÉNA. Le litige sur le bois d'œuvre échappe maintenant quasi complètement au chapitre 19 de l'ALÉNA. Et les tensions en matière de marchés publics, qui devraient relever du chapitre 10 de l'ALÉNA, semblent vouloir se résorber grâce à un accord sectoriel à être convenu entre les États-Unis et le Canada. La relation commerciale canado-américaine est-elle en train de changer de forme?

---

80 *Communautés européennes – Mesures prohibant l'importation et la commercialisation de produits dérivés du phoque (Demande de consultations présentée par le Canada)* (4 novembre 2009), OMC Doc WT/DS400/1, en ligne: OMC <http://docsonline.wto.org/DDFDocuments/u/G/AG/GEN87.doc>. Cette demande de consultations est à distinguer de la demande de consultations déposée par le Canada en 2007 dans l'affaire WT/DS369 et qui visait des mesures belges et néerlandaises prohibant aussi l'importation de produits dérivés du phoque. Il est permis de croire que cette affaire 369 sera solutionnée ou tranchée à l'occasion de l'affaire dont il est question ici.

II   Le Canada et le système financier international en 2009

BERNARD COLAS

L'économie mondiale a traversé en 2008-09 une période d'instabilité financière sans précédent, qui s'est accompagné de la récession économique la plus profonde et de l'effondrement des échanges les plus graves depuis de nombreuses décennies. Ainsi, les divers acteurs du système financier international ont placé comme priorité la relance stable et durable de l'économie mondiale. Néanmoins, la communauté internationale continue à lutter activement contre le blanchiment de capitaux et le financement du terrorisme. Ces actions ont été menées de concert par: (I) le Groupe des 20 (G20); (II) les institutions financières internationales; (III) les organismes de contrôle des établissements financiers; (IV) le groupe d'action financière; et (V) le Joint Forum. Au sein de ces institutions, le Canada joue un rôle prépondérant.

I   LE GROUPE DES 20

Lors du sommet de Pittsburgh, les 24 et 25 septembre 2009, le G20 a posé les bases d'une nouvelle gouvernance économique et financière mondiale. Le contexte de récession mondiale, malgré quelques signes de reprise, astreint la communauté internationale à rester vigilent et notamment à renforcer sa politique de relance de l'économie mondiale. De ce fait, les chefs d'États et de gouvernements ont désigné le G20 comme étant le forum prioritaire de la coopération économique internationale.[1]

Bernard Colas est avocat associé de l'étude Colas Moreira Kazandjian Zikovsky (CMKZ) à Montréal et Docteur en droit. L'auteur remercie Xavier Mageau, LL.M., de la même étude pour son importante contribution à cet article, ainsi que Virginie Dougnac-Galant.

[1] Sommet de Pittsburgh, 24-25 septembre 2009, Déclaration des chefs d'États et de gouvernement, en ligne: <http://www.g20.utoronto.ca/2009/2009 communique0925-fr.html>.

Les axes majeurs traités lors de ce sommet s'inscrivent dans la continuité des thèmes principaux mis en exergue lors du G20 de 2008. En effet, la nécessaire régulation du système financier, la relance ainsi que la refonte de la gouvernance mondiale ont primé lors de ce sommet. Dans un contexte mondial entre la crise et la reprise, les dirigeants du G20 ont souligné la nécessité d'adopter un ensemble de mesures, de règles et de réformes radicales. Se présentant comme le directoire de l'économie mondiale, le Groupe des 20 a créé, lors du Sommet de Londres le 2 avril 2009, le Conseil de stabilité financière (CSF) composé des puissances émergentes afin de coordonner et d'assurer un suivie des progrès du renforcement de la régulation financière. Les dirigeants l'ont notamment mandaté pour effectuer un rapport sur les progrès effectué d'ici le prochain Sommet.

Insistant sur la nécessité de mise en œuvre de réformes radicales et de refonte du système financier afin d'arrêter la diffusion de la crise financière, les chefs d'États et de gouvernements ont décidé d'augmenter significativement les ressources nécessaires. Ainsi, les dirigeants ont décidé d'augmenter les ressources du Fonds monétaires international (FMI). Soulignant la nécessité de renforcer l'institution, ils ont pris des engagements financiers considérables. De ce fait, le Comité monétaire et financier international (CMFI) a approuvé un renforcement notable des capacités de prêt du Fonds. Il a été convenu d'accroître les ressources à la disposition de l'institution de 250 milliards de dollars au moyen d'un financement immédiat de la part des pays membres. Outre ce triplement de la capacité de prêt, les dirigeants ont décidé d'injecter des liquidités supplémentaires dans l'économie mondiale en procédant à une distribution générale de DTS d'un montant de 250 milliards. Affirmant son rôle de grande puissance mondiale, le Canada s'est acquitté de ses engagements en accordant un prêt bilatéral de 10 milliards de dollars américains au Fonds.

Comme cela avait été envisagé lors du précédant sommet de Londres, le FMI sera amené à jouer un rôle primordial quant à l'évaluation des différentes politiques économiques mises en place et verra notamment sa mission renforcée quant à la régulation des activités économiques et financières mondiales. En outre, les grandes puissances économiques se sont accordées sur la réforme du Fonds: cinq pour cent des droits de vote du FMI seront transférés aux pays émergents afin de répondre à l'objectif de renforcement de leur position au sein de la gouvernance de l'institution. Il en est de même pour la Banque mondiale, où les droits de votes des pays émergents seront augmentés d'au moins trois pour cent.

II Les institutions financières internationales

Le contexte de crise financière actuelle a accéléré la mise en œuvre de certains éléments de travail du FMI. En effet, des programmes nationaux et internationaux ont été engagés pour stabiliser le système financier, ce qui a conduit à l'attribution de ressources vers les matières suivantes: promotion des priorités de la surveillance; réforme du dispositif de prêt; renforcement des capacités; soutien aux pays à faible revenu en raison de la flambée des prix des produits alimentaires et pétroliers; et la réforme de la gouvernance de l'institution. La démarche de modernisation, qui s'était accélérée en 2008 avec la restructuration, s'est poursuivie en 2009. Durant cette période de perturbations économiques graves, le Canada a joué un rôle influent[2] au sein du Fonds monétaire internationale (A) et à la Banque mondiale (B).

A LE FONDS MONÉTAIRE INTERNATIONAL (FMI)

Durant l'exercice 2009, la crise financière a continué de se propager à un rythme plus rapide que prévu et conduit à un repli sans précédent de la production et du commerce au niveau mondial. Relevant une défaillance de l'architecture globale et une série de problèmes liés à la réglementation comme facteurs déterminants de la crise financière, le FMI a préconisé l'application à l'échelle nationale et mondiale des mesures prioritaires suivantes: assainir les bilans du secteur financier; reconnaître l'importance du soutien que peut apporter la politique monétaire; apporter à l'échelle mondiale une stimulation budgétaire en 2009 et 2010; et accroître manifestement le financement public international.

Afin de riposter le plus efficacement face à la crise, et de manières à apporter aux pays membres une réponse adéquate, le Conseil d'administration a approuvé plusieurs modifications majeures.

Outre, le renforcement financier majeur de l'institution, le Conseil d'administration, a approuvé une refonte majeure des

---

[2] Le Canada au FMI et à la Banque mondiale — Rapport de 2009 sur les opérations effectuées en vertu de la *Loi sur les accords de Bretton Woods et des accords connexes*, en ligne: <http://www.fin.gc.ca/bretwood/bretwd09-fra.asp>.

instruments de prêts du FMI afin de permettre aux membres d'évaluer précisément l'utilisation optimale des ressources du Fonds. Les représentants canadiens ont appuyé les efforts du FMI, tendant à mettre en place ces outils de prêt modernes, en émettant des propositions de changements. Le Conseil a ainsi donné son accord pour un important réaménagement du dispositif de prêt non concessionnel. Les réformes approuvées sont les suivantes: modernisation de la confidentialité des emprunteurs; instauration d'une nouvelle ligne de crédit modulable; assouplissement des accords de confirmation classique; doublement du plafond normal d'accès aux prêts non concessionnels; simplification des coûts des échéances; et suppression de facilités rarement utilisées.

En plus de la modernisation du dispositif de prêt du FMI, d'autres réformes ont été approuvées, telles que la modernisation de la confidentialité des programmes du FMI pour tous les emprunteurs; la mise en place d'une nouvelle ligne de crédit modulable; ainsi que le doublement des limites d'accès normales aux ressources, qu'elles soient concessionnelles ou pas.

Suite à la revue triennale de la surveillance conclue en octobre 2008, le Conseil d'administration a publié la première Déclaration du FMI sur ses priorités en matière de surveillance. Le Canada a aussi fait entendre sa voix à ce sujet. En effet, le ministre des Finances a prôné l'importance de changements concernant la gouvernance institutionnelle du Fonds afin d'affirmer sa légitimité et crédibilité. Le Conseil a fixé quatre priorités économiques et quatre priorités opérationnelles afin de promouvoir la collaboration multilatérale. Les priorités économiques préconisées par le Fonds sont les suivantes: pallier aux perturbations des marchés financiers; consolider le système financier mondial en modernisant la réglementation et la supervision nationales et internationales; s'adapter aux fluctuations brutales des cours des matières premières; et favoriser une réduction ordonnée des déséquilibres internationaux. Concernant les priorités opérationnelles, il s'agit de l'évaluation des risques, la surveillance du secteur financier et des liens entre économie réelle et sphère financière, privilégier une optique multilatérale dans la surveillance et enfin analyser les taux de change et les risque pour la stabilité externe.

La gouvernance du FMI, thème majeur en 2008, a conservé une place prépondérante en 2009. Ainsi, le CMFI a demandé d'accélérer la réforme des quotes-parts afin de renforcer la représentation des pays émergents et des pays en développement au sein du Fonds.

B   LA BANQUE MONDIALE

L'année 2009 n'est pas sans difficulté pour les pays pauvres qui, malgré les faibles signes de reprise, subissent les conséquences de la récession mondiale, ainsi que des crises alimentaires, énergétiques et financières. De ce fait, la Banque mondiale a aussi consenti des prêts considérables en 2009. En effet, il s'agit d'engagements financiers record pour l'institution et qui représente une forte augmentation par rapport à ceux de 2008.[3]

Là encore, le Canada joue un rôle influent dans le renforcement de l'institution afin que celle-ci dispose de toutes les armes pour faire face à la plus importante crise financière depuis les années 30. Le Canada a offert des contributions financières considérables à l'appui du Programme de liquidité pour le commerce mondial de la Société financière internationale (SFI) et du Mécanisme d'aide aux pays vulnérables du Groupe de la Banque mondiale. Le président de la Banque mondiale, Robert Zoellic, a souligné le rôle prépondérant du Canada en indiquant qu'il était le premier donateur à engager des fonds, à hauteur de 200 millions dollars américains pour contribuer au financement de programmes mis en place par l'institution.[4] Le Canada a aussi contribué au financement des fonds fiduciaires à donateurs multiples à hauteur de 75,6 millions de dollars, ainsi qu'au financement de différentes initiatives d'envergure mondiale[5] à hauteur de 141,9 millions de dollars.

En outre, afin de répondre à des besoins précis liés à la crise et de disposer de ressources supplémentaires pour aider les pays les plus vulnérables, la Banque mondiale a mis en place diverses facilités spécifiques. En l'occurrence, a été créé le Programme d'intervention en réponse à la crise alimentaire mondiale, le Programme mondial pour l'agriculture et la sécurité alimentaire ainsi que le Guichet de financement de ripostes à la crise de l'Association internationale de développement (IDA).

---

[3] Les engagements ont atteint le montant de 60 milliards de dollars américains, ce qui représente une augmentation de 54% par rapport à 2008: Banque Mondiale — Rapport annuel 2009, en ligne: <http://siteresources.worldbank.org/EXTAR2009/Resources/6223977-1253813071839/AR09_Year_in_Review_French.pdf>.

[4] Le Canada au FMI et à la Banque mondiale — Rapport de 2009 sur les opérations effectuées en vertu de la *Loi sur les accords de BrettonWoods et des accords connexes,* *supra* note 2.

[5] Initiatives de portée mondiale: le Fonds mondial de lutte contre le SIDA, la tuberculose et le paludisme (FMLSTP) et le Facilité pour l'environnement mondial (FEM).

Enfin en 2009, le Groupe de la Banque mondiale a continué à affirmer la nécessité de réformer plusieurs domaines, et notamment, la gouvernance interne. Le Canada encourage fortement cette réforme qui faciliterait l'approbation des projets, et ainsi, permettrait au Conseil d'administration de se focaliser sur les enjeux stratégiques.

III Les organismes de contrôle des établissements financiers

A Le comité de Bâle sur le contrôle bancaire

Le comité de Bâle sur le contrôle bancaire (CBCB) est un organe essentiel dans l'élaboration de règles relatives à la surveillance du secteur bancaire. En 2009, la composition du Comité a doublé, il compte 27 juridictions membres et est constitué de hauts responsables de 44 banques et autorités de contrôle, ce qui accroit sa légitimité en tant qu'organe d'élaboration de normes internationales.

Face à la crise financière, le G20 lors du sommet de Pittsburgh a préconisé la refonte du secteur bancaire. Le CBCB a donc établi un programme de réformes pour 2009-10[6] afin de renforcer la réglementation prudentielle ainsi qu'engager des travaux en vue de renforcer la résilience du système bancaire mondial.

Les réformes du Comité de Bâle tendent à renforcer les règlementations en matière de fonds propres et de liquidités[7]. Les propositions de décembre 2009 ont été soumises à consultation à divers acteurs du marché dont les commentaires ont été pris en compte par le Comité et ses groupes de travail. Là encore, il est possible d'affirmer l'implication certaine du Canada au sein du CBCB. En effet, le Bureau du surintendant des institutions financières (BSIF) participe activement aux travaux de ce Comité, il est membre de trois groupes de travail.[8] Tout d'abord, le BSIF travail au sein du Groupe de mise en œuvre des normes (GMN) qui permet aux organismes de surveillance d'échanger des informations et de suivre la

---

6 Réponse du Comité de Bâle à la crise financière: Rapport au Groupe des Vingt — Octobre 2010, en ligne: <http://www.bis.org/publ/bcbs179_fr.pdf>.

7 Introduction de deux ratios de liquidités: le LCR (*Liquidity Coverage Ratio*) et le NSFR (*Net Stable Funding Ratio*): Accords de Bâle III publiés le 16 décembre 2010, *supra* note 1.

8 Bureau du surintendant des institutions financières Canada, *Rapport Annuel 2009-10*, en ligne: <http://www.osfi-bsif.gc.ca/app/DocRepository/1/fra/rapports/bsif/aro910_f.pdf>.

mise en œuvre des normes édictées par le CBCB. En outre, il est membre du Groupe de travail sur la comptabilité (GTC) qui veillent à l'application des normes et pratiques internationales de comptabilité pour renforcer la sûreté et la solidité du système bancaire. Enfin, le BSIF fait partie du Groupe de l'élaboration des politiques (GEP) qui étudie les nouveaux enjeux en matière de surveillance et oriente les politiques en ce sens.

En outre, le CBCB a engagé des travaux dans divers domaines sur des points essentiels pour la résilience des banques. Les sujets traités par le Comité sont les suivants: la révision complète des règles applicables au portefeuille de négociation; le recours aux notations externes; la réponse du Comité à la question des établissements bancaires d'importance systémique; le traitement des grands risques; l'amélioration de la résolution des défaillance bancaire transfrontières; l'actualisation des principes fondamentaux pour un contrôle bancaire efficace; et la mise en œuvre des normes et collaborations renforcées entre les contrôleurs bancaires par le biais de collèges prudentiels. Ces travaux futurs traduisent ainsi l'importance du Comité de Bâle dans la promotion d'un marché monétaire stable.

B   L'ORGANISATION INTERNATIONALE DES COMMISSIONS
    DES VALEURS

Fin 2009, l'organisation internationale des commissions des valeurs (OICV) regroupe 192 membres. La 34ème conférence de l'OICV s'est déroulée du 8 au 11 juin 2009 à Tel Aviv où d'importantes avancées ont été enregistrées dans le traitement des problèmes que connaissent les marchés financiers suite à la crise économique. Parmi les sujets traités, il figure notamment les informations à fournir concernant les titres basés sur des actifs, sur les secteurs non réglementés du marché et sur les produits financiers, sur la réglementation des ventes à découvert, et sur la supervision des fonds spéculatifs (hedge funds). Suite à la conférence, l'OICV a publié un rapport au sein duquel elle édicte des recommandations pour la réglementation des ventes à découvert et la supervision des fonds spéculatifs. En outre, elle a publié un rapport sur l'impact de la crise financière sur les marchés émergents.

De par l'importance des travaux de l'organisation relatifs aux marchés financiers, le Comité exécutif a décidé de mettre en place un groupe de travail "task force" chargé d'examiner son orientation stratégique future.

Les autorités canadiennes en valeurs mobilières (ACVM) ont continué en 2009 à prendre des mesures d'application de la loi afin de renforcer la confiance dans les marchés financiers. En effet, 19 millions de dollars d'actifs ont été gelées par l'ACVM.[9] De plus, en 2010, les membres des ACVM comptent élaborer un protocole d'enquête et de poursuite multi territoriale et former des spécialistes des délits d'initié et de la manipulation de marché.

IV Le groupe d'action financiere (GAFI)

L'année 2009 a été marquée par la crise économique et financière qui risque de rendre plus fragile les systèmes de lutte contre le blanchiment de capitaux et le financement du terrorisme (LBC/FAT) si les États consacrent moins de ressources pour combattre ces phénomènes. De ce fait, le GAFI a engagé un examen des conséquences de la crise sur les efforts de lutte contre le blanchiment de capitaux et financement du terrorisme.

Le recyclage des produits de criminalité étant une préoccupation pour les États et les organismes de règlementation financière, le secteur financier canadien doit pouvoir s'appuyer sur les solides programmes LRPC/FAT. Ainsi, le BSIF poursuit ses programmes d'évaluation, aux fins d'éventuelles corrections, et s'est particulièrement intéressé au secteur bancaire au sein duquel il a relevé certaines lacunes. Le BSIF participe activement aux travaux du GAFI. À la suite du sommet des chefs d'État et de gouvernement du G-20, le GAFI a mis en place un processus visant à déterminer les instances mondiales dont les régimes LRPC/FAT comportent des lacunes stratégiques. Le BSIF est aussi membre du comité consultatif conjoint des secteurs public et privé sur la LRPC/FAT. Ce comité permet de discuter du régime canadien LRPC/FAT.

Depuis 2007, le GAFI analyse les pays et territoires à haut risque et recommande que certaines mesures spécifiques soient mises en œuvre pour pallier à ces phénomènes. En 2008-09, le GAFI a publié une série de déclarations publiques dans lesquelles a été mis en exergue des préoccupations face à des lacunes relevées dans les dispositifs LBC/FAT de certains États. À la suite du sommet des dirigeants G-20, qui ont d'ailleurs salué dans un communiqué publié en septembre 2009 les progrès de l'organisme en la matière, les

---

9 Autorités canadiennes en valeurs mobilières, *Rapport sur l'application de la loi 2009*, en ligne: <http://www.autorites-valeurs-mobilieres.ca/uploadedFiles/General/pdfs_fr/CSAReport09FR%5BFA%5D.pdf>.

dirigeants ont demandé que soit établi une liste des pays et territoires à haut risque et non coopératifs d'ici 2010.

Afin de faire face, à l'échelle mondiale, de la manière la plus adéquate aux nouveaux risques et aux nouvelles menaces en matière de blanchiment de capitaux et de financement du terrorisme, le GAFI a établi des rapports sur les typologies. La réunion des experts du GAFI-XXI, qui s'est déroulée du 18 au 20 novembre 2009, a été organisée conjointement avec le Groupe d'action financière des Caraïbes. Les cinq ateliers ont porté sur les thèmes suivants: zones franches commerciales; nouveaux moyens de paiement; prestataires de services aux sociétés et fiducies; appréciation de la menace mondiale et questions opérationnelles diverses. Ainsi, en octobre 2009, a été publié pour la première fois une nouvelle étude sur les typologies consacrées au blanchiment et au financement du terrorisme dans le secteur des valeurs mobilières. En outre, deux autres nouvelles études sur les typologies sont en cours d'achèvement: un rapport sur les vulnérabilités des zones franches commerciales et un rapport sur les activités de blanchiment de capitaux par le truchement de passeurs de fonds et de changeurs.

Ainsi, les troubles qui découlent de la crise financière ont mis en évidence la nécessité pour le GAFI d'insister sur l'examen ciblé des menaces concernant le blanchiment de capitaux et le financement du terrorisme dans lequel le Canada joue un rôle prépondérant.

V Le joint forum

L'aggravation de la crise financière en 2009 a conduit le Joint Forum à s'intéresser particulièrement à l'identification des risques et notamment à la règlementation des institutions financières. Ainsi, l'année 2009 a été marquée par la publication de trois rapports concernant les structures hors bilan; l'utilisation des notations des agences dans la règlementation; ainsi que le champ et la nature différenciée de la régulation.[10]

La participation active du Canada par le biais du BSIF a été confirmée en 2009. En effet, le BSIF a consolidé ses liens avec les organismes de surveillance étrangers en participant aux discussions internationales relatives à l'établissement de la règlementation ainsi qu'aux collèges internationaux de surveillance et notamment en

---

10 *Rapport annuel de l'AMF*, chapitre 5, "Les relations de l'AMF avec la Place et les institutions nationales, européennes et internationales," en ligne: <http://www.amf-france.org/documents/general/9478_1.pdf>.

concluant des accords de partage de l'information avec les instances de surveillance de pays hôtes qui règlementent d'importantes filiales étrangères de banques et de sociétés d'assurance canadiennes. D'ici 2010, 30 accords de ce type seront conclus et d'autres négociations seront en cours.[11] Ainsi, l'implication du Canada en matière de surveillance financière reste marquée; les institutions financières canadiennes se plient aux exigences de transparence imposée par le Joint Forum.

En outre, en travaillant de concert avec les organismes canadiens de normalisation et l'International Accounting Standards Board (IASB), le BISF tend à influencer les règles comptables internationales qui s'appliquent aux institutions financières canadiennes. Le BSIF a également travaillé en collaboration avec le personnel du Conseil des normes comptables (CNC) sur les dossiers relatifs à l'adoption des Normes internationales d'information financière (IFRS) en 2011. Il est notamment membre du Comité consultatif des normes IFRS. En effet, le BSIF a analysé les conséquences de l'adoption des normes IFRS, pour les entités fédérales, en termes de stratégie et d'obligations redditionnelles. Ainsi, a été publié en octobre 2009 la version provisoire d'un préavis intitulée *Passage des entités fédérales aux normes internationales d'information financière*. La participation active du Canada à la discussion et à l'élaboration de ces normes favorise l'adoption de normes mondiales de qualité et favorise la compréhension de celle-ci.

En 2009, malgré quelques signes de reprises, l'économie mondiale reste ébranlée par la vaste crise financière née sur les marchés des pays avancés en 2007. Ainsi, les institutions financières internationales ont réitéré leurs objectifs de refonte du secteur financier, de surveillance ainsi que de transparence et de renforcement des institutions. Le Canada s'est montré très enclins à collaborer aux fins de réalisations des objectifs, notamment avec la participation active des institutions financières canadiennes sur la scène internationale.

---

[11] Bureau du surintendant des institutions financières Canada, *Rapport Annuel 2009-2010, supra* note 8.

III Investissement

CÉLINE LÉVESQUE

I INTRODUCTION

La chronique de l'année 2009 est d'abord l'occasion de faire une mise à jour au sujet du programme de négociations canadien d'accords bilatéraux portant sur l'investissement (APIE).[1] Le Canada a signé quatre APIE durant cette année en plus d'en négocier plusieurs autres. Par ailleurs, l'étude de deux sentences arbitrales rendues sous le régime du chapitre 11 (Investissement) de l'*Accord de libre-échange nord-américain* (*ALENA*)[2] retient la majeure partie de notre attention. Dans l'affaire *Glamis Gold c United States*,[3] la compagnie canadienne demanderesse a été complètement déboutée dans une décision datant du 8 juin 2009. Cette sentence, qui compte 355 pages, a mis un terme à une affaire qui avait attiré l'attention, car

---

Céline Lévesque est professeure agrégée à la Faculté de droit, Section de droit civil, de l'Université d'Ottawa. L'auteur tient à remercier Florence Sauvé-Lafrance pour sa précieuse assistance de recherche et le Conseil de recherche en sciences humaines du Canada pour son soutien financier.

1 Sur le programme de négociations des APIEs du Canada voir "Programme de négociations des Accords sur la promotion et la protection de l'investissement étranger (APIE) du Canada: Programme d'APIE du Canada" en ligne: Affaires étrangères et Commerce International Canada (MAECI) <http://www.international.gc.ca/trade-agreements-accords-commerciaux/agr-acc/fipa-apie/index.aspx?lang=fra>.

2 *Accord de libre-échange nord-américain entre le gouvernement du Canada, le gouvernement du Mexique et le gouvernement des États-Unis d'Amérique*, 17 décembre 1992, RTCan 1994 n° 2, 32(3) ILM 605 (entrée en vigueur: 1er janvier 1994) [*ALENA*].

3 *Glamis Gold Ltd c United States* (Award, 8 juin 2009) [*Glamis*]. Il est à noter que les sentences arbitrales mentionnées dans cette chronique sont disponibles en ligne: <http://italaw.com/>. Les sites internet des Parties à l'*ALENA* contiennent également les sentences rendues en vertu du ch.11. Voir MAECI, disponible en ligne à: <http://www.international.gc.ca/trade-agreements-accords-commerciaux/disp-diff/nafta.aspx?lang=fra>.

elle soulevait des questions sensibles liées à l'exploitation minière, la protection environnementale et le droit des autochtones.

La sentence rendue le 18 septembre 2009 dans l'affaire *Cargill c Mexico*,[4] quant à elle, complète la trilogie des affaires mexicaines concernant les édulcorants dont les précédents chapitres ont fait l'objet d'une étude comparative dans la chronique de l'année 2008.[5] Cette sentence, qui contredit sur certains points la décision dans l'affaire *ADM c Mexico*[6] et sur d'autres celle dans l'affaire *CPI c Mexico*,[7] contribue au malaise noté l'an dernier quant au risque d'incohérence entre les sentences arbitrales. En définitive, par contre, les trois affaires ont connu la même issue: le Mexique a été condamné à indemniser les investisseurs américains (à hauteur de plus de 168 millions de dollars), car son imposition d'une taxe de 20 pour cent sur les boissons gazeuses qui utilisaient un édulcorant autre que le sucre de canne a été jugé discriminatoire par les tribunaux. Toutefois, le Mexique a uniquement fait une demande d'annulation de la sentence dans l'affaire *Cargill*.[8] Dans sa demande, le Mexique ne conteste pas la conclusion de manquement à l'obligation de traitement national, mais prétend plutôt que le Tribunal a outrepassé ses compétences, notamment en ne respectant pas les limites territoriales prévues à l'*ALENA*.[9]

Par ailleurs, on note une certaine parenté entre les approches des Tribunaux dans les affaires *Cargill* et *Glamis*.[10] Dans le cas de ces Tribunaux, la présence d'un arbitre commun aura su contribuer à

---

[4] *Cargill, Incorporated c Mexico* (Award, 18 septembre 2009) ICSID Case N° ARB(AF)/05/2 [*Cargill*].

[5] Voir C Lévesque, "Chronique de Droit international économique en 2008: Investissement" (2009) XLVII ACDI aux pp 385-410.

[6] *Archer Daniels Midland Company and Tate & Lyle Ingredients Americas, Inc. c Mexico* (Award, 21 novembre 2007) ICSID Case N° ARB(AF)/04/05 [*ADM*].

[7] *Corn Products International, Inc c Mexico* (Decision on Responsibility, 15 janvier 2008) ICSID Case n° ARB(AF)/04/01 [*CPI*].

[8] Voir *United Mexican States v Cargill, Incorporated* (The United Mexican States and Cargill, Incorporated, Notice of Application, In the Matter of an Application to Set Aside an Arbitral Award under Rule 14.05(2) of the Rules of Civil Procedure and Article 34 of the *UNCITRAL Model Law on International Commercial Arbitration, Being the Schedule to the International Commercial Arbitration Act*, RSO 1990, C I.9, As Amended) [2010] ONSC 4656 (Can, SCJ Ont) [*Affaire Cargill, demande d'annulation*].

[9] *Ibid* aux para 7-9.

[10] Le Tribunal dans l'affaire *Glamis, supra* note 3, était constitué des arbitres Michael K Young (président), David D Caron et Kenneth D Hubbard. Dans l'affaire *Cargill, supra* note 4, il s'agissait de Michael Pryles (président), David D Caron et Donald M McRae.

la cohérence des approches, notamment quant à l'interprétation de la norme minimale de traitement à l'article 1105 de l'*ALENA*.[11]

II Les négociations d'accords portant sur l'investissement

Durant l'année 2009, le Canada a signé avec trois membres de l'Union européenne de nouveaux accords qui remplaceront, lors de leur entrée en vigueur, les traités conclus avec ces États dans les années 1990. Ces négociations ont fait suite à la demande de la Commission européenne en 2003, auprès des futurs membres de l'Union, afin d'harmoniser leur APIE avec le Canada en fonction des obligations découlant du droit européen.[12] Cette demande concernait six nouveaux membres, mais en date de 2009, seules les négociations avec la Lettonie,[13] la République tchèque[14] et la Roumanie[15] ont abouti à la signature d'un accord.[16]

---

[11] *ALENA, supra* note 2. Le professeur David Caron (de nationalité américaine) a été nommé par les États-Unis dans l'affaire *Glamis, supra* note 3 au para 188, et par l'investisseur dans l'affaire *Cargill, supra* note 4 au para 21.

[12] Voir, "Négociations portant sur les Accords sur la promotion et la protection des investissements étrangers entre le Canada et 6 pays membres de l'Union européenne: Contexte"en ligne: MAECI <http://www.international.gc.ca/trade-agreements-accords-commerciaux/agr-acc/fipa-apie/eu6-ue6.aspx?lang=fra&menu_id=21> (Négociations portant sur les APIEs).

[13] *Accord entre le gouvernement du Canada et le gouvernement de la République de Lettonie concernant la promotion et la protection des investissements*, 5 mai 2009 [*APIE Canada-Lettonie* (2009)], qui remplace *l'Accord entre le gouvernement du Canada et le gouvernement de la République de la Lettonie pour l'encouragement et la protection des investissements*, 26 avril 1995 (entrée en vigueur: 27 juillet 1995). Les textes des APIEs sont disponibles en ligne: MAECI <http://www.international.gc.ca/trade-agreements-accords-commerciaux/agr-acc/fipa-apie/fipa_list.aspx?lang=fra&menu_id=22>.

[14] *Accord entre le Canada et la République Tchèque concernant la promotion et la protection des investissements*, 6 mai 2009 [*APIE Canada-République Tchèque* (2009)], qui remplace *l'Accord entre le gouvernement du Canada et le gouvernement de la République Fédérale tchèque et Slovaque sur l'encouragement et la protection des investissements*, 15 novembre1990 (entrée en vigueur: 9 mars 1992) qui avait été repris à son compte par la République tchèque.

[15] *Accord entre le gouvernement du Canada et le gouvernement de Roumanie concernant la promotion et la protection réciproque des investissements*, 8 mai 2009 [*APIE Canada-Roumanie* (2009)], qui remplace *l'Accord entre le gouvernement du Canada et le gouvernement de Roumanie pour l'encouragement et la protection des investissements*, 17 avril 1996 (entrée en vigueur: 11 février 1997).

[16] Des négociations sont en cours avec la Hongrie et la Pologne. Un accord a été signé avec la République Slovaque en juillet 2010. Voir Négociations portant sur les APIEs, *supra* note 12.

Ces nouveaux accords sont *sui generis* et ne sont pas susceptibles d'être reproduits en raison du contexte particulier. Ils conservent en grande partie la structure des accords précédents, mais comprennent des dispositions veillant à remplir les obligations des membres de l'Union européenne, ainsi que des mises à jour qui reflètent l'évolution de la pratique du Canada dans ses traités d'investissement.

En ce qui a trait aux exigences de l'Union, pour ne donner que quelques exemples, on trouve dans ces APIEs des modifications à la portée des obligations de traitement national et de la nation la plus favorisée qui ne s'appliquent pas "aux avantages accordés par une Partie contractante conformément à ses obligations en tant que membre d'une union douanière, économique ou monétaire, d'un marché commun ou d'une zone de libre-échange."[17] D'autres exclusions concernent les prescriptions de résultats et la politique agricole européenne.[18] D'autres dispositions reconnaissent les obligations des membres de l'Union en matière de sécurité,[19] ou encore de balance des paiements.[20] De plus, en ce qui concerne les consultations pouvant avoir lieu entre les Parties à l'accord, il est prévu que: "[l]es consultations prévues par le présent article comprennent les consultations se rapportant à des mesures qu'une Partie contractante peut juger nécessaires pour assurer la compatibilité du présent accord avec le *Traité instituant la Communauté européenne.*"[21]

Par ailleurs, plusieurs nouveautés reflètent l'évolution de la pratique du Canada suivant l'adoption de l'APIE-type de 2004.[22] Sur

---

17 Voir *APIE Canada-République tchèque* (2009), *supra* note 14, art IV(2); *APIE Canada-Lettonie* (2009), *supra* note 13, art IV(2); *APIE Canada-Roumanie* (2009), *supra* note 15, art IV(2).

18 Voir *APIE Canada-Roumanie* (2009), *supra* note 15, art V(3); *APIE Canada-Lettonie* (2009), *supra* note 13, art V(3).

19 Voir *APIE Canada-République tchèque* (2009), *supra* note 14, art XV(4); *APIE Canada-Lettonie* (2009), *supra* note 13, art XVIII(4); *APIE Canada-Roumanie* (2009), *supra* note 15, art XVIII(4).

20 Voir *APIE Canada-République tchèque* (2009), *supra* note 14, art XV(3); *APIE Canada-Lettonie* (2009), *supra* note 13, art XVIII(3); *APIE Canada-Roumanie* (2009), *supra* note 15, art XVIII(3).

21 Voir *APIE Canada-République tchèque* (2009), *supra* note 14, art XI(2); *APIE Canada-Lettonie* (2009), *supra* note 13, art XIV(2); *APIE Canada-Roumanie* (2009), *supra* note 15, art XIV(2).

22 Accord-type sur la promotion et la protection des investissements étrangers. Voir "Programme de négociations des Accords de promotion et de protection de

le fond, on note, par exemple, l'ajout de la clarification concernant la norme minimale de traitement (en vertu du droit international coutumier),[23] et d'une annexe visant également à clarifier la définition de l'expropriation indirecte.[24] En matière de règlement des différends et de transparence, on trouve dorénavant dans ces accords des dispositions concernant l'accès du public aux audiences[25] et la possibilité pour un tiers de soumettre des observations au Tribunal.[26]

En juin 2009, le Canada a également signé un APIE avec la Jordanie.[27] Les négociations de cet accord étaient déjà terminées depuis juin 2007, mais la signature a eu lieu en 2009 en même temps que celle d'un accord de libre-échange (qui ne couvre pas les investissements), d'un accord de coopération dans le domaine du travail et d'un accord de coopération dans le domaine de l'environnement.[28] L'APIE est sur le fond et sur la forme très proche de l'APIE-type de 2004 du Canada. Il contient lui aussi 52 articles (couvrant les mêmes sujets) et quatre annexes pour un total dépassant 75 pages. On remarque certaines différences dans le préambule (notamment la référence à la promotion du développement durable), dans les définitions (notamment au sujet de l'expression

---

l'investissement étranger (APIE) du Canada" en ligne: MAECI <http://www.international.gc.ca/trade-agreements-accords-commerciaux/agr-acc/fipa-apie/what_fipa.aspx?lang=fra&menu_id=65>[APIE-type du Canada].

23 *Ibid*, art 5; *APIE Canada-République tchèque* (2009), *supra* note 14, art III(1); *APIE Canada-Lettonie* (2009), *supra* note 13, art II(2); *APIE Canada-Roumanie* (2009), *supra* note 15, art II(2).

24 APIE-type du Canada, *supra* note 22, Annex B.13(1); *APIE Canada-République tchèque* (2009), *supra* note 14, Annexe A; *APIE Canada-Lettonie* (2009), *supra* note 13, Annexe B; *APIE Canada-Roumanie* (2009), *supra* note 15, Annexe B.

25 APIE-type du Canada, *supra* note 24, art 38; *APIE Canada-République tchèque* (2009), *supra* note 14, Annexe B; *APIE Canada-Lettonie* (2009), *supra* note 13, art 1; *APIE Canada-Roumanie* (2009), *supra* note 15, art 1.

26 APIE-type du Canada, *supra* note 24, art 34, 35, 39; *APIE Canada-République tchèque* (2009), *supra* note 14, Annexe B; *APIE Canada-Lettonie* (2009), *supra* note 13, Annexe C; *APIE Canada-Roumanie* (2009), *supra* note 15, art II, III et IV.

27 *Accord entre le Canada et le Royaume Hachémite de Jordanie concernant la promotion et la protection des investissements*, 28 juin 2009 (entrée en vigueur: 14 décembre 2009) [*APIE Canada-Jordanie* (2009)].

28 Voir "Fiche d'information concernant l'Accord sur la promotion et la protection des investissements étrangers (APIE) Canada-Jordanie" en ligne: MAECI <http://www.international.gc.ca/trade-agreements-accords-commerciaux/agr-acc/fipa-apie/jordan-jordanie.aspx?lang=fra>.

"cherche à effectuer," de la double nationalité et du territoire), dans les prescriptions de résultats et dans les exceptions au traitement de la nation la plus favorisée, mais rien de fondamental.[29]

D'autres négociations se sont poursuivies avec plusieurs pays en 2009, dont la Chine, l'Inde, l'Indonésie, la Mongolie, le Vietnam, et le Bahrein.[30] Compte tenu de la durée de certaines de ces négociations, on peut douter que le Canada arrive à atteindre son objectif de doubler le nombre d'APIE en cinq ans.[31]

III L'AFFAIRE *GLAMIS GOLD C UNITED STATES*

A FAITS ET CONTEXTE JURIDIQUE

Glamis Gold Ltd. (Glamis) est une compagnie minière canadienne engagée dans l'exploration, le développement et l'extraction de métaux précieux aux États-Unis et en Amérique latine.[32] De 1994 à 2002, elle a entrepris, à travers une filiale constituée aux États-Unis, l'extraction d'or en Californie dans le cadre de son Projet Impérial.[33] Glamis n'en était pas à ses premières expériences, car, dans les années 1980 et 1990, elle avait notamment exploité avec succès deux mines d'or en Californie.[34] Entre 1987 et 1994, Glamis a acquis un bon nombre de titres miniers et a entrepris un important programme de forage exploratoire afin de vérifier la présence de métaux précieux tels que l'or ou l'argent sur le site du Projet Impérial,[35] un projet d'une superficie de 1 631 acres de terres publiques fédérales.[36] Ce programme de forage lui avait permis de planifier le creusage de trois fosses à ciel ouvert (*open mining pits*) dont deux

---

[29] Voir par ex *APIE Canada-Jordanie* (2009), *supra* note 27, art 1 (t), 1 (w), 1 (ff); 7-8 et à l'annexe III.

[30] Voir "Programme de négociations des Accords sur la promotion et la protection de l'investissement étranger (APIE) du Canada: Programme d'APIE du Canada," MAECI, *supra* note 1.

[31] Voir "Rapport du Canada — 2009 en matière d'accès aux marchés internationaux, Chapitre 11: Investissement" en ligne: MAECI <http://www.international. gc.ca/trade-agreements-accords-commerciaux/cimar-rcami/2009/11. aspx?lang=fra>.

[32] *Glamis, supra* note 3 au para 27.

[33] *Ibid* au para 10.

[34] *Ibid* aux para 28-29.

[35] *Ibid* aux para 32, 85.

[36] *Ibid* au para 31.

seraient remblayées séquentiellement.[37] Vu les coûts importants engendrés par cette opération de remblayage, Glamis n'avait pas prévu de remblayer complètement la troisième fosse.[38] En 2003, toutefois, Glamis, n'ayant pu obtenir les approbations nécessaires à la réalisation de son projet mais ayant dépensé des millions de dollars pour celui-ci, a déposé une plainte contre les États-Unis en vertu de l'*ALENA*.[39]

Glamis fonde sa plainte sur une série d'actions gouvernementales et de multiples et complexes dispositions législatives en lien avec l'exploitation minière, tant au niveau fédéral qu'à celui de l'État de la Californie.[40] De manière générale, les dispositions pertinentes applicables à la région où le Projet Impérial était localisé, visaient un équilibre (en droit et en fait difficile) entre l'encouragement de l'exploitation minière et la protection environnementale et culturelle des lieux. De manière précise, certaines dispositions législatives avaient été adoptées en réponse directe à des inquiétudes quant aux conséquences potentielles du Projet Impérial.[41] D'abord, le procédé d'exploitation retenu par Glamis (*open pit leach pad mining process*) était l'objet de préoccupations accrues du point de vue environnemental.[42] Ensuite, l'emplacement du Projet Impérial posait problème. Les Quéchuans, une tribu amérindienne, prétendaient que le Projet Impérial couvrait des sites sacrés, notamment le sentier *Trail of Dreams*, d'importance religieuse, culturelle et éducative capitale pour la tribu.[43]

Ainsi, dans le but d'empêcher que le plan d'opération de Glamis ne soit approuvé (malgré les droits miniers valides détenus par Glamis), la Californie a modifié avec empressement les dispositions législatives existantes.[44] Plus précisément, des amendements aux *State Mining and Geology Board Regulations,* en vigueur à partir de décembre 2002, de même que le projet de loi no. 22 du Sénat, promulgué en avril 2003, rendaient obligatoire le remblayage des

---

[37] *Ibid* aux para 33-34.

[38] *Ibid* au para 34.

[39] *Ibid* aux para 88, 98, 156, 186.

[40] *Ibid* aux para 36-84.

[41] *Ibid* aux para 140-65.

[42] *Ibid* aux para 10, 178-84.

[43] *Ibid* aux para 105-7.

[44] *Ibid* aux para 166-84.

fosses qu'avait prévu de creuser Glamis,[45] ce qui générait un accroissement des coûts fort considérable pour l'investisseur. En fait, Glamis allèguait que l'obligation de remblayer ses trois fosses transformait son projet, autrement lucratif, en un investissement non rentable.[46]

Glamis a signifié aux États-Unis son intention de déposer une plainte en vertu du chapitre 11 de l'*ALENA* le 21 juillet 2003 et a soumis sa plainte à l'arbitrage en décembre de la même année.[47] Glamis a allégué la violation par les États-Unis de ses obligations en vertu des articles 1105 (norme minimale de traitement) et 1110 (expropriation) de l'*ALENA*. Plus précisément, Glamis a prétendu que le gouvernement fédéral américain avait, à travers diverses actions, retardé illicitement l'analyse de son projet proposé et que, lorsque l'approbation dudit projet avait semblé probable, l'État californien avait adopté des mesures législatives et réglementaires concernant le projet, le rendant non rentable économiquement. En conséquence, Glamis a allégué que les États-Unis, de par des actions fédérales et de l'État de la Californie, avaient exproprié ses titres miniers et ne lui avaient pas accordé un traitement juste et équitable.[48]

B   RAISONNEMENT DU TRIBUNAL

1   *Commentaires introductifs*

Le Tribunal a jugé pertinent, avant de commencer son analyse des allégations de violation de l'*ALENA*, de définir en détails l'étendue de son mandat.[49] Ainsi, le Tribunal a d'abord comparé son mandat à celui d'un tribunal d'arbitrage mis en place sur une base contractuelle pour régler un litige commercial international particulier. Étant donné que les Parties à l'*ALENA* n'avaient pas créé de tribunal permanent, il ne revenait pas aux tribunaux *ad hoc* de réconcilier leurs décisions avec celles rendues précédemment.[50] Toutefois, le

---

[45] *Ibid* aux para 166, 181-84.

[46] Glamis prétend que son Projet Impérial, qui était évalué à 49,1 millions de dollars avant l'adoption des mesures de remblayage, s'est retrouvé avec une valeur négative de 8,9 millions de dollars suite à l'adoption de ces mesures. Voir *ibid* au para 362.

[47] *Ibid* au para 185.

[48] *Ibid* au para 11.

[49] *Ibid* aux para 3-7.

[50] *Ibid* au para 3.

Tribunal a reconnu l'existence d'enjeux systémiques en soulignant que: *"[t]he reality is that Chapter 11 of the NAFTA contains a significant public system of private investment protection ... The ultimate integrity of the Chapter 11 system as a whole requires a modicum of awareness of each of these tribunals for each other and the system as a whole."*[51] Aussi, le Tribunal a affirmé ne pas ignorer les conséquences que pourrait avoir sa décision sur les sentences futures, de même que ses implications systémiques potentielles.[52]

Dans ce contexte, le Tribunal a énuméré ce qu'il considère comme étant cinq principes clés, soit: (1) un tribunal doit se limiter à décider des questions qui se posent dans le différend qui lui est soumis; (2) étant donné que les Parties à l'*ALENA* se sont entendues pour permettre le dépôt d'observations d'*amici curiae*, celles-ci devraient être abordées dans les sentences dans la mesure où elles sont pertinentes pour la résolution du litige (ce qui n'était pas le cas en l'espèce); (3) il est essentiel que le tribunal fournisse des raisons détaillées justifiant ses conclusions — l'intégrité du système en dépend; (4) un tribunal doit présenter son raisonnement de façon claire, mais aussi succincte (ce pourquoi un résumé a été inclus dans la sentence) et (5) un tribunal se doit d'expliquer les raisons pour lesquelles il choisit de s'éloigner des tendances principales découlant des sentences rendues précédemment (et ce malgré l'absence d'une règle de précédent).[53]

2   Objections préliminaires

Les États-Unis ont présenté deux objections préliminaires. Premièrement, ils ont soumis une objection de "maturité" (*ripeness*) en avançant le fait que la demande de Glamis n'était pas mûre pour faire l'objet d'un arbitrage, puisque l'investisseur n'avait pas subi de perte ou de préjudice au moment où il a déposé sa plainte en vertu du chapitre 11. Cette condition découle de l'article 1117(2) qui prévoit que:

Un investisseur d'une Partie, agissant au nom d'une entreprise d'une autre Partie qui est une personne morale que l'investisseur possède ou contrôle directement ou indirectement, peut soumettre à l'arbitrage, en vertu de

---

[51] *Ibid* au para 5.

[52] *Ibid* au para 6.

[53] *Ibid* au para 8.

la présente section, une plainte selon laquelle l'autre Partie a manqué à une obligation découlant

a) de la section A ...
b) ... et que l'entreprise a subi des pertes ou des dommages en raison ou par suite de ce manquement.[54]

Dans le contexte de l'expropriation, une interférence réelle dans le droit de propriété d'un investisseur, et non une simple menace d'expropriation, est donc nécessaire afin qu'une demande puisse être soumise à l'arbitrage.[55] Selon le Tribunal, dans la mesure où la plainte de Glamis concernait le fait que les mesures américaines avaient rendu le Projet Impérial sans valeur *au moment de leur adoption*, et non que ces mesures ne permettraient jamais à Glamis de mettre en avant son Projet Impérial, celle-ci était mûre pour l'arbitrage. Le Tribunal a donc rejeté l'objection des États-Unis.[56]

Deuxièmement, les États-Unis ont allégué que la plainte était prescrite. Comme indiqué précédemment, Glamis fondait sa plainte en vertu de l'article 1105 sur une longue série d'actions gouvernementales et de dispositions législatives. Les États-Unis ont alors soulevé le fait que trois de ces actes gouvernementaux étaient prescrits, puisqu'ils remontaient à plus de trois ans avant que Glamis ait eu connaissance de la violation et des dommages allégués.[57] En effet, l'article 1117(2) prévoit que: "Un investisseur ne pourra déposer une plainte au nom d'une entreprise décrite au paragraphe 1 si plus de trois ans se sont écoulés depuis la date à laquelle l'entreprise a eu ou aurait dû avoir connaissance du manquement allégué et de la perte ou du dommage subi."[58]

À cet égard, le Tribunal a conclu que ces évènements n'ont été évoqués par Glamis que dans le but d'illustrer le contexte factuel dans lequel se sont déroulées les mesures subséquentes, et non en tant que fondement de sa plainte en vertu de l'article 1105 de l'*ALENA*.[59] En conséquence, le Tribunal a également rejeté cette objection des États-Unis.[60]

---

[54] *ALENA, supra* note 2, art 1117(1).
[55] *Glamis, supra* note 3 au para 331.
[56] *Ibid* aux para 13, 342, 352.
[57] *Ibid* au para 13.
[58] *ALENA, supra* note 2, art 1117(2).
[59] *Glamis, supra* note 3 aux para 348-49.
[60] *Ibid* aux para 350-51.

3   *Expropriation: Article 1110*

Il n'était pas contesté que Glamis possédait encore formellement les droits miniers lui ayant été conférés par le gouvernement fédéral.[61] Glamis alléguait plutôt que les actions du gouvernement fédéral et de la Californie avaient eu pour effet d'exproprier ses droits, tant leur valeur avait diminué.[62] Aussi les parties se sont-elles toutes les deux concentrées sur l'évaluation de la valeur du droit de Glamis prétendument exproprié par les États-Unis, de même que sur l'impact des mesures gouvernementales sur la valeur de ce droit. Alors que Glamis utilisait cette évaluation en tant que moyen de détermination de la compensation devant lui être octroyée, les États-Unis s'en servaient plutôt afin de prouver que Glamis possédait encore un droit d'une certaine valeur, réfutant ainsi l'allégation d'expropriation.[63]

Le Tribunal a rejeté les allégations de manquement à l'article 1110, puisqu'il a conclu que les droits miniers de Glamis n'avaient pas été rendus substantiellement sans valeur en raison des actions gouvernementales.[64] Cet article prévoit que:

Aucune des Parties ne pourra, directement ou indirectement, nationaliser ou exproprier un investissement effectué sur son territoire par un investisseur d'une autre Partie, ni prendre une mesure équivalant à la nationalisation ou à l'expropriation d'un tel investissement («expropriation»), sauf:

a) pour une raison d'intérêt public;
b) sur une base non discriminatoire;
c) en conformité avec l'application régulière de la loi et le paragraphe 1105 (1); et
d) moyennant le versement d'une indemnité en conformité avec les paragraphes 2 à 6.[65]

Le Tribunal a jugé qu'il se devait avant tout d'évaluer si les États-Unis avaient privé Glamis de ses droits de propriété.[66] Afin d'évaluer le degré d'interférence des mesures gouvernementales avec le droit de propriété de Glamis, le Tribunal s'est proposé d'avoir recours

---

61 *Ibid* au para 15.
62 *Ibid.*
63 *Ibid* au para 15.
64 *Ibid* au para 14.
65 *ALENA, supra* note 2, art 1110(1).
66 *Glamis, supra* note 3 au para 356.

aux deux critères fréquemment utilisés lors d'une telle analyse, soit la sévérité des conséquences économiques des mesures gouvernementales, de même que leur durée dans le temps. Autrement dit, le Tribunal devait déterminer si l'impact économique de ces mesures était suffisant pour conclure à une privation de droits.[67] Le Tribunal a décrit son approche de la façon suivante: *"To determine whether the Claimant's investment in the Imperial Project has been so radically deprived of its economic value to Claimant as to potentially constitute an expropriation and violation of Article 1110 of the NAFTA, the Tribunal must assess the impact of the complained measures on the value of the Project."*[68]

Glamis prétendait qu'au moment de l'expropriation alléguée, le Projet Impérial avait une valeur de 49,1 millions de dollars, ce que le Tribunal a accepté pour les fins de son analyse.[69] Le Tribunal s'est ensuite livré à de savants calculs (couvrant environ soixante pages) afin de déterminer la perte de valeur engendrée par les mesures de remblayage.[70] Après avoir entre autres déterminé le coût du remblayage nécessaire, la valeur de l'or, le coût des garanties financières requises par les gouvernements fédéral, de l'État californien et de comté, et le taux d'escompte approprié, le Tribunal a conclu que le projet conservait une valeur de plus de 20 millions de dollars et que les mesures gouvernementales n'avaient pas causé un impact économique suffisant pour constituer une expropriation de l'investissement de Glamis.[71] En conséquence, les allégations de manquement à l'article 1110 ont été rejetées.[72]

4   Norme minimale de traitement: Article 1105

Le Tribunal a également rejeté les allégations de violation de l'article 1105.[73] Cet article prévoit que: "Chacune des Parties accordera aux investissements effectués par les investisseurs d'une autre Partie un traitement conforme au droit international, notamment un traitement juste et équitable ainsi qu'une protection et une sécurité intégrales."[74]

---

[67] *Ibid* aux para 356-57.

[68] *Ibid* au para 358.

[69] *Ibid* aux para 17, 362.

[70] *Ibid* aux para 363-535.

[71] *Ibid* aux para 17, 536.

[72] *Ibid* au para 536.

[73] *Ibid* au para 18.

[74] *ALENA, supra* note 2, art 1105(1).

Le Tribunal a constaté que le contenu de cette obligation de traitement juste et équitable doit être interprété en fonction du droit international coutumier.[75] Le Tribunal a précisé que son mandat est distinct de celui d'un tribunal ayant à interpréter une obligation de traitement juste et équitable "autonome," c'est-à-dire à procéder à une interprétation basée uniquement sur la lettre du traité et les règles d'interprétation.[76] Ainsi, en terme de sources du droit, bien que Glamis ait invoqué de nombreuses sentences arbitrales selon lesquelles le traitement juste et équitable inclut désormais des principes fondamentaux tels que *"the duty to act in good faith, due process, transparency and candor, and fairness and protection from arbitrariness,"* le Tribunal a déclaré que celles-ci ne pouvaient servir à prouver l'existence d'une coutume.[77] D'ailleurs, plusieurs sentences arbitrales citées par l'investisseur, notamment la décision dans l'affaire *Tecmed*, comportent une étude d'une clause de traitement juste et équitable qui a été jugée par le tribunal saisi comme étant autonome. En conséquence, ces sentences arbitrales n'étaient pas pertinentes dans l'analyse du Tribunal en l'espèce.[78]

Le Tribunal devait ensuite se tourner vers la question de la portée ou du contenu de l'obligation de traitement juste et équitable en droit international coutumier. Le Tribunal a noté que bien que les deux parties au litige, de même que les deux autres Parties à l'*ALENA*, s'entendaient pour reconnaître que la norme minimale de traitement est au moins celle établie dans l'affaire *Neer*[79] qui date des années 1920, les parties au litige ne s'entendaient toutefois pas sur le point de savoir si, et dans quelle mesure, ce standard avait évolué avec le temps.[80] Puisque le contenu de la coutume était en discussion, il revenait à Glamis d'en faire la preuve.[81] Pour ce faire,

---

75 *Glamis, supra* note 3 au para 19.

76 *Ibid* aux para 19-21, 599, 607.

77 *Ibid* aux para 605-7.

78 *Ibid* aux para 609-10; voir aussi *Tecnicas Medioambientales Tecmed SA c Mexico* (Award, 29 mai 2003) ICSID Case N° ARB(AF)/00/2 [*Tecmed*].

79 *LFH Neer and Pauline Neer (USA) c Mexico* (1926), 4 IRAA 60 [*Neer*]. Le standard avait été formulé de la façon suivante: "*[T]he treatment of an alien, in order to constitute an international delinquency, should amount to an outrage, to bad faith, to wilful neglect of duty, or to an insufficiency of governmental action so far short of international standards that every reasonable and impartial man would readily recognize its insufficiency*" (aux pp 61-62).

80 *Glamis, supra* note 3 aux para 21, 601, 612.

81 *Ibid* aux para 21-22, 600-1.

Glamis devait démontrer, comme dans le cas de toute allégation quant à l'existence d'une coutume, une pratique concordante découlant d'un sentiment d'obligation juridique; ceci pouvant être fait à travers la pratique en matière de traités, certaines déclarations gouvernementales et parfois des plaidoiries.[82]

Le Tribunal a constaté que le standard de traitement juste et équitable en droit international coutumier pouvait avoir évolué de deux façons depuis la décision dans l'affaire *Neer,* soit que (1) la norme minimale de traitement avait dépassé ce qu'elle était en 1926; soit que (2) ce que la communauté internationale considère comme étant *"outrageous"* pouvait avoir évolué avec le temps.[83]

En ce qui concerne le premier type d'évolution, le Tribunal a conclu que bien que les situations soumises aux tribunaux soient aujourd'hui plus variées et complexes qu'elles ne l'étaient, la rigueur du contrôle auquel ceux-ci doivent se livrer n'a pas changé depuis l'affaire *Neer.*[84] Selon le Tribunal, la norme minimale de traitement en vertu du droit international coutumier doit être comprise comme étant un minimum absolu, un plancher en-deçà duquel la communauté internationale ne tolèrera pas la conduite d'un État.[85] Ainsi, le Tribunal affirme que:

> [T]o violate the customary international law minimum standard of treatment codified in Article 1105 of the NAFTA, an act must be sufficiently egregious and shocking — a gross denial of justice, manifest arbitrariness, blatant unfairness, a complete lack of due process, evident discrimination, or a manifest lack of reasons — so as to fall below accepted international standards and constitute a breach of Article 1105(1). Such a breach may be exhibited by a "gross denial of justice or manifest arbitrariness falling below acceptable international standards;" or the creation by the State of objective expectations <u>in order to induce</u> investment and the subsequent repudiation of those expectations.[86]

Toutefois, en ce qui concerne le deuxième type d'évolution de la norme minimale de traitement en droit international coutumier, le Tribunal, après avoir cité la décision dans l'affaire *Mondev,* a déclaré qu'il était fort possible que la communauté internationale s'offusque de nos jours à l'endroit d'actions gouvernementales qui

---

[82] *Ibid* aux para 602-3.

[83] *Ibid* au para 612.

[84] *Ibid* aux para 22, 614-16.

[85] *Ibid* au para 619.

[86] *Ibid* aux para 22, 627 [souligné dans l'original].

auraient autrefois été jugées acceptables.[87] Ainsi, le Tribunal a conclu que ce que la communauté internationale considère comme étant "*outrageous*" a bel et bien évolué avec le temps.

Le Tribunal a ensuite analysé les prétentions spécifiques de Glamis, selon lesquelles font partie des exigences de l'article 1105: (1) l'obligation de protéger les attentes légitimes des investisseurs par la mise en place d'un cadre juridique prévisible et transparent et (2) l'obligation de fournir une protection contre des mesures arbitraires.[88] En ce qui concerne la protection des attentes légitimes des investisseurs, le Tribunal s'est dit être d'accord avec la sentence arbitrale dans l'affaire *Thunderbird*, selon laquelle une violation de l'article 1105 pourrait être reconnue dans le cas où la conduite de l'État a créé des attentes raisonnables et justifiées de la part de l'investisseur qui l'ont amené à agir en se fondant sur cette conduite. Ainsi, un État peut être lié par les attentes objectives qu'il a créées dans le but d'inciter l'investissement.[89] Pour ce qui est de l'obligation de fournir une protection contre des mesures arbitraires, le Tribunal a conclu qu'une mesure présentant un niveau si élevé d'arbitraire qu'elle contrevient à *la* règle de droit, plutôt qu'à *une* règle de droit, pourra constituer une violation de l'article 1105.[90] En conséquence, le Tribunal a déclaré qu'il découle de l'article 1105 une obligation pour les États Parties de ne pas traiter les investisseurs étrangers d'une façon qui soit *manifestement* arbitraire.[91]

Une fois le contenu de l'obligation de traitement juste et équitable défini par le Tribunal, ce dernier s'est livré à une longue analyse pour savoir si les actions du gouvernement fédéral et de l'État de la Californie violaient, individuellement ou collectivement, l'article 1105.[92] Cette étude détaillée de chacune des mesures gouvernementales, prise individuellement, s'est soldée par une réponse négative de la part du Tribunal.[93] Finalement, le Tribunal s'est interrogé sur le point de savoir si ces mesures, bien que ne violant pas l'article

---

87 *Ibid* aux para 22, 613, 616; voir aussi *Mondev International Ltd c United States* (Award, 11 octobre 2002) ICSID Case N° ARB(AF)/99/2 [*Mondev*].

88 *Glamis*, *supra* note 3 aux para 618-26.

89 *Ibid* au para 621; voir aussi *International Thunderbird Gaming Corporation c Mexico* (Award, 26 janvier 2006) au para 147 [*Thunderbird*].

90 *Glamis*, *supra* note 3 au para 625.

91 *Ibid* au para 626.

92 *Ibid* aux para 24, 628-830.

93 *Ibid* au para 26.

1105 de façon individuelle, le violaient lorsque prises collectivement. À cet sujet, le Tribunal a déclaré:

> *The Tribunal determines that, for acts that do not individually violate Article 1105 to nonetheless breach that Article when taken together, there must be some additional quality that exists only when the acts are viewed as a whole, as opposed to individually. It is not clear, in general terms, what such quality would be in all circumstances though, in this factual situation, the Tribunal holds that it cannot see that the conduct as a whole is a violation of the fair and equitable treatment standard.*[94]

Ainsi, le Tribunal a également rejeté la demande de Glamis en vertu de l'article 1105. En définitive, après avoir rejeté en totalité la plainte de l'investisseur, le Tribunal a condamné Glamis à payer les deux tiers des frais d'arbitrage, mais a décidé que chaque partie assumerait ses propres frais de représentation.[95]

C   OBSERVATIONS

De manière générale, il faut noter qu'avec cette sentence, les États-Unis échappent toujours à une première condamnation en vertu du chapitre 11 de l'*ALENA*, en vigueur depuis plus de quinze ans.[96] Il s'agit aussi de la deuxième affaire où des investisseurs canadiens se voient déboutés dans leur contestation de mesures adoptées par la Californie, notamment en matières environnementales.[97] L'affaire *Methanex* avait elle aussi donné lieu à une sentence de plus de 350 pages; ce qui fait d'elles les plus volumineuses de l'histoire du chapitre 11.[98] Dans l'affaire *Glamis*, toutefois, le Tribunal a jugé opportun d'inclure un résumé de sa décision en début de sentence, une façon de faire qui demeure inusitée. L'approche du Tribunal et son interprétation des articles 1105 et 1110 méritent qu'on s'y arrête.

1   Approche du Tribunal

Le soin pris par le Tribunal en début de sentence de préciser son mandat et de définir son approche est tout aussi inusité que son

---

[94] *Ibid* aux para 25, 825-26.

[95] *Ibid* aux para 26, 830-33.

[96] *ALENA, supra* note 2.

[97] Voir *Methanex Corporation c United States* (Final Award of the Tribunal on Jurisdiction and Merits, 3 août 2005) [*Methanex*].

[98] Le Tribunal dans *Glamis* ne cherche pas à s'excuser de la longueur de sa sentence, au contraire. *Glamis, supra* note 3, à la note de bas de page 5 de la sentence. Le Tribunal dans l'affaire *Methanex, supra* note 97 au para 9 avait fait de même.

résumé. Il n'est pas rare pour les tribunaux arbitraux de faire référence en début de sentence au droit applicable et aux règles d'interprétation de la Convention de Vienne sur le droit des traités.[99] Dans cette affaire, le Tribunal a adopté une approche différente et beaucoup plus systémique. Il s'agit peut-être là d'un signe de maturité qui vient avec l'expérience sous le régime du chapitre 11. En effet, en date de 2009, un total de vingt affaires avaient donné lieu à des sentences finales.[100] Aussi, le Tribunal semble avoir ressenti le besoin de situer sa sentence dans un ensemble plus large. Le thème de l'intégrité du système — et la façon de la maintenir — revient à plusieurs endroits.[101] Par ailleurs, on pourrait y voir une tentative de la part du Tribunal de combler le vide existant justement dans un système d'arbitrage *ad hoc*, en traçant la voie aux tribunaux à venir. Au sujet de la question du "précédent," le Tribunal se situe clairement dans le camp de ceux qui estiment que les tribunaux arbitraux doivent se justifier lorsqu'ils décident de s'écarter de la jurisprudence constante.[102]

Deux aspects particuliers de l'approche méritent aussi d'être soulignés, bien qu'ils ne ressortent pas du résumé inclus dans cette chronique. Le premier a trait aux nombreuses références faites par le Tribunal au droit interne américain et le second est lié au degré de déférence dont devraient faire preuve les tribunaux par apport aux décisions d'organes gouvernementaux.

De mémoire, aucune autre sentence arbitrale rendue en vertu du chapitre 11 de l'*ALENA* ne contient autant de références au droit américain (surtout à la jurisprudence) que la sentence dans l'affaire *Glamis*. Pourtant, l'article 1131(1) de l'*ALENA* prévoit clairement qu'"[u]n tribunal établi en vertu de la présente section tranchera les points en litige conformément au présent accord et aux règles applicables du droit international."[103] Bien que le Tribunal semble sensible à la question, il ne s'empêche pas de faire référence au droit américain, souvent en parallèle au droit international, afin de résoudre les questions procédurales autant que celles portant sur

---

99 *Convention de Vienne sur le droit des traités*, 1155 RTNU 331 (23 mai 1969).

100 Voir "NAFTA Chapter 11: Investment," en ligne: MAECI <http://www.international.gc.ca/trade-agreements-accords-commerciaux/disp-diff/nafta.aspx>.

101 Voir *Glamis, supra* note 3, par ex voir aux para 5, 8.

102 Voir *Ibid* au para 8, n 6.

103 *ALENA, supra* note 2, art 1131(1).

le fond.[104] Une explication réside dans les arguments des parties à l'affaire. A quelques reprises, le Tribunal mentionne que les deux parties lui ont soumis des autorités provenant du droit interne américain.[105] Malgré tout, il aurait été préférable que le Tribunal garde ses distances par rapport à la jurisprudence américaine.

L'approche du Tribunal quant à la déférence à accorder aux décisions d'organes gouvernementaux retient aussi notre attention. Des questions similaires s'étaient posées dans l'affaire *Methanex*, car l'investisseur remettait en question les conclusions scientifiques qui avaient fondé la prohibition contestée d'un certain additif à l'essence.[106] Dans ce contexte, les États-Unis avaient plaidé avec conviction que les tribunaux constitués sur le fondement du chapitre 11 ne siégeaient pas en tant que *"super-regulatory body"* ayant l'autorité de remettre en question les décisions des Parties à l'*ALENA* en matières réglementaires ou scientifiques.[107] Dans *Glamis*, les États-Unis ont présenté des arguments similaires au Tribunal en réponse aux allégations de l'investisseur quant au caractère arbitraire, discriminatoire et non transparent de l'évaluation culturelle du Projet Impérial, ainsi que de la décision d'obliger au remblayage pour certaines mines et pas pour d'autres.[108] Le Tribunal s'est dit d'accord avec les États-Unis quant à son rôle limité, notamment quant à l'évaluation culturelle du projet:

In evaluating each of these arguments, the Tribunal is mindful of Respondent's statement that "[i]t is simply not this Tribunal's task to become archaeologists and ethnographers and to draw a definitive conclusion as to the location of the Trail of Dreams." The Tribunal agrees with this statement. It is not the role of this Tribunal, or any international tribunal, to supplant its own judgment of underlying factual material and support for that of a qualified domestic agency.[109]

---

[104] Voir par ex *Glamis, supra* note 3 aux para 219, 233 et 332. De manière générale, voir para 221, 224, 226, 310, 334, 356, 591, 742.

[105] Voir *ibid* par ex aux para 233, 326, 329 et 356.

[106] Voir *Methanex, supra* note 97.

[107] Voir *Methanex c United States*, US Rejoinder, 23 avril 2004, au para 79, en ligne: United States Department of State :<http://www.state.gov/documents/organization/31977.pdf>.

[108] Voir *Glamis, supra* note 3 aux paras 645-50, 679-702, en particulier au para 701.

[109] *Ibid* au para 779 [notes omises]. L'analyse détaillée de la preuve par le Tribunal présente un intérêt certain mais qui dépasse le cadre de cette chronique. Pour une discussion de ces questions (en particulier en lien avec l'affaire *Methanex*), voir C Lévesque, "Science in the Hands of International Investment Tribunals: A Case for 'Scientific Due Process'" (2009) 20 Finnish YB Int'l L 127.

Toutefois, le Tribunal a rejeté l'argument plus large des États-Unis selon lequel la déférence dont font preuve les tribunaux internes (notamment des États-Unis et du Canada) à l'égard des décisions d'organes gouvernementaux est nécessairement applicable aux tribunaux internationaux. Pour le Tribunal, l'idée de déférence se reflète dans la norme de l'article 1105, qu'il est chargé d'appliquer, par le biais de l'adverbe "manifestement" ou du qualificatif "flagrant."[110] Autrement dit, le fait que la norme minimale de traitement est exigeante présuppose un degré de déférence élevé. Cette approche paraît salutaire à deux égards. D'abord, elle permet aux tribunaux arbitraux de se prononcer sur la violation des obligations de l'*ALENA* sans toutefois se transformer en "*science court*" ayant la responsabilité de juger des conclusions scientifiques ou techniques sous-jacentes à une mesure gouvernementale.[111] Ensuite, elle permet d'éviter la confusion, selon nous dangereuse, entre les normes de révision appliquées par les tribunaux en droit administratif interne et les normes de violation des droits des investisseurs dans la sphère internationale (ici, de l'*ALENA*). Il n'y a pas lieu d'importer les normes de droit interne des Parties — même si les États-Unis et le Canada ont adopté des normes porteuses de déférence. Ici, au moins, le Tribunal aura évité l'application du droit administratif américain. Par ailleurs, il importe de mentionner que l'intérêt que présente la question de la déférence dépasse le cadre de l'article 1105 et s'étend notamment à l'interprétation des articles 1102 (traitement national) et 1110 de l'*ALENA* (tel que démontré dans l'affaire *Methanex*).[112]

2   *Interprétation de l'article 1105*

L'interprétation de l'article 1105 par les tribunaux arbitraux a posé des problèmes aux Parties à l'*ALENA* depuis presque les toutes premières sentences arbitrales rendues.[113] En 2001, les Parties

---

[110] *Glamis, supra* note 3 aux para 23, 617; voir aussi les arguments des États-Unis aux para 594-95.

[111] Voir *ibid* au para 594.

[112] *Methanex, supra* note 97.

[113] La chronique de l'année 2000 avait notamment souligné les difficultés présentées par les affaires *Metalclad Corporation c Mexico* (Award, 30 août 2000) ICSID Case N° ARB/AF/97/1 [*Metalclad*]; *S.D. Myers, Inc. c Canada* (Partial Award, 13 novembre 2000) [*S.D. Myers*]. *Pope & Talbot Inc. c Canada* (Award on the Merits of Phase II, 10 avril 2001) [*Pope & Talbot*]. Voir C Lévesque "Chronique de

avaient adopté une interprétation de cet article qui visait notamment "à éclaircir et à réaffirmer" ce qui suit:

L'article 1105(1) prescrit la norme minimale de traitement conforme au droit international coutumier à l'égard des étrangers comme norme minimale de traitement à accorder aux investissements effectués par les investisseurs d'une autre Partie.

Les concepts de "traitement juste et équitable" et de "protection et sécurité intégrales" ne prévoient pas de traitement supplémentaire ou supérieur à celui exigé par la norme minimale de traitement conforme au droit international coutumier à l'égard des étrangers.

La constatation qu'il y a eu violation d'une autre disposition de l'*ALENA* ou d'un accord international distinct ne démontre pas qu'il y ait eu violation de l'article 1105(1).[114]

Cette interprétation n'allait toutefois pas avoir l'effet escompté, car si elle a pu "éclaircir" la norme applicable, son contenu demeurait incertain. Il est alors revenu aux tribunaux subséquents de juger au cas par cas de la portée actuelle de la norme minimale de traitement en droit international coutumier.[115] Une tendance semblait toutefois se dessiner: la norme minimale de traitement était exigeante, c'est-à-dire que le seuil de violation était assez élevé, mais elle avait bel et bien évolué depuis les années 1920 et l'affaire *Neer*.[116] L'affaire *Mondev*, suivie des affaires *ADF* et *Waste Management II*, notamment, avaient remis en question la pertinence de l'affaire

---

Droit international économique en 2000 — Investissement," (2001) XXXIX ACDI 463.

[114] Commission du libre-échange de l'*ALENA*, "Notes d'interprétation de certaines dispositions du chapitre 11 (31 juillet 2001)," en ligne: MAECI <http://www.international.gc.ca/trade-agreements-accords-commerciaux/disp-diff/NAFTA-Interpr.aspx?lang=fr>.

[115] Voir par ex les affaires *Mondev, supra* note 87; *ADF Group Inc. c United States* (Award, 9 janvier 2003) ICSID Case N° ARB(AF)/00/1 [*ADF*]; *Loewen Group, Inc. and Raymond L Loewen c United States* (Award, 26 juin 2003) ICSID Case N° ARB(AF)/98/3 [*Loewen*]; *Waste Management, Inc. c Mexico* (Award, 30 avril 2004) ICSID Case N° ARB(AF)/00/3 [*Waste Management II*]; *Methanex, supra* note 97; *GAMI Investments, Inc. c Mexico* (Final Award, 15 novembre 2004) [*GAMI*]; *Thunderbird, supra* note 89.

[116] *Neer, supra* note 79.

Neer à titre d'étalon de la norme minimale de traitement.[117] Durant cette étape, les Parties à l'*ALENA* avaient notamment été contraintes de reconnaître que le droit international coutumier en matière de protection des étrangers n'était pas "gelé" à l'époque de l'affaire *Neer*.[118]

En 2009, arrive la sentence dans l'affaire *Glamis*.[119] Elle affirme sans ambages que la norme de traitement dans l'affaire *Neer* demeure applicable. Elle affirme aussi qu'il revient à l'investisseur de prouver toute évolution alléguée de la coutume, une tâche que le Tribunal admet être difficile.[120] Ce raisonnement est d'abord frappant en ce qu'il semble être en décalage par rapport aux sentences précédentes, et d'autant plus que les États-Unis n'ont pas plaidé, en l'espèce, que la norme de l'affaire *Neer* était applicable.[121] Au surplus, le Canada et le Mexique avaient quelque peu pris leurs distances par rapport à l'affaire *Neer* — malgré la description ambiguë que fait le Tribunal de leurs positions respectives.[122] Il a pu sembler aussi frappant d'exiger des investisseurs la preuve de la coutume internationale, ce qui pour certains commentateurs, imposait un fardeau impossible à assumer pour une partie privée.

La surprise laissant toutefois place à la réflexion, il semble que cette rupture soit plus apparente que réelle et ce, pour deux motifs principaux. D'abord, le Tribunal dans l'affaire *Glamis* reconnait lui-même que, collectivement, on peut être offusqué plus facilement,

---

117 *Mondev, supra* note 87 aux para 115-16; *ADF, supra* note 115 aux para 179-81; *Waste Management II, supra* note 115 au para 93; voir aussi *GAMI, supra* note 115 au para 95.

118 Voir par ex *ADF, ibid* para 179: "*The FTC Interpretation of 31 July 2001, in the view of the United States, refers to customary international law 'as it exists today'. It is equally important to note that Canada and Mexico accept the view of the United States on this point even as they stress that 'the threshold [for violation of that standard] remains high.' Put in slightly different terms, what customary international law projects is not a static photograph of the minimum standard of treatment of aliens as it stood in 1927 when the Award in the Neer case was rendered*" [notes omises].

119 *Glamis, supra* note 3.

120 *Ibid* au para 602 et s.

121 Voir *Glamis Gold, Inc. c United States*, US Counter-Memorial, 19 septembre 2006, en ligne: US Department of State <http://www.state.gov/documents/organization/73686.pdf> [*Glamis*, US Counter-Memorial].

122 Voir par ex la soumission du Canada (en vertu de l'art 1128 de l'*ALENA*) dans l'affaire *ADF* en date du 19 juillet 2002: "*Canada's position has never been that the customary international law regarding the treatment of aliens was 'frozen in amber at the time of the Neer decision'*" (au para 23) (cité dans *ADF, supra* note 115, n 170).

par rapport à des actions gouvernementales, que dans les années 1920. Il s'agit de l'un des deux types d'évolution admis par le Tribunal.[123] Il est ainsi permis de se demander si les deux points de départ différents dans la jurisprudence ne risquent pas d'aboutir au même résultat: (1) norme élevée intacte, mais mœurs plus exigeantes et (2) norme assouplie avec le temps en raison des mœurs plus exigeantes.

Ensuite, quant au contenu de la norme en droit international coutumier, le Tribunal reconnaît l'obligation de respect des attentes légitimes des investisseurs, sans tenir compte des exigences qu'il a lui-même fixées en matière de preuve. En effet, quatre courts paragraphes auront suffi au Tribunal pour régler cette question par ailleurs controversée. Le Tribunal se réfère principalement à la sentence dans l'affaire *Thunderbird*, qui avait également réglé la question de façon sommaire — en un seul paragraphe, en citant à l'appui "*recent case-law and the good faith principle of international customary law.*"[124] Cette façon de procéder nous permet de douter de la nature exigeante de la preuve de la coutume effectivement requise par le Tribunal.

Qui plus est, cette façon de procéder remet en doute l'énoncé du Tribunal selon lequel la jurisprudence arbitrale n'est pas, en elle-même, une source de droit international coutumier.[125] Cela dit, la sentence a quand même le mérite de distinguer clairement entre la jurisprudence comportant une interprétation de normes dites "autonomes" et celle interprétant la norme minimale de traitement en droit international coutumier.

3   *Interprétation de l'article 1110*

Parmi les articles dont le manquement est le plus souvent allégué, on retrouve l'article 1105 mais aussi l'article 1110 de l'*ALENA*.[126] Le taux de succès des investisseurs, par contre, est beaucoup moindre lorsqu'il s'agit de prouver une expropriation. En date de 2009, un seul Tribunal a reconnu une violation de l'article 1110, dans

---

123 Voir dans cette chronique *supra* note 90 et texte correspondant.

124 *Thunderbird, supra* note 89 au para 147.

125 *Glamis, supra* note 3: "*Arbitral awards, Respondent rightly notes, do not constitute State practice and thus cannot create or prove customary international law. They can, however, serve as illustrations of customary international law if they involve an examination of customary international law, as opposed to a treaty-based, or autonomous, interpretation*" (au para 605) [notes omises].

126 *ALENA, supra* note 2; voir aussi *supra* note 65 et texte correspondant.

l'affaire *Metalclad*.[127] La décision dans l'affaire *Glamis* se situe dans cette mouvance, imposant à l'investisseur la preuve exigeante d'une ingérence importante dans son investissement, mais son raisonnement est à tout le moins surprenant.

Il est coutumier pour les tribunaux, en matière d'expropriation, d'évaluer le degré d'ingérence dans les droits de propriété d'un investisseur dans un investissement. Depuis l'affaire *Pope & Talbot*, souvent citée à cet égard, les tribunaux ont eu tendance à examiner l'effet des mesures alléguées sur la propriété et le contrôle de l'investissement.[128] Ils ont aussi examiné l'impact des mesures sur les attributs de la propriété (*usus, fructus, abusus*).[129] Dans l'affaire *Glamis*, après avoir exposé les principes en usage, le Tribunal s'est rapidement concentré sur l'impact économique des mesures gouvernementales sur la *valeur* du projet Impérial. Ce faisant, il n'a pas jugé nécessaire de se soumettre à l'analyse en trois étapes, tirée du droit américain de l'expropriation (*U.S. takings law*), que les deux parties à l'affaire lui avaient soumise.[130] L'exercice est devenu purement mathématique et comptable: si le projet valait 49 millions de dollars et qu'il en vaut, suite aux mesures de remblayage, plus de 20, Glamis n'a pas été exproprié. Autrement dit, la valeur du projet n'a pas été radicalement réduite.

Ces calculs, toutefois, sont davantage propres à l'évaluation des dommages, à laquelle procède un tribunal une fois qu'il a conclu à l'expropriation, qu'à l'analyse de l'ingérence dans le droit de propriété dans un investissement. Le Tribunal explique — tant bien que mal — sa méthode de la façon suivante:

Thus, to be specific, the Tribunal's goal in this inquiry into Claimant's valuation model is not to determine if there was an expropriation, but to determine if there was not significant economic impact. These are very different inquiries: the first requires definitive cost calculations and a full revision of the discounted cash flow methodologies to determine exactly the value of the Imperial Project post-back filling;

---

127 *Metalclad, supra* note 113.

128 Voir *Pope & Talbot Inc. c Canada* (Interim Award, 26 juin 2000) aux para 100-2.

129 Voir par ex *Marvin Feldman c Mexico* (Award, 16 décembre 2002) ICSID Case N° ARB(AF)/99/1, au para 100 et s; *Waste Management II, supra* note 115 aux para 159-60; *Fireman's Fund Insurance Company c Mexico* (Award, 17 juillet 2006) ICSID Case N° ARB(AF)/02/01, au para 176; *ADM, supra* note 6 aux para 238-51; *CPI, supra* note 7 aux para 82-93.

130 Voir les mémoires des deux parties dans *Glamis*, en ligne: US Department of State <http://www.state.gov/s/l/c10986.htm>.

while the second requires only sufficient calculation to determine if the Project's value is positive.[131]

Sans doute, cette approche reflétait la position des États-Unis qui, très tôt, avaient remis en question les prétentions de Glamis quant à la réduction en valeur de son projet.[132] Il demeure qu'elle soulève plusieurs interrogations. D'abord, elle ne semble pas refléter la règle qui se trouve pourtant dans le *2004 Model BIT* des États-Unis selon laquelle la diminution de valeur n'est pas le facteur déterminant:

The determination of whether an action or series of actions by a Party, in a specific fact situation, constitutes an indirect expropriation, requires a case-by-case, fact-based inquiry that considers, among other factors: (a) the economic impact of the government action, although the fact that an action or series of actions by a Party <u>*has an adverse effect on the economic value of an investment, standing alone, does*</u> <u>*not establish that an indirect expropriation has occurred.*</u>[133]

Cela dit, est-il approprié, dans certains cas, de se concentrer uniquement sur la valeur de l'investissement allégué, en faisant fi d'une analyse plus large des attributs de la propriété? Connaissant les difficultés et les incertitudes notoires liées à l'évaluation des dommages, est-il sage ou même possible de faire dépendre la détermination de l'expropriation de tels calculs? Il aurait été souhaitable que le Tribunal justifie davantage son approche car, si elle est suivie, elle pourrait opérer un changement majeur en droit international de l'expropriation.

IV L'AFFAIRE *CARGILL C MEXICO*

A FAITS ET CONTEXTE JURIDIQUE

Un bref rappel des faits ayant donné naissance à la trilogie des affaires concernant les édulcorants s'impose.[134] Archer Daniels Midland

---

[131] *Glamis, supra* note 3 au para 365.

[132] Voir *Glamis*, US Counter-Memorial, *supra* note 121 à la p 162 et s.

[133] *Treaty between the Government of the United States of America and the Government of [Country] Concerning the Encouragement and Reciprocal Protection of Investment* (*2004 Model BIT*), Annex B Expropriation, en ligne: US Department of State <http://www.state.gov/documents/organization/117601.pdf> [nous soulignons].

[134] Pour une étude plus détaillée des faits, voir Lévesque, *supra* note 5.

Company et Tate & Lyle Ingredients Americas, Inc. (ADM), Corn Products International, Inc. (CPI) et Cargill, Inc. (Cargill) sont des compagnies américaines qui produisent et distribuent du sirop de maïs à haute teneur en fructose (SHTF).[135] Le SHTF est utilisé pour l'édulcoration des boissons gazeuses et des produits alimentaires. Aux États-Unis, le SHTF a graduellement remplacé le sucre comme édulcorant, mais ce n'est pas avant le milieu des années 1980 qu'il est devenu le produit de choix pour sucrer les aliments, et particulièrement les boissons gazeuses. Le SHTF est en effet moins coûteux et plus facile à utiliser que le sucre, parce qu'il se trouve sous forme liquide. Ce n'est qu'au début des années 1990 que des compagnies américaines ont commencé à pénétrer le marché mexicain.[136] ADM et CPI ont toutes deux choisi d'investir dans la production locale de SHTF au Mexique, important à cette fin le maïs jaune des États-Unis. Elles ont aussi exporté le SHTF vers le Mexique à partir de leurs usines de production aux États-Unis.[137] Pour sa part, Cargill a choisi d'uniquement investir dans l'exportation et la distribution du SHTF vers le Mexique à partir de ses usines situées aux États-Unis.[138]

Il importe de rappeler que le commerce du sucre et des sirops avait fait l'objet d'une attention particulière dans le cadre des négociations de l'*ALENA*. Une annexe concernant l'accès aux marchés prévoyait une période de transition de quinze ans vers une libéralisation dans le secteur entre le Mexique et les États-Unis.[139] Le fait, pour une des Parties, d'atteindre le statut de "producteur excédentaire net" de sucre, avait pour conséquence un accès accru en franchise au marché de l'autre. L'excédent net de production était calculé par rapport à la consommation de sucre sur le territoire d'une Partie.[140] Le manque de clarté de cette annexe est rapidement devenu un problème, notamment en ce qui concerne le traitement du SHTF dans le calcul de l'excédent net de production d'une

---

[135] *ADM, supra* note 6 au para 39; *CPI, supra* note 7 au para 27, *Cargill, supra* note 4 aux para 53, 57.

[136] *Cargill, supra* note 4 au para 62; *CPI, supra* note 7 au para 27; *ADM, supra* note 6 au para 55.

[137] *ADM, supra* note 6 aux para 39-40; *CPI, supra* note 7 aux para 26-27.

[138] *Cargill, supra* note 4 au para 79.

[139] *Cargill, supra* note 4 au para 68; *CPI, supra* note 7 aux para 6, 33; *ADM, supra* note 6 au para 59.

[140] *ADM, supra* note 6 au para 59; *CPI, supra* note 7 aux para 6, 33; voir également *ALENA, supra* note 2 à l'Annexe 703.2.

Partie.[141] Malgré un échange de lettres entre le Mexique et les États-Unis dans le but de régler le problème, des désaccords persistaient quant à la teneur de l'accord. Cette mésentente a pris une signification particulière en 1995, lorsque le Mexique est devenu un producteur excédentaire, puisque les Parties ne pouvaient pas s'entendre sur l'ampleur de ce surplus.[142]

Un déséquilibre important s'en est suivi, puisque les producteurs mexicains ne pouvaient pas exporter leur surplus de sucre sans droits de douane aux États-Unis (selon leur point de vue, contrairement aux dispositions de l'*ALENA*), tandis que plus de SHTF était exporté et produit au Mexique, accentuant le surplus de sucre.[143] Le Mexique a porté plainte au plus haut niveau du gouvernement américain, sans résultat.[144] Suite à des démarches de consultations infructueuses, le Mexique a finalement demandé la constitution d'un groupe spécial en vertu du chapitre 20 (règlement des différends entre États) de l'*ALENA*. Cependant, un tel groupe spécial n'a jamais été constitué. Le Mexique a accusé les États-Unis de faire obstacle à la constitution du groupe, alors que les États-Unis ont nié avoir agi à l'encontre de leurs obligations en vertu de l'*ALENA*.[145]

Les mesures contestées par ADM, CPI et Cargill s'inscrivent dans une longue série de mesures adoptées par le Mexique, à partir de 1997, et visant à protéger son industrie du sucre alors en crise. Ces différentes mesures, notamment l'imposition de droits antidumping sur le SHTF importé et l'expropriation d'un certain nombre de raffineries de sucre qui traversaient une période financière difficile, ont donné lieu à des recours multiples en vertu de l'*ALENA* et à l'Organisation mondiale du commerce (OMC).[146]

---

[141] *ADM, supra* note 6 aux para 57-68; *CPI, supra* note 7 au para 34; *Cargill, supra* note 4 aux para 72-73.

[142] *ADM, supra* note 6 au para 69; *CPI, supra* note 7 aux para 82-83; *Cargill, supra* note 4 aux para 82-83.

[143] *ADM, supra* note 6 au para 71; *CPI, supra* note 7 au para 35; *Cargill, supra* note 4 au para 82.

[144] *ADM, supra* note 6 au para 71; *CPI, supra* note 7 au para 37; *Cargill, supra* note 4 au para 85.

[145] *ADM, supra* note 6 aux para 71, 77-79; *CPI, supra* note 7 aux para 37-39; *Cargill, supra* note 4 aux para 77-79.

[146] Pour un exposé détaillé des mesures adoptées par le Mexique, de même que les diverses contestations par les États-Unis et les investisseurs américains affectés par ces mesures, voir Lévesque, *supra* note 5.

En particulier, le 31 décembre 2001, le Mexique a modifié une loi qui imposait une taxe d'accise sur certains biens et services. La modification, qui prenait effet le lendemain, imposait une taxe de 20 pour cent, notamment sur les boissons gazeuses qui utilisaient un édulcorant autre que le sucre de canne (la taxe IEPS).[147] L'impact sur l'industrie du SHTF a été immédiat: plusieurs producteurs de boissons gazeuses ont recommencé à utiliser du sucre et les producteurs et fournisseurs de SHTF ont en conséquences encaissé des pertes importantes.[148] La taxe IEPS est la mesure au cœur des affaires *ADM, CPI* et *Cargill.*

Cargill, en plus de contester cette taxe, s'oppose au décret du gouvernement mexicain, également publié le 31 décembre 2001, instaurant de nouveaux tarifs sur l'importation de SHTF et de nouvelles conditions d'obtention de permis d'importation. En cas de non-respect de ces conditions, les investisseurs étrangers étaient confrontés à un taux d'imposition plusieurs fois supérieur à ceux applicables en vertu de l'*ALENA.*[149] De plus, une controverse quant à la disponibilité de ces permis d'importation a été soulevée. Cargill prétendait que bien qu'un système de permis d'importation ait été mis en place, aucun critère ou procédure pour l'obtention de ceux-ci n'avait été publié par le Secrétaire de l'économie.[150] D'ailleurs, Cargill a dit avoir essuyé un refus à chacune de ses multiples demandes d'obtention de permis d'importation.[151]

ADM, CPI et Cargill ont toutes trois contestées la taxe IEPS au cours des années 2003-2004.[152] Plus précisément dans le cas qui nous intéresse, Cargill a signifié au Mexique son intention de déposer une plainte en vertu du chapitre 11 de l'*ALENA* en septembre 2004 et a soumis sa plainte à l'arbitrage en décembre de la même année.[153] Cargill alléguait la violation des articles 1102 (traitement

---

[147] *ADM, supra* note 6 aux para 81-82; *CPI, supra* note 7 au para 40; *Cargill, supra* note 4 au para 105.

[148] *ADM, supra* note 6 au para 49; *CPI, supra* note 7 au para 44; *Cargill, supra* note 4 au para 107.

[149] *Cargill, supra* note 4 au para 117.

[150] *Ibid* aux para 118-21.

[151] *Ibid* au para 120.

[152] CPI a soumis sa plainte à l'arbitrage en octobre 2003, alors que la plainte d'ADM a suivi en août 2004. Voir *ADM, supra* note 6 aux para 13-15 et *CPI, supra* note 7 au para 15.

[153] *Cargill, Incorporated c Mexico,* Notice of Intent du 30 septembre 2004; *Cargill, Incorporated c Mexico,* Request for an Institution of Arbitration Proceedings du

national), 1103 (traitement de la nation la plus favorisée), 1105, 1106 (prescriptions de résultats) et 1110.[154]

Alors que les plaintes des investisseurs se multipliaient, les États-Unis ont contesté la taxe IEPS devant l'OMC en juin 2004. En octobre 2005, un groupe spécial a jugé que le Mexique n'avait pas respecté ses obligations de traitement national prévues à l'article III du GATT. Il a également rejeté la défense de contre-mesures présentée par la Mexique en vertu de l'article XX du GATT.[155]

Cinq ans après son entrée en vigueur, le Mexique a abrogé sa taxe IEPS le 1er janvier 2007.[156] En définitive, le Tribunal dans l'affaire Cargill a jugé que le Mexique avait manqué à ses obligations en vertu des articles 1102, 1105 et 1106 de l'*ALENA*.[157]

B   RAISONNEMENT DU TRIBUNAL

1   *Objections juridictionnelles*

Le Tribunal dans l'affaire *Cargill* a d'abord traité de ce qu'il décrit comme étant les principales objections juridictionnelles avancées par le Mexique. Celles-ci concernaient en particulier l'emplacement de l'investissement de Cargill, de même que la pertinence du chapitre 11 en rapport avec des mesures gouvernementales affectant le commerce.[158]

Dans sa réflexion, le Tribunal a d'abord souligné que l'*ALENA* traite du commerce de biens et services, et de la protection des investissements dans des chapitres distincts.[159] Après analyse, toutefois, le Tribunal a conclu qu'un chevauchement entre les divers chapitres

---

29 décembre 2004, en ligne: <http://www.economia.gob.mx/swb/work/models/economia/Resource/434/1/images/IV_Cargill_Incorporated_20092804.pdf>.

154 Voir *ALENA, supra* note 2.

155 *ADM, supra* note 6 aux para 87-96; *CPI, supra* note 7 au para 47; *Cargill, supra* note 4 au para 113, citant Organisation Mondiale du Commerce, *Mexique – Mesures fiscales concernant les boissons sans alcool et autres boissons* (*Rapport du Groupe spécial*), OMC Doc WT/DS308/R (2005).

156 *ADM, supra* note 6 aux para 97-99; *CPI, supra* note 7 aux para 43, 48; *Cargill, supra* note 4 au para 124 (il est à noter que la taxe avait été suspendue pour une durée de quelques mois et rétablie par la suite).

157 *Cargill, supra* note 4 aux para 548-52.

158 *Ibid* au para 140.

159 *Ibid* au para 146.

de l'*ALENA* n'était pas exclu et qu'un tel chevauchement ne constitue pas nécessairement une "incompatibilité" qui ferait prévaloir un autre chapitre sur le chapitre 11.[160] Le Tribunal a ensuite conclu que la pertinence de la relation entre l'investissement et le commerce se situe au niveau de l'évaluation des dommages (en particulier à savoir si les ventes à l'exportation pouvaient être compensées), ce qui est, selon lui, une question d'interprétation, et non de compétence.[161]

Au titre de la compétence, le Tribunal a ensuite abordé les différentes dispositions juridictionnelles du chapitre 11, en commençant par l'article 1101. Après avoir noté son accord avec la décision dans l'affaire *Bayview Irrigation District et al v Mexico,* en vertu de laquelle un investisseur d'une Partie doit faire (ou proposer de faire) un investissement dans le territoire d'une autre Partie pour que l'article 1101(1)a) s'applique,[162] le Tribunal dans l'affaire *Cargill* a affirmé qu'en l'espèce, il n'y avait aucun doute que l'investisseur avait effectué un investissement au Mexique à travers une filiale — Cargill de Mexico — qui est une entreprise.[163] De plus, la taxe IEPS était aussi une mesure reliée à un investisseur ou un investissement.[164] Le Mexique a toutefois soulevé une objection juridictionnelle concernant les conditions d'obtention d'un permis d'importation sur la base, *inter alia,* qu'il s'agit d'une mesure concernant le commerce, et non l'investissement.[165] Cette objection a ramené le Tribunal, une fois de plus, à sa discussion sur la relation entre le commerce et l'investissement. Le Tribunal a alors fait référence à l'interprétation par le Tribunal dans l'affaire *Methanex* de l'expression "concernant" contenue à l'article 1101 et a conclu qu'un test de la connexion juridiquement significative (*legally significant connection*) y a été établi. Ainsi, le Tribunal a conclu qu'en empêchant l'importation de SHTF, la mesure a affecté l'investissement de l'investisseur au Mexique.[166] La dernière question sur laquelle s'est penchée le Tribunal sous le titre de l'article 1101 est de savoir si une part de marché véritable ou potentielle est en soi un "investissement" en

---

160 *Ibid* au para 148 (faisant référence à l'article 1112(1) de l'*ALENA, supra* note 2).

161 *Ibid* au para 154.

162 *Ibid* au para 165.

163 *Ibid* au para 167.

164 *Ibid* aux para 168-69.

165 *Ibid* au para 170.

166 *Ibid* aux para 173-75.

vertu de l'article 1139. Le Tribunal a noté que cette question, bien qu'ayant été discutée notamment dans les affaires *Methanex* et *Pope and Talbot,* n'a jamais été résolue.[167] À ce point, le Tribunal a toutefois décliné d'y répondre.

Une fois sa compétence établie, le Tribunal s'est penché sur les différentes allégations de violation de l'*ALENA* par le Mexique.

2   *Traitement national: Article 1102*

Cargill a allégué un manquement à l'obligation de traitement national, puisque la taxe IEPS était imposée sur toutes les boissons gazeuses contenant du SHTF, lequel était totalement fourni par des compagnies américaines. De plus, Cargill a prétendu que les conditions d'octroi du permis d'importation, de même que le refus systématique par le Mexique de lui octroyer un tel permis d'importation, l'ont désavantagée au bénéfice des producteurs de sucre nationaux mexicains.[168] Ainsi, Cargill a affirmé que la taxe IEPS et la mise en place du système de permis d'importation constituaient un traitement moins favorable envers l'investissement comme envers l'investisseur.[169]

L'article 1102(1) de l'*ALENA* prévoit que:

> Chacune des Parties accordera aux investisseurs d'une autre Partie un traitement non moins favorable que celui qu'elle accorde, dans des circonstances analogues, à ses propres investisseurs, en ce qui concerne l'établissement, l'acquisition, l'expansion, la gestion, la direction, l'exploitation et la vente ou autre aliénation d'investissements.[170]

De façon similaire aux Tribunaux dans les affaires *ADM* et *CPI,* le Tribunal dans l'affaire *Cargill* n'a eu aucune difficulté à conclure à un manquement à l'obligation de traitement national. Le Tribunal s'est d'abord penché sur la question de savoir si Cargill se situait dans des circonstances similaires aux producteurs de sucre mexicains et a répondu par l'affirmative. Dans ce cadre, il a décidé que le fait qu'un tribunal de l'OMC ait conclu que le sucre et le SHTF

---

[167] *Ibid* aux para 176-78.

[168] *Ibid* au para 185.

[169] *Ibid* au para 188.

[170] *ALENA, supra* note 2, art 1102(1) (le paragraphe 2 de l'article 1102 prévoit la même obligation mais au profit des "investissements des investisseurs").

sont des produits similaires est pertinent, mais non déterminant, pour les fins de son analyse en vertu de l'article 1102.[171]

De plus, selon le Tribunal, il ne faisait aucun doute qu'en raison de la taxe et des permis d'importation, Cargill a reçu un traitement moins favorable que les fournisseurs de canne à sucre. Ainsi, le Tribunal conclut que cette discrimination était, tant par son intention que son effet, basée sur la nationalité.[172]

Finalement, le Tribunal a rapidement décidé que le traitement "concern[ait] l'établissement, l'acquisition, l'expansion, la gestion, la direction, l'exploitation et la vente ou autre aliénation d'investissements," ce qui n'est d'ailleurs pas contesté par le Mexique.[173] Ainsi, le Tribunal a conclu à une violation par le Mexique du standard de traitement national.[174]

3   Traitement de la nation la plus favorisée: Article 1103

Le Tribunal a rejeté de façon sommaire l'allégation de manquement à l'obligation de traitement de la nation la plus favorisée. L'article 1103(1) prévoit que:

Chacune des Parties accordera aux investisseurs d'une autre Partie un traitement non moins favorable que celui qu'elle accorde, dans des circonstances analogues, aux investisseurs de toute autre Partie ou d'un pays tiers, en ce qui concerne l'établissement, l'acquisition, l'expansion, la gestion, la direction, l'exploitation et la vente ou autre aliénation d'investissements.[175]

Le Tribunal a été en mesure de rapidement réfuter l'argument de Cargill selon lequel le traitement qu'il reçoit peut être comparé à celui reçu par CPI à travers Casco, une filiale canadienne de cet investisseur américain. En effet, Casco est un investissement de CPI en sol canadien, et non en sol mexicain, et ne pouvait donc pas être utilisé comme base de comparaison en vertu de l'article 1103.[176]

---

171 *Cargill, supra* note 4 aux para 194, 211-214; voir aussi l'affaire *Mexique – Mesures fiscales concernant les boissons sans alcool et autres boissons, supra* note 155.

172 *Ibid* aux para 219-21.

173 *Ibid* au para 222.

174 *Ibid* au para 223.

175 *ALENA, supra* note 2, art 1103(1).

176 *Cargill, supra* note 4 au para 233-34.

4   *Norme minimale de traitement: Article 1105*

Consciente que la taxe IEPS ne pouvait constituer la base d'une réclamation en vertu de l'article 1105, Cargill a plutôt fondé sa réclamation sur la longue et implacable campagne anti-SHTF menée par le Mexique.[177] Cependant, Cargill a prétendu que l'instauration du système de permis d'importation, à elle seule, était suffisante pour constituer une violation de l'article 1105.[178]

Le Tribunal a commencé son analyse en affirmant que le contenu de cette obligation est difficile à définir avec précision et que les déclarations des différentes tribunaux arbitraux sur le sujet sont difficilement applicables à des faits particuliers.[179] Le Tribunal a enchaîné en mentionnant qu'il est clairement établi que la référence au "traitement juste et équitable" contenue à l'article 1105 doit être comprise à la lumière du droit international coutumier, ce qui a notamment été affirmé par la Commission du libre-échange de l'*ALENA* en 2001.[180]

Le désaccord entre les parties à l'affaire, par contre, se situait davantage au niveau de la détermination du contenu de la norme minimale de traitement en droit international coutumier.[181] La description de l'approche du Tribunal dans les trois paragraphes qui suivent reprend presque mot pour mot celle du Tribunal dans l'affaire *Glamis*.[182] La présence d'un arbitre commun aux deux affaires explique sans doute cette répétition (bien que la source ne soit pas indiquée). Ainsi, ce Tribunal a lui aussi confirmé que: (1) l'interprétation en vertu du droit international coutumier est distincte de l'interprétation dite "autonome" de la norme de traitement juste et équitable; (2) il revient à la partie qui invoque une coutume d'en faire la preuve (même si cette dernière peut-être difficile à faire); (3) la norme minimale de traitement est au moins la norme de l'affaire *Neer*.[183]

Au sujet de la preuve, le Tribunal a reconnu qu'il puisse être difficile pour Cargill de lui offrir une étude de la pratique récente

---

[177] Voir *ALENA, supra* note 2, art 2103 qui prévoit une exclusion pour les mesures fiscales.

[178] *Cargill, supra* note 4 au para 235.

[179] *Ibid* au para 266.

[180] *Ibid* aux para 267-68.

[181] *Ibid* au para 268.

[182] *Glamis, supra* note 3, en particulier aux para 20-21.

[183] *Cargill, supra* note 4 aux para 270-73.

des États et a donc accepté d'avoir recours à d'autres éléments de preuve de la coutume.[184] Ainsi, le Tribunal a accepté de considérer — avec prudence — diverses déclarations effectuées par les trois États Parties, que ce soit en tant que défendeur ou États tiers lors d'arbitrages en vertu du chapitre 11,[185] de même que l'adoption étendue de formulations identiques dans plusieurs traités signés entre différents États,[186] les écrits d'éminents juristes et les sentences arbitrales.[187]

Cargill a tenté d'établir que le contenu de la norme de traitement minimale, tel que défini dans l'affaire *Tecmed*, reflétait l'état du droit international coutumier. Toutefois, le Tribunal a refusé de considérer cette affaire dans son analyse, puisque le Tribunal dans l'affaire *Tecmed* y avait expressément dit avoir procédé à une interprétation autonome de la disposition du traité d'investissement entre l'Espagne et le Mexique.[188]

Le Tribunal a plutôt jugé pertinent de faire référence aux décisions dans les affaires *Mondev* et *ADF* où les Tribunaux ont reconnu que la norme de traitement minimale en vertu du droit international coutumier est constamment en développement.[189] La question à laquelle le Tribunal se devait de répondre était donc de déterminer ce que le droit international coutumier exigeait d'octroyer — à l'heure actuelle — aux étrangers, en termes de norme minimale de traitement.[190] Après avoir analysé les sentences arbitrales traitant de ce sujet, de même que les éléments de preuve de coutume énumérés précédemment, le Tribunal a noté:

> *The tribunal observes a trend in previous NAFTA awards, not so much to make the holding of Neer arbitration more exacting, but rather to adapt the principle underlying the holding of the Neer arbitration to the more complicated and varied economic positions held by foreign nationals today. Key to this adaptation is that, even as more situations are addressed, the required severity of the conduct as held in Neer is maintained.[191]*

---

184 *Ibid* au para 274.
185 *Ibid* au para 275.
186 *Ibid* au para 276.
187 *Ibid* au para 277.
188 *Ibid* au para 280.
189 *Ibid* au para 281.
190 *Ibid* au para 283.
191 *Ibid* au para 284.

Le Tribunal a également analysé les éléments spécifiques dont Cargill prétendait qu'ils étaient inclus dans la norme minimale de traitement. Le Tribunal a reconnu qu'un degré élevé d'arbitraire pouvait constituer un manquement à l'article 1105, mais a rejeté, en raison du manque de preuve, tant l'obligation de transparence[192] que celle de la garantie d'un environnement stable et prévisible qui ne frustre par les attentes légitimes des investisseurs (du moins lorsqu'elles n'étaient pas fondées sur un contrat ou un quasicontrat).[193]

En conclusion, le Tribunal a résumé la norme de la façon suivante:

> To determine whether an action fails to meet the requirement of fair and equitable treatment, a tribunal must carefully examine whether the complained of measures were grossly unfair, unjust or idiosyncratic; arbitrary beyond a merely inconsistent or questionable application of administrative or legal policy or procedure so as to constitute an unexpected and shocking repudiation of a policy's very purpose and goals, or to otherwise grossly subvert a domestic law or policy for an ulterior motive; or involve an utter lack of due process so as to offend judicial propriety.[194]

Suite à cette analyse, le Tribunal a conclu que la taxe IEPS, de même que les conséquences des droits antidumping ne peuvent pas servir de base à la conclusion d'une violation de l'article 1105, puisque les mesures fiscales sont exclues de l'application de l'article 1105 et que les droits antidumping excèdent la compétence temporelle du Tribunal. Ainsi, le Tribunal ne s'est basé que sur la mise en place du système de permis d'importation, tout en gardant à l'esprit qu'il ne s'agissait que d'une mesure parmi toute une série.[195] Le Tribunal a alors facilement conclu à une violation de l'article 1105, puisque les permis d'importation ne constituaient qu'une mesure parmi plusieurs visant expressément à nuire aux producteurs et fournisseurs américains de SHTF dans le but de persuader le gouvernement américain de modifier sa politique concernant

---

[192] *Ibid* au para 294.

[193] *Ibid* aux para 289-90. Par ailleurs, le Tribunal a refusé de statuer sur l'existence d'une obligation de non-discrimination puisque Cargill n'a appuyé sa position à cet effet que sur les arguments déjà avancés en ce qui a trait aux violations alléguées en vertu des articles 1102 et 1103 au para 295.

[194] *Ibid* au para 296.

[195] *Ibid* au para 297.

l'importation de sucre du Mexique.[196] Il a estimé que cette action avait surpassé la norme de "gross misconduct and [was] more akin to bad faith"[197] Il a aussi jugé que "*willful targeting, by its nature, [was] a manifest injustice.*"[198]

5 *Prescriptions de résultats: Article 1106*

Le Tribunal a commencé son analyse de l'obligation de l'article 1106 en soulignant son accord avec les prétentions des deux parties selon lesquelles il existe peu de lignes directrices quant à l'interprétation de cette disposition en raison de la faible fréquence des réclamations à ce titre.[199]

L'article 1106(3) prévoit que:

Aucune des Parties ne pourra subordonner l'octroi ou le maintien de l'octroi d'un avantage, *en ce qui concerne* un investissement effectué sur son territoire par un investisseur d'une autre Partie ou d'un pays tiers, à l'observation de l'une quelconque des prescriptions suivantes:

(a) atteindre un niveau ou un pourcentage donné de contenu national;
(b) acheter, utiliser ou privilégier les produits produits sur son territoire, ou acheter des produits de producteurs situés sur son territoire.[200]

L'analyse, somme toute sommaire, du Tribunal se résume à ceci: "*the central question in this case is whether a tax on soft drinks containing HFCS can be said to be a measure 'in connection with' an investment relating to the business of supplying HFCS to the soft drink industry.*"[201] Autrement dit, pouvait-il considérer que la taxe IEPS conditionnait l'octroi d'un "avantage" en ce qui concerne l'investissement de Cargill au Mexique, soit Cargill de Mexico?[202] Le Tribunal s'est donc engagé dans une analyse de l'interprétation de l'expression "en ce qui concerne," mais s'est toutefois abstenu de se prononcer, dans l'abstrait, sur le degré d'association nécessaire afin de conclure qu'une mesure est prise "en ce qui concerne" un investissement.

196 *Ibid* aux para 299-305.

197 *Ibid* au para 298.

198 *Ibid* au para 300.

199 *Ibid* au para 313.

200 *ALENA, supra* note 2, art 1106(3) [nous soulignons].

201 *Cargill, supra* note 4 au para 313.

202 *Ibid* au para 313.

En l'espèce, il a jugé que la prescription de résultats est intégralement reliée à l'investissement de l'investisseur.[203] Le Tribunal a donc conclu à la violation de l'article 1106(3) par le Mexique.

6   Expropriation: Article 1110

Le Tribunal a commencé son analyse en s'interrogeant à savoir si Cargill avait fondé sa plainte en vertu de l'article 1110 sur un "investissement" tel que défini à l'article 1139.[204] Cette question était pertinente, puisque Cargill fondait sa demande non pas sur l'expropriation de Cargill de Mexico (clairement un "investissement"), mais bien de son activité commerciale mexicaine liée au SHTF. Ainsi, Cargill ne réclamait pas pour la diminution de la valeur des actifs matériels détenus par Cargill de Mexico, mais plutôt pour des dommages résultant de la perte alléguée de leur utilisation prévue.[205] Le Tribunal a donc défini la question comme étant celle de déterminer d'abord si l'activité commerciale liée au SHTF constituait un investissement en soi, avant de déterminer si cette activité, en tant qu'investissement en vertu de l'article 1139, était susceptible d'expropriation en vertu de l'article 1110.[206]

Après avoir rappelé que la définition d'investissement contenue à l'article 1139 est large et inclusive,[207] le Tribunal s'est livré à un examen de sentences rendues précédemment, notamment dans les affaires *Pope & Talbot* et *Methanex* où il a été décidé que le revenu d'entreprise d'un investissement forme une partie intégrante de la valeur de la propriété sous-jacente.[208] Ainsi, le Tribunal n'a guère eu de difficulté à conclure que des revenus d'entreprise, particulièrement lorsqu'associés à des actifs matériels dans le pays hôte, constituent un élément d'un investissement plus large incluant des actifs matériels ou un investissement en soi.[209]

Dans un deuxième temps, le Tribunal a procédé à l'évaluation du degré d'interférence que les mesures prises par le Mexique ont eu dans l'investissement de Cargill.[210] Il a fondé son analyse non

---

203 *Ibid* au para 317.

204 *ALENA, supra* note 2, art 1110, cité *supra* note 65 et texte correspondant.

205 *Cargill, supra* note 4 au para 350.

206 *Ibid* au para 351.

207 *Ibid* au para 352.

208 *Ibid* aux para 355-57.

209 *Ibid* aux para 353, 358.

210 *Ibid* aux para 359-78.

seulement sur l'activité liée au SHTF, mais sur l'entreprise Cargill de Mexico dans son ensemble.[211] Le Tribunal s'est penché sur la possibilité qu'une atteinte temporaire à la propriété puisse constituer une expropriation en vertu de l'article 1110 de l'*ALENA* et a conclu par la négative. Par conséquent, la plainte de Cargill en vertu de l'article 1110 a été rejetée.[212]

7 *Défense de contre-mesures*

Le Tribunal a ensuite abordé la validité de la défense de contre-mesures avancée par le Mexique. Sur ce point, le Tribunal était intéressé par le raisonnement des Tribunaux dans les affaires *ADM* et *CPI* en raison des importantes implications de la question, de même que des liens étroits entre l'affaire examinée et les deux sentences rendues précédemment.[213] En définitive, le Tribunal a obtenu l'accès à la sentence dans l'affaire *ADM*, alors qu'une note en bas de page mentionne que le Tribunal n'a obtenu l'accès à la sentence dans l'affaire *CPI* que juste avant l'achèvement de la sentence. Le Tribunal souligne donc uniquement au passage que la défense de contremesures a également été rejetée dans l'affaire *CPI*.[214] Après avoir revu et analysé le raisonnement de la majorité et l'opinion concurrente dans l'affaire *ADM*, le Tribunal a énuméré les raisons l'amenant à rejeter la défense de contre-mesures.

Ainsi, le raisonnement du tribunal dans l'affaire *Cargill* est principalement construit en trois temps. Premièrement, le Tribunal constate que les droits des investisseurs en vertu de l'*ALENA* sont similaires à ceux des États tiers en ce qui concerne les contre-mesures.[215] En conséquence, bien que la mise en place d'une contre-mesure à l'encontre des États-Unis affecte probablement les droits de ses ressortissants, cela ne signifie pas qu'elle puisse avoir un effet juridique sur les obligations garanties directement aux investisseurs américains.[216] Deuxièmement, le Tribunal a conclu que les investisseurs ne jouissent pas de simples droits procéduraux en vertu du chapitre 11 — contrairement à ce que la majorité du Tribunal avait jugé dans l'affaire ADM.[217] Troisièmement, le Tribunal a déclaré

---

[211] *Ibid* aux para 366-68.

[212] *Ibid* au para 378.

[213] *Ibid* au para 380.

[214] *Ibid* au para 102.

[215] *Ibid* au para 422.

[216] *Ibid.*

[217] *Ibid* au para 424.

qu'il n'est pas fructueux de tenter de tirer la ligne entre les droits substantiels et les droits procéduraux.[218] Selon le Tribunal, le chapitre 11 a mis en place un cadre dans lequel les investisseurs agissent en leur nom propre et bénéficient des obligations du chapitre. Dans cette optique, le Tribunal a souligné que c'est l'investisseur qui porte plainte, qui engendre la constitution du tribunal, et qui est nommément partie à toutes les étapes de la procédure.[219] Cette situation est fort distincte de celle qui règne en vertu des règles de protection diplomatique où la réclamation appartient à l'État, qui est une partie nommée, et où, en conséquence, la défense de contre-mesures peut être appliquée.[220]

Ainsi, le Tribunal a conclu que la défense de contre-mesures ne pouvait empêcher l'illicéité des actions du Mexique dans le cadre d'une plainte en vertu du chapitre 11 de l'*ALENA*.[221]

8   *Octroi de dommages*

La phase d'évaluation des dommages a fait resurgir la problématique de la définition d'un "investissement", de même que celle de la territorialité. Le Tribunal a décidé que l'approche à adopter afin d'évaluer les dommages était de calculer la valeur actuelle nette des "*lost cash flows,*" ce qui équivaut à calculer la quantité de SHTF que Cargill aurait vendue, n'eût été l'instauration de la taxe IEPS et du système de permis d'importation.[222] Les pertes incluses dans ce calcul couvraient la période de juin 2001 à décembre 2007.[223]

C'est à cette étape que le Tribunal s'est posé la question de savoir si les pertes de Cargill en rapport avec les ventes à l'exportation à partir des États-Unis vers Cargill de Mexico faisaient partie de l'investissement ou si elles étaient des pertes d'exportation distinctes, et donc exclues du calcul des dommages en vertu du chapitre 11. Afin de résoudre cette question, le Tribunal a jugé utile de considérer les profits perdus à la frontière en deux groupes, soit les *upstream losses* (celles attribuables à l'impossibilité pour Cargill de vendre le SHTF à Cargill de Mexico) et les *downstream losses* (celles attribuables

---

[218] *Ibid* au para 426.
[219] *Ibid.*
[220] *Ibid* au para 424.
[221] *Ibid* au para 429.
[222] *Ibid* aux para 444-47.
[223] *Ibid* au para 464.

aux pertes directes de Cargill de Mexico).[224] Après réflexion, le Tribunal a décidé que tant les pertes en amont que les pertes en aval pouvaient être incluses dans le calcul des dommages pouvant être octroyés en vertu du chapitre 11.

Le Tribunal a toutefois été confronté au fait que le Tribunal dans l'affaire *ADM* en était venu à une conclusion contraire en statuant ne pas avoir compétence pour octroyer des dommages relativement à la perte de vente de SHTF produit aux États-Unis et ne pouvant être exporté au Mexique en raison de la taxe IEPS. Afin de se sortir de cette impasse, le Tribunal dans l'affaire *Cargill* a réitéré sa position selon laquelle la définition d'investissement en vertu de l'*ALENA* est large et que le revenu d'entreprise peut être considéré autant comme un investissement en soi que comme un élément formant partie d'un investissement plus vaste.[225] C'est dans ce contexte que le Tribunal a affirmé ce qui suit:

> *With respect to the particular facts of this case, the Tribunal finds that the profits generated by Cargill's sales of HFCS to its subsidiary, Cargill de Mexico, for CdM's marketing, distribution, and re-sale of that HFCS, were so associated with the claimed investment, CdM, as to be compensable under the NAFTA. Cargill's investment in Mexico involved importing HFCS and then selling it to domestic users, principally the soft drink industry. Thus, supplying HFCS to Cargill de Mexico was an inextricable part of Cargill's investment. As a result, in the view of the Tribunal, losses resulting from the inability of Cargill to supply its investment Cargill de Mexico with HFCS are just as much losses to Cargill in respect of its investment in Mexico as losses resulting from the inability of Cargill de Mexico to sell HFCS in Mexico.[226]*

Ainsi, le Tribunal a décrit son approche comme étant "holistique," puisque l'incapacité de Cargill d'exporter n'était que l'autre côté de la médaille de l'incapacité de Cargill de Mexico d'importer.[227] Le Tribunal a également tenté, dans un court paragraphe, de distinguer la situation à l'étude de celle dans l'affaire *ADM* sur la base des faits. En effet, le Tribunal a jugé pertinent de souligner le fait que, contrairement à ADM, qui vend du SHTF produit au Mexique,

---

[224] *Ibid* au para 519.

[225] *Ibid* aux para 521-22.

[226] *Ibid* au para 523.

[227] *Ibid* au para 525.

Cargill de Mexico vend uniquement du SHTF importé de sa société mère située en sol américain.[228] En conséquence, le Tribunal a ordonné au Mexique de payer 77 329 240 $US à Cargill.[229]

C OBSERVATIONS

Après que les sentences dans les affaires *ADM* et *CPI* eurent conclu à la violation de l'obligation de traitement national, le Mexique ne pouvait être surpris de la conclusion au même effet du Tribunal dans l'affaire *Cargill*. Pour le reste, les deux premières sentences avaient révélé un potentiel de raisonnement et de décisions contradictoires et la sentence dans l'affaire *Cargill* n'a pas déçu! Par contre, elle seule a fait l'objet d'une demande d'annulation de la part du Mexique. Des observations sommaires suivent au sujet du risque d'incohérence entre les sentences arbitrales, un thème déjà abordé dans la chronique de 2008,[230] et au sujet de l'approche commune des Tribunaux dans les affaires *Cargill* et *Glamis* en ce qui a trait à l'interprétation de l'article 1105. Par ailleurs, l'aspect le plus controversé de la sentence dans l'affaire *Cargill* retiendra notre attention: est-ce que le Tribunal a outrepassé ses compétences en octroyant des dommages à Cargill pour ses pertes d'exportations aux États-Unis?

I   Risque d'incohérence entre les sentences arbitrales

Comme indiqué dans la chronique de l'année 2008, le risque d'incohérence entre les sentences arbitrales découle notamment de la nature *ad hoc* de l'arbitrage international en matière d'investissement. Les trois affaires mexicaines concernant les édulcorants sont tout de même uniques en leur genre, puisque les plaintes ont toutes été déposées en vertu du même traité, contre la même partie défenderesse, par des investisseurs qui sont producteurs et distributeurs d'un même produit, et qui se plaignent de la même mesure gouvernementale.[231] Qui plus est, les règles d'arbitrage applicables, ainsi que le siège des Tribunaux, étaient les mêmes.[232]

---

[228] *Ibid* au para 524.

[229] *Ibid* au para 559.

[230] Lévesque, *supra* note 5.

[231] *Ibid* à la p 388, 408

[232] Les trois arbitrages étaient soumis au Mécanisme supplémentaire du CIRDI et leur siège était Toronto. Voir *Cargill, supra* note 4; *ADM, supra* note 6; *CPI, supra* note 7.

Ces traits communs, on le sait maintenant, n'ont pas été gage de cohérence. Il faut admettre que les Tribunaux étaient d'accord sur la question de la discrimination et de l'expropriation (même si leurs raisonnements ont fait preuve de certaines divergences). Toutefois, les Tribunaux dans les affaires *ADM* et *Cargill* on conclu à la violation de l'article 1106 tandis que le Tribunal dans l'affaire *CPI* a rejeté cette prétention. Au sujet de la défense de contre-mesures, le Tribunal dans l'affaire *ADM* l'a admise en principe (mais rejetée en l'espèce), tandis que les Tribunaux dans les affaires *CPI* et *Cargill* l'ont rejetée.[233] En ce qui concerne l'évaluation des dommages et la portée du chapitre 11, les Tribunaux dans les affaires *ADM* et *Cargill* ont rendu des décisions contradictoires (voir plus bas).

Bien qu'on ne puisse s'attendre à une cohérence parfaite, ou même la souhaiter en toute hypothèse, l'exemple fourni par ces trois affaires est inquiétant. À ce sujet, même si elle décrit bien le système actuel, la note de bas de pages qui suit, tirée de la sentence dans l'affaire *Glamis,* n'a rien de rassurant:

Given that there is no precedent, a tribunal may depart from even major previous trends. Unlike institutions with a closed docket of cases where consistency between the various claimants is often of paramount importance, the NAFTA regime's effort at consistency is one that both looks backward to major trends in past decided disputes and forward toward disputes that have not yet arisen. The appeal process (in the sense that it corrects a statement of the law) in arbitration runs forward in time over several cases rather than upwards in one particular case until a supreme judicial authority settles a question for a time. It is for these reasons that as a tribunal departs from past major trends, it should indicate the reasons for doing so.[234]

Même en ignorant le problème des affaires qui se déroulent en parallèle (comme celles des édulcorants), ce constat n'est pas de nature à mettre du baume sur les plaies des parties perdantes qui n'ont qu'à se tourner vers l'avenir pour voir une erreur de droit corrigée dans une autre affaire.

2   La cohérence entre les affaires Cargill et Glamis

Au titre de la cohérence, cette fois, il faut prendre note de l'approche commune des Tribunaux dans les affaires *Cargill* et *Glamis* quant

---

[233] Pour une étude détaillée des motifs rendus par les Tribunaux dans les affaires *CPI* et *ADM,* voir Lévesque, *supra* note 5.

[234] *Glamis, supra* note 3 à la note de bas de page 7 (apparaissant au para 8).

à l'interprétation de l'article 1105. Bien que ces deux décisions aient été rendues à environ trois mois d'intervalle en 2009 (ce qui en principe aurait empêché l'influence de l'une sur l'autre), la présence de l'arbitre Caron aura permis d'assurer une certaine cohérence dans l'approche.

Les observations précédentes portant sur l'affaire *Glamis* et la description du raisonnement dans l'affaire *Cargill*, auront déjà permis de remettre en question le caractère véritablement singulier de l'approche de ces Tribunaux au sujet de l'interprétation de l'article 1105. Cela dit, ces tribunaux ont eu le mérite de confirmer les exigences de preuve de la coutume internationale et de dire clairement que les sentences rendues en vertu d'autres traités que l'*ALENA* ne sont utiles que dans la mesure où elles comportent une analyse de l'état de la norme minimale de traitement en droit international coutumier. Sur cette base, ils ont pu notamment écarter la pertinence de l'affaire *Tecmed* — la manne des investisseurs de par le monde.[235]

À tout prendre, le Tribunal dans l'affaire *Cargill* a agi de façon plus conforme à la démarche qu'il avait fixée, en rejetant sommairement, par manque de preuve, les prétentions de l'investisseur quant à l'obligation de transparence et à l'obligation de stabilité et de prévisibilité du régime juridique.

3   Portée du chapitre 11 et évaluation des dommages dans l'affaire Cargill

Étant donné que l'*ALENA* est le premier traité de libre-échange à inclure un chapitre sur l'investissement prévoyant l'arbitrage investisseur-État, la question des relations entre les différents chapitres du traité s'est rapidement posée. Malgré les prétentions des Parties à l'*ALENA*, selon lesquelles une mesure commerciale ne pouvait faire l'objet d'une plainte en vertu du chapitre 11, les tribunaux ont constamment jugé qu'il n'y avait pas d'incompatibilité de principe entre le chapitre 11 et les chapitres 3 (sur le commerce) ou 12 (sur les services).[236] Le Tribunal dans l'affaire *Cargill* en a décidé de même. Malgré cela, les difficultés liées à la relation entre le commerce et l'investissement, et les différentes règles qui y sont applicables, perdurent.

---

[235] Pour une critique de l'affaire *Tecmed*, voir Z Douglas, "Nothing if Not Critical for Investment Treaty Arbitration: *Occidental, Eureko* and *Methanex*" (2006) Arb Int'l 27 aux pp 27-28.

[236] Voir par ex les affaires *S.D. Myers* et *Pope & Talbot*, *supra* note 113.

L'une des difficultés découle des nombreuses ramifications de la question et des perceptions variées des tribunaux à leur égard. Pour ne donner que quelques exemples: (1) Est-ce que le revenu d'entreprise ou l'accès au marché affecté par une mesure commerciale peut constituer un "investissement" en vertu du chapitre 11? (2) Si un investisseur effectue un investissement modeste dans le territoire d'une Partie, afin de faciliter l'exportation de biens, à quels dommages a-t-il droit: aux dommages subis à titre d'investisseur seulement ou aussi à titre d'exportateur? (3) Quel est l'impact de la nature territoriale de la protection offerte aux investisseurs en vertu du chapitre 11? (4) Ces questions relèvent-elles de l'interprétation (par exemple, du domaine de l'évaluation des dommages et de la causalité) ou de la compétence même du Tribunal?

Comme on l'a vu, de telles questions se sont posées dans l'affaire *Cargill* et, avant elle, dans les affaires *ADM* et *CPI*. Avant de poursuivre, il est utile de rappeler une particularité de l'affaire *Cargill* qui la distingue des autres. La différence principale tient au fait que la compagnie Cargill, contrairement à ADM et CPI, ne produit pas de SHTF en sol mexicain. En effet, Cargill a opté pour n'investir que dans l'exportation et la distribution du SHTF vers le Mexique à partir de ses usines situées aux États-Unis.[237] C'est pourquoi Cargill se trouvait gravement affecté par l'instauration du système de permis d'importation, alors que cette mesure n'a pas été abordée dans les deux décisions précédentes.

Il n'en demeure pas moins que les décisions dans les affaires *Cargill* et *ADM* sont contradictoires au sujet de la possibilité pour un investisseur de réclamer les montants correspondant à ses pertes à l'exportation dans son pays d'origine.[238] Le Tribunal dans l'affaire *Cargill,* pourtant au courant de la différence, n'a pas cru bon de se rallier à la décision du Tribunal dans l'affaire *ADM.* Le Tribunal a plutôt mis l'accent sur le fait que la fourniture de SHTF à Cargill de Mexico était une partie inextricable de l'investissement de Cargill. Pour lui, il s'agissait des deux côtés de la médaille.

Du point du vue du gouvernement mexicain, toutefois, l'un des cotés de cette médaille (le coté américain) n'était pas assujetti à la compétence du Tribunal. C'est pourquoi le 25 novembre 2009, le Mexique a fait une demande d'annulation dans l'affaire *Cargill,* au

---

[237] *Cargill, supra* note 4 au para 79.

[238] L'évaluation des dommages dans l'affaire *CPI, supra* note 7, n'étant pas disponible, on ne peut encore faire de comparaison avec le raisonnement dans cette sentence.

motif que la sentence contient des décisions qui dépassent les termes du consentement à l'arbitrage en vertu du chapitre 11 de l'*ALENA*.[239] La demande contient trois arguments, mais le plus important est indéniablement celui lié à l'évaluation des dommages par le Tribunal.[240]

L'issue de cette demande fera nécessairement l'objet d'un commentaire dans une chronique prochaine. Il y a tout de même lieu de noter dès maintenant l'importance systémique des questions posées. Dans le schéma des règles commerciales internationales, à l'OMC ou dans l'*ALENA*, les commerçants victimes de manquement aux obligations internationales des Parties doivent s'en remettre à leur État, qui décide s'il y a lieu ou non d'entreprendre une contestation. Par contre, les investisseurs dans le cadre de l'*ALENA* sont en mesure de porter plainte directement contre un État s'ils se croient victimes d'un manquement à une obligation comprise au chapitre 11 de l'*ALENA*. En conséquence, on peut se demander si la décision dans l'affaire *Cargill* ne remet pas en question la distinction traditionnelle entre les règles commerciales et les règles en matière d'investissement, en permettant à un investisseur d'obtenir une compensation pour les dommages subis par son investissement dans le territoire d'une autre Partie, mais aussi pour ses pertes à l'exportation.

---

[239] *Cargill, demande d'annulation, supra* note 8.

[240] *Ibid* au para 9.

Canadian Practice in International Law / Pratique canadienne en matière de droit international

At the Department of Foreign Affairs and International Trade in 2009–10 / Au ministère des Affaires étrangères et du Commerce international en 2009–10

compiled by / préparé par
ALAN KESSEL

AIR AND SPACE LAW

Convention on International Civil Aviation — Interpretation of Word "Territory"

In a legal opinion dated 21 October 2009, the Legal Branch wrote:

The Convention on International Civil Aviation, done at Chicago on 7 December 1944 [Chicago Convention] sets out the current framework for international air transport. Article 1 of the Chicago Convention declares that:

> The contracting States recognize that every State has complete and exclusive sovereignty over the airspace above its territory.

Article 2 of the Chicago Convention then describes the lateral limits of territorial airspace as follows:

Alan Kessel is the Legal Adviser in the Department of Foreign Affairs and International Trade, Ottawa, Canada. The extracts from official correspondence contained in this survey have been made available by courtesy of the Department of Foreign Affairs and International Trade. Some of the correspondence from which the extracts are given was provided for the general guidance of the enquirer in relation to specific facts that are often not described in full in the extracts within this compilation. The statements of law and practice should not necessarily be regarded as definitive.

> For the purposes of this Convention the territory of a State shall be deemed to be the land areas and territorial waters adjacent thereto under the sovereignty, suzerainty, protection or mandate of such State.

These provisions closely resemble Article 1 of the 1919 Convention Relating to the Regulation of Aerial Navigation, done at Paris on 13 October 1919 [Paris Convention]:

> The High Contracting Parties recognise that every Power has complete and exclusive sovereignty over the air space above its territory.

> For the purpose of the present Convention, the territory of a State shall be understood as including the national territory, both that of the mother country and of the colonies, and the territorial waters adjacent thereto.

The Articles in both the Paris Convention and the Chicago Convention use the word "recognize" indicating that the provisions are intended to be declaratory of existing international law. In fact, an analysis of classical and late Roman Law demonstrates that ownership and use of the airspace above land was a right created in favour of the landowner as far back as Roman times. This was reflected in the work of the glossatores and was embodied in the Latin maxim coined by Accursius of Bologna in the thirteenth century:

> *Cujus est solum, ejus est usque ad coelum et ad inferos* [for whoever owns the soil, it is theirs up to Heaven and down to Hell]

The use of the *cujus est solum* maxim in English domestic law to describe the rights of landowners in the airspace above their land began to appear in the sixteenth century and was common place by the eighteenth century. Coke had this to say about the principle of ownership of airspace:

> ... the earth hath in law a great extent upwards, not only of water, as hath been said, but of ayre and all other things even up to heaven ...

William Blackstone also wrote:

> Land hath also, in its legal signification, an indefinite extent upwards ... So that the word "land" is not only the face of the earth, but everything under it, or over it.

Therefore, in private law ownership of the land included ownership of the space above and below that land. The landowner's rights in that regard were gradually limited by the common law and by statute over the years. However, in the domain of public international law, the State has continued to enjoy unlimited sovereignty in its territorial airspace and it was not seriously questioned that airspace was included in the territory of a State. The only debate surrounding the *cujus est solum* maxim at international law focussed on whether there should exist in air law a right of innocent passage through territorial airspace similar to that which existed in maritime law. The arguments of Grotius and Selden were once again used by those advocating the "freedom of the air" and "sovereignty in national airspace" theories. This time international events intervened to hand the victory to those supporting Selden's views. The military implications of aviation, dramatically illustrated in two world wars, dictated that there could be no right of innocent passage through territorial airspace. States would have absolute and exclusive sovereignty in their territorial airspace. This principle would even be expanded by some States to justify the imposition of Air Defence Identification Zones which extend beyond the lateral limits of State territory described in Article 2 of the Chicago Convention.

Commentaries on Articles 1 and 2 of the Chicago Convention have not hesitated to declare that these provisions define the scope of a State's territory. John Cobb Cooper; an eminent air law pioneer, former Vice-President of Pan American World Airways, adviser to the US government at the Chicago Conference, first General Counsel and architect of the International Air Transport Association (IATA) and first Director of the Institute of International Air Law (now Institute of Air and Space Law) at McGill University; had this to say about territorial airspace:

> The territory of a sovereign State is three dimensional, including within such territory the airspace above its internal and territorial waters.

Ian Brownlie states in his text on public international law:

> ... airspace superjacent to land territory, internal waters, and the territorial sea is in law a part of State territory ...

Professor Bin Cheng explains that:

> The territorial scope of a State's jurisdiction, as recognised and accepted by the contracting States to the Chicago Convention extends, therefore, upwards into space and downwards to the centre of the Earth ...

There can be little doubt that the modern definition of territory includes airspace. A State is competent to exercise jurisdiction within its territory, including airspace as Professor Cheng notes above. The only limit to the upward extent of a State's territory is alluded to by Manfred Lachs, former judge of the International Court of Justice, in his writings:

> *Cuius est solum, eius est usque ad coelum et ad sidera* [derived from the Latin *sidus* for star]; this principle, inherited from Roman Law, was

accepted by international law ... For centuries States faced no practical questions concerning the control over their airspace nor the height to which their sovereignty extended ... Only the first journey of a man-made satellite reopened the issue ...

The Treaty on Principles Governing the Activities of States in the Exploration and Use of Outer Space, including the Moon and Other Celestial Bodies, done at London, Moscow and Washington on 27 January 1967, 610 UNTS, prohibits States from claiming sovereignty over any part of outer space including the Moon or other celestial bodies. Therefore, the coelum ends once you reach outer space and so does State territory.

In the definitions section of Canada's model Air Transport Agreements, the following definition of territory is used:

"Territory" means for each Contracting Party, its land areas (mainland and islands), internal waters and territorial sea as determined by its domestic law, and includes the air space above these areas ...

This provision illustrates that Canada follows the same interpretation of territory as those cited above. Air transport agreements concluded before the model agreement was developed often simply referred to the definition of territory in the Chicago Convention.

International Liability for Damage Caused by Space Objects

In a legal opinion dated 27 May 2010, the Legal Branch wrote:

Article II of the Convention on International Liability for Damage Caused by Space Objects, done at London, Moscow and Washington, DC on 29 March 1972 [the Liability Convention] states as follows:

A launching State shall be absolutely liable to pay compensation for damage caused by its space object on the surface of the Earth or to aircraft in flight.

Article VIII of the Liability Convention specifies which State or States can present a claim for damages referred to in Article II:

1. A State which suffers damage, or whose natural or juridical persons suffer damage, may present to a launching State a claim for compensation for such damage.
2. If the State of nationality has not presented a claim, another State may, in respect of damage sustained in its territory by any natural or juridical person, present a claim to a launching State.
3. If neither the State of nationality nor the State in whose territory the damage was sustained has presented a claim or notified its intention

of presenting a claim, another State may, in respect of damage sustained by its permanent residents, present a claim to a launching State.

Regardless of the impact zone drawn up, the launching State will be liable for damages to Canadian interests wherever such damages occur. Nationality is the primary indicator of which State may present a claim but even damage to foreign nationals in Canadian territory can be the foundation of a Canadian claim under the Liability Convention.

In addition to the provisions of the Liability Convention, Canada also has a basis for a claim under general international law for any violation of its sovereignty, such as an unauthorized trespass into its territory. Articles 1 and 2 of the Convention on International Civil Aviation, done at Chicago on 7 December 1944 [the Chicago Convention] reiterate the principle of customary international law that States have complete sovereignty over their territory, which includes the airspace above the land areas and territorial seas of a State. The Chicago Convention goes on to explain that no foreign State may operate any activity in the airspace of another State without the explicit authorization of that State and then only in accordance with the terms of such authorization. While the Chicago Convention applies primarily to civil aviation, the rule that permission must be sought to enter into the airspace of another State for any purpose is part of customary international law and simply reflects the logical consequence of the sovereignty every State has over its territory. Absent the express authorization of Canada, a foreign State cannot enter into Canadian territory.

Canada grants permission to enter into and cross its territory to aircraft engaged in scheduled air services through bilateral air transport agreements. Aircraft operating non-scheduled air services, also known as charter services, are granted overflight rights by virtue of Article 5 of the Chicago Convention subject to the right of the overflown State to impose conditions on such passage. Foreign State aircraft are granted permission to overfly Canada as well, but in limited circumstances and usually on a case by case basis. Outside of these instances, foreign States have no right of innocent passage through Canadian airspace. Although some academics have suggested that rockets intended for outer space enjoy some sort of right of innocent passage across foreign territory, this does not represent the current state of international law. Furthermore, there is no right which permits a launching State to drop rocket stages onto or through the territory of another State during the launch process. Doing so without permission represents a violation of State sovereignty.

Therefore, it is important for Canada to communicate to foreign States that it is not acceptable to design launches that produce impact areas that include our territory in order to rebut the presumption, hinted at in communications with our Embassy, that international law grants States the right to launch rockets across another State's territory or to drop rocket stages onto or through its territory without permission.

Jurisdiction over Closed Cabin Space of Aircraft

In a legal opinion dated 11 January 2010, the Legal Branch wrote:

> By virtue of Article 1 of the Convention on International Civil Aviation, done at Chicago on 7 December 1944 [the Chicago Convention] a State has complete and exclusive sovereignty in its airspace. The Chicago Convention simply reaffirmed what was, in 1944, already well-established customary international law: the territory of a State includes its airspace.
>
> The Chicago Convention does not create any exception to Article 1 relating to the closed cabin space within an aircraft, wherever it is located, and aircraft do not enjoy any quasi-territorial status under international law. Instead, Article 17 of the Chicago Convention gives an aircraft the nationality of the State in which it is registered but nothing more. Similar to any other national, the aircraft is subject to the laws of the territory through which it travels. A simple yet telling example of this rule in practice is the temporary prohibition of alcohol sales on board aircraft when flying over certain States.
>
> Some confusion regarding this rule of international air law may arise as a result of the application of anti-terrorist/anti-hijacking conventions. Article 3(1) of the Convention on Offences and Certain Other Acts Committed on Board Aircraft, done at Tokyo on 14 September 1963 [the Tokyo Convention] provides a basis for the State of registration to exercise jurisdiction over acts committed on board an aircraft:
>
>> 1. The State of registration of the aircraft is competent to exercise jurisdiction over offences and acts committed on board.
>
> The "acts" mentioned above are those that jeopardize the safety of the aircraft or good order and discipline on board. The competence granted by Article 3(1) of the Tokyo Convention is not exclusive. It does not displace the sovereignty of the over flown State or that State's competence to exercise jurisdiction over an offence. This is reinforced by Article 3(3) of the Tokyo Convention:
>
>> 3. This Convention does not exclude any criminal jurisdiction exercised in accordance with national law.
>
> The Tokyo Convention creates an additional basis for the assumption of jurisdiction to address any gap that existed for offences committed over the High Seas precisely because aircraft do not enjoy the quality of quasi-

territory and no State has jurisdiction in the airspace above the High Seas. The Convention for the Suppression of Unlawful Seizure of Aircraft, done at The Hague on 16 December 1970 [the Hague Convention] takes this principle even further by providing the following basis for the assumption of jurisdiction in Article 4(1)(b):

> (b) when the aircraft on board which the offence is committed lands in its territory with the alleged offender still on board ...

In the case contemplated in 4(1)(b), Canada could take jurisdiction even if the aircraft was registered in a foreign State, destined for a State other than Canada, and the offence was committed over the High Seas or another State. The goal of the Tokyo and Hague Conventions is to ensure that there are no safe havens for offenders and these provisions should not be interpreted so as to rob a State of sovereign jurisdiction over its own territory.

It could be said that the Tokyo and Hague Conventions create a shared or concurrent jurisdiction only over offences committed on board aircraft. Canada has carefully measured its language to ensure that its territorial jurisdiction is respected while not limiting the jurisdiction available to other States relating to offences committed on board. It is for this reason that the words "exclusive jurisdiction" are not used. However, the exclusive applicability of Canadian laws in Canadian airspace is never in doubt.

In conclusion, we must respectfully disagree with the assertion that the internal cabin space is not subject to the domestic law of the country it is in (or over) unless and until the door to the cabin is opened, according to customary international law. No such customary norm could be said to exist given the provisions of the Chicago, Tokyo and Hague Conventions.

DIPLOMATIC LAW

Vienna Convention on Consular Relations — Scope of Paragraph 37(a) — Application in Canadian Law

In a legal opinion dated September 2009, the Legal Bureau wrote:

Is Canada in violation of the Vienna Convention on Consular Relations [VCCR] where [a province] declines to provide a foreign mission with a long form death certificate in the case of a death of [a] national [of the requesting state] in that province?

Several [foreign] embassies have expressed views that Article 37 entitles a foreign mission to all relevant information surrounding the death of [the requesting state's] national in Canada. They ask that the Government of [a province] provide in particular the long form death certificate in respect of a deceased national.

Canada is not in violation of the VCCR should [a province] decline to provide a foreign mission with a long form death certificate in respect of [a] deceased national of the requesting state. Article 37 of the VCCR requires that a consular post be notified of the fact that a death of its national has occurred, if that information is available to the competent authorities. The provision does not contemplate that notification of death be provided in a specific form, and so does not mandate the provision of the long form death certificate.

INTERNATIONAL CRIMINAL LAW

Rome Statute of the International Criminal Court — Review Conference

In remarks made in the General Debate at the Review Conference of the Rome Statute of the International Criminal Court from 31 May to 11 June 2010, the Canadian Legal Adviser said:

In 1998, Canada joined other delegations at the Rome Diplomatic Conference with an ambitious goal — the creation of an independent and effective International Criminal Court [ICC] with jurisdiction over the most serious crimes of concern to the international community. In 2010, we are gathered again, to reflect on the achievements of the past twelve years and to take constructive steps to improve further the Rome Statute system.

Our aim at this Review Conference is to strengthen the Court and to advance the fight against impunity. In doing so, we must look not only at the work of the Court, but also at the roles and responsibilities of States Parties and the opportunities for non-States Parties and members of civil society to assist the work of the Court.

Canada's continuing support for international criminal justice is based on our strong commitment to the rule of law and the principle that those who commit crimes must be held accountable. Within this paradigm, Canada has supported the work of the International Criminal Tribunals for Rwanda and the former Yugoslavia, the Special Court for Sierra Leone, the Special Tribunal for Lebanon, the Extraordinary Chambers in the Courts of Cambodia and, of course, the ICC.

In December 1998, Canada was the 14th country to sign the Rome Statute. In June 2000, Canada enacted the *Crimes Against Humanity and War Crimes Act*, becoming the first country in the world to adopt comprehensive legislation incorporating the obligations of the Rome Statute into its national laws. Canada ratified the Statute the following month.

The enactment of the *Crimes Against Humanity and War Crimes Act* and other associated legislative changes have allowed Canada to cooperate fully with the Court and have ensured that Canada is not — and will not become

— a safe haven for persons involved in genocide, war crimes, crimes against humanity or other reprehensible acts regardless of when or where they occurred. To this end, Canada's first successful prosecution under the *Crimes Against Humanity and War Crimes Act* took place in 2009, and another has been initiated.

It is the duty of every state to exercise its criminal jurisdiction over those responsible for serious crimes. The ICC is a crucial part of the international criminal justice system, but it is also a court of last resort. Where such crimes have occurred, states must ensure accountability through effective and genuine investigations and prosecutions at the national level. In this respect, Canada recognizes that strengthening domestic capacity to investigate and prosecute these crimes is essential to closing the impunity gap.

Canada has supported projects promoting ICC ratification and implementation and has supported programming aimed generally at promoting the rule of law and accountability. For example, Canada has funded the production of manuals on ratification and implementation of the Rome Statute and on cooperation of national criminal justice personnel with the ICC. Canada, with the collaboration of many States Parties, has also undertaken to shepherd the establishment of the Justice Rapid Response mechanism which can assist, when needed, in the investigations of both the Court and national jurisdictions.

While the strengthening of national systems is important, in the instances where the Court takes jurisdiction over crimes — States must fulfill their obligation to cooperate with the Court. States Parties must continue to recognize and protect the independence of the Court and must offer their full diplomatic support to the Court. Further, States Parties must enforce the orders of the Court, particularly through the execution of arrest warrants. This obligation, we would stress, is not limited to the accused's state of nationality.

Over the coming days, we will consider potential amendments to the Rome Statute. On the crime of aggression, there is a divergence of views. Legitimate concerns have been raised and must be addressed in a creative and flexible manner. We must strive to move forward by consensus on these issues — to do otherwise will only weaken the Court and undermine its mandate.

Clearly, there is a strong desire among States Parties to have a successful outcome to this Conference. Canada shares this sentiment, but the success of this Review Conference should be judged qualitatively — any outcomes should (1) serve to promote accountability; (2) strengthen the Court; (3) reinforce the continued commitment of States Parties to the Rome Statute; and (4) encourage the universal acceptance of the Rome Statute. In furtherance of these goals, Canada will be participating actively in the upcoming discussions and negotiations; and we would encourage other delegations to do the same.

Over the past twelve years, much has been invested in the Court and in the Rome Statute system. Significant and important progress has been made in a short time. We look forward to making further progress over the coming weeks, and we are committed to working collaboratively with all delegations at this Conference.

INTERNATIONAL ENVIRONMENTAL LAW

Rotterdam Convention on the Prior Informed Consent Procedure for Certain Hazardous Chemicals and Pesticides in International Trade — Interpretation of Article 5.1

In a legal opinion dated February 2010, the Legal Branch wrote the following:

Article 31 of the Vienna Convention on the Law of Treaties [Vienna Convention] establishes that treaties should be interpreted "in good faith in accordance with the ordinary meaning to be given to the terms of the treaty in their context and in the light of its object and purpose." The context includes the text, its preamble and annexes. Under Article 31 it is further provided that any subsequent practice in the application of the treaty which establishes the agreement of the parties regarding its interpretation may be taken into account as well as any subsequent agreements between the parties regarding the interpretation of the treaty. Finally, under Article 32, recourse can be had to supplementary means of interpretation, including the preparatory work of the treaty and the circumstances of its conclusion where the interpretation according to the ordinary meaning in its context and given subsequent agreements or practice leaves the meaning ambiguous or obscure or leads to an unreasonable result.

The text of Article 5 of the Rotterdam Convention on the Prior Informed Consent Procedure for Certain Hazardous Chemicals and Pesticides in International Trade requires Parties to notify the Secretariat in writing of a final regulatory action as soon as possible, and in any event not later than ninety days after the date on which the final regulatory action has taken effect. (It is not absolutely clear whether the term "has taken effect" is the same as the date of entry into force for that action. A final regulatory action may enter into force on a certain date with specific provisions to take effect on a later date. In this opinion we will not consider this issue further). It is clear from the text of Article 5.1 that Parties are under an obligation to submit a Notification of Final Regulatory Action (NFRA) in a timely manner and not later than ninety days after the final regulatory action has taken effect.

However, the consequence of failure to notify in a timely manner is not addressed anywhere in the text of the Convention or its Annexes. Article 5.1 contains no language that addresses this issue. Article 5.3 establishes an obligation on the Secretariat to verify whether the NFRA contains the information required by Annex I. Annex I does not contain any reference to timeliness. Under Article 5.6 the Chemical Review Committee must review the information in the notifications in accordance with Annex II. Annex II which establishes criteria for listing does not contain any reference to timeliness. We conclude from this review that in the absence of any text establishing consequences for failure to provide notification, the "ordinary meaning" of Article 5 cannot be interpreted as rendering invalid NFRAs provided after the ninety day period.

Further support for the interpretation that failure to submit the NFRA in time does not result in the invalidity of the notification can be drawn from an analysis of the context of Article 5. The objective of the Convention is to promote shared responsibility and cooperative efforts among Parties in the international trade of certain hazardous chemicals in order to protect human health and the environment from potential harm and to contribute to their environmentally sound use, by facilitating information exchange about their characteristics, by providing for a national decision-making process on their import and export and by disseminating these decisions to Parties. A NFRA is in essence information exchange between Parties about certain hazardous chemicals in international trade. It is a cooperative effort and a step towards sharing responsibility. Rendering a notification invalid on the basis of timeliness is not in accordance with the promotion of shared responsibility and cooperative efforts among Parties. Nor is it consistent with facilitating information exchange or disseminating information on national decision making. Thus, interpreting Article 5 in light of the objective does not support the assertion that the late submission of the NFRA would render such NFRA invalid.

The preamble provides support for the emphasis on the protection of human health and the environment. Paragraph 7 of the preamble refers to the desire of Parties to ensure that hazardous chemicals that are exported from their territory are packaged and labelled in a manner that is adequately protective of human health and the environment. Paragraph 11 establishes the determination of the Parties to protect human health and the environment against potentially harmful impacts from certain hazardous chemicals and pesticides in international trade. Limiting or delaying the ability of the Parties to the Convention to review chemicals on the basis of a defect in timeliness is not consistent with the preamble which empha-sizes the need to protect human health and the environment against certain hazardous chemicals and pesticides in international trade.

A further basis of support can be found in Article 31 (3) (b) of the Vienna Convention which refers to state practice in the application of a treaty as a basis for interpretation.

> (3) There shall be taken into account, together with the context:
> ...
> (b) any subsequent practice in the application of the treaty which estab-lishes the agreement of the parties regarding its interpretation.

In the case of the Rotterdam Convention, the practice has been for the CRC to review those NFRAs which meet the information requirements stated in Annex I and assess them on the basis of criteria given in Annex II. The NFRAs, which are available to all Parties, contain information to the CRC on whether or not the notification has been sent within six months of the date of entry into force. This information is found in reading Ques-tion 2.2.3 of the form for Final Notification of the Regulatory Action together with the date of the signature of the Designated National Author-ity. Where the signature is not dated, an estimate can be made from the information found in the Prior Informed Consent circular which establishes when the Secretariat provided the notification. We note that submissions have been late in the past. The CRC has, as a matter of practice, accepted late submissions for review in accordance with Annex II criteria and has made recommendations in respect of chemicals where some of the NFRAs were submitted past the ninety-day period specified in the Convention. From this practice, we draw the conclusion that a plausible argument could be made that the practice of the Parties, demonstrated through the CRC, expresses their understanding that late submission does not invalidate any NFRA on the basis of lack of timeliness. A counter argument could be made that the CRC, being a body that does not include all Parties, is not sufficiently broad to establish a practice. However, as the actions of the CRC are the most relevant to the process, we are of the view that the stronger argument is that the practice of states through the CRC, although it may not be universal, does express the views of many Parties on this issue.

We observe that if any notification that was submitted late was rendered invalid, there would be no remedy to this procedural defect. This inter-pretation would have serious consequences for the Party forwarding the NFRA, as there would be no method by which a Party could resubmit a late notification. A further resubmission would also be beyond the ninety-day requirement. The Party in default would thereby be forever barred from submitting its late notification. This kind of consequence is punitive and would have to be clearly expressed in clear language. It would also severely compromise the effective implementation of the Convention.

We note that Article 17 of the Convention requires that a regime be established to determine non-compliance and the treatment of Parties found to be in non-compliance. However to date such a regime has not been established. The most recent version of the proposed compliance procedure is facilitative in nature. It does not to date include strong punitive measures. However, until the compliance procedure is finalized there remains a possibility that a consequence for lack of timeliness in the submission of final regulatory submissions, could be adopted in the future.

While the treaty has some room for interpretation, a conclusion that a notification is invalid because it is submitted beyond the ninety-day requirement, cannot be drawn from the existing text. The ordinary meaning of the words "and in any event not later than ninety days" does not address the issue of a delay in submitting the NFRA. There is no text anywhere in the Convention including its Annexes that addresses the failure to notify not later than ninety days after the final regulatory action has taken effect. In effect, there is an absence of text dealing with the legal effects of delay.

The context of the treaty including its objectives, and the preamble, supports an interpretation that the late submission of the NFRA does not render such submission invalid. State practice of the Parties, who under the CRC did consider a number of NFRAs submitted after the ninety-day period also supports the interpretation that the Parties do not consider late submission of a NFRA to render that notification invalid. We have not reviewed any preparatory work since the review of the text, given the plain and ordinary meaning of the words dealing with timeliness, in their context, provide a reasonable understanding of the text. We conclude that a NFRA that is submitted late, but meets the requirements of Annex I, should be forwarded to the CRC to consider in accordance with the criteria of Annex II.

INTERNATIONAL HUMAN RIGHTS LAW

Domestic Human Rights Law — Extraterritorial Application — Canadian Approach

In remarks made on 25 March 2010 to the American Society of International Law's 104th annual meeting, a member of the Legal Branch said:

The extra-territorial reach of domestic legal frameworks for the protection of human rights has seen a great deal of attention in Canadian courts over the last few years, as it has in many jurisdictions since 9/11 and the interventions in Afghanistan and Iraq. In Canada, the framework in question is the *Canadian Charter of Rights and Freedoms,* adopted in 1982 and in its substantive protections largely reflective of the International Covenant on Civil and Political Rights.

Four decisions in particular reflect the most recent evolution of Canadian juridical thinking on the extra-territorial application of the *Charter,* although doubtless there are still some aspects to be considered in due course. In the meantime, these cases, which came out over 2½ years and interlock like a puzzle, allow us to extract 10 guiding principles that summarize the Canadian approach as it stands.

The cases in question are *Hape v. R* (SCC, October 2007); *Omar Khadr v. Attorney General et al #1* (SCC, May 2008); *Amnesty International et al v. Chief of Defence Staff et al* (FC (TD), March 2008; FCA, December 2008; leave to SCC denied, May 2009); and *Omar Khadr v. Prime Minister et al #2* (SCC, January 2010). Because of the time constraints of this presentation I will keep to the main findings of interest coming from each one, and only those specific to the question of extra-territoriality.

The *Hape* decision concerned an appeal by the accused from a conviction for money-laundering offences based on investigations carried out by the RCMP in the Turks & Caicos Islands. The investigations were carried out under local law, with the supervision and participation of the local authorities. Hape complained that the searches were carried out without a warrant, in violation of s. 8 of the *Charter* (unreasonable search and seizure). The Court made several important findings, starting with its statement that the *Charter* itself does not expressly impose any territorial limits on its application; any limits on its jurisdictional reach are for the courts to determine [at para. 33]. The court also reiterated a well-established rule in Canadian law, namely that it could look to international law in its interpretation of the *Charter,* based on a (rebuttable) presumption that Canadian law intends to conform with international law.

After determining that — in the absence of conflicting legislation — prohibitive rules of customary international law were adopted into domestic law through the common law [at para. 39], the Court noted that as a result, the principles of territorial sovereignty, sovereign equality and non-intervention had to be taken into account in determining the extra-territorial application of the *Charter* [at para. 46]. Where Canadian law could have an impact on the sovereignty of another state, the principle of comity would bear on its interpretation.

Importantly, the Court also found that the principle of comity did not offer a rationale for another state's breach of international law (this became relevant in the first *Khadr* case). In the Court's own words, that "deference [to comity and respect for sovereignty] ends where clear violations of international law and fundamental human rights begin [at para. 52]," and where

Canadian officers would be "participating in activities that, though authorized by the laws of another state, would cause Canada to be in violation of its international obligations in respect of human rights" [at para. 90].

Referencing the *Lotus* case of the Permanent Court of International Justice as well as *Nicaragua (Merits)*, *Hape* confirms that a state cannot act to enforce its laws within the territory of another state absent that state's consent or any other basis in international law [at para. 68]. The court further clarified that where Canadian officials lack the authority to act in a place where the alleged breach occurred — i.e. where that authority belonged to another state — the *Charter* could not apply [at para. 81]. This argument was revisited in the *Amnesty* case. Accordingly, for Canadian courts, the principle of consent is central to assertions of enforcement jurisdiction — and with the host state's consent, the *Charter* could apply.

On the facts in the *Hape* case, the *Charter* was held not to apply, the search was admitted, and Mr. Hape's conviction stood.

Hape came out just before the Federal Court (Trial Division) was asked to rule whether the *Charter* applied to the transfer by Canadian military forces of detainees — non-Canadians — in Afghanistan to Afghan authorities. In *Amnesty International*, the applicants claimed that such transfer would result in detainees being subject to torture, in violation of s. 7 of the *Charter* (life, liberty and security of the person). Amnesty argued that the limits on extra-territorial application of the *Charter* set out in *Hape* applied to the law enforcement context only and should not be applied in the context of military activities on foreign soil, since military action of necessity impaired the sovereignty of the other state.

The trial judge held that it was neither necessary nor appropriate to decide whether *Hape* should be applied in every instance where Canadian military power was exercised abroad. In the present case, Afghan consent had been given to the presence of Canadian Forces, but not to the application of Canadian law — with the very limited exception of its cessation of jurisdiction over Canadian personnel under a bilateral status of forces arrangement.

The Court embraced the "effective territorial control" test set out by the European Court of Human Rights in *Bankovic*, while dismissing the "effective control of the person" test applied by the House of Lords in *Al Skeini*. Specifically, the judge questioned the link drawn between detention facilities and the "embassy/flag vessel" exceptions to territorial restrictions in that case. Most importantly, she said that "the practical result of applying such a 'control of the person' based test would be problematic in the context of a multinational military effort such as the one in which Canada is currently involved in Afghanistan. Indeed, it would result in a patchwork of different national legal norms applying in relation to detained Afghan citizens in different parts of Afghanistan ... within the territory of a state whose sovereignty the international community has pledged to uphold." Importantly, she found (and the Court of Appeal later concurred) that the absence of *Charter* application did not create a legal gap, since the actions of the Canadian Forces in Afghanistan were at all times governed by international humanitarian law.

Finally, Justice McTavish rejected the notion — which Amnesty sought to derive from what it considered to be the "human rights exception" in *Hape* — that the nature or quality of a *Charter* breach would create extraterritorial jurisdiction where it does not otherwise exist. The Federal Court of Appeal, which confirmed her judgment in December of 2008, concurred very strongly in this finding.

Two months after the Federal Court's ruling in *Amnesty*, the first *Khadr* case came before the Supreme Court of Canada. Omar Khadr is a Canadian national who, at the age of 15, was captured in Afghanistan by US forces in 2002, following an exchange of hostilities with Al Qaida fighters in which he allegedly threw a grenade that killed a US serviceman. He was transferred to U.S. Guantanamo Bay Detention Camp where he has remained since, having been charged under the Military Commissions Act (2006) with murder and attempted murder in violation of the laws of war, material support for terrorism, conspiracy and spying. In 2003 and 2004 Canadian intelligence officials went to GTMO to interview Mr. Khadr. The interviews included the events that had led to Mr. Khadr's capture in Afghanistan, and the Canadian officials shared their findings with US authorities. Mr. Khadr, in this 2008 case, sought to obtain disclosure of all relevant documents from the Canadian Government, believing that they would assist him in the proceedings before the Military Commission.

The Supreme Court of Canada held that the process to which Mr. Khadr was subject at the time the interviews were conducted violated US domestic law and international human rights obligations to which Canada is party; it did so based on the US Supreme Court's own findings in *Rasul v. Bush* and *Hamdan v. Rumsfeld* [at paras. 3, 21ff].

Following its own ruling in *Hape*, the Supreme Court of Canada found that the principles of international law and comity that might otherwise preclude application of the *Charter* to Canadian officials abroad did not apply to the assistance Canadian officials had given to US authorities in Guantanamo Bay, and that accordingly the *Charter* bound Canada — to the extent that the conduct of Canadian officials involved it in a process that violated Canada's international obligations [at paras. 27ff].

The December 2008 Federal Court of Appeal decision in the *Amnesty* case, unlike the trial judge's, had the benefit of the Supreme Court's ruling in *Khadr #1*, but found the very narrow circumstances in that case — a Canadian citizen who obtained disclosure of documents held by Canada and produced by Canadian officials in breach of his rights under the *Charter* — to be "miles apart from the situation where foreigners, with no attachment whatsoever to Canada, are held in Canadian Forces detention facilities in Afghanistan." The Federal Court of Appeal then upheld the trial judge's dismissal of the effective control test, in reliance on *Bankovic*, noting that the CF were not an occupying force, and confirmed that the applicable law was not the *Charter* but international humanitarian law.

Finally we come to the most recent decision, *Khadr #2*. This case relied on essentially the same *Charter* violations found in *Khadr #1*, but added evidence obtained through the disclosure obtained as a result of the first case. This evidence indicated that prior to one of the interviews (in 2004) the applicant had been subjected to a prolonged program of sleep deprivation — the so-called "frequent flier program" — and that his interviewer had knowledge of this but elected to proceed regardless. To remedy the breach of his rights under s. 7 of the *Charter* Khadr asked the Court to compel the Prime Minister of Canada to seek his repatriation from Guantanamo Bay.

The Court made quick work of confirming its earlier decision in *Khadr #1*, and adding that "Canada's active participation in what was at the time [2003-4] an illegal regime has contributed and continues to contribute to Mr. Khadr's current detention" [at para 21]. But while this finding provided the necessary jurisdictional basis for application of the *Charter*, Mr. Khadr still needed to prove that the deprivation of liberty he suffered — as a result of the Government's failure to prevent the downstream use of statements made by Mr. Khadr to Canadian officials — did not accord with the principles of fundamental justice. The court minced few words in determining that "interrogation of a youth, to elicit statements about the most serious criminal charges while detained in these conditions and without access to counsel, and while knowing that the fruits of the interrogations would be shared with US prosecutors, offend the most basic Canadian standards about the treatment of detained youth suspects" [at para. 25].

Finally, the Court found that despite its findings of *Charter* violations, it could not order the Prime Minister to seek Mr. Khadr's repatriation, as had been done at the lower levels. This remedy, the SCC said, fell squarely within the prerogative powers of the Crown to conduct foreign relations, and hence lay outside the constitutional competence of the judiciary. The Court was limited to providing declaratory relief, but noted that its decision would provide the legal framework in which the Government should exercise its function and consider what actions to take in respect of Mr. Khadr [at para. 47].

Interestingly, neither *Hape* nor the two *Khadr* cases provides any analysis concerning the scope of those "international obligations" the breach of which they cite as reason to extend the extra-territorial application of the *Charter*. The Court simply based its findings on Canada's status as a State Party — to the Geneva Conventions, the *International Covenant on Civil and Political Rights* [ICCPR] and other treaties dealing with relevant subject matter — without considering whether the obligations did, in fact, themselves apply to Canada on an extra-territorial basis, and at the material time.

We are all familiar with the restrictions on the scope of the various human rights treaties — all are based on territory, some apply to "all persons in [a state's] territory and under its jurisdiction." Would the ICCPR actually apply to the acts of Canadian officials in Guantanamo Bay? If it does not apply — and on the very face of the treaty it does not — on what exactly did the Supreme Court base its finding that Canadian officials participated in "acts contrary to Canada's international obligations"? Perhaps what the Court should have said is that the test is based on acts that would have been contrary to Canada's international obligations if they had been committed in Canada. That said, this point was not expressly argued, nor considered by the Court.

To conclude, this quartet of recent cases allows us to extract a series of principles which, together, summarize the Canadian approach to the extra-territorial reach of the *Canadian Charter of Rights and Freedoms*. There may well be others, but these are the ones where the decisions most clearly and consistently converge:

1. The *Charter* itself does not expressly impose any territorial limits on its application; any limits on its jurisdictional reach are for the courts to determine;

2. In determining the extra-territorial application of the *Charter*, the principles of territorial sovereignty, sovereign equality, non-intervention and comity have to be taken into account;

3. The *Charter* cannot apply where Canadian officials lack the authority to act in the place where the alleged breach occurred — i.e. where that authority belonged to another state — unless that state has given its consent;

4. The *Charter* could apply extra-territorially in cases where Canada exercises "effective territorial control" (the *Bankovic* test);

5. Applying the "effective control" test as meaning "control over the person" is not appropriate in the context of a multinational military

effort, as this could result in a patchwork of different national legal norms in one place;

6. The nature or quality of an alleged *Charter* breach cannot create extra-territorial jurisdiction where it does not otherwise exist (in other words, no boot-strapping — regardless of the severity of the alleged violations);

7. Deference to the principles of territorial sovereignty, sovereign equality, non-intervention and comity ends where Canadian officers participate in activities that would cause Canada to be in violation of its international human rights obligations;

8. The *Charter* binds Canada extra-territorially but only to the extent that the conduct of Canadian officials involve it in a process that violates Canada's international obligations;

9. A finding that the necessary jurisdictional basis exists for extra-territorial application of the *Charter*, based on the above, still requires the applicant to prove the actual violation of his rights;

10. The remedy for an extra-territorial breach of an individual's *Charter* right must respect the prerogative powers of the Executive to make decisions on matters of foreign relations and defence.

Droits des personnes handicapées

Dans une note de breffage rédigée en janvier 2010, la Direction générale des affaires juridiques a écrit:

La Convention relative aux droits des personnes handicapées protège le droit à l'égalité et à la non-discrimination des personnes handicapées en ce qui touche à l'ensemble des droits de la personne et des libertés fondamentales. La Convention se fonde sur les traités internationaux existants en matière de droits de la personne: elle réaffirme que les personnes handicapées jouissent, sans discrimination et sur la base de l'égalité avec les autres, des droits de la personne et des libertés fondamentales garantis par ces traités.

Les États qui ratifient la Convention acceptent de s'acquitter de certaines obligations prévues par la Convention. Ces obligations comprennent la garantie que des aménagements raisonnables, comme ils le sont définis dans la Convention, sont fournis. Les États parties sont également tenus de promouvoir un environnement favorable afin que les personnes handicapées puissent jouir pleinement de ces droits sur la base de l'égalité avec les autres. La Convention exige en outre que les personnes handicapées, y compris les enfants handicapés, soient consultées et participent à la prise de décisions relatives aux questions les concernant.

INTERNATIONAL INVESTMENT LAW

North American Free Trade Agreement (NAFTA) — Awarding of Costs

In a motion on termination and costs dated 29 April 2010 in the NAFTA Investment Arbitration case *Melvin J. Howard and Centurion Health Corporation v Canada*, the Legal Branch submitted:

Where a Tribunal issues a termination order [for failure to make a deposit under Article 41(4) of the United Nations Commission on International Trade Law [UNCITRAL] Arbitration Rules], Article 40(3) of the UNCITRAL Arbitration Rules requires it to "fix the costs of arbitration referred to in Article 38 and Article 39, paragraph 1, in the text of that order or award." The costs covered by Article 38 include both the cost of the arbitral proceeding and the costs to the parties of legal representation and assistance.

Costs serve the "dual function of reparation and dissuasion," especially in the case of frivolous or vexatious claims. Frivolous investor claims have been a concern in the international community. Indeed, recent amendments to the ICSID Convention and the 2004 Model U.S. bilateral investment treaty permit expedited hearings on claims that are apparently without merit.

No NAFTA tribunal has been faced with the task of making a decision on costs in the context of a termination order being issued as a result of the Claimants' failure to make any effort to progress the arbitration or pay the required deposits to the Tribunal. In each of the NAFTA arbitrations where the Tribunal has had to decide the issue of costs, the claim was pursued in good faith, even if unsuccessfully, by the Claimants until the natural end of the arbitration. Even in such cases, the NAFTA tribunals that have considered the issue have endorsed the "loser pays" principle both with respect to arbitration costs, under Article 40(1), and the costs of legal representation and assistance, under Article 40(2) of the UNCITRAL Arbitration Rules.

Where a termination order is issued because a Claimant failed to advance even the first deposit required by the Tribunal, costs should always be awarded to the Respondent.

North American Free Trade Agreement — Claim for Damages

In its counter-memorial dated 1 December 2009 in the NAFTA Investment Arbitration case *Mobil Investments Inc and Murphy Oil v Canada*, the Legal Branch submitted:

The claim for damages from 2009 until 2036 is not a claim for damages which the Claimants have incurred and which requires the calculation of

lost future profits. For example, this is not a claim for the past expropriation of an investment that requires the calculation of the investment's
future profits to determine the value of the investment on the date of
expropriation. In that circumstance, the damages are incurred on the date
of expropriation, which is in the past.

In contrast, the Claimants seek compensation for damages not yet incurred. They assert that they will incur damages each future year until
2036 through the expenditures which they will be required to make under
the Guidelines. This is a claim for damages which the Claimants assert they
will incur in the future. Such damages cannot be awarded because:

- the award of damages not yet incurred is inconsistent with the NAFTA;
- the award of damages not yet incurred is inconsistent with international
  principles of compensation; and
- such damages are speculative.

Article 1116 is clear that a tribunal may only award compensation for
damages already incurred:

> An investor of a Party may submit to arbitration under this Section
> a claim that another Party has breached an obligation under [Chapter
> Eleven] ... and that the investor has incurred loss or damage by
> reason of, or arising out of, that breach.

The rule that international tribunals only award compensation for damages
already incurred stems from the principle that States are only obliged to
compensate for damages that are sufficiently certain. This principle is
widely recognized. In its seminal statement on reparation in *Factory at
Chorzow*, the Permanent Court of International Justice recognized that
"reparation must ... reestablish the situation which would, in all probability,
have existed if that act had not been committed." Similarly, in *Amoco Finance
Corp v. Iran*, the Iran–US Claims Tribunal observed that "[o]ne of the best
settled rules of the law of international responsibility of States is that no
reparation for speculative or uncertain damage can be awarded. This holds
true for the existence of the damage and of its effect as well." The International Law Commission drew from this jurisprudence to note that
"Tribunals have been reluctant to provide compensation for claims with
inherently speculative elements."

*North American Free Trade Agreement — Minimum Standard of
Treatment*

In its counter-memorial dated 1 December 2009 in the NAFTA
investment arbitration case *Mobil Investments Inc and Murphy Oil v
Canada*, the Legal Branch submitted:

The Claimants have failed to fulfil their burden to prove the minimum standard of treatment includes the protection of an investor's legitimate expectations or the obligation to provide a stable regulatory environment for foreign investments. In any event, it is difficult to see how either obligation could have crystallized into a particular rule of custom. For example, expectations that may be legitimate can arise out of a contract between a State and an investor, but it has been long recognized that a mere breach of contract by the State does not rise to the level of a violation of international law. If it were true that customary international law required States to refrain from regulating in a way that frustrated the expectations of foreign investors, it would be impossible for States to regulate at all. The same can be said for the assertion that States are bound by custom to provide a "stable regulatory framework" for foreign investors. Not only do the cases relied on by the Claimants in support of this purported rule contain no evidence of state practice or *opinio juris*, the implications of such a vague obligation would subject States to endless suits by foreign investors advocating that any change in laws or regulations is "unstable" and thus violates international law.

North American Free Trade Agreement — Annex I Reservations

In a counter-memorial dated 1 December 2009 in the NAFTA Investment Arbitration case *Mobil Investments Inc. and Murphy Oil v Canada,* the Legal Branch wrote:

The R&D Guidelines adopted by the Canada-Newfoundland Offshore Petroleum Board fall within the scope of Canada's Annex I Reservation to Article 1106.

Like all provisions in the Agreement, reservations to the NAFTA must be interpreted according to Article 31 of the Vienna Convention on the Law of Treaties. Article 31 states that "[a] treaty shall be interpreted in good faith in accordance with the ordinary meaning to be given to the terms of the treaty in their context and in the light of its object and purpose." Neither the Article, nor any other part of the Convention, excludes reservations or exceptions from this rule ...

NAFTA Article 1108(1)(a) provides:

Articles 1102, 1103, 1106 and 1107 do not apply to:
(a) any existing non-conforming measure that is maintained by
    (i) a Party at the federal level, as set out in its Schedule to Annex I ...
    (ii) a ... province ... as set out by a Party in its Schedule to Annex I.

Consequently, Article 1108(1)(a) reserves from the scope of Article 1106 "any existing non-conforming measure" listed in Annex I. In that Annex, Canada listed the Accord Acts as an existing measure that is reserved from Article 1106 ...

When reserving the Accord Acts [*Canada-Newfoundland Atlantic Accord Implementation Act*, SC 1987, c 3 and *Canada-Newfoundland and Labrador Atlantic Accord Implementation Newfoundland and Labrador Act*, RSNL 1990, c C-2] from the scope of Article 1106, Canada also reserved any measures subordinate to those Acts. Article 1108(1)(a) provides that "Article ... 1106 ... [does] not apply to any existing non-conforming measure" set out in the schedule to Annex I. The interpretative note to Annex I explains at Article 2(f)(ii) that a "measure cited in the Measures element ... includes any subordinate measure." The Article defines a subordinate measure as a "measure adopted or maintained under the authority of and consistent with the measure [that is expressly reserved]."

Consequently, by reserving the Accord Acts from the scope of Article 1106, Canada also reserved from the scope of the Article any measure adopted under the authority of, and consistent with, those Acts ...

As explained above, Article 1108(1)(a) provides that "Article ... 1106 ... [does] not apply to any existing non-conforming measure that is maintained by a Party at the federal level [or province], as set out in its Schedule to Annex I ..." According to the general definitions for the NAFTA within Chapter 2 of the Agreement, "existing" means "in effect on the date of entry in force of this Agreement." Consequently, only measures which were in effect on the date of entry into force of the NAFTA are expressly listed in Annex I. However, this does not mean that the subordinate measures which are also reserved must be in effect at that date ...

The word "measure" within Article 1108(1)(a) is defined in Annex I as including "any subordinate measure adopted or maintained under the authority of and consistent with the measure [that is expressly reserved]." Consequently, the NAFTA parties not only reserved subordinate measures that existed at the time the NAFTA entered into force and were maintained but also subordinate measures that were adopted after this date.

This distinction is supported by the context of the definition of a subordinate measure. The definition appears in the following provision in the interpretative note to Annex I:

A measure cited in the measures element
(i) means the measure as amended, continued or renewed as of the date of entry into force of this Agreement; and
(ii) includes any subordinate measure adopted or maintained under the authority of and consistent with the measure.

Thus, part (i) of the definition includes only measures "amended, continued or renewed as of the date of entry into force of this Agreement." If the drafters had intended that the measures falling within part (ii) were similarly restricted then they would have added the same restriction. By not restricting part (ii) to subordinate measures "as of the date of entry into force of this Agreement," the drafters clearly expressed an intention that subordinate measures adopted after this date also fell within the definition of "measure."

The distinction between measures adopted and those maintained is reinforced by Article 1108(3) and Annex II. Article 1108(3) enables the NAFTA parties to reserve existing and future measures within particular sectors, which are listed in Annex II. Article 1108(3) provides that "Articles 1102, 1103, 1106 and 1107 do not apply to any measure that a Party adopts or maintains with respect to sectors, subsectors or activities, as set out in its Schedule to Annex II." The interpretative note to Annex II confirms that the word "maintain" refers to existing measures but "adopt" refers to future measures: "[t]he Schedule of a Party sets out, pursuant to Article ... 1108(3) ... the reservations taken by that Party with respect to specific sectors, sub-sectors or activities for which it may maintain existing, or adopt new or more restrictive, measures that do not conform with obligations imposed by ... Article 1106 (Performance Requirements) ..."

The use of the terms "maintain" and "adopt" in Article 1108 demonstrates that a measure which is maintained is one that exists at the time the Agreement entered into force and is maintained after that date. A measure which is adopted is one that came into existence after this date. Consequently, by including within the reservation for Article 1108(1)(a) "any subordinate measure adopted or maintained under the authority of and consistent with the [expressly reserved] measure," the NAFTA reserves both subordinate measures which existed at the date of entry into force of the Agreement as well as those which came into existence afterwards.

INTERNATIONAL TRADE LAW

World Trade Organization (WTO) — Application of International Standards

In a Written Submission to the WTO dated 1 February 2010 in the case of *Korea – Measures Affecting the Importation of Bovine Meat and Meat Products from Canada*, the Legal Branch wrote:

Article 3.1 of the WTO Agreement on the Application of Sanitary and Phytosanitary Measures [SPS Agreement] requires WTO Members to base their sanitary and phytosanitary measures on international standards, guidelines or recommendations, except as otherwise provided for in the SPS Agreement, and in particular Article 3.3.

The term "international standards, guidelines and recommendations" is defined in Annex A.3 of the SPS Agreement. For animal health and zoonoses such as Bovine Spongiform Encephalopathy [BSE], subparagraph (b) of this Annex defines "international standards, guidelines and recommendations" as:

> the standards, guidelines and recommendations developed under the auspices of the International Office of Epizootics.

Given that the SPS Agreement specifically recognizes the International Office of Epizootics, or OIE, as the relevant international standard-setting body, the OIE standards pertaining to BSE are the relevant international standards for the purpose of resolving this dispute.

Chapter 11.6 of the OIE Terrestrial Code pertains specifically to BSE and contains standards for the veterinary authorities of importing and exporting countries to manage the human and animal health risks associated with the presence of the BSE agent in cattle.

Article 11.6.1 sets out the basis for veterinary authorities to impose conditions related to BSE when they authorize the importation or transit of certain commodities. Paragraph 1 lists "safe commodities" for which no BSE-related conditions should be imposed, regardless of the BSE risk status of the cattle population of the exporting country. These safe commodities include, notably:

> (g) deboned skeletal muscle meat (excluding mechanically separated meat) from cattle which were not subjected to a stunning process prior to slaughter, with a device injecting compressed air or gas into the cranial cavity or to a pithing process, and which passed ante-mortem and post-mortem inspections and which has been prepared in a manner to avoid contamination with tissues listed in Article 11.6.14.

Paragraph 2 of Article 11.6.1 indicates that for the importation or transit of other commodities such as bone-in cuts of meat and offals, the veterinary authority of the importing country should require the conditions prescribed in Chapter 11.6 that are relevant to the BSE risk status of the cattle population of the exporting country.

Korea's BSE measures are inconsistent with Article 3.1 of the SPS Agreement because these measures are not *based on* the standards set out in Chapter 11.6 of the OIE Terrestrial Code, including those standards applicable to the BSE risk status of the cattle population of Canada.

The SPS Agreement does not define the term "based on" as used in Article 3.1 of the SPS Agreement. However, the Appellate Body has determined that a measure is "based on" a particular international standard when the standard is used as the "principal constituent" or "fundamental principle" for the purpose of enacting the measure. The Appellate Body has also found that "[a] thing is commonly said to be 'based' on another thing when the former 'stands' or is 'founded' or 'built' upon or 'is supported by' the latter." Finally, the Appellate Body found that — at a minimum — where a measure contradicts the international standard, it cannot be properly concluded that the international standard was used as the "basis for" the measure in question.

Korea's BSE measures are structured on the basis of a total prohibition on the importation of bovine meat and meat products from Canada. By contrast, the OIE Terrestrial Code establishes standards that start from the premise that trade in the listed safe commodities and products made from these commodities should not be restricted and that trade in live cattle and in bovine meat and meat products other than the listed safe commodities should continue, subject to conditions commensurate with the level of BSE risk of the exporting country.

Korea's BSE measures are contrary to the standards set out in Chapter 11.6 of the OIE Terrestrial Code in numerous respects. First, the import prohibition adopted by Korea covers certain products that are listed as safe commodities in Article 11.6.1, namely deboned skeletal muscle meat derived from cattle of any age. Korea's total import prohibition on deboned skeletal muscle meat from Canada is manifestly contrary to the standards of the OIE, which state that no restriction should apply to this commodity, regardless of the BSE risk status of the cattle population of the exporting country.

Second, with regard to the importation of bovine meat and meat products (other than safe commodities) from a country with a controlled BSE risk, such as Canada, Article 11.6.11 sets out the necessary conditions. For example, this provision provides that the veterinary authority of the importing country should require an international veterinary certificate attesting that the cattle from which the meat and meat products are derived passed ante mortem and post mortem inspections, that they were not subject to a stunning or pithing process prior to slaughter, and that the meat and meat products were not contaminated by certain tissues such as Specified Risk Material.

By prohibiting the importation of all bovine meat and meat products from Canada, Korea's BSE measures go far beyond the standards set out in Chapter 11.6. This is obviously the case not only for deboned skeletal muscle meat listed as a safe commodity in Article 11.6.1 of the OIE Terrestrial

Code, but also for all other bovine meat and meat products from Canada.

Moreover, Article 32(1)(3) of the Act on the Prevention of Contagious Animal Diseases, which provides for an import prohibition on beef and beef products derived from cattle 30 months of age and over originating from countries where less than five years has elapsed since the latest case of BSE, is also clearly more restrictive than the standards of the OIE, which do not require that a country be free of BSE for a five-year period before allowing trade in such commodities.

Based on the foregoing, Korea cannot plausibly argue that the OIE standards were used as the "principal constituent" or the "fundamental principle" for its BSE measures or that the latter "stand," are "founded," "built" upon or "supported by" the OIE standards. Consequently, Korea's BSE measures are not "based on" the relevant OIE standards and therefore they do not meet the requirements of Article 3.1 of the SPS Agreement.

WTO Agreement on Technical Barriers to Trade — Less Favourable Treatment Standard under Article 2.1

In Canada's first written submission to the WTO panel in *United States – Certain Country of Origin Labelling Requirements,* dated 23 June 2010, the Legal Branch wrote:

The U.S. measure requiring beef and pork produced from imported livestock to be labelled differently than if produced from U.S.-born livestock [COOL measure] violates Article 2.1 of the WTO Agreement on Technical Barriers to Trade [TBT Agreement] because it accords less favourable treatment to Canadian cattle and hogs than that accorded to "like" U.S. cattle and hogs.

In *EC – Trademarks and Geographical Indications (Australia),* it was determined that to establish a violation of Article 2.1, it must be demonstrated that:

- a measure is a technical regulation;
- the technical regulation applies to "like products"; and
- the technical regulation treats imported products less favourably than like domestic products.

The terms "like product" and "treatment no less favourable" under Article 2.1 have not been interpreted in a panel or Appellate Body report. However, given the textual similarity between Article 2.1 of the TBT Agreement and Article III:4 of GATT 1994, the interpretation of these terms under Article III:4 provides guidance for the interpretation of these terms under the TBT Agreement.

The "less favourable treatment" analysis developed under the GATT 1994 provides the basis for how the term is to be interpreted under the TBT Agreement. This approach is supported by the preamble of the TBT Agreement which provides that one of the purposes of the Agreement is to further the objectives of the GATT 1994.

Article 2.1 requires that imported products be accorded "treatment no less favourable" than the treatment accorded to like products of national origin. In assessing whether less favourable treatment has been accorded to an imported product, the Appellate Body in *Korea – Beef,* Appellate Body Report, at para. 137, found that an examination should be made as to whether a measure "modifies the conditions of competition in the relevant market to the detriment of imported products." Per the *EC – Asbestos* case, a measure may not be applied in a manner that affects the competitive relationship in the marketplace such that the measure "affords[s] protection to domestic production." In *Dominican Republic – Import and Sale of Cigarettes,* the Appellate Body found that a measure accords less favourable treatment to an imported product where it gives the domestic like product "a competitive advantage in the market over imported like products."

The objective of the "treatment no less favourable" requirement is to provide "equality of opportunities" for imported goods per the GATT Panel in *US – Section 337 Tariff Act* case. This concept along with the concept of "conditions of competition" provides the basis for interpreting the "treatment no less favourable" requirement.

In examining the discriminatory effects of the COOL measure, the *Korea – Beef* case is instructive. In *Korea – Beef,* a Korean law required two separate retail distribution channels for beef: one channel for the retail sale of domestic beef and another channel for the retail sale of imported beef. In determining whether the dual retail system modified the conditions of competition in the Korean market to the disadvantage of imported products, the Appellate Body looked at the conditions of competition for domestic and imported beef both prior to and after the introduction of the Korean measure. Given the dominance of domestic beef in the Korean market, there was little practical choice but for Korean retailers to 'choose' to exclusively sell Korean beef to "the virtual exclusion of imported beef from the retail distribution channels." This resulted in a "drastic reduction of commercial opportunity" to sell imported beef through traditional retail channels.

The COOL measure restricts access to the U.S. market, by drastically reducing the commercial opportunities for Canadian-born cattle and hogs. Although U.S. feeding operations and slaughter houses do, in theory, have the ability to 'choose' whether to use Canadian cattle and hogs, and U.S.

retailers have, in theory, the ability to 'choose' to sell Canadian-origin beef and pork, the COOL measure imposes the "necessity of making a choice." As in *Korea – Beef,* the "intervention of some element of private choice" does not absolve the United States of its obligation to ensure that imported cattle and hogs are not subject to less favourable competitive conditions than their like domestic counterparts. And, given the cost implications, there is no real choice at all. The United States has, thus, modified the conditions of competition to the detriment of Canadian-born cattle and hogs contrary to TBT Article 2.1.

WTO Agreement on Technical Barriers to Trade – Article 2.2 – Determining a Measure's Legitimacy and Whether It Is More Trade Restrictive Than Necessary

In Canada's first written submission to the WTO panel in *United States – Certain Country of Origin Labelling Requirements,* dated 23 June 2010, the Legal Branch wrote:

The first sentence of Article 2.2 of the WTO Agreement on Technical Barriers to Trade [TBT Agreement] requires Members to ensure that their technical regulations do not create unnecessary obstacles to international trade. The second sentence then goes on to explain what is meant by this: Members must ensure that their technical regulations are "no more trade-restrictive than necessary to fulfil a legitimate objective." It can be inferred from the text of Article 2.2 that a technical regulation violates Article 2.2 if:

- the objective of the technical regulation is not a legitimate one;
- the technical regulation fails to fulfil the legitimate objective; or
- the technical regulation is more trade restrictive than necessary to fulfil the legitimate objective, taking into account the risks arising from non-fulfilment of the objective.

An examination of the commodities covered by the U.S. measure requiring beef and pork produced from imported livestock to be labelled differently than if produced from U.S.-born livestock [COOL measure] as well as the statements of U.S. lawmakers and industry groups during the development and enactment of the COOL measure demonstrates that its true objective is trade protectionism. Trade protectionism can never be a justifiable or legitimate objective under Article 2.2 of the TBT Agreement.

The phrase "more trade-restrictive than necessary" is not defined in the TBT Agreement and has not been interpreted in a panel or Appellate Body report. Based on the text of Article 2.2, two elements must be established to demonstrate that a technical regulation is "more trade-restrictive than necessary":

* it must restrict trade; and
* the trade restrictiveness of the technical regulation must be greater than necessary to fulfil its legitimate objective.

In the context of Article XI:1 of the GATT 1994, the panel in *India – Autos* interpreted the term "restriction" to mean "any form of limitation imposed on, or in relation to importation." Furthermore, it has been found that the GATT 1994 disciplines on the use of restrictions are meant to protect not "trade flows," but rather the "competitive opportunities of imported products" [see *EC – Bananas III (Article 21.5 – Ecuador II)*, Panel Report, at para. 7.330; *EC – Bananas III (Article 21.5 – US)*, Panel Report at para. 7.677].

Accordingly, measures that are "trade-restrictive" include those that impose any form of limitation of imports, discriminate against imports or deny competitive opportunities to imports.

According to its preamble, one of the purposes of the TBT Agreement is to further the objectives of the GATT. Therefore, the language and jurisprudence of the GATT offer guidance to the interpretation of the TBT Agreement, including Article 2.2. In particular, the interpretation of the word "necessary" under Article XX of the GATT 1994 is relevant to interpreting the phrase "more trade-restrictive than necessary" under Article 2.2 of the TBT Agreement.

According to a long line of adopted GATT and WTO dispute settlement reports, a party cannot justify a measure as "necessary" under Article XX of the GATT 1994 if an alternative measure is available which it could reasonably be expected to employ, and which is not inconsistent with, or is less inconsistent with, other GATT provisions. This reasoning is also applicable to Article 2.2 of the TBT Agreement.

The interpretation of a similar provision in Article 5.6 of the SPS Agreement and its footnote supports this reasoning. Article 5.6 provides, in relevant part, that "when establishing or maintaining sanitary or phytosanitary measures to achieve the appropriate level of sanitary or phytosanitary protection, Members shall ensure that such measures are not more trade-restrictive than required to achieve their appropriate level of sanitary or phytosanitary protection, taking into account technical and economic feasibility." The footnote to Article 5.6 clarifies that "a measure is not more trade restrictive than required unless there is another measure, reasonably available taking into account technical and economic feasibility, that achieves the appropriate level of sanitary or phytosanitary protection and is significantly less restrictive to trade" [see *Agreement on the Application of Sanitary and Phytosanitary Measures* [*SPS Agreement*], Article 5.6, footnote 3]. In *Australia – Salmon*, the Appellate Body, at para. 194, confirmed that, in order to find a violation of SPS Article 5.6, three elements must be established. The three elements are that "there is an SPS measure which: (1) is reasonably available taking into account technical and economic feasibility; (2) achieves the Member's appropriate level of sanitary or phytosanitary protection; and (3) is significantly less restrictive to trade than the SPS measure contested." The Appellate Body observed that the three prongs are cumulative in nature, in that, in order to establish inconsistency, all of them have to be satisfied. And if any of those elements are not fulfilled, the measure in dispute would be consistent with Article 5.6.

LAW OF THE SEA

Conservation and Management of Fish Stocks in the Arctic Ocean

In a briefing note dated 16 June 2010, the Legal Branch wrote:

Under the United Nations Convention on the Law of the Sea [UNCLOS] article 61, the coastal State shall determine the allowable catch of the living resources in its Exclusive Economic Zone [EEZ] and, taking into account the best scientific evidence available to it, shall ensure through proper conservation and management that the maintenance of the living resources in the EEZ is not endangered by overexploitation. In addition, UNCLOS article 63 (1), provides that where stocks occur within the EEZ of two or more coastal States, these States shall seek to agree upon the measures necessary to coordinate and ensure the conservation and development of such stocks. As fish stocks extend to the Arctic high seas, coastal States remain responsible for the management of the portion of the stock found in their EEZ. Finally, pursuant to the United Nations Fish Stock Agreement [UNFSA], in the exercise of their sovereign rights to explore, exploit, conserve and manage straddling fish stocks and highly migratory fish stocks within areas under their national jurisdiction, coastal States must apply *mutatis mutandis* the general principles of UNFSA, including the precautionary approach.

States that eventually fish on the Arctic high seas will be under the duty, pursuant to UNCLOS article 117, to adopt measures for the conservation of the living resources therein. UNCLOS Article 116 further provides that the right of those States to fish on the high seas is subject to the rights of coastal States, including in article 63 (2) and 64. Article 63 (2) provides that where stocks occur both within the EEZ and in an area beyond and adjacent to the zone, the coastal State and the States fishing for such stocks in the adjacent area shall seek to agree upon the measures necessary for the conservation of these stocks in the adjacent area. Article 64 provides that for highly migratory species, the coastal State and other States whose nationals fish in the region for these species shall cooperate with a view to ensuring conservation of such species throughout the region. Consequently, States fishing in the area adjacent to the coastal State's EEZ have a duty to cooperate with the relevant coastal State to conserve and manage straddling stocks and highly migratory stocks whether or not the coastal State is also harvesting such stocks. In addition, pursuant to UNFSA, States fishing on the high seas have a duty to cooperate with coastal States to adopt measures for the high seas that apply the general principles set out in Article 5 and are compatible with and do not undermine the measures adopted by coastal States for areas under national jurisdiction.

Continental Shelf

In a *note verbale* dated 9 November 2009 from Canada to the secretary-general of the United Nations, the Legal Branch wrote:

The Government of Canada rejects any claims by the French Republic to any maritime area, including any areas of continental shelf, beyond the area awarded to the French Republic by the Court of Arbitration in the *Case Concerning the Delimitation of Maritime Areas between Canada and the French Republic* (10 June 1992). Consistent with the 1992 decision, the United Nations Convention on the Law of the Sea and principles of international law, a claim by the French Republic to an area of extended continental shelf off Saint-Pierre and Miquelon cannot arise.

TREATY LAW

Countermeasures

In a legal opinion dated 11 January 2010, the Legal Branch wrote:

The breach of a treaty is an internationally wrongful act. In response to such a wrongful act, in this case a breach of a treaty, the other party to the treaty may terminate the treaty or suspend its operation in whole or in part per article 60 of the Vienna Convention on the Law of Treaties [VCLT]. The party which seeks to suspend the treaty must advise the other party of its claim of a breach and of the measures it proposes to take in response (i.e. suspension of the treaty) per art 65(1) of the VCLT. The notice must give the other party an opportunity to respond and if it objects to the measures, there is a process of consultations, negotiations and dispute settlement that must take place prior to the implementation of the suspension of the treaty [VCLT arts 65(2) and (3), 66]. The obligation to follow this procedure is seldom respected in practice.

A State may also respond to an internationally wrongful act with countermeasures, which consist of a State not performing certain of its international obligations towards the State committing the wrongful act for the purpose of inducing the cessation of the wrong. In *Gabčíkovo-Nagymoros Project (Hungary v Slovakia)*, [1997] ICJ Reports 3 at p 7, paras. 82-87, the International Court of Justice outlined four criteria necessary for the lawful exercise of a countermeasure:

- it must be taken in response to a previous international wrong of another state and directed against that state;
- the injured state must have called on the other state to discontinue its wrongful conduct or make reparation for it;
- the purpose must be to induce the other state to comply with its obligations (i.e., to resolve the dispute, not escalate it); and
- the effects of the countermeasure must be proportionate to the injury suffered, taking account of the rights in question, and therefore the countermeasure must be reversible.

In addition to the criteria above, it has been suggested that there are additional obligations to notify the responsible State of any decision to take countermeasures and to offer to negotiate prior to taking countermeasures [per Draft Articles, art 52]. While the practice of notification of a claim and proposed countermeasures is usually observed, the obligation to negotiate does not form a part of customary international law.

The proportionality of countermeasures is a critical feature as excessive countermeasures are themselves an internationally wrongful act. The assessment of proportionality is heavily fact dependent but the more closely the measure is related to the breach, the more likely it is to be proportionate. There is no need for proportionality to be defined solely by a comparative analysis of the economic injury suffered by the parties. The analysis must also include an evaluation of the importance the governments attach to the interest protected by the treaty or rule. The issue can be examined in the context of a broader policy framework and the ramifications of the breach to that framework.

The arbitral tribunal in the *United States v France* (1978) dispute had to consider the proportionality of the US suspension of all Air France flights to Los Angeles in response to the French denial of change of gauge rights between London and Paris. The tribunal examined the countermeasures in the context of the general air transport policy adopted by the US and implemented into many bilateral air transport agreements to find that the US measures were not "clearly disproportionate when compared to those taken by France." The US Department of Transport cited the 1978 US-France arbitral tribunal conclusions on countermeasures in 1993 in its order reducing Qantas from ten to seven weekly frequencies on the Sydney-Los Angeles route in response to Australia's restrictions on Northwest's fifth freedom traffic between Osaka and Sydney.

Parliamentary Declarations in 2010-11 / Déclarations parlementaires en 2010-11

compiled by / préparé par

ALEXANDRA LOGVIN

STATEMENTS MADE ON THE INTRODUCTION OF LEGISLATION /
DÉCLARATIONS SUR L'INTRODUCTION DE LA LÉGISLATION

S-3 (Tax Conventions Implementation Act, 2010 / Loi de 2010 pour la mise en oeuvre de conventions fiscales)

S-5 (Ensuring Safe Vehicles Imported from Mexico for Canadians Act / Loi assurant aux Canadiens la sécurité des véhicules importés du Mexique

C-2 (Canada–Colombia Free Trade Act / Loi de mise en oeuvre de l'Accord de libre-échange Canada-Colombie)

C-5 (Keeping Canadians Safe (International Transfer of Offenders) Act / Loi visant à assurer la sécurité des Canadiens (tranfèrement international des délinqants))

C-8 (Canada–Jordan Free Trade Act / Loi sur le libre-échange entre le Canada et la Jordanie)

C-11 (Balanced Refugee Reform Act / Loi sur des mesures de réforme équitables concernant les réfugiés)

C-17 (Combating Terrorism Act / Loi sur la lutte contre le terrorisme)

C-42 (Strengthening Aviation Security Act / Loi sur le renforcement de la sûreté aérienne)

C-46 (Canada-Panama Free Trade Act / Loi sur le libre-échange entre le Canada et le Panama)

C-47 (Sustaining Canada's Economic Recovery Act / Loi de soutien de la reprise économique au Canada)

Alexandra Logvin is a lawyer at Fasken Martineau DuMoulin, LLP. The period covered herein corresponds to the third session of the 40th Parliament, 3 March 2010 to 26 March 2011.

C-49 (Keeping Canadians Safe (Preventing Human Smugglers from Abusing Canada's Immigration System Act / Loi visant à empêcher les passeurs d'utiliser abusivement le système d'immigration canadien))

C-61 (Assets of Corrupt Foreign Officials Act / Loi sur le blocage des biens de dirigeants étrangers corrompus)

STATEMENTS IN RESPONSE TO QUESTIONS / DÉCLARATIONS EN RÉPONSE AUX QUESTIONS

ENVIRONMENT / ENVIRONNEMENT

Biodiversity / Biodiversité
Climate change / Changements climatiques
Oil Spills / Marées noires
Radioactive Waste / Déchets radioactifs
Seal Hunt / Chasse au loup-marin
Water / Eau

FOREIGN AFFAIRS / AFFAIRES ÉTRANGÈRES

Afghanistan
Africa / Afrique
Arctic Sovereignty / Souveraineté dans l'Arctique
Canada's International Year / Année internationale du Canada
Egypt / Égypte
Israel / Israël
Libya / Libye
Mexico / Mexique
North Korea / Corée du Nord
Rwanda
Tunisia / Tunisie
UN Security Council / Conseil de sécurité des Nations Unies
United Arab Emirates / Émirats arabes unis

HEALTH / SANTÉ

HUMAN RIGHTS / DROITS DE LA PERSONNE

Burma / Burmanie
Child Care / Garde d'enfants
Sexual Orientation / Orientation sexuelle
Immigration
Iran
Mexico / Mexique
Pakistan

Poverty / Pauvreté
Protecting Canadians Abroad / Protection des Canadiens à
  l'étranger
Religion
Rights of Women / Droits des femmes
  Health / Santé
Self-Determination / Autodétermination
Ukraine
United States / États-Unis

INTERNATIONAL CRIMINAL LAW / DROIT PÉNAL INTERNATIONAL

Corruption
Death penalty / Peine de mort
Genocide / Génocide
Smuggling / Contrebande
Terrorism / Terrorisme

INTERNATIONAL HUMANITARIAN LAW / DROIT INTERNATIONAL
HUMANITAIRE

Humanitarian Intervention and Aid / Aide et intervention
  humanitaire
  International Development / Développement internationale
  Afghanistan / Afghanistan
  Africa / Afrique
  Chile / Chili
  Haiti / Haïti
  Israel / Israël
  Japan / Japon
  Libya / Libye
  Pakistan
Landmines and Cluster Bombs / Mines terrestres et les bombes
  à fragmentation
Nuclear disarmament / Désarmement nucléaire
Refugees / Réfugiés

TRADE AND ECONOMY / COMMERCE ET ÉCONOMIE

Buy Local Policy / Politique d'achat local
Aerospace / Industrie aérospatiale
Agriculture / Agriculture
  Genetically Modified Organisms / Organismes génétiquement
    modifiés
  Supply Management / Gestion de l'offre

Automotive / Secteur de l'automobile
Canada-US Border / Frontière canado-américaine
Canada's Economy / Économie du Canada
Copyright / Droit d'auteur
Dispute Settlement / Règlement des différends
Financial Institutions / Institutions financières
Foreign Investment / Investissement étranger
Labelling / Étiquetage
Manufacturing / Secteur manufacturier
Procurement / Marchés publics
Shipbuilding / Construction navale
Softwood Lumber and Forestry / Bois d'œuvre et forestière
Taxation / Fiscalité
Tourism / Tourisme
Trade Agreements / Accords commerciaux
   Asia / Asie
   Colombia / Colombie
   European Union / Union européenne
   Panama / Panama
Trade and Human Rights / Commerce et les droits de la
   personne
World Trade Organization / Organisation mondiale de commerce

LAW OF THE SEA / DROIT DE LA MER

Fisheries / Pêches
   Access to Foreign Markets / Accès aux marchés étrangers
   Quotas
   Sustainability / Durabilité

SPORTS

STATEMENTS MADE ON THE INTRODUCTION OF LEGISLATION /
DÉCLARATIONS SUR L'INTRODUCTION DE LA LÉGISLATION

BILL S-3: TAX CONVENTIONS IMPLEMENTATION ACT, 2010 / LOI S-3 :
LOI DE 2010 POUR LA MISE EN OEUVRE DE CONVENTIONS FISCALES [1]

---

[1] *An Act to Implement Conventions and Protocols Concluded between Canada and Colombia,
Greece and Turkey for the Avoidance of Double Taxation and the Prevention of Fiscal Evasion with respect to Taxes on Income / Loi mettant en oeuvre des conventions et des protocoles
conclus entre le Canada et la Colombie, la Grèce et la Turquie en vue d'éviter les doubles
impositions et de prévenir l'évasion fiscale en matière d'impôts sur le revenu*, introduced
in the Senate on 23 March 2010 and in the House of Commons on 10 May 2010.
The bill received royal assent on 15 December 2010: SC 2010, c 15.

Mr. Ted Menzies (Parliamentary Secretary to the Minister of Finance):

As this legislation involves Greece, perhaps it is a very relevant time to bring ... the House up to speed on the latest issues in Greece. First and foremost, Canada is concerned about the situation in that country and other threats to the global economy. That is why we have been taking a leadership role within the G7 and the G20 on global financial reform, including Greece.

Over the weekend, the finance minister chaired conference calls ... with G7 finance ministers on that matter. Canada, through the IMF and through our IMF partners, is providing key support to help ensure the situation is contained. The Bank of Canada, working with the central banks around the world, is also helping provide key liquidity to markets.

While we are satisfied that the IMF and the EU actions to date will help address recent market volatility, we remain concerned about the fiscal situation in some countries. Hopefully, in a small way, the passage of Bill S-3 and the Greece-Canada tax treaty within it will help the turnaround in Greece by reducing tax barriers to trade and investment between our two countries. The strong ties between our two countries, bolstered by the large and active Greek Canadian community, will further be strengthened by this legislation as we create better conditions for Greek companies to do business in Canada and for Canadian companies to operate in Greece.

The legislation would implement Canada's recently concluded tax treaties with Greece and Turkey as well as Colombia, tax treaties that would help both prevent unfair double taxation and tax evasion.

Bill S-3 is part of Canada's ongoing effort to update and modernize its network of income tax treaties, which represents one of the most extensive in the world. In fact, Canada has tax treaties in place with nearly 90 countries. Moreover, Canada is continually working on agreements with other jurisdictions.

While Bill S-3 is important legislation, it is largely routine. Indeed, in the 39th Parliament, the House adopted similar legislation related to tax treaties with Finland, Mexico and Korea. In the 38th Parliament ..., legislation concerning tax treaties with Gabon, Ireland, Armenia, Oman and Azerbaijan were also adopted.

Bill S-3 and all the aforementioned similar legislation related to tax treaties are in fact patterned after the OECD model tax convention. This OECD framework is widely accepted in the international community.

As Peter Barnes, the noted former deputy international tax counsel at the U.S. Treasury Department, noted in the OECD *Observer* magazine:

the OECD model has achieved a consensus position as the benchmark against which essentially all tax treaty negotiations take place ... the

OECD Model Tax Convention is a tremendously important tool for smoothing the way of international business and global trade.

Rest assured, the provisions in the three treaties in Bill S-3 comply with the international norms that apply to such treaties ...

Our Conservative government is always working to expand its network of tax agreements with other countries. In order to combat offshore tax evasion, we unveiled a policy in budget 2007 that introduced incentives that have non-treaty countries enter into OECD-modelled tax information exchange agreements with Canada. It also required that all new tax treaties and revisions to existing tax treaties include that standard for tax information exchange.

[N]egotiations on tax information exchange agreements have commenced with more than a dozen jurisdictions. What is more, in August 2009, Canada signed its first tax information exchange agreement with the Netherlands Antilles. That agreement, along with those between Canada and Colombia, Greece and Turkey, all include the OECD standard on international tax information exchange.

We have built on that record in recent years as well. For instance, we have given the Canada Revenue Agency additional resources for international tax audit and enforcement. I believe all members realize and understand that tax treaties are an important tool for improving our system of international taxation.

[T]he tax treaties with Greece, Turkey and Colombia are designed with two key objectives in mind. The first objective is to remove barriers to cross-border trade and investment, most notably the double taxation of income. The second objective is to prevent tax evasion by encouraging cooperation between Canada's tax authorities and those in other countries.

First, we all recognize that removing barriers to trade and investment are paramount in today's global economy. Investors, traders and others with international dealings need to know that the tax implications associated with their activities, both in Canada and abroad, are protected.

Canadians also want to be treated fairly, with consistent tax treatment that is set out from the start. In other words, they want to know the rules of the game and they want to know the rules will not change in the middle of the game.

Bill S-3 will remove uncertainty about the tax implications associated with doing business, working or visiting abroad in Greece, Turkey and Colombia.

These tax treaties will establish a mutual understanding of how those tax regimes will interface with those in Canada. This can only promote certainty and stability, and help produce a better business climate, especially with respect to eliminating double taxation. Nobody wants to have their income taxed twice, nor should it be, but without a tax treaty, that is exactly what could happen. Both countries could claim tax on income without providing the taxpayer with any measure of relief for the tax paid in the other country.

To alleviate the potential for double taxation, tax treaties use two general methods, depending on their particular circumstances. In some cases the exclusive right to tax particular income is granted to the country where the taxpayer resides. In other cases, the taxing right is shared. For example, if a Canadian resident employed by a Canadian company is sent on a short-term assignment, perhaps for three months, to any one of the three treaty countries noted in Bill S-3, Canada has the exclusive right to tax that person's employment income. If, on the other hand, that same person is employed abroad for a longer period of time, say for one year, then the host country can also tax the employment income.

Under the terms of the tax treaty, this individual will be treated fairly. When the individual files his or her taxes, a credit will be provided on the tax that has been paid in that other country, thus avoiding double taxation and keeping the tax system fair.

It has been noted that one way to reduce the potential for double taxation is to reduce withholding taxes. These taxes are a common feature in international taxation. They are levied by a country on certain items of income arising in that country and paid to residents of another country.

The types of income normally subjected to withholding tax would include, for example, interest, dividends and royalties. Withholding taxes are levied on the gross amounts paid to non-residents and represent their final obligations with respect to Canadian income tax.

Without tax treaties, Canada usually taxes this income at a rate of 25%, which is the rate set out under our own legislation, the Income Tax Act. Accordingly, Bill S-3, as with all tax treaties, addresses this issue with numerous withholding rate reductions. Specifically, Bill S-3 will provide for a maximum withholding tax on portfolio dividends paid to non-residents of 15% in the case of Colombia and Greece, and 20% in the case of Turkey.

For dividends paid by subsidiaries to their parent companies, the maximum withholding rate is reduced to 5% in the case of Colombia and Greece, and 15% in the case of Turkey. Withholding rate reductions also apply to royalty, interest and pension payments.

The treaties in Bill S-3 cap the maximum withholding tax rate on interest at 10% in the case of Colombia and Greece, and 15% in the case of Turkey. Each treaty in this bill caps the maximum withholding tax rate of a royalty payment at 10% and on periodic pension payments at 15%.

I mentioned that the tax treaties have two objectives. I have spoken at length about the first objective of removing barriers to cross-border trade and investment by eliminating double taxation. While double taxation is clearly problematic, tax evasion and avoidance are also unfair and economically damaging. The loss of revenue resulting from tax avoidance and evasion obviously negatively affect the efforts of governments to function.

Not only that, tax evasion is blatantly unfair as it places an uneven share of the tax burden on honest taxpayers. That is why the second objective of tax treaties is to encourage co-operation between Canadian tax authorities and those in other countries.

We all appreciate that the best defence against international tax avoidance and evasion is through improved and expanded mechanisms for international co-operation and information sharing. By increasing co-operation between Canada and other countries, in this instance Colombia, Greece and Turkey, we are able to better prevent tax evasion.

Tax treaties are an important tool in protecting Canada's tax base by allowing consultations and information to be exchanged between our two governments. This means that we can better catch those trying to avoid taxes, ensure the integrity of our tax system, and that everyone is taxed equally ...

For instance, in budget 2010 we proposed to address tax planning practices that have developed, which have allowed under particular circumstances a portion of stock-based employment benefits to escape taxation at both personal and corporate levels, by: preventing tax arbitrage opportunities involving leases with government entities, other tax exempt entities or non-residents who are not subject to Canadian taxation; consulting regarding a proposal to require taxpayers to identify aggressive tax planning, which will provide the Canada Revenue Agency with early notice of new and emerging aggressive tax-avoidance schemes; consulting on revised proposals to prevent tax avoidance through the use of offshore trusts or other foreign investment entities; and ensuring that businesses cannot inappropriately capitalize on the differences between the tax systems of Canada and other countries to artificially increase foreign tax credits related to cross-border transactions and, thus, pay less tax.

We also propose to prevent aggressive tax planning by ensuring that income trust conversions into corporations are subject to the same loss utilization rules that currently apply to similar transactions involving only corporations, and finally, to ensure the provisions of the Criminal Code that apply to serious crimes related to money laundering and terrorist financing can be invoked in cases of tax evasion and prosecuted under Canada's tax statutes.

(House of Commons Debates, 13 May 2010, pp. 2764-66)
(Débats de la Chambre des communes, le 13 mai 2010, pp. 2764-66)

BILL S-5: ENSURING SAFE VEHICLES IMPORTED FROM MEXICO FOR
CANADIANS ACT / LOI S-5: LOI ASSURANT AUX CANADIENS LA
SÉCURITÉ DES VÉHICULES IMPORTÉS DU MEXIQUE [2]

Hon. Peter Kent (Minister of State of Foreign Affairs (Americas),
for the Minister of Transport, Infrastructure and Communities):

These changes are being proposed in order to bring Canada into compliance with the automotive provisions of the North American Free Trade Agreement, known as NAFTA. These amendments will address the importation of used vehicles from Mexico in a manner that continues to both preserve the safety of Canadians and to protect our precious environment.

Although the North American Free Trade Agreement was signed in 1993, its provisions on the importation of used vehicles only came into effect on January 1, 2009. These provisions require that Mexico, the United States and Canada allow the importation of used vehicles from one another's countries. The requirement is to be implemented in a phased manner by each of the countries. The allowable importations will start with vehicles that are 10 years old and older. The age threshold for the vehicles will decrease by two years, every two years, until 2019 when countries may not adopt or maintain a prohibition or restriction on imports of used vehicles from each other.

The current wording of the Motor Vehicle Safety Act does not allow for this importation.

The Motor Vehicle Safety Act is the key enabling legislative tool that regulates the manufacture and importation of motor vehicles and motor vehicle equipment in order to reduce the risk of death, injury and damage to property and to the environment. It is the tool that the government uses to provide direction to manufacturers, to importers and to the general public, thus allowing us to work together to continually increase the level of road safety in Canada.

This act sets out a comprehensive minimum safety standard for vehicles manufactured or imported for use into Canada. It also sets the standards for new tires and for equipment used in the restraint of children and disabled persons within the vehicle. The Motor Vehicle Safety Act first came into effect in 1971, and was last amended in 1993.

---

[2] *An Act to Amend the Motor Vehicle Safety Act and the Canadian Environmental Protection Act, 1999 / Loi modifiant la Loi sur la sécurité automobile et la Loi canadienne sur la protection de l'environnement (1999)*, introduced in the Senate on 14 April 2010 and in the House of Commons on 10 June 2010. The bill received royal assent on 23 March 2011: SC 2011, c 1.

The Motor Vehicle Safety Act enables the development of the motor vehicle safety regulations and the Canada motor vehicle safety standards. These regulations and standards help to ensure the current and the ongoing safety of Canadians on our roadways.

The Canadian Environmental Protection Act, 1999, came into force on March 31, 2000, following an extensive parliamentary review of the original 1988 act. The Canadian Environmental Protection Act, 1999, is the government's principal legislative tool to prevent pollution in order to protect the environment and human health. It provides a comprehensive approach to reducing harmful emissions from vehicles and equipment by considering vehicles, engines and fuels as integrated systems.

Even with a modern, efficient piece of legislation such as the Canadian Environmental Protection Act, 1999, amendments are required from time to time to keep pace with various international commitments, such as the North American Free Trade Agreement. We believe it is important to move swiftly to meet our international commitments and to be compliant with the North American Free Trade Agreement. We believe it is also essential to demonstrate our continued good faith and to maintain our reputation with our trading partners.

Both the United States and Mexico have regimes in place that allow for the importation of these used vehicles.

Prior to the automotive provisions of the North American Free Trade Agreement coming into force, the American government already had a program where it considered requests for importation of vehicles from other countries. A determination is made for each individual vehicle to see if it can be modified to meet American safety standards; therefore, its rules did not need to change in order to meet the North American Free Trade Agreement requirements.

On December 22, 2008, the President of Mexico issued a decree allowing for the duty-free entry of used light and heavy-duty weight vehicles from Canada and the United States that are 10 years old or older into Mexico. This decree entered into force on January 1, 2009.

[It is important] for Canada to meet its reciprocal obligations. Making these changes to the Motor Vehicle Safety Act and the Canadian Environmental Protection Act, 1999, will help to fulfill these commitments to our trading partner.

(House of Commons Debates, 6 December 2010, pp. 6862-65)
(Débats de la Chambre des communes, le 6 décembre 2010, pp. 6862-65)

BILL C-2: CANADA–COLOMBIA FREE TRADE AGREEMENT
IMPLEMENTATION ACT / LOI C-2: LOI DE MISE EN OEUVRE DE
L'ACCORD DE LIBRE-ÉCHANGE CANADA–COLOMBIE [3]

Hon. Peter Van Loan (Minister of International Trade):

Our government has indicated the priority that we place on implementing free trade agreements to help Canadian businesses compete in international markets. Today's debate on approval of the Canada-Colombia free trade agreement reflects this objective of creating jobs and opportunities for Canadian workers through trade ...

Our government is committed to pursuing bilateral and multilateral trade relationships that bring continued prosperity to Canadians right here at home. The global economic crisis emphasizes the importance and urgency of expanding trade and investment relations to improve market access.

The Canada-Colombia free trade agreement is one of many efforts by our government to expand opportunities for Canadian business. As members know, we have entered an age of fierce global competition ... Canadian businesses and Canadian workers are up to the challenge of competing internationally ...

The government launched negotiations with Colombia and other Andean partners in June 2007. I am proud to say that we continue working hard to create new opportunities abroad to benefit Canadian workers at home. The Canada-Colombia free trade agreement, along with the related agreements on the environment and labour are an important part of this broader trade agenda.

À l'heure actuelle, le Canada a depuis longtemps des accords de libre-échange avec les États-Unis et le Mexique dans le cadre de l'Accord de libre-échange nord-américain, ainsi qu'avec Israël, le Chili et le Costa Rica. [W]e recently implemented new free trade agreements with the European Free Trade Association and Peru. In 2009, we also signed a free trade agreement with Jordan, which I had the pleasure of tabling in the House today.

---

[3] *An Act to Implement the Free Trade Agreement between Canada and the Republic of Colombia, the Agreement on the Environment between Canada and the Republic of Colombia and the Agreement on Labour Cooperation between Canada and the Republic of Colombia / Loi portant mise en oeuvre de l'Accord de libre-échange entre le Canada et la République de Colombie, de l'Accord sur l'environnement entre le Canada et la République de Colombie et de l'Accord de coopération dans le domaine du travail entre le Canada et la République de Colombie*, introduced in the House of Commons on 10 March 2010. The bill received royal assent on 29 June 2010: SC 2010, c 4.

On August 11, 2009, the government successfully concluded free trade negotiations with Panama. At the announcement of the conclusion of the Panama negotiations, the Prime Minister himself emphasized that Canada's commitment was to stronger trade partnerships.

We are on the right track and are also looking ahead to other important partners in the world. At the Canada-European Union Summit last May, the government launched negotiations toward a comprehensive economic and trade agreement with the European Union. We also remain dedicated to advancing our ongoing free trade negotiations with other partners, including Central American countries, the Caribbean community and the Dominican Republic ...

We are currently working to launch negotiations with new partners, such as Morocco and the Ukraine, and exploring deeper trade ties with India and Japan ...

Our recent economic action plan is making significant investments in our national innovation strategy. We have also cut corporate taxes to make Canada more attractive to business. We have the lowest taxes on new business entrants who are creating jobs, lower taxes on new business than anywhere in the G7. In 2012 we will have the lowest business taxes across the board in the G7.

We have made Canada the first country in the G20 to have a tariff-free zone for a broad range of machinery and equipment for Canadian manufacturers. Eliminating tariffs on new equipment, parts and machinery will help make our manufacturers more innovative, more productive and more cost-competitive. We are helping Canadian companies at home and we will continue to ensure they can compete abroad.

En adoptant cet accord de libre-échange avec la Colombie, nous écoutons ce que les entreprises canadiennes nous disent et nous répondons à leurs besoins pour qu'elles demeurent compétitives. Ce partenariat économique plus étroit avec la Colombie permettra aussi de réduire les droits de douane imposés aux exportateurs canadiens. L'accord de libre-échange Canada-Colombie multipliera également les possibilités offertes aux investisseurs et aux fournisseurs de services canadiens. Pour le Canada, la Colombie est déjà un important partenaire commercial.

In 2009, our two-way merchandise trade totalled $1.335 billion and Colombia is an established and growing market for Canadian exports. Over the past five years, Canadian merchandise exports have grown by over 55%.

La Colombie est également une destination stratégique pour l'investissement canadien. En 2008, la valeur des investissements canadiens en Colombie a atteint approximativement 1,1 milliard de dollars.

However, that is not all. The Colombian market is an exciting one. With 48 million people, Colombia's macroeconomic policy and improved security under its current leadership have generated favourable economic conditions. Colombia's government is committed to reversing years of underinvestment in public infrastructure. Investment in infrastructure has grown from 4% of the country's gross domestic product in 2005 to more than 8% in 2009.

A country like ours, with so much expertise in this area, can offer a lot. These are areas where Canadian companies can compete. In fact, the potential goes far beyond infrastructure and includes other key sectors like agriculture and industrial goods, and services like engineering, mining, energy and financial services. These are all areas where Canada and Canadians excel.

Moreover, those sectors are linchpins of our economy in communities large and small across this great nation, but this agreement is not just about creating opportunities for Canadian business. It is also about strengthening our partnership with Colombia ...

Colombia has demonstrated its continued efforts to curb violence, fight impunity and promote peace and security. This government recognizes that challenges remain in Colombia and is committed to working with Colombia to address those issues.

This government believes that economic growth through free trade, rules-based trade and investment can contribute to alleviating poverty and create new wealth and opportunities for Colombians. We want the business of both nations to grow and expand together. Colombians are looking for and need these kinds of opportunities and they are seeking new partnerships abroad.

The Government of Colombia, like ours, is working hard to acquire new markets for its citizens. In fact, Colombia is moving forward on an ambitious economic agenda that includes free trade agreements with a range of partners. Canada's main competitor in the Colombian market, the United States, has already completed a free trade agreement with Colombia.

Our firms and Canadian workers expect that their government will work for them and put in place trade agreements that address the situation and allow them to compete in international markets on a level playing field. Canadians deserve this. Our government is ensuring that they get the opportunity to compete and succeed in Colombia and around the world.

We cannot put our exporters at a relative disadvantage. The time for Canada to act is now.

Non seulement nous pourrons rivaliser avec les pays européens, mais les entreprises canadiennes auront aussi une occasion importante d'avoir un avantage sur les principaux concurrents américains. Cet accord de libre-échange permettra aux Canadiens de prendre de l'expansion dans cet important marché. C'est tout à fait ce genre de débouchés que les entreprises canadiennes demandent.

I believe it is important for the members of the House to clearly understand the importance of the Colombian market for the business in their regions, for their constituents and, in fact, for all Canadians. Starting on the east coast, the provinces of Nova Scotia, Prince Edward Island, New Brunswick and Newfoundland and Labrador exported about $52.8 million worth of products to Colombia directly benefiting core industries such as oil, paper, paper board and fertilizers. These industries will clearly benefit from freer trade with Colombia.

What about machinery and industrial goods? Personne n'ignore que les fabricants canadiens, et en particulier ceux de l'Ontario et du Québec, coeur industriel du Canada, vivent des temps difficiles ces jours-ci. Our economic recovery is fragile and they need all the opportunities they can get to grow stronger and more competitive ...

The Prairie provinces of Alberta, Saskatchewan and Manitoba will also benefit from the agreement. The immediate removal of Colombian tariffs from such cornerstone crops as wheat, barley and pulses will make these products from the Canadian Prairies even more competitive in the Colombian market. Prairie producers are a cornerstone of our economy. They will see clear benefits from free trade with Colombia.

I should also point out that Canada enjoys significant investment presence in the Colombian market thanks to oil and gas projects. We fully expect this presence to deepen as projects continue to develop.

Our free trade agreement with Colombia would help secure Canadian investments in the region by providing greater predictability and protection for investors. These investment provisions will directly benefit those Alberta firms that are investing in Colombia. British Columbia also stands to benefit, especially B.C.'s mechanical, machinery and paper industries. In fact, many British Columbia companies have told us that they are looking to expand trade with Colombia.

With those kinds of benefits across Canada, it is no wonder that Canadian businesses, investors and producers alike have been calling for closer commercial ties with Colombia for some time now. The time to act is now. Members opposite should listen to Canadians who have been loud and clear.

Colombia has an ambitious and aggressive free trade agenda that includes some key competitors for Canada, competitors like the U.S. and the EU. We need to take steps sooner rather than later to ensure that Canadian exporters, investors and producers in regions and provinces across the country are not put at a disadvantage relative to our competitors.

Our Canadian exporters, investors and producers welcome the opportunity to establish themselves in this market ahead of the competition.

They can compete with the best in the world. Let us give them the opportunity to do so. We have negotiated a good deal for Canadians and Colombians alike.

This agreement would give Colombians greater access and opportunities in the North American market. Colombians would also benefit from a greater range of Canadian products. This agreement would also promote economic development in the region.

(*House of Commons Debates, 24 March 2010, pp. 884-87*)
(*Débats de la Chambre des communes, le 24 mars 2010, pp. 884-87*)

BILL C-5: KEEPING CANADIANS SAFE (INTERNATIONAL TRANSFER OF OFFENDERS ACT) / LOI C-5: LOI VISANT À ASSURER LA SÉCURITÉ DES CANADIENS (TRANSFÈREMENT INTERNATIONAL DES DÉLINQUANTS)[4]

Mr. Dave MacKenzie (Parliamentary Secretary to the Minister of Public Safety):

One of the strongest commitments our government made ... was to make our streets, our playgrounds and our communities safer places for everyone ...

We have passed tough new laws to crack down on crime. We have taken action to ensure that offenders are held accountable and that they serve sentences which reflect the serious nature of their actions. We have given police and law enforcement agencies more of the tools they need to do their job. The legislation before us today builds on this impressive track record while also helping to ensure that the appropriate factors are better taken into account when it comes to considering offender transfer requests.

Today, when a Canadian citizen serving a sentence abroad requests a transfer to Canada, the minister shall take several factors into consideration in assessing these requests. The minister shall, for example, consider whether an offender's return to Canada would constitute a threat to the security of Canada. The minister shall also consider whether the offender has social or family ties in Canada and whether the foreign government or prison system presents a serious threat to the offender's security or human rights. These are important factors.

---

4 *An Act to Amend the International Transfer of Offenders Act / Loi modifiant la Loi sur le transferement international des délinquants*, introduced in the House of Commons on 18 March 2010.

Under the amendments, which our government is proposing, the minister would still be able to consider these factors. Bill C-5 would not change that. What it would do is clarify in the existing International Transfer of Offenders Act that the minister may also take other factors into account when considering requests for offender transfers. Among these additional factors is whether the offender's return to Canada will endanger public safety. Surely that makes sense. All of us want to ensure that our homes and our communities are safe, and that is what Bill C-5 would help to do.

In particular, Bill C-5 would help to ensure that in all transfer decisions due consideration is given to the safety of any member of the offender's family, the safety of children and the safety of victims ...

Our government is committed to ensuring that their voices are heard and their concerns are taken seriously. That is one of our highest priorities and why we have taken action on a number of fronts. We have committed $52 million over four years to enhance the federal victims strategy so the government could better meet the needs of victims. Among other things, we have also created the Office of the Federal Ombudsman for Victims of Crime and given victims the resources to attend parole hearings or seek help if they experience crime while abroad.

Our government has also taken steps to keep our children safe, most recently introducing legislation in the other place to strengthen the Sex Offender Information Registration Act.

Crime places a heavy toll on individual victims, their families, communities and society at large. That is why we need to take action to be sure that the scales of justice are balanced to include victims and some of the more vulnerable members of our society. That is why Bill C-5 is so important.

In addition to ensuring that public safety is a principal consideration of offender transfer requests, Bill C-5 would also provide for the consideration of other factors, many of which are in line with current reforms currently underway within the corrections system. These include whether in the minister's opinion the offender is likely to continue to engage in criminal activity after the transfer, the offender's health and whether the offender has refused to participate in a rehabilitation or reintegration program.

In addition, Bill C-5 notes that the minister may consider whether the offender has accepted responsibility for the events for which he or she has been convicted, including by acknowledging the harm done to victims and to the community, the manner in which the offender will be supervised after the transfer while he or she is serving his or her sentence, and whether the offender has co-operated or has undertaken to co-operate with a law enforcement agency.

As well, the legislation before us today notes that the minister may consider any other factor which he or she considers relevant.

All in all, the legislation before us today would help to ensure that Canadian offenders who request a transfer are treated fairly and equitably while not being allowed to escape accountability if an offence is committed abroad. It is fair, timely and what Canadians want.

(*House of Commons Debates, 16 April 2010, pp. 1590-91*)
(*Débats de la Chambre des communes, le 16 avril 2010, pp. 1590-91*)

BILL C-8: CANADA-JORDAN FREE TRADE ACT / LOI C-8: LOI SUR LE LIBRE-ÉCHANGE ENTRE LE CANADA ET LA JORDANIE[5]

Mr. Gerald Keddy (Parliamentary Secretary to the Minister of International Trade):

This is excellent legislation that would benefit all Canadians and certainly all Jordanians. These agreements are the latest examples of our government's strategy to open doors for Canadian businesses and investors in these challenging economic times. This agreement will be the Canada-Jordan free trade agreement and related agreements on labour cooperation and the environment ...

The fact is that sectors across Canada's economy need the kind of competitive access provided by this free trade agreement. Our companies need to be able to compete and succeed in a global marketplace. The agreement would immediately eliminate tariffs on the vast majority of current Canadian exports to Jordan. To be more precise, the agreement would eliminate all non-agricultural tariffs and the vast majority of agricultural tariffs on our two-way trade.

Farmers would benefit because the agreement would eliminate tariffs on pulse crops, including lentils, chickpeas and beans, frozen french fries, animal feed and various prepared foods. It would also expand opportunities for Canadians in other sectors, including forest products, industrial and electrical machinery, construction equipment and auto parts ...

I want to take a moment to also touch on the Canada-Jordan foreign investment promotion and protection agreement that came into force on December 14 of last year. Signed at the same time as the free trade agreement,

---

5 *An Act to Implement the Free Trade Agreement between Canada and the Hashemite Kingdom of Jordan, the Agreement on the Environment between Canada and the Hashemite Kingdom of Jordan and the Agreement on Labour Cooperation between Canada and the Hashemite Kingdom of Jordan / Loi portant mise en oeuvre de l'Accord de libre-échange entre le Canada et le Royaume hachémite de Jordanie, de l'Accord sur l'environnement entre le Canada et le Royaume hachémite de Jordanie et de l'Accord de coopération dans le domaine du travail entre le Canada et le Royaume hachémite de Jordanie*, introduced in the House of Commons on 24 March 2010.

it will help encourage two-way investment by providing investors in both countries with the clarity and the certainty they need when investing in each other's markets.

Canadian investors are discovering a wealth of opportunities in the Jordanian market. Sectors, like resource extraction, nuclear energy, telecommunications, transportation and infrastructure, all hold much promise for Canadian investors. One need only look at the great success the Potash Corporation of Saskatchewan has found in Jordan. It is now the largest foreign investor in Jordan. We can all also look at the long list of other Canadian companies, like Bombardier and SNC-Lavalin for instance, that have made significant inroads in the Jordanian market ...

The Canada-Jordan FTA is Canada's first ever free trade agreement with an Arab country. The Middle East and the north Africa region are becoming more important to Canadian business.

This agreement with Jordan would give us access to a critical market in the region. We have opened a number of significant doorways into the region and set the stage for Canadian businesses to create even more commercial links throughout the Middle East and north Africa in the years ahead.

However, Canada also believes that deeper commercial engagement need not come at the expense of labour standards or the environment. We think trade and investment can be a positive force for communities worldwide. We are very pleased to include parallel labour and environment agreements as part of the larger package of agreements we have signed with Jordan.

I will start with the labour co-operation agreement. It commits both countries to respect the core labour standards set out by the International Labour Organization, standards that help eliminate child labour, forced labour and workplace discrimination, and that respect freedom of association and the right to bargain collectively. The agreement also commits both countries in providing acceptable minimum employment standards and compensation for occupational injuries and illnesses. I should also add that under this agreement migrant workers would enjoy the same legal protections as nationals, when it comes to working conditions.

In a similar vein, the agreement on the environment commits both countries to pursue high levels of environmental protection and the development and improvement of policies that protect the natural environment. Domestic environmental laws must be respected and enforced. This agreement commits both countries to this goal.

It also commits both countries to ensure that the strong environmental assessment processes are in place, as well as remedies for violating environmental laws. Through the agreement on the environment, our governments are also encouraging businesses to adopt best practices of corporate social responsibility and promote public awareness and engagement. As with the labour agreement, these measures would help ensure that increased trade and investment does not come at the expense of the environment and that businesses can play a positive role in the life of each country.

This is a critical time for Canada's economy. The global economic downturn has hit all nations hard. Our bilateral trade with Jordan, for example, fell from $92 million in 2008 to $82 million in 2009, primarily due to a decline in Canadian exports to Jordan.

We must do the right things to get there. We must continue to take steps to sharpen Canada's competitive edge. The global economy is not going away and one in five Canadian jobs depends upon Canada trading with the rest of the world. We need to continue opening doors to opportunity for our businesses and investors to thrive and prosper today and beyond the current economic downturn. Our free trade agreement with Jordan is an important part of these efforts. So is the foreign investment protection agreement and the two agreements on labour and the environment. Canada needs these tools to be competitive in Jordan.

This free trade agreement resonates with many Canadians. It would eliminate tariffs on Canadian products into this expanding market. In doing so, it would create opportunities for Canadian industries still on the rebound from recent economic turbulence and complement the government's successful strategy to stimulate economic growth for Canadians on all fronts. It would benefit Canadian consumers by eliminating tariffs on virtually all imports from Jordan. In doing all of that, and this is the key, it would also protect the environment and workers' rights.

I cannot mention this fact enough. This is not just a free trade agreement. It has a side agreement on labour co-operation and the environment. They were negotiated in parallel with the free trade agreement and link directly to environmental and labour provisions. Both the environment and the labour agreements contain what the negotiators call a non-derogation clause, meaning that neither Canada nor Jordan may waive or lessen existing environmental and labour laws to encourage trade or investment.

In effect, the parallel labour and environment agreements would help to ensure progress on labour rights and environment protection.

I will begin by elaborating on the agreement on the environment that is included in this agreement.

This agreement commits both countries to pursue high levels of environmental protection and to continue to strive to develop and improve their environmental laws and policies.

Canada and Jordan are committed to complying with and effectively enforcing their domestic environmental laws, ensure that proceedings are available to remedy violations of environmental laws, promote public awareness of environmental laws and policies, put in place environmental impact assessment processes, and encourage the use of voluntary best practices of corporate social responsibility by enterprises.

The agreement on the environment also creates potential avenues for cooperation. Areas of activities would include cooperation on enforcement and compliance, corporate social responsibility and environmental technologies.

The agreement's dispute settlement provisions are forward-looking and progressive.

Members of the public would be able to submit questions to either party on any obligations or cooperative activities under the agreement. Canada and Jordan can undertake consultations to resolve any disagreements and, if need be, the matter can be referred to ministers for resolution.

As a final step, both Jordan and Canada would be able to ask for an independent review panel to investigate situations where they think the other party has failed to effectively enforce its environmental laws. In these circumstances, Canada and Jordan will work to develop an action plan to implement panel recommendations.

Environmental and labour protections are integral to the Canada-Jordan free trade agreement. We all know that the environmental and labour standards can go together and even benefit from free trade. Our free trade agreement with Jordan, along with the parallel agreements on the environment and labour cooperation, ensures that they do.

Finally, in summarizing this agreement, I just want to go over a couple more points.

We know that Canada and Jordan would eliminate all non-agricultural tariffs and most agricultural tariffs and have both committed to reducing non-tariff barriers to trade. Canadian exporters would benefit from enhanced access to the Jordanian market. A Canada-Jordan free trade agreement would also help to level the playing field, vis-à-vis competitors who currently benefit from preferential access against our companies here in Canada.

Under tariff elimination, there would be an elimination of all Jordanian non-agricultural tariffs that currently average 11%. These include tariffs of 10% to 30% on many non-agricultural products of Canadian export interests, including industrial and electrical machinery, auto parts, construction equipment and forest products such as wood building materials and paper. The elimination of the vast majority of Jordan's agricultural tariffs, including key Canadian export interests, such as pulse crops, frozen french fries, various prepared foods and animal feeds, which face high tariffs of as much as 30% [*sic*].

The vast majority of current Canadian exports to Jordan would benefit from the immediate duty-free access to the Jordanian market upon implementation of this free trade agreement. Upon implementation, Canada will immediately eliminate all non-agricultural tariffs on imports originating in Jordan, as well as most agricultural tariffs. As in all of our past free trade agreements, Canada has excluded over-quota supply managed dairy, poultry and ag [*sic*] products from any tariff reductions.

There are also reductions to non-tariff barriers to trade in this agreement, commitments to ensure non-discriminatory treatment of imported goods, provisions to affirm and build on obligations under the WTO Agreement on Technical Barriers to Trade, and an agreement to apply the provisions of the WTO agreement on the application of sanitary and phytosanitary measures in bilateral trade.

A committee on trade in goods and rules of origin would be created as a forum for Canada and Jordan to discuss any goods-related trade issues that arise, including technical barriers to trade.

There would be a bilateral goods trade overview. Canadian exports to Jordan totalled $65.8 million in 2009, up from $31 million in 2003. Our top exports to Jordan in 2009 included vehicles, forest products, machinery, pulse crops, such as lentils and chick peas, ships and boats and plastics. The top exports for the previous year included paper and paperboard, copper wire, pulse crops, machinery and wood pulp. Canadian merchandise imports from Jordan totalled $16.6 million in 2009, up from $6 million in 2003. Top imports included knit and woven apparel, precious stones and metals, mainly jewellery, vegetables and inorganic chemicals.

All our consultations and reviews of this very important agreement show us that trade will not just be expanded, but will be drastically expanded.

(*House of Commons Debates, 29 March 2010, pp. 1029-32*)
(*Débats de la Chambre des communes, le 29 mars 2010, pp. 1029-32*)

BILL C-11: BALANCED REFUGEE REFORM ACT / LOI C-11: LOI SUR DES MESURES DE RÉFORME ÉQUITABLES CONCERNANT LES RÉFUGIÉS [6]

Hon. Jason Kenney (Minister of Citizenship, Immigration and Multiculturalism):

This bill and related reforms would reinforce Canada's humanitarian tradition as a place of refuge for victims of persecution and torture, while improving our asylum system to ensure that it is balanced, fast and fair.

---

6 *An Act to Amend the Immigration and Refugee Protection Act and the Federal Courts Act / Loi modifiant la Loi sur l'immigration et la protection des réfugiés et la Loi sur les Cours fédérales*, introduced in the House of Commons on 30 March 2010. The bill received royal assent on 29 June 2010: SC 2010, c 8.

The bill would ensure faster protection of bona fide refugees, reinforce procedural fairness by implementing a robust refugee appeals division at the IRB and ensure faster removal of those who seek to abuse Canada's generosity by making asylum claims.

Canada has always been a place of refuge for victims of persecution, warfare and oppression. English Canada was founded by refugees fleeing the American revolution, the United Empire Loyalists. Canada was the north star of the underground railroad for escaped slaves from the southern United States.

In 1956, Canada welcomed some 40,000 refugees of Soviet communism fleeing the invasion of Budapest. In 1979 and 1980, Canadian churches and families welcomed some 50,000 Vietnamese or Indochinese boat people, creating the magnificent foundations of our privately sponsored refugee program.

Having said that, there have been moments when we turned our backs on those most urgently in need of our help. We think, of course, of the example of the European Jewish refugees during the Second World War who Canada refused to accept, detailed in the great historical work *None is Too Many* written by Harold Troper and Irving Abella.

We must learn from the mistakes of that period so that we never repeat them. I believe we have learned from those mistakes, because Canada has welcomed some one million refugees to make a new start here in Canada in security and with our protection since the Second World War.

There remain an estimated 10.5 million refugees, according to the UN High Commissioner for Refugees, around the world. Every year, some 20 developed democracies resettle about 100,000 refugees, and from that number Canada annually resettles between 10,000 and 12,000 or 1 out of every 10 refugees resettled globally, second only to the United States with 10 times our population.

The government is also active with our international partners to help those in need. Take, for example, the government's commitment to resettle up to 5,000 Bhutanese refugees from Nepal over several years. We have already welcomed more than 850 Bhutanese refugees in several communities across Canada. In addition, we have also completed the resettlement of more than 3,900 Karens from Thailand.

I was very proud last year to announce a special program to welcome to Canada over the course of three years some 12,000 refugees from the conflict in Iraq. I visited some of these families in Damascus, Syria, last May and I must say I still remain touched and deeply moved after hearing their stories of violence and persecution, often on religious grounds ...

In addition to all those things, we have increased our support for the UNHCR in its important work to help displaced populations on the ground.

In fact, to quote Abraham Abraham, the UNHCR representative to Canada, "Canada, a major settlement country and a major donor to UNHCR activities worldwide, has for the time [*sic*] in its funding of UNHCR's global operations worldwide reached a new level of over $51 million, making this the highest ever annual Canadian grant to the UN refugee agency" ...

In spite of our many achievements ... Canada can and should do more to help those in need of our protection. That is why, as part of this broader package of reform to our refugee systems, including our asylum system, I have announced our intention to increase the number of resettled refugees welcomed to Canada by 2,500 individuals, to 14,000. We would continue to lead the world and set an example for other countries.

I propose, in the context of refugee reform, that we increase by some 20% or $9 million the refugee assistance program to provide initial assistance for the successful integration of government-assisted refugees typically coming from UN camps. I have also announced, as part of these increases and targets, an increase of some 2,000 positions for people to come through the very effective, privately sponsored refugee program ...

There can be no doubt that this government is committed to continuing Canada's proud humanitarian tradition of protecting those in need, but let me turn my attention to the asylum system.

We also have ... a very robust, highly regarded and extraordinarily fair *Charter*-compliant legal system for the consideration of asylum claims made by refugee claimants arriving in Canada. Unfortunately the system has many serious, longstanding problems ... One of the problems is that we have had long, very large backlogs in asylum claims as a permanent feature of the system. The average size of the asylum backlog in our system over the past 10 or 15 years has been 40,000 people waiting for a hearing on their applications for asylum protection in Canada. That means that, typically, people have been waiting about a year to get even a hearing. Right now the backlog is as high as 60,000 people waiting for a decision or a hearing on their applications, meaning that people have to wait 19 months for a hearing. This is not acceptable. We must do better.

If someone manages to escape one of Ahmadinejad's prisons in Iran and he arrives at one of our airports with the scars of torture fresh on his back, we do not offer him a quick pathway to security and protection in Canada. We give him a form and say we will check back with him in 19 months. That is not good enough ...

The truth is this. Too many people try to use our asylum system as a back door to gain entry into Canada, rather than wait patiently to come here through the immigration process. The result is that too many people abuse our system in an effort to jump the immigration queue. There are a number of problems with the current system, which encourage unfounded claims.

How do I make this assessment that there are many unfounded claims? In the last two years, we have seen that some 58% of the claims for asylum made in Canada were subsequently deemed to be unfounded or not in need of our protection. Many of those claims are actually withdrawn by the claimants ...

Of the 2,500 claims made [Hungary], only 3 claims were found to be in need of our protection. Therefore, with six out of ten claims being made, which were subsequently found not to be in need of Canada's protection, and with Canada receiving one of the highest levels of asylum claims in the world with a 60% increase in the number of claims filed between 2006 and 2008, all of this to me indicates that Canada has become, regrettably, a country of choice for those who seek to migrate, not through the normal legal system, but by inventing claims often facilitated by unscrupulous agents and third parties in the immigration industry.

These problems are serious ...What we seek to do in these reforms is to create and reinforce balance that respects our obligation to provide due process that is compliant with the *Charter* and with the United Nations conventions on torture and refugees to asylum claimants, balance that does not restrict access to the asylum system for those who believe they have a need for our protection but balance that will provide faster protection decisions for legitimate refugees while providing faster removals for the many who actually come here seeking to abuse Canada's generosity.

How do we propose to do that? First, there would be an initial information gathering interview that would provide earlier contact with an officer from the IRB than claimants now have. Although these officers would not decide on claims, they would be able to identify claims that appear well founded and could recommend expedited processing for them. What this means for people who have managed to escape persecution is that they would not have to wait a year and a half for protection but could receive it in a matter of weeks ...

The proposed new system would also include, and this is very important, a full appeal for most claimants. Unlike the appeal process proposed in the past and the one dormant in our current legislation, this refugee appeal division, or RAD, would allow for the introduction of new evidence and, in certain circumstances, provide for an oral hearing ...

I will now turn my attention to one of the more contentious aspects of the legislation, which would be to allow for the designation of certain countries as being safe. The nationals from those countries, under these reforms, would still, and I emphasize still, have the same access they currently do to our asylum system. They would still have access to an appeal by our independent judiciary at the Federal Court. They would still have access to a fully *Charter* compliant process that actually exceeds our international obligations but the consideration of those unfounded claims from designated safe countries would move somewhat more expeditiously, reducing the process by about four months by not allowing them to make two appeals, the first one being to the refugee appeal division.

Someone said that this is unfair or inappropriate. No less authority than the UN High Commissioner for Refugees, Antonio Guterres, said here in Ottawa on March 24, "there are indeed safe countries of origin. There are indeed countries in which there is a presumption that refugee claims will probably be not as strong as in other countries." He went on to say that we could not deny access to the initial hearing, which we do not in our proposed reforms, and that it was important to have a fair and transparent process for designating these countries, as do most western European asylum systems whose example we are emulating in these reforms.

I want to be absolutely clear that the proposition is not to create a comprehensive list of all countries designated as safe or unsafe. To the contrary, the criteria would be the following. A country would need to be designated as safe. We propose that this designation process would be in the hands of a panel of senior public servants who would make consultations with UNHCR and would refer to independent human rights supports [*sic*] by NGOs. The criteria would be: if a country is a principal source of asylum claims to Canada, the overwhelming majority of which are unfounded; and if such a country is a signatory to and in compliance with international human rights instruments, which has a strong human rights record and which offers state protection to its citizens, including vulnerable individuals ...

All we are saying is that we need a tool other than the imposition of visas to address those spikes in unfounded claims ...

As I said, these reforms have been broadly endorsed. Eighty-four percent of Canadians say that the government should take steps to reform the refugee determination system. Eighty-one percent of Canadians agree that refugee claims should be dealt with more quickly so that genuine refugees can settle in Canada faster and bogus claimants can be sent home more quick [*sic*]. By a margin of four to one, Canadians agree that more needs to be done to quickly remove from Canada people whose refugee claims are unfounded and rejected.

(*House of Commons Debates, 26 April 2010, pp. 1943-46*)
(*Débats de la Chambre des communes, le 26 avril 2010, pp. 1943-46*)

BILL C-17: COMBATING TERRORISM ACT / LOI C-17: LOI SUR LA
LUTTE CONTRE LE TERRORISME [7]

Hon. Rob Nicholson (Minister of Justice and Attorney General of
Canada):

This bill seeks to reinstate, with additional safeguards, the investigative
hearing and recognizance with conditions provisions that sunsetted in
March 2007 ...

In the March 3, 2010, Speech from the Throne, the government committed to taking steps to safeguard Canada's national security, maintaining
Canada as a peaceful and prosperous country and one of the safest places
in the world in which to live ... There is somewhat of a history in this
place on these powers. These provisions were first introduced in the Anti-
terrorism Act in December 2001 and were subject to a sunset clause.
[T]he ATA also contained a mandatory parliamentary review component,
which led to two separate reviews: one by a Senate special committee and,
in this place, by two subcommittees, the last being the Public Safety and
National Security Subcommittee.

As the committees were winding down their review of the ATA, including
the investigative hearing and the recognizance with conditions powers,
the sunset date on these provisions was fast approaching. As a result, the
government introduced a resolution in the House of Commons that proposed to extend these provisions for three years. Unfortunately, the powers
were not extended by a vote of 159 to 124 and the provisions, therefore,
expired on March 1, 2007.

It is important to recognize that the reports published by the parliamentary committees that reviewed the ATA were generally supportive of the
powers contained in Bill C-17 and called for their extension.

Since that time, attempts have been made by this government to reinstate
these important tools. First, Bill S-3 was introduced in the Senate in the
39th Parliament and contained additional safeguards and technical changes to respond to the recommendations of the committees reviewing the
ATA. The Senate passed Bill S-3 on March 6, 2008, with a few amendments,
but it died on the order paper when the election of 2008 was called.

More recently, in the last session of Parliament, this government again
made efforts at bringing this important piece of legislation back to life,
through Bill C-19. Bill C-19 contained the amendments made by the Senate to the former bill. In summary, these were making mandatory a review

---

[7] *An Act to Amend the Criminal Code (Investigative Hearing and Recognizance with Conditions) / Loi modifiant le Code criminel (investigation et engagement assorti de conditions),*
introduced in the House of Commons on 23 April 2010.

of these provisions by a parliamentary committee within five years; deleting some words in the recognizance with conditions provisions to track *Charter* jurisprudence; and making a technical amendment for consistency. These changes are also now found in Bill C-17.

[T]he investigative hearing and the recognizance with conditions provisions of this bill ... would achieve the appropriate balance between the respect for human rights without compromising effectiveness and utility. First, with the investigative hearing provisions, the courts would be empowered to question, as witnesses, those persons who are reasonably believed to have information about a past or future terrorism offence. The key here is that the person required to attend an investigative hearing is treated as a witness, not someone who is accused of a crime. It is important to note that witnesses could be questioned under this scheme without the commencement of any prosecution.

Earlier, I noted the balance between human rights and security. In this regard, the investigative hearing provision would be equipped with numerous safeguards for witnesses in accordance with the *Charter of Rights* and the *Canadian Bill of Rights* ... First, the attorney general must consent before the investigative hearing can be initiated. Second, an independent judge must agree that an investigative hearing is warranted, finding in particular that it is believed on reasonable grounds that a terrorism offence has been, or will be committed, the information concerning the offence or the location of a suspect is likely to be obtained as a result of the order, and in all cases, reasonable attempts have been made to obtain the information by other means. Previously, this safeguard only applied to future terrorism offences and not past ones. Third, section 707 of the Criminal Code, which sets out the maximum period of time in relation to which an arrested witnesses can be detained at a criminal trial, would apply to a person arrested to attend an investigative hearing. This is a new safeguard that is added to Bill C-17, something that was not in the original legislation. Fourth, the person named in the investigative hearing would have the right to retain and instruct counsel at any stage of the proceeding. Finally, there is a robust prohibition against the state using the information or evidence derived from the information against the person ...

The recognizance with conditions proposal would permit the court to impose on a person such reasonable conditions as the court considers necessary to prevent terrorist activity ...

We all know that terrorism is not a new phenomenon. Since the attacks on the United States in September 2001, the world has witnessed numerous acts of terrorism but, more important, as the recent guilty pleas and convictions in terrorism cases in our country have shown us, Canada is not immune to the threat of terrorism.

We as a government and as parliamentarians have a responsibility to protect our citizens. In doing so, we must provide our law enforcement agencies with the necessary tools to achieve that objective. It is equally our responsibility to do so in a balanced way with due regard for human rights. That was our goal with this reform and I believe that we have achieved it.

The investigative hearing and the recognizance with conditions powers are necessary, effective and reasonable.

(*House of Commons Debates, 20 September 2010, pp. 4079-81*)
(*Débats de la Chambre des communes, le 20 septembre 2010, pp. 4079-81*)

BILL C-42: STRENGTHENING AVIATION SECURITY ACT / LOI C-42: LOI SUR LE RENFORCEMENT DE LA SÛRETÉ AÉRIENNE [8]

Mr. Dave MacKenzie (Parliamentary Secretary to the Minister of Public Safety):

The bill before us today would help to ensure that Canadian business people and tourists who choose to travel by air can continue to access certain destinations in the fastest and most cost-effective way possible while also building on our ongoing efforts to enhance aviation security in conjunction with our international partners.

It also would allow Canadian air carriers to comply with the secure flight regime in the United States by providing passenger information to the Transportation Security Administration 72 hours before departing for destinations such as Latin America or the Caribbean. At the moment, airline carriers themselves are required to match passenger information against U.S. no-fly and selectee terrorist watch lists if their flight destination is to anywhere in the United States.

The previous government passed legislation in 2001 so that Canadian airline carriers could do this, although concerns have subsequently been raised about privacy issues and the number of false matches. Secure flight is expected to reduce the number of false matches by transferring responsibility for watch list matching from the airlines to the Transportation Security Administration for all U.S. domestic flights, as well as for all international flights to the U.S. and those which fly through U.S. air space. The TSA has also developed a comprehensive privacy plan to incorporate privacy laws and practices into all areas of secure flight.

---

[8] *An Act to Amend the Aeronautics Act / Loi modifiant la Loi sur l'aéronautique*, introduced in the House of Commons on 17 June 2010. The bill received royal assent on 23 March 2011: SC 2011, c 9.

The legislation before us today is important for a number of reasons. First, I want to point out that any nation, including the U.S. and Canada, has the sovereign right to control its own air space. International laws do recognize that airlines have the right to fly over any country in the world but they also recognize that each state has a right to regulate aircraft entering into, within or departing from its territory. Moreover, the Chicago Convention expressly recognizes that each state has sovereignty over its own air space. Article 11 of the convention requires compliance with:

> ... the laws and regulations of a contracting State relating to the admission to or departure from its territory of aircraft engaged in international air navigation.

Secure flight is therefore in accordance with the international rules of which Canada is a signatory ... As a sovereign nation, Canada could say that this country will choose not to comply with secure flight rules but that would force Canadian airline companies to access destinations, such as Mexico, by flying outside of American air space, substantially increasing travel times and costs.

The second reason that this legislation before us today is important relates to our commitment to protect the safety and security of Canadians ... Our government has worked to prevent global terrorism. We have strengthened aviation security and taken steps to protect the safety of air travellers through actions and measures, including a new passenger protect program, to keep people who may pose an immediate security threat from boarding commercial flights and a new air cargo security pilot test program. We have introduced legislation to starve terrorists of financing. Our government has openly condemned groups with links to terrorism and has worked with the United Nations and our allies to prevent terrorism.

We have also introduced measures to allow the RCMP to expand criminal background checks for workers with access to secure areas in Canada's airports, people such as baggage handlers, catering crews and airplane groomers and flight crews, among others.

What is more, we took additional steps to strengthen aviation security in the week following December 25, 2009, when there was an attempted terrorist attack on a flight bound for Detroit. Those measures include strengthening explosive trace detection, new full body scanners and steps to develop a passenger behaviour observation program. It included funding of $1.5 billion over five years to help the Canadian Air Transport Security Authority strengthen the security of our aviation system and protect air travellers. It also included a full review into the spending efficiency and structure of Canadian Air Transport Security Authority.

Most recently, our government announced the air cargo security program, a $95.7 million investment that will be phased in over five years building on the air cargo initiative unveiled by the Prime Minister in June 2006. Of course we share views through several multinational discussions on global aviation security ...

We need to continue to strengthen security within our borders. We also need to continue to work with our international partners to ensure not only the safety of Canadians but also the safety and security of our allies and partners. This is what Bill C-42 is all about. It is about working with our partners to enhance international aviation security while also ensuring that individual privacy rights are respected ... Bill C-42 is not a large piece of legislation but it is an important one. It supports the commitment ... to protect the safety and security of air travellers ... to combat terrorist threats both at home and abroad [... and] to ensure that air travel remains safe and that Canadians can access destinations south of the border in the most efficient and cost effective ways possible.

(*House of Commons Debates,* 19 October 2010, pp. 5048-49)
(*Débats de la Chambre des communes, le* 19 octobre 2010, pp. 5048-49)

BILL C-46: CANADA-PANAMA FREE TRADE ACT / LOI C-46: LOI SUR LE LIBRE-ÉCHANGE ENTRE LE CANADA ET LE PANAMA [9]

Hon. Peter Van Loan (Minister of International Trade):

Canada made the big jump into free trade with our free trade agreement with the United States ... Canadians embrace free trade. Our trade with the United States has doubled since that time and our trade with Mexico, as part of the North American Free Trade Agreement, has increased almost five times.

[O]ur government is firmly committed to free trade. However, the United States will remain, certainly for my lifetime, the major priority of Canada in free trade as 70% of our trade is with the United States and it is a relationship we must constantly tend to. We did that when we became the only country in the world to achieve a waiver from the buy American provisions of the U.S. stimulus program, and we continue to stand up for Canadian

---

[9] *An Act to Implement the Free Trade Agreement between Canada and the Republic of Panama, the Agreement on the Environment between Canada and the Republic of Panama and the Agreement on Labour Cooperation between Canada and the Republic of Panama / Loi portant mise en oeuvre de l'Accord de libre-échange entre le Canada et la République du Panama, de l'Accord sur l'environnement entre le Canada et la République du Panama et de l'Accord de coopération dans le domaine du travail entre le Canada et la République du Panama,* introduced in the House of Commons on 23 September 2010.

businesses and protect our access to that critical market. That will remain our number one priority.

However, we have three major initiatives underway: first, the European Union free trade talks; second, our initiative with regard to India, which looks very positive at this point in time; and third, an effort to carve out for Canada a role in the Americas, not dissimilar to the one Australia already has with regard to the Asian marketplace.

We have our existing free trade agreements with Chile and Costa Rica, which are being improved and enhanced by this government. We have the free trade agreement implemented with Peru and the recently passed free trade agreement with Colombia. We have had negotiations with the Dominican Republic, the countries of the Caribbean community, and the Central American four. Altogether, we can see that Canada is working very hard to achieve that special, privileged position of having a dominant free trading position within the Americas.

Indeed, it is as part of that overall strategy of being a key trading country in our hemisphere ... that we also now add the concept of a free trade agreement with Panama. I was very proud and pleased to sign that agreement in May with Roberto Henríquez, my counterpart ...

Panama has had one of the fastest growing economies in the Americas. Its real gross domestic product growth in 2008 was 10.7%. Even during the economic downturn it posted positive growth in 2009. Panama's real gross domestic product is expected to rise even further in 2010.

Panama is also a strategic hub for the region. It is also an important logistical platform for commercial activity. As a link between two great oceans, Panama, and of course the historic and well-understood Panama Canal, is vital to global trade ...

Our exporters have been active in the Panamanian market. In 2009, Canada's two-way merchandise trade with Panama was $132.1 million, and our trade has been largely complementary. Upon implementation of the free trade agreement, things will improve significantly. Panama will immediately lift tariffs on some 99.9% of all non-agricultural imports from Canada, with the remaining tariffs to be phased out over five to 15 years. Tariffs will also be lifted immediately on 94% of Canada's agricultural exports to Panama.

These outcomes directly benefit a number of sectors that already have established business ties in Panama, including agriculture and agri-food products, pharmaceuticals, pulp and paper, vehicles, machinery, and information and communications technology products, among others.

We are also pleased that Panama has recognized Canada's inspection systems for beef and pork and has removed its previous ban on Canadian beef ...

Panama is also an established destination for Canadian direct investment abroad. At the end of 2008, the stock of Canadian direct investment in Panama totalled $93 million ...

Government procurement has also been a key priority in our deepening trade relationship with Panama. One of the key drivers is the ongoing Panama Canal expansion and its associated projects. The Panama Canal makes Panama a natural centre for global trade. In fact, Panama handles 5% of global trade and has some of the world's largest export processing zones. The planned Panama Canal expansion, which is actually under construction, is only reinforcing its position as a nexus for international importers and exporters.

The canal expansion is a $5.3 billion project. It provides numerous opportunities to Canadian businesses through subcontracts and satellite projects, which will be further consolidated by this free trade agreement. We are calling on the opposition to consider and approve this free trade agreement very quickly so that our workers and our businesses can profit from the opportunities that exist right now.

The government procurement provisions in the Canada-Panama free trade agreement guarantee that Canadian suppliers will have non-discriminatory access to a broad range of procurement opportunities, including those under the Panama Canal Authority. Projects, including those associated with the canal expansion, may also lead to increased goods exports from Canadian manufacturers that have expertise in infrastructure.

We are also proud of the work done to protect labour rights and environmental responsibilities. Of course, in general, freer trade and increased prosperity have been shown to aid in improving human development indices. Of course, we have with this agreement, as we have had with others, parallel accords dealing with labour and the environment.

For all these reasons, the Panama agreement is a good deal for Canada, but it is also a good deal because it ensures that Canada remains competitive in the Panamanian marketplace. Panama has an active trade agenda with many partners, including the United States and the European Union. For this reason, time is, as I said, of the essence. Any delay of this bill would hurt Canadian businesses that are eager to compete and capitalize on the opportunities in Panama.

If Canada can establish access to the Panamanian market before our competitors take hold, it will give our companies an advantage, a real foothold, in doing business there.

Panama is also negotiating a trade agreement with Colombia and is exploring trade deals with the European Free Trade Association, the Caribbean community, Peru, Korea, and others ...

Free trade is a reason for Canada's prosperity and Canada's success. It is the reason we are working so ambitiously to put in place opportunities for Canadian workers all around the world. Our free trade agreement with Panama is part of that plan. It is part of our strategic approach to the region of the Americas and to this hemisphere, and it is one reason Canadian workers and businesses can expect to succeed more in the future and enjoy greater prosperity in the future.

(*House of Commons Debates, 29 September 2010, pp. 4545-47*)
(*Débats de la Chambre des communes, le 29 septembre 2010, pp. 4545-47*)

BILL C-47: SUSTAINING CANADA'S ECONOMIC RECOVERY ACT / LOI C-47: LOI DE SOUTIEN DE LA REPRISE ÉCONOMIQUE AU CANADA [10]

Mr. Ted Menzies (Parliamentary Secretary to the Minister of Finance):

This bill represents a key component of Canada's economic action plan, including many important measures from budget 2010, with real support for families, consumers, businesses and taxpayers. We heard last week that nearly 23,000 job-creating projects across Canada, supported under the plan, are currently under way or already completed. The continued implementation of the economic action plan through economic legislation such as sustaining Canada's economic recovery act will help ensure Canada meets the ongoing global economic challenges head on.

Indeed, Canada has met the recent global economic storm with an aggressive and effective response that has served as a model for other countries to follow. Bank of Montreal deputy chief economist Doug Porter has declared that Canada has had "arguably one of the most successful stimulus programs in the industrialized world" ... Let us look at the facts. Canada is the only G7 country to have virtually recouped economic output and private domestic activity lost since the start of the recession. Canada is the only G7 country to have posted significant positive job growth since the summer of 2009, in fact creating almost 430,000 net new jobs since July 2009. Canada's total government net debt to GDP ratio is projected to remain the lowest by far in the G7. What is more, according to the IMF

---

[10] *A Second Act to Implement Certain Provisions of the Budget Tabled in Parliament on March 4, 2010 and Other Measures / Loi no 2 portant exécution de certaines dispositions du budget déposé au Parlement le 4 mars 2010 et mettant en oeuvre d'autres mesures,* introduced in the House of Commons on 30 September 2010. The bill received royal assent on 15 December 2010: SC 2010, c 25.

and the OECD, Canada is expected to be the fastest growing economy in the G7 over the 2010-11 period ...

Internationally, Canada has been held up as a model of strong economic leadership to follow. The BBC said: "As Americans and Europeans face deficits and drastic government cuts, Canada's economy is recovering from only a mild recession. ... The Canadians, it seems, have answers for even the toughest puzzles ... [I]n this economy, we all want to be Canadian."

The *Los Angeles Times* remarked:

> [O]n such critical issues as the deficit, unemployment, immigration and prospering in the global economy, Canada seems to be outper-forming the United States. And in doing so, it is offering examples of successful strategies that Americans might consider ... Canada's financial house is tidy and secure.

The OECD recently commented:

> I think Canada looks good — it shines, actually. Canada could even be considered a safe haven.

All that said, we cannot be complacent or smug. Uncertainty remains. Beyond our borders, the global economic recovery is far from secure. This is especially true in the United States, which is, of course, our largest trad-ing partner, where grave economic challenges persist.

At home too many Canadians are still looking for work. Without a doubt, the economy must remain our priority. Canadians expect nothing less ...

[T]he Sustaining Canada's Economic Recovery Act, an Act that would help Canadian families get ahead by, for instance, indexing the working income tax benefit, as well as by further strengthening federally regulated pension plans and allowing a 10-year carry forward for registered disability savings plan grants and bonds. It is an Act that would help cut red tape for taxpayers by allowing them to request online notices from the Canada Revenue Agency, registered charities with disbursement quota reform and job-creating small businesses by allowing them to file their taxes semi-annually instead of monthly. It is an [A]ct that would help protect consum-ers by improving the complaint process when dealing with banks and the financial services industry. It is an Act that would close down tax loopholes by better targeting tax incentives for employee stock options and addressing aggressive tax planning related to tax-free savings accounts. It is an Act that would promote clean energy with an accelerated capital cost allowance for clean energy generation ... This Act, as a key component in imple-menting Canada's economic action plan, would help keep our economy moving in the right direction. The Act would help protect our economy against the ongoing global economic turmoil during this fragile period and keep Canada's economic advantage.

(*House of Commons Debates,* 7 *October 2010, pp. 4858-60*)
(*Débats de la Chambre des communes, le 7 octobre 2010, pp. 4858-60*)

BILL C-49: PREVENTING HUMAN SMUGGLERS FROM ABUSING CANADA'S IMMIGRATION SYSTEM ACT / LOI C-49: LOI VISANT À EMPÊCHER LES PASSEURS D'UTILISER ABUSIVEMENT LE SYSTÈME D'IMMIGRATION CANADIEN [11]

Hon. Jason Kenney (for the Minister of Public Safety):

Canada is very proud of its long tradition of being a place of migration for people from around the world. We receive more newcomers than any other country in the developed world, 0.8% of our population, every year as new permanent residents.

We are also proud of our long humanitarian tradition of being a place of protection and refuge for victims of persecution and violence, those who need our protection. This goes back long into our history, in fact to the days of the arrival of the United Empire Loyalists, the Black Loyalists, the Underground Railroad, the eastern European refugees before the war, the refugees from Hungary and Soviet and Communist oppression after the war, and, most famously, the over 60,000 Indo Chinese who were welcomed by Canadians in 1979 and 1980. This underscores our long and deep humanitarian tradition as a place of protection.

Canada receives more resettled refugees than any other developed country in the world. This is so important to Canadians that our government announced earlier this year an increase of 20% in the number of resettled refugees who we will receive. That means that, beginning next year, we will welcome some 14,000 refugees in need of our protection each and every year, which is in addition to those who come to Canada making asylum claims that are assessed by our Immigration and Refugee Board and through various appeals and administrative appeals in our legal system.

One of the problems this Parliament recognized was the abuse of that asylum system, which is why Bill C-11, *Balanced Refugee Reform Act*, was adopted unanimously by this Parliament following all party co-operation

---

[11] *An Act to Amend the Immigration and Refugee Protection Act, the Balanced Refugee Reform Act and the Marine Transportation Security Act / Loi modifiant la Loi sur l'immigration et la protection des réfugiés, la Loi sur des mesures de réforme équitables concernant les réfugiés et la Loi sur la sûreté du transport maritime,* introduced in the House of Commons on 21 October 2010.

in the spring in order to significantly speed up the process of refugee determination, providing protection to bona fide refugees and the removal of those who seek to abuse Canada's generosity.

However, Canadians are deeply concerned with a particularly pernicious crime, a crime that exploits vulnerable people in their dream to come to Canada, the dangerous crime of human smuggling. In the past year, it is well known that Canada has received two large vessels on our west coast, together carrying nearly 600 illegal migrants to our shores, people who, based on our intelligence, had paid criminal smuggling syndicates some $50,000 each in order to come to Canada in the most dangerous and exploitative way possible.

The remarkable openness of Canada to immigration in general and refugee protection in particular, which makes possible our very generous approach to immigration, is dependent on public confidence in the system ... Canadians demand an immigration system that is characterized by a sense of fair play and a rule of law ... We know that every year hundreds and potentially thousands of people around the world fall victim to the dangerous ruse of smuggling syndicates ... Bill C-49 proposes ... strong but fair remedies [to combat this].

There are approximately three or four criminal syndicates operating in [Asia] that have a long history of being involved in the arms smuggling trade. Because there has been an end to hostilities in the Sri Lankan civil war, those syndicates have now decided to smuggle and to traffic a different commodity, which is human beings. They have refocused their logistical ability to selling people the opportunity to be smuggled illegally to Canada.

I have been told by our partners in the region that they believe these syndicates have the capacity to deliver several large steel hulled vessels with the ability to bring in each hundreds of illegal smuggled migrants to Canada each year. Prospectively thousands of people are being smuggled to our country in this dangerous fashion ... What we have seen since the arrival of the last smuggling vessel is a fundamental and very disturbing decline in public support for immigration in general and refugee protection in particular ...

[I]t is evident there are legitimate refugees in need of protection in Southeast Asia. It is also true, according to the United Nations High Commissioner for Refugees, that it is always preferable to find a local or regional protection solution for those who are bona fide refugees and to do everything possible to prevent them from being exploited by trafficking syndicates. That is why we have begun preliminary discussions with our international partners, including Australia, which obviously has a great stake in this issue, and with the United Nations High Commissioner for

Refugees to pursue the possibility of some form of regional protection framework in the Southeast Asian region.

In part that would entail encouraging the countries now being used as transit points for smuggling and trafficking to offer at least temporary protection to those deemed by the UN in need of protection and then for countries such as Canada to provide, to some extent, reasonable resettlement opportunities for those deemed to be bona fide refugees, which is something we are pursuing.

However, to be honest, that is a mid to long-term solution. Working on that with the UN and our international partners will not stop the fact that criminal networks in Southeast Asian countries are planning to smuggle their customers to Canada. They are in the process right now. People have already paid their upfront fee and are sitting in waiting positions in parts of Southeast Asia. Vessels have been acquired. Officials have been, shall we say, induced to co-operate with these networks. The operations are not abstract. This is not a possibility. This is not a theory. This is a real and present reality and we must react with real, present and current action to disincentivize the smuggling networks.

It is also true, insofar as we are talking about a flow of illegally smuggled migrants of Tamil origin, that we acknowledge that Canadians have a stake in seeing a just and durable peace in Sri Lanka. We acknowledge that the Tamil people have legitimate aspirations and that they deserve to be protected from violence and persecution. That is why, through the Department of Foreign Affairs, our High Commission in Colombo and through multilateral institutions, we continue to strongly encourage the government of Sri Lanka to make every effort to find a just resolution to the legitimate aspirations of its Tamil minority. That is one important issue. A regional protection framework is another important issue.

Perhaps the most important element in combatting the smuggling is to stop the boats from leaving the transit countries in the first place. That is why our government has directed relevant security and intelligence agencies to increase their presence and capability in the transit countries, partly to assist the transit countries in improving their capacity to detect fraudulent documents and smuggling networks and to gather better and actionable intelligence to prevent people from being loaded on to the vessels in the first place.

In this respect, I would note that two weeks ago the Royal Thai Police detained some 150 individuals who were in the country illegally, without status. Apparently they were planning to board vessels to be smuggled possibly to Canada. Therefore, that work is being done as well. There is increased and improved police and intelligence co-operation in the region among ourselves, the Australians and the transit countries.

However, should a vessel successfully leave a transit country, and we are talking about these leaky, decommissioned cargo vessels that people are loaded onto like cattle to take the dangerous voyage across the Pacific, and arrive in our territorial waters, Canada, after the adoption of Bill C-49, will continue to fully honour our humanitarian, domestic and international legal obligations to provide refugee protection ...

We do need to send a strong message to the smugglers, which is why Bill C-49 proposes strong mandatory minimum prison sentences for those involved in smuggling operations. Those who are involved in smuggling under 50 people would face a mandatory minimum prison sentence of at least 3 years. If there are one of two aggravating factors involved, they would face a mandatory minimum of five years. If the group is over 50 individuals, they could face a mandatory minimum of 5 years unless there was an aggravating factor, such as having put the life or safety of their customers in danger, in which case a 10 year mandatory minimum. We believe this will help to cause the smugglers and the crews that work for them to think twice before targeting Canada for their sordid trade. We also propose massive new penalties for the shipowners.

(*House of Commons Debates,* 27 *October 2010, pp. 5415-18*)
(*Débats de la Chambre des communes, le 27 octobre 2010, pp. 5415-18*)

BILL C-61: ASSETS OF CORRUPT FOREIGN OFFICIALS ACT / LOI C-61: LOI SUR LE BLOCAGE DES BIENS DE DIRIGEANTS ÉTRANGERS CORROMPUS [12]

Mr. Deepak Obhrai (Parliamentary Secretary to the Minister of Foreign Affairs):

[The House has] worked diligently to ensure this bill has a quick passage in the House and becomes law in the shortest possible time. Collectively, members in the House have sent a message that a dictator and his family, including officials associated with the regime, will not find a safe haven in

---

[12] *An Act to Provide for the Taking of Restrictive Measures in respect of the Property of Officials and Former Officials of Foreign States and of Their Family Members / Loi prévoyant la prise de mesures restrictives à l'égard des biens de dirigeants et anciens dirigeants d'États étrangers et de ceux des membres de leur famille,* introduced in the House of Commons on 3 March 2011. The bill received royal assent on 23 March 2011: SC 2011, c 10. Bill C-61 was fast-tracked in the House to third reading with no second reading. See motion by Minister O'Connor, agreed to, 10 March 2011, *Hansard* at p 8870).

Canada for stealing money or assets from their citizens. This bill has all the safeguards required to ensure compliance with all Canadian laws.

(*House of Commons Debates, 10 March 2011, p. 8872*)
(*Débats de la Chambre des communes, le 10 mars 201, p. 8872*)

STATEMENTS IN RESPONSE TO QUESTIONS / DÉCLARATIONS EN RÉPONSE AUX QUESTIONS

ENVIRONMENT / ENVIRONNEMENT

Biodiversity / Biodiversité

M. Bernard Bigras (Rosemont — La Petite-Patrie):

Le Canada a tenté pendant quatre ans de diluer le Protocole de Carthagène sur la biodiversité pour refuser ensuite de le ratifier. Samedi dernier à Nagoya, un nouveau protocole a fait l'objet d'un accord définitif. Ce nouveau protocole définit un régime de responsabilité pour les producteurs d'OGM et de réparation des dommages causés aux écosystèmes. Est-ce que le Canada entend signer et ratifier le nouveau protocole ou va-t-il maintenir l'attitude de fermeture complète qui a été la sienne vis-à-vis du Protocole de Carthagène?

Mr. Mark Warawa (Parliamentary Secretary to the Minister of the Environment):

The importance of the environment and biodiversity and protecting the environment [is well known] to this government. Canada was instrumental in drafting the United Nations Convention on Biological Diversity. We were the first industrialized country to ratify the convention and we hosted the international secretary in Montreal. We have a strong record that we are proud of on the environment.

(*House of Commons Debates, 19 October 2010, p. 5063*)
(*Débats de la Chambre des communes, le 19 octobre 2010, p. 5063*)

Climate Change / Changements climatiques

M. David McGuinty (Ottawa-Sud):

L'Accord de Copenhague stipule qu'il faut réduire les émissions de gaz à effet de serre selon les données scientifiques. Il exige que les mesures soient conformes aux données scientifiques. Les États-Unis et l'Union européenne proposent des augmentations majeures du financement de la recherche sur le climat. Pourquoi le gouvernement conservateur, qui a signé cet accord il y a à peine trois mois, refuse-t-il de renouveler le financement de la

Fondation canadienne pour les sciences du climat et de l'atmosphère? À quoi s'oppose-t-on exactement, sur le plan scientifique?

Hon. Jim Prentice (Minister of the Environment):

The matter my friend raises in the House goes back to 2007-08. [T]he government has agreed with the Copenhagen court. As of today 106 nations agree with the Government of Canada. In addition, more than 90% of the world's emissions are under this agreement. The world supports Copenhagen.

(House of Commons Debates, 15 March 2010, p. 449)
(Débats de la Chambre des communes, le 15 mars 2010, p.449)

Mr. Bruce Hyer (Thunder Bay — Superior North):

A major environmental climate change conference starts in Cochabamba, Bolivia in only three days. More than 70 countries, such as France, Russia and Spain, will be there, including the majority of those least developed nations, those whose populations will bear the heaviest burden from climate change. [W]ho will represent Canada or will our seat at the table be empty again?

Mr. Mark Warawa (Parliamentary Secretary to the Minister of the Environment):

Our government, along with 117 other countries representing over 90% of the world's emissions, have signed on to the Copenhagen accord. This week the IEA executive director, Nobuo Tanaka, praised Canada's recent climate change targets to reduce greenhouse gas emissions by 17% below 2005 levels by 2020. We already know that our emissions are going down. Under this government, we are getting it done.

(House of Commons Debates, 16 April 2010, p. 1607)
(Débats de la Chambre des communes, le 16 avril 2010, p.1607)

M. Bernard Bigras (Rosemont — La Petite-Patrie):

Le dossier de la lutte aux changements climatiques illustre le parti pris des conservateurs en faveur des pétrolières canadiennes au détriment de l'économie verte du Québec. En refusant de mettre en place un plan effi-cace de lutte aux GES, le gouvernement fédéral protège les sables bitumi-neux mais nuit à l'économie québécoise qui tirerait profit d'un marché du carbone à Montréal. Quand le gouvernement conservateur prendra-t-il conscience de tout le tort qu'il cause au Québec et à son économie en refu-sant de s'attaquer aux changements climatiques?

L'hon. Jim Prentice (Ministre de l'Environnement):

Les organisations internationales respectées applaudissent nos efforts. Par exemple, le rapport Pew, de mars 2010, a classé le Canada en sixième position pour les investissements dans les énergies vertes. Aussi, en avril 2010, l'Agence mondiale de l'énergie a félicité l'engagement du Canada à augmenter sa production d'électricité propre. Hier, la même agence a reconnue les efforts importants du Canada pour le développement du stockage du carbone.

(House of Commons Debates, 17 June 2010, p. 4013)
(Débats de la Chambre des communes, le 17 juin 2010, p. 4013)

Oil Spills / Marées noires

Hon. Jack Layton (Toronto — Danforth):

The impact of th[e] environmental [oil spill] catastrophe in the gulf is going to have an impact for decades to come. People all around the world are very concerned ... [T]he G8 [should] put this issue on the agenda. In addition, in the wake of this disaster, Nunavut Tunngavik, Nunavut's land claim organization, has quite naturally asked for a conference on marine safety issues, including the whole question of oil spill response capacity off our Arctic communities. Will the Prime Minister show some leadership and call these two conferences?

Right Hon. Stephen Harper (Prime Minister):

The situation truly is horrific. It is an environmental catastrophe unlike anything we have seen in quite a long time. The behaviour of the companies in question is completely unacceptable and would be completely unacceptable in this country. There are strong rules in Canada. There are rules for relief wells. The National Energy Board does not allow drilling unless it is convinced that the safety of the environment and the safety of workers can be assured. [W]e will continue to enforce stronger environmental standards in this country ... That is the bottom line, and this government will not tolerate the kind of situation we see in the Gulf of Mexico.

(House of Commons Debates, 3 May, 2010, p. 2267)
(Débats de la Chambre des communes, le 3 mai 2010, p. 2267)

Mrs. Tilly O'Neill-Gordon (Miramichi):

[What are] the latest actions taken by our government to assist our American neighbours [in the Gulf of Mexico]?

Hon. Gail Shea (Minister of Fisheries and Oceans):

Canada and the United States have a proud tradition of helping each other in times of need and the situation in the Gulf of Mexico certainly is one of those times. Yesterday I was very proud to announce that the Canadian Coast Guard will provide the Americans with 3,000 metres of oil spill containment boom, in addition to the DFO experts already in the field. Our government will continue to work closely with the United States so that we can ensure and maximize Canada's contribution to the cleanup effort.

(*House of Commons Debates, 7 June 2010, p. 3471*)
(*Débats de la Chambre des communes, le 7 juin 2010, p. 3471*)

Radioactive Waste / Déchets radioactifs

Mr. Nathan Cullen (Skeena — Bulkley Valley):

The current government is now considering a plan to allow the shipping of 1,600 tonnes of radioactive waste across the Great Lakes along the St. Lawrence Seaway. This dangerous plan will threaten our environment with the catastrophic nuclear contamination of our largest waterway. The Canadian Nuclear Safety Commission tried to get this through under the radar with no debate and no consultation. Will the minister demand a full environmental assessment, including public hearings, into this reckless plan?

L'hon. Christian Paradis (ministre des Ressources naturelles):

La Commission canadienne de la sûreté nucléaire a reçu une demande de permis de la part de Bruce Power, justement afin de transporter 16 générateurs de vapeur en Suède. Une audience publique sera tenue par la commission les 28 et 29 septembre prochains. La demande sera étudiée en bonne et due forme.

(*House of Commons Debates, 27 September 2010, p. 4424*)
(*Débats de la Chambre des communes, le 27 septembre 2010, p. 4424*)

Seal Hunt / Chasse au loup-marin

Mrs. Tilly O'Neill-Gordon (Miramichi):

[What are the] developments at the European General Court on the important issue [of the seal hunt]?

Hon. Gail Shea (Minister of Fisheries and Oceans):

Yesterday, the European General Court confirmed that European markets would remain open to Canadian seal products pending further resolution of an Inuit-led court challenge. Our government welcomes this news and will continue to stand with the Inuit and with all Canadian sealers to defend this legitimate industry.

(*House of Commons Debates, 21 October 2010, p. 5186*)
(*Débats de la Chambre des communes, le 21 octobre 2010, p. 5186*)

Water / Eau

Ms. Linda Duncan (Edmonton — Strathcona):

In honour of the United Nations World Water Day, will the government finally table the long promised aboriginal safe drinking water law, a law to ban bulk water exports, and assert federal powers to address serious climate and pollution threats to Canada's precious water?

Hon. Jim Prentice (Minister of the Environment):

This is World Water Day and it draws attention to the excellent work that this government is doing. I am sure the hon. member meant to point out and draw to the country's attention the historic gazetting on Saturday of Canada's first national waste water standards, which will regulate 4,000 facilities across this country, as well as the other investments, in particular those that relate to the Great Lakes. We also announced today the Government of Canada's support for the United Nations GEMS/Water Programme to do important work internationally.

(*House of Commons Debates, 22 March 2010, p. 755*)
(*Débats de la Chambre des communes, le 22 mars 2010, p. 755*)

Mr. Francis Scarpaleggia (Lac-Saint-Louis):

The previous ... government took major steps to protect Canada's freshwater from export, including amending the International Boundary Waters Treaty Act. Why has the Conservative government not acted in any way to protect against the possibility of future exports of this vital Canadian resource?

Hon. Jim Prentice (Minister of the Environment):

We are opposed to any bulk water exports, and our position on that is quite clear. There is an extensive layer of provincial regulations in place right now that deal with this issue ... This past weekend ... this government has brought in [the regulations] to deal with the discharge of municipal sewage into our natural water system. We have been pursuing these regulations for a generation in this country. They would apply to some 4,000 municipal waste water facilities across the country.

(*House of Commons Debates, 29 March 2010, p. 1052*)

(*Débats de la Chambre des communes, le 29 mars 2010, p. 1052*)

FOREIGN AFFAIRS / AFFAIRES ÉTRANGÈRES

Afghanistan

Hon. Ujjal Dosanjh (Vancouver South):

In 2007, Chris Alexander, Canada's former ambassador and deputy UN special representative in Afghanistan, had warned the government that Asadullah Khalid was the culprit behind the murder of five UN workers and possibly behind other attacks on the internationals in Kandahar. Why did the Conservative government continue to protect Khalid from being fired by Karzai? And, why did it continue to pay $12,000 per month to this butcher of Kandahar?

Hon. Peter Kent (Minister of State of Foreign Affairs (Americas)):

The Government of Canada does not appoint governors in Afghanistan. The independent Government of Afghanistan appoints its own governors. This is true today and that was true then. The individual in question, in fact, was removed as governor some time ago ... Military and diplomatic officials spoke to those allegations last fall before the special committee on Afghanistan. The Government of Canada regularly questions the Government of Afghanistan on those and other human rights issues.

(*House of Commons Debates, 13 April 2010, p. 1419*)

(*Débats de la Chambre des communes, le 13 avril 2010, p. 1419*)

Africa / Afrique

M. Jean Dorion (Longueuil — Pierre-Boucher):

Après avoir retiré sept pays africains de la liste prioritaire d'aide publique au développement, le gouvernement se prépare à fermer d'autres ambassades en Afrique. Le ministre des Affaires étrangères peut-il nous confirmer qu'aucune ambassade canadienne en Afrique ne cessera ses activités?

Hon. Peter Kent (Minister of State of Foreign Affairs (Americas)):

Every year the Government of Canada property holdings reviews our embassies abroad. An ongoing program is in place to review property and decisions are made based on value principles applied in these decisions. As part of the ongoing review, 12 to 15 properties every year are sold on average in any given year. The normal practice is to replace them with a more appropriate property.

(*House of Commons Debates, 19 November 2010, p. 6189*)
(*Débats de la Chambre des communes, le 19 novembre 2010, p. 6189*)

Arctic Sovereignty / Souveraineté dans l'Arctique

Mr. James Rajotte (Edmonton — Leduc):

What [is] our government doing to defend Canada's sovereignty in the north?

Hon. Lawrence Cannon (Minister of Foreign Affairs):

Our claim is long-standing [and] is well-established and based on historic title. I will personally be able to reassert Canada's sovereignty at a meeting on the Arctic with the Arctic foreign ministers next week here in Gatineau. We have taken real action with our new Arctic patrol ships.

(*House of Commons Debates, 18 March 2010, p. 649*)
(*Débats de la Chambre des communes, le 18 mars 2010, p. 649*)

Canada's International Year / Année internationale du Canada

Mr. Dean Allison (Niagara West — Glanbrook):

2010 has seen an unprecedented level of Canadian activity on the international stage. From the 2010 Vancouver Winter Olympic and Paralympic Games to the G8 and G20 summits, Canada has played host to the world. Our ... quick responses to natural disasters in Haiti and Pakistan have once again demonstrated the generosity of Canadians. [H]ow is the government carrying forward Canada's international leadership role?

Hon. Lawrence Cannon (Minister of Foreign Affairs):

Last January the Prime Minister ... called 2010 Canada's international year. Canada's strong support for international peace and security includes more than 3,000 troops, as well as police, diplomats, development officers and correctional personnel, serving in a variety of UN-mandated missions around the globe. Yesterday our government was proud to launch Canada's action plan to promote and protect women and girls in international zones of conflict.

(*House of Commons Debates, 6 October 2010, p. 4815*)
(*Débats de la Chambre des communes, le 6 octobre 2010, p. 4815*)

Egypt / Égypte

Hon. Michael Ignatieff (Leader of the Opposition):

As events have unfolded in Egypt ... [w]hat exactly has the government been saying to the authorities in Egypt?

Right Hon. Stephen Harper (Prime Minister):

In North Africa last week that the fundamental basis of this government's foreign policy was the encouragement of freedom, democracy, human rights and the rule of law. Those are the values that we express to all governments around the world. Obviously important events are unfolding in Egypt. We want to see it transition toward the basic values of freedom, democracy, human rights and justice. We want to ensure the transition does not tend toward violence, instability and extremism.

(*House of Commons Debates, 31 January 2011, p. 7424*)
(*Débats de la Chambre des communes, le 31 janvier 2010, p. 7424*)

Israel / Israël

Hon. Bob Rae (Toronto Centre):

Many Canadians have expressed concern about the possibility that potential peace talks between the government of Israel and the Palestinian Authority might be derailed by recent events and recent announcements by the government of Israel. [Has the Prime Minister] in fact discussed this issue with Prime Minister Netanyahu of Israel?

Right Hon. Stephen Harper (Prime Minister):

I have discussed this with Prime Minister Netanyahu, and of course I repeated the Government of Canada's position, as the Minister of Foreign Affairs did last week in collaboration with a number of our allies. Our position on the particular issue at hand is well known. At the same time, I indicated to Prime Minister Netanyahu and would indicate to all involved in this particular conflict that I hope they will all make their best efforts to see their way to resuming peace talks in some form as soon as possible.

(*House of Commons Debates, 16 March 2010, p. 525*)
(*Débats de la Chambre des communes, le 16 mars 2010, p. 525*)

Mme Johanne Deschamps (Laurentides — Labelle):

Le gouvernement conservateur a déploré timidement à l'ONU la décision du premier ministre Netanyahou d'intensifier la colonisation juive par la construction de 1 600 nouveaux logements dans Jérusalem-Est. Le ministre affirmera-t-il clairement au gouvernement israélien que la situation est inacceptable, et s'engagera-t-il à dénoncer toute construction en territoire occupé?

L'hon. Lawrence Cannon (ministre des Affaires étrangères):

Ce matin, à l'occasion de mon témoignage livré devant le comité, j'ai eu la chance d'expliquer très clairement la position canadienne. La position canadienne est fondée sur la négociation entre deux parties, afin qu'il y ait de la stabilité et de la paix entre ces deux sociétés, ces deux États souverains vivant l'un à côté de l'autre, mais aussi sur l'engagement dans un processus de paix. C'est la position du gouvernement du Canada. Comme je l'ai déjà mentionné, nous dénonçons le fait d'étendre la colonie dans Jérusalem-Est.

(*House of Commons Debates, 16 March 2010, p. 532*)
(*Débats de la Chambre des communes, le 16 mars 2010, p. 532*)

Mr. Scott Armstrong (Cumberland — Colchester — Musquodoboit Valley):

The NDP House leader has stated in an interview that she believes the Israeli occupation began in 1948. That is the same date as the creation of the state of Israel. She also has said that she supports the campaign of boycott, divestment and sanctions against the state of Israel. [How] would the [Government] respond to these ... statements?

Mr. Pierre Poilievre (Parliamentary Secretary to the Prime Minister and to the Minister of Intergovernmental Affairs):

[These are] despicable remarks. It was our government under the leadership of this Prime Minister that was the first in the world to cut off international aid to the Hamas regime in Gaza. It was the first to announce it would not participate in the Durban hate festival. Other countries later followed. This government was the first to march out on Mahmoud Ahmadinejad's speech at the United Nations. We were the only country to stand up to an unbalanced Francophonie resolution targeting Israel. This Prime Minister is prepared to stand for what is right, even when it means standing alone.

(*House of Commons Debates, 11 June 2010, p. 3718*)
(*Débats de la Chambre des communes, le 11 juin 2010, p. 3718*)

Mrs. Tilly O'Neill-Gordon (Miramichi):

Yesterday, Liberal candidate Andrew Lang said that Canada needed to stop placating Israel. He says that Canada should criticize Israel for being insufficiently non-violent ... Does the government House leader agree with the Liberals that Canada should lecture Israel on the need to be less violent?

Hon. John Baird (Leader of the Government in the House of Commons):

No, I do not ... Israel is Canada's friend and ally. Our ... government supports Israel in its daily struggle against the anti-Semitic death cults that the Jewish people face each and every day, terrorism wanting to drive them into the sea. Like all countries facing armed terrorist attacks, Israel has the right of self-defence, and our government will always support Israel in the exercise of that right.

(*House of Commons Debates, 8 October 2010, p. 4939*)
(*Débats de la Chambre des communes, le 8 octobre 2010, p. 4939*)

Libya / Libye

Mme Monique Guay (Rivière-du-Nord):

La France et la Grande-Bretagne ont reconnu le Conseil national de transition, regroupant les principales forces d'opposition à Kadhafi. En reconnaissant la validité de ce nouvel interlocuteur politique, elles apportent ainsi un soutien déterminant au peuple libyen, qui lutte pour sa liberté. Le gouvernement conservateur va-t-il clairement couper les ponts avec le régime Kadhafi et entamer des discussions avec le Conseil national de transition?

L'hon. Lawrence Cannon (ministre des Affaires étrangères):

Ce sont des États qui reconnaissent des États. Nous nous sommes engagés à prendre contact avec ce conseil intérimaire afin que nous puissions ouvrir le dialogue. Nous croyons que c'est un interlocuteur valable pour mettre fin, d'une part, aux hostilités en Libye et, d'autre part, pour mettre fin à ce bain de sang que le régime Kadhafi inflige à sa population.

(*House of Commons Debates, 11 March 2011, p. 8960*)
(*Débats de la Chambre des communes, le 11 mars 2011, p. 8960*)

Mexico / Mexique

M. Jean-Yves Laforest (Saint-Maurice — Champlain):

L'ex-ministre Hélène Scherrer est une autre victime du conflit diplomatique opposant le Canada et le Mexique à propos des visas. Elle et son
conjoint ont été refoulés à la frontière car les autorités mexicaines exigent
que les détenteurs de passeports diplomatiques canadiens présentent un
visa. Cette mesure fait suite à la décision du gouvernement conservateur
d'imposer des visas aux ressortissants mexicains. Au lieu de se lancer dans
une guerre diplomatique nuisant au tourisme et aux échanges commerciaux, pourquoi le gouvernement conservateur ne cesse-t-il pas d'imposer
des visas aux ressortissants mexicains?

Hon. Peter Kent (Minister of State of Foreign Affairs (Americas)):

Mexico ... is an important and strategic partner with Canada in North
America, in the hemisphere and around the world. The Government of
Canada made the decision last year to impose visas to protect our refugee
system and in October last year Mexico imposed a visa on those citizens
travelling on diplomatic or official passports. Those holding diplomatic
or official passports have a responsibility to stay informed about restrictions
on their use abroad.

(*House of Commons Debates, 30 April 2010, p. 2215*)
(*Débats de la Chambre des communes, le 30 avril 2010, p. 2215*)

North Korea / Corée du Nord

Mr. Scott Armstrong (Cumberland — Colchester — Musquodoboit Valley):

On March 26, the South Korean ship Cheonan sank in waters near the
northern limit line, claiming the lives of 46 sailors. At the request of the
South Korean government, Canada deployed three experts from the Canadian navy to join the multinational investigation team. In the light of the
conclusions of North Korea's belligerence, what further measures will the
government pursue?

Hon. Lawrence Cannon (Minister of Foreign Affairs):

Canadians can be very proud of our swift response and unwavering commitment in the face of the North Korean aggression and our help to our
friends and allies in South Korea. We condemn North Korea's blatant
disregard and egregious violations of international law. We will take steps
to impose enhanced restriction on trade investment and other bilateral
relations with the regime, including the addition of North Korea to the
area control list.

(*House of Commons Debates, 25 May 2010, p. 2911*)
(*Débats de la Chambre des communes, le 25 mai 2010, p. 2911*)

Rwanda

Mme Francine Lalonde (La Pointe-de-l'Île):

Mercredi, nous avons appris avec stupeur la détention arbitraire au Rwanda de Mme Victoire Ingabire, candidate aux élections présidentielles d'août prochain. Elle cherchait à faire reconnaître son parti, le FDU, fondé en exil, malgré le harcèlement de la police. De plus en plus, on constate que les autorités du Rwanda posent des gestes autoritaires et non démocratiques. Le Canada ne peut pas, à nouveau, rester les bras croisés. Le ministre des Affaires étrangères va-t-il profiter du passage de la Gouverneure générale au Rwanda pour protester vigoureusement contre cette détention arbitraire?

Mr. Deepak Obhrai (Parliamentary Secretary to the Minister of Foreign Affairs):

The visit of the Governor General to Rwanda was a highly successful visit. We will continue monitoring the events in Rwanda as they move forward ... If [this case] requires intervention, the Government of Canada will intervene. I wish to state again that Canada and Rwanda have a very good relationship.

(*House of Commons Debates, 22 April 2010, p. 1861*)
(*Débats de la Chambre des communes, le 22 avril 2010, p. 1861*)

Tunisia / Tunisie

M. Jean Dorion (Longueuil — Pierre-Boucher):

En 2010, sur son site Internet, Exportation et développement Canada invitait les entreprises d'ici à investir en Tunisie, en affirmant que la Tunisie disposait d'un environnement politique et économique stable. Le ministre n'est-il pas inquiet de voir que, peu avant la révolution en Tunisie, ses analystes en arrivaient à une telle conclusion?

Hon. Peter Van Loan (Minister of International Trade):

There have been significant changes in the political environment in Tunisia recently. Canada has enjoyed good export success in the past. Our hope is that as the situation normalizes there in the future, once again that kind of relationship could be established for the benefit of the citizens of both countries.

(*House of Commons Debates, 31 January 2011, p. 7427*)
(*Débats de la Chambre des communes, le 31 janvier 2011, p. 7427*)

M. Jean Dorion (Longueuil — Pierre-Boucher):

L'Union européenne a décidé récemment de geler les avoirs de la famille de l'ex-dictateur tunisien Ben Ali. Le gouvernement entend-il imiter l'Union européenne en gelant les avoirs canadiens de la famille de l'ex-dictateur tunisien, ou préfère-t-il lui donner le temps de placer ces actifs en lieu sûr dans un paradis fiscal?

L'hon. Lawrence Cannon (ministre des Affaires étrangères):

Le gouvernement du Canada travaille en étroite collaboration avec le gouvernement tunisien de façon à ce que nous puissions examiner toutes les options pour geler les avoirs de l'ancien régime tunisien. Présentement, plusieurs options sont sur la table, et dès que nous aurons la confirmation de tout cela, nous allons aller de l'avant.

(*House of Commons Debates, 1 February 2011, p. 7545*)
(*Débats de la Chambre des communes, le 1 février 2011, p. 7545*)

UN Security Council / Conseil de sécurité des Nations Unies

M. Gilles Duceppe (Laurier — Sainte-Marie):

Le premier ministre rencontre aujourd'hui le Secrétaire général des Nations Unies, M. Ban Ki-moon. On sait que l'un des objectifs de cette rencontre est de mousser la candidature du Canada au Conseil de sécurité des Nations Unies. Or, depuis son élection, le gouvernement conservateur est en porte-à-faux avec plusieurs positions de l'ONU. Comment le premier ministre peut-il prétendre au titre de membre du Conseil de sécurité de l'ONU alors qu'il n'a toujours pas signé la Déclaration des Nations Unies sur les droits des peuples autochtones ... [et] n'a posé aucun geste concret ... en matière de changements climatiques?

Le très hon. Stephen Harper (premier ministre):

Au contraire, comme le secrétaire général l'a reconnu, le Canada est l'un des plus grands donateurs et contributeurs aux activités des Nations Unies en matière de sécurité, de droits humains, de développement, de responsabilité et d'imputabilité. Le rôle du Canada au sein des Nations Unies est très important pour notre pays souverain ... [L]e Canada appuie fortement l'Accord de Copenhague, qui est le premier à inclure tous les grands émetteurs.

(House of Commons Debates, 12 May 2010, p. 2683)
(Débats de la Chambre des communes, le 12 mai 2010, p. 2683)

Hon. Michael Ignatieff (Leader of the Opposition):

Pourquoi ce premier ministre a-t-il perdu le siège à l'ONU?

Right Hon. Stephen Harper (Prime Minister):

[T]here is a secret vote at the United Nations. These things are inherently difficult to predict, regardless of the fact that we had secured written approval from the vast majority of the countries. But the fact of the matter is this. Precisely because these things are not predictable, we do not base Canadian foreign policy on them. We act according to Canada's values ... [N]ous avons reçu l'appui écrit de la grande majorité des pays. Ce n'est pas possible de prédire le vote dans un scrutin secret, mais c'est la raison pour laquelle on ne base pas nos décisions de politique étrangère sur de tels votes. On les base sur les principes, les valeurs et les intérêts du Canada et des Canadiens.

(House of Commons Debates, 19 October 2010, p. 5058)
(Débats de la Chambre des communes, le 19 octobre 2010, p. 5058)

United Arab Emirates / Émirats arabes unis

L'hon. John McCallum (Markham — Unionville):

Selon un député conservateur senior, c'est ce premier ministre qui est la cause de l'éviction de nos forces armées de la base de Dubai, et ce, à cause, et je cite: "de sa truculence, de sa brutalité." L'ambassadeur des Émirats m'a personnellement confirmé cette version. Le gouvernement a annulé des rencontres à répétition et a renié ses engagements. Pourquoi les conservateurs traitent-ils un allié du Canada de cette façon?

Hon. Peter Kent (Minister of State of Foreign Affairs (Americas)):

The Government of Canada always chooses arrangements that are in the best interest of Canada and of best value to Canadians ... [W]hat the UAE was offering was not in the best interest of Canada.

(House of Commons Debates, 20 October 2010, p. 5103)
(Débats de la Chambre des communes, le 20 octobre 2010, p. 5103)

HEALTH / SANTÉ

Mr. Malcolm Allen (Welland):

The HVP recall has affected more than 100 products already and could be the largest recall in North American history. Contaminated HVP was distributed for nearly a month and after the contamination was detected, it took another two weeks before Canadians were told. The listeriosis crisis killed 22 Canadians ... Why will the government not make protecting the health of Canadians a priority?

Hon. Gerry Ritz (Minister of Agriculture and Agri-Food and Minister for the Canadian Wheat Board):

The safety of Canadians and the food they eat is a priority for this government. This government reacted immediately when we were notified by the FTA that there was a problem with this Las Vegas-based operation. We immediately started to react. We have since then removed a product off the shelves. We have a tremendous amount of information up on our new website, foodsafety.gc.ca ... $75 million [for food safety] was announced last summer. It is already in play. We have already worked toward hiring the 166 inspectors.

(*House of Commons Debates, 11 March 2010, p. 346*)
(*Débats de la Chambre des communes, le 11 mars 2010, p. 346*)

Ms. Kirsty Duncan (Etobicoke North):

Because of the new tainted meat recall, we find out that plants packaging meat for the U.S. market must be inspected daily in order to meet U.S. standards while plants that package meat for our domestic market get inspected only once a week. Why [does] the government care more about the health of Americans than it does the health of Canadians?

Hon. Gerry Ritz (Minister of Agriculture and Agri-Food and Minister for the Canadian Wheat Board):

I want to assure Canadian consumers that our food supply is safe because absolutely none of that is true. The inspection rate for domestic consumption, as well as for international trade, is exactly the same. It works on a 12-hour cycle.

(*House of Commons Debates, 15 March 2010, p. 450*)
(*Débats de la Chambre des communes, le 15 mars 2010, p. 450*)

Hon. Geoff Regan (Halifax West):

AECL is once again revising the return to service date for the Chalk River reactor, which has not produced isotopes since it was shut down last May.

We heard this week that only 51% of the repairs are done and the remaining welding is extremely technical. In fact, AECL is currently assessing the recommendations from an expert review conducted earlier this week. Will the minister finally admit that there is a growing crisis with the supply of medical isotopes?

Mr. Pierre Lemieux (Parliamentary Secretary to the Minister of Agriculture):

[O]ur government [is frustrated] with the slow progress of this project and the continued delays that are completely unacceptable. The health and safety of Canadians remains our top priority. The security of isotope supply is a global issue requiring a global response. That is why our government led the way in the creation of the high level group on medical isotopes to make the global supply more secure and more predictable ... [I]n May 2008, the Government of Canada accepted the decision of the board of directors of AECL to discontinue the MAPLEs project and that remains the government's view. In terms of action items, our government has told AECL that its highest priority must be to return to service the National Research Universal as quickly and as safely as possible. In addition, the Minister of Health is working with the medical community to manage the supply of available isotopes and maximize its use of alternatives.

(*House of Commons Debates, 19 March 2010, p. 696*)
(*Débats de la Chambre des communes, le 19 mars 2010, p. 696*)

Ms. Kirsty Duncan (Etobicoke North):

Today is World Tuberculosis Day. Tuberculosis is Canada's forgotten disease. The tuberculosis rate among status Indians is 31 times higher than that of non-aboriginal Canadians, and the rate among Inuit is 186 times higher. Why does the government think that sub-Saharan TB rates are acceptable among aboriginal Canadians?

Hon. Leona Aglukkaq (Minister of Health):

As someone from the north, I understand how serious this issue is. Our government takes the health and safety of all citizens very seriously and remains vigilant in the efforts to address tuberculosis. Our government has almost doubled its spending on the prevention and treatment of tuberculosis in aboriginal communities compared to the Liberal Party in the last four years of its time in government. This year alone, we have contributed about $10 million. More than that, we are addressing a number of other areas that will help prevent the spread of tuberculosis, including infrastructure, investment in housing, tobacco, food.

(*House of Commons Debates, 24 March 2010, p. 876*)
(*Débats de la Chambre des communes, le 24 mars 2010, p. 876*)

Ms. Megan Leslie (Halifax):

Suicide is the leading cause of death for first nations youth and the second leading cause of death for youth ages 10 to 24. Countries that have a national suicide prevention strategy, like the U.K. and the U.S., have much lower suicide rates than in Canada. When will the government establish a national suicide prevention strategy for Canada?

Mr. Colin Carrie (Parliamentary Secretary to the Minister of Health):

Suicide is a tragic event and it affects far too many Canadian families. Sixty-five million dollars has been spent to date to implement the national aboriginal youth suicide prevention strategy, and there is more. We committed $285 million in budget 2010 to federal aboriginal health programs in the area of suicide prevention, maternal child health, health human resources and the aboriginal health transition fund.

(*House of Commons Debates, 5 November 2010, p. 5889*)
(*Débats de la Chambre des communes, le 5 novembre 2010, p. 5889*)

HUMAN RIGHTS / DROITS DE LA PERSONNE

Burma / Burmanie

Mr. Rodney Weston (Saint John):

Human rights in Burma have long been a cause for concern for the international community. The military regime in Burma is by far one of the worst and most repressive regimes in the world. Unfortunately, even if Burmese citizens are successful in escaping the terror, many still face starvation and disease in the refugee camps of bordering nations. [W]hat [is] our government doing to help the refugees and migrants fleeing the Burmese regime?

Hon. Bev Oda (Minister of International Cooperation):

It is true that there is a tragedy happening in Burma and the Burmese continue to suffer. We have been supporting the Burmese border area program and it has achieved success by providing service to Burmese people. One million cases of malaria have been treated, 145,000 refugees are receiving service and over 500,000 people have received health care. That is why I am pleased today to announce a renewal of the Burmese border area program by increasing the amount to under $16 million.

(*House of Commons Debates, 11 March 2010, p. 347*)
(*Débats de la Chambre des communes, le 11 mars 2010, p. 347*)

Hon. Jack Layton (Toronto — Danforth):

We extended Canadian citizenship to [Burmese democratic activist Aung San Suu Kyi to Canada] on an honorary basis ... Est-ce que le gouvernement a l'intention de faire suite à l'initiative que nous avons prise et inviter la militante birmane Aung San Suu Kyi au Canada pour recevoir sa citoyenneté?

Hon. John Baird (Leader of the Government in the House of Commons and Minister of the Environment):

Our government, and I think all Canadians, are incredibly pleased that Aung San Suu Kyi has finally been released from house arrest in Burma. Canada has taken very strong sanctions against this repressive regime. [T]he government is ... pleased to continue to work ... on this important issue.

(*House of Commons Debates, 2 December 2010, p. 6749*)
(*Débats de la Chambre des communes, le 2 décembre 2010, p. 6749*)

Child Care / Garde d'enfants

Ms. Olivia Chow (Trinity — Spadina):

International organizations such as the OECD and UNICEF rank Canada dead last in the provision of early learning and child care. When will the government ... create new child care services for families?

Hon. Diane Finley (Minister of Human Resources and Skills Development):

We have created and introduced the universal child care benefit. It offers $100 a month for each child under the age of six, so that parents can get their choice in child care ... [A]nd that alone has lifted 22,000 families, including some 57,000 children, above the poverty line. On top of that, we delivered $250 million to the provinces to help them create spaces, and they have announced over 85,000 of those so far.

(*House of Commons Debates, 17 March 2010, pp. 571-72*)
(*Débats de la Chambre des communes, le 17 mars 2010, pp. 571-72*)

Sexual Orientation / Orientation sexuelle

Mrs. Nina Grewal (Fleetwood — Port Kells):

Recently Canadians were rightly shocked to hear of the sentencing in Malawi of a same-sex couple to 14 years of hard labour. [W]hat actions the government is taking to address this serious abuse of human rights?

Hon. Lawrence Cannon (Minister of Foreign Affairs):

Canada has clearly spoken out against human rights violations on the basis of sexual orientation, both at home, as well as around the world. We strongly condemn the blatant violation of human rights, and of the promotion of freedom and the rule of law. Democracy is an integral part, as we know, of our foreign policy. Canada will continue to encourage its partners, including Malawi, to respect human rights and ensure equal protection under the law without discrimination.

(*House of Commons Debates, 27 May 2010, p. 3004*)
(*Débats de la Chambre des communes, le 27 mai 2010, p. 3004*)

Mr. Bill Siksay (Burnaby — Douglas):

Last week gay rights activist David Kato was murdered in his own home. He was one of 100 Ugandan GLBTT activists targeted by a hateful newspaper campaign inciting vigilantes to "hang them." How has Canada responded?

Hon. Lawrence Cannon (Minister of Foreign Affairs):

We have called upon the Ugandan government to conduct a thorough investigation into the death and to increase the human rights protection of all Ugandans. We passed a unanimous motion in the House and have been very forceful in our determination to ensure that we do protect the rights of all these individuals.

(*House of Commons Debates, 1 February 2011, p. 7547*)
(*Débats de la Chambre des communes, le 1 février 2011, p. 7547*)

Immigration

M. Thierry St-Cyr (Jeanne-Le Ber):

Ce gouvernement prétend qu'il accélère les procédures pour accueillir rapidement des Haïtiens en vertu du programme de regroupement familial. Or les choses traînent en longueur, et on ne sent pas de réelle volonté d'accélérer le traitement des dossiers. Les réfugiés kosovars ont été traités avec plus d'empressement en 1999. Comment le gouvernement peut-il prétendre accélérer les choses, alors que les effectifs de l'ambassade de Port-au-Prince sont encore trop peu nombreux pour répondre à l'accroissement record du nombre de demandes?

L'hon. Jason Kenney (ministre de la Citoyenneté, de l'Immigration et du Multiculturalisme):

Toute la fonction publique, y compris Citoyenneté et Immigration Canada, a fait une démarche incroyable. Faisant face à des défis énormes après le tremblement de terre en Haïti, dont l'accélération du traitement des dossiers de parrainage familial, on a annoncé que tous les dossiers de parrainage de membres de familles de citoyens canadiens ou de résidents permanents qui sont en Haïti seront traités aussitôt que possible. On est en mesure de le faire. On a déjà traité des centaines de dossiers. Notre mission à Port-au-Prince ayant subi des dommages, notre capacité de traitement est limitée à cause du tremblement de terre. Cependant, nous faisons notre possible.

(*House of Commons Debates, 10 March 2010, p. 266*)
(*Débats de la Chambre des communes, le 10 mars 2010, p. 266*)

Hon. Bob Rae (Toronto Centre):

Last week the Minister of Immigration announced a 5% reduction in the family class of people coming to Canada ... How does he justify that kind of ... practice?

Hon. Jason Kenney (Minister of Citizenship, Immigration and Multiculturalism):

The reality is that yesterday I announced that in 2010 we welcomed 281,000 permanent residents to Canada, the largest number in 57 years ... We are welcoming more family members, more economic immigrants. We have announced a 20% increase in the number of refugees that we have resettled. We are getting the job done for newcomers.

(*House of Commons Debates, 14 February 2011, p. 8108*)
(*Débats de la Chambre des communes, le 14 février 2011, p. 8108*)

Iran

Ms. Lois Brown (Newmarket — Aurora):

Canadians are outraged by Iran's treatment of Sakineh Ashtiani, an Iranian woman who faces execution following a process that was completely at odds with international standards and the rule of law. She has been the victim of harassment by judicial authorities, denied due process, and false or coerced confessions have been used against her. Today there are reports that she could be executed as early as Wednesday. Could the minister elaborate on these troubling reports?

Hon. Lawrence Cannon (Minister of Foreign Affairs):

Our government is deeply troubled by reports that Iran may be moving forward with its plans to execute Ms. Ashtiani. The appalling treatment of Ms. Ashtiani is completely out of line with international standards and the rule of law. Once again this year our government has spearheaded a resolution at the UN General Assembly to call out Iran for its egregious human rights violations. Iran's wanton abuse of the rights of its own citizens is completely unacceptable to our government.

(*House of Commons Debates, 2 November 2010, p. 5684*)
(*Débats de la Chambre des communes, le 2 novembre 2010, p. 5684*)

Mexico / Mexique

Mme Johanne Deschamps (Laurentides — Labelle):

Plusieurs syndicats québécois et canadiens manifesteront aujourd'hui en appui aux syndicats mexicains. Il y a encore trop d'atteintes illégales et violentes contre les syndicats mexicains autonomes. [Où est] la ministre?

Hon. Lisa Raitt (Minister of Labour):

I work very closely with my counterparts both in the United States and in Mexico ... I recently returned from Mexico where I had a very meaningful dialogue with the secretary there. We discussed all these issues. I also took the opportunity to meet with Mexican unions as well, to listen to the workers, because that is the best way to hear from the people what is going on in their own country.

(*House of Commons Debates, 15 February 2011, p. 8199*)
(*Débats de la Chambre des communes, le 15 février 2011, p. 8199*)

Pakistan

Hon. Michael Ignatieff (Leader of the Opposition):

[Is] the Prime Minister ... prepared to ... express the shock, outrage, and anger ... at the assassination of Shahbaz Bhatti, a friend of Canada and a passionate defender of religious freedom in Pakistan[?]

Right Hon. Stephen Harper (Prime Minister):

I want to also share in that shock and outrage, and also to express our condolences to the friends, family and colleagues of minister Shahbaz Bhatti, who was a courageous defender of human rights. He was recently in my office. He knew that his life was in jeopardy in his fight against the notorious blasphemy laws and his defence of religious freedom. We call on Pakistani authorities to pursue justice for the killers of minister Bhatti and also to ensure that they continue the fight for religious freedom for both non-Muslims and Muslims alike.

(*House of Commons Debates, 2 March 2011, p. 8540*)
(*Débats de la Chambre des communes, le 2 mars 2011, p. 8540*)

Poverty / Pauvreté

Mr. Tony Martin (Sault Ste. Marie):

Last year the number of Canadians living in poverty increased by 900,000. Are these sad statistics going to be the government's legacy, or will it now start to address the growing impoverishment of our citizens?

Hon. Jim Flaherty (Minister of Finance):

We were well prepared for the recession that came from outside Canada into Canada. We had paid down almost $40 billion in public debt. The most important thing is to protect jobs. We are still concerned with this tentative recovery that the unemployment rate remains above 8%. However, let us remember how well Canada is doing. We have the best fiscal situation in the G7. We have the highest credit rating, the soundest financial system and the strongest growth in the G7 this year and next. Canada is poised to outperform all of its competitors.

(*House of Commons Debates, 4 May 2010, p. 2352*)
(*Débats de la Chambre des communes, le 4 mai 2010, p. 2352*)

Protecting Canadians Abroad / Protection des Canadiens à l'étranger

Hon. Dan McTeague (Pickering — Scarborough East):

For two years, Noah Kirkman has been held in the United States by a county judge who refuses to send this 12-year-old boy back to his family here in Canada. Calgary Child Services has not declared Mr. Kirkman, Mrs. Kirkman or Noah's grandparents, for that matter, unfit to look after him. For two years, Noah has been bounced back and forth between several foster parents and schools, yet this outrageous judicial detention of a Canadian citizen continues. This case flies in the face of the Hague Convention on returning children to their countries of origin. Can the minister explain when he is prepared to act and how long this travesty will continue?

Mr. Deepak Obhrai (Parliamentary Secretary to the Minister of Foreign Affairs):

Consular officials abroad and in Ottawa have been providing consular assistance to the Kirkman family since October 15, 2008. This particular case is in front of the courts. Consular officials abroad and here in Ottawa have respected and will respect the court orders concerning the minor child. If ordered by the court, consular officials abroad and in Ottawa are ready to assist in the child's return to Canada ... [T]he child protection agency is responsible for the protection of minor children. Under international law, this is the court in the U.S.A. As the current matter is in front of the courts, we will abide by the court rules. We will continue abiding by the court rules and if ordered by the court, consular officials abroad and in Ottawa are ready to assist in the child's return to Canada.

(*House of Commons Debates, 15 April 2010, p. 1556*)
(*Débats de la Chambre des communes, le 15 avril 2010, p. 1556*)

L'hon. Dan McTeague (Pickering — Scarborough-Est):

Des centaines de Canadiens sont coincés en Europe depuis plusieurs jours en raison de l'annulation des vols ... Qu'a-t-il fait de notre plan d'urgence?

L'hon. Lawrence Cannon (ministre des Affaires étrangères):

We sympathize with all the travellers who have been inconvenienced by this volcanic eruption but ... it is a natural phenomenon that nobody could have predicted. Canadian officials are closely monitoring the ash cloud and I have directed officials at Canada's embassies overseas to help Canadians in practical ways. We are encouraged by signs that the situation might be improving. As we speak, eight aircraft are flying Canadians home from Europe. Nos ambassades sont sur pied d'alerte pour porter secours et aide à ceux qui en ont grandement besoin, mais nous sommes encouragés par les signes qui commencent à poindre un peu partout.

(House of Commons Debates, 20 April 2010, p. 1735)
(Débats de la Chambre des communes, le 20 avril 2010, p. 1735)

Mr. Wayne Marston (Hamilton East — Stoney Creek):

In January, the Supreme Court of Canada ruled that every minute Omar Khadr sits in a U.S. prison in Guantanamo Bay is a violation of his rights. Omar Khadr was a child soldier of 15 years of age when he was captured. The nature of his detention and the extreme interrogation techniques put to him would not be tolerated here in Canada. As his pretrial begins before a U.S. military tribunal, will the current government finally petition President Obama to send Omar Khadr home?

Hon. Lawrence Cannon (Minister of Foreign Affairs):

Canada recognizes the independence of the U.S. criminal proceedings. We are aware of media reports indicating ongoing discussions between the prosecution and the defence, and I want to point out that the Government of Canada continues to provide consular services to Mr. Khadr.

(House of Commons Debates, 28 April 2010, p. 2078)
(Débats de la Chambre des communes, le 28 avril 2010, p. 2078)

M. Jean-Yves Laforest (Saint-Maurice — Champlain):

Hier, le ministre des Affaires étrangères a rencontré le vice-ministre de l'Intérieur saoudien. Ils ont discuté du cas de Nathalie Morin, cette jeune Québécoise et ses enfants retenus de force à l'étranger par un conjoint violent. [P]eut-il nous dire s'il a, au moins, demandé le rapatriement de Nathalie Morin et de ses enfants?

L'hon. Lawrence Cannon (ministre des Affaires étrangères):

J'ai effectivement soulevé la question, comme je l'ai fait auprès du ministre des Affaires étrangères de l'Arabie Saoudite lorsque j'ai pu voyager dans ce pays au mois d'octobre dernier. Comme de nombreuses autres personnes, nous suivons le dossier de très près. Comme nous avons pu le faire dans de nombreux cas, nous allons offrir tous les services consulaires possibles à cette dame qui est présentement en Arabie Saoudite ... [B]ien sûr, nous nous conformons aux lois canadiennes et nous les respectons de façon intégrale. Je rappelle que dans le cas de Mme Morin, il s'agit d'un dossier familial complexe. Il faut aussi rappeler qu'on doit respecter les lois saoudiennes en vigueur, de même que la Convention de La Haye qui porte sur les jeunes enfants. Dans ce contexte, on fournit tous les services consulaires possibles dans les circonstances.

(House of Commons Debates, 14 May 2010, p. 2843)
(Débats de la Chambre des communes, le 14 mai 2010, p. 2843)

M. Jean Dorion (Longueuil — Pierre-Boucher):

L'Iran vient de condamner un blogueur canadien d'origine iranienne à 19 ans de prison. On l'accuse de "publicité contre la République islamique" pour des propos critiques tenus sur le Web. En plus, le gouvernement iranien refuse qu'Ottawa le visite dans la même prison où la Montréalaise Zahra Kazemi a été tuée en 2003. Quels moyens le gouvernement entend-il prendre pour que l'Iran libère ce blogueur canadien?

Mr. Deepak Obhrai (Parliamentary Secretary to the Minister of Foreign Affairs):

This government has been very active on this file for a while. We are deeply concerned about the news of this potentially severe sentence. Our embassy in Tehran is following up to seek confirmation of these reports. If this is true, it is completely unacceptable and unjustifiable. Canada believes that no one should be punished anywhere for simply exercising one's inherent right to freedom of expression. Our government's position has been very clear. Iran must release Mr. Derakhshan and other journalists who have been unjustifiably detained and sentenced.

(House of Commons Debates, 29 September 2010, p. 4542)
(Débats de la Chambre des communes, le 29 septembre 2010, p. 4542)

Hon. Dan McTeague (Pickering — Scarborough East):

For 15 months Canadian Philip Halliday has languished in a Spanish prison, awaiting his chance to prove his innocence. He is also waiting desperately for much needed gallbladder surgery. He has lost almost 50 pounds. And now we have learned that he is now suffering from very serious liver and kidney diseases, which are in fact leading to substantial unintended consequences. Would the minister responsible for consular affairs finally ask Spanish authorities to provide Mr. Halliday with immediate treatment to save his life?

Hon. Diane Ablonczy (Minister of State of Foreign Affairs (Americas and Consular Affairs)):

We are aware of this case, of course. We are actively providing consular assistance and support to Mr. Halliday. We are in regular contact with his partner here in Canada. We have also requested that Canada's ambassador to Spain be engaged with local authorities to request help for the medical situation that the member mentioned.

(House of Commons Debates, 9 March 2011, p. 8834)
(Débats de la Chambre des communes, le 9 mars 2011, p. 8834)

Religion

Hon. John McKay (Scarborough — Guildwood):

After 35 years of government support, KAIROS had its funding cut off by the Conservative government ... Will the CIDA minister offer a clear explanation for these ... cuts?

Hon. Bev Oda (Minister of International Cooperation):

[T]his government [i]s commit[ed] to effective international assistance. We want to make sure that we are making a difference. We will continue to support religious affiliated groups. In fact, we support 11 of them that are working in 50 countries on projects that are helping people living in poverty. We continue to support good work that will actually make a difference on the ground.

Hon. Jim Abbott (Parliamentary Secretary to the Minister of International Cooperation):

Our government has established priorities that were well publicized. KAIROS, along with every other organization, was aware of what those priorities were. Its application was inadequate and insufficient against the priorities of which it was aware.

(House of Commons Debates, 4-5 March 2010, pp. 59, 94)
(Débats de la Chambre des communes, le 4-5 mars 2010, pp. 59, 94)

Mr. John Weston (West Vancouver — Sunshine Coast — Sea to Sky Country):

Our government learned last Friday of vicious attacks on the Ahmadi Muslims in Lahore, Pakistan ... These acts were clearly motivated by hatred. Victims were targeted based solely on their faith, which is completely unacceptable. [W]hat [is] our government doing to address the issues facing the Ahmadi Muslims in Lahore and attacks on minorities around the world?

Hon. Lawrence Cannon (Minister of Foreign Affairs):

Our government condemns last Friday's barbaric attacks on worshippers at two mosques in Lahore. We are urging Pakistani authorities to ensure equal rights for members of minority communities. We will continue to work with Pakistan and our allies to bring peace and stability to that country.

[We] will be putting forward a motion to the House officially condemning these acts. Our government actively works with countries around the world to promote freedom, democracy, the rule of law and particularly religious freedom.

(House of Commons Debates, 31 May 2010, p. 3156)
(Débats de la Chambre des communes, le 31 mai 2010, p. 3156)

Rights of Women / Droits des femmes

Mrs. Nina Grewal (Fleetwood — Port Kells):

This year, Canada's theme for International Women's Day is "Girls' Rights Matter." [W]hy [did] Canada choose this theme to mark the 100th [International Women's Day] anniversary?

Hon. Rona Ambrose (Minister of Public Works and Government Services and Minister for Status of Women):

This year's theme for International Women's Day is "Girls' Rights Matter." It was chosen because girls across the globe face serious obstacles that must be overcome. A girl who enjoys equality has a greater likelihood of being self-confident and aware of her own potential and being empowered to access education and job opportunities that will contribute to her success. At Status of Women, we have doubled our funding in support of community organizations that want to empower Canadian women and girls.

(House of Commons Debates, 8 March 2011, p.8791)
(Débats de la Chambre des communes, le 8 mars 2011, p.8791)

Health / Santé

Mme Nicole Demers (Laval):

Le gouvernement exclue l'avortement et la contraception des mesures destinées à venir en aide aux femmes et enfants dans les pays les plus pauvres de la planète ... Ce n'est pas pour rien que la ministre a été accueillie froidement à l'ONU. Le gouvernement peut-il mettre de côté son idéologie et s'assurer que toutes les femmes ont accès à l'ensemble des moyens permettant un choix éclairé?

Hon. Bev Oda (Minister of International Cooperation):

Our government has adopted a G8 initiative focused on saving the lives of mothers and children. In fact, when 500,000 women die in pregnancy and childbirth every year and 9 million children every year die before their fifth birthday, it is important that we put our support behind that which has seen the least progress.

(House of Commons Debates, 4 March 2010, p. 62)
(Débats de la Chambre des communes, le 4 mars 2010, p. 62)

Hon. Jack Layton (Toronto — Danforth):

L'Organisation mondiale de la Santé, USAID et Action Canada pour la population et le développement disent tous que la contraception sauve des vies. Le premier ministre est-il d'accord?

Le très hon. Stephen Harper (premier ministre):

La position du gouvernement est claire ... Le gouvernement cherche un dialogue avec les pays du G8 pour sauver des vies, des mères et des enfants dans le monde entier. On ne ferme la porte à aucune option, y compris à la contraception, mais nous ne voulons pas d'un débat, ici ou ailleurs, sur l'avortement.

Mme Alexandra Mendes (Brossard — La Prairie):

Le gouvernement s'engageait formellement à soutenir la planification familiale volontaire lors du G8. Pourquoi aujourd'hui veut-il bloquer l'accès à la contraception des femmes africaines? [C]e gouvernement croit-il aux bienfaits de la contraception?

Hon. Bev Oda (Minister of International Cooperation):

At the G8 the leaders will discuss maternal and child health. [T]here are no doors being closed even including contraception. There will be fulsome discussion and they will chart a way forward to help save the lives of mothers and children.

(House of Commons Debates, 18 March 2010, pp. 644-45)
(Débats de la Chambre des communes, le 18 mars 2010, pp. 644-45)

Ms. Lois Brown (Newmarket — Aurora):

At the MDG summit in New York, the Prime Minister outlined the plans for our maternal health initiative ... [I]t will be critical that our words... ultimately translate into simple realities like food on the table, improved health and a better life for children around the world. What is [the Minister] doing to make good on [this] promise?

Hon. Bev Oda (Minister of International Cooperation):

Too many children's lives throughout the developing world are being lost to diseases that can be prevented, and Canada is taking real action to save lives in developing countries. At the UN, the Prime Minister announced a 20% increase in Canada's support for the Global Fund to Fight AIDS, Tuberculosis and Malaria. Today I am pleased to announce Canada's increased contribution to the Global Alliance for Vaccines and Immunization of $50 million over five years. This will strengthen the immunization systems in developing countries and save lives of children, an important component of Canada's G8 initiative to save the lives of mothers, newborns, and children.

(*House of Commons Debates, 6 October 2010, p. 4815*)
(*Débats de la Chambre des communes, le 6 octobre 2010, p. 4815*)

Self-Determination / Autodétermination

Mme Francine Lalonde (La Pointe-de-l'Île):

Il est décevant de constater que trois des cinq membres du sommet de l'Arctique, dont le Canada, n'ont pas signé la Déclaration des Nations Unies sur les droits des peuples autochtones. Le gouvernement ne devrait-il pas commencer par signer cette déclaration, sans condition, et inviter ses partenaires à faire de même, afin d'obtenir une entente durable sur l'Arctique?

Hon. Peter Kent (Minister of State of Foreign Affairs (Americas)):

Northerners do play a fundamental role in Canada's Arctic sovereignty strategy. The Minister of Foreign Affairs spoke with territorial leaders and leaders of Arctic indigenous organizations before the summit. Today's meeting is specifically for those states that share a coastline with the Arctic Ocean.

(*House of Commons Debates, 29 March 2010, p. 1051*)
(*Débats de la Chambre des communes, le 29 mars 2010, p.1051*)

Ms. Jean Crowder (Nanaimo — Cowichan):

What does the government have against consulting with aboriginal people? Yesterday, a meeting of select foreign ministers from the Arctic Council ended in disaster with Hillary Clinton basically walking out. Why? Because this government failed to invite all stakeholders, including the six permanent indigenous organizations on the council ... Is there a reason that indigenous people were excluded from taking their seats at the conference?

Hon. Peter Kent (Minister of State of Foreign Affairs (Americas)):

Building a strong Canadian north is an essential part of building our nation. The government clearly understands the potential of the north more than any other government before it.

Hon. Chuck Strahl (Minister of Indian Affairs and Northern Development, Federal Interlocutor for Métis and Non-Status Indians and Minister of the Canadian Northern Economic Development Agency):

[Y]esterday was a very good day. I met with Secretary Salazar here. We have had discussions since I was down in Washington last year, talking about ways his government and ours can share best practices on things that we have learned on both sides of the border and errors that have been made on both sides of the border, so that we can make sure we design programs and work with aboriginal people. We have talked about everything from the UN Declaration on the Rights of Indigenous Peoples to the apology that was made here in the House of Commons and many other things. It was the first time ever that the United States government and the Canadian government came to such an agreement. It was a great moment for aboriginals.

(*House of Commons Debates, 30 March 2010, p. 1126*)
(*Débats de la Chambre des communes, le 30 mars 2010, p. 1126*)

Ukraine

Mr. Borys Wrzesnewskyj (Etobicoke Centre):

On September 23 the Prime Minister met Ukrainian President Yanukovych under whom democratic and human rights transgressions are regularly occurring: intimidation of media, restrictions to freedom of assembly, tampering with election rules, secret police even pressuring university rectors to spy on students. [T]he Prime Minister did not make clear that Canada stands united with Ukrainians who demonstrated their will to be a free democratic state during the Orange Revolution. Will he do so on October 25 while meeting with the president in Kyiv?

Hon. Peter Kent (Minister of State of Foreign Affairs (Americas)):

The short answer is yes. We do have concerns about the encroachment of fundamental democratic freedoms in Ukraine, and yes, the Prime Minister will raise those concerns during his visit.

(*House of Commons Debates, 20 October 2010, p. 5107*)
(*Débats de la Chambre des communes, le 20 octobre 2010, p. 5107*)

United States / États-Unis

Mr. Terence Young (Oakville):

[Has there been] any diplomatic progress that has been achieved toward removing U.S. dual national restrictions as they relate to the international traffic in arms regulations following President Obama's speech of last week? As we know, these restrictions prevent many Canadians of ethnic origin from working for Canadian companies involved in projects that include sensitive U.S. products.

Right Hon. Stephen Harper (Prime Minister):

I recently had the opportunity to discuss this issue with Vice President Biden in Vancouver. Since then, President Obama has outlined his intention to work towards resolving the dual national problem. This is a hopeful sign and I am thankful to the administration for this step forward. We will continue to work with our U.S. counterparts to ensure we resolve this issue in a way that respects both our national securities and also the rights of all Canadians to be treated equally under the law.

(*House of Commons Debates, 24 March 2010, pp. 873-74*)
(*Débats de la Chambre des communes, le 24 mars 2010, pp. 873-74*)

INTERNATIONAL CRIMINAL LAW / DROIT PÉNAL INTERNATIONAL

Corruption

M. Gilles Duceppe (Laurier — Sainte-Marie):

À la suite des révélations des médias en octobre 2009, nous avions demandé au premier ministre s'il y avait eu intervention politique dans le dossier Cinar pour empêcher la GRC de porter des accusations au criminel dans ce dossier ... Aujourd'hui, nous apprenons que la Sûreté du Québec, elle, a finalement porté des accusations dans le dossier Cinar. Pourquoi le gouvernement n'a-t-il toujours pas agi dans le dossier Cinar?

Hon. Rob Nicholson (Minister of Justice and Attorney General of Canada):

This matter is before the court.

M. Pierre Paquette (Joliette):

Ce n'est pas ce dossier qui est devant les tribunaux ... La complaisance du gouvernement fédéral face aux paradis fiscaux a facilité le transfert illicite de 120 millions de dollars vers les Bahamas par ces criminels à cravate. Les conservateurs, en signant en 2010 une convention avec les Bahamas, un paradis fiscal notoire, n'ont rien fait pour prévenir de nouvelles fraudes à l'encontre des petits investisseurs. Alors que la communauté internationale se mobilise contre les paradis fiscaux, pourquoi les conservateurs les protègent-ils?

Hon. Keith Ashfield (Minister of National Revenue, Minister of the Atlantic Canada Opportunities Agency and Minister for the Atlantic Gateway):

The government ha[s] taken decisive action to give CRA the tools and resources it needs to aggressively pursue those Canadians who avoid paying their taxes. This includes important measures contained in budget 2010 to close tax loopholes, and the inclusion of proceeds of crime legislation in the Criminal Code. We expect CRA to focus on aggressive audit efforts to find money that is hiding in offshore accounts.

(*House of Commons Debates, 3 March 2011, p. 8620*)
(*Débats de la Chambre des communes, le 3 mars 2011, p. 8620*)

M. Jean Dorion (Longueuil — Pierre-Boucher):

Le gouvernement peut ... utiliser l'article 354 et la partie XII.2 du Code criminel, ainsi que l'article 54 de la Convention des Nations Unies contre la corruption, pour geler immédiatement les avoirs de Ben Ali et de sa famille. Le ministre ... va-t-il procéder immédiatement au gel des biens dérobés au peuple tunisien?

Hon. Rob Nicholson (Minister of Justice and Attorney General of Canada):

I thank the ... member for that legal advice. Of course, he got it completely wrong. We work with Tunisia. We work with other countries. I am very pleased and very proud that the legislation to correct the laws of our country and fill in the gaps will go to committee today[13] ... Let us get it passed by the end of the week.

(*House of Commons Debates, 7 March 2011, p. 8720*)
(*Débats de la Chambre des communes, le 7 mars 2011, p. 8720*)

---

13 Bill C-61, *supra* note 12.

Death Penalty / Peine de mort

Hon. Dan McTeague (Pickering — Scarborough East):

For three years, Mohamed Kohail has been incarcerated in Saudi Arabia for a crime that he did not commit. At his initial trial, he was found guilty and sentenced to death, but the supreme council overruled that verdict and ordered a new trial on the basis of irregularities that denied Mohamed a fair and impartial hearing. Nonetheless, Mohamed could yet again face the death penalty. Will the Prime Minister use the occasion of the G20 summit to ask King Abdallah if Saudi officials will indeed closely monitor the proceedings of the new trial and if Mohamed could at least be released on bail while the second trial is conducted. Could he do the very same for our friend Pavel Kulisek, who is facing the same situation in Mexico?

Mr. Deepak Obhrai (Parliamentary Secretary to the Minister of Foreign Affairs):

Canada has pursued and will continue to pursue all avenues to assist Mohamed and Sultan Kohail. Our government has continuously raised this case with Saudi officials. We continue to raise the case of Mr. Kulisek, as well. We are closely engaged with the Mexican government on that file. We take all these cases very seriously.

(*House of Commons Debates, 17 June 2010, p. 4017*)
(*Débats de la Chambre des communes, le 17 juin 2010, p. 4017*)

Genocide / Génocide

Hon. Irwin Cotler (Mount Royal):

International law authorities and experts in genocide have determined that Iran has already committed the crime of incitement to genocide, prohibited under the genocide convention and international law. [W]ill Canada, as a state party to the genocide convention, undertake its mandated legal responsibilities to prevent such incitement and undertake the modest step of simply referring the matter of the state-sanctioned genocidal incitement to the UN Security Council for deliberation and account?

Hon. Peter Kent (Minister of State of Foreign Affairs (Americas)):

Canada's words and actions at the United Nations and in other world bodies are very clear. We have censured the behaviour of Iran in these areas on any number of violations of human rights. We will continue to participate in international bodies working against these continuing violations by the Iranian regime.

(House of Commons Debates, 4 June 2010, p. 3430)
(Débats de la Chambre des communes, le 4 juin 2010, p. 3430)

Smuggling / Contrebande

Mr. Mike Wallace (Burlington):

Our immigration system has been under attack. Human smugglers are treating our country like a doormat. [What is] our government going [to do] prevent this abuse of our immigration system?

Hon. Jason Kenney (Minister of Citizenship, Immigration and Multiculturalism):

First of all I would like to commend the Thai authorities for their recent successful action to help interdict apparent human smuggling. We know that Thailand has been a transit point for the dangerous exploitation represented by the criminal syndicates running the human smuggling business. We resettle more refugees than any other country in the world on a per capita basis. We receive more immigrants than any other developed country, but we will not allow exploitive human smugglers to violate our immigration laws or compromise the fairness of our immigration system. We will take action against them.

(House of Commons Debates, 18 October 2010, p. 4992)
(Débats de la Chambre des communes, le 18 octobre 2010, p.4992)

M. Nicolas Dufour (Repentigny):

Le déménagement de la douane d'Akwesasne vers Cornwall en juin 2009 a déplacé le trafic du tabac vers le Québec. Selon la GRC, la contrebande de cigarettes a augmenté de 400 p. 100 depuis le déplacement du poste de douane. Le gouvernement fédéral va-t-il ... renforcer la présence policière aux abords du Saint-Laurent pour freiner la contrebande?

Mr. Dave MacKenzie (Parliamentary Secretary to the Minister of Public Safety):

This government and provincial governments along the border have taken up additional roles. The seizure of contraband and illegally produced cigarettes has gone up. [W]e take this issue very seriously. We have been working with our American neighbours to patrol the Great Lakes and this has been a factor in cutting down on that.

(House of Commons Debates, 11 February 2011, p. 8066)
(Débats de la Chambre des communes, le 11 février 2011, p.8066)

Mrs. Patricia Davidson (Sarnia — Lambton):

[What are] Canadian Forces doing in this international fight against illegal drugs?

Hon. Laurie Hawn (Parliamentary Secretary to the Minister of National Defence):

Today we welcome home the crews of HMCS Toronto and two Aurora surveillance planes. They have been working through the past month with the U.S. Coast Guard in the Caribbean Sea on a counter-drug operation called Op CARIBBE. They intercepted 1,650 kilograms of cocaine worth $33 million. The men and women from HMCS Toronto prevented these drugs from entering Canada and other North American communities. Since Op CARIBBE started in 2006, over 1,000 metric tons of illegal drugs have been prevented from entering Canada, the United States and other countries.

(*House of Commons Debates, 18 February 2011, p. 8385*)
(*Débats de la Chambre des communes, le 18 février 2011, p.8385*)

Terrorism / Terrorisme

Mr. Ed Fast (Abbotsford):

Could the Minister of Public Safety tell the House of another important step in the global fight against terrorism?

Hon. Vic Toews (Minister of Public Safety):

Yesterday the government listed al-Shabab as a terrorist group under the Criminal Code of Canada. This is a strong commitment that this government will not tolerate terrorism and is determined that terrorist groups do not receive support from Canadian sources. Listing this group is another example of how we will not dither on taking decisive action to protect Canadians and make our communities safe.

(*House of Commons Debates, 8 March 2010, p. 153*)
(*Débats de la Chambre des communes, le 8 mars 2010, p. 153*)

Hon. Irwin Cotler (Mount Royal):

The Iranian Islamic Revolutionary Guard Corps has been characterized as the leading international sponsor and perpetrator of global terrorism, responsible for the commission of more than 100 terrorist acts spanning every continent, while engaged in the massive domestic repression of its own people. Will the government list the IRGC as a terrorist entity and thereby sanction this epicentre of international terrorist threat and massive domestic repression?

Hon. Peter Kent (Minister of State of Foreign Affairs (Americas)):

This is a matter of ongoing concern obviously for this government. We continue to consider the possibility of such sanction.

(*House of Commons Debates, 4 June 2010, p. 3430*)
(*Débats de la Chambre des communes, le 4 juin 2010, p. 3430*)

INTERNATIONAL HUMANITARIAN LAW / DROIT INTERNATIONAL HUMANITAIRE

Humanitarian Intervention and Aid / Aide et intervention humanitaire

International development / Développement internationale

Mme Lise Zarac (LaSalle — Émard):

Le gouvernement réduira de 4 milliards de dollars sur 5 ans les fonds consacrés au développement international, notamment en coupant le budget de l'ACDI. Le gouvernement admettra-t-il finalement que son incompétence est la cause directe du recul de l'influence du Canada sur la scène internationale?

Hon. Jim Abbott (Parliamentary Secretary to the Minister of International Cooperation):

The fact is we have doubled aid over the last very short period of time by increasing funding year after year by 8%. We are going to maintain that at the level of $5 billion into the future.

Hon. Bev Oda (Minister of International Cooperation):

This government did not cut aid. In fact, we are raising it next year to the highest level ever in Canadian history. We want to ensure that we are really making a difference for those people living in developing countries. We are maximizing the value of our aid dollars. [O]ur food aid will now buy 30% more food than before.

(*House of Commons Debates, 5 and 8 March 2010, pp. 92-93, 148-49*)
(*Débats de la Chambre des communes, le 5 et 8 mars 2010, pp. 92-93, 148-49*)

Mr. Rodney Weston (Saint John):

At the G8 summit in July 2009, the Prime Minister announced that Canada would double its investment in support of sustainable agriculture development by committing an additional $600 million over three years. [W]hat progress has been made?

Hon. Bev Oda (Minister of International Cooperation):

Canada is a strong leader in food aid and food security. The member is quite right. Canada made a commitment that would double its support for developing countries, particularly smallholder farmers and women in developing countries. Today, Canada is announcing a contribution of $230 million to the global agriculture and food security programs.

(*House of Commons Debates, 22 April 2010, p. 1865*)
(*Débats de la Chambre des communes, le 22 avril 2010, p. 1865*)

Mr. Paul Dewar (Ottawa Centre):

[UN] world leaders are meeting this week to review progress on global poverty goals. The U.K. and other countries are keeping their commitments despite tough economic times. Sadly, Canada has been called out as a laggard. Will [this Government] lift the freeze on our foreign aid budget?

Hon. Jim Abbott (Parliamentary Secretary to the Minister of International Cooperation):

I am very proud of Canada's record on the international stage. Canada is playing a part in advancing the millennium development goals. Canada met its commitment to double international assistance to Africa from 2003-04 levels to $2.1 billion in 2008-09. We have forgiven more than $1 billion in debt to the world's poorest country and we are on track to make our commitment to double our international assistance from the 2001-02 levels.

(*House of Commons Debates, 20 September 2010, p. 4103*)
(*Débats de la Chambre des communes, le 20 septembre 2010, p. 4103*)

Afghanistan

L'hon. Jack Layton (Toronto — Danforth):

On apprend que la SCRS a joué un rôle concernant des détenus et leur interrogation. Nous connaissons tous les méthodes brutales de la NSD afghane. Est-ce que le rôle du SCRS est de décider qui a besoin de se faire brasser par les services secrets afghans? Est-ce que c'est ça qui se passe?

Le très hon. Stephen Harper (premier ministre):

Monsieur le Président, le SCRS, comme toutes les agences du gouverne-ment fédéral, respecte ses obligations internationales à cet égard.

Hon. Jack Layton:

Why ... not call a public inquiry to ensure Canadians can have access to the full truth about what has gone on with the transfer of detainees?

Right Hon. Stephen Harper:

The Canadian Security Intelligence Service is not the CIA, but it is Canada's premier intelligence service and of course it respects its international obligations at all times. The opposition has questioned the work of public servants who are responsible for administering access to information. In order to further assure them, I have asked Justice Iacobucci to review their work and he will give a public report.

(*House of Commons Debates, 8 March 2010, p. 148*)
(*Débats de la Chambre des communes, le 8 mars 2010, p. 148*)

Mr. Jack Harris (St. John's East):

We have yet another revelation today that Afghan officials asked the gov-ernment to build a prison where detainees could be held without the risk of torture ... Included in today's revelations was the fact that last year when the National Directorate of Security complained about detainee inspections creating problems, the Conservative government agreed to limit them to once a month at the most and to give plenty of advance notice ... [What is our government response to this?]

Hon. Peter MacKay (Minister of National Defence):

We are talking about events that happened a number of years ago. It is interesting to note that in fact the issue around NATO prisons circulated years ago, but in November 2007 General Ray Henault, a Canadian, then the chair of NATO's military committee, publicly ruled out the creation of NATO prisons. We are there not to build prisons for Afghans; we are there to help them build capacity to do these things for themselves. We will continue to do so. [W]e have invested in Afghan prisons. We continue to monitor prisoners transferred by our forces. We will continue to work to build that capacity.

Hon. Lawrence Cannon (Minister of Foreign Affairs):

There have been over 210 visits by Canadian officials to Afghan detention facilities since the transfer agreement was signed. The most recent unannounced visit by Canadian officials to Afghan detention facilities occurred within the last 10 days. These occur, have occurred and continue to occur on a regular basis. This is the nature of the transfer agreement that we put in place.

(*House of Commons Debates, 17 March 2010, p. 573*)
(*Débats de la Chambre des communes, le 17 mars 2010, p. 573*)

M. Gilles Duceppe (Laurier — Sainte-Marie):

En plein sommet de l'OTAN, le premier ministre a eu le culot de promettre de ne pas poursuivre la mission en Afghanistan au-delà de 2014. Pourtant, le 6 janvier 2010, le premier ministre a déclaré publiquement qu'il n'y aurait pas de présence militaire en Afghanistan au-delà de 2011, à part celle requise pour assurer la protection de l'ambassade canadienne. [E]st-ce que le premier ministre réalise que, du coup, il a perdu toute crédibilité pour la suite des choses et qu'on ne le croit tout simplement plus?

L'hon. Denis Lebel (ministre d'État (Agence de développement économique du Canada pour les régions du Québec)):

Nous avons clairement énoncé, avec nos alliés, que la mission de combat du Canada se terminerait à la fin 2011. C'est très clair depuis le début. Durant la transition, nous continuerons de fournir de l'aide, de nous concentrer sur le développement et d'aider ce pays, tel qu'on l'a mentionné … [N]otre gouvernement est celui qui appuie le plus les forces armées, après une décennie de noirceur, et nous continuerons de le faire. Comme l'a déclaré le premier ministre, ce rôle de formation, qui exclut les combats, fera en sorte que se poursuivent les progrès accomplis à ce jour par les Forces canadiennes. Les sacrifices consentis par nos courageux hommes et femmes en uniforme ont contribué à bâtir un Afghanistan plus sûr, plus stable et plus prospère et qui ne soit plus un refuge pour les terroristes.

(*House of Commons Debates, 22 November 2010, p. 6238*)
(*Débats de la Chambre des communes, le 22 novembre 2010, p. 6238*)

Africa / Afrique

Mme Johanne Deschamps (Laurentides — Labelle):

Le 11 mars dernier, Vues d'Afrique a appris qu'après 25 années de partenariat, l'ACDI mettait fin au financement de ses activités, dont le très renommé festival de cinéma PanAfrica International. Il est déplorable que l'ACDI abandonne une organisation qui a prouvé son efficacité. La [gouvernement] peut-elle nous expliquer en quoi les activités de Vues d'Afrique ne répondent plus aux priorités du gouvernement?

Hon. Bev Oda (Minister of International Cooperation):

This government is about making Canada's international assistance more efficient, more effective and more accountable. As the Minister of Finance said in the budget, programs are being reviewed to get results. When we looked at this program we saw that it did not guarantee complete and maximized access to all Canadians for them to be aware of the product. We believe that our tax dollars can be used more effectively by actually helping people in developing countries.

(*House of Commons Debates, 15 March 2010, p. 454*)
(*Débats de la Chambre des communes, le 15 mars 2010, p. 454*)

Mr. Paul Dewar (Ottawa Centre):

Will the government confirm reports that we will assist in the UN peace-keeping mission in the Congo?

Hon. Peter Kent (Minister of State of Foreign Affairs (Americas)):

The government is proud to stand with strong democracies and against those groups and states that embrace tyranny, hate and terror.

Hon. Peter MacKay (Minister of National Defence):

All members can be extremely proud of the work being done by the men and women in uniform in Afghanistan, as they can be with the work they did in Haiti and the work in Africa in the past. Future deployments of the Canadian Forces will be decided upon by the government in consultation with our capabilities, of course, and with senior leadership in the Canadian Forces. Until the year 2011, we know that the primary commitment to the world is to continue our work in Afghanistan.

(*House of Commons Debates, 29 March 2010, p. 1053*)
(*Débats de la Chambre des communes, le 29 mars 2010, p. 1053*)

Chile / Chili

Mr. Jim Maloway (Elmwood — Transcona):

After the earthquake in Haiti, not only did Canadians donate generously, but the government matched donations and sent aid immediately. Why is the same not happening for Chile?

Hon. Peter Kent (Minister of State of Foreign Affairs (Americas)):

I had the honour of visiting Chile last week for the inauguration. The capacity of this country, a virtual developed country, to respond is very different from that of the government of Haiti. We are awaiting the new government's direction and suggestion of how exactly our assistance might be delivered.

(*House of Commons Debates, 19 March 2010, p. 700*)
(*Débats de la Chambre des communes, le 19 mars 2010, p. 700*)

Haiti / Haïti

Mr. Mike Allen (Tobique — Mactaquac):

Today HMCS Athabaskan begins its return trip to Canada after working since January 19 to provide humanitarian assistance to the people of earthquake-damaged Haiti. This government dispatched the Canadian Forces to provide relief during this crisis. [What was] Canada's response to the disaster in Haiti?

Hon. Peter MacKay (Minister of National Defence):

In fact, within 20 hours, members of the Canadian Forces were on the ground in the wake of the earthquake, assessing needs and delivering help to Haiti. Thanks to this government's purchase of the C-17 aircraft, load after load of equipment and disaster relief was brought to Haiti. Then over 4,000 Canadians were brought home. We built runways, cleared roads, rescued people trapped in buildings, produced over two million litres of water and delivered almost one and a half million meals. Canadian Forces medics treated over 22,000 patients, delivered babies and performed surgeries. All Canadians can be proud of our military, our aid workers and our diplomats who responded so compassionately in Haiti.

Hon. Bev Oda (Minister of International Cooperation):

This government put forward $85 million immediately in the early days following the earthquake. We have also supported Canadian charities. There are over 357 charities in Canada that have received the support of generous Canadians and we know that the humanitarian relief needs are being met. We are now confirming the contributions for the matching fund and the matching fund will go toward recovery and reconstruction in line with the plans of the government.

(*House of Commons Debates, 10-11 March 2010, pp. 267, 347*)
(*Débats de la Chambre des communes, le 10 et 11 mars 2010, pp. 267, 347*)

M. Gilles Duceppe (Laurier — Sainte-Marie):

Le retrait rapide des soldats canadiens d'Haïti cause beaucoup de problèmes. En effet, en quittant le pays après avoir participé à l'effort de reconstruction, les soldats ramènent avec eux du matériel et de la main-d'oeuvre,
ce qui a pour effet de rendre dysfonctionnel ce qui avait commencé à être
fonctionnel, notamment les infrastructures aéroportuaires. Le rythme
de reconstruction a aussi considérablement ralenti. Pourquoi le premier
ministre n'a-t-il pas attendu les conclusions de la Conférence internationale
des pays donateurs pour la reconstruction d'Haïti, qui aura lieu le 31 mars
prochain à New York, avant de retirer ses troupes d'Haïti ... Afin de venir
en aide à Haïti, le Bloc québécois a appuyé l'idée du Conseil de l'industrie
forestière du Québec d'envoyer du bois pour la reconstruction des maisons.
Bien entendu, cela se ferait dans un cadre multilatéral en respectant les
demandes d'Haïti, d'une part, et les règles de l'OMC, d'autre part. Le
gouvernement fédéral entend-il présenter une telle proposition lors de la
Conférence internationale des pays donateurs pour la reconstruction
d'Haïti le 31 mars prochain?

Le très hon. Stephen Harper (premier ministre):

La mission militaire en Haïti n'est pas une mission permanente, à long
terme; c'est une mission d'urgence. Ces soldats ont beaucoup aidé la population, que ce soit dans les hôpitaux ou en lui fournissant de la nourriture
et de l'eau potable. Nous sommes en transition vers une autre mission
humanitaire à long terme et menée par des gens travaillant dans le domaine
du développement ... La communauté internationale continue à travailler
avec le gouvernement d'Haïti à un plan de reconstruction à long terme.
Évidemment, nous considérerons toutes les suggestions et nous verrons
les résultats que donnera la conférence du 31 mars.

(*House of Commons Debates, 24 March 2010, pp. 869-70*)
(*Débats de la Chambre des communes, le 24 mars 2010, pp. 869-70*)

Mr. Mario Silva (Davenport):

For months Haitians have been dealing with a serious outbreak of cholera.
This epidemic has killed over 1,000 people and 10 months after the earthquake, up to one million people still live in tents and lack clean water, the
source of the cholera outbreak. [W]ill the government ... give us an update
on this crisis?

Hon. Bev Oda (Minister of International Cooperation):

We are very concerned. The latest report indicates that 1,100 lives have been lost and 18,000 people have been hospitalized. In fact, it is my pleasure to inform my colleague that today we are adding $4 million to combat this cholera outbreak. We are working with organizations such as the Pan American Health Organization and UNICEF. We will be providing more prevention campaigns, more medical supplies and clean water.

(*House of Commons Debates, 19 November 2010, p. 6190*)
(*Débats de la Chambre des communes, le 19 novembre 2010, p. 6190*)

Israel / Israël

M. Gilles Duceppe (Laurier — Sainte-Marie):

Suite à l'assaut par l'armée israélienne d'une flottille humanitaire se dirigeant vers Gaza, le Conseil de sécurité des Nations Unies a demandé une enquête impartiale, transparente et conforme aux normes internationales afin de faire toute la lumière sur cette terrible tragédie. Le Conseil de sécurité a aussi demandé la libération des prisonniers par les autorités israéliennes. Le gouvernement conservateur appuiera-t-il sans réserve les demandes du Conseil de sécurité des Nations Unies?

Le très hon. Stephen Harper (premier ministre):

La position du Canada est claire. Nous nous attendons à ce que les faits soient présentés par toutes les parties impliquées dans cet incident.

(*House of Commons Debates, 1 June 2010, p. 3262*)
(*Débats de la Chambre des communes, le 1 juin 2010, p. 3262*)

Japan / Japon

Hon. Ralph Goodale (Wascana):

A savage earthquake caused huge damage and many deaths this morning in Japan. The entire Pacific Rim, including the west coast of Canada, is threatened with a tsunami ... [What is] the latest situation including the impact on Canadians in Japan or elsewhere, the tsunami risk to British Columbia, and the steps Canada will take to help all of those anywhere who are suffering as a consequence of this disaster?

Hon. Lawrence Cannon (Minister of Foreign Affairs):

Our thoughts are with all of those affected by this terrible earthquake, the strongest in Japan's history, that has caused widespread infrastructure

damage as well as fatalities. Ce matin, le premier ministre a parlé avec l'ambassadeur du Japon au Canada. Il lui a évidemment communiqué l'offre d'assistance de même que le fait que nos pensées sont avec ceux et celles qui sont touchés par cette terrible tragédie. [N]os officiers de l'ambassade du Canada à Tokyo sont en train de travailler très étroitement avec les collègues.

(*House of Commons Debates, 11 March 2011, p. 8954*)
(*Débats de la Chambre des communes, le 11 mars 2011, p. 8954*)

Libya / Libye

Mr. Stephen Woodworth (Kitchener Centre):

Canadians have been following the dire situation in Libya with great concern. [What is] the government's response to this crisis?

Right Hon. Stephen Harper (Prime Minister):

In light of the trouble and likely ongoing concerns in the region, the HMCS Charlottetown will depart Halifax tomorrow to take part in Canadian and international evacuation operations that are already under way in Libya ... The men and women of our naval forces and the men and women of all of our armed forces have been called upon time and time again to make a difference in difficult situations. We are once again pleased that they are answering the call.

(*House of Commons Debates, 1 March 2011, p. 8506*)
(*Débats de la Chambre des communes, le 1 mars 2011, p 8506*)

M. Steven Blaney (Lévis — Bellechasse):

Compte tenu du climat de violence en Libye et du nombre accru de personnes qui franchissent les frontières pour se rendre en Égypte et en Tunisie, il est clair qu'une aide humanitaire est nécessaire pour celles et ceux qui souffrent à la suite des soulèvements des derniers jours. [Quelles sont] des mesures pour venir en aide à ces victimes et améliorer la situation?

Le très hon. Stephen Harper (premier ministre):

Aujourd'hui, j'ai le plaisir d'annoncer que notre gouvernement réagira immédiatement à la crise humanitaire en Libye en débloquant jusqu'à 5 millions de dollars en aide humanitaire pour des soins médicaux, de la nourriture et des abris. Of course, in order to resolve this growing crisis, we will continue to repeat our calls on the Libyan authorities to end their violence and Mr. Gadhafi to renounce his position and authority.

(*House of Commons Debates*, 2 March 2011, *p.* 8545)
(*Débats de la Chambre des communes, le* 2 *mars* 2011, *p.* 8545)

Pakistan

Mr. Dave Van Kesteren (Chatham-Kent — Essex):

The Pakistan floods have been the worst in recent history. The scale of the disaster has overwhelmed the population. The United Nations estimates that over 20 million people have been affected and almost two million homes have been destroyed. We know the Canadian government has already provided $52 million in flood relief so far. [H]ow much was raised through our Pakistan matching fund program?

Hon. Bev Oda (Minister of International Cooperation):

Once again Canadians have demonstrated their amazing generosity and compassion. Their contributions to the victims of the floods will provide much-needed food aid, emergency medical care, as well as support for the devastated agricultural sector. [I]ndividual Canadians contributed $46.8 million to help the Pakistani people.

(*House of Commons Debates*, 15 *November* 2010, *p.* 5940)
(*Débats de la Chambre des communes, le* 15 *novembre* 2010, *p.* 5940)

Landmines and Cluster Bombs / Mines terrestres et les bombes à fragmentation

Hon. Bryon Wilfert (Richmond Hill):

For decades, the world has looked to Canada for moral leadership on issues of munitions control and disarmament ... Today, however, we learn that the government has reversed this trend and fired Earl Turcotte, one of Canada's leading arms experts, simply because Washington did not like him defending Canadian interests so vigorously. How can the government justify firing a renowned Canadian official who was simply trying to defend Canada's long-standing human rights interests and reputation?

Hon. Lawrence Cannon (Minister of Foreign Affairs):

It is not true. [C]luster munitions pose a grave threat to humanity and to civilians, which indeed is a serious obstacle, obviously, to sustainable development. [W]e are not throwing anybody out of government. The ambassador to Geneva will be the person who will indeed represent Canada's interest at these negotiations and discussions ... Our government was ... pleased to be among the first countries in the world to sign the convention in the month of December.

(*House of Commons Debates, 7 February 2011, p. 7788*)
(*Débats de la Chambre des communes, le 7 février 2011, p. 7788*)

Nuclear Disarmament / Désarmement nucléaire

Mme Francine Lalonde (La Pointe-de-l'Île):

Les ministres des Affaires étrangères du G8 se pencheront sur la menace nucléaire que représentent l'Iran et la Corée du Nord ... [L]e Canada a conclu une entente avec l'Inde, qui n'a pas signé le Traité sur la non-prolifération des armes nucléaires. Le ministre comprend-il qu'il parlerait avec plus d'autorité si son gouvernement était plus vigilant en matière de non-prolifération nucléaire?

Hon. Peter Kent (Minister of State of Foreign Affairs (Americas)):

Canada is committed to promoting international peace and security by working to prevent the spread of nuclear weapons. Canada's policy is rooted in its support of the Treaty on the Non-Proliferation on Nuclear Weapons.

(*House of Commons Debates, 29 March 2010, p. 1051*)
(*Débats de la Chambre des communes, le 29 mars 2010, p. 1051*)

Mr. Phil McColeman (Brant):

One of the stated goals of this week's nuclear security summit in Washington is to ensure that terrorists never get their hands on nuclear weapons. [H]ow is Canada responding to this summit?

Hon. Peter Kent (Minister of State of Foreign Affairs (Americas)):

This government recognizes that the prospect of nuclear material falling into the hands of terrorists is a threat to global security. Yesterday, the Prime Minister announced that Canada would send Canada's weapon grade uranium to U.S. plants where it will be rendered unusable for bombs. By doing so on the first day of the summit, the Prime Minister was sending a strong example for other countries to follow.

(*House of Commons Debates, 13 April 2010, p. 1419*)
(*Débats de la Chambre des communes, le 13 avril 2010, p. 1419*)

Refugees / Réfugiés

Mme Ève-Mary Thaï Thi Lac (Saint-Hyacinthe — Bagot):

Le Haut Commissaire des Nations Unies pour les réfugiés craint que le triage à deux vitesses selon le pays d'origine pénalise certains groupes persécutés en provenance de pays jugés sécuritaires ... Quelles mesures seront mises en place pour ne pas renvoyer des réfugiés qui risquent, par exemple, de subir des mutilations génitales, des mariages forcés ou de la persécution en raison de leur orientation sexuelle?

L'hon. Jason Kenney (ministre de la Citoyenneté, de l'Immigration et du Multiculturalisme):

Demain, je vais déposer à la Chambre un projet de loi portant sur une réforme équilibrée du système d'octroi d'asile. On veut améliorer ce système afin d'offrir de la protection aux victimes de persécution beaucoup plus rapidement et régler la question des demandes d'asile non fondées. Toutes les réformes seront conformes à nos obligations légales internationales et à la Charte canadienne des droits et libertés. Tout le monde pourra déposer une demande d'asile auprès de la CISR. La réforme sera très équilibrée ... Les réformes que je vais suggérer demain seront totalement conformes à toutes nos obligations légales et morales. Je viens d'annoncer que dans le cadre de sa réforme, le Canada va accepter l'établissement de 2 500 réfugiés de plus de partout dans le monde.

(*House of Commons Debates, 29 March 2010, pp. 1051-52*)
(*Débats de la Chambre des ommunes, le 29 mars 2010, pp. 1051-52*)

Ms. Olivia Chow (Trinity — Spadina):

Does the minister honestly believe he has the right to pick and choose which groups should become second-class refugees?

Hon. Jason Kenney (Minister of Citizenship, Immigration and Multiculturalism):

No, I do not and nor do the balanced reforms suggest that. What we have done is to deliver a new refugee appeal division, faster protection for bona fide refugees. They will not have to wait for a year and a half; they will be getting protection within 60 days. There will be faster removal of false claimants. There will no longer be five years of gaming the system; they will be out within a year. There will be public service decision makers, a significant backlog reduction, more resettled refugees from abroad, more support for those refugees to get integrated.

Mrs. Nina Grewal (Fleetwood — Port Kells):

Our government is taking action to avoid a two-tiered immigration system, one for immigrants who wait in line, often for years, to come to Canada and another for those who abuse the asylum system not for protection but to try to get into Canada through the back door. [H]ow will these new reforms fix the two-tiered immigration system and provide better protection for legitimate asylum seekers?

Hon. Jason Kenney:

For too long Canada's asylum system has been broken with huge backlogs, enormous waiting times, a year and a half to get a hearing. What we are doing is finally bringing about balanced reforms that will give protection to bona fide refugees in just a few weeks and that will remove false refugee claimants in less than a year rather than taking several years to game our system. This is a reform that will allow more UN refugees who are in camps abroad to come to Canada and provide them with additional support. It adds more process to protect their rights, the new refugee appeal division. This is in the best tradition of our humanitarian [policy].

(*House of Commons Debates, 30 March 2010, pp. 1127-28*)
(*Débats de la Chambre des communes, le 30 mars 2010, pp. 1127-28*)

TRADE AND ECONOMY / COMMERCE ET ÉCONOMIE

Buy Local Policy / Politique d'achat locale

Ms. Martha Hall Findlay (Willowdale):

The United States is once again threatening protectionist legislation that will significantly harm Canadian businesses and jobs ... What action will the minister take and when?

Mr. Gerald Keddy (Parliamentary Secretary to the Minister of International Trade):

In these difficult economic times, Canadians can count on our government to oppose protectionism and defend free and open trade on the world stage. That includes our close relationship with the United States. We are following this bill closely and working to ensure that Canada's concerns are taken into account by the U.S. lawmakers. It is far from certain whether this bill will become law, but our government will continue to work closely with the Obama administration on issues like this. As a result of our relationship, Canada was the only country in the world to be able to get an exemption from the buy American provisions of the U.S. stimulus program.

(*House of Commons Debates, 24 September 2010, pp. 4371-72*)
(*Débats de la Chambre des communes, le 24 septembre 2010, pp. 4371-72*)

Aerospace / Industrie aérospatiale

Mr. John Cummins (Delta — Richmond East):

Canada has long been a world leader in the space industry ... Last year we saw Dr. Thirsk and Dr. Payette providing expertise and leadership aboard the international space station, essential components of which were manufactured in Canada by MacDonald, Dettwiler and Associates Ltd. This year's budget committed $397 million to develop the RADARSAT Constellation mission. [What] is being done by our Canadian Space Agency?

Hon. Tony Clement (Minister of Industry):

The budget did commit $397 million to develop the RADARSAT Constellation mission to continue the legacy in space that Canada has. One of the astronauts who has done most particularly well is Dr. Robert Thirsk, the first Canadian to launch aboard a Russian Soyuz capsule and play an integral role on a six-month expedition at the international space station. With this mission he has surpassed the total number of days in space of all the other Canadian astronauts combined.

(*House of Commons Debates, 11 May 2010, p. 2649*)
(*Débats de la Chambre des communes, le 11 mai 2010, p. 2649*)

Mr. Terence Young (Oakville):

Today, the Minister of Industry announc[ed] a $300 million investment into a $1 billion project by Pratt & Whitney to develop lighter aircraft engines with more power, better fuel consumption and improved durability. [H]ow [is] the government's continued commitment to research and development keeping Canada at the forefront of the international aerospace industry?

Hon. Tony Clement (Minister of Industry):

We announced a major investment by the Government of Canada through a repayable contribution but also by the industry itself, a $1 billion R and D investment in the aerospace sector. That translates into 700 jobs for research and development and over 2,000 jobs when it comes to the actual production phase. We are in favour of research and development, whether it comes to F-35s or whether it comes to the aerospace industry.

(*House of Commons Debates, 13 December 2010, p. 7137*)
(*Débats de la Chambre des communes, le 13 décembre 2010, p. 7137*)

Agriculture

Genetically Modified Organisms (GMO) / Organismes génétiquement modifiés (OGM)

Mr. Alex Atamanenko (British Columbia Southern Interior):

On March 18, Bulgaria adopted the most restrictive law on GMO released in the European Union. This new law includes a ban on GM wheat. Six other European Union countries, including France and Germany, have imposed bans on growing GM corn. Argentina protects its farmers by analyzing the potential adverse effects of Argentinian GM exports. Will the minister protect Canadian farmers by following Argentina's example?

Mr. Pierre Lemieux (Parliamentary Secretary to the Minister of Agriculture):

Farmers are best positioned to make decisions on what is best for their business, which is why industry must continue to work with our producers to evaluate any new products. Our government understands that in order to be competitive our farmers deserve timely access to the cutting edge inputs they need, but we also understand that our system must be based on sound science. What the [Hon. member] is proposing would put a choke on research and development in the agricultural sector and would diminish the competitiveness of our farmers.

(*House of Commons Debates, 26 March 2010, pp. 999-1000*)
(*Débats de la Chambre des communes, le 26 mars 2010, pp. 999-1000*)

Supply Management / Gestion de l'offre

Mr. Malcolm Allen (Welland):

Canadians are increasingly concerned about their food, where it is coming from, how it is made and whether it is safe. EU representatives are in Ottawa this week for trade negotiations, and the future of Canadian-grown food is in question. Canada's current supply management system ensures fairness for farmers, and it benefits both Canadians and our economy. Will the Minister of International Trade confirm that he has honoured his commitment to Canada's dairy, poultry and egg farmers and taken supply management off the negotiating table?

Hon. Peter Van Loan (Minister of International Trade):

We have been strong supporters of supply management, and we continue to be. That has not prevented us from successfully entering into free trade agreements with the United States, with Colombia and with other countries and having the benefits of the prosperity that have come from that. Our negotiations with the European Union, right now the largest economy in the world, offer us the opportunity for more prosperity, not just for Canadian workers, but also for Canadian farmers. That is why we are pursuing it.

(*House of Commons Debates, 21 April 2010, p. 1784*)
(*Débats de la Chambre des communes, le 21 avril 2010, p. 1784*)

Mr. Peter Julian (Burnaby — New Westminster):

The softwood industry [is] in the infamous softwood sellout. [O]ur ship-building industry [is] sold out in EFTA. The witnesses at the trade committee have stated that now our key supply management sector has been clearly put on the table as part of the Canada-E.U. trade negotiations. Why is the government so eagerly and irresponsibly willing to sacrifice Canada's supply management system?

Hon. Peter Van Loan (Minister of International Trade):

Our government is clearly committed to defending and protecting our supply-managed industries. However, we are also committed to creating trade opportunities for our farmers and workers around the world. That is why we want an agreement with the European Union that will deliver a $12 billion boost to the Canadian economy.

(*House of Commons Debates, 16 June 2010, p. 3922*)
(*Débats de la Chambre des communes, le 16 juin 2010, p. 3922*)

Automotive / Secteur de l'automobile

Mr. Brian Masse (Windsor West):

Toyota is providing rental cars and vehicle pickups to Americans but not to Canadians. A new Toyota research centre is going to the U.S. but not to Canada. Why will the government not stand up for Toyota's Canadian consumers?

Hon. John Baird (Minister of Transport, Infrastructure and Communities):

One of the most important priorities for us at Transport Canada is the safety of Canadian motorists and others who use our roads. At Transport Canada, we will ensure that all legal measures, the full force of Canadian law, are used to ensure that all efforts will be taken to ensure Canadians are safe now and in the future. Canada has a strong record of leading in recalls. We are proud of the work we have done. We welcome the opportunity for hearings so those who are in decision-making positions can be held accountable ... We will work to ensure that all manufacturers and importers are held to the highest standard under Canadian law.

(*House of Commons Debates, 10 March 2010, pp. 268-69*)
(*Débats de la Chambre des communes, le 10 mars 2010, pp. 268-69*)

Mr. Francis Valeriote (Guelph):

Last year GM terminated 240 Canadian dealerships in a process described as being a "mistake" and "arbitrary" by GM's CEO. Under U.S. congressional pressure, 660 U.S. dealerships were reinstated. Guelph's Robinson Pontiac Buick, cited by GM for over 100% sales efficiency in 2009 and having just spent $2 million on upgrades at GM's request, is being closed for no good reason. Why, as a GM shareholder, does the government refuse to take action to protect these Canadian dealerships and the jobs and they represent?

Mr. Mike Lake (Parliamentary Secretary to the Minister of Industry):

That is a question to be asked of GM, not of the Government of Canada. I would point out that the actions taken by this government saved thousands of Canadian jobs in the auto sector. In fact, due to the actions of this Canadian government, we have created over 300,000 new jobs in the last year. We are applauded across the world by every industrialized country for our actions taken. In fact the IMF, the World Economic Forum and the OECD have called Canada a star. The Economist said that we are an economic star.

(*House of Commons Debates, 11 June 2010, p. 3716*)
(*Débats de la Chambre des communes, le 11 juin 2010, p. 3716*)

Canada-US Border / Frontière canado-américaine

Mr. Robert Oliphant (Don Valley West):

[T]he government is engaged in secret backroom negotiations on the so-called perimeter security proposals that could result in vast changes to our sovereign right to determine who gets in and who gets out of our country. After softwood lumber, climate change and F-35s, how can Canadians trust this government to negotiate anything and maintain control of our own borders?

Hon. Peter Kent (Minister of State of Foreign Affairs (Americas)):

Our government always puts the interests of Canada first. [W]e have been focused on creating jobs and promoting economic growth through free, open and secure trade. That means our shared border is open to trade and investment but closed to security and terrorist threats.

(*House of Commons Debates, 13 December 2010, p. 7134*)
(*Débats de la Chambre des communes, le 13 décembre 2010, p. 7134*)

Canada's Economy / Économie du Canada

Mr. James Bezan (Selkirk — Interlake):

[What is] today's IMF economic outlook?

Hon. Jim Flaherty (Minister of Finance):

Today the IMF has forecasted Canada's economic growth will be at the head of the pack for the G7 and all major advanced economies. The IMF has singled out Canada for special praise, saying, "Canada entered the global crisis in good shape, and thus the exit strategy appears less challenging than elsewhere." We have said all along that while not immune from the global recession, we entered it and we exit it in the strongest position in the G7.

(*House of Commons Debates, 21 April 2010, p. 1781*)
(*Débats de la Chambre des communes, le 21 avril 2010, p. 1781*)

Mr. Ron Cannan (Kelowna — Lake Country):

Today the OECD released its spring 2010 economic outlook. According to the report, the Canadian economy is rebounding vigorously, helped by a recovering trade sector and policy measures. [What are] further details about today's positive economic report?

Hon. John Baird (Minister of Transport, Infrastructure and Communities):

The OECD expects this year and next year that Canada will be the fastest growing economy in the entire G7 and also beat the OECD forecasts for economic growth by a very wide margin ... Let me read what the report said. Listen to what one senior OECD official said about the good work on the Canadian economy, "I think Canada looks good — it shines, actually. Canada could even be considered a safe haven."

(House of Commons Debates, 26 May 2010, p. 2953)
(Débats de la Chambre des communes, le 26 mai 2010, p. 2953)

Copyright / Droit d'auteur

Mme Carole Lavallée (Saint-Bruno — Saint-Hubert):

Le Barreau du Québec affirme que le projet de loi C-32 n'est qu'une série "d'amendements à la pièce, sans vision et sans cohérence d'ensemble, reprenant mal des parties de modèles étrangers que l'on sait être déjà désuets." Le bâtonnier du Québec demande au ministre du Patrimoine canadien de refaire ses devoirs car le projet de loi C-32 ne respecte pas les engagements internationaux du Canada. Le ministre va-t-il modifier substantiellement son projet de loi sur le droit d'auteur, comme le demandent le Québec et son barreau?

L'hon. James Moore (ministre du Patrimoine canadien et des Langues officielles):

Le projet de loi C-32 est équitable et responsable. Il reflète les recommandations entendues au pays quand on a fait des consultations sans précédent pour arriver à un projet de loi responsable qui réponde aux besoins des consommateurs comme à ceux des créateurs. [O]ui, ce projet de loi mettra le Canada au premier rang des pays sur la scène internationale pour protéger nos créateurs contre ceux et celles qui s'engagent dans le piratage et qui volent les créateurs. On va s'engager avec l'OMPI et protéger tous les Canadiens.

(House of Commons Debates, 9 December 2010, p. 7028)
(Débats de la Chambre des communes, le 9 décembre 2010, p. 7028)

Dispute Settlement / Règlement des différends

Mr. Charlie Angus (Timmins — James Bay):

We learn that an American, Vito Gallo, is trying to hit up the Canadian taxpayer for $355 million through a NAFTA challenge ... He invested zero dollars in [Canada's economy]. Will the government stand up for Canada?

Hon. Peter Van Loan (Minister of International Trade):

Our government has a very proud record of standing up for Canada and for Canadian workers throughout by taking advantage of the provisions that exist in our North American Free Trade Agreement ... [There have been] a number of very recent successes where Canada has won its cases in that forum. We continue to be successful in that forum. We will continue to stand up for Canadian workers, for policies that are sound, and for jobs and prosperity in Canada as a result of the North American Free Trade Agreement.

(*House of Commons Debates, 6 October 2010, p. 4816*)
(*Débats de la Chambre des communes, le 6 octobre 2010, p. 4816*)

Financial Institutions / Institutions financières

M. Daniel Paillé (Hochelaga):

Des groupes syndicaux et environnementaux réclament, à leur tour, une taxe sur les transactions financières internationales. Dans le même sens, un consensus se dégage au G20 pour taxer les profits gargantuesques des banques afin de répondre à d'éventuelles crises. Quand le ministre des Finances, qui fait cavalier seul, va-t-il cesser de protéger ses amies les banques?

Hon. Jim Flaherty (Minister of Finance):

The world has just been through the most serious credit crisis in at least a generation. Fortunately, in this country, we have a very sound banking system. In fact, the World Economic Forum ranks our banking system as the strongest in the world. No Canadian taxpayers' money had to be put into our banking system. This is not true in the United States, Great Britain, Germany, France and other places. Some of these other countries are looking at taxing their banks. We are looking at alternative forms of accomplishing the same goal. We will continue to work with our international partners.

(*House of Commons Debates, 20 April 2010, p. 1735*)
(*Débats de la Chambre des communes, le 20 avril 2010, p. 1735*)

Foreign Investment / Investissement étranger

Mr. Brian Masse (Windsor West):

The government is rushing to tear up rules that have ensured Canadian innovation built world-class Canadian companies employing thousands across this country. It wants to strip foreign ownership restrictions in key strategic sectors essential for future growth such as satellite, telecom and mining ... It is this ideology that allowed Inco and Falconbridge, Canada's leading mining giants, to be picked off ... by foreign mining firms. The Conservatives welcomed Vale and Xstrata into our country and have done nothing when they have attacked workers and shipped Canadian profits to other jurisdictions ... What does the minister have against Canadian corporate leadership?

Hon. Tony Clement (Minister of Industry):

Absolutely nothing. Indeed, the fact of the matter is that Canadians can compete anywhere in the world against any competition and win that battle. That is what Canadian companies can do and they are doing it right now. They are competing in open markets and we must open our markets as well. If we want more jobs, more innovation, more competitiveness, better prices and more choice for consumers, that requires Canadians and foreign direct investment in measures.

(*House of Commons Debates, 4 March 2010, pp. 61-62*)
(*Débats de la Chambre des communes, le 4 mars 2010, pp.61-62*)

Hon. Jack Layton (Toronto — Danforth):

Opening up telecommunications to foreign ownership will follow along from 10 years where too many of the economic jewels in this country were sold off with the permission of the government ... Dofasco, Stelco, Algoma Steel, IPSCO, Falconbridge, Inco, LionOre, Cognos, Westcoast Energy, Vincor, Molson, Labatt, the Bay, Van Houtte, ATI Technology and Alcan. Why is the Prime Minister now opening up telecommunications?

Right Hon. Stephen Harper (Prime Minister):

At the same time as we have seen some of those acquisitions, we have also seen many acquisitions by Canadian firms internationally as Canadian champions have been emerging. It is one of the reasons that Canada is coming out of the global recession with one of the strongest economies if not the strongest economy in the developed world.

Mr. Mike Lake (Parliamentary Secretary to the Minister of Industry):

This government has a record of standing up for greater competition. Competition creates economic growth, innovation and better options for Canadian consumers. [I]n terms of foreign direct investment in Canada, while there is a lot of focus on the foreign direct investment happening in Canada, which is good, foreign direct investment by Canadian champions abroad was about $135 billion more in 2008 than the direct investment in Canada ... A report of the World Economic Forum in the fall said that Canada would lead the way in the industrialized world in competition, being one of only two industrialized countries to come out of this global recession in a more competitive position than it went in.

(*House of Commons Debates, 11 March 2010, pp. 341-42, 345*)
(*Débats de la Chambre des communes, le 11 mars 2010, pp. 341-42, 345*)

Ms. Chris Charlton (Hamilton Mountain):

Steel slabs made in Hamilton by U.S. Steel are being shipped to the U.S., rolled into coils there and then returned to Hamilton for customers like Honda Canada. U.S. Steel is moving Canadian product 1,500 kilometres for processing in the U.S. when Lake Erie Works, a top-notch Canadian facility in Nanticoke, is left sitting idle. In the Nanticoke plant, 1,100 jobs are on hold while steel is senselessly travelling back and forth across the border. Will the government stop hiding behind its court case and act to help workers now?

Mr. Mike Lake (Parliamentary Secretary to the Minister of Industry):

Canada has a record of standing up for greater competition under this government. In 2008, foreign direct investment in Canada reached $505 billion, while Canadian investments abroad reached $637 billion, almost $130 billion more than direct investment in Canada. Competition creates economic growth. It creates innovation and better options for Canadian consumers.

(*House of Commons Debates, 25 March 2010, p. 947*)
(*Débats de la Chambre des communes, le 25 mars 2010, p.947*)

L'hon. Geoff Regan (Halifax-Ouest):

Le projet de loi budgétaire enlèvera toute assurance qu'Énergie atomique du Canada limitée ne sera pas vendue à des compagnies étrangères ... Veulent-il[] cacher le fait que le premier ministre a déjà décidé de vendre la technologie CANDU?

Hon. Tony Clement (Minister of Industry):

The hon. member raises a question about the application, perhaps, of the Investment Canada Act. What I can say is, based on our considerations, even if the Investment Canada Act is not applicable in this case, this government would review that situation, which is a speculative situation, certainly with the best interests of Canada and Canadians.

Hon. Geoff Regan:

Why are the Conservatives hollowing out another key segment of our economy? Did they learn nothing from the Avro Arrow fiasco?

L'hon. Christian Paradis (ministre des Ressources naturelles):

Les objectifs sont clairs. On veut assurer la sécurité énergétique au Canada, tout en respectant la capacité de payer des contribuables. Il est également important de le faire toujours en vue d'assurer un futur viable à l'industrie nucléaire du Canada. C'est ce qu'on fait, ce n'est pas plus compliqué que cela. Qu'on arrête de brandir des épouvantails et de semer la peur un peu partout. C'est responsable de notre part de restructurer cette compagnie.

(*House of Commons Debates, 30 March 2010, pp. 1123-24*)
(*Débats de la Chambre des communes, le 30 mars 2010, pp. 1123-24*)

Hon. Ralph Goodale (Wascana):

With respect to any possible takeover of the Potash Corporation of Saskatchewan, what is the government's definition of net benefit to Canada? Will the government commit to that and to complete transparency and enforceability in deciding this matter?

Mr. Mike Lake (Parliamentary Secretary to the Minister of Industry):

The government is aware of this proposed transaction and will monitor the situation closely to determine how the Investment Canada Act applies. The acquisition of control by a foreign investor of a Canadian business with assets of $299 million or more is subject to review, and where a transaction is subject to review, the investor must obtain approval of the Minister of Industry prior to implementing the investment. The minister will only approve applications for review where an investment demonstrates that it is likely to be of net benefit to Canada ... [T]his year Canadian international acquisitions exceeded the value of foreign acquisitions by a ratio of 20%. The net benefit review process is rigorous. It involves consultations ... with the affected provinces and territories and other government departments as required.

(*House of Commons Debates, 1 October 2010, pp. 4662-63*)
(*Débats de la Chambre des communes, le 1 octobre 2010, pp. 4662-63*)

Mr. James Lunney (Nanaimo — Alberni):

According to an analysis released yesterday by the OECD, Canada was the leading investment recipient in the first half of this year. [What] measures have been taken ... to make Canada an attractive destination for investment[?]

Mr. Gerald Keddy (Parliamentary Secretary to the Minister of International Trade):

It is another example of the results produced by our government's commitment to make Canada a top destination for foreign investment. That is why we push for such things as the lowest taxes on new business investments of any major economy. In addition to this, Canada has weathered the global economic downturn, with the lowest debt of any major economy [and] the lowest deficit.

(House of Commons Debates, 3 December 2010, pp. 6798-99)
(Débats de la Chambre des communes, le 3 décembre 2010, pp. 6798-99)

Labelling / Étiquetage

M. André Bellavance (Richmond — Arthabaska):

Pendant que le ministre d'État de l'Agriculture mène des consultations depuis deux ans au sujet de la norme de 98 p. 100 pour utiliser la mention "Produit du Canada," le milieu agricole subit les contrecoups de cette politique d'étiquetage que l'UPA qualifie de "confuse, mal faite, qui fait en sorte que le consommateur n'arrive pas à choisir hors de tout doute un produit canadien." Pourquoi le ministre ne met-il pas un terme à cette mascarade en adoptant immédiatement une norme de 85 p. 100, comme le réclament tous les acteurs de l'industrie, le Comité permanent de l'agriculture et de l'agroalimentaire et ses propres fonctionnaires?

M. Pierre Lemieux (secrétaire parlementaire du ministre de l'Agriculture):

Lorsqu'elles vont faire leurs emplettes à l'épicerie, les familles canadiennes recherchent des aliments canadiens. Les nouvelles lignes directrices concernant la mention "Produit du Canada" leur fournissent l'information dont elles ont besoin. Et la conclusion est claire: si la mention "Produit du Canada" figure sur l'étiquette, alors l'aliment qu'elle décrit doit être canadien.

M. André Bellavance:

Le gouvernement conservateur laisse entrer de plus en plus de produits étrangers ne respectant pas les mêmes normes. Quand le ministre va-t-il contrer cette concurrence déloyale en donnant le mandat au Secrétariat à l'accès au marché d'assurer la réciprocité des normes pour les produits importés?

M. Pierre Lemieux:

Les Canadiens savent qu'il est interdit d'apposer la mention "Produit du Canada" lorsque le produit contient des ingrédients étrangers. Les Canadiens voulaient savoir ce que contiennent les aliments qu'ils mangent, et nous avons répondu à leur demande. Nous continuons à consulter l'industrie et les consommateurs afin de nous assurer que les lignes directrices fonctionnent. Le député libéral de Malpeque a dit que la réglementation fournira aux consommateurs des renseignements honnêtes sur le contenu des produits qu'ils achètent et que ces changements pourront également aboutir à une augmentation de la consommation de produits canadiens.

(*House of Commons Debates, 5 November 2010, p. 5886*)
(*Débats de la Chambre des communes, le 5 novembre 2010, p.5886*)

Manufacturing / Secteur manufacturier

Mr. Terence Young (Oakville):

What [is] our government doing to help create jobs in the important manufacturing sector?

Hon. Jim Flaherty (Minister of Finance):

We did highlight today the fact that Canada will become a tariff-free zone for manufacturers as a result of budget 2010. We will eliminate all job-killing tariffs on manufacturing inputs, machinery and equipment, which will make Canada the first country in the G20 to eliminate all manufacturing tariffs. As in many other ways, including fiscal management, the banking sector and the financial sector overall, Canada is leading the way in the G20.

(*House of Commons Debates, 9 March 2010, p. 227*)
(*Débats de la Chambre des communes, le 9 mars 2010, p. 227*)

Procurement / Marchés publics

Ms. Linda Duncan (Edmonton — Strathcona):

By not yet endorsing Edmonton's bid to host Expo 2017, the government is putting Canada's only bid at risk. Edmonton's Expo theme is energy and our planet. It would showcase innovations in clean energy technology and sustainability, initiatives the government claims are among its priorities. Supporting this bid would help deliver on the government's stated clean energy policy. Will the government immediately endorse Edmonton's bid to host Expo 2017 for Canada?

Hon. James Moore (Minister of Canadian Heritage and Official Languages):

We are aware that the City of Edmonton has put together a proposal to host Expo in 2017. As a matter of fact, Mayor Mandel was in Ottawa last week, and the Minister of Finance and I met with him. [W]e are doing our due diligence on this project. We are concerned about the large price tag associated with this.

(*House of Commons Debates, 17 November 2010, p. 6066*)
(*Débats de la Chambre des communes, le 17 novembre 2010, p. 6066*)

Shipbuilding / Construction navale

Mr. Malcolm Allen (Welland):

The Canadian shipbuilding industry was already nervous when it learned of secret talks being held with the U.K. over naval shipbuilding. Now we have learned that the government has gone to Germany and Spain for ship designs when our own navy has developed plans for replacement vessels ... Will the minister commit to involving the industry in any talks with foreign governments and will he commit to keeping Canadian shipbuilding jobs in Canada?

Mr. Jacques Gourde (Parliamentary Secretary to the Minister of Public Works and Government Services and for Official Languages):

Our National Shipbuilding Procurement Strategy establishes a long-term relationship with the Canadian shipbuilding industry to renew Canada's federal fleet.

(*House of Commons Debates, 11 March 2011, p. 8960*)
(*Débats de la Chambre des communes, le 11 mars 2011, p. 8960*)

Softwood Lumber and Forestry / Bois d'œuvre et forestière

Mr. Anthony Rota (Nipissing — Timiskaming):

Why is our lumber industry forced to pay for the government's incompetence through yet another tax increase in budget 2010?

Hon. Peter Van Loan (Minister of International Trade):

The softwood lumber agreement continues to provide tremendous benefits for Canada. As a result of the softwood lumber agreement, $5 billion in taxes that had been collected by the Americans were repatriated to Canadian businesses. There is a reason the softwood lumber agreement continues to have the strong support of all the provinces and the industry, and that it is a good agreement that works in the best interests of Canadian softwood lumber companies and workers ... L'Accord sur le bois d'oeuvre résineux fonctionne bien depuis plus de trois ans. Il a assuré un accès au marché américain [et] procuré la certitude voulue à l'industrie.

(*House of Commons Debates, 30 March 2010, p. 1127*)
(*Débats de la Chambre des communes, le 30 mars 2010, p. 1127*)

Mr. Peter Julian (Burnaby — New Westminster):

[The 2006 softwood lumber agreement] expires in two years. Is the government planning to renew the agreement?

Hon. Peter Van Loan (Minister of International Trade):

We are very pleased with the progress of the softwood lumber agreement. In fact, we just recently had a decision where the U.S. contested some programs in Quebec and Ontario and the arbitration ruled that 97% of those American claims were rejected ... That is because of the softwood lumber agreement, which is providing stability, jobs and certainty for our Canadian industry.

(*House of Commons Debates, 1 February 2011, p. 7546*)
(*Débats de la Chambre des communes, le 1 février 2011, p. 7546*)

Taxation / Fiscalité

Ms. Chris Charlton (Hamilton Mountain):

Yesterday Bank of Canada governor Mark Carney blamed business leaders for Canada's "abysmal" productivity record ... Will the finance minister admit that sweeping corporate tax cuts have failed to stimulate productivity, and will he instead adopt a plan of targeted assistance in key sectors to protect and create jobs?

Hon. Jim Flaherty (Minister of Finance):

By 2013 we will have one of the lowest corporate tax rates, between the provinces and the territories, in the G7. We have the lowest overall tax rate on new business investment in the G7 by this year, 2010. This is important for business in Canada, for small and medium size businesses to create jobs in our country.

(*House of Commons Debates, 25 March 2010, p. 947*)
(*Débats de la Chambre des communes, le 25 mars 2010, p. 947*)

M. Gilles Duceppe (Laurier — Sainte-Marie):

On apprend que dans le dernier budget, le gouvernement a ouvert une brèche qui permettrait à davantage d'entreprises de bénéficier des paradis fiscaux, donc d'éviter de payer leur juste part d'impôts ... Il nous dit que ce gouvernement s'attaque aux paradis fiscaux. Or il veut négocier un traité de libre-échange avec le Panama, qui est justement sur la liste des paradis fiscaux émise par l'OCDE. Comment peut-on demander à ses concitoyens de se serrer la ceinture et signer en même temps un traité avec un pays qui est sur la liste des paradis fiscaux émise par l'OCDE? Comment le gouvernement ose-t-il demander aux contribuables de faire des efforts alors qu'il laisse certaines entreprises s'en tirer sans payer d'impôts sur la vente d'actions?

L'hon. Christian Paradis (ministre des Ressources naturelles):

Dans le budget de 2010, on a fermé près de 10 échappatoires fiscales afin d'assurer l'équité fiscale pour tous les Canadiens. On travaille activement avec nos partenaires internationaux afin de mettre fin à tous les paradis fiscaux, notamment en améliorant nos ententes d'échange de renseignements fiscaux avec d'autres pays et en consacrant plus de ressources à Revenu Canada pour la vérification des dossiers fiscaux. Ils pourraient bien appuyer le budget ... 10 échappatoires fiscales ont été stoppées. De plus, le budget de 2010 apporte des changements qui permettront aux entreprises canadiennes d'attirer des capitaux étrangers. Cela fera aussi augmenter la productivité au Canada et soutiendra la concurrence internationale.

(*House of Commons Debates, 29 March 2010, p. 1049*)
(*Débats de la Chambre des communes, le 29 mars 2010, p.1049*)

Tourism / Tourisme

Hon. Helena Guergis (Simcoe — Grey):

A cost-competitive transportation sector is a key component of the travel and tourism industry, generating billions in tax revenues. Canada's existing airline policies have resulted in a drop from 8th to 15th place among the world's most visited destinations. Our tourist deficit has risen dramatically from $1 billion to $14.5 billion, and 2.5 million Canadians are now going to U.S. airports in order to travel on less expensive airline tickets. When will the government live up to its commitment to eliminate or cut airport rents and excise fuel taxes so Canada can become globally competitive and a more affordable destination?

Hon. Chuck Strahl (Minister of Transport, Infrastructure and Communities):

Things such as airport rents are important. After we took office, we reduced the rents for airports by half. They have been cut in half from what they were up to in 2005. So there are some savings there ... [T]he Senate committee ... is starting a study on the whole airline industry, as well. [I]ts members [will] look at not only things such as airport rents but also the governance structure of the airport authorities themselves and other issues. It is a pretty wide-open study, but I think right now we are in that mode where it is time to re-examine the policies for Canada. We want it to be very competitive.

(*House of Commons Debates, 21 October 2010, p. 5189*)
(*Débats de la Chambre des communes, le 21 octobre 2010, p. 5189*)

Mr. Dave Van Kesteren (Chatham-Kent — Essex):

Canada was recognized as the number one country brand in the world by the Country Brand Index. "Canada: Keep Exploring" is now the most recognized tourism brand. [H]ow [have] investments in the tourism industry helped put Canada in the number one spot?

Hon. Rob Moore (Minister of State (Small Business and Tourism)):

This is truly an incredible achievement and shows that our government's investments are paying off. Since we took office in 2006, Canada has leap-frogged from 12th place to 1st place on the Country Brand Index. Our goal is to make Canada a top tourism destination, from hosting the 2010 Vancouver Olympic and Paralympic Games to approved destination status with China. This year has been Canada's year and our government is delivering strong results for tourism.

(*House of Commons Debates, 5 November 2010, p. 5888*)
(*Débats de la Chambre des communes, le 5 novembre 2010, p. 5888*)

Trade Agreements / Accords commerciaux

Mrs. Kelly Block (Saskatoon — Rosetown — Biggar):

What steps [is the] government [is] taking to stand up against protectionism and to promote free trade for the benefit of all Canadians?

Hon. Peter Van Loan (Minister of International Trade):

Our government believes firmly that opening foreign markets to Canadian goods and services is the best way to assist Canadian businesses and workers in creating jobs and prosperity for this country. Our recent achievement of an agreement on a waiver from the buy American policies is evidence of our policy at work and of the strong relationship we have built with the Obama administration, which leads our greatest trading partner. Later today I will be reintroducing in the House our Canada–Colombia free trade agreement, another opportunity for us to open markets to the high quality products produced by Canadian workers and businesses. We can compete and succeed.

(*House of Commons Debates, 10 March 2010, p. 269*)
(*Débats de la Chambre des communes, le 10 mars 2010, p. 269*)

Asia / Asie

Hon. Scott Brison (Kings — Hants):

The trans-Pacific partnership is the biggest multilateral free trade deal in the region right now. It includes some of Canada's biggest allies, including the U.S., Australia and New Zealand. Canada is a Pacific nation but we are not even at the table. Why not? ... What is the government doing right now to fight the U.S. veto against Canada's participation in these vital trans-Pacific trade talks?

Hon. Peter Van Loan (Minister of International Trade):

Canada sees Asia as a very important part of our emerging trade patterns. Of course we encourage what we see happening with the trans-Pacific partnership. Any move toward freer trade is a positive development as far as we are concerned. We continue to have discussions with the members of the trans-Pacific partnership to determine what kind of role would be appropriate for us and if it does make sense for Canada to participate. We will continue those ongoing bilateral discussions ... We will continue to work constructively to determine if it makes sense for Canada to have a role, how we can best contribute to the advancement of the trans-Pacific partnership. As for the relationship with the United States, we are very proud of our trading relationships. NAFTA has been good for Canada. What is more, with our delivery of a deal, a waiver from buy America, we have reinforced once again that Canada has a special trading relationship with the United States that no other country in the world has.

(*House of Commons Debates, 12 April 2010, pp. 1347-48*)
(*Débats de la Chambre des communes, le 12 avril 2010, pp. 1347-48*)

Colombia / Colombie

M. Jean-Yves Laforest (Saint-Maurice — Champlain):

Alors que plusieurs projets valables de libre-échange sont sur la table, comme que celui avec la Jordanie, le gouvernement presse le Parlement d'adopter le controversé projet d'accord entre le Canada et la Colombie. L'idée d'accélérer inconditionnellement les échanges économiques avec un pays ayant un bien triste bilan en matière de droits de la personne a pourtant soulevé l'indignation au Québec et au Canada. Pourquoi le gouvernement ... s'entête-t-il à faire adopter [cet accord ?]

Mr. Gerald Keddy (Parliamentary Secretary to the Minister of International Trade):

[T]his agreement is a good agreement for Canadian workers. It is a good agreement for Quebec workers. It is a good agreement for industry throughout this country from coast to coast to coast. It will provide jobs and opportunity not just for Canadian workers, but also badly needed jobs and opportunity for Colombian workers. It will give us an edge on the competition. Other countries around the world, including the European free trade countries and Norway, have already signed free trade agreements with Colombia and we are just playing catch-up.

(*House of Commons Debates, 12 March 2010, p. 396*)
(*Débats de la Chambre des communes, le 12 mars 2010, p. 396*)

European Union / Union européenne

M. André Bellavance (Richmond — Arthabaska):

En 2006, le gouvernement avait refusé de se joindre aux négociations pour un accord de libre-échange transpacifique à cause des menaces que cela faisait peser sur la gestion de l'offre. Or maintenant, le Canada serait disposé à participer à ces négociations. Est-ce à dire que le gouvernement, comme il l'a fait lors des négociations entamées avec l'Union européenne, est prêt à faire des compromis sur la gestion de l'offre?

L'hon. Jean-Pierre Blackburn (ministre des Anciens Combattants et ministre d'État (Agriculture)):

Dans le discours du Trône, le gouvernement a pu clarifier très clairement sa position à l'égard de la gestion de l'offre. Nous appuyons les agriculteurs et nous entendons protéger la gestion de l'offre tant dans les discussions avec l'Union européenne que dans les négociations d'accords de libre-échange.

(*House of Commons Debates, 13 April 2010, p. 1421*)
(*Débats de la Chambre des communes, le 13 avril 2010, p. 1421*)

M. Jean-Yves Laforest (Saint-Maurice — Champlain):

Selon le négociateur en chef du Canada, les négociations pour un accord économique et commercial global avec l'Europe progressent rapidement et les pourparlers sont à mi-chemin d'un échéancier qui se termine en 2011. Le ministre du Commerce international conviendra-t-il qu'il est plus que temps de rendre publics les documents préliminaires et le mandat de négociation de ce que lui-même considère comme l'entente commerciale la plus ambitieuse jamais envisagée?

Mr. Gerald Keddy (Parliamentary Secretary to the Minister of International Trade):

This is certainly a time of economic uncertainty and this government is working to open new doors for Canadian business. The economic agreement that we are hopefully signing with the European Union has the potential to increase trade between Canada and Europe by $12 billion and to provide jobs and opportunities not just for Canadians and not just for Europeans, but to set a standard for the rest of the world to follow.

(*House of Commons Debates, 4 May 2010, p. 2353*)
(*Débats de la Chambre des communes, le 4 mai 2010, p. 2353*)

Ms. Dona Cadman (Surrey North):

[What are] the efforts our government is taking to diversify trading opportunities for Canadian businesses and workers?

Hon. Peter Van Loan (Minister of International Trade):

Our government is focused on economic recovery and delivering jobs for Canadians. That is why this week we launched the fifth round of negotiations for a free trade deal with the European Union. Two-thirds of our economy is trade-based. That is one of the reasons that Canada has been successful in weathering the economic storm and posting the strongest economic growth of any major developed economy, any of the G7 countries. We are focused on continuing that with trade negotiations under way with close to 50 countries right now.

(*House of Commons Debates, 19 October 2010, p. 5062*)
(*Débats de la Chambre des communes, le 19 octobre 2010, p. 5062*)

M. Pablo Rodriguez (Honoré-Mercier):

Le ministre va-t-il ... exiger l'exemption culturelle dans ... le cadre de nos négociations avec l'Union européenne?

Mr. Gerald Keddy (Parliamentary Secretary to the Minister of International Trade):

We are seeking the normal cultural exemption that we seek in all of our trade agreements and we are confident that the 27 members of the European Union will be seeking similar cultural exemptions.

(*House of Commons Debates, 22 October 2010, p. 5231*)
(*Débats de la Chambre des communes, le 22 octobre 2010, p. 5231*)

Panama

M. Jean-Yves Laforest (Saint-Maurice — Champlain):

Comment le ministre peut-il défendre un accord avec le Panama, un paradis fiscal qui figure sur la liste de l'OCDE des 11 États qui ne respectent pas leur engagement à échanger des renseignements fiscaux?

Hon. Peter Van Loan (Minister of International Trade):

The government of Panama has made a commitment to follow the OECD requirements for transparency and tax information sharing. We encourage that and we are there to help them do it. However, it is important for us to create opportunities for Canadian workers and Canadian companies to succeed by trading everywhere but especially in the Americas where we are carving out a special role with free trade agreements with Colombia ... Peru, Mexico, Costa Rica and further negotiations under way ... Our priority is to deliver jobs and prosperity for Canadians and we are entering into these agreements in order to do that. In fact, by bringing Panama more and more into that system, we are doing, what so many other countries, including those in the European Union are doing, we are delivering results for Canadian workers.

(*House of Commons Debates, 5 October 2010, p. 4777*)
(*Débats de la Chambre des communes, le 5 octobre 2010, p. 4777*)

Trade and Human Rights / Commerce et les droits de la personne

Mr. Peter Julian (Burnaby — New Westminster):

The Colombian trade deal has taken a sad new twist ... Unbelievably, the Colombian government gets to grade itself on its human rights record ... Why is the government still flogging this amoral deal that repudiates Canadian values?

Hon. Peter Van Loan (Minister of International Trade):

Our government has always been prepared to advance human rights while advancing our trade agenda ... Certainly we are very concerned about the rights of Colombians and that is why in this trade agreement we have parallel provisions relating to labour, which cover human rights, and also with regard to the environment and protecting the rights of the people of Colombia. We believe that by engaging through trade, we can advance the progress made by the Colombian government in advancing human rights.

(*House of Commons Debates, 25 March 2010, p. 949*)
(*Débats de la Chambre des communes, le 25 mars 2010, p.949*)

Mme Monique Guay (Rivière-du-Nord):

Au Honduras, depuis le coup d'État de 2009, des militants pour les droits de la personne sont toujours emprisonnés, des femmes sont violées et des enseignants sont assassinés. Comment le ministre du Commerce international peut-il ainsi faire abstraction du non-respect des droits de la personne et continuer à donner son appui à ces dirigeants sans scrupules en négociant avec eux un accord de libre-échange?

Mr. Gerald Keddy (Parliamentary Secretary to the Minister of International Trade):

The Government of Canada believes that engagement rather than isolationism is the best way of supporting change in Honduras. Canada works with like-minded countries, international organizations and governments worldwide to support improved respect for human rights and international humanitarian law and to lay the foundations for peace. Free trade between

Canada and Honduras will benefit not just Canadians, but Hondurans alike.

(*House of Commons Debates, 11 March 2011, p. 8960*)
(*Débats de la Chambre des communes, le 11 mars 2011, p.8960*)

World Trade Organization (WTO) / Organisation mondiale du Commerce (OMC)

Mr. Blaine Calkins (Wetaskiwin):

[What are] the latest steps taken to protect the traditional livelihoods of our Canadian sealers?

Hon. Gail Shea (Minister of Fisheries and Oceans):

We believe the EU ban on Canadian seal products is inconsistent with the EU's international trade obligations. That is why today our government formally requested a WTO dispute settlement panel. [We are] firmly committed to protecting traditional markets and to opening new markets for Canadian seal products. We will continue to defend Canada's sealing industry and the coastal and northern communities that depend on the seal hunt.

(*House of Commons Debates, 11 February 2011, p. 8066*)
(*Débats de la Chambre des communes, le 11 février 2011, p. 8066*)

LAW OF THE SEA / DROIT DE LA MER

Fisheries / Pêches

Access to foreign markets / Accès aux marchés étrangers

Mr. James Lunney (Nanaimo — Alberni):

Maintaining market access is essential for Canada's hard-working fishermen. Eighty-five per cent of our seafood products are exported abroad. With these markets increasingly demanding certification that fish are caught from a sustainably managed fishery ... what [is] the government doing to ensure that our fishing industry maintains access to these essential foreign markets?

Hon. Gail Shea (Minister of Fisheries and Oceans):

Our government recognizes the need to protect the livelihood of our fishing communities. Budget 2010 provided $7.2 million over two years to support a new catch certification program. Through this program, Fisheries and Oceans will issue certificates to exporters, ensuring that Canadian fish products can be traced back to their origin and back to sustainable fisheries. The European market alone is worth approximately $500 million annually to the Canadian fish and seafood industry, so this is a very sound investment. Our Conservative government proudly supports the fishing industry.

(House of Commons Debates, 12 March 2010, p. 397)
(Débats de la Chambre des communes, le 12 mars 2010, p. 397)

Mrs. Tilly O'Neill-Gordon (Miramichi):

For generations Atlantic Canadian fishermen have looked south to sell their products in the lucrative New England market ... [What was been done] at the International Boston Seafood Show and [what is] our government's support for Canadian fishermen?

Hon. Gail Shea (Minister of Fisheries and Oceans):

I was very pleased to attend the International Boston Seafood Show. I can say that I was certainly very proud to be a Canadian. There I heard firsthand not just from Americans but also from global buyers that there is increasing demand for our Canadian seafood, because it is high quality and our fishers have a reputation for producing the best seafood in the world. It was also evident that Canada is a leader in the emerging trend of traceability and eco-certification. With our historic investments in lobster marketing and new initiatives such as traceability and catch certification, our Canadian fishing industry stands to emerge from this global recession.

(House of Commons Debates, 15 March 2010, pp. 454-55)
(Débats de la Chambre des communes, le 15 mars 2010, pp. 454-55)

Quotas

Hon. Gerry Byrne (Humber — St. Barbe — Baie Verte):

The gulf crab fishery is made up of both traditional and new entrants alike. In recent years, former groundfish-dependent fleets were allowed entry into area 12, but when the minister announced the 63% reductions in quota this year, rather than cutting the newer entrants first, a policy known as last in, first out, all shared the cuts proportionately and all shared the remaining quota, regardless of when they entered the fishery. Will the minister confirm that she will be consistent and apply this same decision to northern shrimp, should quota reductions occur in that fishery?

Mr. Randy Kamp (Parliamentary Secretary to the Minister of Fisheries and Oceans):

These decisions are always difficult decisions, especially when a quota is cut. These decisions are reached after considerable consultation with industry and science. That is what was done in this case. We are following the precautionary approach and we will continue to do so ... At this point there is no plan to provide some financial assistance, but we do allow some flexibility in the rules governing how the fishery is implemented, and we will assist harvesters in that way. The standing committee unanimously supported a motion to take a look at the crab issue in Atlantic Canada. Perhaps these issues will be raised there.

(House of Commons Debates, 23 April 2010, p. 1912)
(Débats de la Chambre des communes, le 23 avril 2010, p. 1912)

Sustainability / Durabilité

Mr. Scott Armstrong (Cumberland — Colchester — Musquodoboit Valley):

Canadians care deeply about the future of the Atlantic bluefin tuna and our government shares the concerns of experts around the world about the conservation of this important species. [What is] the most recent development on this important file, on which Canada continues to show international leadership?

Hon. Gail Shea (Minister of Fisheries and Oceans):

The Canadian bluefin tuna fishery is a model of sustainability for the world. At meetings in Doha, in March, the world was put on notice that the time for talk was over and urgent action was needed now to protect this species. At international meetings next week, our government will continue to show leadership on this file and press our international tuna fishing partners to follow the example of Canadian fishers, who strictly adhere to sustainable fishing practices and protect the future of this fishery.

(House of Commons Debates, 28 May 2010, p. 3103)
(Débats de la Chambre des communes, le 28 mai 2010, p. 3103)

SPORTS

Mr. Ed Fast (Abbotsford):

Yesterday marked the official end of the 2010 Olympic and Paralympic Games. [What has been] the success of the 2010 Olympic and Paralympic Games?

Hon. James Moore (Minister of Canadian Heritage and Official Languages):

From the torch relay, which was the longest torch relay in Olympic history at over 46,000 kilometres and involved over 90% of Canadians from coast to coast to coast, to the great Canadian athletes, like Brian McKeever, Jen Heil, Alexandre Bilodeau and Joannie Rochette who are now known not only in Canada but internationally, to the cultural Olympiad which saw over 3,000 artists perform at over 300 venues all across the country, to the infrastructure legacies of the Canada Line and the Richmond Oval, to everything that was the Olympic Games, we are so proud of the success of this event. This shows what a great country can do. When the federal government, provincial governments, four host first nations and everybody gets together and puts on a great event, Canada can shine on the world stage like never before.

(House of Commons Debates, 22 March 2010, pp. 749-50)
(Débats de la Chambre des communes, le 22 mars 2010, pp. 749-50)

Treaty Action Taken by Canada in 2009 / Mesures prises par le Canada en matière de traités en 2009

compiled by/préparé par
JACQUELINE CARON

BILATERAL

Bahamas
Agreement between the Government of Canada and the Government of the Commonwealth of the Bahamas regarding the Sharing of Forfeited or Confiscated Assets or Their Equivalent Sums. *Signed:* Nassau, 12 March 2009. *Entered into force:* 20 October 2009.

People's Republic of China
Protocol amending the Agreement between the Government of Canada and the Government of the People's Republic of China on Maritime Transport. *Signed:* Ottawa, 6 May 2009. *Entered into force:* 4 December 2009.

Czech Republic
Agreement between Canada and the Czech Republic for the Promotion and Protection of Investments. *Signed:* Prague, 6 May 2009.

Denmark
Exchange of Notes constituting an Agreement to Amend the Agreement between the Government of Canada and the Government of the Kingdom of Denmark relating to the Delimitation of the Continental Shelf between Greenland and Canada done at Ottawa on 17 December 1973. *Signed by Denmark:* Copenhagen, 5 April 2004. *Signed by Canada:* Copenhagen, 20 April 2004. *Entered into force:* 16 December 2009.

European Community
Agreement on Civil Aviation Safety between Canada and the European Community. *Signed:* Prague, 6 May 2009.

Agreement on Air Transport between Canada and the European Community and Its Member States. *Signed by the European Community and its Member States:* Brussels, 17 December 2009. *Signed by Canada:* Ottawa, 18 December 2009.

Estonia
Agreement between the Government of Canada and the Government of the Republic of Estonia Concerning Youth Exchanges. *Signed:* Tallinn, 14 December 2009. *Entered into force:* 1 August 2010.

Jacqueline Caron is Treaty Registrar in the Legal Affairs Bureau of the Department of Foreign Affairs and International Trade / Jacqueline Caron est Greffier des Traités, Direction générale des affaires juridiques, Ministère des Affaires étrangères et du Commerce international.

Greece
Convention between Canada and the Hellenic Republic for the Avoidance of Double Taxation and the Prevention of Fiscal Evasion with Respect to Taxes on Income and on Capital. *Signed:* Athens, 29 June 2009. *Entered into force:* 16 December 2010.

Iceland
Agreement on Agriculture between Canada and the Republic of Iceland. *Signed:* Davos, 26 January 2008. *Entered into force:* 1 July 2009.

Jordan
Agreement between the Government of Canada and the Government of the Hashemite Kingdom of Jordan for Co-operation in the Peaceful Uses of Nuclear Energy. *Signed:* Amman, 17 February 2009. *Entered into force:* 16 June 2009. CTS 2009/9.

Agreement between Canada and the Hashemite Kingdom of Jordan for the Promotion and Protection of Investments. *Signed:* Amman, 28 June 2009. *Entered into force:* 14 December 2009.

Free Trade Agreement between Canada and the Hashemite Kingdom of Jordan. *Signed:* Amman, 28 June 2009.

Agreement on the Environment between Canada and the Hashemite Kingdom of Jordan. *Signed:* Amman, 28 June 2009.

Agreement on Labour Cooperation between Canada and the Hashemite Kingdom of Jordan. *Signed:* Amman, 28 June 2009.

Kyrgyzstan
Agreement between the Government of Canada and the Government of the Kyrgyz Republic Concerning Cooperation in the Field of Biological Security

and Biological Safety. *Signed:* Bishkek, 22 August 2008. *Entered into force:* 8 April 2009. CTS 2009/8.

Latvia
Agreement between the Government of Canada and the Government of the Republic of Latvia for the Promotion and Protection of Investments. *Signed:* Riga, 5 May 2009.

Lithuania
Agreement between the Government of Canada and the Government of the Republic of Lithuania Concerning Youth Exchanges. *Signed:* Vilnius, 19 November 2009. *Entered into force:* 1 October 2010.

Macedonia
Agreement on Social Security between Canada and the Republic of Macedonia. *Signed:* Ottawa, 26 August 2009.

Netherlands
Exchange of Notes Constituting an Amendment to the Agreement between the Government of Canada and the Government of the Kingdom of the Netherlands on Mutual Administrative Assistance in Customs Matters, done in Ottawa on 14 August 2007. *Signed by Canada:* Ottawa, 30 March 2009. *Signed by the Netherlands:* Ottawa, 28 April 2009. *Entered into force:* 1 December 2010.

Agreement between the Government of Canada and the Government of the Kingdom of the Netherlands in Respect of the Netherlands Antilles on Exchange of Information on Tax Matters. *Signed:* Vancouver, 29 August 2009. *Entered into force:* 1 January 2011.

New Zealand
Agreement between the Government of Canada and the Government of New Zealand on Air Transport. *Signed:* Singapore, 21 July 2009.

Norway

Agreement on Agriculture between Canada and the Kingdom of Norway. *Signed:* Davos, 26 January 2008. *Entered into force:* 1 July 2009. CTS 2009/5.

Peru

Free Trade Agreement between Canada and the Republic of Peru. *Signed:* Lima, 29 May 2008. *Entered into force:* 1 August 2009.

Agreement on the Environment between Canada and the Republic of Peru. *Signed:* Lima, 29 May 2008. *Entered into force:* 1 August 2009. CTS 2009/16.

Agreement on Labour Cooperation between Canada and the Republic of Peru. *Signed:* Lima, 29 May 2008. *Entered into force:* 1 August 2009. CTS 2009/17.

Poland

Agreement on Social Security between Canada and the Republic of Poland. *Signed:* Warsaw, 2 April 2008. *Entered into force:* 1 October 2009. CTS 2009/13.

Agreement between the Government of Canada and the Government of the Republic of Poland Concerning the Promotion of Mobility of Young Citizens. *Signed:* Warsaw, 14 July 2008. *Entered into force:* 1 August 2009. CTS 2009/12.

Romania

Agreement between the Government of Canada and the Government of Romania for the Promotion and Reciprocal Protection of Investments. *Signed:* Bucharest, 8 May 2009.

Agreement on Social Security between Canada and Romania. *Signed:* Ottawa, 19 November 2009.

Russian Federation

Exchange of Notes between the Government of Canada and the Government of the Russian Federation Constituting an Additional Agreement to the Agreement between the Government of Canada and the Government of the Union of Soviet Socialist Republics for Cooperation in the Peaceful Uses of Nuclear Energy, done on 20 November 1989. *Signed by the Russian Federation:* Ottawa, 23 April 2008. *Signed by Canada:* Ottawa, 6 May 2008. *Entered into force:* 3 June 2009. CTS 2009/10.

Slovenia

Agreement between Canada and the Republic of Slovenia Concerning Youth Mobility. *Signed:* Ljubljana, 22 October 2009. *Entered into force:* 1 July 2010.

South Africa

Agreement between the Government of Canada and the Government of the Republic of South Africa regarding Mutual Assistance between Their Customs Administrations. *Signed:* Johannesburg, 30 October 2009. *Entered into force:* 9 November 2010.

Spain

Agreement between Canada and Spain on Youth Mobility Programs. *Signed:* Ottawa, 10 March 2009. *Entered into force:* 1 August 2009. CTS 2009/11.

Switzerland

Agreement on Agriculture between Canada and the Swiss Confederation. *Signed:* Davos, 26 January 2008. *Entered into force:* 1 July 2009. CTS 2009/6.

Turkey

Agreement between Canada and the Republic of Turkey for the Avoidance of Double Taxation and the Prevention of Fiscal Evasion with Respect to Taxes on Income and on Capital. *Signed:* Ottawa, 14 July 2009. *Entered into force:* 4 May 2011.

United Nations
Agreement between the United Nations and the Government of Canada Contributing Resources to the United Nations — African Union Mission in Darfur (UNAMID). *Signed:* New York, 9 July 2009.

United States of America
Exchange of Letters constituting an Agreement between the Government of Canada and the Government of the United States of America Amending Appendix 6 of Annex 300-B, Textiles and Apparel Goods, of the North American Free Trade Agreement between the Government of Canada, the Government of the United States of America and the Government of the United Mexican States. *Signed by the United States of America:* Washington, 29 May 2008. *Signed by Canada:* Ottawa, 21 July 2008. *Entered into force:* 1 July 2009.

Agreement between the Government of Canada and the Government of the United States of America on Emergency Management Cooperation. *Signed:* Washington, 12 December 2008. *Entered into force:* 7 July 2009. CTS 2009/14.

Agreement between the Government of Canada and the Government of the United States of America on Cooperation in Comprehensive Civil Emergency Planning and Management. *Signed:* Ottawa, 28 April 1986. *Entered into force:* 28 April 1986. *Terminated:* 7 July 2009. CTS 1986/36.

Exchange of Notes constituting an Agreement to Renew for an Indeterminate Period and Amend the Agreement between the Government of Canada and the Government of the

United States of America on Cooperation in Comprehensive Civil Emergency Planning and Management, done at Ottawa on 28 April 1986. *Signed by Canada:* Washington, 19 December 1997 and 2 December 1998. *Signed by the United States of America:* Washington, 17 March 1998. *Entered into force:* 2 December 1998. *Terminated:* 7 July 2009. CTS 1998/36.

Exchange of Notes between the Government of Canada and the Government of the United States of America relating to Annex IV of the Treaty between the Government of Canada and the Government of the United States of America Concerning Pacific Salmon. *Signed:* Washington, 23 December 2008. *Entered into force:* 1 January 2009. CTS 2009/7.

Exchange of Notes amending the Agreement between the Government of Canada and the Government of the United States of America for the Establishment of a Binational Educational Exchange Foundation. *Signed by Canada:* Ottawa, 8 May 2009. *Signed by the United States of America:* Ottawa, 22 May 2009. *Entered into force:* 23 October 2009.

Framework Agreement on Integrated Cross-Border Maritime Law Enforcement Operations between the Government of Canada and the Government of the United States of America. *Signed:* Detroit, 26 May 2009.

Exchange of Notes between the Government of Canada and the Government of the United States of America Concluding Amendments to the Treaty between the Government of Canada and the Government of the United States of America on Pacific Coast Albacore Tuna Vessels and Port Privileges. *Signed:* Washington, 12

June 2009. *Entered into force:* 8 March 2010.

Framework Agreement between the Government of Canada and the Government of the United States of America for Cooperation in the Exploration and Use of Outer Space for Peaceful Purposes. *Signed:* Washington, 9 September 2009. *Entered into force:* 11 May 2010.

MULTILATERAL

Aviation
Amendments to the Limits of Liability under the Convention for the Unification of Certain Rules for International Carriage by Air, done at Montreal on 28 May 1999, Montreal, 30 June 2009. *Entered into force for Canada:* 30 December 2009.

Defence
Protocol to the North Atlantic Treaty on the Accession of the Republic of Albania, Brussels, 9 July 2008. *Signed by Canada:* 9 July 2008. *Accepted by Canada:* 16 January 2009. *Entered into force for Canada:* 27 March 2009.

Protocol to the North Atlantic Treaty on the Accession of the Republic of Croatia, Brussels, 9 July 2008. *Signed by Canada:* 9 July 2008. *Accepted by Canada:* 16 January 2009. *Entered into force for Canada:* 30 March 2009.

Disarmament
Protocol on Explosive Remnants of War to the Convention on Prohibitions or Restrictions on the Use of Certain Conventional Weapons Which May Be Deemed to Be Excessively Injurious or to Have Indiscriminate Effects (Protocol V), Geneva, 28 November 2003. *Accepted by Canada:* 19 May 2009. *Entered into force for Canada:* 19 November 2009.

Finance
Amendment of the Articles of Agreement of the International Bank for Reconstruction and Development, Washington, 30 January 2009. *Signed by Canada:* 30 January 2009.

Fisheries
Amendment to the Convention on Future Multilateral Cooperation in the Northwest Atlantic Fisheries, Lisbon, 28 September 2007. *Accepted by Canada:* 11 December 2009.

Convention for the Strengthening of the Inter-American Tropical Tuna Commission Established by the 1949 Convention between the United States of America and the Republic of Costa Rica, Washington, 14 November 2003. *Signed by Canada:* 22 December 2004. *Ratified by Canada:* 3 June 2009. *Entered into force for Canada:* 27 August 2010.

Narcotics
Amendments to Annex I and Annex II of the International Convention against Doping in Sport, Paris, 16 November 2008. *Entered into force for Canada:* 1 January 2009. CTS 2009/2.

Navigation
Protocol of Amendments to the Convention on the International Hydrographic Organization, Monaco, 14 April 2005. *Approved by Canada:* 28 May 2009.

International Convention on Civil Liability for Bunker Oil Pollution Damage, 2001, London, 23 March 2001. *Signed by Canada:* 27 September 2002. *Acceded to by Canada:* 2 October 2009. *Entered into force for Canada:* 2 January 2010.

Protocol of 2003 to the International Convention on the Establishment of an International Fund for Compensation for Oil Pollution Damage, 1992, London, 16 May 2003. *Acceded to by Canada:* 2 October 2009. *Entered into force for Canada:* 2 January 2010.

Post
Acts of the XXIth Congress of the Postal Union of the Americas, Spain and Portugal, Santiago, 21 August 2009. *Signed by Canada:* 21 August 2009.

Trade
Protocol Amending the Agreement on Trade-Related Aspects of Intellectual Property Rights, Geneva, 6 December 2005. *Accepted by Canada:* 16 June 2009.

Free Trade Agreement between Canada and the States of the European Free Trade Association (Iceland, Liechtenstein, Norway and Switzerland), Davos, 26 January 2008. *Signed by Canada:* 26 January 2008. *Ratified by Canada:* 30 April 2009. *Entered into force for Canada:* 1 July 2009. CTS 2009/3.

Exchange of Letters Constituting an Agreement between the Government of Canada, the Government of the United Mexican States and the Government of the United States of America, Amending Annex 401 of the North American Free Trade Agreement between the Government of Canada, the Government of the United Mexican States and the Government of the United States of America, Mexico, Ottawa and Washington, 11 April 2008. *Signed by Canada:* 11 April 2008. *Entered into force for Canada:* 1 September 2009.

Exchange of Letters Constituting an Agreement between the Government of Canada, the Government of the United Mexican States and the Government of the United States of America Rectifying Annex 300-B, Annex 308.1, Annex 401, Annex 403.1 and the Uni-

form Regulations for Chapter Four of the North American Free Trade Agreement, Mexico, Ottawa, Washington, 24 April 2009. *Signed by the United States of America:* 9 April 2009. *Signed by the United Mexican States:* 13 April 2009. *Signed by Canada:* 24 April 2009. *Entered into force for Canada:* 1 September 2009.

Tropical Timber
International Tropical Timber Agreement, 2006, Geneva, 27 January 2006. *Signed by Canada:* 2 March 2009. *Ratified by Canada:* 19 November 2009.

BILATÉRAUX

Afrique du Sud
Accord entre le gouvernement du Canada et le gouvernement de la République d'Afrique du Sud concernant l'assistance mutuelle entre leurs administrations des douanes. *Signé:* Johannesburg, le 30 octobre 2009. *Entré en vigueur:* le 9 novembre 2010.

Bahamas
Accord entre le gouvernement du Canada et le gouvernement du Commonwealth des Bahamas concernant le partage des biens confisqués ou des sommes d'argent équivalentes. *Signé:* Nassau, le 12 mars 2009. *Entré en vigueur:* le 20 octobre 2009.

Communauté européenne
Accord sur la sécurité de l'aviation civile entre le Canada et la Communauté européenne. *Signé:* Prague, le 6 mai 2009.

Accord sur le transport aérien entre le Canada et la Communauté européenne et ses États membres. *Signé par la Communauté européenne et ses États membres:* Bruxelles, le 17 décembre 2009. *Signé par le Canada:* Ottawa, le 18 décembre 2009.

République populaire de Chine
Protocole modifiant l'Accord sur le transport maritime entre le gouvernement du Canada et le gouvernement de la République populaire de Chine. *Signé:* Ottawa, le 6 mai 2009. *Entré en vigueur:* le 4 décembre 2009.

Danemark
Échange de notes constituant un Accord modifiant l'Accord entre le gouvernement du Canada et le gouvernement du Royaume du Danemark relatif à la délimitation du plateau continental entre le Groenland et le Canada fait à Ottawa le 17 décembre 1973. *Signé par le Danemark:* Copenhague, le 5 avril 2004. *Signé par le Canada:* Copenhague, le 20 avril 2004. *Entré en vigueur:* le 16 décembre 2009.

Espagne
Accord entre le Canada et l'Espagne relatif aux programmes de mobilité des jeunes. *Signé:* Ottawa, le 10 mars 2009. *Entré en vigueur:* le 1er août 2009. RTC 2009/11.

Estonie
Accord entre le gouvernement du Canada et le gouvernement de la République d'Estonie relatif aux échanges jeunesse. *Signé:* Tallinn, le 14 décembre 2009. *Entré en vigueur:* le 1er août 2010.

États-Unis
Échange de lettres constituant un Accord entre le gouvernement du Canada et le gouvernement des États-Unis d'Amérique modifiant l'Appendice 6 de l'Annexe 300-B, Produits textiles et vêtements, de l'Accord de libre-échange nord-américain entre le gouvernement du Canada, le gouvernement des États-Unis d'Amérique et le gouvernement des États-Unis du Mexique. *Signé par les États-Unis:* le 29 mai 2008. *Signé par le Canada:* le 21 juillet 2008. *Entré en vigueur:* le 1er juillet 2009.

Accord de coopération entre le gouvernement du Canada et le gouvernement des États-Unis d'Amérique concernant la gestion des urgences. *Signé:* Washington, le 12 décembre 2008. *Entré en vigueur:* le 7 juillet 2009. RTC 2009/14.

Accord de coopération entre le gouvernement du Canada et le gouvernement des États-Unis d'Amérique concernant la planification et la gestion civiles d'urgence sur une base globale. *Signé:* Ottawa, le 28 avril 1986. *Entré en vigueur:* le 28 avril 1986. *Pris fin:* le 7 juillet 2009. RTC 1986/36.

Échange de notes constituant un Accord reconduisant pour une période indéterminée et modifiant l'Accord de coopération entre le gouvernement du Canada et le gouvernement des États-Unis d'Amérique concernant la planification et la gestion civiles d'urgence sur une base globale, conclu à Ottawa le 28 avril 1986. *Signé par le Canada:* Washington, le 19 décembre 1997 et le 2 décembre 1998. *Signé par les États-Unis:* Washington, le 17 mars 1998. *Entré en vigueur:* le 2 décembre 1998. *Pris fin:* le 7 juillet 2009. RTC 1998/36.

Échange de notes entre le gouvernement du Canada et le gouvernement des États-Unis d'Amérique relatif à l'Annexe IV du Traité entre le gouvernement du Canada et le gouvernement des États-Unis d'Amérique concernant le saumon du Pacifique. *Signé:* Washington, le 23 décembre 2008. *Entré en vigueur:* le 1er janvier 2009. RTC 2009/7.

Échange de notes modifiant l'Accord entre le gouvernement du Canada et le gouvernement des États-Unis d'Amérique portant création d'une fondation binationale pour les échanges dans le domaine de l'éducation. *Signé par le Canada:* Ottawa, le 8 mai 2009. *Signé par les États-Unis:* Ottawa, le 22 mai 2009. *Entré en vigueur:* le 23 octobre 2009.

Accord cadre sur les opérations intégrées transfrontalières maritimes d'application de la loi entre le gouvernement du Canada et le gouvernement des États-Unis d'Amérique. *Signé:* Détroit, le 26 mai 2009.

Échange de notes entre le gouvernement du Canada et le gouvernement des États-Unis d'Amérique concluant les amendements au Traité entre le gouvernement du Canada et le gouvernement des États-Unis d'Amérique concernant les thoniers (thon blanc) du Pacifique et leurs privilèges portuaires. *Signé:* Washington, le 12 juin 2009. *Entré en vigueur:* le 8 mars 2010.

Accord cadre de coopération entre le gouvernement du Canada et le gouvernement des États-Unis d'Amérique relatif à l'exploration et à l'utilisation de l'espace extra-atmosphérique à des fins pacifiques. *Signé:* Washington, le 9 septembre 2009. *Entré en vigueur:* le 11 mai 2010.

Grèce
Convention entre le Canada et la République hellénique en vue d'éviter les doubles impositions et de prévenir l'évasion fiscale en matière d'impôts sur le revenu et sur la fortune. *Signée:* Athènes, le 29 juin 2009. *Entrée en vigueur:* le 16 décembre 2010.

Islande
Accord sur l'agriculture entre le Canada et la République d'Islande. *Signé:* Davos, le 26 janvier 2008. *Entré en vigueur:* le 1er juillet 2009.

Jordanie
Accord de coopération entre le gouvernement du Canada et le gouvernement du Royaume hachémite de Jordanie concernant les utilisations pacifiques de l'énergie nucléaire. *Signé:* Amman, le 17 février 2009. *Entré en vigueur:* le 16 juin 2009. RTC 2009/9.

Accord entre le Canada et le Royaume hachémite de Jordanie concernant la promotion et la protection des investissements. *Signé:* Amman, le 28 juin 2009. *Entré en vigueur:* le 14 décembre 2009.

Accord de libre-échange entre le Canada et le Royaume hachémite de Jordanie. *Signé:* Amman, le 28 juin 2009.

Accord sur l'environnement entre le Canada et le Royaume hachémite de Jordanie. *Signé:* Amman, le 28 juin 2009.

Accord de coopération dans le domaine du travail entre le Canada et le Royaume hachémite de Jordanie. *Signé:* Amman, le 28 juin 2009.

Kirghizistan
Accord entre le gouvernement du Canada et le gouvernement de la République kirghize concernant la coopération en matière de biosûreté et de biosécurité. *Signé:* Bichkek, le 22 août 2008. *Entré en vigueur:* le 8 avril 2009. RTC 2009/8.

Lettonie
Accord entre le gouvernement du Canada et le gouvernement de la République de Lettonie concernant la promotion et la protection des investissements. *Signé:* Riga, le 5 mai 2009.

Lituanie
Accord entre le gouvernement du Canada et le gouvernement de la République de Lituanie relatif aux échanges jeunesse. *Signé:* Vilnius, le 19 novembre 2009. *Entré en vigueur:* le 1er octobre 2010.

Macédoine
Accord sur la sécurité sociale entre le Canada et la République de Macédoine. *Signé:* Ottawa, le 26 août 2009.

Norvège
Accord sur l'agriculture entre le Canada et le Royaume de Norvège. *Signé:* le 26 janvier 2008. *Entré en vigueur:* le 1er juillet 2009. RTC 2009/5.

Nouvelle-Zélande
Accord sur le transport aérien entre le gouvernement du Canada et le gouvernement de la Nouvelle-Zélande. *Signé:* Singapour, le 21 juillet 2009.

Organisation des Nations Unies
Accord entre l'Organisation des Nations Unies et le gouvernement du Canada relatif aux contributions de ressources à la Mission des Nations Unies et de l'Union africaine au Darfour (l'UNAMID). *Signé:* New York, le 9 juillet 2009.

Pays-Bas
Échange de notes constituant un amendement à l'Accord d'assistance mutuelle administrative en matière douanière entre le gouvernement du Canada et le gouvernement du Royaume des Pays-Bas, fait à Ottawa le 14 août 2007. *Signé par le Canada:* Ottawa, le 30 mars 2009. *Signé par les Pays-Bas:* Ottawa, le 28 avril 2009. *Entré en vigueur:* le 1er décembre 2010.

Accord entre le gouvernement du Canada et le gouvernement du Royaume des Pays-Bas en ce qui concerne les Antilles néerlandaises sur l'échange de renseignements en matière fiscale. *Signé:* Vancouver, le 29 août 2009. *Entré en vigueur:* le 1er janvier 2011.

Pérou
Accord de libre-échange entre le Canada et la République du Pérou. *Signé:*

Lima, le 29 mai 2008. *Entré en vigueur:* le 1er août 2009.

Accord sur l'environnement entre le Canada et la République du Pérou. *Signé:* Lima, le 29 mai 2008. *Entré en vigueur:* le 1er août 2009. RTC 2009/16.

Accord de coopération dans le domaine du travail entre le Canada et la République du Pérou. *Signé:* Lima, le 29 mai 2008. *Entré en vigueur:* le 1er août 2009. RTC 2009/17.

Pologne
Accord sur la sécurité sociale entre le Canada et la République de Pologne. *Signé:* Varsovie, le 2 avril 2008. *Entré en vigueur:* le 1er octobre 2009. RTC 2009/13.

Accord entre le gouvernement du Canada et le gouvernement de la République de Pologne concernant la promotion de la mobilité des jeunes citoyens. *Signé:* Varsovie, le 14 juillet 2008. *Entré en vigueur:* le 1er août 2009. RTC 2009/12.

République tchèque
Accord entre le Canada et la République tchèque concernant la promotion et la protection des investissements. *Signé:* Prague, le 6 mai 2009.

Roumanie
Accord entre le gouvernement du Canada et le gouvernement de Roumanie concernant la promotion et la protection réciproque des investissements. *Signé:* Bucarest, le 8 mai 2009.

Accord de sécurité sociale entre le Canada et la Roumanie. *Signé:* Ottawa, le 19 novembre 2009.

Fédération de Russie
Échange de notes entre le gouvernement du Canada et le gouvernement

de la Fédération de Russie constituant un Accord additionnel à l'Accord de coopération entre le gouvernement du Canada et le gouvernement de l'Union des Républiques socialistes soviétiques concernant les utilisations pacifiques de l'énergie nucléaire, fait le 20 novembre 1989. *Signé par la Fédération de Russie:* Ottawa, le 23 avril 2008. *Signé par le Canada:* Ottawa, le 6 mai 2008. *Entré en vigueur:* le 3 juin 2009.

Slovénie
Accord entre le Canada et la République de Slovénie concernant la mobilité des jeunes. *Signé:* Ljubljana, le 22 octobre 2009. *Entré en vigueur:* le 1er juillet 2010.

Suisse
Accord sur l'agriculture entre le Canada et la Confédération suisse. *Signé:* Davos, le 26 janvier 2008. *Entré en vigueur:* le 1er juillet 2009. RTC 2009/6.

Turquie
Accord entre le Canada et la République de Turquie en vue d'éviter les doubles impositions et de prévenir l'évasion fiscale en matière d'impôts sur le revenu et sur la fortune. *Signé:* Ottawa, le 14 juillet 2009. *Entré en vigueur:* le 4 mai 2011.

MULTILATÉRAUX

Aviation
Amendements aux limites de responsabilité établies dans le cadre de la Convention pour l'unification de certaines règles relatives au transport aérien international, faite à Montréal le 28 mai 1999, Montréal, 30 juin 2009. *Entrés en vigueur pour le Canada:* le 30 décembre 2009.

Bois tropicaux
Accord international de 2006 sur les bois tropicaux, Genève, 27 janvier 2006. *Signé par le Canada:* le 2 mars 2009. *Ratifié par le Canada:* le 19 novembre 2009.

Commerce
Protocole portant amendement de l'accord sur les aspects des droits de propriété intellectuelle qui touchent au commerce, Genève, 6 décembre 2005. *Accepté par le Canada:* le 16 juin 2009.

Échange de lettres constituant un Accord entre le gouvernement du Canada, le gouvernement des États-Unis du Mexique et le gouvernement des États-Unis d'Amérique, modifiant l'Annexe 401 de l'Accord de libre-échange nord-américain entre le gouvernement du Canada, le gouvernement des États-Unis du Mexique et le gouvernement des États-Unis d'Amérique, Mexico, Ottawa, Washington, 11 avril 2008. *Signé par le Canada:* le 11 avril 2008. *Entré en vigueur pour le Canada:* le 1er septembre 2009.

Échange de lettres constituant un Accord entre le gouvernement du Canada, le gouvernement des États-Unis du Mexique et le gouvernement des États-Unis d'Amérique rectifiant l'annexe 300-B, l'annexe 308.1, l'annexe 401, l'annexe 403.1 et la Réglementation uniforme du chapitre quatre de l'Accord de libre-échange nord-américain. *Signé par les États-Unis:* le 9 avril 2009. *Signé par les États-Unis du Mexique:* le 13 avril 2009. *Signé par le Canada:* le 24 avril 2009. *Entré en vigueur pour le Canada:* le 1er septembre 2009.

Accord de libre-échange entre le Canada et les États de l'Association européenne de libre-échange (Islande, Liechtenstein, Norvège et Suisse), Davos, 26 janvier 2008. *Signé par le Canada:* le 26 janvier 2008. *Ratifié par le Canada:* le 30 avril 2009. *Entré en vigueur pour le Canada:* le 1er juillet 2009.

Défense
Protocole au Traité de l'Atlantique Nord sur l'accession de la République d'Albanie, Bruxelles, 9 juillet 2008. *Signé par le Canada:* le 9 juillet 2008. *Accepté par le Canada:* le 16 janvier 2009. *Entré en vigueur pour le Canada:* le 27 mars 2009.

Protocole au Traité de l'Atlantique Nord sur l'accession de la République de Croatie, Bruxelles, 9 juillet 2008. *Signé par le Canada:* le 9 juillet 2008. *Accepté par le Canada:* le 16 janvier 2009. *Entré en vigueur pour le Canada:* le 30 mars 2009.

Désarmement
Protocole relatif aux restes explosifs de guerre à la Convention sur l'interdiction ou la limitation de l'emploi de certaines armes classiques qui peuvent être considérées comme produisant des effets traumatiques excessifs ou comme frappant sans discrimination (Protocole V), Genève, 28 novembre 2003. *Accepté par le Canada:* le 19 mai 2009. *Entré en vigueur pour le Canada:* le 19 novembre 2009.

Finances
Amendement des Statuts de la Banque internationale pour la reconstruction et le développement, Washington, 30 janvier 2009. *Signé par le Canada:* le 30 janvier 2009.

Navigation
Protocole visant à modifier la Convention relative à l'Organisation hydrographique internationale, Monaco, 14 avril 2005. *Approuvé par le Canada:* le 28 mai 2009.

Convention internationale de 2001 sur la responsabilité civile pour les dommages dus à la pollution par les hydrocarbures de soute, Londres, 23 mars 2001. *Signée par le Canada:* le 27 sep-

tembre 2002. *Adhérée par le Canada:* le 2 octobre 2009. *Entrée en vigueur pour le Canada:* le 2 janvier 2010.

Protocole de 2003 à la Convention internationale de 1992 portant création d'un fonds international d'indemnisation pour les dommages dus à la pollution par les hydrocarbures, Londres, 16 mai 2003. *Adhéré par le Canada:* le 2 octobre 2009. *Entré en vigueur pour le Canada:* le 2 janvier 2010.

Pêches
Amendement à la Convention sur la future coopération multilatérale dans les pêches de l'Atlantique du Nord-Ouest, Lisbonne, 28 septembre 2007. *Accepté par le Canada:* le 11 décembre 2009.

Convention relative au renforcement de la Commission interaméricaine du thon tropical établie par la Convention de 1949 entre les États-Unis d'Amérique et la République du Costa Rica, Washington, 14 novembre 2003. *Signée par le Canada:* le 22 décembre 2004. *Ratifiée par le Canada:* le 3 juin 2009. *Entrée en vigueur pour le Canada:* le 27 août 2010.

Poste
Actes du XXIe Congrès de l'Union postale des Amériques, de l'Espagne et du Portugal, Santiago, 21 août 2009. *Signés par le Canada:* le 21 août 2009.

Stupéfiants
Amendements à l'annexe I et à l'annexe II de la Convention internationale contre le dopage dans le sport, Paris, 16 novembre 2008. *Entrés en vigueur pour le Canada:* le 1er janvier 2009. RTC 2009/2.

Cases / Jurisprudence

Canadian Cases in
Public International Law in 2009-10 /
Jurisprudence canadienne en matière de
droit international public en 2009-10

compiled by / préparé par

GIB VAN ERT

Charter *and international law — homelessness*

Victoria (City) v Adams, 2009 BCCA 563 (9 December 2009). Court of Appeal for British Columbia.

This was an appeal from a summary trial decision challenging the constitutionality of a municipal prohibition on erecting temporary overhead shelters, such as tents, in public parks. The claimants were homeless and contended that the prohibition, which consisted of certain bylaws combined with a municipal enforcement policy, violated their constitutional rights to life, liberty, and security of the person under section 7 of the *Canadian Charter of Rights and Freedoms*.[1] The trial judge, Ross J., agreed. The effect of her decision was to permit the homeless of Victoria to erect temporary overhead shelters while sleeping outdoors in public parks and streets.

Before turning to the appeal, it is necessary to review in part the decision at first instance, which considered at some length international instruments relating to housing and an adequate standard of living.[2] Ross J. quoted and considered art. 25(1) of the 1948 *Universal Declaration of Human Rights*,[3] arts. 2(1) and 11(1) of the

Gib van Ert is of the British Columbia Bar and an associate in Hunter Litigation Chambers, Vancouver.

[1] *Canadian Charter of Rights and Freedoms*, Part I of the *Constitution Act, 1982*, being Schedule B of the *Canada Act 1982* (UK) 1982, c 11 [*Charter*].

[2] *Victoria (City) v Adams*, 2008 BCSC 1363 at paras 85-100 [*Adams*].

[3] *Universal Declaration of Human Rights*, GA Res 217 A (III), UN Doc A/810.

1966 *International Covenant on Economic, Social and Cultural Rights*,[4] arts. 3, 11, and 39 of the 1996 Habitat Agenda[5] of the United Nations Human Settlements Programme (UN-HABITAT), and General Comment 4 of the UN Committee on Economic, Social and Cultural Rights.[6] Ross J. considered these instruments in response to objections by the city of Victoria and the attorney general of British Columbia (intervening) that the claims advanced did not fall within the scope of section 7 of the *Charter*. The learned judge relied on these international instruments as recognition of "adequate housing as a fundamental right"[7] and concluded from them that the right to adequate housing is "enshrined ... as a fundamental principle of international law."[8]

The attorney general submitted that the international instruments to which Canada is a party did not assist because they "do not have a normative effect," not being equivalent to domestic law and not having the power of law unless implemented by domestic legislation. The attorney general also cited the *National Corn Growers* case[9] as authority that treaties and other international agreements may be referred to as an interpretive aid only where the legislation in question is ambiguous.[10] Ross J. rejected this submission, saying that the defendants (respondents in the appeal) were not seeking to enforce the international instruments but only to use them as aids to interpreting the meaning and scope of rights under the *Charter*. Ross J. also observed, quite pointedly, that the federal government has twice told the UN that section 7 must be interpreted consistently with Canada's international obligations:

The federal government has expressed the view that s. 7 of the *Charter* must be interpreted in a manner consistent with Canada's obligations under the *Covenant* to not deprive persons of the basic necessities of life, in its

---

4 *International Covenant on Economic, Social and Cultural Rights,* [1976] Can TS no 46.

5 Habitat Agenda, UN Doc A/Conf 165/14 (14 June 1996).

6 ICESCR General Comment 4 on the Right to Adequate Housing (Art. 11(1)), 6th session, 13 December 1991.

7 *Adams, supra* note 2 at para 85.

8 *Ibid* at para 90.

9 *National Corn Growers Association v Canada (Import Tribunal)*, [1990] 2 SCR 817 [*National Corn Growers*].

10 On the difficulty with this characterization of *National Corn Growers*, see the summary of *Canadian Security Intelligence Service Act (Canada) (Re)*, 2008 FC 301, in volume 46 (2008) of this *Yearbook*.

response to a question from the Committee on Economic, Social, and Cultural Rights: Summary Record of the 5th Meeting, ESC, 8th Sess., 5th Mtg., U.N. Doc. E/C.12/1993/SR.5 (25 May 1993). The question arose from the report submitted to the Committee by Canada in 1993, pursuant to its *Covenant* obligations. The federal government assured the Committee at para. 21 that:

> While the guarantee of security of the person under section 7 of the Charter might not lead to a right to a certain type of social assistance, it ensured that persons were not deprived of the basic necessities of life.

This position was again asserted in 1998: Government of Canada "Federal Responses," *Review of Canada's Third Report on the Implementation of the International Covenant on Economic, Social, and Cultural Rights* (November 1998), online: Canadian Heritage, Human Rights Program, <http://www.pch.gc.ca/progs/pdp-hrp/docs/cesc/responses/fd_e.cfm>. The Committee asked whether the answer given in 1993 was still the position of all Canadian governments. In reply, the federal government gave the following answer at Question 53:

> The Supreme Court of Canada has stated that section 7 of the Charter may be interpreted to include the rights protected under the *Covenant* (see decision of *Slaight Communications v. Davidson* [1989] 1 S.C.R. 1038). *The Supreme Court has also held section 7 as guaranteeing that people are not to be deprived of basic necessities* (see decision of *Irwin Toy v. A.-G. Québec*, [1989] 1 S.C.R. 927). *The Government of Canada is bound by these interpretations of section 7 of the Charter.*[11]

RossJ. concluded that "while the various international instruments do not form part of the domestic law of Canada, they should inform the interpretation of the *Charter* and in this case, the scope and content of s. 7." She later observed that international human rights instruments can inform a court's understanding of the principles of fundamental justice.[12]

The Court of Appeal's decision, which was attributed to the Court as a whole, did not include any express consideration of the international position. Nevertheless the Court noted RossJ.'s references to international instruments to which Canada is a party and strongly endorsed her treatment of them, saying:

---

[11] *Adams, supra* note 2 at paras 98-9 [emphasis added].

[12] *Ibid* at paras 100, 161-2.

There is no issue raised on the appeal with respect to the trial judge's reference to international instruments as an aid to interpreting the *Charter*. Nor could there be. The use of international instruments to aid in the interpretation of the meaning and scope of rights under the *Charter*, and in particular the rights protected under s. 7 and the principles of fundamental justice, is well-established in Canadian jurisprudence. In support of referring to international human rights instruments as an interpretative aid, the trial judge cited, among other authorities, *Baker v. Canada (Minister of Citizenship and Immigration)*, [1999] 2 S.C.R. 817 at para 70; *United States v. Burns*, 2001 SCC 7, [2001] 1 S.C.R. 283 at para. 80; and *Suresh v. Canada (Minister of Citizenship and Immigration)*, 2002 SCC 1, [2002] 1 S.C.R. 3 at para. 46; see also *Health Services and Support – Facilities Subsector Bargaining Assn. v. British Columbia*, 2007 SCC 27, [2007] 2 S.C.R. 391 at para 69.[13]

The Court upheld Ross J.'s decision for the most part, allowing the appeal only to vary her order somewhat with respect to remedy. The Court agreed with the trial judge that homelessness was a justiciable issue despite the fact that it engages complex policy decisions on the allocation of public resources.[14] The Court observed that "the homeless represent some of the most vulnerable and marginalized members of our society."[15] The Court rejected the city of Victoria's submission that the decision at trial imposed a positive benefit on the respondents, saying that the decision only required the city to refrain from legislating in a manner that interferes with the section 7 rights of the homeless.[16] Noting the uncontradicted and unopposed expert evidence at trial that compliance with the city's bylaws exposed homeless people to a risk of serious harm including death from hypothermia, the Court affirmed the trial judge's conclusion that prohibiting the homeless from protecting themselves from the elements, in circumstances where there is no practicable shelter alternative, is a significant interference with their dignity and independence constituting interference with the right to life, liberty, and security of the person.[17] The Court agreed with the trial judge's conclusion that the deprivation of the respondents' rights was overbroad and therefore

---

[13] *Victoria (City) v Adams*, 2009 BCCA 563 at para 35 [*Adams* 2009].

[14] *Ibid* at paras 63-9.

[15] *Ibid* at para 75.

[16] *Ibid* at paras 90-97.

[17] *Ibid* at paras 102-10.

not in accordance with the principles of fundamental justice. (The Court disagreed with Ross J.'s conclusion that the impugned legislation was also arbitrary, but nothing turned on this in light of the conclusion on overbreadth.)[18] Having accepted the trial judge's conclusion on overbreadth, the Court unsurprisingly went on to agree that the infringement of the respondents' rights was not minimally impairing and therefore could not be saved under section 1 of the *Charter*. On the issue of remedy, the Court again agreed with the trial judge that the proper remedy was a declaration that the impugned bylaws are of no force or effect pursuant to section 52(1) of the *Constitution Act, 1982*.[19] Notably, the Court approved the trial judge's order of special (that is, solicitor and client) costs of the trial on the basis that it was public interest litigation, a concept upon which the Court elaborated at some length.[20]

While there is little in the way of international legal analysis in the appeal decision, it is nevertheless notable to readers of the *Yearbook* in two ways. First, it is an instance of an appellate court in a Western democracy taking note of a so-called "positive" or "second-generation" right, namely the right to adequate housing. It is impossible to know how important the international recognition of this right was to the Court of Appeal's decision, but the trial judge appears to have given some significant weight to it. Second, the endorsement of the trial court's approach by the Court of Appeal is further evidence of how unassailable reference to international human rights law has become in *Charter* cases. There seems to be little governments can gain now, at least in British Columbia and likely elsewhere, by contending that international law is somehow an irrelevant or impermissible consideration in *Charter* cases. Instead, governments should be prepared to make substantive submissions on the meaning of the relevant international norms and their application or otherwise to the facts of particular cases.

Security — espionage — jurisdiction to grant warrants to spy in foreign countries

Canadian Security Intelligence Service Act (Canada) (Re), 2009 FC 1058 (5 October 2009). Federal Court.

---

18 *Ibid* at paras 111-24.

19 *Constitution Act, 1982*, being Schedule B of the *Canada Act 1982* (UK) 1982, c 11.

20 *Adams* 2009, *supra* note 13 at paras 167-93.

In *Re Canadian Security Intelligence Service Act*,[21] Blanchard J. held that the *Canadian Security Intelligence Services Act* (*CSIS Act*)[22] did not confer jurisdiction on the Federal Court to issue extraterritorial warrants — that is, warrants to investigate the activities of persons outside of Canada. In the present case, the Canadian Security Intelligence Service (CSIS) invited the Court to revisit this question and to distinguish Blanchard J.'s decision on the basis of (1) a more complete description of the facts relating to the activities necessary to permit the interception of communications and information and (2) a different legal argument. Mosley J. was persuaded by the CSIS's submissions. He distinguished Blanchard J.'s decision and issued the warrant. His public reasons for doing so are reviewed here, but they have been heavily redacted, apparently for security reasons, and are not easy to follow.

The case before Mosley J. involved two Canadian citizens suspected of activities constituting threats to the security of Canada. What those activities were is not explained in the reasons. The suspects had already been the subject of warrants authorizing intrusive investigation techniques and information collection within Canada. The CSIS now urgently sought an additional warrant pertaining to activities the suspects would, it was believed, engage in while travelling outside Canada. To succeed, the CSIS had to persuade the Court not to follow Blanchard J.'s 2007 decision that such warrants could not be granted. Blanchard J. had had the benefit of an *amicus curiae* to assist him. Mosley J. considered whether an *amicus curiae* ought to be appointed here too but decided that given the urgency of the situation (which is not explained) he ought not to delay the issuance of the warrant by hearing from anyone other than the CSIS. He noted that the issue had been thoroughly canvassed in the proceedings before Blanchard J.

Section 21 of the act gives a judge jurisdiction to authorize the CSIS to intercept communications and to obtain information while investigating a "threat to the security of Canada." This phrase is defined in section 2 of the *CSIS Act* as including "activities within or relating to Canada." The CSIS argued that the acts necessary to permit the proposed interception of communications and obtaining of information would take place entirely within Canada. They would be performed with the assistance of the Communications Security

---

[21] *Re Canadian Security Intelligence Service Act*, 2008 FC 301 (noted in the 2008 *Yearbook*).

[22] *Canadian Security Intelligence Services Act*, RSC 1985, c C-25.

Establishment (CSE), an agency authorized by statute to acquire and use information from the global information infrastructure for the purpose of providing foreign intelligence to the government of Canada. The CSE is prohibited from directing its activities at Canadian citizens and permanent residents or at any person in Canada, except where providing technical and operations assistance to federal law enforcement and security agencies. In the present case, the CSE could only assist the CSIS if the CSIS obtained a warrant under section 21 of the *CSIS Act.* The evidence was that CSE's interceptions of communications would be controlled from within Canada.

No issue of the Court's jurisdiction to issue the warrant arose in the case at bar, according to the CSIS, because every activity affecting the ability to intercept the suspects' communications would take place in Canada, and information seized would only be "obtained" where it would first be read, namely in Canada. The CSIS argued that it was not seeking a warrant authorizing activities abroad but one authorizing investigative activities to be conducted within Canada.

Mosley J. noted that the application before Blanchard J. sought authority to install, maintain, or remove anything in the foreign jurisdiction required to (apparently — although this is not entirely clear due to redactions in Mosley J.'s reasons) intercept the communications, information, and records sought. By contrast, the draft warrant before Mosley J. only sought authority to do things "from Canada."[23] Mosley J. found little difficulty authorizing the interception of communications, noting that there is no geographical limitation in the *CSIS Act* that restricts the interception of communications to those that either originate or are intended to be received in Canada and that the interception of communications being transmitted presented little difficulty so long as the signals are intercepted from within Canada.[24] As for the seizure of information, Mosley J. observed that if the location of the interception must be construed as occurring abroad, the court would have no jurisdiction to authorize such activities. How Mosley J. overcame this difficulty is unclear — this portion of his reasons is heavily redacted.[25] Reliance was placed on US jurisprudence holding that a judge has jurisdiction

---

[23] *Canadian Security Intelligence Service Act (Canada) (Re)*, 2009 FC 1058 at paras 42-3 [*Re CSIS Act*].

[24] *Ibid* at paras 46-47.

[25] *Ibid* at paras 48-58.

to authorize the interception of communications where the first location at which the communication will be listened to is within the judge's territorial jurisdiction. Mosley J. reiterated that the application before Blanchard J. contemplated intrusive activities in foreign jurisdictions not sought in the present application.[26] He also noted a recent Federal Court of Appeal decision observing that information may notionally reside in more than one place.[27] Mosley J. concluded that there were "sufficient factual and legal grounds to distinguish this application from that which was before Justice Blanchard" and that what the CSIS proposed did not "constitute the enforcement of Canada's laws abroad but rather the exercise of jurisdiction here relating to the protection of Canada's security."[28]

Mosley J. went on to make a number of observations about international comity, extraterritorial investigative measures in criminal proceedings, and the 2001 *Convention on Cybercrime*,[29] to which, Mosley J. noted, Canada is a signatory but not yet a party. These observations are interesting, but their relevance to the case at bar is unclear, probably due to redactions in the reasons. The learned judge notes that crossborder computer searches to obtain evidence in the investigation of foreign-based attacks on domestic computer systems "are perceived to violate the territorial sovereignty of the country where the data is located, absent consent"[30] and that under Article 32 of the convention transborder access to stored computer data is permitted with consent or where the data is publicly available.[31] If this observation is intended to allay fears that the warrant Mosley J. issued violates international law by permitting the CSIS, assisted by the CSE, to access foreign computers (for instance, to read e-mails), it fails to do so, for (as Mosley J. himself observes) Canada has not ratified the convention and, in any case, the convention does not provide a means by which information may be collected abroad for national security purposes.[32] Mosley J. goes on

---

26 *Ibid* at para 65.

27 *Ibid* at para 65, citing *eBay Canada Ltd v Minister of National Revenue*, 2008 FCA 348.

28 *Re CSIS Act, supra* note 23 at para 66.

29 *Convention on Cybercrime*, 23 November 2001, 2296 UNTS 167, ETS 185.

30 *Re CSIS Act, supra* note 23 at para 69.

31 *Ibid* at para 70.

32 *Ibid* at paras 71-72.

to observe that "[t]he norms of territorial sovereignty do not preclude the collection of information by one nation in the territory of another country, in contrast to the exercise of its enforcement jurisdiction."[33] That observation seems at odds with Mosley J.'s previous observation about the perceived illegality of crossborder computer searches.

It is hard to know what to make of this decision. More to the point, it is hard to know what decision was made. This is due to the extensive redactions, the necessity of which may be doubted. Surely a way could have been found to publish this decision without disclosing anything that might prejudice the investigation and without obscuring Mosley J.'s reasoning, which is, after all, the crucial part of reasons for judgment. It is to be hoped that this decision will soon be released in an unredacted, or at least less redacted, form.

Another concern arises from the way this case was presented to the court. The consequences of Blanchard J.'s 2008 decision for the CSIS's activities must have been immediately apparent to it. There can be no doubt that lawyers for the CSIS began considering without delay how practically to comply with the decision and also how to challenge it. Yet rather than bring the issues before the Court of Appeal (by means of an appeal or, if necessary, a reference), or to some other forum that would allow careful review with the benefit of argument on all sides, the CSIS appears not to have taken the matter back to the court until there was, or was alleged to be, a grave risk to national security hanging in the balance. This application was filed on 24 January 2009 and heard on 26 January. Understandably in the circumstances, Mosley J. thought it best to do without an *amicus curiae*, for fear of slowing down the proceedings. He ought not to have been placed in this predicament in the first place. The result is two apparently conflicting decisions from the Federal Court on an important question of national and international law.

Extradition — record of the case — presumption of conformity with international law

United States and Canada (Minister of Justice) v Anekwu, 2009 SCC 41 (24 September 2009). Supreme Court of Canada.

Anekwu was sought by the United States for trial on charges relating to telemarketing fraud. The minister of justice made committal and surrender orders. Anekwu appealed the committal order and sought

---

[33] *Ibid* at para 74.

judicial review of the surrender order. He challenged the validity of the orders, contending that they were contrary to the requirement in section 32(2) of the *Extradition Act*[34] that Canadian-gathered evidence in support of an extradition request satisfy the rules of evidence under Canadian law. The alleged frailty in the evidence was that it was hearsay.

In accordance with the procedure set out in the *Extradition Act*, the attorney general, on behalf of the plaintiffs, sought a committal order from the Supreme Court of British Columbia supported by a record of the case prepared by the United States. The record of the case was duly certified and contained "a document summarizing the evidence available to the extradition partner for use in the prosecution" (see section 33(1)) of the act). The summary described evidence gathered in both the United States and Canada. The Canadian-gathered evidence included various corporate and business records that were not filed but only described in the summary — that is, the evidence was hearsay. Anekwu's objection to the admissibility of this evidence was rejected at first instance[35] but succeeded by a majority in the Court of Appeal, Chiasson J.A. dissenting.[36]

Charron J. for the Supreme Court of Canada allowed the appeal. The question turned on the proper interpretation of section 32(2) of the *Extradition Act* in the context of sections 32 and 33 generally. Those sections are as follows:

---

32 (1) Subject to subsection (2) evidence that would otherwise be admissible under Canadian law shall be admitted as evidence at an extradition hearing. The following shall also be admitted as evidence, even if it would not otherwise be admissible under Canadian law:

    (a) the contents of the documents contained in the record of the case certified under subsection 33(3);

32 (1) Sont admis comme faisant preuve au cours de l'audition de la demande, sous réserve du paragraphe (2), les éléments de preuve admissibles en vertu du droit canadien ainsi que les éléments de preuve suivants même si le droit canadien ne prévoit pas par ailleurs leur admissibilité :

    (a) le contenu des documents qui font partie du dossier d'extradition certifié en conformité avec le paragraphe 33(3);

---

[34] *Extradition Act*, SC 1999, c 18.

[35] *United States and Canada (Minister of Justice) v Anekwu*, 2006 BCSC 1363.

[36] *United States and Canada (Minister of Justice) v Anekwu*, 2008 BCCA 138.

(b) the contents of the documents that are submitted in conformity with the terms of an extradition agreement; and

(c) evidence adduced by the person sought for extradition that is relevant to the tests set out in subsection 29(1) if the judge considers it reliable.

(2) Evidence gathered in Canada must satisfy the rules of evidence under Canadian law in order to be admitted.

33 (1) The record of the case must include

(a) in the case of a person sought for the purpose of prosecution, a document summarizing the evidence available to the extradition partner for use in the prosecution; and

(b) in the case of a person sought for the imposition or enforcement of a sentence,

(i) a copy of the document that records the conviction of the person, and

(ii) a document describing the conduct for which the person was convicted.

(2) A record of the case may include other relevant documents, including documents respecting the identification of the person sought for extradition.

(3) A record of the case may not be admitted unless

(a) in the case of a person sought for the purpose of prosecution, a judicial or prosecuting authority of the extradition

(b) le contenu des documents présentés en conformité avec un accord;

(c) les éléments de preuve présentés par l'intéressé qui sont pertinents pour l'application du paragraphe 29(1) et que le juge estime dignes de foi.

(2) Les éléments de preuve obtenus au Canada sont admis en conformité avec le droit canadien.

33 (1) Le dossier d'extradition comporte obligatoirement :

(a) dans le cas d'une extradition en vue d'un procès, un résumé des éléments de preuve dont dispose le partenaire aux fins de poursuite;

(b) dans le cas d'une extradition en vue d'infliger une peine à l'intéressé ou de la lui faire purger, les éléments suivants:

(i) une copie de la déclaration de culpabilité,

(ii) la description des actes qui ont donné lieu à la déclaration de culpabilité.

(2) Le dossier peut aussi comprendre des documents établissant l'identité de l'intéressé et tout autre document pertinent.

(3) Le dossier n'est admissible en preuve que si:

(a) dans le cas d'une extradition en vue d'un procès, une autorité judiciaire ou un poursuivant du partenaire certifie,

partner certifies that the evidence summarized or contained in the record of the case is available for trial and

(i) is sufficient under the law of the extradition partner to justify prosecution, or

(ii) was gathered according to the law of the extradition partner; or

(b) in the case of a person sought for the imposition or enforcement of a sentence, a judicial, prosecuting or correctional authority of the extradition partner certifies that the documents in the record of the case are accurate.

(4) No authentication of documents is required unless a relevant extradition agreement provides otherwise.

(5) For the purposes of this section, a record of the case includes any supplement added to it.

d'une part, que les éléments de preuve résumés au dossier ou contenus dans celui-ci sont disponibles pour le procès et, d'autre part, soit que la preuve est suffisante pour justifier la poursuite en vertu du droit du partenaire, soit qu'elle a été recueillie conformément à ce droit;

(b) dans le cas d'une extradition en vue d'infliger une peine à l'intéressé ou de la lui faire purger, l'autorité judiciaire, un fonctionnaire du système correctionnel ou un poursuivant du partenaire certifie que les documents au dossier sont exacts.

(4) Sauf disposition contraire d'un accord, les documents n'ont pas à être authentifiés.

(5) Font partie du dossier les documents qui y sont ajoutés par la suite.

Charron J. noted that the language of section 32(2) on its own "reveals no ambiguity" and "mandates compliance with domestic rules of evidence in respect of evidence gathered on Canadian soil." In the context of its related provisions, however, section 32(2)'s meaning is less clear.[37] The interpretive question was how to reconcile the summary of the evidence provided for under section 33(1) with the strictures of the hearsay rule, which, of course, is one of the "rules of evidence under Canadian law."

Charron J. agreed with Chiasson J.A. in the Court of Appeal and also with the similar reasoning of Moldaver J.A. in *United States of*

---

[37] *United States and Canada (Minister of Justice) v Anekwu*, 2009 SCC 41 at paras 13-14 [*Anekwu*].

America v McDowell,[38] that the *Extradition Act* required a two-step approach to Canadian-gathered evidence. The evidence may first be presented to the extradition judge as part of the record of the case, in the form required under section 33. As such, it is presumptively admissible under section 32(1). Section 32(2) then requires the Court to scrutinize Canadian-gathered evidence for compliance with Canadian law.[39] The evidence may be presented in summary form and can be relied on by the extradition judge if, in substance, it would be admissible in a Canadian court.[40]

This approach, in Charron J.'s view, "achieves a proper balance between the liberty interests of the person sought and the international principle of comity." The learned judge explained:

It is a well-established principle of statutory interpretation that in interpreting domestic legislation, courts should strive to arrive at a construction which conforms with Canada's treaty obligations: see, e.g., *R. v. Hape*, 2007 SCC 26, [2007] 2 S.C.R. 292, at para. 53. In the extradition context, the requirement that Canadian-gathered evidence comply with Canadian rules of evidence is unlikely to give rise to particular difficulties with respect to most evidentiary rules, including privilege, the expert opinion rule, or the rule against bad character evidence. The same cannot be said, however, of the hearsay rule.

Adherence to the strictures of the hearsay rule in the extradition context would require, as a general rule, that witnesses be called to give *viva voce* evidence resulting in inevitable delays, increased expenses, and potentially lengthy cross-examinations in a hearing that is neither intended as a vehicle for disclosure nor as a forum to adjudicate on the merits of the foreign prosecution. Traditional adherence to the rule could occasion protracted *voir dires* to determine whether evidence presented in hearsay form falls into one of the recognized exceptions to the rule or meets the twin criteria of necessity and reliability. In my view, Moldaver J.A. rightly concluded in *McDowell* that traditional adherence to the hearsay rule "would be to allow form to triumph over substance and lead to expensive, time-consuming hearings that would disable Canada from complying with its international obligations in a prompt and efficient manner: see *United States of America v. Dynar*, [1997] 2 S.C.R. 462, at para. 122.[41]

---

38 *United States and Canada (Minister of Justice) v McDowell*, (2004), 183 CCC (3d) 149 (Ont CA) [McDowell].

39 *Anekwu, supra* note 37 at para 21.

40 *Ibid* at para 23.

41 *Ibid* at para 17.

Hence, such an interpretation should be avoided.[42]

Charron J. went on to note that extradition proceedings must not be equated with the criminal trial process for extradition procedure, unlike criminal procedure, is founded on the concepts of reciprocity, comity, and respect for differences in other jurisdictions.[43] Later in her reasons, Charron J. quoted again from Moldaver J.A. in *McDowell* as follows:

Insisting that evidence gathered in Canada comply substantively with our rules of evidence is one thing; insisting that it take a certain form is quite another. The latter does nothing to preserve or protect the integrity of our justice system and it creates a barrier to the prompt and efficient discharge of our international obligations.[44]

This judgment is another admirable instance of the Supreme Court of Canada reconciling a problem of statutory interpretation by reference to the presumption of conformity with international law. In this instance, the conformity sought is not with any particular treaty but with the extradition process generally and the principle of comity that underlies it.

Charter — *torture of Guantanamo Bay detainee — foreign affairs prerogative*

Canada (Prime Minister) v Khadr, 2010 SCC 3 (29 January 2010). Supreme Court of Canada.

It is perhaps the most notorious fact of contemporary Canadian law that Canadian national Omar Khadr was fifteen years old when taken prisoner by American forces in Afghanistan in July 2002. He was held without trial at the US prison in Guantanamo Bay, Cuba, for eight years on charges of killing an American soldier and conspiring with Al-Qaeda to commit acts of murder and terrorism. In October 2010 (after the judgment now being considered), he was sentenced to forty years in prison after pleading guilty in a deal that will cap his remaining jail time at eight years. He is the last national of a Western country still imprisoned in Guantanamo, for the reason that Canada has never sought his repatriation.

---

[42] *Ibid* at paras 25-6.

[43] *Ibid* at paras 27, quoting *Kindler v Canada (Minister of Justice),* [1991] 2 SCR 779 at 844-5.

[44] *Anekwu, supra* note 37 at para 30, quoting *McDowell, supra* note 38 at para 23.

The present case arose from Khadr's legal challenge to the Canadian government's refusal to seek repatriation. The prime minister, Steven Harper, announced the decision not to seek Khadr's repatriation during a July 2008 interview. In a judicial review proceeding before O'Reilly J.,[45] Khadr alleged that this decision infringed his section 7 rights. O'Reilly J. agreed. In particular, he relied on the government's admissions that Khadr had been subjected by US authorities to a sleep deprivation regime known by its perpetrators as the "frequent flyer program" and that Canadian authorities knew of this abuse in the spring of 2004 (when Khadr was seventeen) yet proceeded to interrogate him. O'Reilly J. concluded that, in the circumstances, no remedy other than an order requiring Canada to request Khadr's repatriation was capable of mitigating the effect of the *Charter* violation he had suffered. The Federal Court of Appeal upheld the decision (per Evans and Sharlow JJ.A., Nadon J.A. dissenting).[46]

The details of the "frequent flyer program" are pointedly omitted from the Supreme Court of Canada's judgment, but O'Reilly J. explained it in his reasons as a scheme to deprive Khadr of rest and sleep by moving him to a new location every three hours over a period of weeks. The learned judge quoted the following March 2004 report from the Department of Foreign Affairs and International Trade:

In an effort to make him more amenable and willing to talk, [blank] has placed [Khadr] on the "frequent flyer program." [F]or the three weeks before [the] visit, [Khadr] has not been permitted more than three hours in any one location. At three hours' interval he is moved to another cell block, thus denying him uninterrupted sleep and a continued change in neighbours. He will soon be placed in isolation for up to three weeks and then he will be interviewed again.[47]

O'Reilly J. went on to note[48] that the Supreme Court of Israel has found that sleep deprivation for the purpose of "breaking" a suspect is unlawful and that in *Khadr v Canada (Attorney General)*,[49] Mosley

---

45 *Khadr v Canada (Attorney General)*, 2009 FC 405 [*Khadr* FC].

46 *Khadr v Canada (Attorney General)*, 2009 FCA 246 [*Khadr* FCA].

47 *Khadr* FC, *supra* note 45 at paras 11, 15.

48 *Ibid* at para 56.

49 *Khadr v Canada (Attorney General)*, 2008 FC 807.

J. concluded that the subjection of Khadr to sleep deprivation techniques offended the 1984 *Convention against Torture and Other Cruel, Inhuman or Degrading Treatment or Punishment.*[50]

In a judgment attributed only to "the Court," the Supreme Court of Canada began by considering whether the *Charter* applies to the conduct of Canadian officials in this instance. This conduct consisted of interrogating Khadr despite knowing that he had been subjected to US sleep deprivation techniques. (The reasons of the Court deftly avoid describing these techniques as torture, or even as cruel, inhuman, or degrading treatment or punishment. The most the Court will say is that Khadr's statements to Canadian officials were obtained in "oppressive circumstances"[51] and that "these conditions" offended "the most basic Canadian standards about the treatment of detained youth suspects."[52]) Applying its unorthodox analysis of extraterritoriality in *R v Hape*[53] and *Khadr No. 1*,[54] the Court confirmed that the *Charter* applies to the actions of Canadian officials at Guantanamo Bay, despite the supposed extraterritoriality, because the Supreme Court of the United States has held that the Guantanamo regime constitutes a clear violation of fundamental human rights protected by international law.[55]

Having established that the *Charter* applies, the Court moved quickly through the section 7 analysis. It noted that Canadian officials repeatedly questioned Khadr about the central events at issue in his prosecution, extracting statements from him that could prove inculpatory in the US proceedings against him. The Court concluded that it is "reasonable to infer from the uncontradicted evidence before us that the statements taken by Canadian officials are contributing to the continued detention of Mr. Khadr, thereby impacting his liberty and security interests" and that "Canada's active participation in what was at the time an illegal regime has contributed and continues to contribute to Mr. Khadr's current detention."[56] Turning to the principles of fundamental justice, the Court

---

50 *Convention against Torture and Other Cruel, Inhuman or Degrading Treatment or Punishment*, 1987 Can TS no 36.

51 *Canada (Prime Minister) v Khadr*, 2010 SCC 3 at para 20 [*Khadr* SCC].

52 *Ibid* at para 25.

53 *R. v Hape*, 2007 SCC 26; noted in the 2007 *Yearbook*.

54 *Khadr No 1*, 2008 SCC 28; noted in the 2008 *Yearbook*.

55 *Khadr* SCC, *supra* note 51 at para 16.

56 *Ibid* at paras 20-21.

reaffirmed that such principles "take into account Canada's obligations and values, as expressed in the various sources of international human rights law by which Canada is bound."[57] The Court concluded that Canada's conduct did not conform to the principles of fundamental justice. The statements taken by Canadian officials were "obtained through participation in a regime which was known at the time to have refused detainees the right to challenge the legality of detention by way of *habeas corpus*."[58] The Court reiterated its conclusion in *Khadr No. 1* that Canada's participation in Guantanamo Bay "clearly violated Canada's binding international obligations" — again, as in *Khadr No. 1*, without identifying which obligations had been violated or what the violations consist in.[59] The Court then added, almost as an afterthought, that Canada's March 2004 "interview" of Khadr "was conducted knowing that Mr. Khadr had been subjected to three weeks of scheduled sleep deprivation, a measure described by the U.S. Military Commission ... as designed to 'make [detainees] more compliant and break down their resistance to interrogation.'"[60]

The Court concluded that Khadr's section 7 rights had been "violated."[61] I note the use of the term "violated," instead of "infringed," because the Court's rights analysis ended there, with no consideration given to whether the infringement might be justified under section 1 of the *Charter* (as the government had argued unsuccessfully before the Federal Court of Appeal). While commentators have sometimes speculated that an infringement of section 7 could never be justified under section 1, the Court has said that a section 7 breach could be validated under section 1 in exceptional circumstances "such as natural disasters, the outbreak of war, epidemics and the like."[62] Yet here the Court elided the concepts of infringement and violation, further emphasizing the difficulty governments will face in attempting to justify breaches of section 7 under section 1.

57 *Ibid* at paras 23.

58 *Ibid* at para 24.

59 *Ibid* at para 24.

60 *Ibid* at para 24.

61 *Ibid* at para 26.

62 *Re BC Motor Vehicle Act*, [1985] 2 SCR 486 at 518; *New Brunswick (Minister of Health and Community Services) v G(J)*, [1999] 3 SCR 46 at para 99; *Suresh v Canada (Minister of Citizenship and Immigration)*, 2002 SCC 1 at para 78.

On the crucial issue of remedy, the Court identified two questions: (1) was the remedy sought (and granted in the courts below) sufficiently connected to the breach and (2) was the remedy precluded by the fact that it touches upon the Crown prerogative over foreign affairs?[63] The Court answered the first question affirmatively, finding that Canadian officials contributed to Khadr's detention by virtue of their interrogations of him at Guantanamo Bay "knowing Mr. Khadr was a youth, did not have access to legal counsel or *habeas corpus* at the time and, at the time of the interview in March 2004, had been subjected to improper treatment by the U.S. authorities."[64] The Court therefore concluded that the breach of Khadr's section 7 rights remained ongoing and that "the remedy sought could potentially vindicate those rights."[65]

It was in answer to the second question that the Court shied away from the bold relief granted by the courts below. The government argued that courts have no power under the Constitution to require the executive branch to do anything in the area of foreign policy. In considering this submission, the Court described the prerogative power of the Crown to conduct foreign affairs as "a limited source of non-statutory administrative power accorded by the common law to the Crown"[66] — one that had not been displaced by statute.[67] The Court affirmed previous decisions to the effect that prerogative powers are not exempt from constitutional scrutiny, whether under the *Charter* or other constitutional norms, or simply for the purpose of determining whether the asserted prerogative power exists.[68] The Court continued:

This said, judicial review of the exercise of the prerogative power for constitutionality remains sensitive to the fact that the executive branch of government is responsible for decisions under this power, and that the executive is better placed to make such decisions within a range of constitutional options. The government must have flexibility in deciding how

---

63 *Khadr* SCC, *supra* note 51 at para 27.

64 *Ibid* at para 30.

65 *Ibid* at para 30.

66 *Ibid* at para 34.

67 *Ibid* at para 35. In particular, the prerogative has not been displaced by section 10 of the *Department of Foreign Affairs and International Trade Act*, RSC 1985, c E-22 (as amended).

68 *Khadr* SCC, *supra* note 51 at para 36.

its duties under the power are to be discharged ... But it is for the courts to determine the legal and constitutional limits within which such decisions are to be taken. It follows that in the case of refusal by a government to abide by constitutional constraints, courts are empowered to make orders ensuring that the government's foreign affairs prerogative is exercised in accordance with the constitution.[69]

Despite this, the Court went on to find that in this case O'Reilly J. had misdirected himself in exercising the courts' narrow power to review and intervene on matters of foreign affairs to ensure the constitutionality of executive action. How O'Reilly J. misdirected himself is not clearly stated, however. The Court expressed the concern that O'Reilly J.'s remedy "gives too little weight to the constitutional responsibility of the executive to make decisions on matters of foreign affairs in the context of complex and ever-changing circumstances, taking into account Canada's broader national interests,"[70] but does not say why that is so. The Court did not explain, for instance, what national interest Canada has that is broader than the imperative not to be complicit in cruel, inhuman, or degrading treatment of children contrary to international law. Instead, the Court passed quickly on to an attempt to distinguish the present case from *United States v Burns*[71] on the basis that in this case, because Khadr is not under the control of the Canadian government, "the likelihood that the proposed remedy will be effective is unclear" and "the impact on Canadian foreign relations of a repatriation request cannot properly be assessed by the Court."[72]

The Court then complained of the supposed inadequacy of the record, which "gives a necessarily incomplete picture of the range of considerations currently faced by the government in assessing Mr. Khadr's request. We do not know what negotiations may have taken place, or will take place, between the U.S. and Canadian governments over the fate of Mr. Khadr." This criticism is profoundly unfair to Khadr, for he would face immense difficulty in obtaining such evidence even if he were not stranded in a US naval prison in Cuba. Any deficiency in the record in such a case is attributable to the government party. The Court has effectively given

---

[69] *Ibid* at para 37.

[70] *Ibid* at para 39.

[71] *United States v Burns*, 2001 SCC 7.

[72] *Khadr* SCC, *supra* note 51 at para 43.

the government a trump card, for the adequacy of the record on questions of foreign diplomacy is almost entirely within its control.

On this thin reasoning, the Court concluded that the proper relief is not an order that the government request Khadr's repatriation but a mere declaration that

through the conduct of Canadian officials in the course of interrogations in 2003-2004, as established on the evidence before us, Canada actively participated in a process contrary to Canada's international human rights obligations and contributed to Mr. Khadr's ongoing detention so as to deprive him of his right to liberty and security of the person guaranteed by s. 7 of the *Charter*, contrary to the principles of fundamental justice.[73]

Or as the Court put it elsewhere in its reasons, "the appropriate remedy is to declare that, on the record before the Court, Canada infringed Mr. Khadr's s. 7 rights, and to leave it to the government to decide how best to respond to this judgment in light of current information, its responsibility for foreign affairs, and in conformity with the *Charter*."[74] This is like leaving the fox to decide how best to guard the henhouse. As I write, over a year has passed since the Court made its declaration, and we now know the government's response to it: deafening silence, broken only perhaps by muted celebration of the astonishing victory it secured over Khadr by means of this anaemic judgment. While the Court rightly noted the effectiveness of declarations of unconstitutionality in general,[75] the ineffectiveness of mere declaratory relief in Khadr's case ought to have been abundantly obvious to the Court. It did not take hindsight to see that the remedy fashioned for Khadr in this case would prove to be no remedy at all.

Left unstated throughout this decision is the fact that Khadr has been subjected to torture, or at least cruel, inhuman, or degrading treatment contrary to Canadian treaty obligations and general international law. Both O'Reilly J. and the Federal Court of Appeal gave serious consideration to the illegality of Khadr's treatment at international law. Both courts invoked and considered the *Convention against Torture* and the *Convention on the Rights of the Child*. By contrast, the word "torture" appears only once in the Supreme Court

73 *Ibid* at para 48.
74 *Ibid* at para 39.
75 *Ibid* at para 46.

of Canada's decision, and there only in a citation of a decision by a US military commission. Rather than confronting the nature and legal significance of the wrong Khadr has suffered — at American hands but with Canadian complicity — the Court repeatedly downplays the importance of Khadr's mistreatment and emphasizes instead its own decision in *Khadr No. 1* to the effect that Guantanamo Bay is a bad place because the US Supreme Court said so. *Khadr No. 2* will ease the sleep of those Canadian politicians and diplomats complicit in Khadr's nightmare, but it ought to cause Canada's international lawyers and human rights advocates to lose some.

Enforcement of international arbitral awards — limitation periods — treaty interpretation

Yugraneft Corporation v Rexx Management Corporation, 2010 SCC 19 (20 May 2010). Supreme Court of Canada.

Yugraneft is a Russian corporation concerned with oilfields. Rexx is an Alberta corporation from which Yugraneft purchased materials. A contract dispute arose and was arbitrated before the International Commercial Arbitration Court at the Chamber of Commerce and Industry of the Russian Federation. In September 2002, the arbitral tribunal ordered Rexx to pay nearly US $1 billion in damages. In January 2006, Yugraneft applied to the Alberta Court of Queen's Bench for recognition and enforcement of the award. The court dismissed the application[76] on the ground that it was time-barred under the two-year limitation period in section 3 of the Alberta *Limitations Act*.[77] The Court of Appeal upheld the ruling.[78]

Rothstein J. for the Supreme Court of Canada dismissed the appeal. He began with a review of the *Convention on the Recognition and Enforcement of Foreign Arbitral Awards* (*New York Convention*)[79] and the UNCITRAL *Model Law on International Commercial Arbitration* (*Model Law*),[80] both of which, he noted, are incorporated into Alberta law

---

76 *Yugraneft Corporation v Rexx Management Corporation*, 2007 ABQB 450.

77 *Limitations Act*, RSA 2000, c L-12.

78 *Yugraneft Corporation v Rexx Management Corporation*, 2008 ABCA 274.

79 *Convention on the Recognition and Enforcement of Foreign Arbitral Awards*, 1958, [1986] Can TS no 43.

80 UNCITRAL Model Law on International Commercial Arbitration, UN Doc A/40/17, ann. 1 (1985).

by the *International Commercial Arbitration Act*.[81] The learned judge observed that the convention requires all contracting states (of which Canada is one) to recognize and enforce arbitral awards made in the territory of another state, whether or not they are party to the convention, except in cases covered by Article V. As for the Model Law, Rothstein J. noted that it is not a treaty, describing it instead as a codification of international best practices intended to serve as an example for domestic legislation. The *Model Law* has been adopted, with some modifications, by every jurisdiction in Canada. Like Article V of the *New York Convention*, Article 36 of the *Model Law* limits the grounds on which enforcement of an international arbitral award may be refused. Rothstein J. concluded that there is "no doubt that Alberta is required to recognize and enforce eligible foreign arbitral awards."[82] The question before the Court was what limitation period, if any, applies to this obligation.

The threshold question, said Rothstein J., was whether any limitation period can apply, for neither the convention nor the *Model Law* expressly imposes one. Yet Article III of the convention provides that recognition and enforcement shall be in accordance with the rules of procedure of the territory where the award is relied upon. Rothstein J. observed that in the common law tradition — unlike the civil law — limitation periods are generally conceived as procedural in nature. "If limitation periods are characterized as being procedural in nature for the purposes of the Convention," wrote the learned judge, "then recognition and enforcement of a foreign arbitral award may lawfully be refused on the ground that it is time-barred."[83] The parties agreed that Article III allowed contracting states to impose a time limit on recognition and enforcement. Yet that was not enough for Rothstein J., who deftly noted that whether Alberta was in conformity with the convention is not determined by the consent of the parties.[84] Rather, the Court had to ascertain if there was a legal basis for the application of local limitation periods under the convention.

This exercise required interpretation of the convention that, Rothstein J. noted, is governed by the interpretive rules set out in the 1969 *Vienna Convention on the Law of Treaties* (*Vienna Convention*).[85]

---

[81] *International Commercial Arbitration Act*, RSA 2000, c I-5.

[82] *Yugraneft Corporation v Rexx Management Corporation*, 2010 SCC 19 at para 12 [*Yugraneft*].

[83] *Ibid* at para 16.

[84] *Ibid* at para 17.

[85] *Vienna Convention on the Law of Treaties*, [1980] Can TS no 37.

Beginning with the *New York Convention*'s context and purpose, Rothstein J. observed that it was designed to be applied in a large number of states and thus across a multitude of legal systems.[86] When the convention was drafted (explained the learned judge), it was well known that various states characterized limitation periods in different ways and that states in the common law tradition generally regarded them as procedural. Rothstein J. therefore found significance in the fact that the convention's drafters did not restrict a state's ability to impose time limits on recognition and enforcement proceedings.[87] The learned judge then considered subsequent state practice as described in a 2008 study showing that fifty-three contracting states, both common law and civil, subject the recognition and enforcement of foreign arbitral awards to some kind of time limit.[88] Finally, Rothstein J. made brief reference to scholarly commentary suggesting, in his view, that the application of local time limits to recognition and enforcement proceedings is not controversial.[89] This discussion is another commendable example of the Supreme Court of Canada endeavouring to construe treaties according to Article 31 of the *Vienna Convention*.[90]

Rothstein J. next addressed two arguments against the application of Alberta limitations law to foreign arbitral awards. The first argument relied on the Supreme Court of Canada's decision in *Tolofson v Jensen*,[91] to the effect that, in the conflict of laws context, limitation periods should generally be treated as substantive rather than procedural. This was not determinative, explained Rothstein J., because the question before the Court was not how Canadian law characterizes limitation periods but whether local time limits intended to apply to the recognition and enforcement of foreign arbitral awards fall within the ambit of "rules of procedure" as that phrase is used in Article III of the convention. The answer was yes, for the convention takes a permissive approach to the applicability of local limitation periods. Thus, if the local legislature intended to impose limitation periods on recognition and enforcement proceedings,

---

86 *Yugraneft, supra* note 82 at para 19.

87 *Ibid* at para 20.

88 *Ibid* at para 21.

89 *Ibid* at para 22.

90 See also *Pushpanathan v Canada (Minister of Citizenship and Immigration)*, [1998] 1 SCR 982; *Crown Forest Industries Ltd v Canada*, [1995] 2 SCR 802.

91 *Tolofson v Jensen*, [1994] 3 SCR 1022.

the Court would construe them as rules of procedure for the purposes of Article III.[92]

The second argument considered and rejected by Rothstein J. relied on that part of Article III that provides that "[t]here shall not be imposed substantially more onerous conditions or higher fees or charges on the recognition or enforcement of arbitral awards to which the Convention applies than are imposed on the recognition or enforcement of domestic arbitral awards." An intervenor argued that the phrase "domestic arbitral awards" must mean any award rendered within Canada, such that no Canadian province can impose a limitation period more onerous than the most generous available anywhere else in Canada for domestic awards. Since both British Columbia and Quebec provide for ten-year limitation periods on the recognition and enforcement of provincially rendered arbitral awards, Alberta (it was said) is prohibited under the convention from imposing a shorter period on foreign arbitral awards. Rothstein J. rejected this argument as contrary to both Canadian federalism, and the convention that "was intended to be respectful of the internal constitutional order of federal states like Canada."[93] Rothstein J. pointed to Article XI as tempering the international obligations of federal states and therefore disagreed with the intervenor's contention that to apply Alberta's limitation period to foreign arbitral awards would place Canada in violation of the convention. Furthermore, Rothstein J. noted the convention's distinction between contracting states (here, Canada) and the territory where the award is relied upon (here, Alberta). All the convention requires is that Alberta provide foreign awards with treatment as generous as that given to domestic awards rendered in Alberta.[94]

The next question for the Court was whether Alberta law subjects the recognition and enforcement of foreign arbitral awards to a limitation period and, if so, what the applicable period is. After reviewing three Alberta enactments, Rothstein J. concluded that only the *Limitations Act* might apply. This act did not expressly exclude Yugraneft's award from its scope and was in fact intended to create a comprehensive and exhaustive limitations scheme applicable to all causes of action except those expressly excluded by the act or covered by other legislation. Rothstein J. held that an

[92] *Yugraneft, supra* note 82 at paras 27-8.

[93] *Ibid* at para 32.

[94] *Ibid* at para 33.

application for recognition and enforcement of a foreign arbitral award is an application for a "remedial order" within the meaning of the act and is subject to the general two-year limitation period applicable to most causes of action under section 3.[95]

This limitation period is subject to a discoverability rule, meaning that a claim is only barred two years after the claimant first knew or ought to have known that (1) the injury for which it seeks a remedial order had occurred; (2) the injury was attributable to the conduct of the defendant; and (3) the injury, assuming liability on the part of the defendant, warrants bringing the proceeding. The injury Yugraneft had suffered was characterized under the act as "non-performance of an obligation," namely Rexx's obligation to pay the arbitral award.[96] Neither party made submissions on the point, and Rothstein J. agreed with their apparent assumption that if the two-year limitation period applied Yugraneft was out of time. Rothstein J. nevertheless made some interesting observations about the application of the limitation period to Yugraneft's award. In his view, the date of issuance of the award ought not to be considered as the date of Rexx's non-performance of its obligation to pay. The *Model Law* provides that a party to an arbitration has three months to apply to the local courts to have an award set aside. Rothstein J. suggested that "until that deadline has passed, the arbitral award may not have the requisite degree of finality to form the basis of an application for recognition and enforcement under the Convention."[97] In those circumstances, Rothstein J. held that the Alberta limitation period will not be triggered until the possibility that the award might be set aside by the local (here, Russian) courts has been foreclosed. However, even with this extra three months, Yugraneft's Alberta enforcement proceedings were time-barred.[98]

Rothstein J.'s reasons concluded, intriguingly, with a brief reference to Rexx's argument that the award's enforcement ought to be refused under the convention on the ground that it was tainted by fraud. Having found that Yugraneft was time-barred, Rothstein J. refrained from ruling on this issue.[99]

---

[95] See *ibid* at paras 35-45.

[96] *Ibid* at para 50.

[97] *Ibid* at para 54.

[98] *Ibid* at para 56; see also paras 57-63.

[99] *Ibid* at para 64.

National security — inadmissible persons — evidence obtained through torture or cruel, inhuman, or degrading treatment or punishment

Re Mahjoub, 2010 FC 787 (9 June 2010). Federal Court.

Mahjoub was the subject of a certificate stating that he was inadmissible to Canada on grounds of security. The certificate was referred to the Federal Court pursuant to section 77 of the *Immigration and Refugee Protection Act*[100] for determination of its reasonableness. Prior to the reasonableness hearing, Mahjoub applied to exclude from evidence information relied on by the government on the ground that it was obtained as a result of the use of torture or cruel, inhuman, or degrading treatment or punishment (CIDT), pursuant to section 83(1.1) which reads:

For the purposes of paragraph (1)(h), reliable and appropriate evidence does not include information that is believed on reasonable grounds to have been obtained as a result of the use of torture within the meaning of section 269.1 of the *Criminal Code*, or cruel, inhuman or degrading treatment or punishment within the meaning of the *Convention against Torture*.

Pour l'application de l'alinéa (1)h), sont exclus des éléments de preuve dignes de foi et utiles les renseignements dont il existe des motifs raisonnables de croire qu'ils ont été obtenus par suite du recours à la torture, au sens de l'article 269.1 du *Code criminel*, ou à d'autres peines ou traitements cruels, inhumains ou dégradants, au sens de la *Convention contre la torture*.

Mahjoub sought to invoke this provision to exclude from evidence information obtained by the government from foreign agencies, which, were there reasonable grounds to believe, had obtained it through acts of torture or CIDT.

This is another Federal Court security decision that has been significantly redacted. It is clear that Egypt is at least one of the states at issue. Other states may be as well. The identity of the foreign agency or agencies at issue is not disclosed.

The Court (Blanchard J.) heard expert evidence from eight witnesses: two on behalf of the Canadian Security Intelligence Service (CSIS) and six experts on behalf of Mahjoub. The latter evidence was directed generally at Egypt's poor human rights record (particularly with respect to its domestic intelligence service), the practice

---

[100] *Immigration and Refugee Protection Act*, SC 2001, c 27, as amended.

of US authorities in the so-called war on terror, and information sharing among Canadian and foreign intelligence agencies.

Blanchard J. began by attempting to define CIDT, which, as he noted, is not specifically defined in the 1984 *Convention against Torture* (*CAT*).[101] To do so, Blanchard J. turned to the work of the Committee against Torture. He noted that the committee has not expressly defined CIDT and that it has only once found a violation of the CIDT right (art. 16).[102] Yet the committee has provided numerous examples of what it considers to be CIDT in its conclusions and recommendations on the compliance of states parties. Blanchard J. reproduced several such examples, saying that they "provide guidance as to the meaning of CIDT" under the *CAT*.[103] The Court also relied on the observation of Manfred Nowak, UN special rapporteur on torture and other cruel, inhuman, or degrading treatment or punishment, that the distinction between CIDT and torture is not the intensity of the pain or suffering inflicted but "the purpose of the conduct, the intention of the perpetrator and the powerlessness of the victim." Blanchard J. went on to quote Nowak's definition of CIDT as "the infliction of pain or suffering, whether physical or mental, which aims at humiliating the victim" even where the pain or suffering inflicted is not severe.[104]

Blanchard J. then turned to the standard and burden of proof. The standard set out in section 83(1.1) is "reasonable grounds to believe" that information was obtained by the use of torture or CIDT. This standard was explained by the Supreme Court of Canada in *Mugesera v Canada (Minister of Citizenship and Immigration)*[105] as requiring something more than mere suspicion but less than the civil standard of proof on the balance of probabilities. What is required is an objective basis for the belief that is based on compelling and credible information.[106]

While the standard of proof is set out in the legislation, the burden of proof is not. Each side submitted that the burden rested with the

---

[101] *Convention against Torture*, [1987] Can TS no 36.

[102] *Re Mahjoub*, 2010 FC 787 at para 25, citing *Hajrizi Dzemajl v Yugoslavia* (2000), UN Doc CAT/C/29/D/161/2000.

[103] *Re Mahjoub*, *supra* note 102 at para 26.

[104] *Ibid* at para 28.

[105] *Mugesera v Canada (Minister of Citizenship and Immigration)*, 2005 SCC 40 at para 114.

[106] *Re Mahjoub*, *supra* note 102 at paras 29-30.

other. Blanchard J. began by noting the general principles that relevant evidence is admissible unless subject to an exclusionary rule and that the party seeking to introduce evidence must satisfy the court as to its admissibility. Here, the government must satisfy the court of the admissibility of information relied on in the security intelligence report concerning Majhoub. However, section 83(1)(h) provides that the court may receive into evidence anything that, in the judge's opinion, is reliable and appropriate, even if inadmissible in a court of law. Here, too, however, the burden rests with the government: it must satisfy the court that information inadmissible in a court of law is both reliable and appropriate in order for it to be admitted in evidence in a security certificate proceeding.[107] Section 83(1.1) provides that information that is believed on reasonable grounds to have been obtained by torture or CIDT is not reliable and appropriate. The burden of establishing reasonable grounds rests with the government. Blanchard J. quoted with approval the observation of Lord Hope of Craighead in *A & Ors v Secretary of State for the Home Department*[108] that "it would be wholly unrealistic to expect the detainee to prove anything, as he is denied access to so much of the information that is to be used against him." While the named person has the obligation to raise the issue of torture or CIDT, he need only show a plausible connection between the use of torture or CIDT and the information proffered by the government.[109]

The Court then considered whether derivative evidence — that is, physical evidence discovered as a result of an unlawfully obtained statement, is also excluded pursuant to section 83. The government contended that it was not. Blanchard J. disagreed. He postulated three propositions: first, information obtained as a result of the use of torture is inherently unreliable; second, the exclusion of such information in court proceedings effectively discourages the use of torture; third, the admission of such evidence is antithetical to and damages the integrity of the judicial proceeding.[110] Blanchard J. then noted that the parliamentary record made clear that derivative evidence was intended to be captured by the provisions. This is reflected in the choice of the word "information" in section 83(1.1),

---

107 *Ibid* at paras 41-6.

108 *A & Ors v Secretary of State for the Home Department*, [2005] UKHL 71 at para 116.

109 *Re Mahjoub, supra* note 102 at paras 47-59.

110 *Ibid* at para 66.

which is broader than "statement" as used in Article 15 of the *CAT* and section 269.1 (4) of the *Criminal Code.*[111]

Turning now to the substance of Majhoub's argument against the admissibility of the government's evidence, the government contended that CSIS guidelines and policies were sufficient to ensure that information obtained by it is admissible in security certificate proceedings. The government led evidence of CSIS directives and practices to avoid complicity in the use of torture. Majhoub replied that notwithstanding its policy, CSIS will never know whether information obtained by it was the result of torture. Blanchard J. held that CSIS policies and practices do not provide for an effective mechanism to ensure that information obtained from torture or CIDT is excluded from evidence adduced by the government in court. In particular, the learned judge noted that CSIS's profiles of foreign agencies are often at odds with what is reported by human rights organizations and that CSIS does not have the means to investigate independently whether its information was obtained from torture.[112] The government also contended that information that is general in nature is more likely not to be from torture and that the reliability of information, as shown by corroboration, is an indicator that it was not obtained by torture. Blanchard J. rejected these submissions.[113]

After addressing these various preliminary points, the Court came to analyzing the evidence before it. This part of the reasons is where the redactions occur, and in some cases they are so extensive as to make parts of the judgment unintelligible. We know, however, that Blanchard J. accepted Mahjoub's evidence that torture is used systematically somewhere or other at some period or other.[114] The Court relies on unspecified reports of Human Rights Watch and Amnesty International in reaching this conclusion — reports that are almost certainly public, which leaves one wondering why the Court felt obliged to omit the torturers' identities from the reasons. An example of these omissions is illustrative:

[XXX] [The evidence called on behalf of Mr. Mahjoub is clear.] [XXX] not only [XXX] with impunity, but [XXX] torture as primary means of

---

111 *Criminal Code*, RSC 1985, c C-46. See *Re Mahjoub*, *supra* note 102 at paras 60-72.

112 *Re Mahjoub*, *supra* note 102 at paras 90-3.

113 *Ibid* at paras 104-15.

114 *Ibid* at para 133.

gathering information and intelligence [XXX] I am satisfied that the evidence establishes that, at the time information relied on by the Ministers in the case against Mr. Mahjoub was gathered, torture was used systemically [XXX] on persons detained or under [XXX] control. In my view, Mr. Mahjoub has offered a plausible connection between the use of torture and CIDT in [XXX] and the unsourced information, originating from [XXX] proffered by the Ministers.

The Ministers led very little evidence to counter the evidence of the experts in respect to the systematic use of torture in [XXX]. I have not been persuaded otherwise by the Ministers' evidence adduced in closed session, which consists of the [XXX] and the testimony of [XXX]

The Agency Profiles [XXX] for the years in question rely on reports issued by Amnesty International. A review of the Amnesty International reports for the years at issue all indicate that torture is practiced [XXX] with impunity and that its use was systematic. The Service's conclusion [XXX] is unsupported by the Amnesty International reports. Further, the undisputed evidence is that the Service has no capacity to independently investigate allegations of torture. I therefore find the Service's assessment of [XXX] to be of little probative value.[115]

The thrust of this reasoning appears reassuring, even commendable. Reading through these redactions, however, one is left wondering what is really being protected — Canada's national security or its foreign relations.

Given the extensive redactions throughout Blanchard J.'s consideration of the evidence of torture and CIDT, little more can be usefully said than this: the learned judge concluded that there were reasonable grounds to believe that information collected from the interrogation of an unidentified person, and the convictions of Mahjoub and others in an Egyptian trial were obtained by the use of torture. This evidence was therefore held to be inadmissible pursuant to section 83(1)(h) and 83(1.1) of the *Immigration and Refugee Protection Act*.[116] Even with the regrettable, and in some cases doubtful, redactions, Blanchard J.'s reasons are an important vindication of the human right to be free from torture and cruelty.

---

[115] *Ibid* at paras 154-56.

[116] *Immigration and Refugee Protection Act*, SC 2001, c 27.

Canadian Cases in Private International Law in 2010 / Jurisprudence canadienne en matière de droit international privé en 2010

compiled by / préparé par

JOOST BLOM

JURISDICTION / COMPÉTENCE DES TRIBUNAUX

Common Law and Federal

Jurisdiction *in personam*

Non-resident defendant — claim essentially financial — jurisdiction simpliciter found to exist — jurisdiction not declined

McDermott Gulf Operating Co v Oceanografia Sociedad Anonima de Capital Variable (2010), 290 NSR (2d) 118, 2010 NSSC 118

McDermott, a Panamanian company, brought an action claiming about US$5 million, allegedly owed on a charter-party of M.V. *Bold Endurance*, registered in Barbados. The manager of the charter was Secunda, a Nova Scotia company. The charterer was a Louisiana company, Con-Dive, which contracted to use the ship in offshore drilling operations entirely in the territorial waters of Mexico. The charter party included a choice of law clause and a forum selection clause in favour of Nova Scotia.

Con-Dive supplied the vessel to a Mexican company, OSA, which used it in carrying out a pipeline construction and repair contract for Pemex, the Mexican national oil company, and it was OSA that used the vessel throughout the charter term. McDermott suspended operation of the vessel after Con-Dive and OSA, which had been paying hire on Con-Dive's behalf, failed to make payments under the charter party. McDermott and Secunda commenced an action in the United States District Court in Alabama against Con-Dive, OSA, and Yanez, a Mexican citizen who was the owner of Con-Dive and a principal figure in OSA, making essentially the same claims

Joost Blom is in the Faculty of Law at the University of British Columbia.

as were subsequently made in the Nova Scotia action against the same three parties. OSA had not accepted the jurisdiction of the District Court and, at the time of the present proceeding, that court had not decided whether it had jurisdiction over the plaintiffs' claims.

The defendant OSA moved for a stay or dismissal of the Nova Scotia action on the basis that the court lacked territorial competence under the *Court Jurisdiction and Proceedings Transfer Act* (*CJPTA*),[1] or, alternatively, the court should decline jurisdiction on the basis of *forum non conveniens.*

Duncan J. held that at the jurisdictional stage, the facts supporting jurisdiction are not to be found by weighing the opposing submissions of the parties; the plaintiff's version of the facts must be accepted as long as it has a reasonable basis in the record.

On the question whether OSA was bound by the clause in the charter party selecting Nova Scotia as the forum for disputes arising out of the agreement, the judge held that the pleaded facts did not support the conclusion that OSA had itself assumed as against Mc-Dermott the obligations under Con-Dive's charter party. Facts to support OSA's having done so might emerge at trial, but at this stage such a finding could not be made. Therefore, there was no territorial competence in the claim against OSA based on an agreement that the court had jurisdiction.[2]

The other possible basis for territorial competence was that a real and substantial connection existed between Nova Scotia and the facts on which the proceeding was based.[3] None of the presumed real and substantial connections in section 11 applied. The only such arguable connection was that the claim concerned contractual obligations and, by its express terms, the contract was governed by Nova Scotia law.[4] As with the forum selection clause, however, this argument was negated by the lack of any basis for finding that OSA was bound by the charter party's terms. It was therefore incumbent on the plaintiffs to show that a real and substantial connection was in fact present.

The judge held that such a connection was present and that the court therefore had territorial competence. The plaintiffs' claim

---

[1] *Court Jurisdiction and Proceedings Transfer Act*, SNS 2003 (2d Sess), c 2 [*CJPTA*].

[2] *Ibid*, s 4(c).

[3] *Ibid*, s 4(e).

[4] *Ibid*, s 11(e)(ii).

was connected to Nova Scotia in that the charter party was drafted with the intention that Nova Scotia would be the place where disputes under it were litigated; many of the plaintiffs' witnesses would be from Nova Scotia; many of the communications with OSA emanated from there; and the injury to the plaintiffs from non-payment of the accounts occurred, *inter alia*, in Nova Scotia. OSA knew that it was dealing with a Nova Scotia-based manager of the vessel and that the terms of the charter party contained a forum selection clause in favour of Nova Scotia. OSA was making payments based on the terms of the charter party and never objected to application of those terms. OSA took the benefit of that agreement to allow it to continue operations after Con-Dive defaulted on payments of hire, and it could not now say that it was unfair that the plaintiffs sought to attach the obligations of the agreement to it.

OSA had, moreover, relied upon the non-proprietary nature of McDermott's and Secunda's rights under Canadian maritime law in persuading the federal court in Alabama to release the vessel from arrest. By doing so, OSA had implicitly accepted that the choice of law in the charter party applied to its own position. This was not binding on OSA in the Nova Scotia litigation, but it was a factor in assessing whether it would be unfair to take jurisdiction over the claims against OSA. There was also possible unfairness to the plaintiffs in holding against jurisdiction because it was unclear from the material before the Court whether a Mexican court would have jurisdiction over the plaintiffs' claims. A further factor was that the claims against OSA largely overlapped with the claims against the other two defendants, Con-Dive and Yanez, who were bound by the charter party to defend the claims against them in Nova Scotia. Taking jurisdiction would avoid the plaintiffs' having to make their claims before the courts of two countries.

Having concluded it had territorial competence, the Court went on to hold that it should not exercise its discretion to decline jurisdiction under section 12 of the *CJPTA*. OSA had not met the onus of establishing that Mexico was a clearly more appropriate forum than Nova Scotia.

Note. In considering the fairness aspects of taking or not taking jurisdiction, the judge followed *Muscutt v Courcelles*.[5] The role fairness should play in the jurisdiction *simpliciter* inquiry (or territorial competence, to use the *CJPTA* term) was somewhat revised by the

[5] *Muscutt v Courcelles* (2002), 213 DLR (4th) 577 (Ont CA).

Ontario Court of Appeal in *Van Breda v Village Resorts Ltd,* noted below under *Non-resident defendant — claim arising out of personal injury or damage to property or reputation — jurisdiction* simpliciter *found to exist on basis of real and substantial connection — jurisdiction not declined.* The role that the *Muscutt/Van Breda* methodology should play in provinces that have adopted the *CJPTA* is still unclear. The Nova Scotia courts have applied it, but the position in British Columbia is largely against applying it (see *Stanway v Wyeth Pharmaceuticals Inc*).6

Applying the *Muscutt/Van Breda* approach, jurisdiction *simpliciter* was found, and jurisdiction was not declined, in the following cases: *Roadtrek Motorhomes Ltd v Aralex Acoustics Ltd* (Ontario buyer claiming against British Columbia seller of goods; real and substantial connection presumed under *Van Breda* because the contract was made in Ontario);7 *Salus Marine Wear Inc v Queen Charlotte Lodge Ltd* (Ontario seller suing British Columbia buyer for failure to pay for goods supplied; Court took into account that seller could not afford to litigate in British Columbia);8 and *Stubbs v ATS International BV* (plaintiff suing an Ontario company and a Michigan company, both of which employed him, for wrongful dismissal and failure to transfer shares to him; related claims against a Netherlands parent company and an associated foundation held to have a real and substantial connection with Ontario).9

Non-resident defendant — claim essentially financial — jurisdiction simpliciter *found to exist but jurisdiction declined*

Note. A claim by the Alberta-resident purchaser of shares in a British Columbia company from a British Columbia-resident vendor was held more appropriately heard in British Columbia. The share purchase contract was governed by Alberta law, but the litigation concerned the valuation of a business located in British Columbia, which could best be dealt with by the British Columbia court in which the vendors had already brought declaratory proceedings: *Dirtt Environmental Solutions Ltd v Almond.*10 A claim that an employee's

---

6 *Stanway v Wyeth Pharmaceuticals Inc.* (2009), 314 DLR (4th) 618, 2009 BCCA 592, leave to appeal to SCC ref'd 27 May 2009, noted at (2009) 47 CYIL 608.

7 *Roadtrek Motorhomes Ltd v Aralex Acoustics Ltd.,* 2010 ONCA 878.

8 *Salus Marine Wear Inc v Queen Charlotte Lodge Ltd.,* 2010 ONSC 3063.

9 *Stubbs v ATS International BV* (2010), 272 OAC 386, 2010 ONCA 879.

10 *Dirtt Environmental Solutions Ltd v Almond,* 2010 ABQB 499.

wife, resident in Florida, had illegally copied the hard drive of her husband's laptop computer, which belonged to the plaintiff Nova Scotia-based employer, was held more appropriately heard in Florida, partly because only a court there could effectively enforce an injunction against the wife: *Armco Capital Inc v Armoyan*.[11]

Non-resident defendant — claim essentially financial — jurisdiction simpliciter *found not to exist*

North America Steamships Ltd v HBC Hamburg Bulk Carriers GmbH (2010), [2011] 1 WWR 618, 2010 BCCA 501

NASL, a British Columbia company based in that province, went bankrupt as a result of unsuccessfully engaging in forward freight swap agreements, which are a form of a derivative financial instrument that offers a hedge against the future price of freight shipping capacity. In this action, the trustee claimed money owing under one of these agreements, which had been made via a German broker with the defendant, a German counterparty. The agreement was governed by English law and payments under it were to be made as the receiving party might direct. NASL had directed that payments to it be made to an account in Hong Kong. Upon the bankruptcy, the trustee directed that payments were henceforth to be made to an account in Vancouver. The defendant took the position that it had validly terminated the agreement, just before the bankruptcy, for NASL's breach of its solvency obligation under the contract. The plaintiff relied on an order made later under the *Companies' Creditors Arrangement Act*[12] that was said retroactively to have barred NASL's creditors, including HBC, from refusing to perform their obligations towards NASL.

The defendant had no presence in British Columbia and argued that the court lacked jurisdiction *simpliciter* over the claim. The Chambers judge found that jurisdiction *simpliciter* was established on the basis of one of the presumed real and substantial connections defined by the *CJPTA*,[13] namely, where the claim concerns contractual obligations and those obligations, to a substantial extent, were to be performed in the province.[14] The obligations in ques-

---

11 *Armco Capital Inc v Armoyan* (2010), 289 NSR (2d) 201, 2010 NSSC 02.

12 *Companies' Creditors Arrangement Act*, RSC 1985, c. C-36.

13 *CJPTA, supra* note 1.

14 *Ibid*, s 10(e)(i). The decision of the Chambers judge is noted at (2009) 46 CYIL 607-8.

tion, she held, were the payments that were to be made to NASL in Vancouver. She held the claims also concerned a business carried on in the province, which provided a second presumed connection under section 10(h) of the *CJPTA*.

The Court of Appeal reversed the Chambers judge's decision. The test in section 10(e)(i) was not directed at where obligations were to be performed as of the time of the breach but, instead, where obligations were to be performed under the contract taken as a whole. The place of payment only became British Columbia after the trustee entered the picture. Before then, the agreement had very little connection with British Columbia apart from NASL's residence, and it was well established that the plaintiff's residence *per se* was not a substantial connection for the purpose of jurisdiction *simpliciter*. Nor did the claim "concern a business carried on" in British Columbia, a phrase that had a narrower meaning than "arises out of business dealings." Neither presumption therefore applied, and no real and substantial connection with the province could be said to exist otherwise.

Note. The following cases also held that the court lacked jurisdiction *simpliciter. Laboratoires Quinton Internationale S v Biss* (no jurisdiction in respect of Canadian firm's counterclaims against a foreign company, alleging breaches of Canadian trademarks legislation that occurred outside Canada);[15] *Genco Resources Ltd v MacInnis* (plaintiff British Columbia company suing its employee, a Canadian citizen long resident in Mexico, for breaches of the contract under which he worked for it in Mexico);[16] *Broman v Machida Mack Shewchuk Meagher LLP* (claims by British Columbia-resident plaintiff and his British Columbia law firm against an Alberta law firm retained to represent the plaintiff in a personal injury suit in Alberta arising out of an accident there; proceedings ordered transferred to the Alberta court under the *CJPTA*);[17] *Magnum Integrated Technologies Inc v Integrated Industrial Systems* (company that recently moved its business to Canada claimed against United States competitor for passing-off and infringement of trademarks committed outside Canada);[18] *Lazer-Tech Ltd v Dejeray* (action by Ontario creditor of

---

[15] *Laboratoires Quinton Internationale S v Biss*, 2010 FC 358.

[16] *Genco Resources Ltd v MacInnis*, 2010 BCSC 1342 (Master).

[17] *Broman v Machida Mack Shewchuk Meagher LLP*, 2010 BCSC 760.

[18] *Magnum Integrated Technologies Inc v Integrated Industrial Systems* (2010), 84 CPR (4th) 211, 2010 ONSC 3389.

insolvent British Columbia company against individuals who, in British Columbia, engineered a fraudulent conveyance of assets from the insolvent company to third parties);[19] *Unity Life of Canada v Worthington Emond Beaudin services financières inc* (Ontario-based insurance company suing former employees of its agent in four other provinces for misuse, in those provinces, of its confidential information and inducing customers to break contracts with it);[20] and *Oleet Processing Ltd v Puratone Corp* (Saskatchewan company claiming against Manitoba buyer for breach of sale of goods contract; no presumed real and substantial connection under the *CJPTA* and no other connection).[21]

Non-resident defendant — claim arising out of personal injury or damage to property or reputation — jurisdiction simpliciter found to exist on basis of real and substantial connection — jurisdiction not declined

Van Breda v Village Resorts Ltd (2010), 316 DLR (4th) 201, 2010 ONCA 84, leave to appeal to SCC granted, 8 July 2010

In two cases, consolidated on appeal, Ontario residents brought an action in Ontario claiming damages for personal injuries (in one case) and for a death (in the other) that occurred at holiday resorts in Cuba. Both resorts were owned by Cuban companies and managed by Club Resorts, incorporated in the Cayman Islands and part of the SuperClubs group of companies, which operated holiday resorts in various Caribbean countries. Village Resorts, a member of the same group, owned the trademarks used in marketing the resorts. In both cases, Club Resorts and Village Resorts (the defendants) sought a dismissal of the action on the ground that the Ontario court lacked jurisdiction or a stay of proceedings on the basis of *forum non conveniens*. The motions judge in each case had upheld jurisdiction and denied a stay.

The Ontario Court of Appeal affirmed these decisions. The court sat as a panel of five in order to re-examine its decision in *Muscutt v Courcelles*,[22] and Sharpe J.A. gave the judgment of the court in this case as he had in *Muscutt*. In *Muscutt*, the court had said that

19 *Lazer-Tech Ltd v Dejeray*, 2010 ONSC 1662.

20 *Unity Life of Canada v Worthington Emond Beaudin Services Financières Inc*, 2010 ONCA 283, aff'g (2009), 96 OR (3d) 769 (SCJ), noted at (2009) 47 CYIL 608.

21 *Oleet Processing Ltd v Puratone Corp.* (2010), 352 Sask R 190, 2010 SKQB 69.

22 *Muscutt v Courcelles*, *supra* note 5.

jurisdiction *simpliciter*, as distinct from the discretion to decline jurisdiction, was to be decided on the basis of eight factors that were relevant to the jurisdictional criterion of a real and substantial connection between the litigation and the province. The court decided in *Van Breda* that this methodology needed to be clarified and reformulated but not scrapped.

The court adopted into the common law a device used in the *CJPTA*, which originated with the Uniform Law Conference of Canada and is in force in British Columbia, Nova Scotia, and Saskatchewan. The *CJPTA* lists certain types of claims that are presumed to have a real and substantial connection with the province unless the defendant shows otherwise (see the *North America Steamships* case noted immediately above). The *CJPTA* list was derived from the categories of cases in which most provinces' rules of court have allowed service on a non-resident defendant without leave. The court held that, projecting the *CJPTA* approach back onto the rules of court, a real and substantial connection should be presumed if a case fell within one of the grounds on which service *ex juris* was authorized without leave under Civil Procedure Rule 17.02.[23] However, two of the service *ex juris* grounds did not support the presumption of a real and substantial connection, namely, those in subrule (h) (a claim arising out of damage sustained in Ontario from a tort or breach of contract committed elsewhere) and subrule (o) (a claim against a person outside Ontario who is a necessary or proper party to a proceeding against a person in Ontario). These had not been taken up by the drafters of the *CJPTA* and had given rise to jurisdictional challenges in practice.

In addition to embracing presumptions, the court held that, of the eight *Muscutt* factors, only two, the connection that the plaintiff's claim has with the forum and the connection of the defendant to the forum, are the core of the test. The remaining factors were not to be given independent weight equivalent to the core factors but were analytic tools to assist the court in assessing the significance of the connections between the forum, the claim, and the defendant. Thus, the potential unfairness to the defendant of taking jurisdiction and the potential unfairness to the plaintiff of not taking jurisdiction (factors three and four) could not be used to overcome the lack of a real and substantial connection. They were relevant only to assessing the relevance, quality, and strength of the connections that made up the core test. The involvement of other parties

---

[23] *Rules of Civil Procedure*, RRO 1990, Reg 194, r 17.02.

to the suit (factor five) was relevant as support, in some cases, for a real and substantial connection. The court's willingness to recognize and enforce an extra-provincial judgment rendered on the same jurisdictional basis (factor six) was not a factor to be balanced with others but was an important general legal principle that disciplined the assumption of jurisdiction against extra-provincial defendants. Similarly, whether the litigation is interprovincial or international in nature (factor seven) had no weight in itself but was a general principle of law that shaped and guided the analysis. Comity and the standards of jurisdiction, recognition, and enforcement prevailing elsewhere (factor eight) were also relevant legal principles to be taken into account, not as having an independent role, but as relevant to the assessment of real and substantial connection.

The court approved, in *obiter*, of another feature of the *CJPTA*, the "forum of necessity" provision (section 6) that enables a court to take jurisdiction, despite the lack of any ground for territorial competence, if there is no court elsewhere in which the plaintiff is able, or ought reasonably to be required, to bring the proceeding. This was declared to be law in Ontario. Where there was no other forum in which the plaintiff could reasonably seek relief, there was a residual discretion to assume jurisdiction.

In one of the two cases before the court (*Van Breda* itself), the holiday had been booked directly with one of the defendant companies by the victim of the accident and her partner through an Ontario agency that provided sports instructors (the partner was a professional squash player) on short contracts to Caribbean resorts. Since this contract was made in Ontario, it satisfied one of the grounds for service *ex juris* without leave (Rule 17.02(f)(i)) and so raised a presumption of a real and substantial connection. The presumption was not rebutted, especially in light of the fact that the defendants promoted their resorts in the Canadian market. In the other case (*Charron*), the way the trip was booked did not give rise to a contract made in Ontario because the booking was made through a Canadian intermediary company. However, the real and substantial connection with Ontario was positively shown to have been present. Here, again, a major consideration was the defendants' efforts to promote their resorts to Ontario residents.

In neither case had the defendants persuaded the motions judge that Cuba was a more appropriate forum for the litigation than Ontario. The plaintiffs had witnesses from Ontario. Some witnesses from Cuba might have to testify, but this could perhaps be done without their having to travel to Ontario. The defendants were not

Cuban companies and there was evidence that they were insured against liability in Ontario lawsuits. The motions judges' decisions on *forum non conveniens*, which were exercises of discretion, should not be interfered with.

Note. At the time of writing, the Supreme Court of Canada had heard the appeal in this case but not yet delivered judgment. It had also heard the appeal in *Black v Breeden*,[24] which upheld the motions judge's decision.[25] In this case, a prominent businessman, formerly resident in Ontario, was held entitled to bring a libel action in Ontario against directors of the company of which he had formerly been the dominant shareholder. The directors, pursuant to United States securities laws, had published on the Internet and elsewhere a report on the plaintiff's dealings with the company that was highly critical of the plaintiff's probity. The Court of Appeal, applying the *Van Breda* methodology, held there was a presumed real and substantial connection with Ontario, namely, the tort of libel that, according to the plaintiff's claim, was committed in Ontario because the material was published there. (A claim based on a tort committed in the jurisdiction is a ground for service *ex juris* without leave.[26]) The presumption was not rebutted. The plaintiff had legitimate reasons for seeking to vindicate his reputation in Ontario, where the libel laws were more favourable to his claim than in the United States, and so the motions judge had properly refused to decline jurisdiction on *forum non conveniens* grounds.

Other cases in which jurisdiction *simpliciter* was found to exist, and jurisdiction was not declined, were *Dilkas v Red Seal Tours Inc* (Ontario tourist claiming for injuries in accident on Mexican tour bus being operated under a contract with an Ontario tour operator that was governed by Ontario law);[27] *Cardinali v Strait* (Ontario residents injured in automobile accident in Michigan involving residents of Michigan; unfairness to the plaintiffs of denying jurisdiction referred to as a factor);[28] *Dennis v Farrell* (British Columbia resident injured in British Columbia automobile accident but later moved to Ontario; the only issue was damages);[29] and *Braconnier v*

---

[24] *Black v Breeden* (2010), 321 DLR (4th) 659, 2010 ONCA 547.

[25] Noted at (2009) 46 CYIL 613.

[26] *Rules of Civil Procedure, supra* note 23, r 17.02(g).

[27] *Dilkas v Red Seal Tours Inc* (2010), 325 DLR (4th) 301, 2010 ONCA 634.

[28] *Cardinali v Strait*, 2010 ONSC 2503.

[29] *Dennis v Farrell* (2010), 84 CCLI (4th) 64, 2010 ONSC 2401.

Maheux (Ontario resident's claim for personal injuries suffered from a fall in the house in Quebec in which the plaintiff's daughter lived as the defendant's tenant; unfairness of denying jurisdiction considered a factor).[30]

Non-resident defendant — claim arising out of personal injury or damage to property or reputation — jurisdiction simpliciter *found to exist on basis of forum of necessity*

Josephson v Balfour Recreation Commission (2010), 10 BCLR (5th) 369, 2010 BCSC 603

The plaintiff and the defendant, friends who both lived in the state of Idaho, were playing golf in Nelson, British Columbia, when the plaintiff was injured in an accident with the golf cart that the defendant was driving. The plaintiff was taken to a local hospital and then transferred to a hospital in Idaho. He eventually became quadriplegic. The defendant, whom the plaintiff sued in British Columbia, commenced third party proceedings against the Idaho hospital where the plaintiff had been treated and the physicians who had treated him, alleging their negligent treatment was partly to blame for the plaintiff's condition. The Idaho third parties (the "Idaho doctors") applied for dismissal of the defendant's third party claims against them on the ground that the court lacked jurisdiction over the claims. It was accepted by both sides that under Idaho law, the defendant had no claim for contribution or indemnity against the Idaho doctors, because only the patient could sue for medical malpractice. Idaho had abolished joint and several liability and replaced it with several liability alone; and the defendant's claim was in any event out of time.

The court held there was no presumed real and substantial connection with British Columbia under section 10 of the *CJPTA*.[31] The defendant could also not prove that a real and substantial connection existed on the pleaded facts. The Idaho doctors could not reasonably have foreseen that their practice of medicine in Idaho on an Idaho resident would have legal consequences for them in British Columbia. The fact that the medical treatment was made necessary by an accident in British Columbia did not supply a real and substantial connection between the claim against the Idaho doctors and the province.

---

[30] *Braconnier v Maheux*, 2010 ONSC 1524.

[31] *CJPTA, supra* note 1.

The court nevertheless exercised its discretion under section 6 of the *CJPTA* to take jurisdiction. The friend found himself a defendant in an action in British Columbia and was forced by the plaintiff's action to bring a third party claim against the Idaho hospital and doctors. It was unfair to deny him the ability to adjudicate the liability of the Idaho doctors in British Columbia because there was no other court in which he could commence the proceeding (section 6(a)). It was wrong to suggest, as the Idaho doctors did, that the Idaho courts were open to the defendant and the difficulty was only that his claim would fail there. Other cases had held that the expiry of a limitation period in the other forum was no ground for acting as "forum of necessity," but this case was different. The defendant's claim was not recognized in Idaho at all. In addition, the claim was closely connected to the plaintiff's claim against the defendant, which was being litigated in British Columbia.

Note. It is open to question whether the forum of necessity provision is properly invoked when the difficulty is not that the plaintiff is unjustly excluded from recourse to the foreign court, but that the plaintiff has no prospect of success in that court. The judge referred to Quebec decisions that interpreted Article 3136 of the *Code civil du Québec*,[32] which was one of the models for *CJPTA* section 6. These decisions stressed the narrow and very exceptional character of the jurisdiction that Article 3136 was intended to confer, but the judge did not advert to that aspect of the cases. Leave to appeal her jurisdictional decision was granted,[33] but the appeal is understood to have been settled.

If the case against the Idaho doctors had come to trial in British Columbia, the defendant would have had to overcome an argument that Idaho law governs liability for acts or omissions committed in Idaho,[34] and his claim for contribution, on the basis that the doctors committed a wrong against the plaintiff there, must fail. The counter-argument might have been that the Idaho doctors did commit a wrong against the plaintiff under Idaho law. The fact that the plaintiff, who under Idaho law was the only one who could do so, had not made the malpractice claim in Idaho should not prevent a British Columbia court from finding that the doctors' liability to

---

[32] *Code civil du Québec*, LQ 1991, ch 64 [*CcQ*].

[33] *Josephson v Balfour Recreation Commission*, 2010 BCCA 339.

[34] *Tolofson v Jensen*, [1994] 3 SCR 1022 [*Tolofson*].

the plaintiff nevertheless existed under Idaho law, which would then trigger the defendant's right of contribution under British Columbia law.

Non-resident defendant — claim arising out of personal injury or damage to property or reputation — jurisdiction simpliciter *found not to exist*

Note. Challenges to jurisdiction *simpliciter* succeeded in *Bellefontaine v Purdue Frederick Inc* (named plaintiffs in class action against drug manufacturer did not reside in the province and had not been prescribed the drug in the province (*CJPTA*));[35] *Kahlon v Cheecham* (plaintiff now resident in Ontario suing for injuries suffered in Alberta road accident, with liability in issue);[36] and *Wall Estate v GlaxoSmithKline Inc* (claims against drug distributor and other foreign companies not shown to have any connection to Saskatchewan (*CJPTA*)).[37]

Declining jurisdiction *in personam*

Forum selection clause

Note. The contract between a professional baseball team in Ontario and the Can-Am League, to which it belonged, provided that any disputes arising out of the contract must be resolved in North Carolina and were subject to arbitration. The team sued the league in Ontario for having terminated its membership and drawing down a letter of credit the team had given it. The league's attornment to the court's jurisdiction, by filing a notice of intent to defend and a statement of defence, was held not to preclude the defendant from relying on the clause nor to constitute "strong cause" for refusing to enforce the clause: *Momentous.ca Corp v Canadian American Association of Professional Baseball Ltd.*[38] The court emphasized that the "strong cause" test for overriding a forum selection clause is much more stringent than a *forum non conveniens* test. The same court had made the same point in *Expedition Helicopters Inc v Honeywell Inc.*[39]

---

[35] *Bellefontaine v Purdue Frederick Inc.* (2010), 292 NSR (2d) 290, 2010 NSCA 58.

[36] *Kahlon v Cheecham*, 2010 ONSC 1957.

[37] *Wall Estate v GlaxoSmithKline Inc*, 2010 SKQB 351.

[38] *Momentous.ca Corp v Canadian American Association of Professional Baseball Ltd* (2010), 325 DLR (4th) 685, 2010 ONCA 722, leave to appeal to SCC granted, 19 May 2011.

[39] *Expedition Helicopters Inc v Honeywell Inc* (2010), 319 DLR (4th) 316, 2010 ONCA 351, leave to appeal to SCC refused, 25 November 2010.

(Ontario action by Ontario owner of helicopter that crashed in Saskatchewan suing American manufacturer of the engine, exclusive choice of Arizona forum in contract between owner and manufacturer enforced).

The "strong cause" test was also applied, and the forum selection clause enforced, in *Liebrecht v Lieder*.[40] The contract was one with a German lawyer for performance of services in Germany and included express choices of German law and a German forum; British Columbia legislation guaranteeing the client's right to have a judge tax a lawyer's bill did not apply.

Resident defendant — claim essentially financial — forum non conveniens

Henry Estate v Henry, 2010 MBQB 267

A Manitoba resident was sued by two of his siblings, one of whom resided in Quebec and the other in California, in respect of his alleged misappropriation of property said to have belonged to the estate of their deceased mother, who had died in Jamaica. There were five other siblings, of whom three lived in Manitoba, one in Ontario, and one in Texas. The plaintiffs were the executors of the mother's estate. The court held that it had jurisdiction *simpliciter*. Aside from the defendant's residence, the location of the assets and the alleged misconduct with respect to them supplied a real and substantial connection to the province. On *forum non conveniens*, the court did not give great weight to the fact that one of the issues was likely to be the mother's testamentary capacity, which would require witnesses from Jamaica. Most of these, according to the plaintiffs' evidence, were prepared to testify by live video-conference. Half the siblings, including the defendant, lived in Manitoba. There was no evidence that a court in Jamaica would hear the claim against the defendant and, even if it did, the judgment might well not be enforceable in Manitoba and the plaintiffs would have to re-litigate. The plaintiffs also had a legitimate advantage if the proceeding took place in Manitoba, namely security for recovery of any judgment, given that they had obtained the payment into court of the proceeds of the sale of the assets in question.

---

[40] *Liebrecht v Lieder*, 2010 BCSC 1548.

Non-resident defendant — claim essentially financial — related proceedings in foreign court

Note. In *Eurofase Inc v FDV-Firme Di Vetro SpA*,[41] the Ontario proceeding was stayed pending the outcome of Italian proceedings that, if they resulted in judgment, would substantially reduce the issues in the Ontario action. By contrast, a stay was denied in *Bedessee Imports Ltd v Guyana Sugar Corp*.[42] A Guyanese government minister and a state corporation were sued in Ontario and New York in respect of statements that allegedly disparaged the plaintiff's wares. The Ontario court refused to stay the proceeding because the New York action might well be unable to give relief in respect of claims that the plaintiff made for contravention of Canadian trademarks legislation. See also *Dirtt Environmental Solutions Ltd v Almond*,[43] noted above under Jurisdiction *in personam: Non-resident defendant — claim essentially financial — jurisdiction* simpliciter *exists but jurisdiction declined.*

Class actions

Certification — jurisdiction simpliciter *in respect of the claim — forum non conveniens*

Note: Bellefontaine v Purdue Frederick Inc[44] (see above under Jurisdiction *in personam; Non-resident defendant — claim arising out of personal injury or damage to property or reputation — jurisdiction* simpliciter *found not to exist*) dealt with individuals who were excluded as representative plaintiffs in a class action against a pharmaceutical company because their claims lacked a real and substantial connection with Nova Scotia. Whether the claims by the remaining representative plaintiffs should be certified on the basis of a national class was a matter to be decided at the certification stage. *Wall Estate v GlaxoSmithKline Inc*[45] (see above) refused to certify a class action against five foreign drug companies because the pleaded facts did not show a real and substantial connection between the claims against them and Saskatchewan. The claims against those defendants were

[41] *Eurofase Inc v FDV-Firme Di Vetro SpA*, 2010 ONSC 5277.
[42] *Bedessee Imports Ltd v Guyana Sugar Corp* (2010), 329 DLR (4th) 382, 2010 ONCA 719, leave to appeal to SCC refused, 14 April 2011.
[43] *Dirtt Environmental Solutions Ltd v Almond*, *supra* note 10.
[44] *Bellefontaine v Purdue Frederick Inc*, *supra* note 35.
[45] *Wall Estate v GlaxoSmithKline Inc*, *supra* note 37.

dismissed. In *Frey v BCE Inc*,[46] the court gave leave to appeal from the certification of a class action against various mobile telephone companies, alleging they had overcharged their customers. Jurisdiction *simpliciter* and *forum non conveniens* were the issues that were held to meet the requirements of merit and importance.

Administration and Succession

Note. See *Henry Estate v Henry*, noted above under Declining jurisdiction *in personam*; *Resident defendant — claim essentially financial — forum non conveniens*; and *Davies v Collins*, noted below under CHOICE OF LAW; *Common Law and Federal*; Property; *Succession — will — essential validity*.

Bankruptcy and Insolvency

Bankruptcy protection — foreign order — recognition

Note. See *Re Xerium Technologies Inc*,[47] noted below under FOREIGN JUDGMENTS; *Common Law and Federal*; Bankruptcy and Insolvency; *Cross-border insolvency — bankruptcy protection orders made abroad — co-ordinated action by Canadian court*.

Matrimonial Causes

Divorce — declining jurisdiction

Cheng v Liu (2010), 83 RFL (6th) 62, 2010 ONSC 2221

The father, who had immigrated from China to Canada in 2002, met the mother, who lived in China, over the Internet in 2006. That year, during a brief visit by the father to China, the mother became pregnant. The father returned to China later that year for a one-day visit to marry her. Their daughter was born early in 2007. The father visited the mother and daughter briefly at the end of 2007 and decided to end the relationship. He withdrew the application he had made to sponsor their immigration to Canada. He had no further contact with them until, in March 2009, the mother began a divorce proceeding in Ontario, claiming custody, child and spousal support, and property division. The father retained counsel, who informed the mother's counsel that she would bring a motion to determine jurisdiction. A few weeks later, the father brought an

---

[46] *Frey v BCE Inc*, 2010 SKCA 37.

[47] *Re Xerium Technologies Inc.* (2010), 71 CBR (5th) 300, 2010 ONSC 3974.

application in China for divorce, division of property, custody, and child support. He now sought to have the mother's proceeding in Ontario stayed.

The judge held, first, that the Ontario court had jurisdiction because, as required by section 3(1) of the *Divorce Act*,[48] one party, in this case the respondent father, had been ordinarily resident in Ontario for more than one year immediately preceding the presentation of the mother's petition. However, both section 6 of the *Divorce Act* and section 22 of the *Children's Law Reform Act*[49] (which governs custody other than as corollary relief under the *Divorce Act*), permitted or required the court to decline jurisdiction on custody and access issues if the child was not resident in Ontario, because the child's best interests could most appropriately be determined where the child normally resided. The mother conceded that custody and access must be adjudicated in China. Property division, according to section 15 of the *Family Law Act*,[50] was governed by the law of the parties' last common habitual residence or, if there was no last common habitual residence, the law of Ontario. The parties' marital relationship, however brief, had occurred exclusively in China, and so an Ontario court would be required to apply Chinese law to property division. Rather than have a split proceeding, with custody and access being heard in China and the rest in Canada, though with Chinese law applying to the property issues, it was more appropriate that the proceedings take place entirely in China. The risk that the father might not obey any support orders made by the Chinese court was dealt with by granting the stay on condition that the husband comply promptly with all procedural and substantive orders of the courts of China in the case now pending there between the parties.

Support obligations — interjurisdictional enforcement of support orders

Trylinski-Branson v Branson (2010), 326 DLR (4th) 59, 2010 ABCA 322

The wife and husband were married in Calgary in 1986 but lived from then until their separation in 1994 in Australia. Since the separation, the wife had lived in Alberta with their three children. She applied to vary a consent child support order made by an

---

[48] *Divorce Act*, RSC 1985, c 3 (2d Supp).

[49] *Children's Law Reform Act*, RSO 1990, c C-12.

[50] *Family Law Act*, RSO 1990, c F-3.

Australian court in 1995 and served the husband with a Notice to Disclose, which the Alberta court subsequently ordered the husband to comply with. The husband challenged the court's jurisdiction to require him to make disclosure. The court held against him and ordered disclosure, and the Court of Appeal upheld the Judge's order. In 2003, between the initial order and the decision on appeal, the *Interjurisdictional Support Orders Act* (*IJSOA*) came into force.[51] The Chambers judge in 2005 made a final order under section 35 of the *IJSOA*, varying the Australian support order.

The Court of Appeal allowed the husband's appeal from this order. Section 35 says that the court can "vary a support order registered in Alberta" (the Australian order had been registered) where both the applicant and the respondent "accept the Alberta court's jurisdiction." This meant the parties must accept the court's jurisdiction to vary the support order on a final basis. Merely attorning to the Alberta court's jurisdiction to make a provisional order, which the Chambers judge held the husband had done by making a formal offer, was not the same thing as accepting the court's jurisdiction for the purposes of making a final order. To hold it was would contravene the scheme of the *IJSOA* and discourage respondents from attempting to settle the amount of a provisional order. Nor did the fact that the husband was served with the Notice to Disclose, while he was temporarily in Alberta, vest jurisdiction in the court to make a final order under section 35. At common law, it would give the court jurisdiction to make a fresh support order, but to make a new order conflicting with the Australian order would be contrary to the purpose of the *IJSOA*, which was not to displace the jurisdiction of the original court but to facilitate amendment of the orders of that court when one of the parties has left the jurisdiction. The Chambers judge's order was declared a provisional order only, which, after being updated by the court below, could be sent to Australia for confirmation.

Note. Where the other jurisdiction has also enacted the *IJSOA*, the two-stage provisional order-final order procedure is simplified by allowing the support application to be forwarded directly to the other jurisdiction, where the respondent resides, for determination by a court there. In *Lei v Kwan*,[52] the provisional order procedure was necessary because Quebec, the other jurisdiction, had not

---

[51] *Interjurisdictional Support Orders Act*, RSA 2000, c I-3.5.

[52] *Lei v Kwan* (2010), 328 DLR (4th) 553, 2010 MBCA 108.

enacted the *IJSOA*. The motions judge had refused to make a provisional order because, under Quebec law (as she held), the petitioner had no right to support because she was not married to the respondent. The Court of Appeal held that at the provisional order stage, the foreign law is not applied. The scheme of the act made it clear that only the court of a receiving state should interpret and determine the local law. A provisional order therefore should have been made.

Infants and Children

Custody — jurisdiction

Note. When custody is sought ancillary to divorce, the court's jurisdiction under the *Divorce Act*[53] determines jurisdiction in custody, although the court can decline jurisdiction on the basis of *forum non conveniens*: see *Roco v Roco*[54] and *Bullecer v Mayangat*,[55] two very similar cases in which jurisdiction was not declined, although the children of the marriage were resident with a grandparent in the Philippines. *Campbell v Campbell*[56] is an example where the Ontario court, to which the father had applied for custody, communicated with the court in Utah to which the mother had applied for custody, before either court decided on jurisdiction. After the judges' exchange of information, the Utah court decided it would not take jurisdiction and the Ontario court then decided that it would. See also *Shortridge-Tsuchiya v Tsuchiya*, noted immediately below.

Child abduction

Shortridge-Tsuchiya v Tsuchiya (2010), 315 DLR (4th) 498, 2010 BCCA 61, leave to appeal to SCC refused, 8 July 2010

The mother was a Canadian who met and, in 2000, married the father, a resident of Japan, while she was teaching English in Japan. Their son was born in 2001. The parties lived their married life in Japan until, in 2007, the father advised the mother he intended to seek a divorce. Before the third mediation session, which Japanese law required prior to a divorce, the mother left Japan with the son,

---

[53] *Divorce Act, supra* note 48.
[54] *Roco v Roco*, 2010 ABQB 683.
[55] *Bullecer v Mayangat*, 2010 ABQB 680.
[56] *Campbell v Campbell*, 2010 ONSC 4363.

without informing the father, and moved to British Columbia to live with her parents. She commenced an action in British Columbia in November 2008 seeking custody and guardianship of the child, and child and spousal support. The following day, the father brought a proceeding in Japan for divorce and custody. He withdrew his proceedings for divorce in February 2009 on the advice of his Japanese counsel, who said there was no point in pursuing the action while the child was subject to outstanding proceedings in British Columbia. In April 2009, he applied to the British Columbia Court under Part 3 of the *Family Relations Act*[57] for, *inter alia*, an order that the court "decline to exercise its territorial competence in the proceeding" brought by the mother.

The Chamber's judge noted that Japan was not a signatory to the *Hague Convention on the Civil Aspects of International Child Abduction* (*Hague Convention*).[58] He held that the court lacked jurisdiction *simpliciter*. The child's habitual residence was still Japan, and the grounds for taking jurisdiction over a non-resident child under section 44(1)(b) of the *Family Relations Act* were not met. The evidence available in British Columbia concerning the child's best interests was not, as paragraph (ii) requires, "substantial." Also, although subparagraph (v) requires the child to have a real and substantial connection with British Columbia, the child's connection in this case, though real, was not substantial. Even if the judge had jurisdiction he would decline to exercise it, partly on the ground that one of the purposes of the jurisdictional rules in the act is to discourage a parent from abducting a child, as the mother had done in this case.

The Court of Appeal disagreed with the judge's analysis of jurisdiction *simpliciter*. Section 44(1) states that a court "must exercise its jurisdiction ... only if" the stipulated factors — habitual residence of the child under paragraph (a) or the list of factors under (b) — are present. This did not create jurisdiction. It only provided for the circumstances in which the court was required to exercise it (subject to the discretion to decline jurisdiction under section 46). Even if the section 44 criteria were absent, a court would have jurisdiction as long as there was a real and substantial connection

---

[57] *Family Relations Act*, RSBC 1996, c 128.

[58] *Hague Convention on the Civil Aspects of International Child Abduction*, 25 October, 1980, Hague XXVIII (in force 1 December 1983) [*Hague Convention*].

with the province, as would be the case if exercising jurisdiction was necessary to prevent harm to the child (section 45) or the court's *parens patriae* jurisdiction was engaged.

However, even if the court had jurisdiction over custody, the judge was right to decline jurisdiction in favour of having custody determined in Japan. The factors in section 11 of the *CJPTA*[59] applied, and, as they were not exhaustive, the court was able to consider the purposes of Part 3 of the *Family Relations Act*, including the best interests of the child and — considerations common to both statutes — avoiding conflicting decisions and discouraging the wrongful removal of children from one jurisdiction to another. The judge had taken the right factors into account in exercising his discretion. The mother argued that the judge should have given more weight to the difficulty she would have in enforcing any British Columbia court order in Japan, since it was not a signatory to the *Hague Convention*. It was incongruous that it was she who sought the benefits associated with the *Hague Convention* in circumstances in which her removal of the child from Japan had been wrongful and, had the convention applied, the father could probably have secured an order for the return of the child. The mother had not been exercising her own right to custody or lawful mobility rights in the interests of the child. Her own evidence showed that she believed she faced a lengthy and difficult custody battle in the Japanese courts and chose to deceive the father as to her plans in order to avoid confrontation and ensure that she would be successful in leaving the country. This was precisely the sort of conduct that Part 3 of the *Family Relations Act* was designed to deter.

One judge dissented on the ground that the judge should not have declined jurisdiction, particularly because there was no evidence that the mother's rights under any British Columbia court order would be enforceable in the Japanese courts. It was not clear that there was any effective way to prevent the father from simply taking the child if the child was returned to Japan.

Kubera v Kubera (2010), 317 DLR (4th) 307, 2010 BCCA 118

The court upheld the Chamber's judge's refusal to order the return of a child to Poland under the *Hague Convention*,[60] notwithstanding

---

[59] *CJPTA, supra* note 1.

[60] *Hague Convention, supra* note 58.

that the mother had wrongfully retained the child in Canada since 2004. Since the proceedings were commenced more than a year after the wrongful retention, it was open to a court to refuse to return the child if it was "now settled in its new environment" (the exception in Article 12). Settlement, for the purposes of this provision, included both a physical element, relating to being established in a community, and an emotional element, relating to security and stability. The actual circumstances of the child were to be considered, including the likely effect of uprooting a child who has already been the victim of one international relocation. The inquiry must be "child-centric" because the purpose is to focus on the child's best interests, not to pass judgment on the behaviour of the parents. Wrongful concealment or delay of the proceedings by a parent was relevant only so far as it interfered with the child's ability to settle in the new environment and community.

One of the key questions argued on the appeal was whether the "settlement" of the child was to be assessed as of the time of the hearing or the time when the proceeding for return was commenced (April 2006). The "now settled" language in Article 12 supported the former reading. A determination of whether a child is settled in the new environment can occur only after the court conducting the hearing has found that the child has been "wrongfully removed or retained." As a result, any decision or demonstration regarding the child's settlement would have to occur at the time of the hearing. The French version of the convention used the present tense (*"s'est intégré"*), which also suggested an assessment as of the time of the hearing. This view was also consistent with cases in the United Kingdom and Australia and with the policy of the convention to base decisions on a child's actual circumstances.

Any delay or deception by the respondent parent that prevented commencement of the proceedings until the one-year period in Article 12 had elapsed and so brought the case potentially within the exception should be considered on a case-by-case basis as it relates to the underlying objectives of the convention. There had been such behaviour in this case on the mother's part, because she deceived the father about her intention to return to Poland for six months after her wrongful retention began, which was in May 2004, when her visa extension ran out and she stayed in Canada based on a refugee claim. However, nothing prevented the father from applying after that point. The Chamber's judge's conclusion that the degree of settlement of the child now outweighed the general deterrent value of an order for return should stand.

Note. In *Abib v Abib*,[61] a daughter was ordered returned to the United Kingdom under the *Hague Convention*. Although the family had travelled together to Canada, this had not, on the facts, been a change of their habitual residence from the United Kingdom. The judge's refusal to apply the Article 12 exception should not be interfered with.

Québec

Action personnelle

Compétence territoriale — naissance du droit d'action — préjudice

Bombardier inc c Air liquide Canada inc, 2010 QCCS 4051, autorisation d'appel à la Cour d'appel du Québec refusée, 2010 QCCA 1631

Air Liquide Welding France (ALWF) demande le renvoi à l'arbitrage du litige l'opposant à Bombardier, qui réclame d'Air liquide Canada (ALC) la somme de 5 709 897 $ à titre de dommages-intérêts. Bombardier allègue qu'elle a acheté d'ALC du fil à souder pour la fabrication de bogies de train de métro, et que le fil serait atteint de vice de fabrication. Bombardier a ajouté ALWF à titre de co-défenderesse au motif que c'est cette dernière qui a fabriqué le fil à souder. ALC et ALWF sont des sociétés liées. ALWF prétend qu'une clause d'arbitrage le lie à ALC. De plus, plaide ALWF, une clause d'élection de droit prévoit que le droit français régit leurs relations. Selon ALWF, toujours en application du droit français, ladite clause d'arbitrage est opposable à Bombardier suivant l'effet des contrats translatifs de propriété. ALWF demande le rejet de l'action de Bombardier vu l'incompétence des tribunaux québécois puisque c'est le droit français qui s'applique. Bombardier soutient que son recours est étranger aux factures échangées entre ALWF et ALC et que c'est le droit québécois qui s'applique. Toujours selon Bombardier, les règles du droit international privé en matière de responsabilité du fabricant prévoient que le choix de la loi applicable revient à la victime, donc à Bombardier en l'occurrence. La Cour rejette la requête d'ALWF. L'article 1730 *CcQ*[62] permet à l'acquéreur d'un bien de poursuivre le fabricant au même titre que le vendeur sur la base de la garantie légale à laquelle il est tenu envers l'acquéreur. Le fabricant est perçu comme le codébiteur des

---

[61] *Abib v Abib*, 2010 ONCA 827.

[62] *CcQ*, *supra* note 32.

obligations envers l'acquéreur. Or, le fabricant est soumis à la garantie légale de qualité aux mêmes conditions que le vendeur. Ajouter un codéfendeur (le fabricant) trouve donc sa source dans le *CcQ* et non dans un contrat ou bon de commande ou autre document entre le fabricant et le vendeur du bien. La relation tripartite est donc légale et non conventionnelle. Lorsque l'acquéreur d'un bien intente un recours direct contre le fabricant, les dispositions du droit international privé lui accordent le choix du forum, selon l'article 3128 *CcQ*. Le bien a été acquis au Québec et Bombardier avait donc le choix et pouvait choisir le Québec comme forum pour le litige. D'ailleurs, l'article 3148 *CcQ* prévoit plusieurs facteurs de rattachement. Bombardier et ALC ont choisi le Québec comme forum compétent, le contrat entre elles a été fait au Québec et les biens ont été achetés et livrés au Québec. Le préjudice a aussi été subi au même endroit.

Il n'y a pas une clause d'arbitrage entre Bombardier et ALC mais elle existe dans certains cas entre ALC et ALWF. Cette clause n'a jamais été portée à l'attention de, ou acceptée par, Bombardier. Les conditions requises pour que le Tribunal soit obligé de renvoyer le dossier à un arbitre pour que ce dernier statue sur la validité de la clause d'arbitrage ne sont pas remplies. La clause est inopposable à Bombardier.

Compétence territoriale — forum non conveniens

Bil'in (Village Council) c Green Park International Inc (2010), 322 DLR (4th) 232, 2010 QCCA 1455, autorisation d'appel à la CSC refusée le 3 mars 2011

Two Quebec companies, Green Park and Green Mount, began constructing residential buildings in the village of Bil'in in the West Bank, territory occupied by Israel since 1967. The buildings were to be occupied by Israeli citizens. The village council, and individuals who were said to have owned the land in question, brought an action in Quebec against the two companies and their principal shareholder, Laroche, claiming a declaration that the defendants' activities made them complicit in Israel's violation of Article 49(6) of the *Geneva Convention Relative to the Protection of Civilian Persons in Time of War* (*Geneva Convention IV*)[63] and of other international

---

[63] *Geneva Convention Relative to the Protection of Civilian Persons in Time of War,* 12 August, 1949, 75 UNTS 287 (in force 21 October 1950).

conventions and customary international law. The defendants applied for a stay of proceedings on the ground of *forum non conveniens*, which was granted by the Superior Court judge.[64]

There was no reason to interfere with the exercise by the court below of its discretion to decline jurisdiction under Article 3135 of the *CcQ* (*forum non conveniens*). It was correct that the provision requires "exceptional" circumstances to do so, but the judge had a basis for finding that the criterion was met.

The judge had not erred in taking into account that ownership of the land in question would be an issue in any Quebec proceeding because it was clear that the interest of some of the plaintiffs to sue depended on their ownership of the property. Nor had he erred in rejecting the plaintiffs' contention that their claim was outside the jurisdiction of the High Court of Justice in Israel — that assertion was unsupported by the evidence. Nor had he erred in holding that the plaintiffs had not made good their claim that, even if it heard the case, the High Court would refuse to decide it as non-justiciable.

The judge had not misapplied the factors relevant to *forum non conveniens* as identified in *Spar Aerospace Ltd v American Mobile Satellite Corp*.[65] There was no doubt that the residence of the parties and the witnesses, the location of material evidence, the execution of the work, the location of the defendants' assets, and the need to have the judgment recognized in another jurisdiction, all pointed to Israel as the more appropriate forum. The plaintiffs argued that the judge's characterization of the connection with Quebec as "superficial" was wrong, given that the principal party behind the defendant corporations chose to incorporate in Quebec because of tax benefits and should not now be able to avoid the obligations arising from his choice. That was true as far as it went, but the fact remained that the dispute pitted citizens of the West Bank against corporations carrying out work in the West Bank in compliance with the law applicable in the West Bank. It required a great deal of imagination to claim that the action had a serious connection with Quebec.

---

[64] Decision noted at (2009) 47 CYIL 631.

[65] *Spar Aerospace Ltd v American Mobile Satellite Corp.*, [2002] 4 SCR 205, 2002 SCC 78 at para 71.

Litispendance

Jugement étranger pas encore reconnu au Québec — article 3137 CcQ

Samson c Banque canadienne impériale de commerce, 2010 QCCA 604

Avant de faire cession volontaire de ses biens en mai 2006, Sky High œuvrait dans le milieu cinématographique. À l'occasion de ses opérations commerciales aux États-Unis, celle-ci obtient de la banque une ouverture de crédit en devise américaine de 2 700 000 $ et une autre de 2 376 017 $, cette fois en devise canadienne. En janvier 2005, faute par Sky High d'honorer ses obligations, la banque dépose devant la Cour supérieure une procédure en délaissement forcé (article 2667 *CcQ*). Sky High évite l'exécution en signant une transaction (article 2631 *CcQ*) à laquelle interviennent Carl et Armand Samson à titre de cautions de l'emprunt en dollars canadiens. En décembre 2005, devant la United States District Court en Illinois, Sky High et Carl Samson sont poursuivis en justice par deux sociétés américaines. Celles-ci adjoignent la banque comme défenderesse pour assurer, le cas échéant, l'exécution de leur jugement. Elles formulent à l'égard de Carl Samson plusieurs griefs, dont un voulant que ce dernier ait falsifié la signature de Kempf, l'un de leurs administrateurs. Devant le tribunal de l'Illinois, la banque choisit de réclamer à Carl Samson des dommages-intérêts en réparation du préjudice que lui a causé la conduite fautive de ce dernier. Les deux sociétés américaines et la banque obtiennent contre Carl Samson un jugement par défaut lui condamnant à payer à la banque 3 345 620 $ américains. En mars 2008, en application des articles 3155 et suivants du *CcQ*, la banque demande à la Cour supérieure de reconnaitre le jugement rendu par le tribunal de l'Illinois.

En janvier 2009, la banque obtint de la Cour supérieure un jugement condamnant Carl et Armand Samson à lui payer 581 706 $. Ceux-ci ont porté ce jugement en appel. L'un des moyens était que le jugement de première instance était de la même nature que celui prononcé par le tribunal en l'Illinois. À l'avis des appelants, sa reconnaissance au Québec, non encore acquise, conduit à une double condamnation de Carl Samson à l'égard du prêt en dollars canadiens. Ils invoquent la litispendance internationale.

La Cour rejette l'appel. En matière de litispendance internationale, l'article 3137 du *CcQ* confère aux tribunaux québécois une certaine discrétion. (Le tribunal "peut, quand une action est introduite devant elle, surseoir à statuer si une autre action entre les mêmes parties, fondée sur les mêmes faits et ayant le même objet, est déjà pendante devant une autorité étrangère, pourvu qu'elle puisse donner lieu à une décision pouvant être reconnue au Québec, ou si une telle décision a déjà été rendue par une autorité étrangère".) Cette discrétion est largement tributaire des circonstances. Le jugement rendu par le tribunal américain n'étant pas encore reconnu au Québec, les appelants peuvent toujours s'opposer à ce qu'il devienne exécutoire en invoquant des moyens de défense prévus à l'article 3155 *CcQ*. La condamnation prononcée par le tribunal étranger à l'égard de Carl Samson repose, du moins en partie, sur le même fondement que celui du jugement de première instance, soit le défaut de rembourser le prêt en dollars canadiens. En elle-même, cette situation ne permet toutefois pas de remettre en question le bien-fondé du jugement de première instance. Les appelants pourront toujours, devant le tribunal de l'*exequatur*, invoquer la condamnation prononcée dans le présent dossier.

Note. Voir aussi *Bombardier inc c Fastwing Investment Holdings Ltd*[66] (action au Texas n'était pas pendante lors du dépôt des procédures au Québec, et en tout cas le tribunal québécois était le forum naturel du litige et ne doit pas exercer sa discrétion d'ordonner la suspension des procédures selon l'article 3137 *CcQ*).

Enfants et mineurs

Garde — enlèvement d'enfants — Convention de la Haye

Droit de la famille — 102375, 2010 QCCS 4390

The petitioner presented a motion under the *Act Respecting the Civil Aspects of International and Interprovincial Child Abduction*,[67] which, *inter alia*, implements the *Hague Convention*,[68] for the return of his daughter from Mexico. The daughter was born in 2005 in Mexico and was brought to Quebec by her mother in 2008, when the mother fled Mexico and claimed refugee status in Canada, which was still pending. The father alleged that the mother wrongfully removed the daughter from her habitual residence in Mexico. The mother had been in a lesbian relationship with her present partner, S, since 2006. She and the father separated that year, and, in 2007, the father instituted divorce proceedings in Mexico. Provisional custody

---

[66] *Bombardier Inc c Fastwing Investment Holdings Ltd*, 2010 QCCS 6665.

[67] *Act Respecting the Civil Aspects of International and Interprovincial Child Abduction*, RSQ, c A-23.01 [Quebec Act].

[68] *Hague Convention, supra* note 58.

was given to the mother. He also subsequently filed a criminal complaint against the mother for the corruption and exploitation of a minor.

It was this, together with the father's evident unwillingness to let her have access to the daughter, that led her, with the daughter, to leave the state where the parties lived and go into hiding elsewhere in Mexico. After the mother and daughter, using a false passport for the daughter, had left Mexico, the father obtained a modification of the provisional custody order to give provisional custody to himself, largely on the basis that the mother's homosexuality endangered the daughter by increasing the risk that she would become lesbian herself. A divorce was subsequently granted, and permanent custody awarded to the father, with similar reasons supporting the custody decision. Some time later, an appeal court, reversing an acquittal at first instance, held the mother guilty of the crime of corrupting her daughter. The mother, on bad legal advice, had not participated in the criminal proceeding at any stage. Before the Quebec court, she denied the allegations in the criminal complaint as distortions or lies. Extradition proceedings were commenced in Mexico.

The mother's wrongful removal of the child from Mexico was conceded. In asking the court to refuse to order the return of her daughter to Mexico, the mother relied on Article 20(2) of the *Quebec Act*, corresponding to Article 12(2) of the *Hague Convention*, alleging that the child had become settled or integrated into Quebec and Canadian society and that her life would be disrupted by having to return. She also relied on the exception in Article 21(2) of the *Quebec Act* (Article 13(b) of the *Hague Convention*), stating that if the child was returned, there was a grave risk that she would be exposed to psychological harm or otherwise placed in an intolerable situation.

The court held that the grounds for the "now settled" exception had not been established. The child was only five and had lived in two towns in Quebec during her twenty-three months in Canada. The "grave risk" exception, however, was made out. If the daughter returned to Mexico, she would most probably be living with her father while her mother was imprisoned, surrounded by relatives who feared or discriminated against homosexuals and who had a very negative opinion of her mother. There was a serious and clear risk of alienation of the child from her mother or of placing her in a severe conflict of loyalties. There was no doubt that, should this occur, the daughter would not only be placed in an intolerable situation but would also risk psychological and emotional harm. The father's promise to stop the criminal proceedings in Mexico if the child were ordered returned was not persuasive because the criminal process was really beyond his control. No authority in Mexico gave any guarantee or assurance that the mother would not be imprisoned if she returned to Mexico.

Because the return of the child would naturally involve the return of the mother, who would certainly never abandon her daughter, and given that there was a grave risk that the mother would be incarcerated for an indefinite or prolonged period, the child would be deprived of the care, protection, and attention of her mother, a clear infringement of Article 39 of the Quebec *Charter of Human Rights and Freedoms* (Quebec *Charter*).[69] Moreover, given the mother's legal circumstances in Mexico, to order the return of the child and, as a result, the mother would be contrary to the rights of equal treatment and non-discrimination based on sex or sexual orientation enshrined in section 15 of the *Canadian Charter of Rights and Freedoms*[70] and Article 10 of the Quebec *Charter*.

PROCEDURE / PROCÉDURE

Common Law and Federal

Commencement of Proceedings

Service of process

Note. Service upon an officer of a Canadian company was held not to constitute service upon French and United States companies that were part of the same corporate group. There was insufficient evidence before the court as to the business the foreign companies did in Alberta, or the individual's relationship to them, to support service as having been on "an agent, manager, office manager or other representative [of the foreign defendant] resident and carrying on his business within the jurisdiction" (rule 20 of the *Alberta Rules of Court*[71]): *Venture Helicopters Ltd v European Aeronautic Defence*

---

69 *Charter of Human Rights and Freedoms*, RSQ, c C-12 [*Quebec Charter*].

70 *Canadian Charter of Rights and Freedoms*, Part I of the *Constitution Act, 1982*, being Schedule B to the *Canada Act 1982* (UK) 1982, c 11 [*Charter*].

71 *Alberta Rules of Court*, Alta Reg 390/1968.

& Space Co Eads NV.[72] It was immaterial that the Alberta proceeding had in fact come to the companies' attention.

FOREIGN JUDGMENTS / JUGEMENTS ÉTRANGERS

Common Law and Federal

Conditions for Recognition or Enforcement

Jurisdiction of the original court — subject matter jurisdiction — res judicata

Note. In *Stern Estate v Solehdin*,[73] an action to enforce *in personam* judgments of a United States Bankruptcy Court in Louisiana, made against the guarantors of the bankrupt company's debts, was defended on the basis that the court lacked subject matter jurisdiction. The court held that the judgment debtors had raised and argued this issue before the original court itself and could not relitigate it now. They could have appealed in Louisiana but failed to do so. The expert evidence showed that the judgments were enforceable in Louisiana.

Enforcement of the Canadian Judgments and Decrees Act *— original court's jurisdiction not an issue*

Note. The uniform *Enforcement of Canadian Judgments and Decrees Act* (*ECJDA*),[74] enacted in one version or another in seven Canadian jurisdictions, operates in most of them alongside the older *Reciprocal Enforcement of Judgments Act* (*REJA*).[75] The main difference between them, when it comes to enforcing a judgment from another province, is that the *ECJDA* expressly precludes a judgment debtor from arguing that the original court lacked jurisdiction. The *REJA* includes jurisdictional criteria that more or less replicate those at common law. In *Vanden Brink v Russell*,[76] a judgment debtor tried to argue that the jurisdictional criteria in the *REJA* could somehow

---

[72] *Venture Helicopters Ltd v European Aeronautic Defence & Space Co Eads NV,* 2010 ABQB 633.

[73] *Stern Estate v Solehdin* (2010), 65 CBR (5th) 283, 2010 ONSC 1012, aff'd 2011 ONCA 286.

[74] *Enforcement of Canadian Judgments and Decrees Act,* SBC 2003, c 29.

[75] *Reciprocal Enforcement of Judgments Act,* RSA 2000, c R-6 [*REJA*].

[76] *Vanden Brink v Russell,* 2010 BCSC 337.

be relied upon even if the creditor applied to register the judgment under the *ECJDA*. The argument went down to inevitable defeat.

Defences to Recognition or Enforcement

Fraud

Lang v Lapp (2010), 327 DLR (4th) 372, 2010 BCCA 517

For some years, a Canadian recording artist resident in California and her United States companies with offices in California (collectively the "plaintiff") had a contract with an individual resident in British Columbia and her British Columbia company (collectively the "defendant") to act as the plaintiff's business manager. In November 2005, the plaintiff commenced an action in California state court against the defendant, claiming breach of fiduciary duty and other causes of action arising from the relationship. The defendant was served with the complaint. Counsel on her behalf filed a motion to quash service and then withdrew it. Some time later, the defendant's counsel filed a *forum non conveniens* motion that was heard in April 2006 and dismissed. Subsequently, the defendant's California counsel filed an answer to the complaint but took no further steps before withdrawing. When the defendant failed to comply with the California court's discovery orders, the plaintiff applied to have the complaint struck out as a "terminating sanction" for non-compliance. The defendant then delivered a motion to adjourn the trial of the action, which had been set for February 2007.

In January 2007, the California court granted the order for terminating sanctions and struck out the defendant's answer. The plaintiff then applied to prove the damages suffered. This was done at a hearing in March 2007, at which the court gave default judgment against the defendant in the amount of US $1.9 million. In May 2007, the plaintiff brought an action in British Columbia to enforce the judgment. The defendant pleaded by way of defence that she had not attorned to the jurisdiction of the California court, that there was no real and substantial connection between the litigation and California, that the proceedings violated natural justice, and that enforcement would be contrary to public policy. A Chambers judge struck out all of these defences as unarguable on the facts. The defendant then amended her statement of defence to raise the argument that the California judgment was obtained by fraud, both as to the jurisdiction and as to the merits. This defence was rejected by the Chamber's judge.

The Court of Appeal agreed with the defendant's contention, based on *Beals v Saldanha*,[77] that fraud going to the jurisdiction of the original court was not subject to the "due diligence" requirement that applied to fraud going to the merits. That is, fraud going to the jurisdiction could be raised, notwithstanding that the defendant could have raised the issue before the foreign court. However, the defence failed on the facts. The Chamber's judge had had ample evidence on which to find that the California court was not misled. In any event, the defendant's allegations of fraud related to the plaintiff's submissions at the hearing on her *forum non conveniens* motion. That motion was an invitation to the court to exercise its discretion to decline the jurisdiction that it had. When her counsel withdrew the motion to quash service, the defendant had effectively conceded that the California court had jurisdiction. The court's decision in favour of exercising jurisdiction was properly to be regarded as an element of the court's decision on the merits of the case. If the defendant was dissatisfied with that decision, the proper course was to appeal it or otherwise have it reconsidered in that jurisdiction. It would not conform to principles of international comity to permit the defendant to litigate issues of fact or law that could have been addressed in the foreign jurisdiction.

As for the argument based on fraud going to the merits of the foreign judgment, it also failed. Here the "due diligence" requirement did apply, and it was relevant to undefended as well as defended judgments. There was nothing the defendant now raised, as evidence of fraud, that could not have been raised before the California court.

Note. Fraud going to the foreign court's jurisdiction was also rejected on the facts in *Cabaniss v Cabaniss*.[78]

Lack of meaningful opportunity to defend

United States of America v Yemec (2010), 320 DLR (4th) 96, 2010 ONCA 414

The defendants operated a lottery ticket reselling business out of Toronto that marketed to customers in the United States. The business was legal under Canadian law as it then stood because it was not operating a lottery, only reselling tickets. (The law changed by

---

[77] *Beals v Saldanha*, [2003] 3 SCR 416, 2003 SCC 72.
[78] *Cabaniss v Cabaniss* (2010), 7 BCLR (5th) 266, 2010 BCCA 348.

the time of these proceedings to make it illegal.) However, the United States Federal Trade Commission (FTC) took steps to shut the defendants' business down in the United States. It obtained a court decision that the defendants were violating an FTC regulation by not warning their customers that use of the mails to send lottery tickets might be illegal. The defendants were never charged under the laws about use of the mails. The United States also obtained a summary judgment in federal District Court in Illinois for a permanent injunction against the defendants and payment of US $19 million in consumer redress and other relief. An appeal to the United States Court of Appeals for the Seventh Circuit was dismissed.

The United States brought an action in Ontario for (1) damages suffered by United States residents from the defendants' activities and (2) enforcement of the injunction and the US $19 million judgment. In October 2002, the United States obtained Mareva and Anton Piller orders in Ontario that effectively ended the defendants' business by seizing all their computers and records. These orders were set aside a year later when it appeared that the basis on which they were granted, affidavit evidence of the defendants' targeting seniors, was in fact untrue. There was no evidence of fraud or of a risk of flight and dissipation of assets. Now the defendants applied to have the United States' damages undertaking, given as a condition of obtaining the interlocutory orders, enforced. The United States responded by applying for summary judgment on the US $19 million foreign judgment. The motion's judge held that the damages undertaking should be enforced (with damages to be assessed), that summary judgment on the United States District Court's judgment should be denied because of a possible "new defence" of lack of a meaningful opportunity to defend, and that the United States did not have standing to make damages claims on behalf of its residents.

The Court of Appeal upheld the judge's decision that the damages undertaking was enforceable but granted summary judgment on enforcement of the District Court judgment. It also held that the District Court's order of a permanent injunction should be enforced. The United States did not pursue its claim for damages on behalf of its residents because those were included in the now enforceable foreign judgment.

On enforcement of the money judgment, the motion's judge had thought there was an arguable defence that the defendants had no reasonable opportunity to defend, owing to having been stymied in their operations by the invalidly obtained Mareva and Anton Piller orders. The Court of Appeal held there was no such "new" defence because the argument was indistinguishable from the established defence of violation of natural justice. The court had held likewise in relation to a very similar argument, based on lack of a reasonable opportunity to be heard in *King v Drabinsky*.[79] There had been no violation of natural justice in the United States proceedings. The defendants had a full opportunity to defend both at trial and in a *de novo* appeal. They retained a lawyer and paid him $120,000 in legal fees. The United States and Ontario orders permitted the defendant to seek access to frozen assets to pay legal fees. The effect of the Anton Piller order was mitigated by the prompt return of the computers to the defendants. The United States had sought and obtained the defendants' consent before reviewing, for the purpose of the District Court proceeding, documents seized under the Anton Piller order. A number of the arguments based on alleged unfairness were raised before the United States court and found to lack substance. On all of the evidence, there was no suggestion of any unfairness to the defendants in the United States summary judgment proceeding. Perhaps most crucially, the defendants had not raised natural justice or denial of a meaningful opportunity to be heard in their appeal to the Seventh Circuit Court of Appeals.

Before the Court of Appeal, the defendants raised the argument for the first time that the permanent injunction granted by the District Court should not be enforced. The injunction restrained them from "engaging in, participating in, or assisting in the telemarketing, in any manner, of any product or service to any person in the US." This was said not to meet the criteria for enforcement of foreign non-monetary orders as laid down in *Pro Swing Inc v Elta Golf Inc*.[80] The Court of Appeal disagreed. The terms of the order were simple, clear, and specific. The extension to all telemarketing activities, not just reselling lottery tickets, was reasonable in view of the District Court's conclusion that the defendants had engaged in deceptive practices contrary to US law. Enforcement of the order placed no undue burden on the Canadian legal system. It did not expose the defendants to unforeseen obligations. The order did

---

[79] *King v Drabinsky* (2008), 295 DLR (4th) 727, 2008 ONCA 586, leave to appeal to SCC refused 12 February 2009, noted at (2008) 46 CYIL 699.

[80] *Pro Swing Inc v Elta Golf Inc.*, [2006] 2 SCR 612, 2006 SCC 52.

require the defendants to disclose the identity of third parties, namely their customers, but since this was for the purpose of distributing the damages, it was unlikely the customers would object. Lastly, enforcement of the United States court order was consistent with the type of orders that would be allowed for domestic litigants.

Means of Enforcement

Limitation period

Note. A foreign judgment was held subject to the general two-year limitation period for enforcing civil claims, as provided in the *Limitations Act.*[81] It was not an "order of a court, or any other order that may be enforced in the same way as an order of a court" within section 16(1)(b) of the act, which is not subject to a limitation period. Foreign money judgments have always been assimilated to debts rather than to domestic court orders: *Commission de la construction du Québec v Access Rigging Services Inc.*[82] See also *Yugraneft Corp v Rexx Management Corp*, noted later under CHOICE OF LAW; *Common Law and Federal;* Characterization; *Substance and procedure — limitation period — enforcement of arbitral award.*

Bankruptcy and Insolvency

Cross-border insolvency — bankruptcy protection orders made abroad — co-ordinated action by a Canadian court

Note. The cross-border insolvency provisions in Part IV of the *Companies' Creditors Arrangement Act,*[83] added in 2005, were applied in *Re Xerium Technologies Inc.*[84] The court held it had not only the jurisdiction but also a duty to grant recognition in Canada to court orders in the United States implementing measures under Chapter 11 of the US bankruptcy laws. The recognition sought was precisely the kind of comity in international insolvency contemplated by Part IV.

---

[81] *Limitations Act,* SO 2002, c 24, Schedule B.

[82] *Commission de la construction du Québec v Access Rigging Services Inc.,* 2010 ONSC 5897.

[83] *Companies' Creditors Arrangement Act, supra* note 12.

[84] *Re Xerium Technologies Inc, supra* note 47.

Arbitral Awards

Defences to recognition or enforcement

Note. In *Znamensky Selekcionno-Gibridny Center LLC v Donaldson International Livestock Ltd,*[85] a Russian company sought to enforce against the defendant, a Canadian company, two arbitral awards made by the International Commercial Arbitration Court at the Chamber of Commerce and Industry of the Russian Federation. The defendant raised a number of defences under Article 36 of the UNCITRAL Model Law on International Commercial Arbitration, as implemented by the *International Commercial Arbitration Act.*[86] They all related to the allegation that the defendant had been unable to present its case before the tribunal because of death threats made against its personnel. The application judge had rejected the defences and held the awards enforceable, on the basis that the issue of the death threats was *res judicata.* An earlier decision of the Court of Appeal, which affirmed a motion judge's refusal of an injunction to restrain the Russian arbitral proceeding, was said to give rise to an issue estoppel. In the present case, the Court of Appeal held that issue estoppel did not arise on the facts and that, even if it had, it would have been appropriate to exercise the court's discretion not to apply it because to do so would work an injustice. The judgment was set aside and the enforcement application remitted for a fresh determination.

Québec

Immunité de juridiction

Moyen d'irrecevabilité — immunité des États

Kuwait Airways Corp c Irak, [2010] 2 RCS 571, 2010 CSC 40

Lors de l'invasion et de l'occupation du Koweit en 1990, le gouvernement irakien ordonna à sa société d'État de transport aérien, IAC, de s'emparer des avions et de l'équipement de la société aérienne KAC. Après la guerre, KAC recouvra seulement une partie de ses avions. KAC prit action en Angleterre contre IAC pour se faire indemniser. Après des procédures longues, KAC obtint une

---

85 *Znamensky Selekcionno-Gibridny Center LLC v Donaldson International Livestock Ltd* (2010), 90 CPC (4th) 163, 2010 ONCA 303.

86 *International Commercial Arbitration Act,* RSO 1990, c I.9.

condamnation de plus d'un milliard de dollars canadiens contre IAC. Alléguant que l'Irak avait contrôlé, financé et surveillé la défense d'IAC tout au long des procédures marquées de parjures et de manœuvres par IAC et l'Irak pour tromper les tribunaux britanniques, KAC réclama en outre de l'Irak des dépens qui s'élevaient à environ 84 millions de dollars canadiens. En 2008, la High Court of Justice condamna l'Irak à payer le montant réclamé. Selon le juge anglais, les actes accomplis par l'Irak dans le contrôle de la défense d'IAC ne constituaient pas des actes de souveraineté, mais se situaient plutôt, pour l'application de la *State Immunity Act 1978* (R.-U.), dans le cadre de l'exception commerciale au principe de l'immunité de juridiction des États.

KAC demanda la reconnaissance judiciaire de ce jugement devant la Cour supérieure du Québec. L'Irak, invoquant la *Loi sur l'immunité des États*,[87] requit le rejet de la demande de reconnaissance judiciaire au motif que les actes qui lui étaient reprochés constituaient des actes de souveraineté et qu'elle bénéficiait en conséquence de l'immunité de juridiction reconnue par la loi canadienne. La Cour supérieure rejeta la demande de reconnaissance judiciaire et la Cour d'appel rejeta l'appel. Selon ces tribunaux, la participation de l'Irak dans le procès engagé contre IAC en Angleterre ne se situait pas dans le cadre de l'exception commerciale à l'immunité de juridiction établie dans la *LIÉ*.

La Cour suprême a accueilli le pourvoi. La *LIÉ* s'applique à une demande de reconnaissance judiciaire d'un jugement étranger. L'article 3076 *CcQ*[88] spécifie que les dispositions du Code relatives au droit international privé, y compris celles qui portent sur la reconnaissance judiciaire des décisions étrangères, s'appliquent sous réserve des règles de droit en vigueur au Québec et dont l'application s'impose en raison de leur but particulier. Ces règles comprennent la *LIÉ*. De plus, une demande d'*exequatur* constitue une demande en justice qui donne ouverture à un débat contradictoire régi par les règles générales de la procédure civile, comme le prévoient les articles 785 et 786 du *Code de procédure civile*.[89] Il s'agit donc d'une "instance" ou "*proceedings*" au sujet de laquelle l'immunité de juridiction reconnue par l'article 3 de la *LIÉ* s'applique. Comme l'Irak est un État, elle bénéficie en principe de l'immunité.

---

87 *Loi sur l'immunité des États*, LRC 1985, c S-18 [*LIÉ*].

88 *CcQ, supra* note 32.

89 *Code de procédure civile*, LRQ, ch C-25.

Même si le tribunal anglais a rendu sa propre décision sur la question, celle-ci n'a pas force de chose jugée au Canada. Il appartient à KAC d'établir, sous le régime du droit canadien, qu'elle peut invoquer une exception à cette immunité. Cependant, le tribunal saisi de la demande doit respecter les limites du rôle dévolu à l'autorité québécoise à l'occasion de l'examen d'une demande d'*exequatur*. Il ne peut reprendre l'étude du fond de la décision (article 3158 *CcQ*).

Dans la présente affaire, l'immunité de juridiction reconnue par l'article 3 de la *LIÉ* ne pouvait être invoquée par l'Irak, car l'exception de commercialité prévue par l'article 5 s'appliquait. Il faut retenir les conclusions de fait du juge anglais selon lesquelles l'Irak a été le maître d'œuvre de nombreux actes de fabrication de faux, de dissimulation de preuve et de mensonges, qui ont induit les tribunaux anglais en erreur. En outre, le litige dans lequel l'Irak est intervenue pour défendre IAC portait sur la rétention des avions de KAC après leur saisie. Or, aucun lien n'existe entre ce litige commercial et l'acte souverain qui constituait la saisie initiale des avions.

Conditions de reconnaissance et exécution

Ordre public

Facebook inc c Guerbuez, 2010 QCCS 4649, autorisation d'appel à la Cour d'appel du Québec refusée, 2011 QCCA 268

Facebook demande la reconnaissance et l'exécution d'un jugement rendu en 2008 par un tribunal de Californie. Ce jugement condamne Guerbuez à payer à Facebook une somme de 873 277 200 $ américains en dommages suite à 4 366 386 violations à une loi américaine portant sur le commerce électronique.[90] Les 4 366 386 faits reprochés à Guerbuez sont principalement l'envoi de "pourriels" (courriels non sollicités), ainsi que l'appropriation non autorisée de données lors d'intrusions aux comptes d'utilisateurs de Facebook. La somme que Guerbuez est condamné à payer consistait des dommages compensatoires et préalables en vertu de cette loi au montant de 100 $ américains pour chacune des 4 366 386 violations à la loi, et des dommages majorés, limités à une fois les dommages compensatoires. La condamnation recherchée par Facebook, au Québec, totalise 1 068 928 721,46 $ canadiens, compte tenu du

---

[90] *Can-Spam Act*, 15 U.C § 7701 *et seq.*

taux de change en vigueur au moment où le jugement a eu l'autorité de chose jugée en Californie. Ce jugement comprend également différentes ordonnances d'injonction permanente contre Guerbuez lui ordonnant de cesser certains actes en relation avec Facebook. Guerbuez fait valoir que la condamnation est incompatible avec l'ordre public, tel qu'il est entendu dans les relations internationales, vu le montant exagéré des sommes octroyées par le tribunal californien, dont il ne pouvait soupçonner l'importance au moment de la signification des procédures.

La Cour a décidé que le jugement californien doit être reconnu et déclaré exécutoire au Québec.

La demande de reconnaissance de l'injonction permanente n'est pas contestée par Guerbuez. Dans *Pro Swing inc c Elta Golf Inc*,[91] la Cour suprême mentionne que le *CcQ*[92] ne distingue pas entre jugement pécuniaire et non pécuniaire. Il s'agit ici d'un jugement final qui remplit toutes les conditions prévues au *CcQ*.

La demande, telle que signifiée à Guerbuez, lui permettait de mesurer l'ampleur du risque financier auquel il était exposé. Les différents articles de loi invoqués par Facebook conjugués au nombre impressionnant de pourriels ou contraventions apparaissant à la demande devaient inciter Guerbuez à s'informer afin de circonscrire et connaître le risque auquel il s'exposait. Guerbuez n'explique pas pourquoi il a choisi de ne pas comparaître ni contester l'action de Facebook en Californie. Il ne mentionne pas non plus s'il a fait des démarches lui permettant de connaître l'importance des sommes réclamées ou la procédure et le droit applicables à une telle demande. Il a eu la possibilité de connaître l'ampleur des conclusions recherchées contre lui et il ne peut se plaindre de ne pas l'avoir fait lorsque Facebook en demande la reconnaissance au Québec.

Selon Guerbuez, la nature des dommages et l'importance du montant accordé par le tribunal étranger sont contraires à l'ordre public et constituent l'une des exceptions prévues à l'article 3155(5) *CcQ*. La Cour suprême a dit, dans *Beals c Saldanha*,[93] que les dommages-intérêts punitifs aux États-Unis sont souvent extraordinairement élevés par rapport à ceux accordés dans d'autres pays, mais cette approche n'a en soi rien de contraire aux notions d'équité

---

[91] *Pro Swing inc c Elta Golf Inc, supra* note 80.

[92] *CcQ, supra* note 32.

[93] *Beals c Saldanha, supra* note 77, para 225.

fondamentale canadiennes; elle représente simplement un choix stratégique différent qui assure aux demandeurs américains une protection dont ils ne devraient pas nécessairement être privés du seul fait que les biens du défendeur sont situés au Canada. Ici, la loi californienne en vertu de laquelle les dommages préalables et majorés ont été accordés vise à dénoncer un comportement qui suscite la réprobation non seulement aux États-Unis et au Canada, mais également partout dans le monde. C'est après avoir constaté le comportement intentionnel et répété de Guerbuez qu'une telle ordonnance a été rendue. Il ne s'agit pas d'une condamnation arbitraire. Il n'y a pas lieu de permettre à Guerbuez de se soustraire aux conséquences de ses gestes et contraventions à différentes lois. Il serait plutôt contraire à l'ordre public que le Québec lui permette d'échapper à la reconnaissance des droits valablement acquis par Facebook en Californie. S'il en était ainsi, cela permettrait que toute une série d'infractions via l'Internet se fasse en toute impunité et que les revenus provenant de telles activités soient insaisissables au Québec.

CHOICE OF LAW (INCLUDING STATUS OF PERSONS) / CONFLITS DE LOIS (Y COMPRIS STATUT PERSONNEL)

Common Law and Federal

Characterization

Substance and procedure — limitation period — enforcement of arbitral award

Yugraneft Corp v Rexx Management Corp, [2010] 1 SCR 649, 2010 SCC 19

On 6 September 2002, a Russian tribunal gave an award ordering the defendant to pay the plaintiff US $952,614.43 in damages. On 27 January 2006, the plaintiff applied to the Alberta Court of Queen's Bench for enforcement of the award under the *International Commercial Arbitration Act*,[94] which implements both the 1958 *Convention on the Recognition and Enforcement of Foreign Arbitral Awards* (*New York Convention*) and the UNCITRAL *Model Law on International Commercial Arbitration* (*Model Law*).[95] The judge refused enforcement

---

[94] *International Commercial Arbitration Act*, RSA 2000, c I-5.

[95] *Convention on the Recognition and Enforcement of Foreign Arbitral Awards, 1958*, [1986] Can TS no 43 [*New York Convention*]. *UNCITRAL Model Law on International Commercial Arbitration*, UN Doc A/40/17, ann 1 (1985).

on the ground that the application was statute-barred under the two-year limitation period in section 3 of the *Limitations Act*,[96] and the Court of Appeal affirmed the decision.

The Supreme Court of Canada dismissed the plaintiff's appeal. Since neither the *New York Convention* nor the *Model Law* includes a limitation provision, a threshold question was whether any limitation period applied to the Alberta courts' obligation, imposed by both these instruments, to enforce foreign arbitral awards. Article III of the convention says that recognition and enforcement shall be "in accordance with the rules of procedure of the territory in which enforcement is sought." Although, under Canadian conflicts principles, limitation periods are regarded as substantive rather than procedural rules,[97] the expression "procedural" as used in Article III should be read as encompassing limitation provisions, whatever their characterization might be for other purposes.

When the *New York Convention* was drafted, it was well known that various states characterized limitation periods in different ways and that common law jurisdictions generally treated them as procedural in nature. Since the drafters did not include any restriction on a state's ability to impose time limits on recognition and enforcement proceedings, it could be inferred that they intended to take a permissive approach. State practice confirmed this interpretation since, according to a recent International Chamber of Commerce study, fifty-three states, both common law and civil law, definitely or probably subject the recognition and enforcement of foreign arbitral awards to some kind of time limit. The writings of scholars also assume that the convention allows states to do so.

One of the arbitral organizations that appeared as intervenors relied on another part of Article III, which prohibits a state from imposing "substantially more onerous conditions" on the recognition of foreign arbitral awards than it does in respect of domestic awards. This was said to prevent application to foreign arbitral awards of a limitation period shorter than the longest period applicable to domestic awards anywhere in Canada, which was ten years (Alberta's was two years). This argument contradicted Canada's federal constitution, under which enforcement of awards was a provincial matter. It also overlooked Article XI of the convention, which recognized that in "non-unitary" states, jurisdiction over the subject matter of the treaty might lie with a sub-national entity.

[96] *Limitations Act*, RSA 2000, c L-12.

[97] See *Tolofson, supra* note 34.

The way being clear to apply Alberta limitations law, the Court turned to what the applicable rule was. The only relevant statute was the *Limitations Act*, whose purpose was to streamline the law of limitations by limiting the number of exceptions and providing a uniform two-year limitation period for most actions. The act, in section 12, made it clear that the Alberta limitation period applied even if, as a matter of the conflict of laws, a foreign limitation period also applied. The act was therefore intended to be pervasive. It applied to all claims for a "remedial order" as defined (section 2(1)). There was no indication of any intent to exclude the enforcement of foreign arbitral awards from the broad concept of "remedial order."

The plaintiff argued that an arbitral award fell under section 11 of the *Limitations Act*, which provides a ten-year period for enforcing a "judgment or order for the payment of money." This argument failed because an arbitral award, unlike a local judgment, owes its existence to the will of the parties alone, without the intervention of a judicial system, and is not directly enforceable. Nor did the Court accept the argument that the act was ambiguous as to whether foreign arbitral awards fitted under section 3 or section 11, such that the plaintiff should get the benefit of the longer period. The act was not ambiguous. Moreover, arbitral awards from reciprocating states have only a six-year limitation period under the *REJA*,[98] and it would be anomalous if awards from non-reciprocating states, such as Russia, were entitled to a longer limitation period than those from reciprocating states under the *REJA*.

Lastly, the Court considered the effect of the *Limitations Act* rule (section 3(2)) that the period begins only when the plaintiff has actual or imputed knowledge that the injury has occurred, that it was attributable to the conduct of the defendant, and that it warrants bringing a proceeding. In this context, the period began to run when the plaintiff not only knew that the defendant was refusing to pay the award but also that the defendant's right to appeal the award (before which an enforcement proceeding in Alberta was arguably not warranted) had expired. Under the *Model Law*, which is also the law of Russia, the unsuccessful party has three months from receipt of the award to commence proceedings to set the award aside (Article 34(3)). The time for applying in Russia to set the award aside had therefore expired in early December 2002, which meant that the Alberta limitation period had expired in early December 2004, and the plaintiff's action was out of time.

---

98 *REJA, supra* note 75.

Note 1. In *Bank of America v Maas*,[99] an express choice of Michigan law to govern a contract had the consequence, according to the conflicts rule in section 23 of the *Limitations Act*,[100] that Michigan limitations law would also apply because it was substantive in nature.[101] The choice of law clause was held not to constitute an agreement in advance to vary or exclude a limitation period, which would be nullified according to section 22(1) of the act. The latter rule clearly referred only to exclusions of a limitation period when Ontario law was applicable.

Note 2. The conditions for obtaining an interlocutory injunction in Ontario against a breach of a non-competition covenant were held governed by Ontario law, not Ohio law as the law that governed the contractual obligations: *Telesis Technologies Inc v Sure Controls Systems Inc.*[102] The court contemplated (at para. 9) that the parties might have agreed that Ohio law would determine the conditions for interlocutory relief.

Contracts

No agreed choice

EE Hobbs & Associates Ltd v Whitesand First Nation (2010), 253 Man R (2d) 33, 2010 MBQB 89

Hobbs, a federally incorporated consulting firm, was engaged by the Whitesand First Nation to do socio-historical research and assist Whitesand in pursuing a compensation claim against Ontario Hydro, the province of Ontario, and Canada for improper use of its traditional lands in Ontario. In addition to an hourly rate of compensation, Hobbs was to receive 3 percent of the value of any financial settlement ultimately concluded. After Whitesand's claims were settled in 2009, Hobbs sought payment of the lump sum. When Whitesand demurred, Hobbs invoked an arbitration clause in the consulting contract, which provided that any dispute about billings or the terms of the contract "would be resolved by an arbitrator appointed by agreement between us." Hobbs nominated an arbitrator who was rejected by Whitesand. Hobbs then issued a notice of

99 *Bank of America v Maas*, 2010 ONSC 4546, aff'd 2010 ONCA 833.

100 SO 2002, c 24.

101 Echoing *Tolofson v Jensen, supra* note 34.

102 *Telesis Technologies Inc v Sure Controls Systems Inc.*, 2010 ONSC 5288.

application to the Manitoba Queen's Bench, requesting that the court appoint an arbitrator under the *Arbitration Act*.[103] Shortly afterwards, Whitesand applied to the Ontario Superior Court of Justice in Thunder Bay for the appointment of a different arbitrator under the *Arbitration Act, 1991*.[104] Whitesand acknowledged that the Manitoba court had jurisdiction *simpliciter* to appoint an arbitrator but argued that it was *forum non conveniens* for resolution of that matter because the Ontario court was the more appropriate one to make the appointment.

Although the parties argued the case on the basis of *forum non conveniens*, the judge preferred to base his decision on a choice of law analysis as to which province's statute applied. The proper law of the consulting contract was the law of Ontario, as the system of law with which it had the closest and most real connection. Whitesand was an Indian band with its traditional lands and reserve situated in Ontario; the work Hobbs was to perform related to claims made by Whitesand against Ontario Hydro and Ontario; the negotiations for the agreement took place in Thunder Bay; and the agreement was signed by Whitesand's chief at the Whitesand First Nation in Ontario. Hobbs's research also had a strong Ontario connection. Even if, as Hobbs asserted, much of the "leg work" was done in the Hudson's Bay Company archives in Winnipeg, that would not override the Ontario connection to the project. The finished product was intended for use in Ontario. The two Hobbs supervisors on the project were resident in Ottawa, Ontario, at the time of the contract, and Hobbs's head office was also there. The fact that Hobbs had since moved its head office to Winnipeg did not have a bearing on the proper law of the contract, which had to be determined on the basis of the situation at the time the contract was made.

Since Ontario law governed the contract, the Ontario *Arbitration Act* applied. The court given the power under that act to appoint an arbitrator was the court in Ontario. Even if the decision had been made on *forum non conveniens* grounds, the result would have been the same.

Insurance — automobile — interjurisdictional arrangements

Note. Reciprocal arrangements are in place among the automobile insurance regulators in each province and state in North America

---

[103] *Arbitration Act*, CCSM, c A120.

[104] *Arbitration Act, 1991*, SO 1991, c 17.

for the recognition of certificates of insurance issued in each other's jurisdiction, so that drivers do not need to obtain separate insurance when they enter the province. This is implemented by requiring each out-of-province insurer that issues such a certificate to file a power of attorney and undertaking with the regulator. By this document, the insurer is obliged, if there has been an accident in the province, to appear in proceedings in the province's courts; not to raise any defence that would not be available to the insurer if the contract had been entered into in the province; and to pay any judgment up to the policy limit, but to an amount not less than the local minimum compulsory coverage. In *Moldovan v Insurance Corp of British Columbia*,[105] the terms of the document were held to prevent an out-of-province insurer from denying liability for the no-fault accident benefits that ICBC (the universal automobile insurer in the province) was required to provide by Part 7 of the *Insurance (Vehicle) Regulation* made pursuant to the *Insurance (Vehicle) Act*.[106] It did not, however, entitle the insurer to the benefit of the two-year limitation period that applied specifically (under section 103 of the regulation) to claims against ICBC.

Torts

Workers' compensation legislation — bar to civil action

MacDougall v Nova Scotia (Workers' Compensation Appeals Tribunal) (2010), 299 NSR (2d) 106, 2010 NSCA 92

The defendant, a Nova Scotia resident, while driving in Newfoundland in the course of her work for her Nova Scotia-based employer, was covered by the *Workers' Compensation Act*.[107] She was involved in an accident in which a fellow employee, who was a passenger, was killed. The dependents of the deceased employee brought an action against the defendant in Nova Scotia. She contended that the action was barred under section 28(1) of the act. The Nova Scotia statute bars actions against a co-employee, whereas the equivalent statute in Newfoundland permits the injured party to elect between claiming workers' compensation benefits and suing the co-employee.

The court held that the plaintiffs' rights were to be determined by Newfoundland law because, under section 27(1) of the Nova

---

105 *Moldovan v Insurance Corp of British Columbia* (2010), [2011] ILR I-5085, 2010 BCSC 1778.

106 *Insurance (Vehicle) Act*, RSBC 1996, c 231.

107 *Workers' Compensation Act*, SNS 1994-95, c 10.

Scotia act, if a worker injured outside Nova Scotia is entitled to "compensation" pursuant to the law of the place of injury and under the Nova Scotia scheme, the worker may choose to "be compensated according to either the laws of the jurisdiction where the accident occurred" or the Nova Scotia act. "Compensation," in section 27(1), should not be read as referring exclusively to workers' compensation benefits. The better interpretation was that opting to sue the co-employee, as Newfoundland law permitted, did qualify as a choice to "be compensated according to" that law. Such an interpretation was also in accord with choice of law principles in tort, according to which the governing law is that of the place of the accident. The action against the deceased's co-employee was therefore not barred by the act.

Property

Succession — wills — essential validity

Davies v Collins (2010), 297 NSR (2d) 136, 2010 NSSC 457

While on his deathbed in Trinidad and Tobago (Trinidad) in 2007, the testator, who was domiciled in Nova Scotia, married Ms. Collins, with whom he had been living for seven years. Ms. Collins obtained a grant of administration of his estate from a court in Trinidad on the basis that the deceased died intestate. Ms. Davies, who had been divorced from the deceased in 2001 and lived in Nova Scotia, applied to the court to have the grant of administration revoked based on a will that the deceased had made in Nova Scotia in 1989. On the basis of an expert opinion that the marriage to Ms. Collins would be considered under Nova Scotia law to have revoked the will, the Trinidad court dismissed Ms. Davies' claim. Ms. Davies' subsequent application in Nova Scotia for probate of the will was refused by the registrar on the ground that the deceased was not resident in Nova Scotia when he died, and the court in Trinidad had granted administration of his estate to Ms. Collins.[108] Ms. Davies now sought a declaration from the Nova Scotia court that the will had not been revoked.

The court held that it had jurisdiction under the *Probate Act* to hear Ms. Davies' claim. The evidence showed that the marriage to Ms. Collins was both formally and essentially valid according to both Trinidad law and Nova Scotia law. It was, however, a deathbed marriage, or marriage *in extremis*, which has a distinct status under the

[108] *Probate Act*, SNS 2000, c 3, s 29.

law of Trinidad. Whereas marriage generally revokes a will, a marriage *in extremis* does not. By contrast, the proper interpretation of section 17 of the Nova Scotia *Wills Act*[109] was that the revocation of a will by marriage does not depend on whether it was contemplated or intended that the marriage would have that effect. The legislative history showed that the purpose of the rule was to favour the testator's new family over the old. The Trinidad marriage, even if a marriage *in extremis*, therefore operated under section 17 to revoke the will, assuming that the law of Nova Scotia applied to the issue.

The next question was whether the issue of the revocation of the will was to be characterized as one of succession or, as Ms. Davies contended, one of matrimonial law. It concerned not the validity or form of the marriage but, rather, the effect of the marriage on the will. That indicated it was succession rather than matrimonial law. However, it was unclear what the succession choice of law rule on the point was. There was a dearth of authority and a diversity of scholarly opinion on the principles that should apply to determine the question whether marriage revoked a will. The judge considered extensively the cases and the opinions of authors. He concluded that the choice of law rule should not distinguish between a will as it applies to immovables and as it applies to movables. The effect of marriage on the will should be the same for both. (The estate here included both.) The rule should be to apply the law of the deceased's domicile at the time of the alleged revoking event, the marriage. Since the parties agreed that the deceased was domiciled in Nova Scotia at the time of his deathbed marriage, the law of Nova Scotia applied, and the will was revoked.

The court also held that the Trinidad court's decision to the same effect, applying Nova Scotia law based on the expert opinion, had made the issue *res judicata*, but the court should exercise its discretion to give Ms. Davies the benefit of a declaration by a Nova Scotia court.

Note. The decision above is understood to be under appeal.

Matrimonial Causes

Divorce — recognition of foreign decree

Zhang v Lin (2010), [2011] 4 WWR 556, 2010 ABQB 420

The husband and wife were married in China and lived for about fourteen years in Alberta. In February 2008, the husband moved

---

[109] *Wills Act*, RSNS 1989, c 505.

from Alberta to Texas. The husband began divorce proceedings in Texas in August 2008, when he had lived there ten days short of the six months' residence in the state that under Texas law was required to establish the court's jurisdiction. In September 2008, the wife commenced divorce proceedings in Alberta. In October 2008, the husband, who was unrepresented, filed a statement of defence to the wife's divorce action in which, among other things, he said he would accept that he would pay $836 a month until May 2014 for support of their son, who was then twenty-one and planning medical studies in Alberta. In January 2009, the Texas court granted a divorce that did not require the husband to pay child support for the couple's adult child or spousal support and that made an unequal distribution of matrimonial property. In 2009, he left Texas and was currently living in Virginia. In the present proceedings, the wife, whose income was much less than her husband's, applied for a declaration that the Texas divorce was not recognized in Alberta and, if that application succeeded, for an order for child and spousal support and for related relief.

The court held that the Texas divorce should not be recognized. It did not meet the statutory recognition rule in section 22(1) of the *Divorce Act*[110] because neither party was ordinarily resident in Texas for at least one year before the commencement of the divorce proceeding. As for the common law grounds for recognition, preserved by section 22(3), one was domicile in the foreign jurisdiction. That did not apply because the husband had not proved he had the requisite intention to remain permanently in Texas when he applied for the divorce. He remained domiciled in Alberta at that point. This ruled out applying another common law ground, namely that the divorce was recognized in the country of his domicile. Nor would a Canadian court have had jurisdiction under parallel facts, which was a further common law ground. Lastly, a foreign divorce could be recognized on the basis of a real and substantial connection with the country that granted the divorce. The court thought that the husband did have such a connection, since he had moved to Texas to live and become employed there.

However, the court denied the divorce recognition on the ground of public policy. The family's ties over the last decade were all with Alberta. There was no evidence that the husband moved to Texas to evade Canadian law, but it was clear that the effect of the Texas decree was very different from the possible effect of a decree in

---

[110] *Divorce Act, supra* note 48.

Alberta. The ability in some circumstances to obtain support for adult children was an important component of Canadian divorce laws, whereas it appeared to be impossible in Texan proceedings. Support for a former spouse was likewise an important component of Canadian divorce law, based on well-settled policy. The clear difference in treatment of child and spousal support between Texas law and Canadian law justified Canada's non-recognition of a Texas divorce in the circumstances here.

The court went on to direct a trial of the issues of support for the adult son and for the wife. A division of property could follow a determination of those issues.

Note. It is unusual for a divorce to be denied recognition on the ground of public policy, if for no other reason than that the "limping marriage" it creates is generally an undesirable outcome. It also seems doubtful whether the differences between Texan and Canadian law engaged fundamental Canadian conceptions of morality, which is the usual criterion for the defence of public policy. The case may have been coloured by the fact that the basis for recognizing the Texas divorce was marginal, given that the husband had been in Texas for just under six months when he filed for divorce, less even than the minimum period for jurisdiction under Texas law. (There was no suggestion that the Texan court had been misled as to the period of residence; it was possible the court had waived the minimum requirement.) Non-recognition preserved the Alberta court's ability to deal with child and spousal support, since jurisdiction depended on the parties' still being married. And, of course, the "limping marriage" problem created by non-recognition would be resolved as soon as the Alberta court itself granted a divorce.

In *Martinez v Basail*,[111] a couple who had emigrated from Cuba to Canada, but remained Cuban citizens, were divorced in Cuba, and the man subsequently married in Cuba another woman whom he had met there. He sought a declaration in Ontario that the divorce from his first wife was recognized in Canada, and the first wife supported his application. The court granted the declaration, reasoning that the divorce was entitled to recognition on the basis of the "real and substantial connection" test also used in *Zhang v Lin*. The parties had lived in Cuba most of their lives, they were married there, they were still Cuban citizens at the time of the divorce, their one child was born there, and the wife's family still lived there.

---

[111] *Martinez v Basail*, 2010 ONSC 2038.

Québec

Statut personnel

Ordonnance étrangère désignant une femme comme administratrice des biens de son mari — force exécutoire au Québec

R (R) c G (An), 2010 QCCS 5314

En 1994, l'intimée, la femme de A.R., a été nommée "Guardian of the person of A.R." et "Trustee of the Estate of A.R." à la suite d'une décision de la Surrogate Court de l'Alberta. A.R. et le fils mineur du couple ont été gravement blessés dans un accident en Alberta et sont invalides depuis. La désignation de l'intimée comme "Trustee" était nécessaire afin que l'intimée puisse représenter son mari dans l'action en justice intentée en Alberta contre les auteurs de l'accident. L'intimée et A.R. sont actuellement en instance de divorce. Vu la séparation du couple et les procédures de divorce, le requérant R.R., père de A.R., a été nommé tuteur à son fils par une décision du greffier de la Cour supérieure en 2010. Il demande que l'intimée soit forcée de rendre compte de son administration.

La Cour décide que le jugement de l'Alberta n'a pas besoin de l'*exequatur* et que la reddition de compte peut être ordonnée par le Tribunal. En tout temps pertinent, les époux sont domiciliés au Québec. L'état et la capacité d'une personne physique sont régis par la loi de son domicile. Le régime juridique des majeurs protégés est régi par la loi du domicile des personnes qui en font l'objet. Dans les deux cas, il s'agit de la loi québécoise. En l'espèce, l'intimée s'est plutôt adressée au Tribunal albertain pour se faire nommer "Trustee of the Estate of A.R.," vraisemblablement par commodité, puisque c'est dans cette province que l'action a été intentée. Elle a accepté cette charge. La reddition de compte est une conséquence de l'acceptation de cette charge. Les décisions étrangères relatives à l'état et à la capacité des personnes physiques produisent de plein droit leurs effets au Québec, et n'ont pas besoin de l'*exequatur* des tribunaux québécois. Cette notion s'explique en raison de la présomption d'efficacité dont jouissent les jugements étrangers au Québec. Il ne s'agit pas ici d'un acte d'exécution sur des biens ou de coercition sur des personnes, qui requiert généralement une action en exemplification. La reddition de compte est certes une mesure d'exécution, mais il s'agit d'exécution volontaire comme la réception de caution ou de délaissement volontaire. Si le rendant ne rend pas compte, l'oyant le fait à sa place. L'instance vise à établir le reliquat de la gestion s'il en est. La Cour ordonne à l'intimée de rendre compte de l'administration des sommes reçues à titre d'administrateur du patrimoine d'A.R.

Book Reviews / Recensions de livres

Domestic Violence and International Law. By Bonita Meyersfeld. Oxford: Hart Publishing, 2010. 368 pages.

It is now well recognized that international law has become an important arena for advancing women's human rights. While generally regarded as a "late bloomer" in social justice terms, international law has been the focus of tremendous analysis and reform by feminist lawyers, activists, judges, scholars, diplomats, and their allies within academic and practitioner circles. The result of this feminist focus on international law can be seen on many levels: from the profusion of new human rights instruments and the explosion in the number of non-governmental organizations (NGOs) working on women's equality, to the more formalized institutional developments, such as the newly constituted United Nations entity, "UN Women." Within the academy, the impact of feminist interventions has been no less dramatic. Many of the core fields within international law have been the subject of sustained feminist analysis from the laws of war to environmental law. There is now even a daily blog, entitled *Intlawgrrls,* which addresses developments relating to women and international law.

Two of the most prolific scholars advancing feminist engagement with international law, Hilary Charlesworth and Christine Chinkin, have outlined some possible future directions for feminist scholarship and activism on international law in the conclusion to their now iconic book, *The Boundaries of International Law.*[1] Feminist international lawyers, they write, "should use existing mechanisms

---

[1] Hilary Charlesworth and C.M. Chinkin, *The Boundaries of International Law: A Feminist Analysis* (Manchester: Manchester University Press, 2000) at 336.

and principles wherever possible to improve women's lives."[2] This quote could mean a focus on law reform so that law "more adequately responds to concerns of women."[3] However, it could also mean an engagement with "the Grotian project of redrawing the boundaries of international law by challenging and questioning the 'objectivity' of the international legal system and its hierarchy based on gender."[4]

Bonita Meyersfeld's volume *Domestic Violence and International Law* clearly falls within the first category of feminist engagement with international law: enhancing the regulatory capacity of international law to better respond to the needs of women.[5] Meyersfeld's objective in this detailed and wide-ranging study is to compile all international and regional developments pertaining to domestic violence as a human rights concern. Next, she argues for, and nudges onward, the development of an international legal norm against domestic violence. This book is, thus, both a detailed study of an issue within international law and an outline for future law reform and advocacy.

At over 300 pages and only four chapters, *Domestic Violence and International Law* is first and foremost a rich resource of legal material. The first chapter summarizes Meyersfeld's canvassing of the international and regional systems and provides a very useful overview of international law developments on violence against women. Meyersfeld includes treaty and United Nations (UN) General Assembly initiatives, the work of special rapporteurs, the undertakings of the UN secretary-general, and the work of several related UN bodies. Her objective in the first chapter is to take the measure of international law in order to determine whether there is a norm prohibiting domestic violence as a human rights violation. She concludes that there is evidence such a norm is emerging but that it "needs to be developed and matured."[6]

The second chapter focuses on the need to frame domestic violence as a human rights issue. Meyersfeld sets herself a difficult task in outlining the many aspects of domestic violence that have implications for its possible international legal condemnation. This

---

2 *Ibid.*

3 *Ibid.*

4 *Ibid.*

5 Bonita Meyersfeld, *Domestic Violence and International Law* (Oxford: Hart, 2010).

6 *Ibid* at 107.

chapter ranges from a discussion of the systemic elements of intimate violence to the complex issues arising from the use of state-level criminal law as a mechanism for responding to domestic violence. However, as I will explain further in this review, I am not entirely sure Meyersfeld's analysis succeeds in painting a coherent picture of how these various issues would be reconciled within an international norm prohibiting domestic violence.

In Chapter 3, the author provides an overview of legal doctrines pertaining to state responsibility and recent developments in the area of due diligence. If there is a norm prohibiting domestic violence as a human rights violation, both state responsibility and the state's obligation to exercise due diligence in ensuring full protection of the law will provide the legal scaffolding on which responsibility and prevention will be constructed. This much shorter and tightly focused chapter provides a useful summary of current developments in due diligence that might be useful for teachers of international human rights law.

The book concludes with a lengthy chapter where the author seeks to answer the question: why international law? For which reasons would one turn to international law to find or generate a norm against domestic violence? Meyersfeld offers several compelling answers. For her, international law is an important arena — not in terms of its (in)ability to compel compliance but, rather, because it is a means for enunciating norms "to which states can aspire and on which individuals can rely in holding their governments to account."[7] She identifies these two qualities as the "expressive value" of international law and its "implementing capability." "Expressivism" is generally used in legal scholarship to describe the phenomenon by which social meanings are communicated and interpreted through legal processes. For Meyersfeld, the articulation of different forms of harm in international law is part of the means by which new norms may be generated and international consensus, solidified. International law is, therefore, an important arena for combating domestic violence because it can "improve the way we understand and respond to domestic violence."[8] Meyersfeld's instincts in this regard are apt. The richness of international law is often lost within analyses that are narrowly preoccupied with questions regarding compliance. Meyersfeld's objectives in mapping the terrain for the recognition of a norm against domestic violence are

---

[7] *Ibid* at 253.

[8] *Ibid* at 266.

also sound and well executed. There is nothing to argue with, in my view, the scholarly objectives advanced in this volume.

Where I part company with Meyersfeld, however, is at her argument structure. While the fourth chapter makes a compelling case for the expressivism of international law, the book is not organized around an exploration of this expressivism in the area of violence against women but, rather, around the existence of a norm against domestic violence. Meyersfeld's analysis, particularly in the first half of the book, is marshalled around a rather traditional set of arguments, exploring, in effect, the question: is there or is there not a norm? While there is nothing wrong with this approach, it does not capture the rich possibilities of international law's "expressive value," to use Meyersfeld's terminology.

For example, in the first chapter, Meyersfeld's lengthy detailing of international and regional developments in the area of violence against women makes almost no reference to the incredible amount of activism by NGOs that have led to those results. Legal developments are thus listed as though they somehow unfolded magically in a political vacuum. Had Meyersfeld taken her analysis to the next step and considered how NGO activism and the expansion of UN conferences as sites of law reform may have shaped the emergence of a domestic violence norm, she may have been able to engage more specifically with the second aspect of Charlesworth and Chinkin's typology of the feminist project — to engage "the Grotian project of redrawing the boundaries of international law."

My second concern with Meyersfeld's approach is in the absence of references to social science literature on violence against women and domestic violence. The portrayal of domestic violence as a human rights problem unfolds in bits and pieces throughout the 300 pages of her analysis, and there is no sustained discussion of the meaning of "domestic violence." Furthermore, legal instruments and legal scholarship, mostly from the United States, form the main sources of information about domestic violence. As a result, the second chapter, which outlines the human rights dimensions of domestic violence, is much less persuasive. The chapter raises a significant number of important issues and demonstrates Meyersfeld's grasp of this complex social problem. However, it portrays only a limited picture of domestic violence as it is experienced globally. Over the course of the text, the most detailed narratives of domestic violence come exclusively from one source — a handful of judgments from the European Court of Human Rights. A more comprehensive discussion of domestic violence in its different manifestations would have significantly enhanced Meyersfeld's arguments about the human rights dimensions of this difficult social problem.

The inclusion of social science literature would also have enabled the author to explore, in more detail, international law's expressive potential in the area of domestic violence — that is, the potential to articulate shared values and social consensus. A focus on expressivism invites, as the author notes, a move away from the very limited "is it law or isn't it?" question to a set of questions about what international law is communicating. What values and what types of consensus can we see in these various aspects of international law's functioning? Focusing on these questions would raise another set of queries for feminist scholars and activists: in what way is domestic violence understood as an international law issue? What does the recognition of domestic violence as a form of gendered harm mean for the ways in which law can (and should) respond? What does the recognition of domestic violence as a legal problem mean for the disciplinary *boundaries* of law? These questions invite a closer reading of law's expressivism and would also be instrumental in shaping future, feminist-inspired, international law reform projects.

Meyersfeld's volume is a valuable contribution to the development of international law. She makes a strong case that domestic violence against women, in all of its complexity, is and should be condemned through international law and international legal institutions. This is an argument that should be aired widely throughout international legal circles.

DORIS BUSS

Associate Professor, Department of Law, Carleton University

The International Criminal Court: A Commentary on the Rome Statute. By William A. Schabas. Oxford: Oxford University Press, 2010. 1,336 pages.

The founding of the International Criminal Court (ICC) in 1998 is generally regarded as the pinnacle of a post-Second World War international criminal justice project, designed to operationalize the international community's desire for response, accountability, and deterrence for mass human rights violations. The path from Nuremburg to The Hague, as has been said, was long and winding, and it is also well documented that the Rome negotiations in the summer of 1998 were among the most intense and politically charged in recent history. The result, the *Rome Statute of the International Criminal Court* (*Rome Statute*), may be one of the most important international instruments ever concluded.[1] It is one of the most complex treaties, designed to establish a court and provide at least the basic framework for its jurisdiction, applicable law, rules of evidence and procedure, and overall administration. The process of determining whether cases are, in the language of the *Rome Statute*, admissible, is no less intricate. This complexity is amplified by the level of political nuance that drove the Rome conference, which resulted in many of the statute's provisions being vague, ambiguous, or amenable to varying interpretations.

For this reason, as well as general interest in the subject matter, an enormous body of literature has been generated about the court and the *Rome Statute*, including several article-by-article examinations of the treaty itself. Much of this literature was written or contributed to by William Schabas, a well-known Canadian and international human rights scholar and director of the Irish Centre for Human Rights at the National University of Ireland, Galway. Schabas, one of the court's most ardent supporters and thoughtful critics, has now produced his own much-anticipated article-by-article analysis of the *Rome Statute*, entitled *The International Criminal Court: A Commentary on the Rome Statute*.[2]

For anyone who follows the literature on the ICC, this book is an indispensable title in an ocean of similar, but often less worthy, literature. To some extent, its antecedents are in Schabas' earlier book, *An Introduction to the International Criminal Court*, which is widely used and is about to be released in its fourth edition. However, *A Commentary on the Rome Statute* is a much more ambitious work, comprising a thorough examination of each article of the *Rome Statute* with notes on the drafting process, doctrinal legal analysis, and erudite commentary.

The book begins with a detailed, amply-footnoted, twenty-seven-page "Historical Introduction." Here, Schabas reviews the development of the notion of individual criminal liability under international law and its direct enforcement, moving efficiently from the post-First World War attempts to prosecute international crimes through to

---

[1] *Rome Statute of the International Criminal Court*, 1 July 2002, UN Doc A/CONF.183/9 (2002).

[2] William A Schabas, *The International Criminal Court: A Commentary on the Rome Statute* (Oxford: Oxford University Press, 2010).

the Nuremburg trials, the post-war work of the International Law Commission (ILC), and, finally, the drafting and negotiation of the *Rome Statute* itself. Close attention to the historical record reveals that, despite popular perception, work on the ICC project had been ongoing for some years prior to its so-called revival by the United Nations: "This was not, in other words, a sudden discovery of the General Assembly in 1989."[3] Interestingly, Schabas observes that the tension between an independent court and its sovereign state members, which has emerged as a major point of conflict since the court's founding, was not only in play in Rome but was also foreshadowed in the initial work of the ILC's working group as early as 1994. This kind of observation is, in fact, characteristic of the entire book. Schabas is careful to trace the development of various trends, themes, and ideas and illustrates how they manifest either in the *Rome Statute* itself, or in the overall legal and political context surrounding the court.

Thereafter, each article of the *Rome Statute*, including the preamble, receives a full summary and analytical treatment under a number of headings. The first section, "Introductory Comments," ranges from one-sentence descriptions of the provision being discussed, to the comparative (for example, the description of how judges have been appointed to various international criminal tribunals, in the introduction to Article 36) and even the critical (for example, a pointed remark about the misleading quality of Article 15's title, "Prosecutor"). This is followed by a section called "Drafting of the Provision," which recounts the genesis of the provision in question, any attention or controversy it attracted during the Rome negotiations, and sometimes very detailed accounts of state positions, interpretations, or reactions. This latter segment is a valuable source of information for future interpretation by both the ICC and other courts. The next section is "Analysis and Interpretation," which typically provides an in-depth examination of the article by both paragraph and sub-paragraph. At the end of each article's treatment is a useful and often extensive bibliography of scholarship on the provision or its general subject matter.

The real meat of the work is contained in the "Analysis and Interpretation" sections for each article, and it is these parts of the book that will be of most interest to its target audience of jurists, practitioners, and academics. The real value is the depth and breadth of the analysis and interpretation, reflecting Schabas' many

---

[3] *Ibid* at 11.

years of work on both the ICC and in international criminal law in general. He eschews providing simple summaries and explanations, offering instead international law analysis that is both textual and contextual and that, importantly for work on this topic, maintains a broader perspective on the legal and the political. He naturally draws links between the *Rome Statute*'s provisions and their legislative/negotiating history but consistently draws out connections and disconnection between the treaty (as well as the elements of crimes and the rules of procedure and evidence) and the broader corpus of international criminal law, both customary and treaty-based. Rulings of the ICC's chambers and written statements by the prosecutor are incorporated where available, with Schabas providing both skepticism and attention to divisions and controversies. He cites extensively the jurisprudence of the ad hoc and other criminal tribunals, including national courts, as well as illustrating the necessary linkages with international human rights law, the law of state responsibility, the law of treaty interpretation, and the general principles of international law. Historical points are carefully grounded in the documentary records of the United Nations and the court itself. The distressingly vast literature on each topic is mined with great precision and to great effect, grounding the analysis while illustrating the outer edges of consensus and controversy. Yet, for the most part, the discussion stays lively and efficient and never strays into the kind of moribund excursus displayed by some similar works.

A good example of the high quality of the "analysis and interpretation" comes in a subsection on the vexed issue of the "state or organizational policy" requirement (or lack thereof) for crimes against humanity, found in the analysis of Article 7. Tracing the controversy back to the decision of the Nuremburg tribunal and the ILC's 1950s work on the *Code of Offences against the Peace and Security of Mankind*, Schabas explores the tension between the "no such requirement" position advocated by the International Criminal Tribunal of Yugoslavia Appeals Chamber and the codification of a "state or organizational policy" element in Article 7(2)(a) of the *Rome Statute*. Invoking law, commentary, and policy, he presents a compelling argument in favour of such a requirement, criticizing the selectivity of those who argue the former position. However, he also critiques the position of the ICC's Pre-Trial Chamber I, which interpreted the requirement broadly enough to include "either ... groups of persons who govern a specific territory or by any organization with the capability to commit a widespread or systematic attack against a civilian population."[4] Schabas forcefully criticizes the breadth of this interpretation: "[I]n subsequent cases upon mature reflection judges at the Court may see the dangers in such an open-ended approach, which encompasses organized crime, motorcycle gangs, and perhaps even serial killers within its ambit."[5]

As the foregoing passage indicates, and as with all of his work, Schabas is nothing if not knowledgeable, opinionated, and controversial. However, in *A Commentary on the Rome Statute*, his tone is reflective in places, and he displays principled thoughtfulness and a willingness to re-scrutinize his earlier positions. Where he had previously criticized the court for its slow movement of proceedings, in the preface he refers to the "high expectations" of the court (explicitly including his own) "that were perhaps, in hindsight, unreasonable" and notes "a tendency to underestimate the political challenges to the work of a permanent court with general jurisdiction."[6] He is similarly less aggressive on the issue of state "self-referral" under Article 14, which he has criticized harshly in the past. He also retreats slightly from his previous position regarding admissibility of cases under Article 17, in which he criticized as judicial activism the Pre-Trial Chamber's initial findings that "inactivity" by states that had jurisdiction over crimes would create a presumption of admissibility. Schabas maintains that this "inactivity" test contravenes the only logical interpretation that Article 17 bears, a view recently challenged with some heat by other expert commentators.[7] However, in *A Commentary on the Rome Statute*, he concedes that his version of the textual interpretation "defies common sense," and he appears to be satisfied with the court's position. He does not directly engage with Darryl Robinson's critique referenced earlier, though it appears that Robinson's article did not appear until after Schabas' manuscript was complete. It is emblematic of his intellectual generosity, perhaps, that Robinson's article appeared in a journal edited by Schabas. On the whole, Schabas is moderate with his own views and is careful to give relatively equal time to the various sides of the important debates.

The text has some limitations. As with any work in this rapidly changing field, it is already out of date in some respects, particularly

---

[4] *Ibid* at 150.

[5] *Ibid* at 151.

[6] *Ibid* at vii.

[7] Darryl Robinson, "The Mysterious Mysteriousness of Complementarity" (2010) 21 Crim LF 67.

given that the ICC's review conference was held in Kampala, Uganda, in the summer of 2010. The developments that occurred there, especially the adoption of a definition of the crime of aggression and a mechanism for bringing it into force, leave that part of *A Commentary on the Rome Statute* sorely wanting. Similarly, the discussion of Article 13 would certainly be enhanced by an examination of the UN Security Council's recent referral of the Libya situation to the court. However, all of this will simply provide grist for subsequent editions, a fact perhaps underscored by Oxford University Press's choice to launch the book at the review conference. The book might also have benefited from further editing, as there are occasional typos and (obviously inadvertent) grammatical errors. However, in a work of this size and density (1,250+ pages), this is a minor quibble.

In general, *A Commentary on the Rome Statute* will undoubtedly have a long shelf life as one of the most authoritative reference books on the ICC. Naturally, some of Schabas' interpretations are speculative, and much of the writing represents his own prescriptive views, but that is to be expected given the fact that the court's work is still largely prospective. This is a giant of a work, from a giant in the field.

Robert J. Currie
Associate Professor, Schulich School of Law, Dalhousie University

International and Transnational Criminal Law. By Robert J. Currie. Toronto: Irwin Law, 2010. 647 pages.

In a world where advances in technology and transportation have shattered the notion that crime is local, Robert J. Currie's book, *International and Transnational Criminal Law,* eloquently explores the complex and rapidly evolving fields of law known as "international criminal law" (ICL) and "transnational criminal law" (TCL).[1] Unlike some texts in international law, which rely on excerpts from international instruments to convey their message, this book studiously synthesizes complex subject matter into readily digestible points. In so doing, the author presents the salient features of these areas of law in a manner that allows the reader to appreciate the interplay between the emerging streams in a style that is

---

[1] Robert J Currie, *International and Transnational Criminal Law* (Toronto: Irwin Law, 2010).

eminently accessible to teachers, students, practitioners, judges, and policy makers alike.

Currie's overview of the history, developments, linkages, and nuances that define these emerging bodies of law conveys the fact that international and domestic law must constantly evolve to effectively respond to globalized crime. Accordingly, the book provides the reader with a set of tools that he or she can draw upon to understand the interplay between domestic and international law, as modern criminals look to exploit weaknesses in criminal law regimes between states, which, in turn, work to tighten the net around criminal activity with improved laws, enforcement, and co-operation.

An underlying theme in Currie's book is that in order for one to appreciate ICL and TCL in a meaningful way, one must understand the historical, philosophical, and legal foundations of these bodies of law. Currie sets the stage for his examination of ICL and TCL by highlighting the evolution of international law from a largely consensual system of rules governing state interactions, to a body of law that can hold individuals directly liable for international crimes, or indirectly liable through domestic law regimes for transnational crimes of international and domestic concern. As part of the *Essentials of Canadian Law* series, this book explores these areas of law with a focus on Canada. By exploring the nexus between these bodies of international law and Canadian domestic law, Currie describes how Canada's criminal law regime has adapted to respond to global crime. In so doing, the author leads his reader through this process seamlessly, each chapter building on the previous.

The first half of the book focuses on the gradual evolution of the state-centric concept of sovereignty. Attention is paid to the development of treaty and customary international law in holding individuals liable for horrendous crimes committed not only against the criminal laws of a single state but also against international law and, thus, the entire world community. Chapter 1 begins with a definition of ICL and TCL and examines how their development as bodies of law is impacted by different enforcement regimes, international co-operation, human rights, sources of law, and, ultimately, by the emergence of individual liability in international law. Chapter 2 considers the jurisdiction of states to prosecute ICL and TCL. Chapters 3 and 4 describe the core crimes of ICL — genocide, crimes against humanity, war crimes, and aggression — and their direct enforcement through international and internationalized criminal courts set up to deal with these crimes, such as the Nuremberg and

Tokyo tribunals, the UN ad hoc tribunals, and the International Criminal Court.

In keeping with the book's Canadian focus, Chapter 5 focuses on the prosecution of international crimes by Canadian courts from 1945 to 1999 and following the adoption of the *Crimes against Humanity and War Crimes Act* in 2000.[2] Notably, Currie's examination of the act is extremely detailed. He highlights the ways in which the act was designed to overcome the inadequacies of the Canadian legal regime for prosecuting war crimes as well as to implement Canada's obligations under the *Rome Statute of the International Criminal Court*.[3] Against this background, the author discusses the case of Désiré Munyaneza, a Rwandan national who was arrested in Canada in 2005 and found guilty in 2009 of two counts each of genocide and crimes against humanity, as well as three counts of war crimes linked to the Rwandan genocide of 1994. Currie deftly analyzes how the Canadian decision to convict a Rwandan national under the principle of universal jurisdiction, including the court's reliance on international treaties and the jurisprudence of the international criminal tribunals for Yugoslavia and Rwanda, is evidence of the fact that international criminal law and domestic criminal law complement one another.

The second half of the book moves from the study of direct criminal liability under international law to an examination of crimes with international characteristics that states prosecute under their domestic criminal law systems. Chapter 6 is devoted to discussing the so-called "other international crimes" of torture, piracy, and slavery and apartheid, noting that whereas they cannot be prosecuted directly under international law, they are sufficiently egregious to merit domestic prosecution of the perpetrators wherever they may go, so as to ensure that they can find no safe havens. In his assessment of these crimes, Currie describes their history and requisite elements, as well as the measures that Canada has put in place to criminalize these offences. The chapter ends with an invitation to the reader to consider whether terrorism could be considered an international crime or a transnational crime of international concern — the author adopts the latter view.

In his treatment of transnational crimes of international concern and transnational crimes of domestic concern, Currie reviews the

---

2 *Crimes against Humanity and War Crimes Act*, SC 2000, c 24.

3 *Rome Statute of the International Criminal Court*, 1 July 2002, UN Doc A/CONF.183/9 (2002).

major international law regimes dealing with drug trafficking, terrorism, transnational organized crime, corruption, and cybercrime. Owing to the vast scope of the TCL, however, the author's evaluation of this area is, understandably, quite survey-like, highlighting the applicable international law and the implementing legislation in Canada. Chapter 7, for example, focuses on transnational crimes of international concern by examining the "suppression conventions" for a wide number of crimes, including transnational organized crime, drug trafficking, terrorism, child sex-tourism, money laundering, and cybercrime. Whereas Currie notes that these conventions commonly require states' parties to criminalize certain acts, exert jurisdiction in an expansive manner, and ensure that an offender is prosecuted directly or extradited for prosecution, the vastness of this area of the law limits his analysis to concise descriptions of the applicable international law and Canada's implementing legislation. In this sense, the book is an excellent introduction to the law and a wonderful starting point for further investigation by the reader.

Chapters 8-10 supplement Currie's survey of transnational criminal law by describing in detail the practical measures undertaken in Canada in order to implement its obligations to prevent and combat transnational crime. Chapter 8 describes in detail the approach that Canadian law and jurisprudence have taken to prevent transnational crimes of domestic concern, including Canadian courts' application of the *Libman* test to determine their jurisdiction to prosecute domestic crimes involving the jurisdiction of more than one state. Chapters 9 and 10 provide a detailed examination of Canada's extradition and mutual legal assistance regime, followed by an analysis of how Canada's human rights obligations affect cooperation with other states for extraditions, deportations, and mutual legal assistance. For the latter, Currie gives a detailed examination, questioning whether the *Canadian Charter of Rights and Freedoms* can apply extraterritorially, and he includes a discussion of the fall-out resulting from the Supreme Court of Canada's approach to extraterritorial jurisdiction in *R v Hape*.

Finally, Chapter 11 brings this impressive book to a close with an examination of immunity from prosecution before international tribunals, domestic courts, and within Canadian law. Currie's work is an invaluable resource that will be welcomed by those with an interest in international and transnational criminal law. In addition to the comprehensive research and practical examples that inform this book, Currie's ability to translate a very complex area of law into easily understood concepts will ensure that this book remains authoritative and relevant for years to come.

Marcus Davies
Legal Officer, Criminal, Security and Diplomatic Law Division,
*Foreign Affairs and International Trade Canada**

Reflections on the UN Declaration on the Rights of Indigenous Peoples. Edited by Stephen Allen and Alexandra Xanthaki. Oxford and Portland, OR: Hart Publishing, 2011. 620 pages.

This collection of twenty-two essays, edited by two faculty members at Brunel Law School in the United Kingdom, aims to serve as the first in-depth academic analysis of the 2007 *United Nations Declaration on the Rights of Indigenous Peoples* (*Declaration on Indigenous Peoples*), focusing on the contributions made to international and national law and policy by the adoption of this declaratory text as well as the challenges ahead, most notably the challenge of implementation.[1] The collection was inspired, in the words of its editors, by a "perceived need to examine the Declaration critically and to situate it within the context of international law."[2] Efforts are also made to engage with "some difficult questions regarding the content and the status of the Declaration in international law" while also exploring "the Declaration's normative resonance for international law" and "the ways in which it could be used to prompt and shape institutional action and influence the development of national laws and policies on indigenous issues."[3]

Overall, the collection achieves its aims and is a solid contribution to the debate and discussion concerning the *Declaration on Indigenous Peoples*'s utility, although there are inconsistencies between the contributions on the question of the declaration's status in law, including the status of either the entire declaration or most of its

---

* The views expressed in this review are personal and not the official views of Foreign Affairs and International Trade Canada.

1 *United Nations Declaration on the Rights of Indigenous Peoples,* GA Res 61/295, UN Doc A/RES/61/295 (2007) [*Declaration on Indigenous Peoples*].

2 Stephen Allen and Alexandra Xanthaki, eds, *Reflections on the UN Declaration on the Rights of Indigenous Peoples* (Oxford: Hart Publishing, 2011) at 2.

3 *Ibid.*

provisions under customary international law. Nevertheless, the collection provides the reader with a useful and timely reference work on the declaration as well as a thoughtful review of its key substantive aspects, including the issues of land rights, rights to participation, and the right of self-determination as well as a discussion of the interconnection between indigenous and minority rights.

Several perspectives are represented within the collection, although there is no contribution written expressly from a state perspective, and none from a representative of a state that voted against the *Declaration on Indigenous Peoples*'s adoption in 2007.[4] Instead, the editors have chosen to include contributions by "the main protagonists in the Declaration's development, indigenous representatives, and field-leading academics."[5] With the latter being perhaps an unwise turn of phrase that opens the door to unnecessary debate and an appraisal as to who is not a contributor to the collection — most notably Arizona law professor S. James Anaya (who also serves as the current UN special rapporteur on the rights of indigenous peoples).

This book is divided into four sections. The first section provides what the editors refer to as "institutional perspectives," with particular reference to the United Nations as the institution that fostered the development of the *Declaration on Indigenous Peoples* over many years. This section begins with a useful historical account of the UN system's engagement with the task of drafting the declaration, written from the perspective of a key protagonist, the former chairperson-rapporteur of the Working Group on Indigenous Populations, Erica-Irene Daes. This chapter also provides some insight into the interventions made by states as the declaration developed over the years, which provides context for understanding the explanations of position later lodged by states upon the text's

---

4   As is well known, Australia, Canada, New Zealand, and the United States voted against the declaration's adoption in the UN General Assembly on 13 September 2007. Beginning with Australia on 3 April 2009, followed by New Zealand on 19 April 2010, Canada on 12 November 2010, and the United States on 16 December 2010, all four opposing states have now expressed support for the principles found within the declaration, while reiterating that the declaration is a nonbinding text. There are indications within the Allen and Xanthaki collection that Australia's and New Zealand's turn-around were known to the editors and contributing authors (see, for example, Allen and Xanthaki, *supra* note 2 at 123, n 4), but there is no specific analysis within the volume as to the impact of the about-face on the question of the declaration's status in law.

5   Allen and Xanthaki, *supra* note 2 at 2.

adoption in 2007. This section also contains a contribution by Patrick Thornberry, writing in his role as a member of the Committee on the Elimination of All Forms of Racial Discrimination and clearly demonstrating how at least one UN human rights treaty-monitoring body has used its position and processes to help shepherd through the declaration's implementation, notwithstanding the absence of an express mandate for such a role.[6] This essay is a useful read for those interested more generally in the UN human rights treaty monitoring system and its evolution, as is the chapter by Andrew Erueti tracing the contribution of the International Labour Organization and its role in encouraging the international indigenous movement. The first section also contains a contribution focused on litigation invoking the declaration in a variety of domestic and international courts, but the contribution lacks the objectivity needed to provide due consideration to opposing arguments. The authors also do not explain persuasively why one domestic court should heed another domestic court's decision to rely upon the declaration.

The second section focuses on "thematic perspectives" with a view to provide a critical review of the issues of status and implementation, including a considered review of the *Declaration on Indigenous Peoples*'s standing under international law. The section begins with an essay by the former UN Special Rapporteur Rodolfo Stavenhagen discussing the "implementation gap" that exists between legislation and practice in the field of indigenous rights. This is followed by a short essay by McGill University law professor H. Patrick Glenn on the ironies of the declaration, noting the use of Western law to advance the indigenous cause as well as the irony that the four states that voted against the declaration's adoption are among the most active in developing domestic laws and policies. Also within this second section is one of the volume's most interesting contributions, specifically an essay by noted Canadian political philosopher Will Kymlicka on the implications of the declaration's adoption for minority rights. This section also contains a useful account of the utility of UN General Assembly resolutions by Brunel Law School lecturer Emmanuel Voyiakis, noting the importance

---

[6] An interesting counter-point is found in the preceding chapter by Julian Burger, the former head of the Indigenous Peoples' Programme at the Office of the United Nations High Commissioner for Human Rights, who notes that the declaration has had little influence in the universal periodic review procedure with respect to either monitoring or recommendations for actions. *Ibid* at 56.

of the voting record, including statements, and a thoughtful essay by editor Stephen Allen on the declaration's non-binding status, emphasizing that the declaration's value is in its contribution to politics and not law.

As for the third section, here the reader finds several contributions organized under the heading of "substantive perspectives," aimed at analyzing the key provisions of the *Declaration on Indigenous Peoples*, albeit with a leaning towards the advocate's perspective. The seven-essay contributions in the third section provide the reader with detailed discussions of such contested topics as the meaning of free, prior, and informed consent, the existence of collective human rights (including rights to land, territories, and resources), and the exercise of the right of self-determination by indigenous peoples. There are also chapters examining the right to development, the recognition of cultural rights and indigenous women's rights, and the intellectual property rights associated with traditional and indigenous knowledge. While each chapter provides a useful reference guide to the relevant collection of treaty body views and recommendations, domestic court cases, and international decisions for each particular topic, the third section would have made a stronger overall contribution if there had been a consistent attempt by each author to refer also to the statements of position made by states during the declaration's drafting and eventually upon the text's adoption in 2007. Such statements, as explained by Voyiakis in his contribution in the second section, serve as useful expressions of state intent. Mention is also needed of the changes made to the proposed declaration text to secure its adoption in 2007, especially the preambular changes that were made to satisfy the concerns of African states and the import of these changes, if any, for the application of the declaration's main provisions.

The final section of the collection is focused on "regional perspectives," with the strongest contribution being a chapter by Spanish researcher Luis Rodríguez-Pinero on the influence and operational effect of the declaration within the inter-American human rights system and its impact on the drafting of a future "American Declaration on the Rights of Indigenous Peoples" under the auspices of the Organization of American States. An African Union perspective on the *Declaration on Indigenous Peoples* is then provided by Bristol University law professor Rachel Murray, which makes a useful point about the role of the African Commission on Human and Peoples' Rights but does not provide an analysis of the changes made to the 2006 version of the declaration that were intended to address the concerns of African states. The remaining chapters in the fourth section focus on the significance (or lack thereof) of the declaration for the Inuit in the Arctic, the Saami in Scandinavia, and the indigenous communities of present-day Pakistan, with the chapter on the Saami serving as a useful update for interested readers on the development of a future Saami convention between Finland, Norway, and Sweden. A chapter discussing recent developments in Japan would have been a welcome inclusion.

One important aspect that is missing from this collection is an in-depth discussion of the *Declaration on Indigenous Peoples'* prospects as a precursor to the drafting of a legally binding treaty on the rights of indigenous peoples.[7] Historically, within the field of international human rights law, the adoption by states of a general non-binding declaratory text, almost always by consensus, serves as the starting point or foundation for the negotiation of a more specific and legally binding treaty on the same subject. This practice is well illustrated by the adoption by the UN General Assembly of the *Universal Declaration of Human Rights*,[8] which was then followed by many years of negotiations before the eventual adoption in 1966 of the now widely ratified *International Covenant on Civil and Political Rights*[9] and the *International Covenant on Economic, Social and Cultural Rights*.[10] Other examples of the practice of adopting a declaratory text to solidify support before negotiating a treaty include the 1963 adoption of the *United Nations Declaration on the Elimination of All Forms of Racial Discrimination*,[11] which was followed by the adoption in 1965 of the *International Convention on the Elimination of All Forms of Racial Discrimination*,[12] the 1967 adoption of a *Declaration on the*

---

[7] Some of the collection's authors, such as Rodolfo Stavenhagen (at 151) and Javaid Rehman (at 584), anticipate the negotiation of a future convention, but the topic is not discussed in detail.

[8] *Universal Declaration of Human Rights*, GA Res 217A (III) (1948).

[9] *International Covenant on Civil and Political Rights*, 16 December 1966, 999 UNTS 171, Can TS 1976 No 47 (entered into force 23 March 1976).

[10] *International Covenant on Economic, Social and Cultural Rights*, 16 December 1966, 993 UNTS 3, Can TS 1976 No 46 (entered into force 3 January 1976).

[11] *United Nations Declaration on the Elimination of All Forms of Racial Discrimination*, GA Res 1904 (XVIII) (1963).

[12] *International Convention on the Elimination of All Forms of Racial Discrimination*, 21 December 1965, 660 UNTS 195, Can TS 1970 No 28 (entered into force 4 January 1969).

Elimination of Discrimination against Women,[13] followed by the adoption in 1979 of the *Convention on the Elimination of All Forms of Discrimination against Women*,[14] and the 1959 adoption of a *Declaration on the Rights of the Child*,[15] followed by the much later adoption of the *Convention on the Rights of the Child* in 1989.[16] In each case, the adoption by consensus of a short declaratory text listing general principles provided the foundation or agreement-in-principle that helped guide subsequent negotiations towards the finalization and adoption of a legally binding treaty text.

Recent treaty negotiations suggest that this practice still finds favour among states, with the adoption of a new *International Convention for the Protection of All Persons from Enforced Disappearance*[17] having gained some assistance by the earlier adoption of a *Declaration on the Protection of All Persons from Enforced Disappearance* in 1992.[18] This example also makes for a suitable comparison with the subject matter under discussion since the promotion of a final text for a convention on enforced disappearances by what was then a brand new Human Rights Council[19] coincided with the council's adoption of a proposed text for an indigenous rights declaration.[20] Consensus greeted the convention text at both the Human Rights Council and before the UN General Assembly, whereas the text of the indigenous rights declaration was met with dissent at both the Human

---

[13] *Declaration on the Elimination of Discrimination against Women*, GA Res 2263 (XXII) (1967).

[14] *Convention on the Elimination of All Forms of Discrimination against Women*, 18 December 1979, 1249 UNTS 13, Can TS 1982 No 31 (entered into force 3 September 1981).

[15] *Declaration on the Rights of the Child*, GA Res 1386 (XVI) (1959).

[16] *Convention on the Rights of the Child*, 20 November 1989, 1577 UNTS 3, Can TS 1992 No 3 (entered into force 2 September 1990).

[17] *International Convention for the Protection of All Persons from Enforced Disappearance*, 20 December 2006, UN Doc A/61/488 (2006) (entered into force 23 December 2010).

[18] *Declaration on the Protection of All Persons from Enforced Disappearance*, GA Res 47/133, UN Doc A/RES/47/133 (1992).

[19] See *International Convention for the Protection of All Persons from Enforced Disappearance*, Human Rights Council (HRC) Res 1/1 of 29 June 2006, reprinted in *Report of the Human Rights Council*, UN Doc A/61/53 (2006) at 3-17.

[20] *Working Group of the Commission on Human Rights to Elaborate a Draft Declaration in Accordance with Paragraph 5 of the General Assembly Resolution 49/214 of 23 December 1994*, HRC Res 1/2 of 29 June 2006, reprinted in *Report of the Human Rights Council*, UN Doc A/61/53 (2006) at 18-27.

Rights Council and the UN General Assembly,[21] suggesting that the declaration may not provide a sufficiently strong foundation for the successful negotiation of an indigenous rights treaty. For these reasons, I suggest that this aspect would have been worth including as a topic of inquiry in the Allen and Xanthaki collection, but I mention this more as a missed opportunity and not as a fundamental flaw with the collection.

JOANNA HARRINGTON
Professor, Faculty of Law, University of Alberta

Human Rights and the Ethics of Globalization. By Daniel E. Lee and
Elizabeth J. Lee. Cambridge: Cambridge University Press. 280
pages.

OVERVIEW OF THE BOOK

Human Rights and the Ethics of Globalization is an introduction to the ethical issues faced by multinational enterprises (MNEs) conducting business in developing countries.[1] The authors address the issues of outsourcing and its impact on the labour markets of developed countries investing in countries with poor human rights records, the role of MNEs and consumers in promoting fair trade, and concession agreements between MNEs and developing countries. The authors use a philosophical approach to address these issues. They conclude with a brief consideration of the ways to enforce compliance with the ethical obligations they set out for MNEs.

The book is divided into three main parts. The first sets out the philosophical basis of the authors' approach to human rights, which is based on a natural rights approach as articulated by Immanuel Kant.[2] This framework is then applied to determine our responsibility

---

[21] The resolution concerning the indigenous rights declaration was adopted at the Human Rights Council by a recorded vote of thirty votes to two (Canada and the Russian Federation), with twelve abstentions (*ibid*) and at the UN General Assembly by a recorded vote of 143 (corrected to 144) votes to four, with eleven abstentions (UN Doc A/61/PV.107 (2007) at 18-19). For further discussion, see Joanna Harrington, "Canada and the United Nations Human Rights Council: Dissent and Division" (2010) 60 UNBLJ 78 at 78-115.

---

[1] Daniel E Lee and Elizabeth J Lee, *Human Rights and the Ethics of Globalization* (New York: Cambridge University Press, 2010).

[2] *Ibid* at xiv.

for those in distant places — for example, our responsibility for those harmed by MNEs operating abroad. The authors conclude this part with a discussion on balancing the imperatives of a corporation, whose duties are principally owed to investors, with the corporation's obligations to others affected by its activities, such as customers, employees, suppliers, and the communities in which the corporation does business.

The second part of the book consists of case studies on the ethics of doing business in China, Liberia, Ethiopia, and Mexico. These case studies do not follow a consistent pattern. The first is primarily an account of some ongoing human rights issues in China, including Chinese policies on reproductive rights, religious freedom, and workers' rights. The authors address the obligations of MNEs doing business in China to advocate for a North American conception of human rights in that country. The Liberia and Ethiopia case studies focus on ethical issues that arise from concession agreements between MNEs and the host state (Liberia — rubber industry) as well as the obligations of MNEs and consumers to ensure fair trade in commodities (Ethiopia — coffee industry). The last study deals with the issue of outsourcing by examining the impacts of shifting production facilities from the United States to Mexico. The authors use this final case study to investigate the impact of outsourcing on both American and Mexican workers, and they formulate some guidelines for companies engaged in outsourcing.

Finally, the third part of the book provides a short overview of various mechanisms for enforcing the human rights obligations of MNEs, followed by a more detailed analysis of the American *Aliens Tort Claim Act* (*ATCA*) as a means of enforcing the compliance of American companies with human rights and environmental protection norms.[3] The focus is primarily on recent case law in American courts interpreting the scope of protection for human rights and environmental abuses under the act. However, there is some evaluation of the change in policy between the government of George W. Bush, which the authors feel generally opposed the use of the *ATCA* to force companies to comply with international human rights and environmental law norms,[4] and the Obama administration, which the authors anticipate will be more open to the use of the *ATCA*.[5]

---

[3] *Aliens Tort Claim Act*, 28 USC §1350 [*ATCA*].

[4] Lee and Lee, *supra* note 1 at 230.

[5] *Ibid* at 231.

SHORT ASSESSMENT

This book will be of little use to legal scholars or international law-yers. It appears to be principally aimed at students of undergraduate business ethics courses, as it offers a simple — at times, even sim-plistic — introduction to the philosophical basis of the ethical obli-gations of businesses operating in foreign countries. While the virtue of the book is its straightforward presentation of these obligations based on Kantian philosophy, the authors fail to consider alterna-tives to a natural rights approach to human rights such as welfare-based ethics (for example, utilitarianism), and they do not consider the critical literature on globalization or the literature on develop-ment and post-colonial studies.

The book is also limited in terms of the legal mechanisms dis-cussed for enforcing compliance with human rights norms and promoting the protection of the environment. Lee and Lee advocate greater use of voluntary compliance mechanisms (that is, norms of corporate social responsibility voluntarily adopted by businesses operating in developing countries),[6] greater monitoring of compli-ance with these voluntary codes,[7] and, in extreme cases, litigation under the *ATCA*.[8] There is no consideration of the work of the UN secretary-general's special representative on business and human rights. There is also no discussion of social and environmental impact assessments or the various ways that impact assessments can be used to promote the protection of human rights and the environ-ment. There is no assessment of the effectiveness of voluntary codes.

The authors flit between consideration of the ethical obligations of MNEs operating in developing countries, consumers buying products produced by MNEs, and the duties of those who regulate MNEs, either at the international or national level. Although a desire to consider the obligations of all of these actors is admirable, the failure to consider the different classes of actors in a systematic way makes it difficult to fully understand the challenges that global-ization poses for each class. It is likewise difficult to understand which enforcement mechanisms are more or less suitable for each type of actor. For instance, the *ATCA* does not seem a likely candi-date for enforcing the ethical obligations of consumers to buy fair trade products. It also does not provide a useful tool for inter-national legal regulation.

6   *Ibid* at 243.

7   *Ibid* at 244.

8   *Ibid* at 245.

The final chapter of the book is the only section that deals extensively with law. Here, the authors focus mainly on whether the *ATCA* can be used to enforce compliance with human rights and environmental law norms. Thus, the only chapter that actually deals with law does not really deal specifically with international law but, rather, with a uniquely American approach to transnational law for regulating multinational corporations accused of human rights violations or the degradation of the environment contrary to international law. Only American jurisprudence is considered in this chapter, and the discussion adds nothing to the existing literature in the area. Indeed, this last chapter takes the form of a rather superficial legal memo, outlining the elements of a claim under the *ATCA* and the recent case law interpreting the act's application. It falls far short of works such as that of François Larocque's masterful book *Civil Actions for Uncivilized Acts,*which fits the *ATCA* into the context of other similar mechanisms that exist in jurisdictions outside the United States.[9]

The Ethical Implications of Globalization

The impetus for *Human Rights and the Ethics of Globalization* is the phenomenon of globalization. We are enmeshed in a web of interactions with those in distant places in ways that were never possible before, and this feeling of closeness must surely engender new ethical responsibilities. However, despite the intuitive appeal of the link between globalization and ethical responsibility, the authors do not build a convincing case for a link between globalization and increased moral responsibility.

First, the authors never define "globalization." In the prologue, they use examples such as McDonald's expansion of their business to Argentina, Aruba, Bahrain, Bolivia, Chile, Costa Rica, Ecuador, Egypt, India, Indonesia, Jamaica, Japan, Korea, Kuwait, Malaysia, Malta, New Zealand, Nicaragua, Pakistan, Paraguay, Saudi Arabia, Singapore, Tahiti, Taiwan, and other countries to capture the phenomenon of globalization.[10] However, while the increasing availability of the Big Mac in every corner of the world is a phenomenon commonly associated with globalization in the media and in popular

---

[9] Francois Larocque, *Civil Actions for Uncivilized Acts: The Adjudicative Jurisdiction of Common Law Courts in Transnational Human Rights Proceedings* (Toronto: Irwin Law, 2010).

[10] Lee and Lee, *supra* note 1 at ix.

culture, no specific definition of "globalization" is provided. Does globalization refer to the spread of "empire" — that is, an anonymous network of institutions that enforce compliance with capitalist structures?[11] Is it a process of "closer economic integration of the countries of the world through the increased flow of goods and services, capital, and even labor"?[12] Is it the decreasing significance of the nation state in an international world?[13] Or does it refer more generally to the "web" of social, economic, and informational relations in which each of us is increasingly embedded in the modern era?[14] A definition of "globalization" is critical if the authors are to successfully explain how their conception of human rights and the ethical obligations of MNEs can respond to the challenges of globalization.

The authors hint at a characterization of globalization in Chapter 2, "Near Neighbors, Distant Neighbors, and the Ethics of Globalization," which deals with the different obligations to those living near to us, as opposed to those living far away. Lee and Lee note that our different obligations form "concentric circles," with each circle defined by a different level of ethical obligation.[15] Parents have greater responsibilities to their children than to the children of those in distant places.[16] Thus, the circle of responsibility containing our children is closer to us than the circle of responsibility containing the children of others. The authors note that globalization affects these circles by expanding and contracting them. Globalization brings those far away "closer" to us — not physically, but ethically.[17] However, having acknowledged that globalization does not bring others *physically* closer to us, Lee and Lee do not explain what the increasing nearness of globalization consists of or by which mechanism it affects the circles of responsibility.

The authors try to address the effects of globalization on our ethical responsibilities by considering globalization as the expansion

---

11 Antonio Negri and Michael Hardt, *Empire* (Cambridge, MA: Harvard University Press, 2000).

12 Joseph E Stiglitz, *Globalization and Its Discontents* (New York: Norton, 2002) at 4.

13 Jan Aart Scholte, *Globalization: A Critical Introduction* (New York: St. Martin's Press, 2000).

14 On the "web" as the defining feature of globalization, see Thomas L Friedman, *The Lexus and the Olive Tree* (New York: Anchor Books, 2000) at 8.

15 Lee and Lee, *supra* note 1 at 47.

16 *Ibid.*

17 *Ibid* at 46.

of the network of employment relations linking workers in distant places to companies operating in our own country. As MNEs employ more people abroad, the reach of the employer-employee relationship extends. Consequently, through employment contracts, employers from developed countries confer on employees in developing countries certain legal rights. Employers are also obliged to respect the "inherent" rights of an employee, such as the right to a safe work environment free from harassment.[18]

However, is this the extent of the consequences of globalization? Does it simply increase the number of people tied to MNEs located in developed countries due to an expansion of the employer-employee relationship? Or does globalization also affect the *quality* of ethical obligations — that is, does initiating an employment relationship with a poor person in a developing country lead to different ethical responsibilities than those that exist between an employer and employee in Canada, the United States, or Europe?

The Lees answer this question as follows:

Because contractual rights and inherent relational rights stem from relationships of various sorts, our obligations related to them typically involve near neighbors, rather than distant neighbors. It might be added, however, that the very nature of globalization is such that distant neighbors in many cases become near neighbors. When Firestone established rubber plantations in Liberia under the terms of the 1926 concession agreement, Liberians — at least those hired by Firestone and those living in the areas in which the rubber plantations are located — became for them near neighbors. The same is true for the companies that have built factories or opened retail outlets in China, Mexico, or any of a number of other countries in which various multinational corporations have established operations.[19]

The authors seem to be arguing that by "globalizing," or expanding business to distant places, the workers in those places become more like family members for the employer, thus affecting the quality and content of our ethical obligations to them. But then they quickly qualify this argument: "This is not to suggest that with globalization everyone becomes a near neighbor. Even in an age of Internet and other forms of telecommunications, there are some who remain distant."[20] The authors now seem to be arguing

18 *Ibid* at 44-45.

19 *Ibid* at 46.

20 *Ibid*.

that globalization does not change the quality or content of ethical obligations of companies to employees — employees will never become as close as family members. Employees of Firestone in Liberia are "near neighbors" like Firestone's employees in the United States. However, if globalization does not affect the content of ethical obligations, in what sense can globalization be said to bring "distant neighbors nearer to us?"[21] Is the only effect of globalization to create employer-employee relations between companies and employees separated by greater distances?

A better definition of "globalization" would have helped the authors explain how it affects the concentric circles of obligation. Does it shrink or expand some circles by increasing the number of employer-employee relationships as businesses expand to more countries? Or does it change the nature or content of ethical obligations because of the different circumstances in which employees in developing countries live and work — conditions that are often very different from those in developed countries?

KANTIAN ETHICS: AN ADEQUATE JUSTIFICATION FOR THE ETHICAL OBLIGATIONS OF AN MNE?

One of the cornerstones of the Lee and Lee's argument is that the Kantian natural law approach to human rights is superior to other ethical theories. Moreover, it is the only theory that provides a coherent interpretation of human rights. In their view, much talk about human rights reduces to "nothing more than a rhetorical device used to advance a particular position."[22] Documents that promote or protect human rights may inspire us, but most do not specify who is responsible for fulfilling a particular human right.[23] In the eyes of the authors, there can be no meaningful right without a statement of who is responsible for respecting and fulfilling it.

To remedy this deficiency, the authors seek to restrict the extent of human rights to negative rights. They use, as their starting point, one of Kant's categorical imperatives: never use others merely as a means to your own ends.[24] They interpret this to mean that we should never forget that every human being is of equal value.[25] And

[21] *Ibid.*

[22] *Ibid* at 18.

[23] *Ibid* at 31.

[24] *Ibid* at 55-56 and 181.

[25] *Ibid* at 56.

although they are not clear on the link between the categorical imperative and business ethics, they derive the following rules of business ethics from it:

- The right to life is the most basic right.
- It is a natural right — a right common to all in virtue of our humanity — rather than a right conferred on us contingently by others.[26]
- Most rights are negative — that is, they are universal duties to forebear from harming others.
- Positive rights will be protected only if, like the right to vote, they are necessary for securing negative rights.[27]
- We should only recognize rights for which we can identify the person specifically responsible for fulfilling them.[28]

It is hard to see how these five conclusions follow from the Kantian categorical imperative.

Moreover, the authors never consider alternatives to a natural rights theory. For instance, there is no consideration of utilitarian ethics. In my view, a discussion of alternatives to Kantian ethics would have strengthened the authors' argument in favour of a natural rights approach, particularly in a book on business ethics, since utilitarianism is often considered to provide the intellectual backbone of free market capitalism.

Having set out the philosophical basis of business ethics, the Lees turn next to identifying the individuals to whom MNEs have moral responsibilities. They argue that it follows from their account of rights that MNEs have obligations to all those who "have a stake in what a company does."[29] According to Lee and Lee, this includes shareholders, customers, employees, suppliers, and the community in which the facility is located.[30] It is unclear how this follows from a natural rights justification for human rights. If the basis of most rights is natural right, then it seems that MNEs owe an obligation to all based solely on their humanity rather than on the closeness of each individual's relationship to the corporation.

Finally, it is unclear how the Kantian categorical imperative is compatible with the Lees' view that the profitability of a company

---

[26] *Ibid* at 30.

[27] *Ibid* at 32-33.

[28] *Ibid*.

[29] *Ibid* at 58.

[30] *Ibid*.

limits its ethical obligations. The authors state that "[t]he reality is that without maintaining profitability, business enterprises cannot in any meaningful way serve any of the constituencies noted previously."[31] However, this seems to subordinate ethical obligations to the survival of the MNE. It is based on the view that MNEs are an essential means of providing for the well-being of shareholders, customers, employees, suppliers, and the community. But this seems to be a questionable claim. Some communities might be better off without a new MNE, and it might, arguably, be the duty of that enterprise to close down its operations, however profitable, if the net result of the operation is creating more harm than good.

Doing Business with China: An Ethical Obligation to Advocate for Human Rights Protection?

In their case study of China, Lee and Lee raise, by implication, many ethical issues for those conducting business abroad. What are the responsibilities of MNEs when deciding whether to do business in China, which, the Lees argue, has a poor human rights record? If they establish a business there, what is the nature of their obligations to their employees? Should they be involved in promoting human rights in China generally? How does globalization affect these relationships beyond merely creating the possibility of doing business in China?

The Lees review three areas in which China has, they argue, failed to respect human rights: reproductive rights, religious freedom, and workers' rights. The chapter is mostly a brief survey of China's current policies regarding these topics. There is, unfortunately, no evaluation of the literature that considers criticism of China's human rights record as hypocritical or one-sided.[32] Moreover, only the section on workers' rights is directly relevant to what the Lees identify as the effects of globalization, namely creating employment relationships between MNEs and those in distant lands.

The Lees' proposal in regard to the rights of workers is that MNEs doing business in China should voluntarily draft a code of conduct based on the Global Sullivan Principles, a set of principles developed for American firms doing business in apartheid South Africa and later broadened, in 1997, to deal with MNEs doing

---

[31] *Ibid* at 61.

[32] See, eg, Randall Peerenboom, "Assessing Human Rights in China: Why the Double Standard?" (2005) 38 Cornell Int'l LJ 71.

business throughout the world.[33] This is a concrete proposal, and the Lees go on to explain how it could be elaborated in order to adapt the Global Sullivan Principles to companies doing business in China.

Some elaboration on the compatibility of the Global Sullivan Principles with a natural rights view of the obligations of MNEs operating abroad would have been helpful. Many of the guidelines suggested by the authors go beyond the negative conception of human rights that were presented earlier in the book. For instance, the authors advocate for employers to take responsibility for "improving the quality of life for employees outside the workplace."[34] It seems that this responsibility is a positive obligation rather than a negative obligation to prevent harming others.

The Lees base employers' obligations to assist communities where their employees live on prudential concerns. They reject Milton Friedman's view that, as all of the assets of the corporation belong to shareholders, it is up to them as individuals, and not up to the firm as a collective, to determine which charitable causes to support with the company's assets.[35] Instead, they recognize that MNEs have the same responsibilities as all citizens to support cultural and social programs in the community.[36] However, in order to limit this broad obligation to support the community, the Lees argue that MNEs are only obliged to support community measures with positive externalities for the business. If the measure will ultimately benefit the business, if it is a measure of which potential customers will approve,[37] and if it is practical to implement, then a MNE may be justified in putting it into practice. I find it difficult to understand how this kind of utilitarian argument is compatible with a natural rights view.

Take, for example, the authors contention that companies may rank which community improvements they support based on the availability of resources. Such a ranking, they argue, is compatible with Kant's view that "ought implies can," which they interpret to mean that "in order to claim in any meaningful way that someone is obligated to do something, it must be possible for that person to

---

33 For information on the Global Sullivan Principles, see <http://www.thesullivan-foundation.org/about/global_sullivan_principles>.

34 Lee and Lee, *supra* note 1 at 108.

35 *Ibid* at 74.

36 *Ibid*.

37 *Ibid* at 74-75.

do what is suggested that he or she ought to do."[38] However, this seems to be a misinterpretation of Kant. In *Theory and Practice,* Kant writes that one has a duty to fulfil one's moral aims unless it is "demonstrably impossible" to fulfil these aims.[39] This concession on Kant's part is a far cry from saying, as the Lees suggest, that the moral responsibilities of MNEs are limited by their obligation to make profits for their investors and that they are justified in ranking charitable contributions to community organizations based on the resources available to them. Surely, respect for human rights might require MNEs to go beyond what is practical or affordable.

The *ATCA:* A Cure for All Ailments?

This chapter may be the one most relevant to lawyers and legal academics because it contains the most in-depth consideration of legal issues relating to globalization and MNEs. However, it fits poorly into the overall framework of the book. Most of the book focuses on ethical issues that arise from doing business in distant places. In contrast, this chapter focuses on legal enforcement mechanisms, leaving one to consider the relationship between ethical duties and legal enforcement mechanisms. Are ethical duties such as treating workers well and protecting the environment the kinds of duties that we can or should enforce through law? These and other questions about the relationship between ethics and the law are left unanswered.

The authors' focus on the *ATCA* limits the book's sole chapter on law to an examination of a remedy available only in the United States. In order to make this book relevant to a wider audience, it would have been helpful for the authors to consider whether the *ATCA* should be a model for other countries: should other countries pass legislation similar to the *ATCA* in order to enforce compliance with the ethical obligations of MNEs?

The style of this chapter is inconsistent with the rest of the book. While previous chapters deal with theoretical and philosophical issues, this chapter reads as a legal memo, summarizing case law decided under the *ATCA*. To better integrate the chapter into the book, it would have been interesting to consider theoretical issues such as the rationale for the *ATCA*, which has its roots in the late eighteenth century. Was it intended to protect the United States against war by providing a remedy for foreign nationals seeking to enforce international law? Was it hoped that the *ATCA* would ensure American diplomats would be safe from reprisal for perceived American violations of international law? Or was it intended to ensure that there are remedies for violations of international law, regardless of the benefits this might have for the United States as a means of fulfilling the cosmopolitan ideals of the Enlightenment that were current at the end of the eigtheenth century?[40] Answering these questions might help to understand how the *ATCA* and its underlying philosophy fit with the ethical ideals discussed in *Human Rights and the Ethics of Globalization*. The short paragraph where the authors address the purpose of the *ATCA* does little to connect the act with the philosophical justifications for the ethical obligations of MNEs examined earlier in the book.[41]

Another issue not fully addressed by the authors is whether the ethical duties they impose on MNEs are the kinds of duties that can be enforced under the *ATCA*. For instance, Larocque suggests that "to be actionable under the *ATCA*, the impugned conduct must contravene well-established, highly defined, and widely accepted international norms."[42] Which activities of MNEs operating abroad would constitute violations of the international legal norms that are enforceable under the *ATCA*? Larocque suggests that the jurisprudence interpreting the *ATCA* only applies to violations by MNEs of prohibitions on piracy, slavery, genocide, and crimes against humanity.[43] Lee and Lee define the international norms enforceable under the *ATCA* more broadly, claiming that international law evolves over time.[44] However, they do not explain whether the current state of international law covers the ethical obligations that they claim MNEs must fulfil. Can the *ATCA* be used to enforce the failure of a MNE operating in China to provide a "safe work environment and appropriate levels of compensation?"Can it be used to "ensure that their suppliers comply with appropriate ethical standards?"[45] Will

---

[38] *Ibid* at 77 (Lee and Lee refer to the *Critique of Pure Reason*, Doc. A807/B835).

[39] Immanuel Kant, "On the Common Saying: 'This May Be True in Theory, but It Does Not Apply in Practice,'" in Hans Siegbert Reiss, ed, *Kant: Political Writings*, 2nd edition, translated by Hugh Barr Nisbet (Cambridge: Cambridge University Press, 1991) at 61 and 89.

[40] See Larocque, *supra* note 9 at 27-40, for a full consideration of these justifications for the *ATCA*.

[41] Lee and Lee, *supra* note 1 at 210.

[42] Larocque, *supra* note 9 at 52.

[43] *Ibid* at 68.

[44] Lee and Lee, *supra* note 1 at 219.

[45] *Ibid* at 113.

the *ATCA* encourage Firestone to follow the terms of the concession agreement it signed with Liberia in 2008, which includes clauses that require it to provide funds for local schools, housing for employees, and assurances of preferential hiring for Liberians with the necessary job skills?[46] If the answer is no, as I suspect it is, then the authors' recourse to the *ATCA* as a means of enforcing compliance with human rights and international environmental law norms is very limited, covering very few of the ethical obligations they seek to impose on MNEs.

Another aspect of the same question is the legal personality of MNEs. There is considerable debate in international law about the legal status of corporations. The authors do not recognize this issue, though it strikes at the heart of the utility of the *ATCA* for enforcing human rights and environmental law norms.

CONCLUSION

Human Rights and the Ethics of Globalization addresses a number of important topics in international business, including the ethics of outsourcing, the conditions of fair trade, issues that arise when MNEs operate in states with poor human rights records (such as China), and the duties of a MNE operating in a state with poor rule of law institutions (such as Liberia). The book is valuable because it targets issues of interest to the general public that arise out of transnational business operations. The authors use a clear and straightforward presentation style and rely on four concrete case studies to illustrate their theoretical arguments.

The main problem with this book is that the authors fail to adequately justify the superiority of the philosophical framework they present. The reader is left wondering why natural law is the proper basis for ethics in a globalized world. Other alternatives such as welfare-based ethical theories are not considered, nor are the weaknesses of the natural law approach. The authors fail to define the phenomenon of globalization that raises novel ethical issues and that is the focus of the book. A definition is essential in order to understand the "new reality" of the globalized world. Without a clear understanding of the way in which globalization has changed business transactions, it is difficult to assess whether a natural law approach is well suited to addressing these issues.

The case studies do not follow from the first three theoretical chapters of the book. It is difficult to see how the authors' conclusions

---

[46] *Ibid* at 136.

about doing business in China or Liberia or in relation to consumer choice between fair trade and non-fair-trade coffee are derived from Kantian ethics. This undermines the utility of the book as a practical illustration of how to put Kant's categorical imperative into effect in a globalized world. Finally, the book has little legal content, and even where law is proposed as a mechanism for enforcing human rights and environmental norms the analysis is not thorough enough. Moreover, the authors do not consider whether the law is the proper tool for enforcing compliance with ethical obligations. Finally, their focus on the *ATCA* does not provide a truly global solution, as it deals with a uniquely American approach, and the authors do not fully explore which of the ethical obligations identified earlier in the book are actually enforceable under the *ATCA*. The latter is essential to support the authors' claim that the *ATCA* is an effective way for ensuring MNE compliance with international human rights and environmental law norms.

GRAHAM MAYEDA
Associate Professor, Faculty of Law, University of Ottawa

The Justiciability of International Disputes: The Advisory Opinion on Israel's Security Fence as a Case Study. By Solon Solomon. Nijmegen, The Netherlands: Wolf Legal Publishers, 2009. 212 pages.

A study of the 760-kilometre barrier being constructed by Israel, roughly dividing the Palestinian territories from Israel, is almost certain to be seen as favouring a specific perspective. This is also true of any examination of Israeli settlements in those territories. The topics seem to defy impartiality, as is evident from the heated diplomatic fallout as a result of the Obama administration's renewed focus on Israeli settlements in its first year in office. Anything said on this topic — at multilateral conferences, in the media, and especially by judicial tribunals — will be regarded as taking one side or the other.

The book under review is no exception.[1] One would reasonably expect from an author who served in the Knesset Legal Department and was, as the back cover to the book suggests, in charge

---

[1] Solon Solomon, *The Justiciability of International Disputes: The Advisory Opinion on Israel's Security Fence as a Case Study* (Nijmegen, The Netherlands: Wolf Legal Publishers, 2009).

of international and constitutional issues, a spirited defence of the
Israeli position on the International Court of Justice's (ICJ) advisory
opinion on the legality of the barrier. This caveat aside, it is clear
that Solomon provides a critical, yet sober, rationale throughout
this volume, not only arguing from the point of view of an Israeli
official but also challenging the ICJ decision from two interesting
perspectives: as a scholar of legal history and as an analyst of the
"competing" evaluation and conclusions of another tribunal, the
Israel Supreme Court. As will be recalled, the latter is highly regarded internationally for the profundity and meticulousness of its
approach and recognized, moreover, for the fact that it often draws
its legal theories from Supreme Court of Canada jurisprudence.

The ICJ's 2004 advisory decision responded to a UN General
Assembly request to examine the legal consequences of the construction of the separation wall. In brief, the court held that the
specific route chosen by Israel, which extended, in part, into Palestinian territory behind the pre-1967 "Green Line," violated a number of international obligations by the occupying power and
infringed on the rights of Palestinians, including the right to free
movement, the capacity to pursue their livelihood, unimpeded, and
their entitlement to self-determination. In addition, by impinging
on their travel and economic base, as well as safeguarding Israeli
settlements in the territories, the wall encouraged the exit of Palestinians and risked causing irreversible changes to the demographic
make-up of the Palestinians within the area of occupation. The
court also acknowledged

certain fears ... that the route of the wall will prejudge the future frontier
between Israel and Palestine and that the construction of the wall and its
associated regime create a "fait accompli" on the ground that could well
become permanent ... and ... would be tantamount to de facto
annexation.[2]

The ICJ ruled that the barrier was, therefore, contrary to international law and urged all states not to recognize the "situation
resulting from" its construction and not to extend assistance that
would maintain the situation. It also recommended that the UN

---

[2] *Legal Consequences of the Construction of a Wall in the Occupied Palestinian Territory*
(Advisory Opinion), Judgment of 9 July 2004, (2004) 43 ILM 1999 at para 121.

General Assembly and Security Council consider action "to bring to an end to the illegal situation."[3]

In reaching its conclusions, the ICJ rejected a number of propositions put forward by Israel challenging the court's jurisdiction and contesting the notion that an advisory opinion was appropriate in the framework of a conflict situation between two belligerents (Israel and the Palestinians). Israel argued that humanitarian law granted its citizens protection in a conflict situation where violent actions against its citizens originated in the territories. The wall was meant to address this situation. In this regard, Israel also averred that the Palestinian authority, the actual party seeking a remedy, failed to come to the court with "clean hands" (the principle of *nullus commodum capere potest de sua injuria*: no one can take advantage of his own wrong). The court rejected these pleas. In response to Israel's clean hands contention, for example, the ICJ held that the argument was not relevant since the UN General Assembly, not a particular state or entity, had requested the advisory opinion.

Despite Israel's ultimate refusal to participate in the proceedings, and the absence of evidence such as topographical studies that were available to the Supreme Court of Israel, the ICJ stated that it had sufficient information on which to rely in making its findings. Unlike adversary proceedings before the court where the parties are required to prove their claims, Israel was not obligated to either take part in the proceedings or furnish evidence. In the sole dissenting opinion to the ruling, Justice Thomas Buergenthal observed that the "Court may not draw any adverse evidentiary conclusions from Israel's failure to supply [evidence supporting its claim regarding the legality of the wall] or assume, without fully inquiring into the matter, that the information before it is sufficient to support its sweeping legal conclusions."[4]

In his book, a reproduction of his LL.M. thesis for the Faculty of Law at the Hebrew University in Jerusalem, Solomon submits that in the interests of international peace and justice and out of respect for international law, the ICJ should have exercised both restraint and prudence and demurred from the consideration of this case. In legal terms, it should have declared the issue as contentious, thus unsuitable for an advisory opinion and non-justiciable.

The top-heavy vote in support of the ICJ's finding — fourteen judges in favour, one against (Buergenthal) — would appear to

---

3 *Ibid* at para 160.

4 *Ibid* at 245.

undermine the author's assertion that the topic of the wall is not justiciable by the court. However, the overwhelming vote against Israel, one of the major parties in the overarching dispute that gave rise to the issue, may demonstrate an additional, non-legal element: the extent to which the court's deliberations mirror the disproportionate number of attacks to which the state of Israel has been subjected to other UN bodies (UN General Assembly, Human Rights Council, and so on) in recent history. The political dimension of the decision is further defined by the puzzling presence on the court of Judge Nabil Elaraby (former foreign minister of Egypt and, presently, secretary-general of the Arab League), who was his government's permanent representative to the UN and participated in deliberations that led to the UN General Assembly request to the ICJ on the Israeli barrier. Whether the perception of politicized content in this case is accepted as valid and whether this is considered to be sufficient to render the case non-justiciable, viewed after an interval of almost a decade, it does raise an enticing question. Did the court's findings promote the cause of peace in the Middle East or would its demurral from considering the issue have advanced the process by stimulating the parties to struggle more vigorously towards negotiating their differences, including the issue of the security barrier?

In arguing that the court ought to have abstained from this case, the author traces the development of the "justiciability doctrine" in both the global context (from ancient Greece to the modern era) and in domestic jurisdictions, such as the United States, Canada, and Germany. The notion that political and other considerations alter the nature of what appears on the surface to be a legal question (and, thus, more appropriately addressed by bilateral discussions between the parties involved) is reviewed in detail with reference to a number of theoretical concepts that have emerged over time. For example, the author analyzes the four-legged justiciability doctrine in the United States, where the possibility of adjudicating certain cases is weighed with respect to standing, ripeness, mootness, and the "political question" doctrine. The book also makes a courageous, although not always clear, attempt at explaining the different elements of the justiciability *stricto sensu* and *lato sensu* dichotomy. The somewhat impenetrable discussion here may have to do more with editing problems than with the content of the review, as mentioned later in this review.

A thorough and engaging analysis is furnished on the "competing" Supreme Court of Israel decision in the 2004 case *Beit Sourik*

Village Council v The Government of Israel.[5] As the author admits, there "is no exact parallelism between national and international jurisdictions, partly because of the ... difficulty of the latter to win the trust of ... international players."[6] However, the aforementioned prestige of the national court, the measured approach it takes in its rulings, and the fact that it had before it material from the Israeli authorities unavailable to the world court suggests that it is worthy of attention, and, indeed, that the ICJ would have benefitted at least from a reference to the case. Taking note of the domestic high court decision might have at least persuaded Israel to reconsider its dismissal of the international court's opinion. The *Beit Sourik* ruling, which was issued several days before the ICJ decision in 2004, includes the following language in its conclusion that undoubtedly resonated with Israeli authorities and might have not been lost on the ears of ICJ judges:

Our task is difficult. We are members of Israeli society. Although we are sometimes in an ivory tower, that tower is the heart of Jerusalem, which is not infrequently struck by ruthless terror. We are aware of the killing and destruction wrought by terror against the state and its citizens. As any other Israelis, we too recognize the need to defend the country and its citizens against the wounds inflicted by terror. We are aware that in the short term, this judgment [which ordered the alteration of part of the route of the security barrier] will not make the state's struggle against those rising up against it easier. But we are judges. When we sit in judgment, we are subject to judgment ... we are convinced that at the end of the day, a struggle according to the law will strengthen her power and her spirit. There is no security without law.[7]

To be sure, the two tribunals did not address an identical spectrum of issues. The ICJ, for instance, examined the entire barrier as a result of the declared illegality of Israeli settlements within the territories. The Supreme Court of Israel reviewed a forty-kilometre stretch of the barrier and ordered a rerouting of part of the fence because of disproportionate injuries caused to Palestinians along its length, damage that "constitute[d] a severe violation of the rights

---

5 *Beit Sourik Village Council v The Government of Israel,* Case HCJ 2056/04, Supreme Court of Israel, 30 May 2004 [*BeitSourik*].

6 Solomon, *supra* note 1 at 143.

7 *Beit Sourik, supra* note 5 at para 86.

of the local inhabitants [and does not satisfy] the humanitarian provisions of the Hague regulations and of the Fourth Geneva Convention."[8] While considering these international instruments, the Israeli court, unlike the ICJ, did not draw links with the lawfulness of the settlements.

Recognizing these differences, nevertheless, the author provides a useful contribution by, as it were, lifting the separation fence between the two decisions and juxtaposing the different methodologies and substantive approaches adopted by the two tribunals. In this regard, a discussion of the Israeli court's three-part proportionality test guiding its evaluation of whether administrative measures are valid will engage readers who are familiar with Supreme Court of Canada jurisprudence. Of interest, as well, will be insights into the thought patterns of this national court, which, as the author notes, recently "has opened its gates to every issue of constitutional implication and to every petitioner."[9]

While this book is a serious and scholarly approach to a significant issue that has agitated the world community, it is regrettably marred by some presentational problems. The publisher has failed to align some page margins and numbers. Vertical black lines on some pages indicate that the work may have been photocopied rather than printed in the original and, at least in the review volume, pages 132-33 have disappeared altogether. In addition, while the author demonstrates a more than adequate command of the written language, syntactical and grammatical errors abound (improper use of prepositions, inappropriate terms or idioms, incorrect tenses, and spelling mistakes). Several sentences, amounting to over 120 words each, do not facilitate clarity. Many of these problems appear to stem from the fact that English is not the author's mother tongue, and his usage is sometimes based on expressions familiar to Hebrew speakers. A good editor and a publisher able to pay greater attention to print quality could overcome these difficulties effectively.

These problems do not, however, fatally detract from the overall analytical quality and seriousness of this book. In the introduction to this volume, the author quotes the inscription on the façade of the Peace Palace at The Hague — *pacis tutela apud judicem* — the fostering of peace is the task of the judge. In essence, this treatise is a useful tool to help the reader contemplate whether in its ad-

---

[8] *Ibid* at para 76.

[9] Solomon, *supra* note 1 at 38.

visory opinion of 9 July 2004 the ICJ has, in fact, achieved that objective.

AHARON MAYNE
Middle East and Islamic Studies, Hebrew University

Legitimacy and Legality in International Law. By Jutta Brunnée and Stephen Toope. Cambridge: Cambridge University Press, 2010.

International law emerged as a distinct discipline in the nineteenth century, at a time when legal positivism dominated the common law tradition. A child of these times, it reflected the positivist construction of domestic law. To do so, it looked for a substitute for the domestic sovereign and found it in the collectivity of sovereign and equal states. Furthermore, preserving the logic of positivism, it sought a rule of recognition in sources theory to identify the formal expressions of states' consent to its rules.

Two centuries later, international law is still dominated by this mindset, despite its shortcomings both as a theory of obligation and as a factual description of the functioning of the international legal system. As noted in the latest edition of D.J. Harris's *Cases and Materials on International Law,*

[t]he above materials concerning custom are based upon the voluntarist or consensual theory of the nature of international law, by which states are bound only by that to which they consent. Although this is a theory that presents certain theoretical problems, it remains the one to which the [International Court of Justice] ICJ adheres and one from which, not surprisingly, states do not appear to dissent in their practice. If the theory may involve an element of fiction, it is not easy to find a substitute that is both more intellectually defensible and as serviceable as a working hypothesis.

This may be the substitute. In their latest book, Jutta Brunnée and Stephen Toope provide a compelling intellectual defence of an alternative theory of international law and demonstrate how the theory works in practice. They have introduced this theory, their "interactional account" of international law, in previous publications. However, *Legality and Legitimacy in International Law* is a comprehensive and fine-tuned account, placing "interactional law" on a solid foundation of legal theory and international law's neighbouring disciplines, particularly international relations theory. The first half of the book explains and defends "interactional law" as a theory of international law; the second half demonstrates its serviceability by applying it to three detailed and comprehensive case studies on climate change, the prohibition on torture, and the prohibition on the use of force.

The process that Brunnée and Toope see at work in the creation and maintenance of international law involves three interlinked stages. The first is a "shared understanding" that develops within a community, which arises from the mutual engagement of its members.[1] The consequence of this construction of "community" is that its members are those who do, in fact, engage with the community, rather than just those entities with a particular status, such as statehood itself. Norms will form from the shared understandings of this community, but they will be *legal* norms only if they meet eight particular criteria. To these criteria, Brunnée and Toope add one more step before we can speak of "interactional" international law. There must be an ongoing practice of legality that confirms and sustains the norm created by the community. The first half of the book fleshes out this process, describing how a "shared understanding" comes into being, the role of the criteria that create "law," and why the third step, the practice of legality, is necessary.

Borrowing the term "shared understandings" from constructivist international relations theory,[2] Brunnée and Toope describe the phenomenon as "collectively held background, norms or practices,"[3] which are generated and maintained by social interaction. Central to their argument is the mutuality of the members of the community and the structure through which they communicate.[4] Drawing on scholarship from constructivist international relations theory and social learning theory, Brunnée and Toope argue that subjects of law "learn" their collective understandings by participating in society. These understandings then affect the subjects' subsequent experience and mould their further experiences as well as their sense of identity.[5] The authors emphasize that at this early stage of

---

[1] Jutta Brunnée and Stephen Toope, *Legitimacy and Legality in International Law* (Cambridge: Cambridge University Press, 2010) at 80.

[2] *Ibid* at 24.

[3] *Ibid* at 64.

[4] *Ibid* at 63.

[5] *Ibid* at 62.

norm development, shared understandings are value-neutral, and they can be both positive and negative.[6]

When legal norms develop, however, a minimal moral content is established. Here the authors draw on Lon Fuller, who saw his eight essential requirements as the "internal morality" of law. They require that the rules of law be (1) general; (2) promulgated; (3) prospective; (4) clear; and (5) not internally contradictory. Furthermore, they (6) may not demand the impossible; and (7) must remain relatively consistent over time. Finally, (8) the official application of the law must comply with the rules as promulgated.[7] This last criterion, congruency, seems, in a domestic system, to govern the vertical relationship between officials and citizens. Brunnée and Toope adjust the wording slightly for the international setting. They point out that the congruency requirement, in fact, ensures the reciprocal fulfilment of duties, thereby preserving a horizontal relationship between law maker and subject as well as a reciprocal relationship between the subjects themselves.[8] In their analysis, the congruency criterion requires practice in conformity with the rules by all subjects of international law.[9]

Following Fuller, Brunnée and Toope argue that norms that meet these requirements will generate their own fidelity. This is the central claim of the book: obligation, the binding power of law, is internal to law and does not derive from formal or external factors. Furthermore, the authors emphasize that only those norms that are produced by their "interactional framework," including Fuller's eight requirements, have the capacity to generate fidelity and obligation. This is a strong and moral claim, as the authors underscore,[10] creating the clearest break with the positivist account of international law. However, Brunnée and Toope have difficulty distinguishing their analysis from natural law, primarily because the substantive commitment entailed by Fuller's eight prerequisites is thin.[11] Interactional law does not entail any agreement on goals but is primarily an agreement on the process whereby goals can be

---

[6] *Ibid* at 63.

[7] *Ibid* at 26 (paraphrasing Lon Fuller, *The Morality of Law*, revised edition (New Haven, CT: Yale University Press, 1965) at 39.

[8] Brunnée and Toope, *supra* note 1 at 38-39, 352.

[9] *Ibid* at 352.

[10] *Ibid* at 53.

[11] *Ibid* at 29ff.

negotiated — a process that ensures the autonomy of its subjects, provides a structure for their communication, and ensures the reciprocity of their interaction with one another. This process is well demonstrated in the chapter on climate change. The moral value of this legal infrastructure lies in its support for the agency of the subjects of law — that is, its capacity to allow its subjects to "reason with law and make choices about their own lives."[12] By promoting this basic moral purpose, such an infrastructure generates fidelity "to the rule of law itself and not merely to specific rules."[13]

The authors call obligation the "value-added" of law,[14] but they acknowledge that Fuller himself paid little attention to the distinction between social and other norms.[15] For the formation and maintenance of "interactional law," Brunnée and Toope, therefore, require a third stage — the ongoing "practice of legality." Two aspects of this third stage seem to raise problems. The first is its close relationship with Fuller's legality criteria. By the authors' own description, the practice of legality is adherence to the criteria of legality[16] — in particular, the practice of legality enjoys a close relationship with the congruency criterion.[17] This notion could cast doubt on what Brunnée and Toope are adding to Fuller's requirements and puts the distinction between the second and third stages of interactional norm-creation into question.

The second problem is suggested by the ubiquitous presence of "practice" throughout the analysis. Practice appears in the authors' concept of "shared understandings," in Fuller's congruency requirement, and in the practice of legality. Its presence in all of the stages of norm creation could suggest that the interactional stages of norm creation are insufficiently distinguishable. A related complaint might be that the interactional configuration is unnecessarily complicated, especially for lawyers used to the apparently clear form of treaties or the simple division of custom into practice and *opinio juris*.

There are, however, two difficulties with the seeming simplicity of traditional, positivist international law. The first is that it is not,

---

[12] *Ibid* at 29-30.

[13] *Ibid* at 53.

[14] *Ibid* at 77.

[15] *Ibid* at 26-27.

[16] *Ibid* at 27.

[17] *Ibid* at 283.

in fact, simple. For example, indeterminacy in the very definition of custom[18] has allowed for such widely differing interpretations that the whole category has long been bemoaned as a catch-all basket of norms, bearing no relation to the orthodox definition of the concept.[19] Norms are still confidently claimed to be rules of custom when there is overwhelming state practice against them, when bodies other than states provide the only examples of practice, or even when there is no attempt to establish that they are supported by practice and *opinio juris* at all. But even where the formal validity of a source can clearly be established — for example, when the prerequisites for a valid treaty are met — mainstream theories often fail to reflect the reality of the international arena. For instance, they do not explain why soft law — "non-valid" law — can be more effective than formally valid treaties.

Brunnée and Toope praise Fuller for his "intensely practical" approach to legal theory, and they follow his lead in this book by suggesting a normative process, which accurately reflects the reality of international relations.[20] The value of their own account is demonstrated by its solid grounding in international relations theory and sociology and by the case studies, which the authors conduct in the second half of the book. The case studies make it clear why practice is present at every stage of the analysis — law arises, is maintained, or falls away in communities of practice. There is no moment in which time is frozen. Indeed, the authors do not even suggest that the three stages of norm development involve different kinds of practice.[21] Instead, the legal import of that practice changes over time because of the nature of the norms that emerge from

---

[18] See Martti Koskenniemi, *From Apology to Utopia: The Structure of International Legal Argument,* reprint with new epilogue (Cambridge: Cambridge University Press, 2005). Koskenniemi famously explained that each element of custom — that is, practice and *opinio juris* — can be found only by reference to the other element, making the entire definition of customary international law self-referential and indeterminate.

[19] Robert Jennings, in Bin Cheng, ed, *International Law: Teaching and Practice* (London: Stevens, 1982) at 5.

[20] Brunnée and Toope, *supra* note 1 at 21.

[21] *Ibid* at 352. Brunnée and Toope's treatment of the term "practice of legality" is depicted as an ongoing project by which shared understandings can be "expanded" and "embedded" in legal practice — a use of the term that recognizes that such a practice is needed through all of the stages of the development of a norm.

them, from weak "shared understandings" to procedural or substantive norms. The authors' analysis also reveals the necessity of the third step: law can be lost. For law, it is not enough that a norm comes into existence through Fuller's eight criteria — it must be maintained and strengthened in the same way. This point is made very effectively in the case studies, where the authors demonstrate how the prohibitions on torture and the use of force are weakened by contrary practice and changing shared understandings.

The clarity of positivism is ostensibly achieved by its factual, inductive inquiry into state practice and its careful distinction between this factual element and any moral requirement. Ironically, however, it loses both normative and descriptive clarity in the process. The interactional account, on the other hand, makes no attempt to divorce the normative element from the practice. Similarly, there is no attempt to distinguish practice and *opinio juris*.[22] It is the nature of the norms emerging from the practice — not the psychological element behind the practice — that gives them their special status as norms of law. And yet interactional law, with all of its moral content, produces a better description of the reality on the ground.

Brunnée and Toope introduce their book with a discussion of the prevailing influence of positivism in international law and the realist school of international relations theory. They suggest that this line of scholarship has led to the denigration of international law, either because international law was dismissed as irrelevant or because it was distorted to fit the domestic image.[23] The authors' analysis suggests that "interactional" international law reveals quintessential elements of all law as well as tools to deal with diversity and conflict. Fuller's vision, for example, allows for thin or merely procedural norms that can protect the pluralism of the global community, while providing the communicative tools that will enable such a community to grow together. Despite this exciting vision, the interactional perspective is not unrealistically optimistic about its subject, as the authors' examination of the prohibition on torture, in particular, demonstrates. Indeed, Brunnée and Toope point out that individuals and organizations have the capacity to do the "hard work"[24] of international law themselves and that, without this hard work, particular norms may not survive.

---

[22] *Ibid* at 47. Indeed, Brunnée and Toope see *opinio juris* as a form of entrenched practice.

[23] *Ibid* at 6.

[24] *Ibid* at 355.

Notwithstanding its close relationship with neighbouring disciplines and its firm grounding in the work of Lon Fuller, this book presents an original and radical approach that will severely threaten the authority enjoyed by positivist international law for the last 200 years. It may not be applicable in all fora. Harris' observation, earlier, suggests that the International Court of Justice is unlikely to use this theory in its deliberations. States, too, may wish to avoid it, and its activist tone may startle both courts and lawyers who wish to preserve the objective aura of positivism. However, love it or hate it, you cannot ignore it. *Legitimacy and Legality in International Law* provides not only a powerful proposal for approaching international law but also a compelling account of how this body of law functions. International lawyers need these tools.

CATHLEEN H. POWELL
Senior Lecturer in Public Law, Faculty of Law, University of Cape Town

Analytical Index / Index analytique

—

THE CANADIAN YEARBOOK OF
INTERNATIONAL LAW

2010

ANNUAIRE CANADIEN
DE DROIT INTERNATIONAL

(A) Article; (NC) Notes and Comments; (Ch) Chronique;
(P) Practice; (C) Cases; (BR) Book Review

(A) Article; (NC) Notes et commentaires; (Ch) Chronique;
(P) Pratique; (C) Jurisprudence; (BR) Recension de livre

Index of Cases /
Index de la jurisprudence

―